An
Introduction
to the
Psychology
of Hearing

Sixth Edition

An Introduction to the Psychology of Hearing

Sixth Edition

Brian C. J. Moore

Department of Experimental Psychology
University of Cambridge
Downing Street
Cambridge CB2 3EB
United Kingdom

United Kingdom – North America – Japan
India – Malaysia – China

Emerald Group Publishing Limited
Howard House, Wagon Lane, Bingley BD16 1WA, UK

First edition 1977

Copyright © 2012 Emerald Group Publishing Limited

Reprints and permission service
Contact: booksandseries@emeraldinsight.com

British Library Cataloguing in Publication Data
A catalogue record for this book is available from the British Library

ISBN: 978-1-78052-038-4

Emerald Group Publishing
Limited, Howard House,
Environmental Management
System has been certified by
ISOQAR to ISO 14001:2004
standards

Awarded in recognition of
Emerald's production
department's adherence to
quality systems and processes
when preparing scholarly
journals for print

INVESTOR IN PEOPLE

To Hedwig

CONTENTS

2 Absolute Thresholds   57

3 Frequency Selectivity, Masking, and the Critical Band   67

6 Pitch Perception

8 Auditory Pattern and Object Perception   283

PREFACE

In this edition, I have updated all of the chapters, and added new sections on a variety of topics that seemed to me to be of general interest. As for previous editions, I have tried to delete equivalent amounts of "less interesting" or "less topical" material to keep the overall length of the book about the same as before.

In the United Kingdom this book is suitable for advanced undergraduate and master's level courses in psychology, speech and hearing sciences, audiology, and audio engineering. In the United States the book might be found a little difficult for undergraduate psychologists, but it would be well suited to graduate courses in perception. The book is suitable for those in the United States and elsewhere taking undergraduate and graduate level courses in subjects with a greater emphasis on hearing, such as audiology, and speech and hearing science. The book may also be useful for researchers and professionals involved in sound and hearing, for example, audio engineers, otologists, hearing-aid designers, audiologists, and hearing-aid dispensers. To make the book as useful as possible, I have given extensive references to original research papers.

I thank all those who have contributed in various ways to earlier editions and the present edition of this book. These include: Michael Akeroyd, José Alcántara, Alan Allport, Tom Baer, Peter Bailey, Mahnaz Baldry, Wynford Bellin, Ian Cannell, Max Coltheart, Roy Davis, Dave Emmerich, Larry Feth,

Shigeto Furukawa, Brian Glasberg, Hedwig Gockel, John Gundry, Mark Haggard, Roy Hammans, Sarah Hawkins, Laurie Heller, Martina Huss, Rachel Keen, Kay Knights, Tony Marcel, Dave Martin, Robert Milroy, Carol Moore, Bernard Moulden, Bernard O'Loughlin, Ken Ohgushi, Andrew Oxenham, Roy Patterson, Robert Peters, Chris Plack, David Raab, Marina Rose, Gregory Schooneveldt, Aleksander Sek, Michael Shailer, Pat Sheldon, Paul Scott, Susan Scott, Anne Sherman, Barbara Shinn-Cunningham, Andrew Simpson, Thomas Stainsby, Michael Stone, Quentin Summerfield, Mark Terry, Deborah Vickers, and Paul Whittle.

Brian C. J. Moore
Cambridge, 2011

CHAPTER 1

The Nature of Sound and the Structure and Function of the Auditory System

1 INTRODUCTION

One of the general aims of this book is to specify, as far as possible, the relationships between the characteristics of the sounds that enter the ear and the sensations that they produce. Wherever possible these relationships will be specified in terms of the underlying mechanisms. In other words, the goal is to understand what the auditory system does *and* how it works. It is not always possible to fulfill both of these objectives. While some aspects of auditory perception can be explained by reference to the anatomy or physiology of the auditory system, knowledge in this respect is not usually as precise or as far reaching as would be desired. Often the results of perceptual studies provide evidence about the kind of things that are occurring in the auditory system, but it is not possible to specify the detailed physiological mechanisms that are involved. Sometimes the results of psychophysical experiments can be used to determine if a particular type of neural coding (see later), which in principle could convey information about a sound, is actually involved in the perception or discrimination of that sound. Before specifying underlying mechanisms, however, it is necessary to know something about the physical nature of sounds, and of the basic anatomy and physiology of the auditory system. That is the purpose of this chapter.

2 THE PHYSICAL CHARACTERISTICS OF SOUNDS

2A THE NATURE OF SOUND

Sound originates from the vibration of an object. This vibration is impressed upon the surrounding medium (usually air) as a pattern of changes in pressure. The atmospheric particles, or molecules, are squeezed closer together than normal (called condensation) and then pulled farther apart than normal (called rarefaction). The sound wave moves outward from the vibrating body, but the molecules do not advance with the wave: they vibrate about an average resting place. The vibrations occur along an axis that is aligned with the direction in which the sound is propagating. This form of wave is known as a "longitudinal wave". The sound wave generally weakens as it moves away from the source, and also may be subject to reflections and refractions caused by walls or objects in its path. Thus, the sound "image" reaching the ear differs somewhat from that initially generated.

One of the simplest types of sound is the sine wave, also known as a sinusoid, which has the waveform (pressure variation plotted against time) shown in Fig. 1.1. This wave is simple both from the physical and mathematical point of view and from the point of view of the auditory system. It happens that sinusoids produce particularly simple responses in the auditory system and that they have a very clean or "pure" sound, like that of a tuning fork. Thus, they are also called simple tones or pure tones. To describe a sinusoid, three things must be specified: the frequency, or the number of times per second the waveform repeats itself (specified in Hertz, where 1 Hertz (Hz) = 1 cycle/s); the amplitude, or the amount of pressure variation about the mean; and the phase, which corresponds to the portion of the cycle through which the wave has advanced in relation to some fixed point in time. As the wave goes through one complete cycle, the phase changes by $360°$, which is equivalent to 2π radians. For continuous sinusoids, phase is only important when considering the relationship between two or more different waves. The time taken for one complete cycle of the waveform is called the

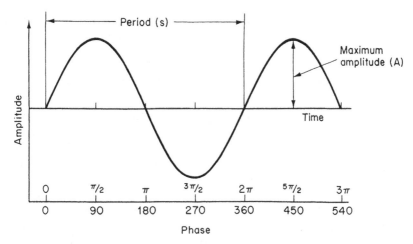

FIGURE 1.1   The waveform of a sine wave or sinusoidal vibration. Only 1.5 cycles are shown, although the waveform should be pictured as repeating indefinitely. The instantaneous amplitude is given by the expression $A \sin(2\pi f t)$, where $t =$ time, $f =$ frequency, and $A =$ maximum amplitude. Phase is indicated along the bottom, using as a reference point the first zero-crossing of the wave. Phase may be measured in degrees or in radians. One complete cycle corresponds to $360°$ or 2π radians.

period, which is the reciprocal of the frequency. For example, a 500-Hz sinusoid has a period of 2 ms.

A sine wave is not the only kind of sound that repeats regularly. Many of the sounds encountered in everyday life, such as those produced by musical instruments and certain speech sounds, also show such regularity and, hence, are called periodic sounds. Although these sounds are generally more complex than sinusoids, they share a common subjective characteristic with sinusoids in that they have pitches. Pitch may be defined as "that attribute of auditory sensation in terms of which sounds may be ordered on a scale extending from low to high" (ANSI, 1994b). Variations in pitch create a sense of melody. A sound that evokes a pitch is often called a "tone", especially when the pitch has a clear musical quality. In general, tones are periodic, but this is not always the case.

The pitch of a sound is related to its repetition rate and, hence, in the case of a sinusoid, to its frequency. It should be emphasized that pitch is a subjective attribute of a stimulus, and as such cannot be measured directly. However, for a sinusoid, the pitch is closely related to the frequency; the higher the frequency, the higher the pitch. For a more complex sound, the pitch is often investigated by asking the subject to adjust a sinusoid so that it has the same pitch as the complex sound. The frequency of the sinusoid is then taken as a measure of the pitch of the complex sound.

2B Fourier Analysis and Spectral Representations

Although all sounds can be specified by their variation in pressure with time, it is often more convenient, and more meaningful, to specify them in a different way when the sounds are complex. This method is based on a theorem by Fourier, who proved that almost any complex waveform can be analyzed, or broken down, into a series of sinusoids with specific frequencies, amplitudes, and phases. This is done using a mathematical procedure called the Fourier transform. The analysis is called Fourier analysis, and each sinusoid is called a (Fourier) component of the complex sound. The complex waveform can be produced by adding together all of the component sinusoids. A complex tone can thus be defined as a tone composed of a number of simple tones, or sinusoids.

The simplest type of complex tone to which Fourier analysis can be applied is one that is periodic. Such a tone is composed of a number of sinusoids, each of which has a frequency that is an integer multiple of the frequency of a common (not necessarily present) fundamental component. The fundamental component thus has the lowest frequency of any of the components in the complex tone, and it may be said to form the "foundation" for the other components. The fundamental component has a frequency equal to the repetition rate of the complex waveform as a whole. The frequency components of the complex tone are known as harmonics and are numbered, the fundamental being given harmonic number 1. Thus, for example, a note of A3 played on the piano has a fundamental component or first harmonic with a frequency of 220 Hz, a second harmonic with a frequency of 440 Hz, a third harmonic with a frequency of 660 Hz, etc. The nth harmonic has a frequency that is n times the fundamental frequency. The fundamental frequency is often denoted F0. An illustration of how a complex tone can be built up from a series of sinusoids is given in Fig. 1.2. Note that, in this example, the even harmonics (the second, fourth, sixth, etc.) are missing or, equivalently, have zero amplitude. Sometimes musicians refer to harmonics above the fundamental as "overtones". The first overtone is the second harmonic, the second overtone is the third harmonic, and so on.

One of the reasons for representing sounds in this way is that humans do seem to be able to hear the harmonics of a periodic sound wave individually to a limited extent. For example, Mersenne (1636) stated that "the string, struck and sounded freely makes at least five sounds at the same time, the first of which is the natural sound of the string and serves as the foundation for the

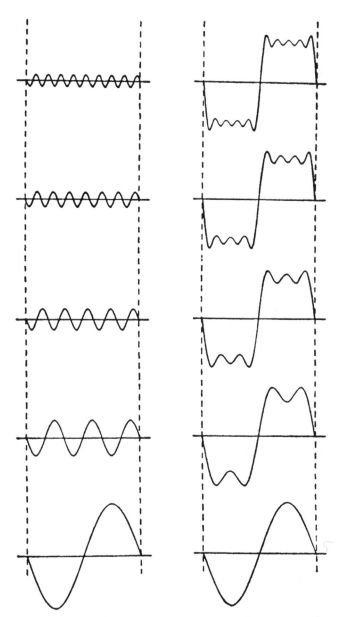

FIGURE 1.2   An illustration of how a complex waveform (a square wave) can be built up from a series of sinusoidal components. The square wave is composed of odd harmonics only, and the 1st, 3rd, 5th, 7th, and 9th harmonics are shown on the left. The series on the right shows progressive changes from a simple sine wave as each component is added. If enough additional harmonics, with appropriate amplitudes and phases, were added, the composite wave would approach a perfectly square shape. From Newman (1948), by permission of John Wiley, New York.

rest...". The fact that pitches can be heard corresponding to the individual sinusoidal components of a complex tone is known as Ohm's acoustical law, after the German physicist Georg Ohm (1789–1854). Normally, when we are presented with a complex tone, we do not listen in this way; rather, we hear a single pitch corresponding to the repetition rate of the whole sound. Nevertheless, we do appear to be able to hear out the lower harmonics of a complex sound to some extent (see Chapters 3 and 6 for further discussion of this). When we are presented with two simultaneous pure tones, whose frequencies are not too close, then these are often heard as two separate tones each with its own pitch, rather than as a single complex sound. Thus, our perception corresponds to the analysis of the sound in terms of its Fourier components. Notice that our perception of color is quite different; if lights of two different frequencies (or wavelengths) are mixed, we see a single color corresponding to the mixture, rather than seeing two component hues.

The structure of a sound, in terms of its frequency components, is often represented by its magnitude spectrum, a plot of sound amplitude, energy, or power as a function of frequency. These are called the amplitude spectrum, energy spectrum, or power spectrum (see Section C for a description of the relationship between amplitude, energy, and power). Examples of magnitude spectra are given in Fig. 1.3. For periodic sounds of long duration, the energy falls at specific discrete frequencies and the spectrum is known as a line spectrum. The first three examples are of this type. The sinusoid, by definition, consists of a single frequency component. The square wave, as shown in Fig. 1.2, consists of the odd harmonics (the first, third, fifth, etc.) of the fundamental component (1 kHz in this example), and the amplitudes of the harmonics decrease with increasing harmonic number. The train of brief pulses, or clicks, contains all the harmonics of the fundamental at equal amplitude. However, since each pulse contains only a small amount of energy, and since there are many harmonics, each harmonic has a low amplitude.

For sounds that are not periodic, such as white noise (a hissing sound), the spectrum can still be obtained by use of Fourier analysis. Non-periodic sounds can still have line spectra, for example, a mixture of two nonharmonically related sinusoids. The term partial is used to describe any discrete sinusoidal component of a complex sound, whether it is a harmonic or not. More commonly, non-periodic sounds have continuous spectra; the energy is spread over certain frequency bands, rather than being concentrated at particular frequencies. The last three examples are of this type. The single pulse, or click, and the white noise both have flat amplitude spectra; the amplitude does not vary as a function of frequency (this is only true for very brief clicks). Although the pulse and the noise have spectra of the same shape, the amplitude of the spectrum of the pulse is lower, since it contains much

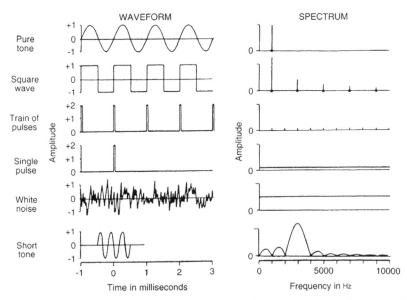

FIGURE 1.3   On the left are shown the waveforms of some common auditory stimuli, and on the right are the corresponding spectra. The periodic stimuli (pure tone, square wave, and train of pulses) have line spectra, while the non-periodic stimuli (single pulse, white noise, and short tone burst) have continuous spectra.

less energy than the noise. The pulse and the noise differ in their phase spectra, which represent the phases of the components as a function of frequency (not shown in the figure). For the noise, the phases of the components are randomly distributed. For the pulse, the components all have a phase of 90° at time zero. This is known as cosine phase, and it means that each component is at its peak amplitude at time zero. The result is that at this time the components all add, whereas at other times they cancel.

The final example shows a short burst of a sinusoid, often called a tone pulse or tone burst. The magnitude spectrum of a sinusoid is only a line if the sinusoid lasts for an extremely long time. For tone pulses of short duration, the magnitude spectrum contains energy over a range of frequencies around the nominal frequency of the sinusoid. This spread of energy increases as the duration of the tone pulse is shortened. Corresponding changes occur in our perception of such tone pulses; as a tone pulse is shortened in duration, it sounds less tone-like and more click-like.

The mathematical techniques used in calculating spectra by Fourier analysis in theory require the waveform to last an infinite time. In practical situations, this is impossible. Also, it is obvious that the ear does not take infinite time to analyze sounds. In many situations it is useful to take a segment of a sound and assume that the waveform has zero value outside the time limits of the segment. This process is often described as applying a "window" to the sound; only the portion of the waveform falling within the window is "seen". An example, for a 1-kHz sinusoidal signal and a 10-ms window, is given in Fig. 1.4. The Fourier transform of the windowed sample can then be calculated, giving what is called the short-term spectrum of the sound. This is shown in the middle-right panel of Fig. 1.4. The spectrum contains energy over a considerable range of frequencies. This is partly a consequence of the sharp discontinuities in the waveform introduced by applying the window. To reduce this effect, it is possible to use a window that is a kind of weighting function that tapers off near the edges; more weight is given to the waveform at the center of the window than at the edges. An example is shown in the bottom-left panel of Fig. 1.4. The resulting spectrum, shown in the bottom-right panel of Fig. 1.4, spreads over a smaller range of frequencies than when a "rectangular" window is used.

Typical window lengths are between 5 and 200 ms. The frequency resolution that is possible depends on the duration of the window and also on the window "shape" (the weighting function). As a rough rule of thumb, the frequency resolution is equal to the reciprocal of the window duration. For example, a duration of 10 ms (0.01 s) would give a frequency resolution of 100 Hz, meaning that two frequency components separated by 100 Hz would just be visible as separate peaks in the spectrum.

For complex sounds such as speech, it is useful to analyze the sounds using a succession of windows that may overlap in time, so that changes in the short-term spectrum with time can be calculated. Examples of this approach are given in Chapter 9.

As mentioned above, the magnitude spectrum of continuous white noise is, in theory, flat. However, in practice, the Fourier transform has to be calculated for a particular sample of the noise. Any such sample of "white" noise does not have a flat magnitude spectrum. It is only when the spectrum is averaged over a long period of time that it becomes flat.

Whenever a stimulus is changed abruptly (e.g., by a change in intensity or a change in frequency), a spread in spectral energy occurs. For example, the short-term spectrum of a continuous sinusoid has most of its energy concentrated around the nominal frequency of the sinusoid (see Fig. 1.4). However, if the intensity of the sinusoid is changed abruptly, the short-term spectrum for a window centered on the change is much broader. This spreading of spectral energy over frequency is often called "energy splatter". Energy splatter can be reduced by slowing down the rate of change (e.g., by switching tones on and off gradually), but it cannot be completely eliminated.

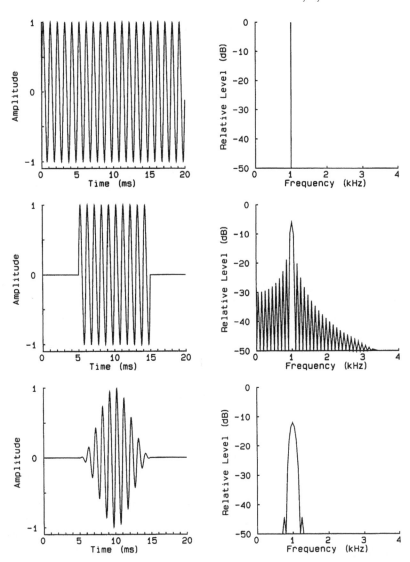

FIGURE 1.4   The top-left panel shows part of the waveform of a 1-kHz sinusoid. The waveform should be pictured as continuing indefinitely. The spectrum, shown in the top-right panel, contains a single line at 1 kHz. The middle-left panel shows a segment of the 1-kHz sinusoid obtained by applying a 10-ms-long rectangular window. The middle-right panel shows the spectrum of the windowed sample of the sinusoid. It contains multiple peaks and dips spread over a wide frequency range, although the biggest peak is still at 1 kHz. The bottom-left panel shows the effect of applying a weighting function to the sinusoid that tapers off at the edges. The bottom-right panel shows the spectrum of the waveform in the bottom left.

2C The Measurement of Sound Level

The instruments used to measure the magnitudes of sounds, such as microphones, normally respond to changes in air pressure. However, sound magnitudes are often specified in terms of intensity, which is the sound energy transmitted per second (i.e., the power) through a unit area in a sound field. For a medium such as air, there is a simple relationship between the pressure variation of a plane (flat-fronted) sound wave in a free field (i.e., in the absence of reflected sound) and the acoustic intensity; intensity is proportional to the square of the pressure variation.

It turns out that the auditory system can deal with a huge range of sound intensities (see Chapter 4). This makes it inconvenient to deal with sound intensities directly. Instead, a logarithmic scale expressing the ratio of two intensities is used. One intensity, I_0, is chosen as a reference and the other intensity, I_1, is expressed relative to this. One Bel corresponds to a ratio of intensities of 10:1. Thus, the number of Bels corresponding to a given intensity ratio is obtained by taking the logarithm to the base 10 of that intensity ratio. For example, an intensity ratio of 100:1 corresponds to 2 Bels. The Bel corresponds to a rather large ratio of intensities for everyday use, and to obtain units of more convenient size, the Bel is divided into 10 decibels (dB). Thus, the number of decibels corresponding to a given ratio of acoustic intensity is:

$$\text{number of decibels} = 10\log_{10}\left(\frac{I_1}{I_0}\right). \tag{1.1}$$

When the magnitude of a sound is specified in decibels, it is customary to use the word "level" to refer to its magnitude. Notice that a given number of decibels represents an intensity or power ratio, not an absolute intensity. To specify the absolute intensity of a sound it is necessary to state that the intensity of the sound, I_1, is X dB above or below some reference intensity, I_0. The reference intensity most commonly used, for sounds in air, is 10^{-12} W/m^2 (watts per square meter), which is equivalent to a pressure of 2×10^{-5} N/m^2 or 20 μPa (micropascal). A sound level specified using this reference level is referred to as a sound pressure level (SPL). Thus, a sound at 60 dB SPL is 60 dB higher in level than the reference level of 0 dB and has an intensity of 10^{-6} W/m^2. Notice that multiplying (or dividing) the ratio of intensities by 10 increases (or decreases) the number of decibels by 10. It is also convenient to remember that a two-fold change in intensity corresponds to a change in level of 3 dB (because the logarithm of 2 is approximately 0.3).

The reference sound level, 0 dB SPL, is a low sound level that was chosen to be close to the average absolute threshold of humans for a 1000-Hz sinusoid.

The absolute threshold is the minimum detectable level of a sound in the absence of any other external sounds (the manner of presentation of the sound and method of determining detectability must be specified; see Chapter 2). In fact, the average absolute threshold at 1000 Hz is about 6.5 dB SPL (when listening with one ear). Sometimes it is convenient to choose as a reference level the absolute threshold of a subject for the sound being used. A sound level specified in this way is referred to as a sensation level (SL). Thus, for a given subject, a sound at 60 dB SL will be 60 dB above the absolute threshold of that subject for that sound. The physical intensity corresponding to a given SL will, of course, differ from subject to subject and from sound to sound.

Finally, it is useful to adapt the decibel notation so that it expresses ratios of pressure as well as ratios of intensity. This may be done by recalling that intensity is proportional to the square of pressure. If one sound has an intensity of I_1 and a pressure P_1, and a second sound has an intensity I_2 and pressure P_2, then the difference in level between them is:

$$\text{number of decibels} = 10\log_{10}\left(\frac{I_1}{I_2}\right) = 10\log_{10}\left(\frac{P_1}{P_2}\right)^2 = 20\log_{10}\left(\frac{P_1}{P_2}\right). \quad (1.2)$$

Thus, a 10-fold increase in pressure corresponds to a 100-fold increase in intensity and is represented by +20 dB. Table 1.1 gives some examples of

TABLE 1.1.   The relationship between decibels, intensity ratios, and pressure ratios

Sound level (dB SPL)	Intensity ratio (I/I_0)	Pressure ratio (P/P_0)	Typical example
140	10^{14}	10^7	Gunshot at close range
120	10^{12}	10^6	Loud rock group
100	10^{10}	10^5	Shouting at close range
80	10^8	10^4	Busy street
70	10^7	3160	Normal conversation
50	10^5	316	Quiet conversation
30	10^3	31.6	Soft whisper
20	10^2	10	Country area at night
6.5	4.5	2.1	Mean absolute threshold at 1 kHz
3	2	1.4	
0	1	1	Reference level
−10	0.1	0.316	

Sound levels in dB SPL are expressed relative to a reference intensity I_0 of 10^{-12} W/m^2. This is equivalent to a pressure of 20 µPa.

intensity and pressure ratios, and also indicates sound levels, in dB SPL, corresponding to various common sounds.

For sounds with discrete spectra, or line spectra, the sound level can be specified either as the overall (total) level or in terms of the levels of the individual components. The total level can be calculated from the total intensity of the sound, which in turn is proportional to the mean-square pressure (measured as the deviation from normal atmospheric pressure). If it is desired to calculate levels in terms of pressure, then the pressure of the sound must be expressed as its root-mean-square (RMS) value. The RMS value is obtained by squaring the instantaneous pressure values, taking the average of all of the squared values (which gives a measure proportional to intensity), and then taking the square root of the result.

For sounds with continuous spectra, the overall level can also be specified, but to indicate how the energy is distributed over frequency another measure is needed. This measure is obtained by specifying the total energy, power, or intensity between certain frequency limits, that is, over a certain band of frequencies. Conventionally, a bandwidth of 1 Hz is chosen. The energy in this one-Hertz-wide band, at a given frequency, is known as the energy density. For a continuous noise, one can also specify the energy per unit time (the power) or the energy per unit time per unit area (the intensity) in this one-Hertz-wide band. The term noise "power density" is used to refer to both of these, although the latter would be more correctly described as the "intensity density". When the noise intensity density is expressed in decibels relative to the standard reference intensity of 10^{-12} W/m^2 (equivalent to 20 μPa), it is known as the spectrum level. Thus, a noise may be characterized by its spectrum level as a function of frequency. A white noise has a spectrum level that does not vary with frequency. Another type of noise that is sometimes used in auditory research is called pink noise. This has a spectrum level that decreases by 3 dB (corresponding to a halving of noise power density) for each doubling in frequency.

2D BEATS

When two sinusoids with slightly different frequencies are added together, they resemble a single sinusoid with frequency equal to the mean frequency of the two sinusoids but whose amplitude fluctuates at a regular rate. These fluctuations in amplitude are known as "beats". Beats occur because of the changing phase relationship between the two sinusoids, which causes them alternately to reinforce and cancel one another. When they are in phase (i.e., when their peaks coincide) they add, while when they are 180° out of phase (the peaks in one coinciding with the minima in the other) they cancel. The resulting amplitude fluctuations occur at a rate equal to the frequency difference between the two tones. For example, if two sinusoids with frequencies 1000 and 1002 Hz are added together, two beats occur each second. Slow beats like this result in audible loudness fluctuations. Chapters 3 and 5 give examples of the role of beats in psychoacoustic experiments.

3 THE CONCEPT OF LINEARITY

One concept that is widely used in auditory research is that of linearity. The auditory system is often conceived as being made up of a series of stages, the output of a given stage forming the input to the next. Each of these stages can be considered as a device or system, with an input and an output. For a system to be linear, the following two conditions must be satisfied:

(1)   If the input to the system is changed in magnitude by a factor k, then the output should also change in magnitude by a factor k, but be otherwise unaltered. This condition is called "homogeneity". For example, if the input is doubled, then the output is doubled, but without any change in the form of the output. Thus, a plot of the output as a function of the input would be a straight line passing through the origin (zero input gives zero output)—hence the term linear system. Such a plot is called an input–output function. An example of such a function is given in panel (a) of Fig. 1.5.

(2)   The output of the system in response to a number of independent inputs presented simultaneously should be equal to the sum of the outputs that would have been obtained if each input was presented alone. For example, if the response to input A is X, and the response to input B is Y, then the response to A and B together is simply X + Y. This condition is known as "superposition".

When describing a system as linear, it is usually assumed that the system is time-invariant. This means that the input–output function does not change over time. For example, if the input is I, and the output is O, the relationship between the input and the output would be:

$$O = cI \qquad (1.3)$$

where c is a constant that does not vary with time.

When a sinusoid is used as an input to a linear system, the output is a sinusoid of the same frequency. This is illustrated in panel (b) of Fig. 1.5. The amplitude and phase of the output may, however, be different from those of

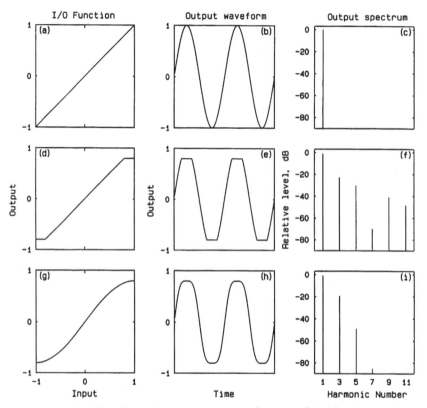

FIGURE 1.5   The left column shows input–output functions for: (a) a linear system; (d) a nonlinear system with "hard" peak clipping; and (g) a nonlinear system with more progressive "saturation". The middle column shows outputs from these systems in response to a sinusoidal input. The third column shows spectra of the outputs.

the input. Assume that the input is a single sinusoid, whose waveform as a function of time, $I(t)$, can be described by:

$$I(t) = A \, \sin(2\pi f t), \tag{1.4}$$

where A is the peak amplitude of the input and f is the frequency in Hz. The output as a function of time, $O(t)$, could then be represented by:

$$O(t) = G \times A \, \sin(2\pi f t + \phi), \tag{1.5}$$

where G is a constant representing the amplitude ratio between the input and output, and ϕ is a constant representing the phase shift between the input and output. G is referred to as the gain of the system. Often, it is expressed in decibels, that is, as $20\log_{10}(G)$.

Since the output of a linear system in response to a sinusoidal input is itself sinusoidal, the spectrum of the output, by definition, consists of a single frequency component. This is illustrated in panel (c) of Fig. 1.5. More generally, the output of a linear system never contains frequency components that were not present in the input signal. The response of a linear system may, however, vary with the frequency of the input sinusoid. This is equivalent to saying that the constants G and ϕ in Eq. 1.5 can vary with the input frequency.

In practice, many devices or systems are linear provided that the input is not too large. Excessive inputs may cause the system to become nonlinear; more details are given later on. Such a system is usually called linear, even though it can become nonlinear under extreme conditions. As an example, consider a loudspeaker. The input is a voltage and the output is a movement of the cone of the loudspeaker that can produce audible sound waves. For the types of inputs that are typically used for a loudspeaker, the response is approximately linear; the conditions of homogeneity and superposition are obeyed. If the input voltage varies in a sinusoidal manner, the movement of the cone is almost sinusoidal. However, if the frequency of the input is changed, holding the magnitude of the input constant, the magnitude of the movement of the cone may vary. In this case, the loudspeaker does not have a "flat" frequency response; G may vary with frequency. Similarly, ϕ may vary with frequency. Other examples of systems that usually operate in a nearly linear way are microphones, amplifiers, and the output transducers used in hearing aids (often called "receivers").

When waveforms other than sinusoids are applied as the input to a linear system, the output waveform often differs from that of the input. For example, if the input to a linear system is a square wave, the output is not necessarily a square wave. This is one reason for the popularity of sinusoids in auditory research; sinusoids are the only waveforms that are always "preserved" by a linear system. However, if a system is linear, then it is relatively easy to predict its output for any arbitrary complex input. As a first step, the output is measured as a function of frequency for a sinusoidal input. Essentially, the values of G and ϕ are determined as a function of the input frequency. To predict the output for a complex input, a Fourier analysis of the input is performed. This gives a description of the input in terms of the amplitudes and phases of its sinusoidal components. The output in response to each of the sinusoidal components comprising the input can then be calculated. Finally, using the principle of superposition, the output in response to the whole complex can be calculated as the sum of the outputs in response to its individual sinusoidal components. This is a powerful method, and it gives another reason for using sinusoids as stimuli.

As mentioned earlier, many linear systems become nonlinear if the input is made large enough. An example is shown in panel (d) of Fig. 1.5. The input–output function is linear over a large part of its range, but it flattens out for large positive or negative values of the input. This is sometimes called "saturation" or "peak clipping", and it can occur in systems such as transistor amplifiers and condenser microphones. In the example shown, the clipping is symmetrical, in that it occurs at the same absolute value for positive and negative values of the input. When a sinusoid is used as input to such a system, and the peak amplitude of the sinusoid, A, is sufficiently large, the output is no longer sinusoidal. This is illustrated in panel (e) of Fig. 1.5. The output is periodic, with the same period as the input sinusoid, but the waveform is distorted. In this case, the output contains frequency components that are not present in the input. This is illustrated in panel (f) of Fig. 1.5. In general, the output of a nonlinear system in response to a single sinusoid at the input contains one or more components (sinusoids) with frequencies that are integer multiples of the frequency of the input. These components are thus harmonics of the input frequency, and the nonlinear system is said to introduce harmonic distortion. For example, if the input was a sinusoid with a frequency of 500 Hz, the output might still contain a component with this frequency, but components with other frequencies might be present too, for example, 1000, 1500, 2000, ... Hz.

Another example of a nonlinear input–output function is shown in panel (g) of Fig. 1.5. In this case, the function does not show "hard" clipping, but the slope becomes more shallow when the absolute value of the input or output exceeds a certain value. This type of input–output function can occur in valve (tube) amplifiers, moving coil microphones, and loudspeakers, and it can also occur in the auditory system. The output waveform, shown in panel (h) of Fig. 1.5, is less distorted than when hard clipping occurs, and the output spectrum, shown in panel (i), reveals less harmonic distortion.

If the input to a nonlinear system consists of two sinusoids, then the output may contain components with frequencies corresponding to the sum and difference of the two input frequencies, and their harmonics, as well as the original sinusoidal components that were present in the input. These extra components are said to result from intermodulation distortion. For example, if the input contains two sinusoids with frequencies f_1 and f_2, the output may contain components with frequencies f_1-f_2, f_1+f_2, $2f_1-f_2$, $2f_2-f_1$, etc. These components are referred to as intermodulation distortion products, and, in the case of the auditory system, they are also called combination tones.

When a system is nonlinear, the response to complex inputs cannot generally be predicted from the responses to the sinusoidal components comprising the inputs. Thus, the characteristics of the system must be investigated using both sinusoidal and complex inputs.

Often, the input and output magnitudes of a system are plotted on logarithmic axes (the decibel scale is an example). In that case, the input and output magnitudes are not specified as instantaneous values (e.g., as the instantaneous voltage in the case of an electrical signal). Generally, instantaneous magnitudes can have both positive and negative values, but it is not possible to take the logarithm of zero or a negative number. Instead, a measure of the input and output magnitude is averaged over a certain time, and the magnitude is expressed as a quantity that cannot have a negative value. Typically, both the input and output are specified in terms of their power (related to the mean-square value) or their root-mean-square (RMS) value. Sometimes, the peak amplitude may be used. For a linear system, the condition of homogeneity still applies to such measures. For example, if the input power is doubled, the output power is also doubled. When plotted on "log–log" axes, the input–output function of a linear system is a straight line with a slope of unity. To see why this is the case, take the logarithm of both sides of Eq. 1.3 ($O = cI$). This gives:

$$\log(O) = \log(cI) = \log(c) + \log(I). \tag{1.6}$$

The value of $\log(c)$ is itself a constant. Therefore, since $\log(O)$ is simply equal to $\log(I)$ plus a constant, the slope of the line relating $\log(O)$ to $\log(I)$ must be unity. In a nonlinear system, the slope of the input–output function on logarithmic axes differs from unity. Say, for example, that the output is proportional to the square of the input:

$$O = cI^2. \tag{1.7}$$

Taking logarithms of both sides gives:

$$\log(O) = \log(cI^2) = \log(c) + 2\log(I). \tag{1.8}$$

In this case, the slope of the input–output function on logarithmic axes is two. When the slope of the input–output function is greater than one, the nonlinearity is referred to as expansive. If the output were proportional to the square root of the input ($O = cI^{0.5}$), the slope of the function would be 0.5. When the slope of the input–output function is less than one, the nonlinearity is referred to as compressive. Examples of input–output functions plotted on log–log axes will be presented later in this chapter, in connection with the response of the basilar membrane within the cochlea.

4 FILTERS AND THEIR PROPERTIES

In many psychoacoustic experiments the experimenter may wish to manipulate the spectra of the stimuli in some way. For example, it may be desired to remove certain frequency components from a complex stimulus, while leaving other components unchanged. In practice, this is often achieved by altering the electrical signal before it is converted into sound by a loudspeaker or headphone. The electronic devices that are used to manipulate the spectrum of a signal are known as filters. Filters may also be applied to digital representations of the signal, before the signals are converted to sound (Rosen and Howell, 2010). Filters are generally linear devices, so in response to a sinusoidal input, the output is a sinusoid of the same frequency. However, they are designed so that at their outputs some frequencies are attenuated more than others. A highpass filter attenuates frequency components below a certain cutoff frequency, but does not affect components above this frequency. A lowpass filter does the reverse. A bandpass filter has two cutoff frequencies, passing components between those two frequencies, and attenuating components outside this passband. A bandstop filter also has two cutoff frequencies, but it attenuates components between these two frequencies, leaving other components intact. Such filters may be used not only for manipulating stimuli, but also for analyzing them.

Bandpass filters are of particular interest, not only because of their widespread use for signal analysis, but also because one stage of the peripheral auditory system is often likened to a bank of bandpass filters, each of which has a different center frequency, so that the whole range of audible frequencies is covered. This concept will be used extensively later in this book, so it is instructive to consider the properties of filters in some detail.

In practice, it is not possible to design filters with infinitely sharp cutoffs, although modern digital filters can come close to achieving this. Instead, there is a range of frequencies over which some components are reduced in level, but not entirely removed. Thus, to specify a filter it is necessary to define both the cutoff frequency (or frequencies) and the slope of the filter response curve. Some typical filter characteristics are illustrated in Fig. 1.6. The cutoff frequency is usually defined as the frequency at which the output of the filter has fallen by 3 dB relative to the output in the passband. This corresponds to a reduction in power or intensity by a factor of 2, and a reduction in amplitude (or voltage for an electronic filter) by a factor of $\sqrt{2}$ (see Table 1.1). For a bandpass filter, the range of frequencies between the two cutoffs defines the bandwidth of the filter. This is called the −3-dB bandwidth, the 3-dB-down bandwidth or (equivalently) the half-power bandwidth. Sometimes, for simplicity, it is just called the 3-dB bandwidth. When a bandwidth is given without specifying dB limits, it is generally assumed that the 3-dB-down points were used.

An alternative measure of bandwidth is the equivalent rectangular bandwidth (ERB). The ERB of a given filter is equal to the bandwidth of a perfect rectangular filter that has a transmission in its passband equal to the maximum transmission of the specified filter and transmits the same power of white noise as the specified filter. The ERB can be determined graphically if

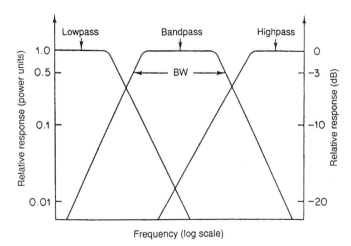

FIGURE 1.6 Typical characteristics for three types of filters: lowpass, bandpass, and highpass. The input to each filter is a sinusoid of variable frequency but constant magnitude. The output of each filter is plotted relative to the input, as a function of frequency. The left ordinate gives the ratio of the output to the input in linear power units. The right ordinate gives that ratio in dB.

the filter responses are plotted with axes of linear power versus linear frequency. The rectangular filter is adjusted to have the same maximum height as the given filter, and its width is adjusted so that it has the same area as the given filter. The bandwidth of the rectangular filter is then equal to the ERB of the given filter.

The response characteristics of electronic filters outside their passbands can often be approximated as straight lines when they are plotted on dB versus log-frequency coordinates. Thus, it is useful to express the slopes of filters in units such that equal frequency ratios represent equal amounts. One unit that does this is the octave. An octave corresponds to a frequency ratio of 2:1. Thus, if a lowpass filter has a slope of 24 dB/octave, this means that the output outside the passband decreases by 24 dB each time the frequency is doubled. Sometimes it is not possible to measure the response of a filter over a frequency range as large as an octave. Thus, it is necessary to work out the proportion of an octave corresponding to any given frequency ratio. Consider two frequencies, f_1 and f_2, where $f_2 > f_1$. Their relative frequency, expressed as a certain number of octaves, n, is given by the relation:

$$\frac{f_2}{f_1} = 2^n \qquad (1.9)$$

where n may be a fraction or a whole number of octaves. Taking the logarithm on both sides of this equation gives:

$$\log_{10}\left(\frac{f_2}{f_1}\right) = n \times 0.301 \tag{1.10}$$

from which it is possible to calculate n given f_2/f_1 and vice versa.

Sometimes the bandwidths of bandpass filters are expressed in octaves. In this case, the two frequencies involved are the upper and lower cutoffs of the filter, that is, the 3-dB-down points. One type of filter in common use has a bandwidth of 1/3 octave. For such a filter, the upper cutoff has a frequency 1.26 times that of the lower cutoff.

If a signal with a "flat" spectrum, such as white noise or a single brief click, is passed through a filter, the magnitude spectrum of the output of the filter has the same shape (i.e., is the same function of frequency) as the filter characteristic. Thus, one can also talk about a highpass noise, a bandpass click, and so on. A stimulus whose spectrum covers a wide frequency range is often referred to as broadband. Any alteration of the spectrum of a signal by filtering also produces a corresponding alteration in the waveform of the signal, and usually an alteration in the way it is perceived. For example, if white noise is passed through a narrow bandpass filter, the waveform at the output of the filter resembles a sinusoid that is fluctuating in amplitude from moment to moment. This narrowband noise has a tone-like quality, with a pitch corresponding to the center frequency of the filter.

The response of a filter to a single brief click, or impulse, can be very informative. In fact this response, known as the impulse response, completely defines the filter characteristic when the filter is linear. Since a click has a flat magnitude spectrum, the spectrum of the output of the filter, namely the impulse response, has the same shape as the filter characteristic. Hence the filter characteristic, or shape, can be obtained by calculating the Fourier transform of the impulse response.

Figure 1.7 shows a series of impulse responses from filters having passbands centered at 1 kHz, but with various bandwidths. For the narrowest filter (top) the response looks like a sinusoid that builds up and decays smoothly and that has a frequency close to 1 kHz. This is described as a "ringing" response, and it is similar to what is heard when a wine glass is tapped with a spoon. The filter "rings" at its own preferred frequency. As the filter bandwidth increases, the frequency of the ringing becomes less regular, and the duration of the response decreases. For the widest filter bandwidth, the impulse response has a waveform resembling that of the input impulse. For an infinitely wide filter, the output would exactly match the input

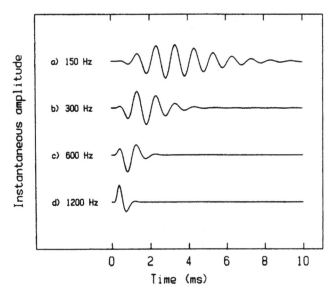

FIGURE 1.7   The responses of filters with various bandwidths to a brief impulse. All filters had a center frequency of 1 kHz, and the bandwidth is indicated to the left of each trace. The responses are not drawn to scale. The peak amplitude of the response actually increases as the filter bandwidth increases.

(provided that the filter delayed all frequency components by an equal time; this is equivalent to saying that the filter has a linear phase response). Figure 1.7 illustrates a general limitation of analyzing sounds with filters. The narrower the bandwidth of a filter, and the steeper its slopes, the longer is its response time. Thus, an increase in the resolution of individual frequency components can only be obtained at the expense of a loss of resolution in time.

If a filter with a narrow bandwidth is excited with a series of impulses, then the response to one impulse may not have died away before the next impulse occurs. Thus, the impulse responses merge. If, for example, an impulse occurs every 2 ms (repetition rate 500 pulses/s), then for the narrowest filter in Fig. 1.7, the merged impulse responses would form a continuous sinusoid with a frequency of 1 kHz. In effect, the filter has "picked out" the second harmonic of the pulse train and is responding mainly to that harmonic. Filters with different center frequencies respond to different harmonics in the pulse train. However, if the bandwidth of the filter is not sufficiently narrow, it responds to more than one harmonic. The waveform at the output is not then sinusoidal, but fluctuates at a rate equal to the repetition rate of the pulse train. When the filter bandwidth is very wide, then a series of isolated impulse responses occurs. These phenomena are illustrated in Fig. 6.6 and are discussed in detail in Chapter 6.

5 HEADPHONES

In psychoacoustic research, sounds are often delivered via headphones. These come in three basic designs: circumaural headphones fit over and around the ears, usually having quite large cushions; supra-aural headphones have cushions that lie on top of the ears; insert headphones sit at the entrance to the ear canal or are inserted into the ear canal. Insert headphones are also called earphones. They may fit loosely, or they may form a seal in the ear canal, so that the sound generated by the earphones does not escape from the ear canal.

One important characteristic of headphones is their frequency response, which can be specified as the sound level (in dB SPL) produced at the eardrum by a sinusoidal signal of fixed voltage, plotted as a function of the frequency of the sinusoid. The response close to the eardrum can be measured with a miniature microphone. Some headphones intended for research purposes are designed to have a "flat" frequency response; the sound level at the eardrum for a fixed voltage at the input is independent of frequency over a certain frequency range. An example is the Etymōtic Research ER2 insert earphone, which is sealed in the ear canal and has a flat response (varying less than $\pm 2\,\mathrm{dB}$) over the range 100–14,000 Hz. However, most headphones do not have a flat frequency response. One design goal adopted by some manufacturers is that the response at the eardrum should be similar to that produced by a loudspeaker with a flat response, when the response at the eardrum is averaged for many different directions of the loudspeaker relative to the head. This is equivalent to what is called a "diffuse-field" response. It leads to a natural sound quality when listening to speech or music signals. Some examples are the Etymōtic Research ER4 and ER6 insert earphones and the Sennheiser HD650 circumaural headphone. The response at the eardrum for a headphone with a diffuse-field response is flat at low frequencies, but shows a peak with a magnitude of 12–15 dB for frequencies around 2.5–3 kHz. The reason for this is described in Chapter 2 (see Fig. 2.2).

Some headphones, especially those used to evaluate hearing in the clinic, have neither a flat response nor a diffuse-field response. However, the response usually varies smoothly and slowly with frequency. Examples are the Sennheiser HDA200 circumaural headphone, the Telephonics TDH39, TDH49, and TDH50 supa-aural headphones and the Etymōtic Research ER3 and ER5 insert earphones.

6 BASIC STRUCTURE AND FUNCTION OF THE AUDITORY SYSTEM

6A THE OUTER AND MIDDLE EAR

The peripheral part of the auditory system of most mammals is rather similar. In this section I start by considering the human auditory system, but later I draw examples from studies of other mammals. Figure 1.8 shows the structure of the peripheral part of the human auditory system. The outer ear is composed of the pinna (the visible part) and the auditory canal or meatus. The pinna significantly modifies the incoming sound, particularly at high frequencies, and this is important in our ability to localize sounds (see Chapter 7). Sound travels down the meatus and causes the eardrum, or tympanic membrane, to vibrate. These vibrations are transmitted through the middle ear by three small bones, the ossicles, to a membrane-covered opening in the bony wall of the inner ear. The part of the inner ear concerned with

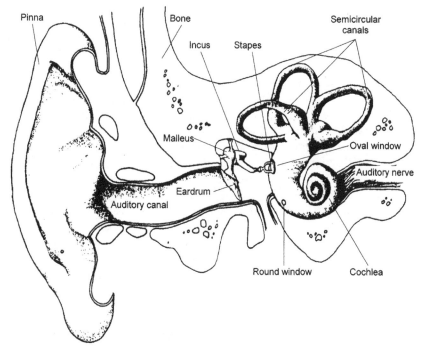

FIGURE 1.8   Illustration of the structure of the peripheral auditory system showing the outer, middle, and inner ear. Redrawn from *Human Information Processing*, by Lindsay and Norman (1972), by permission of the authors.

hearing is the spiral-shaped cochlea (the semi-circular canals are concerned with balance). The three bones, which are the smallest bones in the body, are called the malleus, incus, and stapes. The corresponding popular names are the hammer, anvil, and stirrup. The stapes lies on top of a membrane-covered opening in the cochlea called the oval window. There is a second membrane-covered opening called the round window. When the oval window moves inwards, the round window moves outwards, and vice versa.

The most important function of the middle ear is to ensure the efficient transfer of sound from the air to the fluids in the cochlea. The transfer of sound into the cochlea depends on the difference between the sound pressure applied to the oval window and that applied to the round window. If the sound were to impinge directly onto the oval and round windows, the pressure would be almost the same at the two windows and most of the sound would simply be reflected, rather than entering the cochlea. The middle ear magnifies the pressure applied to the oval window. This is accomplished mainly by the difference in effective areas of the eardrum and the oval window, and to a small extent by the lever action of the ossicles. As a result, there is a pressure difference between the oval and round windows and sound is transmitted more effectively into the cochlea. Technically, the middle ear acts as an impedance-matching device or transformer. Transmission of sound through the middle ear is most efficient at middle frequencies (500–5000 Hz) (Puria et al., 1997; Aibara et al., 2001).

The ossicles have minute muscles attached to them that contract upon exposure to intense sounds. This contraction, known as the middle ear reflex, is probably mediated by neural centers in the brainstem. The reflex reduces the transmission of sound through the middle ear, but only for frequencies below about 1.5 kHz, although it can be activated by higher frequencies than this. The reflex may help to prevent damage to the delicate structures of the cochlea. However, the activation of the reflex is too slow to provide any protection against impulsive sounds, such as gunshots or hammer blows. Two other functions have been suggested for the reflex. The first is the reduction of the audibility of self-generated sounds, particularly speech. The reflex is activated just before vocalization. The second is a reduction of the masking of middle and high frequencies by lower ones, a function that is particularly important at high sound levels (Liberman and Guinan, 1998) (see Fig. 3.10 and the associated discussion of the "upward spread of masking" in Chapter 3, Section 5).

6B The Inner Ear and the Basilar Membrane

An understanding of the functioning of the cochlea can provide insight into many aspects of auditory perception. The cochlea is shaped like the spiral shell of a snail. However, the spiral shape does not appear to have any functional significance (except for saving space), and the cochlea is often described as if the spiral had been "unwound". The cochlea is filled with almost incompressible fluids, and it also has bony rigid walls. It is divided along its length by two membranes, Reissner's membrane and the basilar membrane (BM). It is the motion of the BM in response to sound that is of primary interest. The start of the cochlea, where the oval window is situated, is known as the base, while the other end, the inner tip, is known as the apex. It is also common to refer to the basal end and the apical end, respectively. At the apex there is a small opening (the helicotrema) between the BM and the walls of the cochlea that connects the two outer chambers of the cochlea, the scala vestibuli and the scala tympani. This eliminates static or very low-frequency pressure differences between the two chambers, preventing large movements of the BM that would otherwise occur with changes in air pressure, for example produced by changes in elevation.

When the oval window is set in motion by movement of the stapes, a pressure difference is applied across the BM, and this causes the BM to move. The pressure difference and the pattern of motion on the BM take some time to develop, and they vary along the length of the BM. The response of the BM to sinusoidal stimulation takes the form of a traveling wave that moves along the BM from the base toward the apex. The amplitude of the wave increases at first and then decreases rather abruptly with increasing distance from the basal end. The basic form of the wave is illustrated in Fig. 1.9, which shows schematically the instantaneous displacement of the BM (derived from a cochlear model) for four successive instants in time in response to a low-frequency sinusoid. The dashed line joining the amplitude peaks is called the spatial envelope. The distance between peaks or zero-crossings in the wave decreases as the wave travels along, and the spatial envelope shows a peak at a particular position on the BM.

The response of the BM to sounds of different frequencies is strongly affected by its mechanical properties, which vary considerably from base to apex. At the base it is relatively narrow and stiff, while at the apex it is wider and much less stiff. As a result, the position of the peak in the pattern of vibration differs according to the frequency of stimulation. High-frequency sounds produce maximum displacement of the BM near the base, with little movement on the remainder of the membrane. Low-frequency sounds produce a pattern of vibration that extends all the way along the BM, but reaches a maximum before the apex. Figure 1.10 shows the spatial envelopes of the patterns of vibration for several different low-frequency sinusoids (from von Békésy, 1960). Although it is now known that responses on the BM are more sharply tuned than shown in this figure (and in Fig. 1.9), the figure does illustrate the important point that sounds of different frequencies produce

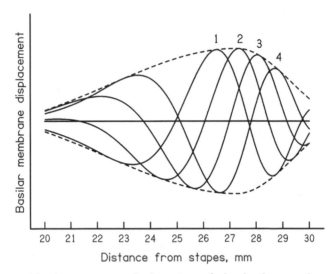

FIGURE 1.9 The instantaneous displacement of the basilar membrane at four successive instants in time, derived from a cochlear model. The pattern moves from left to right, building up gradually with distance and decaying rapidly beyond the point of maximal displacement. The dashed line represents the envelope traced out by the amplitude peaks in the waveform.

maximum displacement at different places along the BM. In effect the cochlea is behaving like a Fourier analyzer, although with a less than perfect frequency-analyzing power. The frequency that gives maximum response at a particular point on the BM is known as the characteristic frequency (CF) for that place.

In response to steady sinusoidal stimulation, each point on the BM vibrates in an approximately sinusoidal manner with a frequency equal to that of the input waveform. For example, if a 1000-Hz sinusoid is applied, each point on the BM for which there is a detectable amount of movement vibrates at that frequency. Some parts of the BM vibrate with a greater amplitude than others, and there are differences in the phase of the vibration at different points along the BM, but the frequency of vibration of each point is the same. This is true whatever the frequency of the input waveform, provided it is a single sinusoid within the audible range of frequencies.

A number of different methods may be used to specify the "sharpness" of tuning of the patterns of vibration on the BM. These methods make it possible to describe quantitatively the frequency resolution of the BM, that is, its ability to separate sounds of differing frequencies. Most of the recent data are based on measurements of the responses of a single point on the BM to

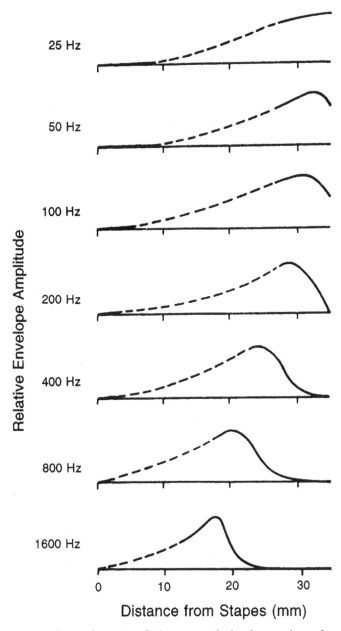

FIGURE 1.10 Envelopes of patterns of vibration on the basilar membrane for a number of low-frequency sinusoids. Solid lines indicate the results of actual measurements, while the dashed lines are von Békésy's extrapolations. Redrawn from *Experiments in Hearing*, by von Békésy (1960), used with the permission of McGraw-Hill.

sinusoids of differing frequency. The measures obtained are analogous to those used with electronic filters, as described in Section 4. Each point on the BM can be considered as a bandpass filter with a certain center frequency (corresponding to the CF) and bandwidth, and with slopes outside the passband. Thus, measures such as the 3-dB bandwidth, and slopes in dB/ octave, can be applied to the BM. Often it is difficult to measure the 3-dB bandwidth accurately, and a measure taken further down from the passband is used. The most common measure is the 10-dB bandwidth, which is the difference between the two frequencies at which the response has fallen by 10 dB. For many types of filters, and for the response of the BM, the bandwidth is not constant, but increases roughly in proportion with CF. Thus, it is sometimes useful to use the relative bandwidth, which is the bandwidth divided by the CF. The reciprocal of the relative bandwidth gives a measure of the sharpness of tuning, known as Q (for quality factor). Normally it is assumed that the 3-dB bandwidth is used to define Q. However, it is quite common in measurements of BM responses, and neural responses (see later), to use the 10-dB bandwidth. In this case the measure of sharpness of tuning is described as Q_{10dB}. A Q value of 4.35 corresponds to a bandwidth of 1/3 octave.

Most of the pioneering work on patterns of vibration along the BM was done by von Békésy (1947). His technique involved the use of a light microscope and stroboscopic illumination to measure the vibration amplitude at many points along the BM in human cadaver ears. For practical reasons his measurements were limited to the apical end of the BM, so he measured mainly low-frequency responses. The "tuning curves" found by von Békésy were rather broad. The relative bandwidth was about 0.6 in the frequency range observed. However, there are a number of difficulties associated with the technique used by von Békésy. First, the vibration amplitudes had to be at least of the order of one wavelength of visible light, which required very high sound levels—about 140 dB SPL. The vibration of the BM is now believed to be nonlinear, so it is not valid to extrapolate from these high levels to more normal sound levels. Second, the frequency-analyzing mechanism is now known to be physiologically vulnerable, so cadaver ears give markedly atypical responses.

Recent measurements of BM vibration, using different techniques in living animals, have shown that the BM is much more sharply tuned than found by von Békésy. In one technique, using an effect called the Mössbauer effect, a radioactive source of gamma rays, of very small mass and physical dimensions, is placed upon the BM. Changes in the velocity of this source, produced by motion of the BM, can be detected as a change in the wavelength of the emitted radiation. This is an example of a Doppler shift, like the drop in pitch of a train whistle as it passes you. A second technique involves placing a small mirror on the surface of the BM and shining a laser beam onto the mirror. The interference between the incident and reflected light can be used to determine the motion of the mirror; hence the name "laser interferometry". A third technique involves placing glass microbeads on the BM and measuring the Doppler shift of laser light reflected from the beads, a technique called "Doppler-shift laser velocimetry". In some work, it has been possible to use laser light reflected from the BM or nearby structures without the use of mirrors or reflective beads (Cooper, 1999; Jacob et al., 2009).

Results using these techniques in live animals have shown that the sharpness of tuning of the BM depends critically on the physiological condition of the animal; the better the condition, the sharper is the tuning (Khanna and Leonard, 1982; Sellick et al., 1982; Leonard and Khanna, 1984; Robles et al., 1986; Ruggero, 1992). Nowadays, the physiological status of the cochlea is often monitored by placing an electrode in or near the auditory nerve and measuring the combined responses of the neurons to tone bursts or clicks; this response is known as the compound action potential (AP or CAP). The lowest sound level at which an AP can be detected is called the AP threshold. Usually, the BM is sharply tuned when the AP threshold is low, indicating good physiological condition.

An example is given in Fig. 1.11, which shows the input sound level (in dB SPL) required to produce a constant velocity of motion at a particular point on the BM, as a function of stimulus frequency (data from Sellick et al., 1982). This is sometimes called a "constant velocity tuning curve". At the beginning of the experiment, when AP thresholds were low, a very sharp tuning curve was obtained (open circles). As the condition of the animal deteriorated, the tuning became broader, and postmortem (filled squares) the sound level required to produce the criterion response increased markedly around the tip.

In a normal, healthy ear each point on the BM is sharply tuned, responding with high sensitivity to a limited range of frequencies, and requiring higher and higher sound intensities to produce a response as the signal frequency is moved outside that range. Q_{10dB} values are typically in the range 3–10, corresponding to bandwidths of 1/2–1/8 octave. It seems likely that the sharp tuning and high sensitivity reflect an active process; that is, they do not result simply from the mechanical properties of the BM and surrounding fluid, but depend on biological structures actively influencing the mechanics. For reviews, see Yates (1995) and Robles and Ruggero (2001). The structures that play this role are the outer hair cells, which will be described later.

BM vibration in a healthy ear is nonlinear; the magnitude of the response does not grow directly in proportion with the magnitude of the input (Rhode, 1971; Rhode and Robles, 1974; Sellick et al., 1982; Robles et al., 1986; Ruggero, 1992). This is illustrated in Fig. 1.12, which shows what are referred to as input–output functions of the BM for a place with a CF of 8 kHz (from

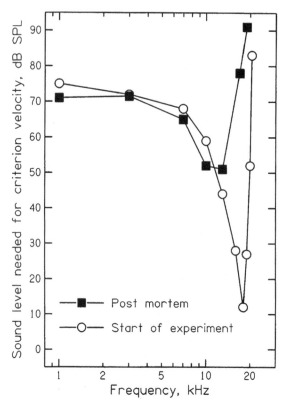

FIGURE 1.11   Tuning curves measured at a single point on the basilar membrane. Each curve shows the input sound level required to produce a constant velocity on the basilar membrane, plotted as a function of stimulus frequency. The curve marked by open circles was obtained at the start of the experiment when the animal was in good physiological condition. The curve marked by filled squares was obtained postmortem. Data from Sellick *et al.* (1982).

Robles *et al.*, 1986). A series of curves is shown; each curve represents a particular stimulating frequency, indicated by a number (in kHz) close to the curve. The output (velocity of vibration) is plotted on a log scale as a function of the input sound level (in dB SPL). If the responses were linear, the functions would be parallel to the dashed line. Two functions are shown for a CF tone (8 kHz), one (at higher levels) obtained about 1 h after the other. The slight shift between the two was probably caused by a deterioration in the condition of the animal.

While the function for the CF tone is almost linear for very low input sound levels (below 20 dB SPL) and approaches linearity for high input sound levels

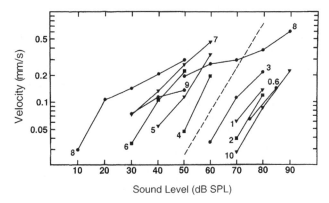

FIGURE 1.12   Input–output functions for a place on the BM with CF = 8 kHz. The stimulating frequency, in kHz, is indicated by a number close to each curve. The dashed line indicates the slope that would be obtained if the responses were linear (velocity directly proportional to sound pressure). Redrawn from Robles *et al.* (1986).

(above 90 dB SPL, not shown in the figure), the function has a very shallow slope at mid-range levels. This indicates a compressive nonlinearity; a large range of input sound levels is compressed into a smaller range of responses on the BM. The form of this function can be explained, at least crudely, in the following way. At low and medium sound levels, the active mechanism amplifies the response on the BM. The amplification (gain) may be 50 dB or more. For very low input sound levels, below 20–30 dB SPL, the gain is roughly constant and at its maximal value. As the sound level increases, the gain progressively reduces. Thus, the response grows more slowly than it would in a linear system. When the sound level is sufficiently high, around 90 dB SPL, the active mechanism is unable to contribute any gain, and the response becomes linear.

At the basal end of the BM, the nonlinearity mainly occurs when the stimulating frequency is close to the CF of the point on the BM that is being monitored. For stimuli with frequencies well away from the CF, the responses are more linear. Hence, the curves for frequencies of 7 and 9 kHz (close to CF) show shallow slopes, while the curves for frequencies below 7 kHz and above 9 kHz show steeper (linear) slopes. Effectively, the compression occurs only around the peak of the response pattern on the BM. As a result, the peak in the pattern flattens out at high sound levels, which partly accounts for the broad tuning observed by von Békésy. The nonlinearity decreases as the physiological condition of the cochlea worsens, and after death the responses are linear. This suggests that the active process responsible for sharp tuning and high sensitivity on the BM is also responsible for the nonlinearity.

At the apical end of the BM, the pattern of responses is somewhat different. Compressive responses have been observed in some studies, mainly using the chinchilla as an experimental animal (Cooper and Rhode, 1995; Rhode and Cooper, 1996). However, the amount of compression appears to be less than at the basal end. Also, the amount of compression does not appear to depend strongly on the frequency of the input relative to CF; the responses to tones of all frequencies are compressed more or less equally. There is still much uncertainty about BM responses at the apex of the cochlea, and indeed at regions intermediate between the apex and the base, as these regions are relatively inaccessible, and direct observation of BM movement is difficult. For reviews, see Ulfendahl (1997), Robles and Ruggero (2001), and Pickles (2008).

So far I have described the responses of the BM to steady sinusoidal stimulation. While there are some disagreements about the details of the patterns of vibration, it is now beyond doubt that a sinusoid produces a pattern with a maximum whose position depends on frequency. In other words, there is a frequency-to-place conversion. The situation with other types of sounds is somewhat more complex. Consider first the case of two sinusoids, of different frequencies, presented simultaneously. The pattern that occurs depends on the frequency separation of the two tones. If this is very large, then the two tones produce two, effectively separate, patterns of vibration. Each produces a maximum at the place on the BM that would have been excited most had that tone been presented alone. Thus, the response of the BM to a low-frequency tone is essentially unaffected by a high-frequency tone, and vice versa. In this kind of situation the BM behaves like a Fourier analyzer, breaking down the complex sound into its sinusoidal components. When the two tones are closer in frequency, however, the patterns of vibration on the BM interact, so that some points on the BM respond to both of the tones. At those points, the displacement of the BM as a function of time is not sinusoidal, but is a complex waveform resulting from the interference of the two tones. When the two tones are sufficiently close in frequency, there is no longer a separate maximum in the pattern of vibration for each of the component tones; instead, there is a single, broader maximum. Thus, in a sense, the BM has failed to resolve the individual frequency components. Chapter 3 describes how the frequency-resolving power of the auditory system, as observed psychoacoustically, is also limited.

The position on the BM that is excited most by a given frequency varies approximately with the logarithm of frequency, for frequencies above 500 Hz. Further, the relative bandwidths of the patterns of vibration on the BM in response to sinusoidal stimulation are approximately constant in this frequency range. This means that the frequency separation necessary for the resolution of two tones is proportional to center frequency.

The response of the BM to a sudden change in sound pressure (a step function) or to a short impulse (a single click) is very different from the response to a sinusoid. The spectra of these stimuli contain a wide range of frequencies, so responses occur all along the BM. What happens is that a "traveling bulge" is set up on the BM, and travels all the way along it. A number of workers have investigated the response of a single point on the BM in response to a brief click; this is called the "impulse response". Figure 1.13 shows impulse responses taken from the data of Recio *et al.* (1998). They look like damped, or decaying, sinusoidal oscillations and resemble the impulse response of a bandpass filter (see Fig. 1.7), although the decay is not quite monotonic. In the left panel, responses are plotted on a scale of absolute velocity. As expected, the response magnitude increases with increasing click level. In the right panel, responses are plotted *relative* to the click pressure.

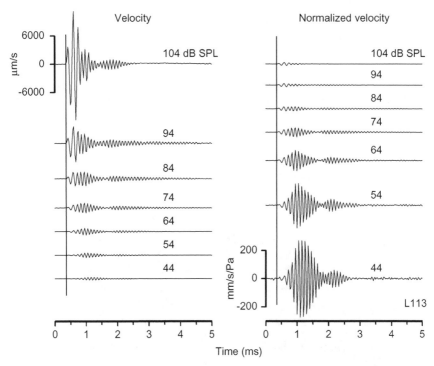

FIGURE 1.13   The response of a point on the basilar membrane with CF = 10 kHz to short impulses (clicks) at various levels. In the left panel, responses are plotted on a scale of absolute velocity. In the right panel, responses are plotted *relative* to the click pressure. The response becomes relatively greater as the click level decreases. From Recio *et al.* (1998), by permission of the authors.

The response becomes relatively greater as the click level decreases. This reflects the nonlinear input–output function of the BM, as shown in Fig. 1.12. The frequency of the oscillation in the impulse responses corresponds approximately to the CF of the point on the BM that is being studied. The basal end of the BM, which responds best to high frequencies, shows a high-frequency oscillation (as in Fig. 1.13), while the apical end, which responds best to low frequencies, shows a low-frequency oscillation. Thus, the waveform as a function of time varies continuously with position along the BM. Chapter 7 describes how this pattern of responses affects our ability to localize sounds of a transient character.

6C THE TRANSDUCTION PROCESS AND THE HAIR CELLS

Between the BM and the tectorial membrane are hair cells, which form part of a structure called the organ of Corti (see Fig. 1.14). The hair cells are divided into two groups by an arch known as the tunnel of Corti. Those on the side of the arch closest to the outside of the cochlea are known as outer hair cells, and they are arranged in three rows in the cat and up to five rows in humans. The hair cells on the other side of the arch form a single row and are known as inner hair cells. In humans, there are about 12,000 outer hair cells, each with about 140 "hairs" (more correctly called stereocilia) protruding from it, while there are about 3500 inner hair cells, each with about 40 stereocilia (Wright et al., 1987).

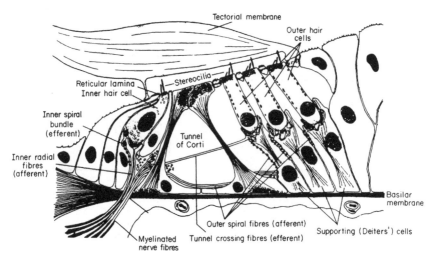

FIGURE 1.14 Cross section of the cochlea, showing the basilar membrane, the tectorial membrane, and the organ of Corti.

The tectorial membrane, which has a gelatinous structure, lies above the stereocilia. It appears that the stereocilia of the outer hair cells actually make contact with the tectorial membrane, but this may not be true for the inner hair cells. The tectorial membrane appears to be effectively hinged at one side (the left in Fig. 1.14), so that, when the BM moves up and down, a shearing motion is created between the BM and the tectorial membrane. As a result, the stereocilia at the tops of the hair cells are displaced.

The inner hair cells act to transduce mechanical movements into neural activity. The stereocilia are joined by fine links called "tip links" (Pickles *et al.*, 1987). Deflection of the stereocilia is thought to apply tension to these links, causing opening of what are called "transduction channels". This leads to a flow of potassium ions into the hair cell, which alters the voltage difference between the inside and outside of the hair cell. This in turn leads to a release of neurotransmitter and the initiation of action potentials in the neurons of the auditory nerve. The great majority of afferent neurons, which carry information from the cochlea to higher levels of the auditory system, connect to inner hair cells; each inner hair cell is contacted by about 20 neurons (Spoendlin, 1970). Thus, most, if not all, information about sounds is conveyed via the inner hair cells.

The main role of the outer hair cells may be actively to influence the mechanics of the cochlea, so as to produce high sensitivity and sharp tuning. The outer hair cells have a motor function, both the hair bundle at the tip and the hair cell body moving in response to electrical and chemical stimulation (Brownell, 1983; Ashmore, 1987; Benser *et al.*, 1996; Hudspeth, 1997; Eguiluz *et al.*, 2000). Supporting the idea that the outer hair cells play an active role in influencing cochlear mechanics, drugs or other agents that selectively affect the operation of the outer hair cells result in a loss of sharp tuning and a reduction of sensitivity of the BM (Ruggero and Rich, 1991). Furthermore, it is likely that this action of the outer hair cells is partly under the control of higher centers of the auditory system. There are about 1800 efferent nerve fibers that carry information from the auditory system to the cochlea, most of them originating in the superior olivary complex of the brainstem (see Section 8). Many of these efferent fibers make contact with the outer hair cells, and thus can affect their activity (Liberman and Guinan, 1998; Kujawa and Liberman, 2001). It appears that even the earliest stages in the analysis of auditory signals are partly under the control of higher centers.

6D Otoacoustic Emissions

Evidence supporting the idea that there are active biological processes influencing cochlear mechanics has come from a remarkable phenomenon first reported by Kemp (1978), although predicted by Gold (1948) many years earlier. If a low-level click is applied to the ear, then it is possible to detect sound coming out of the ear, using a microphone sealed into the ear canal. The early part of this sound appears to come from reflections in the middle ear, but some sound can be detected for delays from 5 to 60 ms following the instant of click presentation. These delays are far too long to be attributed to the middle ear, and they almost certainly result from activity in the cochlea itself. The sounds are known as "evoked otoacoustic emissions", although they have also been called "Kemp echoes" and "cochlear echoes".

Since Kemp's discovery, there has been a considerable amount of work studying this phenomenon. Although the input click in Kemp's experiment contained energy over a wide range of frequencies, only certain frequencies were present in the emitted sound. Kemp suggested that the reflections are generated at points on the BM, or in the transduction mechanism, where there is a sharp gradient or discontinuity in the mechanical or electrical properties. The response is nonlinear, in that the emission does not have an intensity in direct proportion to the input intensity. In fact, the relative level of the emission is greatest at low sound levels; the emission typically grows about 3 dB for each 10 dB increase in input level. This nonlinear behavior can be used to distinguish the response arising from the cochlea from the middle ear response; the latter behaves in a linear manner. Sometimes the amount of energy coming from the cochlea at a given frequency may exceed that which was present in the input click (Burns et al., 1998). This led Kemp and others to suggest that otoacoustic emissions reflect an active process of biological amplification.

Otoacoustic emissions can be very stable in a given individual, both in waveform and frequency content, but each ear gives its own characteristic response. Responses tend to be strongest between 500 and 2500 Hz, probably because transmission from the cochlea back through the middle ear is most efficient in this range. Emissions can be measured for brief tone bursts as well as clicks, and it is even possible to detect an emitted component in response to continuous stimulation with pure tones. The emission in response to a particular component in a stimulus can be suppressed if the ear is stimulated more strongly at a neighboring frequency (see also Section 7F). By presenting neighboring tones at a variety of frequencies and adjusting their levels, it is possible to map out equal suppression contours. These contours have the same general shape as tuning curves on the BM (Fig. 1.11). This lends strong support to the notion that the emissions are generated within the cochlea.

Otoacoustic emissions are usually observed only in ears that are in good physiological condition. Human ears with even moderate pathology of cochlear origin usually show no detectable emissions (Gorga et al., 1997).

Emissions are also abolished in ears that have been exposed to intense sounds or to drugs that adversely affect the operation of the cochlea (McFadden and Plattsmier, 1984). In such cases, the emissions may return after a period of recovery. This suggests that the emissions are linked to a physiologically vulnerable process, just like the process that is responsible for the sharp tuning and high sensitivity of the BM. The measurement of emissions may provide a sensitive way of monitoring the physiological state of the cochlea, and emissions are increasingly being used for the screening of infants for hearing disorders (Grandori and Lutman, 1999; Sergi et al., 2001) and for the early detection of cochlear disorders in adults (Avan and Bonfils, 2005; Montoya et al., 2008; Marshall et al., 2009).

When the ear is stimulated with two tones with frequencies f_1 and f_2 (where $f_2 > f_1$), then an echo may be detected with frequency $2f_1 - f_2$ (Kim et al., 1980). It turns out that subjects often also report hearing a tone with a pitch corresponding to the frequency $2f_1 - f_2$. Such a tone is called a combination tone. This particular combination tone has been frequently observed in auditory research (see Chapters 3 and 6), and it indicates a significant nonlinearity in the auditory system. Its presence as an emission implies that it evokes physical vibration on the BM, and it has, in fact, been observed in BM responses (Robles et al., 1991). The level of the combination tone, relative to the level of the primary tones in the ear canal, can be reversibly reduced by exposing the ear to a fatiguing tone of 80–90 dB SPL at a frequency near or slightly below the primary frequencies (see Chapter 4, Section 8, for a discussion of fatigue). Again this indicates that the nonlinear aspect of cochlear function is physiologically vulnerable.

Sometimes transient stimulation induces a sustained oscillation at a particular frequency, and the subject may report hearing this oscillation as a tonal sensation. The phenomenon of hearing sound in the absence of external stimulation is known as tinnitus. It appears that tinnitus may arise from abnormal activity at several different points in the auditory system, but in a few cases it corresponds to mechanical activity in the cochlea (Penner, 1992). Many ears emit sounds in the absence of any input and these can be detected in the ear canal (Zurek, 1981). Such sounds are called "spontaneous otoacoustic emissions", and their existence indicates that there is a source of energy within the cochlea that is capable of generating sounds.

In summary, while the exact mechanism by which otoacoustic emissions are generated is not understood, there is agreement that they are connected with active processes occurring inside the cochlea. These processes have a strong nonlinear component, they are biologically active, they are physiologically vulnerable, and they appear to be responsible for the sensitivity and sharp tuning of the BM.

7 NEURAL RESPONSES IN THE AUDITORY NERVE

The approximately 30,000 neurons in each auditory nerve carry information from the cochlea to the central nervous system. Each neuron conveys information in the form of brief pulses of an electrical signal that travels along the axon of the neuron; the pulses are called action potentials, nerve impulses, or spikes. When a spike is generated, this is sometimes described as the neuron "firing". For a given neuron, each spike has a fixed size, and information is carried only by the number and timing of the spikes. Most studies of activity in the auditory nerve have used electrodes with very fine tips, known as microelectrodes. These record the spikes in single auditory nerve fibers (often called single units). Three general results have emerged, which seem to hold for most mammals. First, the fibers show background or spontaneous spikes in the absence of sound stimulation. Spontaneous spike rates range from close to 0 up to about 150 per second. Second, the fibers respond better to some frequencies than to others; they show frequency selectivity. Finally, the fibers show phase locking; spikes tend to occur at a particular phase of the stimulating waveform, so that there is a temporal regularity in the spike pattern of a neuron in response to a periodic stimulus. These phenomena are described next.

7A SPONTANEOUS SPIKE RATES AND THRESHOLDS

Liberman (1978) showed that auditory nerve fibers could be classified into three groups on the basis of their spontaneous rates. About 61% of fibers have high spontaneous rates (18–250 spikes per second); 23% have medium rates (0.5–18 spikes per second); and 16% have low spontaneous rates (less than 0.5 spikes per second). The spontaneous rates are correlated with the position and size of the synapses on the inner hair cells. High spontaneous rates are associated with large synapses, primarily located on the side of the inner hair cells facing the outer hair cells. Low spontaneous rates are associated with smaller synapses on the opposite side of the hair cells. The threshold of a neuron is the lowest sound level at which a change in response of the neuron can be measured. High spontaneous rates tend to be associated with low thresholds and vice versa. The most sensitive neurons may have thresholds close to 0 dB SPL, whereas the least sensitive neurons may have thresholds of 80 dB SPL or more.

7B TUNING CURVES AND ISO-RATE CONTOURS

The frequency selectivity of a single nerve fiber is often illustrated by a tuning curve, which shows the fiber's threshold as a function of frequency. This curve is also known as the frequency-threshold curve (FTC). The stimuli are usually tone bursts, rather than continuous tones, so that changes in spike rate are more easily detected. The frequency at which the threshold of the fiber is lowest is called the characteristic frequency. Some typical tuning curves are presented in Fig. 1.15. On the logarithmic frequency scale used, the tuning curves are generally steeper on the high-frequency side than on the low-frequency side. It is usually assumed that the frequency selectivity of single auditory nerve fibers occurs because each fiber responds to vibration at one place along the BM. Experiments tracing single neurons whose tuning curves had been determined directly confirm this supposition (Liberman, 1982b). Furthermore, CFs are distributed in an orderly manner in the auditory nerve. Fibers with high CFs are found in the periphery of the nerve bundle, and there is an orderly decrease in CF toward the center of the nerve bundle (Kiang et al., 1965). This kind of organization is known as tonotopic organization, and it indicates that the place representation of frequency along the BM is preserved as a place representation in the auditory nerve. The sharpness of tuning of the BM is essentially the same as the sharpness of tuning of single neurons in the auditory nerve (Khanna and Leonard, 1982; Sellick et al., 1982; Robles et al., 1986).

To provide a description of the characteristics of single fibers at levels above threshold, iso-rate contours can be plotted. To determine an iso-rate contour, the intensity of a sinusoid required to produce a predetermined spike rate in

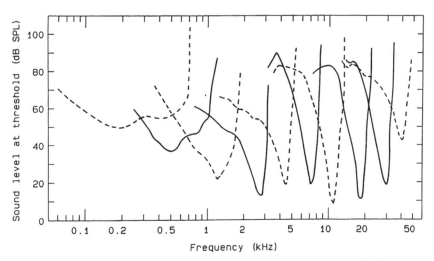

FIGURE 1.15 A sample of tuning curves (also called frequency–threshold curves) obtained from single neurons in the auditory nerve of anesthetized cats. Each curve shows results for one neuron. The sound level required for threshold is plotted as a function of the stimulus frequency (logarithmic scale). Redrawn from Palmer (1987).

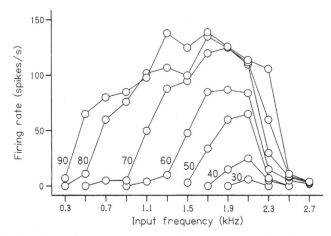

FIGURE 1.16   Iso-intensity contours for a single nerve fiber in the auditory nerve of an anaesthetized squirrel monkey. The number next to each curve indicates the sound level (dB SPL) used to obtain that curve. Note that the frequency producing maximal firing varies as a function of level. Data from Rose *et al.* (1971).

the neuron is plotted as a function of the frequency of the sinusoid. The resulting curves are generally similar in shape to tuning curves, although they sometimes broaden at high sound levels. An alternative method is to record spike rates at equal sound levels as a function of tone frequency. The resulting curves (iso-intensity contours) generally vary in shape according to the sound level chosen and differ considerably from tuning curves (see Fig. 1.16). The interpretation of iso-intensity contours is difficult, because their shape depends on how the rate of spikes of the nerve fiber varies with intensity; this is not usually a linear function (see later). However, it is of interest that for some fibers the frequency that gives maximal spike rate varies as a function of level. This poses some problems for one of the theories of pitch perception discussed in Chapter 6.

7C RATE VERSUS LEVEL FUNCTIONS

Figure 1.17 shows schematically how the rate of discharge for three auditory nerve fibers changes as a function of stimulus level. The curves are called rate versus level functions. In each case, the stimulus was a sinusoid at the CF of the neuron. Consider first the curve labeled (a). This curve is typical of what is observed for neurons with high spontaneous spike rates. Above a certain sound level the neuron no longer responds to increases in sound level with an increase

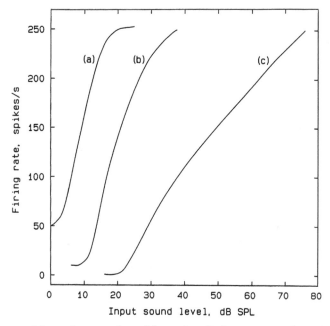

FIGURE 1.17 Schematic examples of how the discharge rates of single auditory neurons vary as a function of stimulus level. The curves are called rate versus level functions. In each case, the stimulus was a sinusoid at the CF of the neuron. Curves (a), (b), and (c) are typical of what is observed for neurons with high, medium, and low spontaneous firing rates, respectively.

in spike rate; the neuron is said to be saturated. The range of sound levels between threshold and the level at which saturation occurs is called the dynamic range. For neurons with high spontaneous rates, this range is often quite small, about 15–30 dB. Curve (b) is typical of what is observed for neurons with medium spontaneous spike rates. The threshold is slightly higher than for (a) and the dynamic range is slightly wider. Curve (c) is typical of what is observed for neurons with low spontaneous spike rates. The threshold is higher than for (b). The spike rate at first increases fairly rapidly with increasing sound level, but then the rate of increase slows down. The spike rate continues to increase gradually with increasing sound level over a wide range of levels. This is called "sloping saturation" (Sachs and Abbas, 1974).

The different shapes of rate versus level functions can be understood in terms of two functions (Yates, 1990; Patuzzi, 1992). This is illustrated in Fig. 1.18. The first function is the input–output function on the BM, illustrated schematically in the top-right panel. The second is the function relating BM displacement or velocity to the rate of spike generation (action

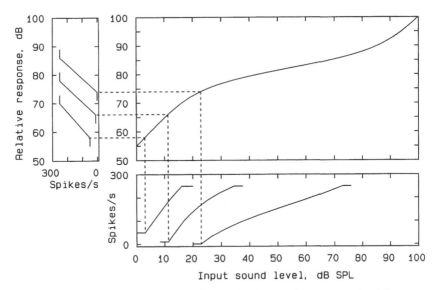

FIGURE 1.18 Schematic illustration of how the shapes of rate versus level functions can be accounted for in terms of the basilar membrane input–output function (top-right panel) and the functions relating neural spike rate (spikes/s) to amplitude of vibration on the basilar membrane (top-left panel). Three such functions are shown, corresponding to synapses with different sensitivities. The resulting three rate versus level functions are shown in the bottom panel. Adapted from Patuzzi (1992).

potentials per second, spikes/s) for the particular neuron under consideration. This is illustrated in the top-left panel of Fig. 1.18. This second function is similar in form for different neurons, except that spontaneous spike rates are higher for neurons with lower thresholds. All three of the functions in the top-left panel show saturation when the BM amplitude is a certain factor above the value required for threshold (in practice, saturation spike rates vary somewhat across neurons).

The variation across neurons probably depends mainly on the type of synapse, as discussed earlier. Neurons with low thresholds have large sensitive synapses. They start to respond at very low sound levels, where the input–output function on the BM is nearly linear. As the sound level increases, the BM displacement increases in a linear manner, and the neuron saturates relatively early, giving a small dynamic range, as shown by the left-most curve in the lower panel of Fig. 1.18. Neurons with higher thresholds have less sensitive synapses. They respond over the range of sound levels where the BM input–output function shows a strong compressive nonlinearity. Hence, a large increase in sound level is needed to increase the BM displacement to the point where the neuron saturates, and the neuron has a wide dynamic range, as shown by the right-most curve in the lower panel.

7D Neural Excitation Patterns

Although the technique of recording from single auditory neurons has provided valuable evidence about the coding of sounds in the auditory system, it does not reveal anything about the pattern of neural responses over different auditory neurons or about possible interactions or mutual dependencies in the spike patterns of different auditory neurons. A considerable advance has come from studies of the responses of many single neurons within one experimental animal to a limited set of stimuli (Pfeiffer and Kim, 1975; Kim and Molnar, 1979; Young and Sachs, 1979; Sachs and Young, 1980; Young, 2008). These studies have shown that in response to a single, low-level, sinusoid there is a high spike rate in neurons with CFs close to the tone frequency, with spike rate dropping off for CFs on either side of this. However, at higher sound levels the picture is more complicated. As a result of neural saturation, there may be a more or less uniform high spike rate over a wide range of CFs, with spike rate only falling off at CFs far removed from the stimulus frequency. Some implications of this are discussed in Chapters 3 and 4.

The distribution of spike rate as a function of CF is sometimes called the "excitation pattern". However, characterizing the spike rate is difficult, since both spontaneous and maximum spike rates vary considerably, even in neurons with similar CFs. Thus, at best, it is only possible to represent what happens in an "average" neuron at a given CF. This problem can be partially overcome by representing excitation patterns in a different way, specifically in terms of the effective *input* level at each CF; this is known as the excitation level. Imagine that it is desired to determine the excitation level produced by a sound S for a neuron with a specific CF. To do this, the sound S is alternated with a sinusoid whose frequency is equal to the CF, and the level of the CF tone is adjusted until it produces the same number of spikes/s as the sound S. The level found in this way is an estimate of the excitation level produced by S at this CF. The estimate is similar for neurons with different sensitivities (but the same CF), provided that the stimulus is above threshold for each neuron, and provided that the neurons are not saturated. If this process is repeated for neurons with different CFs, then the resulting excitation level plotted as a function of CF is the excitation pattern.

In summary, the excitation pattern is a representation of the effective amount of excitation produced by a stimulus as a function of CF and is plotted as effective level (in dB) against CF. Normally the CF is plotted on a

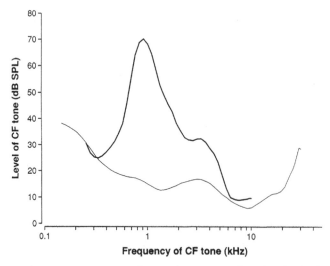

FIGURE 1.19 An excitation pattern for a 1-kHz sinusoid with a level of 70 dB SPL, determined from the responses of single neurons in the auditory nerve of the cat. For each neuron, the CF was determined and the 1-kHz, 70-dB SPL sinusoid was alternated with a second sinusoid at the CF of the neuron. The level of the CF tone was adjusted to determine the level at which the response to the CF tone was almost the same as the response to the fixed 1-kHz tone. This was repeated for neurons with many different CFs. The resulting level of the CF tone is plotted as a function of the frequency of the CF tone (thick curve), giving the desired excitation pattern. The thin curve indicates the threshold at CF of the most sensitive neurons as a function of CF. The origin of the small "bump" around 3 kHz is not clear; it may reflect some characteristic of the transmission of sound through the outer and middle ear. From B. Delgutte (personal communication).

logarithmic scale, roughly in accord with the way that frequency appears to be represented on the BM. Excitation patterns have been determined in this way by Bertrand Delgutte (personal communication). An example is shown in Fig. 1.19. Chapter 3 describes psychoacoustic techniques for determining excitation patterns like this for people. Such excitation patterns can be considered as an internal representation of the spectrum of the stimulus.

7E PHASE LOCKING

So far I have described only the changes in rate of spikes that occur in response to a given stimulus. However, information about the stimulus is also carried in the temporal patterning of the neural spikes. In response to a pure tone, the nerve spikes tend to be phase locked or synchronized to the stimulating waveform. A given nerve fiber does not necessarily fire on every cycle of the stimulus, but, when spikes do occur, they occur at roughly the same phase of the waveform each time. Thus, the time intervals between spikes are (approximately) integer multiples of the period of the stimulating waveform. For example, a 500-Hz sinusoid has a period of 2 ms, and the intervals between nerve spikes evoked by such a tone are close to 2, 4, 6, 8 ms, etc. A neuron does not fire in a regular manner, so there are not exactly 500, or 250, or 125 spikes/s. However, information about the period of the stimulating waveform is carried unambiguously in the temporal pattern of spikes of single neurons. Phase locking is just what would be expected as a result of the transduction process. Deflection of the stereocilia on the inner hair cells produced by movement of the BM toward the tectorial membrane leads to neural excitation. No excitation occurs when the BM moves in the opposite direction (this description is actually oversimplified; see, for example, Ruggero et al., 1986).

One way to demonstrate phase locking in a single auditory nerve fiber is to plot a histogram of the time intervals between successive nerve spikes. Several such interspike interval (ISI) histograms are shown in Fig. 1.20, for a neuron

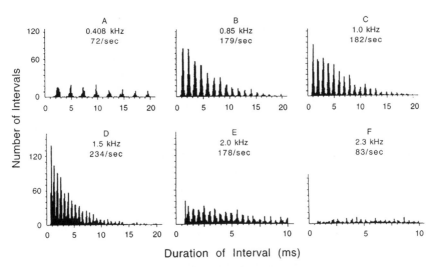

FIGURE 1.20 Interspike interval histograms for a single auditory neuron (in the squirrel monkey) with a CF of 1.6 kHz. The frequency of the stimulating tone and the mean response rate in spikes per second are indicated above each histogram. All tones had a level of 80 dB SPL and a duration of 1 s. Notice that the time scales in E and F differ from those in A–D. Redrawn from Rose et al. (1971), by permission of the authors.

with a CF of 1.6 kHz. For each of the different stimulating frequencies (from 0.408 to 2.3 kHz in this case), the intervals between nerve spikes lie predominantly at integer multiples of the period of the stimulating tone. These intervals are indicated by dots below each abscissa. Thus, although the neuron does not fire on every cycle of the stimulus, the distribution of time intervals between spikes depends closely on the frequency of the stimulus. Note that for the higher stimulus frequencies, such as 2 kHz, the first peak in the ISI histogram does not occur at the period corresponding to the frequency (e.g., 0.5 ms). This happens because of an effect called neural refractoriness. When a spike has occurred, there is a period called the absolute refractory period, typically lasting 0.5–0.75 ms, during which another spike cannot be generated. Following that, there is a period called the relative refractory period, lasting 2–3 ms, during which a spike can occur, but with reduced probability.

Phase locking does not occur over the whole range of audible frequencies. The upper frequency limit lies at about 4–5 kHz, although it varies somewhat across species (Rose et al., 1968; Palmer and Russell, 1986), and weak phase locking may occur for frequencies up to 10 kHz (Heinz et al., 2001a). The upper limit is not determined by the maximum spike rates of neurons. Rather, it is determined by the precision with which the initiation of a nerve impulse is linked to a particular phase of the stimulus. There is variability in the exact instant of initiation of a nerve impulse. At high frequencies this variability becomes comparable with the period of the waveform, so above a certain frequency the spikes are "smeared out" over the whole period of the waveform, instead of occurring primarily at a particular phase. This smearing is responsible for the loss of phase locking above 4–5 kHz.

There is still considerable controversy over the extent to which information carried in the timing of neural impulses is actually used in perceptual processes. It is accepted that the ability to localize sounds depends in part on a comparison of the temporal information from the two ears, but the relevance of temporal information in masking and in pitch perception is still hotly debated. These problems are discussed in detail in Chapters 3 and 6.

7F TWO-TONE SUPPRESSION

So far I have discussed the responses of auditory neurons to single pure tones. One of the reasons for using pure tones as stimuli is that given earlier: if the peripheral auditory system could be characterized as approximately linear, then the response to a complex stimulus could be calculated as the linear sum of the responses to the sinusoidal (Fourier) components of the stimulus (see Section 3). Although neural responses themselves are clearly nonlinear (showing, for example, thresholds and saturation), they sometimes behave as though the system driving them were linear. In other situations the behavior is clearly nonlinear, so it is necessary to investigate directly the neural responses to complex stimuli to understand how the properties of these complex stimuli are coded in the auditory system.

Auditory nerve responses to two tones have been investigated by a number of workers. One striking finding is that the tone-driven activity of a single fiber in response to one tone can be suppressed by the presence of a second tone. This was originally called two-tone inhibition (Sachs and Kiang, 1968), although the term "two-tone suppression" is now generally preferred, since the effect does not appear to involve neural inhibition. The effect is illustrated in Fig. 1.21. Typically the phenomenon is investigated by presenting a tone at, or close to, the CF of a neuron and at a level about 10 dB above the absolute threshold of the neuron for a CF tone; the frequency and level of this tone are

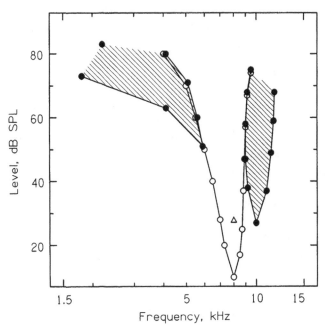

FIGURE 1.21   The open circles show the tuning curve (threshold versus frequency) of a single neuron with a CF at 8 kHz. The neuron was stimulated with a tone at CF and just above threshold (indicated by the open triangle). A second tone was then added, and its frequency and intensity were varied. Any tone within the shaded areas bounded by the solid circles reduced the response to the tone at CF by 20% or more. These are the suppression areas. Data from Arthur et al. (1971).

indicated by the triangle in Fig. 1.21. A second tone is then presented, its frequency and intensity are varied, and the effects of this on the response of the neuron are noted. When the frequency and intensity of the second tone fall within the excitatory area bounded by the tuning curve, it usually produces an increase in spike rate. However, when it falls just outside that area, the response to the first tone is reduced or suppressed. The effect is usually greatest in two suppression regions at frequencies slightly above or below the area of the neuron's excitatory response to a single tone. The suppression effect begins and ceases very rapidly, within a few milliseconds of the onset and termination of the second tone (Arthur et al., 1971). Thus, it is unlikely that the suppression depends on neural interconnections. In fact, there is good evidence that suppression occurs on the BM (Rhode and Robles, 1974; Ruggero et al., 1992; Rhode and Cooper, 1993).

The effects of two-tone stimulation on temporal patterns of neural spikes have also been studied. For tones that are nonharmonically related, Hind et al. (1967) found that discharges may be phase locked to one tone, or to the other, or to both tones simultaneously. Which of these occurs is determined by the intensities of the two tones and their frequencies in relation to the "response area" of the fiber. When phase locking occurs to only one tone of a pair, each of which is effective when acting alone, the temporal structure of the response may be indistinguishable from that which occurs when that tone is presented alone. Further, the discharge rate may be similar to the value produced by that tone alone. Thus, the dominant tone appears to "capture" the response of the neuron. I discuss in Chapter 3 the possibility that this "capture effect" underlies the masking of one sound by another. Notice that the "capture effect" is probably another manifestation of two-tone suppression. The tone that is suppressed ceases to contribute to the pattern of phase locking, and the neuron responds as if only the suppressing tone was present. Suppression measured by phase locking can be shown even if the suppressor is within the excitatory response area of the neuron. However, suppression of response rate is normally seen only when the suppressor is outside or at the edges of the response area. Otherwise the suppressor itself evokes an excitatory response, and produces an increase in spike rate.

7G Phase Locking to Complex Sounds

Brugge et al. (1969) investigated auditory nerve responses to pairs of tones with simple frequency ratios (i.e., harmonically related tones). They drew the following conclusions: (1) auditory nerve fibers are excited by deflections of the BM in only one direction; (2) the spikes occur at times that correspond to displacement of the BM toward the tectorial membrane; and (3) the effective stimulating waveform can be approximated by addition of the component sinusoids, although the required amplitude and phase relations usually cannot be taken directly from the actual stimulus parameters. The results of Brugge *et al.* (1969) indicate that interactions between two tones may take place even when their frequencies are quite widely separated (frequency ratios between the two tones of up to 7:1 were used).

Javel (1980) investigated the responses of single auditory neurons to stimuli consisting of three successive high harmonics of a complex tone. He showed that a portion of the neural activity was phase locked to the overall repetition rate of the stimulus (equal to the absent fundamental frequency). I discuss in Chapter 6 the possibility that such temporal coding is responsible for the pitch of complex tones.

The responses of auditory neurons to clicks are closely related to the corresponding patterns of vibration that occur on the BM (see Section 6B and Fig. 1.13). Such responses are often plotted in the form of post-stimulus time (PST) histograms. To determine a PST histogram, the click is presented many times, and the numbers of spikes occurring at various times after the instant of click presentation are counted. These are then plotted in the form of a histogram, with the instant of click presentation being taken as time zero (see Fig. 1.22). It may be seen that spikes tend to occur at certain preferred

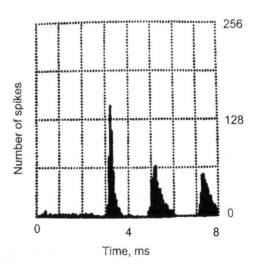

FIGURE 1.22 A post-stimulus-time (PST) histogram showing the number of nerve spikes occurring in response to a click, presented repeatedly, as a function of the time delay from the instant of presentation of the click. The time interval between peaks in the histogram corresponds to the reciprocal of the CF of the neuron (540 Hz). Redrawn from Kiang *et al.* (1965), by permission of the author and MIT Press.

intervals after the presentation of the click, as indicated by the peaks in the histogram. The multiple peaks presumably occur because the response of the BM to a click is a damped or decaying oscillation (see Fig. 1.13). Spikes tend to occur at a particular phase of this damped oscillation. The time intervals between the peaks correspond to the reciprocal of the CF of the neuron. If the polarity of the click is reversed (e.g., from rarefaction to condensation), the pattern is shifted in time, and peaks now appear where dips were located. The latency of the first peak is shortest for rarefaction clicks, again indicating that the excitation of hair cells occurs when the BM is deflected toward the tectorial membrane. These factors are particularly relevant to our ability to locate sounds of a transient character (see Chapter 7).

7H ADAPTATION

When a sound is first turned on, the neural spike rate in response to that sound is initially high, but rapidly declines (Kiang *et al.*, 1965). This effect, called adaptation, is illustrated by the PST histogram for a single neuron in Fig. 1.23 (data from Smith and Brachman, 1980). The signal was an 80-ms burst of broadband noise, which was turned on and off abruptly and had a

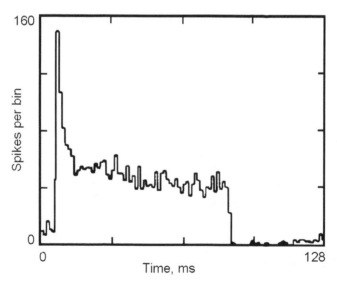

FIGURE 1.23   PST histogram for a single neuron in response to an 80-ms burst of broadband noise, which was turned on and off abruptly and had a level of 53 dB SPL. Data from Smith and Brachman (1980).

level of 53 dB SPL. Before the sound was turned on, the neuron showed a medium amount of spontaneous activity. When the sound was turned on, the spike rate increased rapidly and then declined, initially at a fast rate, and then at a slower rate. After the sound was turned off, the spike rate decreased below the spontaneous rate for a short time, and then recovered. Experiments using long sounds have shown that adaptation continues for several seconds or even minutes after the onset of the sound (Javel, 1996).

8 NEURAL RESPONSES AT HIGHER LEVELS IN THE AUDITORY SYSTEM

In the visual system it is known that neurons respond preferentially to certain features of the stimulus, such as lines of a particular orientation, movement, or color. There seems to be a hierarchy of specialized neural detectors (sometimes called feature detectors) (Hubel and Wiesel, 1968; Zeki, 2001). The information in the optic nerve is recoded and processed at different points in the visual system, and the responses of cortical neurons are very different from those in the optic nerve.

Much the same thing seems to happen in the auditory system, except that, at the level of the brainstem and cortex, it is much less clear what the crucial features of the stimulus are that will produce responses from a given neuron or set of neurons (Gaese, 2001; Kaas and Collins, 2001; Morosan et al., 2001). In addition, the anatomy of the auditory system is exceedingly complex, and many of the neural pathways within and between the various nuclei in the auditory system have yet to be investigated in detail. It is beyond the scope of this book to give more than the briefest description of recent research on the neurophysiology of higher centers in the auditory system. I briefly describe some properties of cortical neurons, and introduce other data later in the book, when they have some relevance to the mechanism or process under discussion. For reviews, see Palmer (1995) and Hall et al. (2003). Some of the more important neural centers or nuclei in the auditory pathway are illustrated in Fig. 1.24.

It is likely that the cortex is concerned with analyzing more complex aspects of stimuli than simple frequency or intensity. Many cortical neurons do not respond to steady pure tones at all, and the tuning properties of those that do respond to pure tones tend to differ from those found in primary auditory neurons. Some neurons show non-monotonic rate versus level functions, different neurons having different "best" sound levels (Pfingst and O'Conner, 1981). Abeles and Goldstein (1972) found three different types of tuning properties: narrow, broad, and multirange (responding to a number of

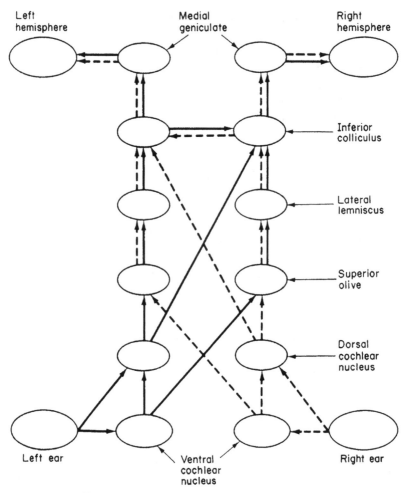

FIGURE 1.24   An illustration of the most important pathways and nuclei from the ear
to the auditory cortex. The nuclei illustrated are located in the brainstem.

preferred frequencies). They considered that this suggested a hierarchical
organization, with several narrow-range neurons converging on to one
multirange neuron. The cortex is tonotopically organized, but there are
multiple "maps", each devoted to analysis of specific stimulus features other
than frequency (Palmer, 1995; Cheung *et al.*, 2001; Tian *et al.*, 2001).

   Evans (1968), using mostly unanesthetized cats, reported that 20% of
cortical neurons respond only to complex stimuli such as clicks, bursts of
noise, or "kissing" sounds. Of those neurons that would respond to tonal

stimuli, 10% would only do so if the tone frequency was changing. Whitfield and Evans (1965) reported that frequency-modulated tones (see Fig. 3.7) were very effective stimuli for the majority of neurons responding to tones. Many neurons exhibited responses that were preferential to certain directions of frequency change. These neurons have been called "frequency sweep detectors". Some neurons respond preferentially to particular rates of modulation or to particular rates of frequency sweep. For other neurons, repetition rate and duration of tonal stimuli were critical parameters. Of all neurons studied, 17% responded only to the onset of a tonal stimulus, while 10% responded only to the termination and 2% responded to both onset and termination. Over 50% of neurons were preferentially or specifically sensitive to particular locations of the sound source in space. This general finding has been confirmed and extended by Brugge and Merzenich (1973) for restrained, unanesthetized monkeys. They found that many neurons were sensitive to interaural (between the ears) time or intensity differences. At low frequencies, spike count was a periodic function of interaural time delay. In several microelectrode penetrations, neighboring cells were most sensitive to the same interaural delay. Some cells were sensitive to small interaural shifts in SPL over a range of about 20 dB. Chapter 7 describes how the features of the stimuli to which these cells are responsive are crucial in our ability to localize sounds. Bendor and Wang (2005) described a region of the marmoset cortex in which neurons were tuned to specific pitches of sounds; see Chapter 6 for a description of the perception of pitch.

9 GENERAL SUMMARY AND CONCLUSIONS

Sound consists of variations in pressure as a function of time. It is often convenient to analyze a complex pressure wave into its sinusoidal frequency components. Periodic sounds can be shown by Fourier analysis to have line spectra containing harmonics of the fundamental component. This component has a frequency equal to the repetition rate of the whole complex. Nonperiodic sounds can be analyzed using the Fourier transform. They have continuous spectra, in which the energy is distributed over a frequency range, rather than being concentrated at discrete frequencies.

Sound levels are usually measured using the decibel scale. This is a logarithmic measure that expresses the ratio of two intensities. When the reference intensity is chosen to be 10^{-12} W/m^2 (equivalent to a sound pressure of 20 μPa), the level has units of dB sound pressure level (dB SPL). When the reference intensity is the absolute threshold for a given sound and a given subject, the units are dB sensation level (dB SL).

The auditory system is often conceived as being composed of a series of successive stages. A stage is linear if it satisfies the conditions of superposition and homogeneity. The response of a linear system to a complex input can be calculated as the sum of the responses to the individual sinusoidal components of that input. Some stages of the auditory system appear to be approximately linear (e.g., the middle ear), but others are distinctly nonlinear.

A filter is a device that passes certain frequency components, but attenuates others. Filters can be used both for the manipulation of stimuli and for their analysis. Highpass, lowpass, bandpass, and bandstop filters can be characterized by their cutoff frequencies, usually measured at the 3-dB-down points on their response functions, and by their slopes in dB/octave. The bandwidth of a bandpass filter is equal to the frequency range between the two 3-dB-down points.

Headphones vary in the frequency response that they produce at the eardrum. A few are designed to produce a flat response, some have a diffuse-field response, and some do not fit either of these categories.

The peripheral auditory system is composed of the outer, middle, and inner ear. The middle ear acts as an impedance-matching transformer to improve the efficiency of the transfer of energy between the air and the fluid-filled cochlea. A membrane called the basilar membrane runs along the length of the cochlea, dividing it into two chambers. Sounds produce traveling waves along the BM, and for each frequency there is a maximum in the pattern of vibration at a specific place. Low frequencies produce maximum vibration close to the apex, and high frequencies produce maximum vibration close to the base. The BM thus acts as a Fourier analyzer, or filter bank, splitting complex sounds into their component frequencies. The sharp tuning of the BM is physiologically vulnerable.

Movement of the BM causes a displacement of the stereocilia at the tips of the hair cells that lie within the organ of Corti on the BM, and this leads to action potentials within the nerve fibers of the auditory nerve. Most afferent nerve fibers contact the inner hair cells. The outer hair cells actively influence the vibration patterns on the BM, contributing to the sharp tuning and high sensitivity. They also seem to be involved in producing certain nonlinearities in the response and in the production of otoacoustic emissions. The action of the outer hair cells may be influenced by efferent neurons carrying signals from the brainstem.

Most nerve fibers of the auditory nerve show spontaneous activity in the absence of sound, but spontaneous spike rates vary markedly across neurons. Each neuron has a threshold, a level below which it does not respond, and a saturation level, above which increases in intensity produce no change in response. High spontaneous rates tend to be associated with low thresholds and small dynamic ranges. The threshold of a given fiber is lowest for one frequency, called the characteristic frequency (CF), and increases for frequencies on either side of this. The plot of threshold versus frequency is called the frequency-threshold curve or tuning curve. Single nerve fibers give tuning curves that are similar to those measured for single points on the BM.

The temporal pattern of the spikes within a given neuron can also carry information about the stimulus. Nerve spikes tend to occur at a particular phase of the stimulating waveform, an effect known as phase locking. Phase locking becomes very weak for frequencies above 4–5 kHz.

Sometimes the response of a single neuron to a sinusoidal tone may be reduced by a second tone, even when the second tone alone produces no response in the neuron. This is known as two-tone suppression, and it is an example of a nonlinear process in the peripheral auditory system.

Neural spike rates are relatively high when a sound is first turned on, but decrease over time, an effect called adaptation. Just after a sound is turned off, the spike rate may drop below the spontaneous rate.

The responses of neurons at higher levels of the auditory system have not been studied as thoroughly as responses in the auditory nerve. Some neurons in the auditory cortex appear to respond only to complex stimuli, or to stimuli with time-varying characteristics.

FURTHER RESOURCES

The following provide information on the physics of sound as related to hearing:

Green, D. M. (1978). *An Introduction to Hearing.* Hillsdale, NJ: Erlbaum.
Hartmann, W. M. (1997). *Signals, Sound, and Sensation.* Woodbury, New York: AIP Press.
Rosen, S., and Howell, P. (2010). *Signals and Systems for Speech and Hearing* (2nd Ed). Bingley, UK: Emerald.

Several animations relating to wave motion and beats can be found at:

http://paws.kettering.edu/~drussell/demos.html

The physiology of the auditory system is reviewed in:

Yates, G. K. (1995). Cochlear structure and function. In B. C. J. Moore (Ed.), *Hearing.* San Diego, CA: Academic Press.
Palmer, A. R. (1995). Neural signal processing. In B. C. J. Moore (Ed.), *Hearing.* San Diego, CA: Academic Press.
Pickles, J. O. (2008). *An Introduction to the Physiology of Hearing* (3rd Ed.). Bingley, UK: Emerald.

An extensive review of cochlear mechanics can be found in:

Robles, L., and Ruggero, M. A. (2001). Mechanics of the mammalian cochlea. *Physiol. Rev., 81,* 1305–1352.

A compact disc (CD) of auditory demonstrations has been produced by A. J. M. Houtsma, T. D. Rossing and W. M. Wagenaars (1987). Demonstrations 4, 5, 6, and 32 are especially relevant to this chapter. The CD is available from the Acoustical Society of America (ASA). The price is $23 for ASA members and $41 for non-members.

Animated illustrations of the auditory system can be found at:

http://www.neurophys.wisc.edu/animations

CHAPTER 2

Absolute Thresholds

1 INTRODUCTION

This chapter describes the ability of the auditory system to detect weak sounds when no other sounds are present. Chapter 3 describes the ability to detect one sound in the presence of one or more background sounds. In the great majority of studies of this type, the test signals have been sinusoidal tones.

2 ABSOLUTE THRESHOLDS FOR LONG-DURATION TONES

The absolute threshold of a sound is the minimum detectable level of that sound in the absence of any other external sounds. It is important to define the way in which the physical intensity of the threshold stimulus is measured, and two methods have been in common use. One method measures the sound pressure at some point close to the entrance of the ear canal or inside the ear canal, using a small "probe" microphone. Ideally, the measurement is made very close to the eardrum. In all cases it is necessary to specify the exact position of the microphone, since small changes in its position can markedly affect the results at high frequencies. The threshold so determined is called the minimum audible pressure (MAP). The sounds are usually, but not always, delivered by headphone.

The other method uses sounds delivered by a loudspeaker, usually in a large anechoic chamber (a room whose walls, floor, and ceiling are highly sound absorbing). The measurement of sound level is made after the listener is removed from the sound field, at the point that had been occupied by the center of the listener's head. The threshold determined in this way is called the minimum audible field (MAF).

Figure 2.1 shows estimates of the MAP, with sound level specified close to the eardrum, published by Killion (1978) and estimates of the MAF, published in an ISO standard (ISO 389-7, 2005). In both cases, the thresholds are plotted as a function of the frequency of a sinusoidal test signal with

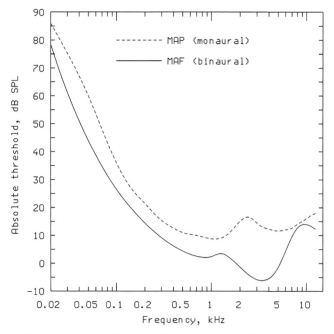

FIGURE 2.1 The minimum audible sound level plotted as a function of frequency. The solid curve shows the minimum audible field (MAF) for binaural listening published in an ISO standard (ISO 389-7, 2005). The dashed curve shows the minimum audible pressure (MAP) for monaural listening.

reasonably long duration (greater than 200 ms). Note that the MAP estimates are for monaural listening and the MAF estimates are for binaural listening. On average, thresholds are about 2 dB lower when two ears are used as against one. Both curves represent the average data from many young listeners with normal hearing. It should be noted, however, that individual subjects may have thresholds as much as 20 dB above or below the mean at a specific frequency and still be considered as "normal".

The "audibility curves" for the MAP and MAF are somewhat differently shaped, since the head, the pinna, and the meatus have an influence on the sound field. The MAP curve shows only minor peaks and dips (± 5 dB) for frequencies between about 0.2 and 13 kHz, whereas the MAF curve shows a distinct dip around 3–4 kHz and a peak around 8–9 kHz. The difference is derived mainly from a broad resonance produced by the meatus and pinna. Figure 2.2 shows the difference in sound level between the free field (i.e., the sound level measured in the absence of a head at the point corresponding to

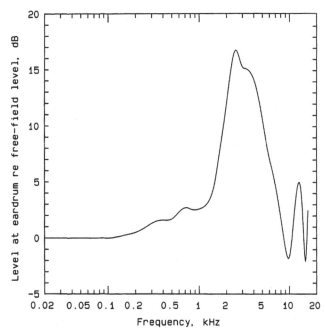

FIGURE 2.2 The difference between the sound level measured at the eardrum (for a sound coming from the frontal direction) and the sound level in the free field at the point corresponding to the center of the listener's head. Data from Shaw (1974).

the center of where the head would be) and the eardrum; data are taken from Shaw (1974). The sound level at the eardrum is enhanced markedly for frequencies in the range 1.5–6 kHz, with a maximum enhancement at 3 kHz of about 15 dB. The enhancement around 3 kHz occurs whatever the angle of incidence of the sound relative to the head. However, the pattern of results at higher frequencies depends markedly on the angle of incidence; see Chapter 7 for details. Also, the pattern of results for frequencies from 1000 Hz upward can vary markedly across individuals. The individual variability is greatest above 6 kHz.

For both the MAP and MAF, thresholds increase rapidly at very high and very low frequencies. This effect depends at least partly on the transmission characteristic of the middle ear. Transmission is most efficient for midrange frequencies and drops off markedly at very low and very high frequencies (Rosowski, 1991; Puria et al., 1997; Aibara et al., 2001). At low frequencies, MAPs, measured under headphones, are greater than MAFs, by between 5 and 10 dB. A number of scientists have shown that this is due to physiological noise of vascular origin, which is "trapped" within the meatus when earphones are worn (Anderson and Whittle, 1971; Soderquist and Lindsey, 1972). The level of this low-frequency "physiological noise" varies with the leakage of air around the headphone (this depends in part on headband pressure), with the volume of the subject's meatus, and with the strength of their heart beat. These sources of variability are lessened when circumaural headphones (which fit around the pinnae) rather than supra-aural headphones (which lie over and flatten the pinnae) are used. "Open-ear" headphones, which do not seal the ear canal, can considerably reduce low-frequency physiological noise.

The highest audible frequency varies considerably with the age of the subject (see Section 3). Young children can often hear tones as high as 20 kHz, but for most adults threshold rises rapidly above about 15 kHz. There seems to be no particular low-frequency limit to our hearing. Whittle et al. (1972) measured thresholds for frequencies from 50 down to 3.15 Hz and showed that their results formed a continuum with the results at higher frequencies. However, for the 3.15-Hz signal, the threshold level was about 120 dB SPL. It has been suggested (Johnson and Gierke, 1974) that sounds below about 16 Hz are not heard in the normal sense, but are detected by virtue of the distortion products (harmonics) that they produce after passing through the middle ear, or by vibration of the body. However, this view is not generally accepted (Møller and Pedersen, 2004). According to Møller and Pedersen (2004), sinusoids with frequencies below 20 Hz are generally detected via the ear rather than as vibrations on the body, but below 20 Hz the sound no longer appears tonal, but has a discontinuous character, and may be perceived as a feeling of pressure at the eardrums. The frequency of 20 Hz is close to the lowest frequency that evokes a pitch sensation for complex sounds (Krumbholz et al., 2000; Pressnitzer et al., 2001).

To a first approximation, it appears that the cochlea is equally sensitive to all frequencies above 500 Hz; the shapes of the MAF and MAP curves arise largely from the effects of transmission of sounds through the outer and middle ear (Puria et al., 1997; Moore et al., 1997; Glasberg and Moore, 2006). However, for frequencies below 500 Hz, the sensitivity of the cochlea appears to decrease somewhat, partly because of reduced amplification from the active mechanism, and partly because the helicotrema (an opening at the basal end of the cochlea that links the scala vestibuli and the scala tympani) reduces pressure variations across the basilar membrane at very low frequencies (Moore et al., 1997; Cheatham and Dallos, 2001; Jurado and Moore, 2010; Jurado et al., 2011).

In many practical situations our ability to detect faint sounds is limited not by our absolute sensitivity to those sounds but by the level of ambient noise. In other words, detection depends upon the masked threshold rather than the absolute threshold; see Chapter 3 for information about masking and masked thresholds. In such cases, the threshold as a function of frequency depends upon the character of the ambient noise (e.g., frequency content, level, and whether intermittent or continuous). The effects of these variables are discussed in detail in Chapter 3.

3 THE AUDIOGRAM AND HEARING LOSS

A third method of specifying absolute thresholds is commonly used when measuring hearing in clinical situations, for example, when a hearing impairment is suspected; thresholds are specified relative to the average threshold at each frequency for young, healthy listeners with "normal" hearing. In this case, the sound level is usually specified relative to standardized values produced by a specific earphone in a specific coupler. A coupler is a device that contains a cavity or series of cavities and a microphone for measuring the sound produced by the earphone. The preferred earphone varies from one country to another. For example, the Telephonics TDH49 or TDH50, or the Etymōtic Research ER3 or ER5 are often used in the UK and USA, while the Beyer DT48 is used in Germany. Thresholds specified in this way have units dB HL (hearing level) in Europe or dB HTL (hearing threshold level) in the USA. For example, a threshold of 40 dB HL at 1 kHz would mean that the person had a threshold that was 40 dB higher than "normal" at that frequency. In psychoacoustic work, thresholds are normally plotted with threshold increasing upward, as in Fig. 2.1.

However, in audiology, threshold elevations are shown as hearing losses, plotted downward. The average "normal" threshold is represented as a horizontal line at the top of the plot, and the degree of hearing loss is indicated by how much the threshold falls below this line. This type of plot is called an *audiogram*. Figure 2.3 compares an audiogram for a hypothetical hearing-impaired person with a "flat" hearing loss, with a plot of the same thresholds expressed as MAP values. Notice that, although the audiogram is flat, the corresponding MAP curve is not flat. Note also that thresholds in dB HL can be negative. For example, a threshold of -10 dB simply means that the individual is 10 dB more sensitive than the average.

Hearing losses may be broadly categorized into two main types. The first type, conductive hearing loss, occurs when there is a problem, usually in the middle ear, that reduces the transmission of sound to the cochlea. For example, viscous fluid may build up in the middle ear as a result of infection (otitis media), or the stapes may be immobilized as a result of growth of bone over the oval window (otosclerosis). Sometimes a conductive loss is produced by wax (cerumen) in the ear canal. In general, a conductive loss can be regarded as resulting in an attenuation of the incoming sound. The difficulty experienced by the sufferer can be well predicted from the elevation in absolute threshold. A hearing aid is usually quite effective in such cases, and surgery can also be effective.

The second type of hearing loss is called sensorineural hearing loss, although it is also inaccurately known as "nerve deafness". Sensorineural hearing loss most commonly arises from a defect in the cochlea, and is then known as a cochlear loss. However, sensorineural hearing loss may also arise as a result of defects in the auditory nerve or higher centers in the auditory system. Hearing loss due to neural disturbances occurring at a higher point in the auditory pathway than the cochlea is known as retrocochlear loss. The particular difficulties experienced by the sufferer, and the types of symptoms exhibited, depend on which part of the system is affected.

Often, the extent of the hearing loss increases with frequency, especially in the elderly. Hearing loss associated with aging is called presbyacusis (presbycusis in the USA). One measure of overall hearing loss is the threshold in dB HL averaged for the frequencies 0.5, 1, 2, and 4 kHz. The data presented by Davis (1995), based on a large scale survey in the UK, indicate that for listeners in the age range 61–71 years, 51% had a hearing loss greater than 20 dB and 11% had a hearing loss greater than 40 dB. For listeners in the age range 71–80 years, 74% had a hearing loss greater than 20 dB and 30% had a hearing loss greater than 40 dB. If the average threshold at high frequencies (4, 6, and 8 kHz) is used as a measure, the proportions are even greater. For example, for listeners in the age range 71–80 years, 98% had a hearing loss greater than 20 dB and 81% had a hearing loss greater than 40 dB.

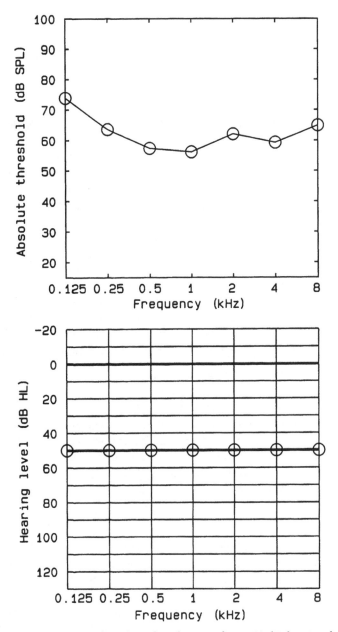

FIGURE 2.3 Comparison of a clinical audiogram for a 50-dB hearing loss at all frequencies (bottom) and the absolute threshold curve for the same hearing loss plotted in terms of the MAP (top).

People with sensorineural hearing loss often have difficulty in understanding speech, especially in noisy environments, and the condition is usually not completely alleviated by using a hearing aid (Moore, 2007). Most sensorineural losses cannot be treated through surgery.

4 TEMPORAL INTEGRATION AND MULTIPLE LOOKS

It has been known for many years (Exner, 1876) that the absolute thresholds of sounds depend upon duration. The studies of absolute threshold that were described earlier were all carried out with sounds, usually tone bursts, of relatively long duration. For durations exceeding about 500 ms, the sound intensity at threshold is roughly independent of duration. However, for durations less than about 200 ms, the sound intensity necessary for detection increases as duration decreases (remember that intensity is a measure of energy per unit time). Many scientists have investigated the relation between threshold and duration for tone pulses, over a wide range of frequencies and durations. The early work of Hughes (1946) and Garner and Miller (1947) indicated that, over a reasonable range of durations, the ear appears to integrate the energy of the stimulus over time in the detection of short-duration tone bursts. If this was true, the following formula would hold:

$$I \times t = \text{constant}$$

where, I is the threshold intensity for a tone pulse of duration t. In other words, the threshold would depend only on the total amount of energy in the stimulus and not on how that energy was distributed over time. The value of the constant would, however, vary with frequency, just as the absolute threshold for long-duration tones varies with frequency. In practice, the results are fitted better by the expression:

$$(I - I_L) \times t = I_L \times \tau = \text{constant}$$

where, I_L is the threshold intensity for a long-duration tone pulse. Notice that in this formula it is not the product of time and intensity that is constant, but the product of time and the amount by which the intensity exceeds the value I_L. Garner and Miller (1947) interpreted I_L as the minimum intensity that is an effective stimulus for the ear. They assumed that only intensities above this minimum value are integrated linearly by the ear.

Thresholds as a function of duration are often plotted on dB versus log-duration coordinates. When plotted in this way, linear energy integration is indicated by the data falling on a straight line with a slope of -3 dB per doubling of duration. Although the average data for a group of subjects typically give a slope close to this value, the slopes for individual subjects can differ significantly from −3 dB per doubling. This suggests that it would be unwise to ascribe too much significance to the average slope. It seems very unlikely that the auditory system would actually integrate stimulus energy; it is almost certainly neural activity that is integrated (Zwislocki, 1960; Penner, 1972). It may also be the case that the auditory system does not actually perform an operation analogous to integration. Rather, it may be that the threshold intensity decreases with increasing duration because a longer stimulus provides more detection opportunities (more chances to detect the stimulus through repeated sampling). This idea is sometimes called "multiple looks" (Viemeister and Wakefield, 1991).

An illustration that the detection of signals involves more than integration over a relatively long time interval is provided by an experiment of Viemeister and Wakefield (1991). They investigated the detection of either a single 1-kHz tone pip or two tone pips separated by 100 ms. The tone pips were presented in a background of noise, but the noise contained gaps at times when the signals might occur, as illustrated in Fig. 2.4 (dashed line). The tone pip (solid line) was presented during either the first gap or the second gap, or both gaps; within a block of trials, this did not change. They also explored the effect of changing the noise level between the two gaps. During the 50-ms interval centered between the gaps, the level was either increased by 6 dB (as in Fig. 2.4), left unchanged, or decreased by 6 dB; again, within a block of trials, this did not change. The

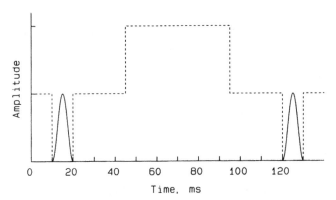

FIGURE 2.4   Schematic illustration of the stimuli used by Viemeister and Wakefield (1991). The envelope of the masker is denoted by a dashed line and that of the signal by a solid line. The signal could occur in the first gap in the noise, in the second gap, or in both gaps (as illustrated). The noise level between the gaps was either constant, decreased by 6 dB, or increased by 6 dB (as illustrated).

results showed that the threshold for detecting the pair of tone pips was about 2.5 dB lower than the threshold for detecting either the first tone pip or the second tone pip. Thus, subjects must have combined information from the two tone pips. If this was accomplished by simple integration over a relatively long time interval, the results should have been strongly affected by the level of the noise between the two gaps. In fact, the thresholds, both for the single tone pips and for the pairs of pips, were almost unaffected by the level of the noise between the two gaps. These results are inconsistent with the idea that detection of the tone pips was mediated by a simple long-term integration process.

There has been some controversy over whether temporal integration varies with frequency. Florentine *et al.* (1988) found that changes in threshold with stimulus duration were similar for frequencies of 250, 1000 and 4000 Hz. However, they found that the rate of change of threshold with duration was slightly less at 14,000 Hz than at the lower frequencies tested.

5 GENERAL CONCLUSIONS

Absolute threshold curves show that we are most sensitive to middle frequencies (1000–5000 Hz). At least part of this sensitivity arises from the action of the outer and middle ear. Our absolute sensitivity is such that our ability to detect faint sounds would normally be limited by environmental noises, rather than by limits in the system itself. There is, however, considerable variability between different individuals, and thresholds 20 dB on either side of the mean are still considered as "normal". Hearing losses with age are most marked at high frequencies.

For durations up to a few hundred milliseconds, the threshold for detecting sounds decreases with increasing duration. This has sometimes been interpreted as indicating that the auditory system acts as an energy integrator. However, it seems more likely that the change with duration occurs because a longer stimulus provides more chances to detect the stimulus through repeated sampling. This idea is sometimes called "multiple looks".

FURTHER READING

A comprehensive summary of how absolute thresholds are affected by age, sex, and social factors is presented in

Davis, A. (1995). *Hearing in Adults.* London: Whurr.

CHAPTER 3

Frequency Selectivity,
Masking, and the Critical Band

1 INTRODUCTION

This chapter is concerned with the frequency selectivity of the auditory system. This refers to the ability to resolve or separate the sinusoidal components in a complex sound. For example, if we listen to two tuning forks that are struck simultaneously, one tuned to C (262 Hz) and one tuned to A (440 Hz), we hear two separate tones, each with its own pitch. Frequency selectivity is also referred to as frequency resolution and frequency analysis. Frequency selectivity plays a role in many aspects of auditory perception. However, it is often demonstrated and measured by studying masking. It is a matter of everyday experience that one sound may be made inaudible by the presence of other sounds. Thus, music from a car radio may mask the sound of the car's engine, if the volume control is turned up sufficiently. Masking has been defined (ANSI, 1994a) as

1. The process by which the threshold of audibility for one sound is raised by the presence of another (masking) sound.

2. The amount by which the threshold of audibility of a sound is raised by the presence of another (masking) sound, expressed in decibels.

It has been known for many years that a signal is most easily masked by a sound having frequency components close to, or the same as, those of the signal (Mayer, 1894; Wegel and Lane, 1924). This led to the idea that our ability to separate the components of a complex sound depends, at least in part, on the frequency analysis that takes place on the BM. This idea will be elaborated later in this chapter. It also led to the idea that masking reflects the limits of frequency selectivity: if the selectivity of the ear is insufficient to separate the signal and the masker, then masking occurs. Thus, masking can be used to quantify frequency selectivity. Hence, much of this chapter will be devoted to studies of masking.

An important physical parameter that affects masking is time. Most of this chapter is devoted to simultaneous masking, in which the signal is presented at the same time as the masker. Later on I discuss forward masking, in which the signal is masked by a preceding masker, and backward masking, in which the masker follows the signal.

2 THE CRITICAL BAND CONCEPT AND THE POWER SPECTRUM MODEL

In a now-classic experiment, Fletcher (1940) measured the threshold for detecting a sinusoidal signal as a function of the bandwidth of a band-pass noise masker. The noise was always centered at the signal frequency, and the noise power density was held constant. Thus, the total noise power increased as the bandwidth increased. This experiment has been repeated several times since then. An example of the results is given in Fig. 3.1. The threshold of the signal increases at first as the noise bandwidth increases, but then flattens off; further increases in noise bandwidth do not change the signal threshold significantly, although the noise becomes markedly louder as its bandwidth increases.

To account for these results, Fletcher (1940), following Helmholtz (1863), suggested that the peripheral auditory system behaves as if it contains a bank of band-pass filters, with overlapping passbands. These filters are now called the "auditory filters". Fletcher thought that the BM provided the basis for the auditory filters. Each location on the BM responds to a limited range of frequencies, so each different point corresponds to a filter with a different center frequency. More recent data are broadly consistent with this point of view (Moore, 1986; Evans et al., 1989).

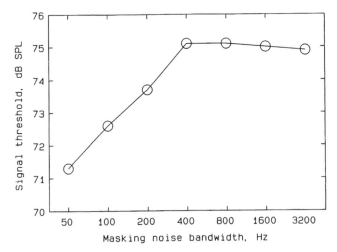

FIGURE 3.1 The threshold for detecting a 2000-Hz sinusoidal signal plotted as a function of the bandwidth of a noise masker centered at 2000 Hz. The threshold of the signal at first increases with increasing masker bandwidth and then remains constant. Based on unpublished data obtained in my laboratory.

When trying to detect a signal in a noise background, the listener is assumed to make use of an auditory filter with a center frequency close to that of the signal. This filter passes the signal but removes a great deal of the noise. Only the components in the noise that pass through the filter have any effect in masking the signal. It is usually assumed that the threshold for the signal is determined by the amount of noise passing through the filter; specifically, threshold is assumed to correspond to a certain signal-to-noise ratio at the output of the filter. This set of assumptions has come to be known as the "power spectrum model" of masking (Patterson and Moore, 1986), because the stimuli are represented by their long-term power spectra, that is, the relative phases of the components and the short-term fluctuations in the masker are ignored. It will be shown later that the assumptions of this model do not always hold, but the model works well in many situations.

In the band-widening experiment described above, increases in noise bandwidth result in more noise passing through the auditory filter, provided the noise bandwidth is less than the filter bandwidth. However, once the noise bandwidth exceeds the filter bandwidth, further increases in noise bandwidth do not increase the noise passing through the filter. Fletcher called the bandwidth at which the signal threshold ceased to increase the "critical bandwidth", which is often abbreviated as CB.

In analyzing the results of his experiment, Fletcher made a simplifying assumption. He assumed that the shape of the auditory filter could be approximated as a simple rectangle, with a flat top and vertical edges. For such a filter, all components within the passband of the filter are passed equally, and all components outside the passband are removed. If the auditory filter were rectangular, the width of its passband would be equal to the CB described above. The term "critical band" is often used to refer to this hypothetical rectangular filter. In fact, Fletcher was well aware that the filters in the ear are not rectangular in shape. However, the assumption of a rectangular shape is convenient for calculating the masking produced by a broadband noise.

Fletcher pointed out that the value of the CB could be estimated indirectly, by measuring the threshold of a tone in broadband white noise, given the following hypotheses:

1. Only a narrow band of frequencies surrounding the tone—those falling within the CB—contribute to the masking of the tone.
2. When the noise just masks the tone, the power of the tone, P, divided by the power of the noise inside the CB is a constant, K.

The value of K is often regarded as a measure of the efficiency of the detection process following the auditory filter. Its value may vary from one person to another.

As described in Chapter 1, noise power is usually specified in terms of the power in a band of frequencies 1 Hz wide (say from 1000 to 1001 Hz). This is called the noise power density and is denoted by the symbol N_o. For a white noise, N_o is independent of frequency, so the total noise power falling in a CB that is W Hz wide is $N_o \times W$. According to Fletcher's second hypothesis,

$$P/(W \times N_o) = K$$

and so

$$W = P/(K \times N_o).$$

Given that the value of N_o is known, by measuring P and by estimating K it is possible to estimate W.

The first hypothesis follows directly from Fletcher's experiment, although, as will be explained later, it is only an approximation. To estimate the value of the constant K, Fletcher measured the threshold for a tone in a band of noise whose width was less than the estimated CB. In this case, K equals the ratio of the power of the tone to the power of the noise, because all of the noise passes through the auditory filter. Fletcher estimated that K was equal to 1, so the value of W should be equal to P/N_o. The ratio P/N_o is now usually known as the critical ratio. Unfortunately, Fletcher's estimate of K has turned out not to be accurate. More recent experiments show that K is typically about 0.4 (Scharf, 1970), although its exact value depends on the method used to measure threshold. Thus, at most frequencies, the critical ratio is about 0.4 times the value of the CB estimated by more direct methods such as the band-widening experiment. However, K varies somewhat with center frequency, so the critical ratio does not give a correct indication of how the CB varies with center frequency (Patterson and Moore, 1986; Peters and Moore, 1992a,b; Moore et al., 1997). Also, K varies across individuals, so the critical ratio does not give a direct estimate of the CB for individuals.

Since Fletcher first described the CB concept, many different experiments have shown that listeners' responses to complex sounds differ according to whether the stimuli have bandwidths greater than or less than the CB. Furthermore, these different experiments give reasonably similar estimates both of the absolute width of the CB and of the way the CB varies as a function of frequency. However, there are some significant discrepancies, particularly at low frequencies. Many of the recent estimates of the CB are based on the results of masking experiments, which are used to calculate the equivalent rectangular bandwidth (ERB) of the auditory filter (see Chapter 1, Section 4, and this Chapter, Section 3B). The ERB may be regarded as a measure of the CB. However, to distinguish the relatively recent measurements from the "older" ones (Zwicker, 1961), the recent ones will be described as ERBs.

Fletcher was well aware that the auditory filter was not rectangular. He knew that a tone or narrow band of noise can mask another tone for frequency separations considerably exceeding the CB. The critical band should be considered as a filter with a rounded top and sloping edges; the CB then becomes a measure of the "effective" bandwidth of this filter. I next describe some attempts to measure the characteristics of the auditory filter, or, in other words, to derive the shape of the auditory filter.

3 ESTIMATING THE SHAPE OF THE AUDITORY FILTER

Most methods for estimating the shape of the auditory filter at a given center frequency are based on the assumptions of the power spectrum model of masking. The detection threshold of a signal whose frequency is fixed is measured in the presence of a masker whose spectral content is varied. It is assumed, as a first approximation, that the signal is detected using the single auditory filter that is centered on the frequency of the signal and that threshold corresponds to a constant ratio of signal power to masker power at the output of that filter. The methods described below are both based on these assumptions.

3A Psychophysical Tuning Curves

One method involves a procedure that is analogous in many ways to the determination of a neural tuning curve, and the resulting function is often called a psychophysical tuning curve (PTC). To determine a PTC, the signal is fixed in level, usually at a very low level, say, 10 dB SL. The masker can be either a sinusoid or a narrow band of noise. When a sinusoid is used, beats occur between the signal and the masker, and these can provide a cue as to the presence of the signal. The effectiveness of this cue varies with the frequency separation of the signal and the masker, because slow beats (which occur at small frequency separations) are more easily detected than rapid beats (see Chapter 5). This varying sensitivity to beats violates one of the assumptions of the power spectrum model of masking. This problem can be reduced by using a narrowband noise masker, because such a masker has inherent fluctuations in amplitude that make it harder to detect the beats (Dau *et al.*, 1997a; Moore *et al.*, 1998). Thus, noise is generally preferred (Kluk and Moore, 2004).

For each of several masker frequencies, the level of the masker needed just to mask the signal is determined. Because the signal is at a low level, it is assumed that it produces activity primarily at the output of one auditory filter. It is assumed further that, at threshold, the masker produces a constant output from that filter, in order to mask the fixed signal. Thus, the PTC indicates the masker level required to produce a fixed output from the auditory filter as a function of frequency. Normally, the shape of a physical filter is determined by plotting the output from the filter for an input varying in frequency and fixed in level (see Chapter 1, Section 4 and Fig. 1.6). However, if the filter is linear, the two methods give the same result; on a dB scale, one is an inverted version of the other. Thus, assuming linearity, the shape of the auditory filter can be obtained simply by inverting the PTC. Examples of some PTCs are given in Fig. 3.2.

The PTCs in Fig. 3.2 are very similar in general form to the neural tuning curves in Fig. 1.15. Remember that the neural tuning curves are obtained by determining the level of a tone required to produce a fixed output from a single neuron, as a function of the tone's frequency. The similarities in the procedures and the results encourage the belief that the basic frequency selectivity of the auditory system is established at the level of the auditory nerve and that the shape of the human auditory filter (or PTC) corresponds to the shape of the neural tuning curve. However, there is a need for caution in reaching this conclusion. In the determination of the neural tuning curve, only one tone is present at a time, whereas for the PTC, the masker and the signal are presented simultaneously. This turns out to be an important point, and I return to it later.

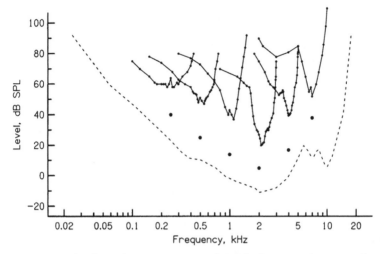

FIGURE 3.2 Psychophysical tuning curves (PTCs) determined in simultaneous masking using sinusoidal signals at 10 dB SL. For each curve, the solid circle below it indicates the frequency and the level of the signal. The masker was a sinusoid that had a fixed starting phase relationship to the 50-ms signal. The masker level required for threshold is plotted as a function of masker frequency on a logarithmic scale. The dashed line shows the absolute threshold for detecting the signal. Data from Vogten (1974).

Another problem is that the neural tuning curve is derived from a single neuron, whereas the PTC inevitably involves activity over a group of neurons with slightly different CFs. It may be the case that the listener does not attend to just one filter. When the masker frequency is above the signal frequency, the listener would do better to attend to a filter centered just below the signal frequency. Since the auditory filters have relatively flat tops and sloping edges, the "off-frequency" filter will considerably attenuate the masker at the filter output, while only slightly attenuating the signal. By using this filter, the listener can improve performance. This is known as "off-frequency listening" or "off-place listening", and there is now good evidence that humans do indeed listen "off frequency" when it is advantageous to do so. The result of off-frequency listening is that the PTC has a sharper tip than would be obtained if only one auditory filter was involved (Johnson-Davies and Patterson, 1979; O'Loughlin and Moore, 1981).

One way to limit off-frequency listening is to add to the masker a fixed, low-level noise with a spectral notch centered at the signal frequency (O'Loughlin and Moore, 1981; Moore et al., 1984a). Such a masker should make it disadvantageous to use an auditory filter whose center frequency is shifted much from the signal frequency. The effect of using such a noise, in addition to the variable narrowband masker, is to broaden the tip of the PTC; the slopes of the skirts are relatively unaffected.

3B THE NOTCHED-NOISE METHOD

Patterson (1976) has described an ingenious method of determining auditory filter shape that prevents off-frequency listening. The method is illustrated in Fig. 3.3. The signal (indicated by the bold vertical line) is fixed in frequency, and the masker is a noise with a bandstop or notch centered at the signal frequency. The deviation of each edge of the noise from the center frequency is denoted by Δf. The width of the notch is varied, and the threshold of the signal is determined as a function of notch width. Since the notch is placed symmetrically around the signal frequency, the method cannot reveal asymmetries in the auditory filter, and the analysis assumes that the filter is symmetric on a linear frequency scale. This assumption appears reasonable, at least for the top part of the filter and at moderate sound levels, because PTCs are quite symmetric around the tips (when plotted on a linear frequency scale). For a signal symmetrically placed in a bandstop noise (BSN), the optimum signal-to-masker ratio at the output of the auditory filter is achieved with a filter centered at the signal frequency, as illustrated in Fig. 3.3. Using a filter not centered at the signal frequency reduces the amount of noise passing

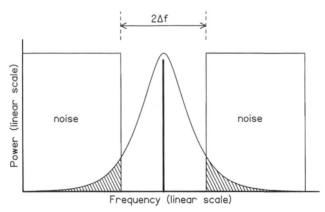

FIGURE 3.3 Schematic illustration of the technique used by Patterson (1976) to determine the shape of the auditory filter. The threshold for detecting the sinusoidal signal is measured as a function of the width of a spectral notch in the noise masker. The amount of noise passing through the auditory filter centered at the signal frequency is proportional to the shaded areas.

through the filter from one of the noise bands, but this is more than offset by the increase in noise from the other band.

As the width of the spectral notch is increased, less and less noise passes through the auditory filter. Thus, the threshold of the signal drops. The amount of noise passing through the auditory filter is proportional to the area under the filter in the frequency range covered by the noise. This is shown as the shaded areas in Fig. 3.3. Assuming that threshold corresponds to a constant signal-to-masker ratio at the output of the filter, the change in signal threshold with notch width indicates how the area under the filter varies with Δf. The area under a function between certain limits is obtained by integrating the value of the function over those limits. Hence by differentiating the function relating threshold to Δf, the relative response of the filter at that value of Δf is obtained. In other words, the relative response of the filter for a given deviation, Δf, from the center frequency is equal to the slope of the function relating signal threshold to notch width, at that value of Δf.

A typical auditory filter derived using this method is shown in Fig. 3.4. The figure shows the relative response of the filter to different input frequencies,

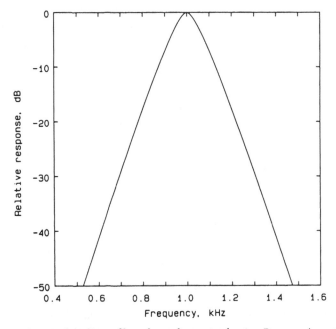

FIGURE 3.4 A typical auditory filter shape determined using Patterson's method. The filter is centered at 1 kHz. The relative response of the filter (in dB) is plotted as a function of frequency.

assuming that the gain of the filter at its tip is 0 dB. The gain is defined as the output level minus the input level, when both are expressed in dB (see Chapter 1, Section 3). The filter has a rounded top and quite steep skirts. Unlike a rectangular filter, a filter with this shape cannot be completely specified with a single number, the CB. However, some sort of summary statistic is useful, and one common measure is the bandwidth of the filter at which the response has fallen by a factor of two in power, that is, by 3 dB (see Chapter 1, Section 4). The 3-dB bandwidths of the auditory filters derived using Patterson's method are typically between 10% and 15% of the center frequency. An alternative measure is the ERB (see Chapter 1, Section 4). The ERBs of the auditory filters derived using Patterson's method are typically between 11% and 17% of the center frequency. In what follows, the mean value of the ERB of the auditory filter measured using moderate sound levels for young people with normal hearing is denoted ERB_N. An equation describing the value of the ERB_N as a function of center frequency, F, is (Glasberg and Moore, 1990):

$$ERB_N = 24.7(4.37F + 1)$$

In this equation, the value of ERB_N is specified in Hz, but F is in kHz.

Figure 3.5 shows the value of ERB_N estimated using the notched-noise method in many different laboratories. It also shows the function defined by the above equation, which fits the data well, and the "old" CB function (Zwicker, 1961; Zwicker and Terhardt, 1980), which fits markedly less well at low frequencies. It should be noted that, when the "old" function was proposed (Zwicker, 1961), the data at low frequencies were sparse, and the estimates of the CB were largely based on "indirect" measures such as the critical ratio (Section 2) and the critical modulation frequency (CMF, described later). Moore and Sek (1995a) have argued that most "direct" measures show a continuing decrease in bandwidth as the center frequency decreases below 500 Hz.

Sometimes it is useful to plot psychoacoustical data on a frequency scale related to ERB_N. Essentially, the value of ERB_N is used as the unit of frequency. For example, the value of ERB_N for a center frequency of 1 kHz is about 130 Hz, and so an increase in frequency from 935 to 1065 Hz represents a step of one ERB_N. This scale is called the ERB_N-number scale. A formula relating ERB_N number to frequency is (Glasberg and Moore, 1990):

$$ERB_N \text{ number} = 21.4 \log_{10}(4.37F + 1),$$

where F is frequency in kHz. This scale is conceptually similar to the Bark scale proposed by Zwicker and Terhardt (1980) and the mel scale of pitch (described in Chapter 6, Section 3E), although it differs somewhat in numerical values. For brevity, ERB_N number is denoted by the unit "Cam",

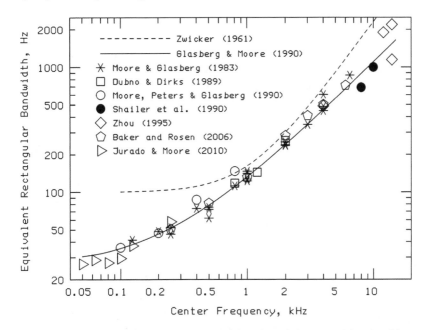

FIGURE 3.5   The dashed curve shows the "old" value of the critical bandwidth as a function of frequency (Zwicker, 1961). The solid curve shows the value of ERB_N of the auditory filter as a function of frequency. The solid curve was obtained by combining the results of several experiments using Patterson's notched-noise method of estimating the auditory filter shape. Data are taken from Moore and Glasberg (1983b), Dubno and Dirks (1989), Moore et al. (1990), Shailer et al. (1990), Zhou (1995), Baker and Rosen (2006, data for the signal level of 30 dB SPL), and Jurado and Moore (2010).

following a suggestion of Hartmann (1997b). For example, a frequency of 1000 Hz corresponds to 15.59 Cams on the ERB_N-number scale.

Patterson's method has been extended to include conditions where the spectral notch in the noise is placed asymmetrically about the signal frequency. This allows the measurement of any asymmetry in the auditory filter, but the analysis of the results is more difficult and has to take off-frequency listening into account (Patterson and Nimmo-Smith, 1980). It is beyond the scope of this book to give details of the method of analysis; the interested reader is referred to Patterson and Moore (1986), Moore and Glasberg (1987), Glasberg and Moore (1990), Baker and Rosen (2006), and Unoki et al. (2006).

If the auditory filter were linear, then its shape would not vary with the level of the noise used to measure it. However, this is not the case. The filter becomes broader with increasing level, especially on the low-frequency side. One way of conceptualizing the changes with level is based on the idea that there is a shallow "tail" filter, determined by the "passive" properties of the BM and surrounding structures, and a sharper "tip" filter dependent on the active mechanism in the cochlea (Glasberg and Moore, 2000; Lopez-Poveda and Meddis, 2001; Zhang et al., 2001; Unoki et al., 2006). At low sound levels, the active component has a strong influence, and sharp tuning is observed, at least around the "tip" of the filter. As the level is increased, the gain of the active tip filter decreases and the passive filter plays a greater role. Thus, the tuning becomes broader with increasing level.

There has been some controversy about what aspect of stimulus level determines the filter shape. Often, auditory filter shapes have been measured using a fixed noise power density, based on the implicit assumption that the masker level determines the shape of the filter. When several fixed noise levels are used, the data for each noise level being analyzed separately, the derived filter tends to become broader on the low-frequency side as the level increases (Lutfi and Patterson, 1984; Patterson and Moore, 1986; Moore and Glasberg, 1987; Glasberg and Moore, 1990; Rosen et al., 1992, 1998); changes on the high-frequency side are smaller and are not consistent across studies.

Rosen and his coworkers (Rosen et al., 1992, 1998; Baker et al., 1998; Baker and Rosen, 2006) have proposed a method for deriving auditory filter shapes from notched-noise data in which several different levels are used within the same experiment. They found that the data were fitted better when it was assumed that the filter shape depended on the signal level rather than the masker spectrum level. The broadening of the low-frequency side of the filter with increasing level could be well described by a change in the gain of the tip filter relative to that of the tail filter. Glasberg and Moore (2000) conducted a similar analysis, where the filter shape was assumed to depend either on the signal level or on the masker level per ERB_N. The data were fitted best when the gain of the tip filter was assumed to be a function of the signal level. The filter shapes showed a level dependence that qualitatively resembled the level dependence of filtering on the BM. The maximum gain of the tip filter tended to increase with increasing center frequency up to 1 kHz, but to remain roughly constant for higher frequencies.

Figure 3.6 is based on the analyses of Glasberg and Moore (2000). It illustrates how the shape of the auditory filter centered at 2000 Hz varies with the frequency of a sinusoidal input, for several different input levels. The upper panel shows the responses of the filters plotted as normalized gain, that is, the gain is assumed to be 0 dB at the tip. In this panel, the gain for frequencies well below the center frequency is negative (the output level is lower than the input level), but the gain at these frequencies *increases* with increasing level. However, it would be more in accord with what is observed

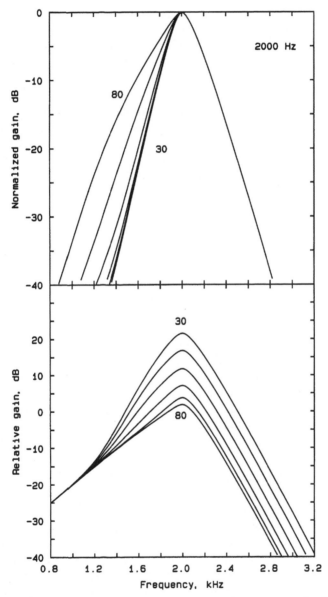

FIGURE 3.6 The shape of the auditory filter centered at 2000 Hz, for levels of a sinusoidal input ranging from 30 dB to 80 dB SPL. The upper panel shows the output of the filter when the output is normalized to have a gain at the tip of 0 dB for every input level. The lower panel shows the filter shapes as gains without this normalization, but assuming that the gain at the tip approaches 0 dB for high-input levels.

on the BM to assume that the gain is fixed for frequencies well below the center frequency and that the gain at the center frequency decreases with increasing level (Ruggero *et al.*, 1997; Rosen *et al.*, 1998). Recall that, at least for high CFs, the input-output function of the BM is linear for frequencies well below CF, but is compressive for frequencies close to CF.

The lower panel in Fig. 3.6 shows filter responses in terms of gain, assuming that the gain of the tip filter approaches 0 dB for a signal at its center frequency for high input levels. When plotted in this way, the gain for input frequencies well below the center frequency is invariant with level, which is consistent with what is observed on the BM. The gain at the center frequency decreases with increasing input level, consistent with a progressively reducing gain from the active mechanism with increasing level.

4 OTHER PHENOMENA REFLECTING AUDITORY FILTERING

Effects reflecting auditory filtering have been observed in many different types of experiments. Some of these are described later. When they were first conducted, many of these experiments were thought to provide direct estimates of the auditory filter bandwidth. However, most of them do not provide accurate estimates of ERB_N, because of various complicating factors (discussed later). Nevertheless, they are described here because the results are undoubtedly influenced by the filtering that takes place in the cochlea. One other phenomenon that depends on auditory filtering, the effect of bandwidth on loudness, is discussed in Chapter 4.

4A THE THRESHOLD OF COMPLEX SOUNDS

When several sinusoidal tones are presented together, a sound may be heard even when each tone in isolation would be below threshold. Gässler (1954) measured the threshold for detecting multitone complexes consisting of evenly spaced sinusoids. The complexes were presented both in quiet and in a special background noise, chosen to give the same masked threshold for each component in the signal. As the number of tones in a complex was increased, the threshold, specified in terms of total energy, remained constant until the overall spacing of the tones reached a certain value, assumed to correspond to the CB. Thereafter the threshold increased. The CB for a center frequency of 1000 Hz was estimated to be about 180 Hz. Gässler suggested that if all of the components in a complex sound fall within the passband of a single auditory filter, the energies of the individual components are summed, and the threshold for detecting that sound is determined by the summed energy. When the components are distributed over a wider frequency range than this, then only information from a single auditory filter is used, and detection is less good.

More recent data are not in agreement with those of Gässler. For example, Spiegel (1981) measured the threshold for detecting a noise signal of variable bandwidth centered at 1000 Hz in a broadband background noise masker. The threshold for detecting the signal, plotted as a function of bandwidth, did not show a break point corresponding to the CB, but increased monotonically as the bandwidth increased beyond 50 Hz. Spiegel suggested that the ear is capable of integration over bandwidths much greater than the auditory filter bandwidth. Other results clearly confirm this (Buus et al., 1986; Langhans and Kohlrausch, 1992). For example, Buus et al. (1986) showed that multiple widely spaced sinusoidal components presented in background noise were more detectable than any of the individual components.

4B Two-Tone Masking

Zwicker (1954) measured the threshold for detecting a narrow band of noise, of center frequency f, in the presence of two sinusoidal tones, with frequencies on either side of f. The bandwidth of the noise signal was typically about one CB (160 Hz for $f = 1000$ Hz). He increased the frequency separation of the two tones, starting with a small separation, and found that threshold for detecting the noise signal remained constant until the separation reached a critical value, after which it fell sharply. He took this critical value to be an estimate of the CB. Unfortunately the interpretation of this experiment is complicated. One problem is that the lower of the two tones may interact with the noise band to produce combination products; these are frequency components not present in the stimulus applied to the ear, and they result largely from a nonlinear process in the cochlea (see Chapter 1, Section 6B and Chapter 6, Section 5A). The listener may detect these combination products even though the signal itself is inaudible. When precautions are taken to mask the distortion products, then the threshold for detecting the signal does not show an abrupt decrease, but decreases smoothly with increasing frequency separation between the two tones (Patterson and Henning, 1977; Glasberg et al., 1984). This is consistent with the idea that the auditory filters have rounded tops and sloping skirts, rather than being rectangular. For an extensive review of results obtained using two-tone maskers, the reader is referred to Rabinowitz et al. (1980).

4C Sensitivity to Phase and the Critical Modulation Frequency

The sounds encountered in everyday life often change in frequency and amplitude from moment to moment. In the laboratory, the perception of such sounds is often studied using either frequency-modulated or amplitude-modulated sine waves. Such waves consist of a carrier frequency (a sine wave) upon which some other signal is impressed. With sinusoidal amplitude modulation (AM), the carrier's amplitude is varied so as to follow the magnitude of a modulating sine wave, while the carrier frequency remains unchanged. With sinusoidal frequency modulation (FM), the carrier's instantaneous frequency is varied in proportion to the modulating signal's magnitude, but the amplitude remains constant. The two types of waveform are illustrated in Fig. 3.7. The expression describing an amplitude-modulated sine wave with carrier frequency f_c and modulating frequency g is:

$$(1 + m \sin 2\pi g t) \sin 2\pi f_c t$$

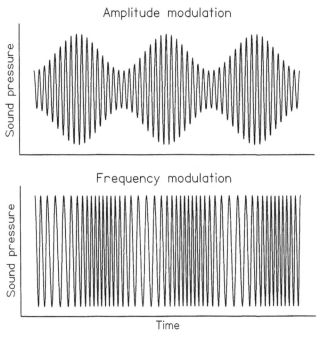

FIGURE 3.7 Waveforms of an amplitude-modulated wave (upper trace) and a frequency-modulated wave (lower trace).

where t is time, and m is a constant determining the amount of modulation; m is referred to as the modulation index. When $m = 1$, the wave is said to be 100% modulated.

The corresponding expression describing a frequency-modulated sine wave is:

$$\sin(2\pi f_c t - \beta \cos 2\pi g t)$$

where β is a constant determining the amount of modulation; β is usually referred to as the modulation index.

These complex waveforms can be analyzed into a series of sinusoidal components. For an AM wave, the results of the analysis are very simple: the spectrum contains just three frequency components with frequencies $f_c - g$, f_c and $f_c + g$. The components above and below the carrier frequency are often called "sidebands". For an FM wave, the spectrum often contains many components, but if β is small, then the FM wave can also be considered as consisting of three components with frequencies $f_c - g$, f_c and $f_c + g$. In some experiments, an approximation to an FM wave has been constructed by adding together three sinusoidal components with appropriate frequencies, amplitudes, and phases. Such an approximation is referred to as a quasi-frequency-modulated (QFM) wave. When the modulation indices for AM and QFM are numerically equal $(m = \beta)$, and when the carrier frequencies and modulation frequencies are the same, the components of an AM wave and a QFM wave are identical in frequency and amplitude, the only difference between them being in the relative phase of the components. If, then, the two types of wave are perceived differently, the difference is likely to arise from a sensitivity to the relative phase of the components. Equivalently, one might say that listeners are sensitive to the difference in time pattern of the sounds.

When g is relatively low, say 5 Hz, an AM sound is heard as a pure tone that is fluctuating in loudness, whereas an FM sound is heard as a pure tone that is fluctuating in pitch. Thus, we are clearly sensitive to the difference in relative phase of the components. As g is increased, the sensation changes to one of "roughness" for AM tones (Terhardt, 1974a) and a rapid "trill" or "vibrato" for FM tones (Miller and Heise, 1950; Gockel et al., 2001). However, when g is sufficiently large, the sensation becomes "smooth" once more. At this point, the sinusoidal components are resolved in the ear, and it may be possible to hear two or three pitches corresponding to the frequencies of the individual components (see later for more information about the ability to "hear out" individual components in complex tones). When the components are resolved, we appear to be relatively insensitive to the relative phases of the components, and AM and QFM tones sound very similar.

Zwicker (1952), Schorer (1986), and Sek (1994) have measured one aspect of the perception of AM and QFM tones, namely, the just-detectable amounts of AM or FM, for various rates of modulation. They found that, for high rates of modulation, where the frequency components were widely spaced, the detectability of AM and QFM was equal when the components in each type of wave were of equal amplitude ($m = \beta$). In this case, the detection threshold is probably determined by the ability to detect one or both of the spectral sidebands. However, for low rates of modulation, when all three components fell within a narrow frequency range, AM could be detected when the relative levels of the sidebands were lower than for a wave with a just-detectable amount of QFM ($m < \beta$). This is illustrated in the upper panel of Fig. 3.8 for a carrier frequency of 1000 Hz. Thus, for small frequency separations of the

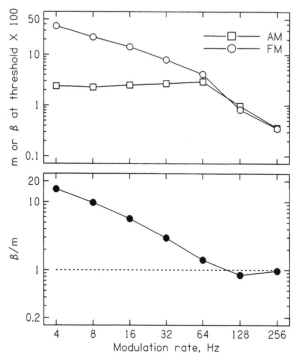

FIGURE 3.8 The upper panel shows thresholds for detecting sinusoidal amplitude modulation or frequency modulation of a 1000-Hz carrier, expressed in terms of the respective modulation indices, m and β, and plotted as a function of modulation rate. To obtain convenient numbers, the thresholds have been multiplied by 100. The lower panel shows the ratio β/m, plotted on a logarithmic scale. The modulation rate at which the ratio first reaches unity (dashed line) is called the critical modulation frequency (CMF). In this example, the CMF is about 90 Hz. Data from Sek (1994).

components, subjects appear to be sensitive to the relative phases of the components, while for wide frequency separations they are not.

If the threshold for detecting modulation is expressed in terms of the modulation index, m or β, the ratio β/m decreases as the modulation frequency increases and approaches an asymptotic value of unity. This is illustrated in the lower panel of Fig. 3.8. The modulation frequency at which the ratio first becomes unity is called the critical modulation frequency (CMF). Zwicker (1952) and Schorer (1986) assumed that we are only sensitive to the relative phases of the components when all three components fall within a CB. They suggested that the CMF corresponds to half the value of the CB; essentially, the CMF was assumed to be reached when the overall stimulus bandwidth reached the CB. If this is correct, then the CMF may be regarded as providing an estimate of the CB at the carrier frequency.

Further analysis suggests that this interpretation of the results may not be completely correct. For low modulation rates, the subject appears to detect the modulation itself; subjects report hearing a fluctuation in loudness (for AM) or pitch (for QFM). For higher rates, subjects do not hear the modulation *per se*; rather, the task seems to depend on detection of the lower or upper sideband in the presence of the component at the carrier frequency, which acts as a masker (Hartmann and Hnath, 1982; Moore and Sek, 1992; Sek and Moore, 1994). The CMF appears to correspond to the point where the threshold for detecting the modulation first starts to depend on the ability to detect a sideband in the spectrum. The threshold for detecting a sideband depends more on the selectivity of auditory filters centered close to the frequency of that sideband than on the selectivity of the auditory filter centered on the carrier frequency. Furthermore, the detectability of the sideband may be influenced by factors not connected with frequency selectivity, such as the efficiency of the detection process following auditory filtering. This efficiency may well vary with center frequency, just as it does for the detection of tones in noise. Thus, like the critical ratio described earlier, the CMF does not provide a direct measure of the CB.

It also appears to be incorrect to assume that changes in the relative phase of the components in a complex sound are only detectable when those components lie within a CB. In cases where all components are well above threshold, subjects can detect phase changes between the components in complex sounds in which the components are separated by considerably more than a CB (Craig and Jeffress, 1962; Blauert and Laws, 1978; Patterson, 1987a). The detection of these phase changes may depend partly on the ability to compare the time patterns at the outputs of different auditory filters, although it appears that we are not very sensitive to such across-channel time differences (Uppenkamp *et al.*, 2001). This topic is discussed further in Chapter 5.

4D THE AUDIBILITY OF PARTIALS IN COMPLEX TONES

According to Ohm's (1843) acoustical law, we are able to hear pitches corresponding to the individual sinusoidal components in a complex periodic sound. In other words, we can "hear out" the individual partials. Plomp (1964a) and Plomp and Mimpen (1968) used complex tones with 12 sinusoidal components to investigate the limits of this ability. The listener was presented with two comparison tones, one of which was of the same frequency as a partial in the complex; the other lay halfway between that frequency and the frequency of the adjacent higher or lower partial. The listener had to judge which of these two tones was a component of the complex. Plomp used two types of complex: a harmonic complex containing harmonics 1 to 12, where the frequencies of the components were integer multiples of that of the fundamental, and a nonharmonic complex, where the frequencies of the components were mistuned from simple frequency ratios. He found that for both kinds of complex, only the first 5–8 components could be heard out. Fig. 3.9 shows Plomp's results, plotted in terms of the frequency

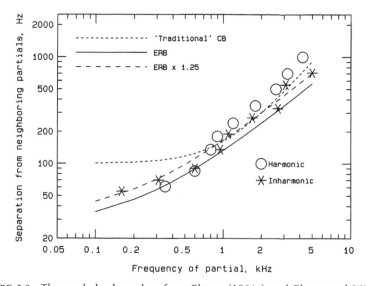

FIGURE 3.9 The symbols show data from Plomp (1964a) and Plomp and Mimpen (1968) on the audibility of partials in complex tones. They show the frequency separation of a partial from neighboring partials necessary for that partial to be heard out with 75% accuracy, plotted as a function of the frequency of the partial. The short-dashed curve shows the "traditional" function relating the critical bandwidth to center frequency. The solid curve shows ERB_N plotted as a function of frequency (see Section 3B). The long-dashed curve shows ERB_N multiplied by 1.25.

separation between a given partial and neighboring partials necessary for that partial be heard out with 75% accuracy.

If it is assumed that a partial will only be heard out when it is separated from its neighbor by at least one CB, then the results can be used to estimate the CB. Above 1000 Hz, the estimates obtained in this way coincided with other CB measures available at that time (Zwicker, 1961). These "traditional" estimates are shown as the short-dashed line in Fig. 3.9. Below 1000 Hz, the estimates of the CB based on Plomp's results were about two-thirds as large as the traditional estimates. However, Plomp's data are consistent with more recent estimates of the CB at low frequencies. The solid line in Fig. 3.9 shows the value of ERB_N. The long-dashed line shows the value of ERB_N multiplied by 1.25. This line fits the data rather well. Thus, Plomp's data are consistent with the hypothesis that a partial can be heard out from neighboring partials when it is separated from those partials by 1.25 times ERB_N.

Moore and Ohgushi (1993) examined the ability of musically trained subjects to hear out individual partials in complex tones with partials uniformly spaced on the Cam scale. Cam spacings of 0.75, 1.0, 1.25, 1.5, and 2 were used, and the central component always had a frequency of 1000 Hz. On each trial, subjects heard a pure tone (the "probe") followed by a complex tone. The probe was close in frequency to one of the partials in the complex but was mistuned downward by 4.5% on half the trials (at random) and mistuned upward by 4.5% on the other half. The task of the subject was to indicate whether the probe was higher or lower in frequency than the nearest partial in the complex. The partial that was "probed" varied randomly from trial to trial. If auditory filtering was the only factor affecting performance on this task, then scores for a given Cam spacing should be similar for each component in the complex sound.

Scores for the highest and lowest components in the complexes were generally high for all component spacings, although they worsened somewhat for Cam spacings of 0.75 and 1.0. Similarly, Plomp (1964a) found that the partials in a two-tone complex could be heard out at smaller frequency separations than were found for multitone complexes. Thus, components at the "edges" of a complex are more easily heard out than "inner" components. Some possible reasons for this are discussed later.

Scores for the inner components were close to chance level for the 0.75-Cam spacing and improved progressively as the spacing was increased from 1 to 2. For Cam spacings of 1.25 or less, the scores did not change smoothly with component frequency; marked irregularities were observed, as well as systematic errors. Moore and Ohgushi suggested that these resulted from irregularities in the transmission of sound through the middle ear (Aibara et al., 2001); such irregularities could change the relative levels of the components, making some components more prominent than others and therefore easier to hear out. Overall, the results of Moore and Ohgushi are consistent with the idea that partials can be heard out with about 75% accuracy when the partials are separated by about 1.25 Cam.

A similar experiment to that of Moore and Ohgushi (1993) was conducted by Moore et al. (2006), but using a wider range of component frequencies and using two levels. Moore et al. found that performance worsened with increasing level, consistent with the idea that the auditory filters broaden with increasing level. They also found that performance worsened for components whose frequencies were above about 3000 Hz. A component with a frequency of 6973 Hz could not be heard out with an accuracy of 75% even when it was separated from neighboring components by 3 Cams. They proposed that the ability to hear out components depends partly on information derived from phase locking and that this information becomes less precise at high frequencies; see Chapter 1, Section 7E.

It seems likely that the ability to hear out partials in a complex sound depends in part on factors other than pure frequency resolution. Soderquist (1970) compared musicians and nonmusicians in a task very similar to that of Plomp and found that the musicians were markedly superior. This result could mean that musicians have narrower auditory filters than nonmusicians. However, Fine and Moore (1993) showed that ERBs, as estimated in a notched-noise masking experiment, did not differ for musicians and nonmusicians. Musicians may be able to perform the task based on less sensory evidence than nonmusicians. In other words, the former may have greater efficiency in performing the task.

4E INTERIM SUMMARY

The examples given above show that the effects of auditory filtering are revealed in a great variety of different experiments. By and large, the results of the different experiments give reasonably consistent estimates of the value of the auditory filter bandwidth. However, it is also clear that most of the experiments do not show a distinct break point corresponding to the CB or the ERB. Rather, the pattern of results changes smoothly and continuously as a function of bandwidth, as would be expected given that the auditory filter has a rounded top and sloping edges.

4F SOME GENERAL OBSERVATIONS ON AUDITORY FILTERS

One question we may ask is whether the listener can only attend to one auditory filter at a time. The answer to this is obviously no, because many of the complex signals that we can perceive and recognize have bandwidths much greater than ERB_N; speech is a prime example of this. Indeed, the perception of timbre depends, at least in part, on the relative response of different auditory filters (see Chapter 8). Furthermore, as described later, the detection of a signal in a masker can sometimes depend on a comparison of the outputs of different auditory filters. Finally, it has already been pointed out that the ear is capable of integration over bandwidths much greater than ERB_N.

In spite of this, it is often possible to predict whether a complex sound will be detected in a given background noise by calculating the detection thresholds of the most prominent frequency components. If the shape of the auditory filter centered on each component is known, then the signal-to-noise ratio at the output of the filter can be calculated. If this ratio exceeds some criterion amount in any filter, then the signal will be detected. For medium frequencies, the criterion amount corresponds to a signal-to-noise ratio of about 1/2.5 or -4 dB; the signal will be detected if its level is not more than 4 dB below that of the noise at the output of the filter. This model has practical applications, because it allows the prediction of appropriate levels for warning signals in factories and aircraft (Patterson and Milroy, 1980). A more recent model (Moore et al., 1997; Glasberg and Moore, 2005) allows more accurate predictions of the threshold for detecting complex signals, because it takes into account the ability of the auditory system to combine information from different auditory filters.

Another question that arises is whether there is only a discrete number of auditory filters, each one adjacent to its neighbors, or whether there is a continuous series of overlapping filters. For convenience, data relating to critical bands have often been presented as though the former were the case. For example, Scharf (1970) presented a table showing CBs for 24 successive critical bands, the upper cutoff frequency (UCF) for each band being the same as the lower cutoff for the next highest band. Although this method of presentation is convenient, it seems clear that auditory filters are continuous rather than discrete; there has been no experimental evidence for any discontinuity or break between different filters. Thus, we may talk about the CB or ERB around any frequency in the audible range that we care to choose.

5 MASKING PATTERNS AND EXCITATION PATTERNS

So far, I have discussed masking experiments in which the frequency of the signal is held constant, while the masker is varied. These experiments are appropriate for estimating the shape of the auditory filter at a given center frequency. However, many of the early experiments on masking did the opposite; the signal frequency was varied while the masker was held constant.

Wegel and Lane (1924) published the first systematic investigation of the masking of one pure tone by another. They determined the threshold for detecting a signal with adjustable frequency in the presence of a masker with fixed frequency and intensity. The graph plotting masked threshold as a function of the frequency of the signal is known as a masking pattern, or sometimes as a masked audiogram. The results of Wegel and Lane were complicated by the occurrence of beats when the signal and the masker were close together in frequency. To reduce this problem, later experimenters (Egan and Hake, 1950; Greenwood, 1961a; Moore et al., 1998; Zwicker and Fastl, 1999; Alcántara et al., 2000) have used a narrow band of noise as either the signal or the masker. Such a noise has "built in" amplitude and frequency variations and does not produce regular beats when added to a tone.

The masking patterns obtained in these experiments show steep slopes on the low-frequency side of between 80 dB and 240 dB/octave for a pure-tone masker and 55–190 dB/octave for a narrowband noise masker. The slopes on the high-frequency side are less steep and depend on the level of the masker. A typical set of results is shown in Fig. 3.10. Notice that on the high-frequency side, the slopes of the curves become shallower at high levels. Thus,

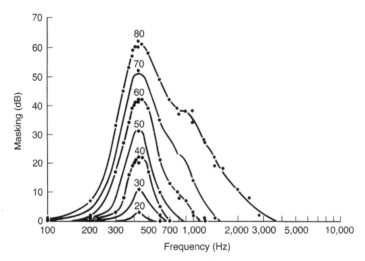

FIGURE 3.10 Masking patterns (masked audiograms) for a narrow band of noise centered at 410 Hz. Each curve shows the elevation in threshold of a pure-tone signal as a function of signal frequency. The overall noise level for each curve is indicated in the figure. Adapted from Egan and Hake (1950), by permission of the authors and J. Acoust. Soc. Am.

if the level of a low-frequency masker is increased by, say, 10 dB, the masked threshold of a high-frequency signal is elevated by more than 10 dB; the amount of masking grows nonlinearly on the high-frequency side. This has been called the "upward spread of masking".

The masking patterns do not reflect the use of a single auditory filter. Rather, for each signal frequency, the listener uses a filter centered close to the signal frequency. Thus, the auditory filter is shifted as the signal frequency is altered. One way of interpreting the masking pattern is as a crude indicator of the excitation pattern of the masker (see Chapter 1, Section 7D). The signal is detected when the excitation it produces is a constant proportion of the excitation produced by the masker at CFs close to the signal frequency. Thus, the threshold of the signal as a function of frequency is proportional to the masker excitation level. The masking pattern should be parallel to the excitation pattern of the masker, but shifted vertically by a small amount. In practice, the situation is not so straightforward, because the shape of the masking pattern is influenced by factors such as off-frequency listening and the detection of combination tones produced by the interaction of the signal and the masker.

Moore and Glasberg (1983b) described a way of deriving the shapes of excitation patterns using the concept of the auditory filter. They suggested that the excitation pattern of a given sound can be thought of as the output of the auditory filters, plotted as a function of their center frequency. This idea is illustrated in Fig. 3.11. The upper portion of the figure shows auditory filter shapes for five center frequencies. The filters are plotted with a gain of 0 dB at their tips. Each filter is symmetrical on the linear frequency scale used, but the bandwidths of the filters increase with increasing center frequency, as illustrated in Fig. 3.5. The dashed line represents a 1-kHz sinusoidal signal whose excitation pattern is to be derived. The lower panel shows the output from each filter in response to the 1-kHz signal, plotted as a function of the center frequency of each filter; this is the desired excitation pattern.

To see how this pattern is derived, consider the output from the filter with the lowest center frequency. This has a relative output in response to the 1-kHz tone of about −40 dB, as indicated by point "a" in the upper panel. In the lower panel, this gives rise to the point "a" on the excitation pattern; the point has an ordinate value of −40 dB and is positioned on the abscissa at a frequency corresponding to the center frequency of the lowest filter illustrated. The relative outputs of the other filters are indicated, in order of increasing center frequency, by points "b" to "e", and each leads to a corresponding point on the excitation pattern. The complete excitation pattern was derived by calculating the filter outputs for filters spaced at 10-Hz intervals. In deriving the excitation pattern, excitation levels were expressed relative to the level at the tip of the pattern, which was arbitrarily labeled

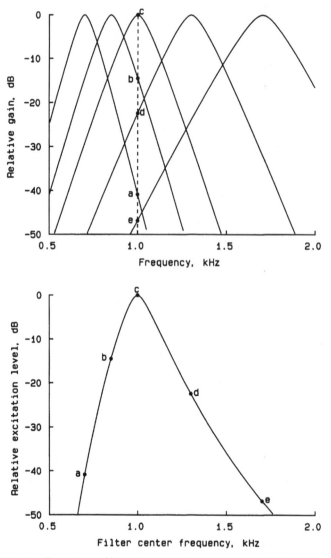

FIGURE 3.11 An illustration of how the excitation pattern of a 1-kHz sinusoid can be derived by calculating the outputs of the auditory filters as a function of their center frequency. The top half shows five auditory filters, centered at different frequencies, and the bottom half shows the calculated excitation pattern. See text for details. From Moore and Glasberg (1983b).

as 0 dB. To calculate the excitation pattern for a 1-kHz tone with a level of, say, 60 dB, the level at the tip would be labeled as 60 dB, and all other excitation levels would correspondingly be increased by 60 dB.

Note that although the auditory filters were assumed to be symmetric on a linear frequency scale, the derived excitation pattern is asymmetric. This happens because ERB$_N$ increases with increasing center frequency. Note also that the excitation pattern has the same general form as the masking patterns shown in Fig. 3.10. This method of deriving excitation patterns is easily extended to the case where the auditory filters are asymmetric (Moore and Glasberg, 1987). However, while it is the lower side of the auditory filter that gets less steep with increasing level (see Fig. 3.6), it is the upper side of the masking pattern and the upper side of the excitation pattern that become less steep with increasing level. This happens because the upper side of the excitation pattern is determined by the lower side of the auditory filter and vice versa.

Figure 3.12 shows excitation patterns for a 1-kHz sinusoid at levels from 20 to 90 dB, calculated in a manner similar to that described above, but this time plotted on a logarithmic frequency scale. The excitation patterns have the same general form as the masking patterns shown in Fig. 3.10 and show the

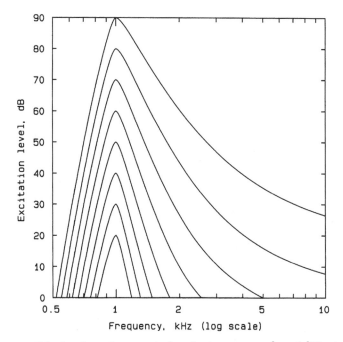

FIGURE 3.12 Calculated psychoacoustical excitation patterns for a 1-kHz sinusoid at levels ranging from 20 dB to 90 dB SPL in 10 dB steps.

same nonlinear expansive growth on the high-frequency side. In calculating the excitation patterns in this figure, it was assumed that the auditory filters had a gain of 0 dB at their tips for all input levels. However, as argued earlier, the gain at the tip probably decreases with increasing input level, as shown in the lower panel of Fig. 3.6. In a sense, the excitation patterns in Fig. 3.12 are misleading; they probably do not directly reflect the magnitude of BM responses. On the BM, the magnitude of response at the tip of the excitation pattern grows in a compressive manner with increasing sound level, whereas the magnitude of response on the high-frequency side grows linearly. This effect is not directly revealed in masking patterns such as those in Fig. 3.10, because the masked threshold depends mainly on the signal-to-masker *ratio* at the output of the auditory filter.

6 THE NATURE OF THE AUDITORY FILTER AND MECHANISMS OF MASKING

6A THE ORIGIN OF THE AUDITORY FILTER

The physiological basis of the auditory filter is still uncertain, although the frequency analysis observed on the BM is almost certainly involved. Indeed, there are many similarities between the frequency selectivity measured on the BM and the frequency selectivity measured psychophysically (Moore, 1986). The CB, or the ERB_N of the auditory filter, corresponds roughly to a constant distance along the BM (Greenwood, 1961b, 1990; Moore, 1986); in humans, each ERB_N corresponds to about 0.9 mm, regardless of the center frequency. Furthermore, the ERB of the auditory filter measured behaviorally in animals corresponds reasonably well with the ERB of tuning curves measured for single neurons of the auditory nerve in the same species. This is illustrated in Fig. 3.13 (Evans *et al.*, 1989). Behavioral ERBs were measured using notched noise or BSN, as described in Section 3B, and using a different type of noise, comb-filtered noise (CFN). However, the extent to which behavioral measures of the tuning match physiological measures is still a matter of some controversy; see Ruggero and Temchin (2005) and Shera *et al.* (2010).

6B TEMPORAL EFFECTS

Although it seems likely that the frequency selectivity of the auditory system is largely determined in the cochlea, it is possible that there are neural

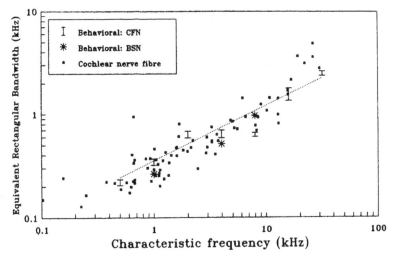

FIGURE 3.13   A comparison of ERBs estimated from behavioral masking experiments and from neurophysiological measurements of the tuning curves of single neurons in the auditory nerve. All data were obtained from guinea pigs. There is a good correspondence between behavioral and neural data. From Evans *et al.* (1989) by permission of the authors.

processes that play a role. If this is the case, then frequency selectivity might take some time to develop. Thus, the CB or ERB measured with very brief signals should be greater than that measured with longer signals.

The data relevant to this issue are not clear cut. Some studies have indicated that the CB does not develop over time. Moore *et al.* (1987) estimated the shape of the auditory filter using the notched-noise method (see Section 3B). The signal was a 20-ms 1-kHz tone presented at the start, the temporal center, or the end of the 400-ms masker. The auditory filter shapes derived from the results did not change significantly with signal delay, suggesting that the selectivity of the auditory filter does not develop over time. On the other hand, measures of frequency selectivity obtained with tonal maskers and signals do show a development of frequency selectivity with time (Bacon and Viemeister, 1985a; Bacon and Moore, 1986a,b, 1987), especially when the masker frequency is above the signal frequency.

One temporal effect in masking that has been studied extensively is called the "overshoot" effect (Zwicker, 1965). The threshold for detecting a brief signal in noise is greater if the signal is presented near the masker onset, or turned on and off synchronously with an equally brief masker, than if the signal is presented after a long onset delay, or in a continuous masker. The effect is greatest (10–15 dB) when the masker covers a broad frequency range, the signal has a high frequency, and the masker is at a moderate level (Bacon, 1990; von Klitzing and Kohlrausch, 1994; Oxenham and Moore, 1995b). Frequency components in the masker above the signal frequency are important in producing the effect (McFadden, 1989; Schmidt and Zwicker, 1991). The fact that the signal threshold is higher at the masker onset could be interpreted in terms of a broader auditory filter at the masker onset. However, the broadening would have to be very large indeed to account for the large effect observed for brief high-frequency signals; according to the power spectrum model, the ERB of the auditory filter would have to be broader by a factor of 10 to account for a 10-dB threshold elevation at the masker onset. Such a large broadening seems implausible.

At present, the mechanisms underlying the overshoot effect, and the development of frequency selectivity over time found by Bacon and coworkers, are not well understood. The results could be interpreted in terms of a peripheral filter whose high-frequency skirt is broader at the onset of the masker. However, it is equally possible to argue that peripheral filtering processes do not develop over time and that the effects depend on more central processes (Bacon and Moore, 1987). Several researchers have suggested that overshoot is connected in some way with the active mechanism in the cochlea (von Klitzing and Kohlrausch, 1994; Oxenham and Moore, 1995b; Bacon and Liu, 2000; Strickland, 2001; Summers, 2001). This may occur through the operation of the efferent system, which is a system of neural projections from the brain stem and cortex to "lower" levels, including the cochlea (see Chapter 1, Section 6C). The efferent signals may regulate the gain and sharpness of tuning provided by the active mechanism (Guinan, 2006), thus influencing the detection of brief tones in noise (Strickland, 2008).

A different kind of temporal effect in masking occurs when the masker waveform has a high "peak factor"; this is the ratio of the peak value of the waveform to its RMS value (see Chapter 1, Section 2C, for the definition of RMS value). More precisely, the important thing is the peak factor of the waveform evoked by the masker on the BM. A waveform with a high peak factor can be described as highly modulated, containing high peaks and deep "dips". When a masker produces a waveform with a high peak factor on the BM, signals can be detected during the dips in the masker, a process sometimes called "dip listening". As a result, the threshold for detecting a signal can be much lower than for a masker with a low peak factor.

An example of this is provided by a study of Kohlrausch and Sander (1995). They used as maskers complex tones containing many equal-amplitude harmonics of a 100-Hz fundamental. The starting phase, θ_n, of the nth harmonic was determined according to equations described by Schroeder (1970):

$$\theta_n = +\pi n(n-1)/N \text{ or } \theta_n = -\pi n(n-1)/N$$

where N is the number of harmonics in the complex sound. In this equation, if a plus sign is used (Schroeder-positive phase), the starting phase increases progressively with increasing harmonic number, whereas if a minus sign is used (Schroeder-negative phase), the starting phase decreases progressively with increasing harmonic number. Both of these phases give waveforms with almost flat envelopes; one waveform is a time-reversed version of the other (see Fig. 3.14). The Schroeder-negative wave is like a repeated upward frequency sweep (up chirp), whereas the Schroeder-positive wave is like a repeated downward frequency sweep (down chirp).

Kohlrausch and Sander (1995) presented evidence that the two waveforms give very different responses on the BM at a place tuned to 1100 Hz; the Schroeder-positive phase leads to a high peak factor, whereas the Schroeder-negative phase leads to a low peak factor. They showed this by using the complex tones as maskers and measuring the threshold for detecting a very brief 1100-Hz sinusoidal signal presented at various times during the 10-ms period of the masker. For the Schroeder-negative phase, the threshold of the signal varied little with the time of presentation. For the Schroeder-positive phase, the threshold varied over a considerable range, indicating that the internal representation of the masker was fluctuating

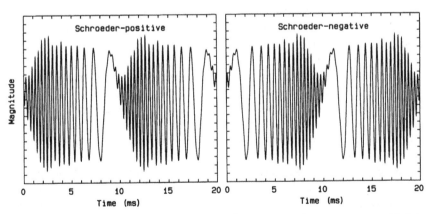

FIGURE 3.14 Waveforms of harmonic complex tones with components added in Schroeder-positive phase (left) or Schroeder-negative phase (right).

within one period. The lowest threshold in the Schroeder-positive-phase masker was much lower than the lowest threshold in the Schroeder-negative-phase masker. When long-duration signals are used, the detection threshold is also lower in a Schroeder-positive-phase masker than in a Schroeder-negative-phase masker (Smith et al., 1986; Summers and Leek, 1997; Oxenham and Dau, 2001).

The difference in BM response to Schroeder-positive- and Schroeder-negative-phase maskers occurs because, at a given place on the BM (e.g., the place tuned to 1100 Hz), high frequencies are delayed relative to low frequencies. In the masker with Schroeder-positive phase, the high frequencies are advanced in time relative to low frequencies. The advance in time of the high frequencies in the stimulus effectively cancels the delay on the BM, and therefore, on the BM, all components in the masker are aligned in time and have roughly the same phase. This means that the peaks in instantaneous amplitude of the components nearly coincide, giving a waveform with a high peak factor. In contrast, the high-frequency components in the Schroeder-negative-phase masker are delayed in time relative to the low-frequency components, and this delay simply adds to the delay on the BM. Hence, the waveform evoked on the BM by the Schroeder-negative-phase masker has a low peak factor.

Phase effects in masking have been observed for other types of maskers. For example, when all of the sinusoidal components in a harmonic complex masker start with 90° phase (also called cosine phase), a waveform with a very high peak factor results (see Chapter 1, Section 2B), and the waveform evoked on the BM also has a high peak factor (Duifhuis, 1970). In contrast, if the components are added with random starting phase, the peak factor is much lower. The threshold for detecting a sinusoidal signal or a signal composed of a band of noise is lower in a cosine-phase masker than in a random-phase masker (Mehrgardt and Schroeder, 1983; Gockel et al., 2002; Alcántara et al., 2003).

The advantage obtained from dip listening may depend partly on the compression that occurs on the BM. As a result of the compression, low-amplitude portions of the waveform on the BM are amplified more than high-amplitude portions, so any signal appearing in the dips is automatically enhanced (Horst et al., 1990). Summers and Leek (1998) have shown that differences in the masking produced by Schroeder-positive-phase and Schroeder-negative-phase maskers are much smaller than normal for subjects with cochlear hearing loss. As such hearing loss often results in loss of compression on the BM (Moore and Oxenham, 1998), this is consistent with the idea that dip listening depends partly on cochlear compression. Finally, it should be noted that the existence of these phase effects in masking is inconsistent with the power spectrum model of masking described earlier, because in that model, the relative phases of the components in the masker are assumed not to influence masking.

6C THE MECHANISM OF MASKING—SWAMPING OR SUPPRESSION?

There are two common conceptions of the mechanism by which masking occurs. The first is that masking involves the swamping of the neural activity evoked by the signal. If the masker produces a significant amount of activity in the channels (auditory filters or critical bands) that would normally respond to the signal, then the activity added by the signal may be undetectable. Consider, for example, the case of a tone together with wideband white noise. When a mid-frequency tone is at its masked threshold, the level of the tone is about 4 dB less than the level of the noise at the output of the auditory filter centered at the frequency of the tone. The combined excitation produced by the tone plus noise is about 1.5 dB higher in level than that produced by the noise alone. Thus, one might argue that 1.5 dB represents the minimum increment in excitation necessary for detection of the tone. If the tone is much lower in level than the noise passing through the auditory filter, then it produces a negligible increment in excitation. For example, if the difference in level is 20 dB, the increment in level is less than 0.05 dB. Thus, the excitation produced by the tone is "swamped" by that produced by the masker.

Note that the task required of the subject may differ somewhat according to the manner of stimulus presentation. For a steady tone presented in a continuous background noise, the subject would have to detect that the excitation at one center frequency exceeded that at surrounding center frequencies, that is, that there was a peak in the pattern of excitation (Greenwood, 1961a; Schubert, 1969). If, on the other hand, the tone was interrupted or presented intermittently, the subject might detect changes in the output of a single auditory filter centered at the frequency of the tone. This might make the task somewhat easier. In either case, this type of masking only occurs if the masker produces excitation at the outputs of the auditory filters that would otherwise respond to the signal.

Another possible mechanism of masking is that the masker suppresses the activity that the signal would evoke if presented alone (Delgutte, 1988, 1990). This mechanism might apply when the signal frequency is well above or below the masker frequency. It is most easily explained by analogy with the "two-tone suppression" observed in single neurons of the auditory nerve, which was described in Chapter 1, Section 7F. The neural response to a tone at the CF of a neuron may be suppressed by a tone that does not itself produce excitatory activity in that neuron. The suppression may be sufficient to drive the firing rate of the neuron down to its spontaneous rate, and it may be argued that this corresponds to the masking of the tone at CF. More generally, a masking sound might produce both excitation and suppression in the neurons responding to the signal, and masking might correspond to a mixture of swamping and suppression (Delgutte, 1990; Moore and Vickers, 1997; Gifford and Bacon, 2000).

If simultaneous masking is influenced by suppression of the signal by the masker, then the auditory filter shapes estimated from PTCs or using the notched-noise method may be broader than the "true" underlying filters (Wightman *et al.*, 1977; Heinz *et al.*, 2002; Moore, 2002; Shera *et al.*, 2002). I return to this point later.

6D THE NEURAL CODE USED FOR SIGNAL DETECTION

So far I have discussed the basis of the auditory filter and the mechanism by which the neural activity evoked by the signal might be "masked". I turn now to a consideration of what aspect of the neural activity evoked by the signal might be used for detection. The most common assumption is that the amount of activity is critical and that neural firing rates are the important variables (Delgutte, 1990, 1996; Heinz *et al.*, 2002). However, an alternative possibility is that information in the temporal patterns of neural firing, in other words phase locking, is used (Moore, 1975; Carney *et al.*, 2002). In response to a complex stimulus, the pattern of phase locking observed in a given neuron depends on which components in the stimulus are most effective in driving that neuron. Recordings of the responses of many different auditory neurons within the same animal indicate that information about the relative levels of components in complex sounds is contained in the time patterns of neural impulses, even at sound levels sufficient to produce saturation in the majority of neurons (Kim and Molnar, 1979; Sachs and Young, 1980). In general, the temporal patterns of response are dominated by the most prominent frequency components in the complex stimulus, with the result that there may be little or no phase locking to weak components that are close in frequency to stronger ones. Thus, it seems reasonable to suggest that a tone (with a frequency below about 5 kHz) will be masked when the subject cannot detect its effect on the time pattern of nerve impulses evoked by the stimulus as a whole.

This argument can easily be applied to the masking of a tone by wideband noise. A tone evokes neural firings with a well-defined temporal pattern; the time intervals between successive nerve spikes are close to integer multiples of the period of the tone. A noise evokes, in the same neurons, a much less regular pattern of neural firings. Thus, a tone may be detected when the neurons responding to it show a certain degree of temporal regularity in their patterns of firing. If the temporal regularity is less than this amount, the tone will be masked. Notice that the neurons involved in the detection of the tone are those with CFs close to the frequency of the tone. The action of the auditory filter is important in reducing the contribution of the noise to the neural responses, and the neurons with CFs close to the tone frequency are the ones showing the greatest degree of temporal regularity. Carney *et al.* (2002) have proposed a specific mechanism for "decoding" the temporal information, based on neurons that detect coincidences in the nerve spikes evoked by neurons with slightly different CFs.

The idea that we use the temporal patterns of neural firing to analyze complex stimuli can provide an explanation for the discrepancies observed by Plomp (1964a) in human subjects' abilities to hear out partials in two-tone complexes and multitone complexes. As described earlier, Plomp's results show that a partial can just be heard out from a multitone complex if it is separated from neighboring partials by about 1.25 Cams. However, for a two-tone complex, the partials can be heard out for separations less than this. Similarly, Moore and Ohgushi (1993) and Moore *et al.* (2006) found that the "edge" partials in an inharmonic complex tone were easier to hear out than the "inner" partials. Figure 3.15 shows excitation patterns for a two-tone complex and a multitone complex. For a multitone complex, the excitation at CFs corresponding to the higher "inner" partials arises from the interaction of several components of comparable effectiveness. Thus, there is no CF where the temporal pattern of response is determined primarily by one component. However, for a two-tone complex, there are certain CFs where the temporal pattern of response is dominated by one or the other of the component tones; this occurs at CFs just below and above the frequencies of the two tones. Thus, the temporal patterns of firing in these neurons could signal the individual pitches of the component tones. This could explain why partials are more easily "heard out" from a two-tone complex than a multitone complex. Consistent with this explanation, an edge partial is not easier to hear out than an inner partial when its frequency lies above 5 kHz (Moore *et al.*, 2006), a frequency at which phase locking would be weak or absent.

Another possible cue that may be used for detection of a tone in noise is the change in the envelope produced by adding the tone to the noise. The envelope fluctuates less when the tone is present than when it is absent (Schooneveldt and Moore, 1989). This cue may be particularly important when the cue of a change in overall level is made unreliable by making the overall level of the tone plus noise vary randomly from trial to trial (Kidd *et al.*, 1989; Richards, 1992; Richards and Nekrich, 1993).

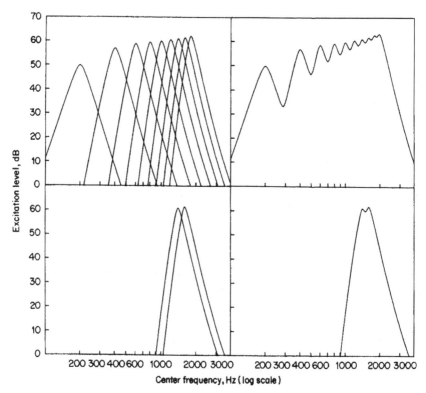

FIGURE 3.15   The top-left panel shows the excitation pattern for each harmonic in a complex tone containing the first nine harmonics of a 200-Hz fundamental. The top-right panel shows the excitation pattern resulting from adding the nine harmonics together. The bottom-left panel shows the excitation patterns for the seventh and eighth harmonics separately, and the bottom-right panel shows the excitation pattern resulting from adding those two harmonics. For the two-tone complex, neurons with CFs below 1400 Hz would be phase locked primarily to the lower of the two harmonics, whereas neurons with CFs above 1600 Hz would be phase locked primarily to the upper of the two harmonics.

7   COMODULATION MASKING RELEASE: SPECTRO-TEMPORAL PATTERN ANALYSIS IN HEARING

The power spectrum model of masking is based on the assumption that, when trying to detect a sinusoidal signal of a given frequency in the presence of a masking sound, the listener makes use of the output of a single auditory filter centered close to the signal frequency. This model works well in many situations, but it clearly fails in others. In particular, there is good evidence that listeners sometimes make comparisons across auditory filters, rather than listening through a single filter. Furthermore, temporal fluctuations of the masker can have important effects. This section reviews evidence for across-filter comparisons, emphasizing the importance of the temporal properties of the stimuli and interpreting the results in terms of pattern analysis in the auditory system.

7A INITIAL DEMONSTRATIONS OF COMODULATION MASKING RELEASE

Hall *et al.* (1984) were among the first to demonstrate that across-filter comparisons could enhance the detection of a sinusoidal signal in a fluctuating noise masker. The crucial feature for achieving this enhancement was that the fluctuations should be coherent or correlated across different frequency bands. In one of their experiments, the threshold for detecting a 1-kHz, 400-ms sinusoidal signal was measured as a function of the bandwidth of a noise masker, keeping the spectrum level constant. The masker was centered at 1 kHz. They used two types of masker. One was a random noise; this has irregular fluctuations in amplitude, and the fluctuations are independent in different frequency regions. The other was a random noise that was modulated in amplitude at an irregular, low rate; a noise low-pass filtered at 50 Hz was used as a modulator. The modulation resulted in fluctuations in the amplitude of the noise that were the same in different frequency regions. This across-frequency coherence was called "comodulation" by Hall *et al.* (1984). Figure 3.16 shows the results of this experiment.

For the random noise (denoted by R), the signal threshold increases as the masker bandwidth increases up to about 100–200 Hz and then remains constant. This is exactly as expected from the power spectrum model of masking (see Section 2 and Fig. 3.1). The auditory filter at this center frequency has a bandwidth of about 130 Hz. Hence, for noise bandwidths up to 130 Hz, increasing the bandwidth results in more noise passing through the filter. However, increasing the bandwidth beyond 130 Hz does not increase the noise passing through the filter, and therefore threshold does not increase. The pattern for the modulated noise (denoted by M) is quite different. For noise bandwidths greater than 100 Hz, the signal threshold decreases as the bandwidth increases. This suggests that subjects can compare the outputs of different auditory filters to enhance signal detection. The fact that the decrease in threshold with increasing bandwidth only occurs with the modulated noise indicates that fluctuations in the masker are critical and that

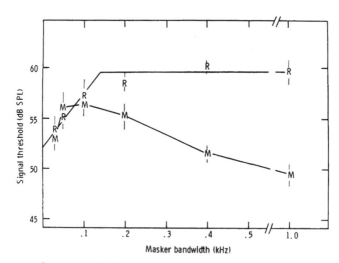

FIGURE 3.16   The points labeled "R" are thresholds for detecting a 1-kHz signal centered in a band of random noise, plotted as a function of the bandwidth of the noise. The points labeled "M" are the thresholds obtained when the noise was amplitude modulated at an irregular, low rate. For bandwidths of 0.1 kHz or more, the thresholds in the modulated noise decrease with increasing bandwidth. This is an example of comodulation masking release (CMR). From Hall *et al.* (1984), by permission of the authors and *J. Acoust. Soc. Am.*

the fluctuations need to be correlated across frequency bands. Hence, this phenomenon has been called "comodulation masking release" (CMR).

Another way in which CMR can be demonstrated is by using narrow bands of noise, which have inherent relatively slow amplitude fluctuations. One band, the on-frequency band, is centered at the signal frequency. A second band, the flanking band, is centered away from the signal frequency. If the flanking band is uncorrelated with the on-frequency band, then when it is added to the on-frequency band, either it has no effect on the signal threshold or it increases the signal threshold slightly. However, when the envelope of the flanking band is correlated with that of the on-frequency band (i.e., it has the same pattern of fluctuation over time), the flanking band can produce a release from masking, a CMR (Hall *et al.*, 1984; Cohen and Schubert, 1987; Schooneveldt and Moore, 1987). The release from masking can occur even if the signal and on-frequency band are presented to one ear and the flanking band is presented to the other ear (Cohen and Schubert, 1987; Schooneveldt and Moore, 1987). The magnitude of the CMR is usually defined as the difference in signal threshold for the condition with the uncorrelated flanking band and the condition with the correlated flanking band.

7B The Role of Within-Channel Cues

CMR is usually assumed to depend on comparisons of the outputs of different auditory filters. However, Schooneveldt and Moore (1987, 1989) have shown that modulation of a masker can produce a release from masking even when the masker's bandwidth is less than the auditory filter bandwidth. This release from masking cannot arise from comparisons of the outputs of different auditory filters. Rather, it results from a cue or cues available in the output of a single auditory filter. Schooneveldt and Moore called such cues "within-channel cues". One example of such a cue is a change in the pattern of envelope modulation that occurs when the signal is added to the masker; the envelope fluctuates less and the minima in the envelope tend to be less deep when the signal is present. This cue appears to be used in band-widening experiments of the type illustrated in Fig. 3.16 (Verhey et al., 1999), but it can only be used when the signal duration is greater than about 100 ms (Schooneveldt and Moore, 1989).

Within-channel cues make it easy to overestimate the magnitude of CMR resulting from across-filter comparisons. However, the cues do not appear to be important for brief signals in band-widening experiments or when the on-frequency and flanking bands are widely separated in frequency (Schooneveldt and Moore, 1987; Dau et al., 2009). They also do not occur when the on-frequency and flanking bands are presented to opposite ears. Hence, results for these conditions can be used to estimate the magnitude of the CMR resulting from across-filter comparisons.

7C Factors Influencing the Magnitude of CMR

CMR measured in band-widening experiments (as in Fig. 3.16) occurs over a wide range of signal frequencies (500–4000 Hz) and does not vary greatly with signal frequency (Haggard et al., 1990). CMR is largest when the modulation of the masker is at a low rate and when the masker covers a wide frequency range (Carlyon et al., 1989). For signal durations of 100 ms or less, for which within-channel cues probably have little effect, CMR can be as large as 11 dB.

When CMR is measured using an on-frequency band and a flanking band, it generally falls in the range 1–6 dB when the flanking band is distant in frequency from the on-frequency band; this probably reflects a CMR resulting from across-filter comparisons. The release from masking can be as large as 14 dB when the flanking band is close in frequency to the on-frequency band, but in this case, within-channel cues probably influence the results. CMR measured with a flanking band presented in the opposite ear to the signal plus masker varies little with center frequency, but it is a little larger for flanking bands close to the signal frequency than for flanking bands farther away (Hall *et al.*, 1990). Thus, there may be a proximity effect separate from the effect of within-channel cues.

CMR measured with an on-frequency band and a flanking band tends to increase as the width of the bands of noise is decreased (Schooneveldt and Moore, 1987). This is probably a consequence of the fact that the rate of envelope fluctuations decreases as the bandwidth decreases; slow fluctuations lead to large CMR. CMR also increases if more than one flanking band is used (Hall *et al.*, 1990). When many bands are used, CMR can be as large as 16 dB (Moore and Shailer, 1991).

7D Models to Explain CMR

Models to explain CMR can be divided into two general categories. Those in the first category are based on the assumption that the auditory system compares envelope modulation patterns at the outputs of auditory filters tuned to different center frequencies (Piechowiak *et al.*, 2007). For a comodulated masker without a signal, the modulation pattern is similar for all of the filters that are active. When a signal is added, the modulation pattern at the output of the auditory filter tuned to the signal frequency is altered. Thus, the presence of the signal is indicated by a disparity in the modulation pattern across different filters. The auditory system may be sensitive to this disparity.

A second category of model (Buus, 1985; Buus *et al.*, 1996) is based on the assumption that the envelope fluctuations at the outputs of auditory filters tuned away from the signal frequency tell the listener the optimum times to listen for the signal, that is, during the minima in the masker envelope. The signal-to-masker ratio is usually greatest during the masker minima, and the flanking band may help to indicate the exact times of the minima. This is called the dip-listening model. Note that these models are not mutually exclusive.

7E Experimental Tests of the Models

Richards (1987) tested the idea that the auditory system can detect disparities in envelope modulation patterns at the outputs of different auditory filters by requiring subjects to distinguish two stimuli. One stimulus consisted of two comodulated bands of noise, that is, two bands with the same envelope fluctuations. The other stimulus consisted of two bands with independent envelopes. Subjects were able to perform this task, indicating that across-filter disparities in modulation pattern can be detected. However, Moore and Emmerich (1990) found that performance on a similar task improved when the bandwidth of the noise bands was increased, which is the opposite of what is found in CMR experiments. This suggests that different mechanisms are involved in the detection of envelope disparities and in CMR.

Hall and Grose (1988) demonstrated that disparities in modulation patterns across filters are not necessary to get a CMR. They used an on-frequency band and a flanking band as maskers, but the signal was a band of noise identical to the on-frequency band. Thus, the addition of the signal to the on-frequency band merely resulted in a change of overall level, without changing the modulation pattern. They found a significant CMR. As well as indicating that a disparity in across-filter modulation patterns is not necessary to produce a CMR, the results also show that dip-listening is not necessary; for this particular signal, the signal-to-noise ratio is not greater at the masker minima than at the masker maxima. The results indicate that across-filter disparities in overall level are sufficient to produce a CMR. This finding is not consistent with either of the simple types of model of CMR described earlier.

In another experiment, Hall and Grose (1988) used a sinusoidal signal, but the level of the flanking band was varied randomly from one stimulus to the next. This would disrupt any cue related to across-filter differences in overall level. A substantial CMR was found, indicating that across-filter-level differences are not necessary to produce a CMR. Presumably in this experiment, the signal was detected either by dip-listening or by detecting across-filter disparities in modulation pattern.

Grose and Hall (1989) used as a masker a series of sinusoidal components that were sinusoidally amplitude modulated (SAM) at a 10-Hz rate. The modulation was either in phase for all of the components (coherent modulation) or had a quasi-random phase for each component (incoherent modulation). The signal was a sinusoid coincident in frequency with the middle component of the masker. The difference in threshold for detecting a signal presented in the two maskers gives a measure of CMR. Grose and Hall investigated the effect of presenting the signal as a series of brief tone pips that occurred either at minima or at maxima in the envelope of the center component of the masker. In the case of the masker with coherent modulation, the addition of the signal at either minima or maxima would have resulted in an across-filter envelope disparity. However, a CMR was found only in the former case. Similar results were reported by Moore et al. (1990). These results support the dip-listening model.

The results of these and other experiments (Fantini et al., 1993) suggest that CMR does not depend on any single cue or mechanism. Rather, it reflects the operation of flexible mechanisms that can exploit a variety of cues or combination of cues depending on the specific stimuli used.

7F GENERAL IMPLICATIONS OF CMR

It seems likely that across-filter comparisons of temporal envelopes are a general feature of auditory pattern analysis, which may play an important role in extracting signals from noisy backgrounds or separating competing sources of sound. As pointed out by Hall *et al.* (1984), "Many real-life auditory stimuli have intensity peaks and valleys as a function of time in which intensity trajectories are highly correlated across frequency. This is true of speech, of interfering noise such as 'cafeteria' noise, and of many other kinds of environmental stimuli". The experiments reviewed earlier suggest that we can exploit these coherent envelope fluctuations very effectively and that substantial reductions in signal threshold can result. Other ways in which we separate competing sound sources are discussed in Chapter 8.

Sometimes, the detection (or discrimination) of modulation on one carrier frequency can be impaired by the presence of modulation on another carrier frequency, even when the second carrier is well separated in frequency from the first. This is an across-channel interference effect known as modulation detection (or discrimination) interference (MDI) (Yost *et al.*, 1989). It is discussed more fully in Chapter 5.

8 PROFILE ANALYSIS

Green and his colleagues (Green, 1988) have carried out a series of experiments demonstrating that, even for stimuli without distinct envelope fluctuations, subjects are able to compare the outputs of different auditory filters to enhance the detection of a signal. They investigated the ability to detect an increment in the level of one component in a complex sound (usually the central component) relative to the level of the other components; the other components are called the "background". Usually the complex sound has been composed of a series of equal-amplitude sinusoidal components, uniformly spaced on a logarithmic frequency scale. To prevent subjects from performing the task by monitoring the magnitude of the output of the single auditory filter centered at the frequency of the incremented component, the overall level of the whole stimulus was varied randomly (roved) from one stimulus to the next, over a relatively large range (typically about 40 dB). This makes the magnitude of the output of any single filter an unreliable cue to the presence of the signal.

Subjects were able to detect changes in the relative level of the signal of only 1–2 dB. Such small thresholds could not be obtained by monitoring the magnitude of the output of a single auditory filter. Green and his colleagues have argued that subjects performed the task by detecting a change in the shape or profile of the spectrum of the sound; hence the name "profile analysis". In other words, subjects can compare the outputs of different auditory filters and can detect when the output of one changes relative to that of others, even when the overall level is varied.

Green (1988) has given an extensive description of the main properties of profile analysis. Profile analysis is most effective when

1. The background has a large spectral range. For example, for a 1000-Hz signal, the threshold is lower when the background extends from 200 to 5000 Hz than when it extends from 724 to 1380 Hz.
2. There are many rather than few components within the spectral range of the background. Thus, increasing the number of components in the background leads to a decrease in the signal threshold. However, there is a limit to this effect. If some of the background components fall close to the signal frequency, then they may have a masking effect on the signal. Thus, making the background too "dense" (i.e., having many closely spaced components) can result in an increase in signal threshold.
3. The signal falls well within the frequency range of the background; threshold tends to rise when the signal is at the edge of the frequency range of the background.
4. The level of the signal component is similar to or slightly above the levels of the components in the background.
5. The background is composed of components with equal levels rather than levels that differ from component to component.

The first two aspects of profile analysis described above resemble CMR; recall that CMR is larger when the masker covers a wide frequency range or when several flanking bands are used. Indeed, profile analysis may be regarded as a special case of CMR, where the masker fluctuates randomly in level across stimuli but not within stimuli.

In one sense, the phenomenon of profile analysis is not surprising. It has been known for many years that one of the main factors determining the timbre or quality of a sound is its spectral shape; this is discussed in more detail in Chapter 8. Our everyday experience tells us that we can recognize and distinguish familiar sounds, such as the different vowels, regardless of the levels of those sounds. When we do this, we are distinguishing different spectral shapes in the face of variations in overall level. This is functionally the same as profile analysis. The experiments on profile analysis can be regarded as a way of quantifying the limits of our ability to distinguish changes in spectral shape.

9 NONSIMULTANEOUS MASKING

"Simultaneous masking" is the term used to describe situations where the masker is present throughout the presentation time of the signal. However, masking can also occur when the signal is presented just before or after the masker. This is called nonsimultaneous masking and it is studied using brief signals, often called "probes". Two basic types of nonsimultaneous masking can be distinguished: (1) backward masking, in which the probe precedes the masker (also known as pre-stimulatory masking or just pre-masking); and (2) forward masking, in which the probe follows the masker (also known as poststimulatory masking or just post-masking). Forward masking is just one of three conceptually distinct processes that may affect the threshold of a probe presented after another sound; the other two are adaptation and fatigue, which are discussed in Chapter 4. Forward masking is distinguished from adaptation and fatigue primarily by the fact that it occurs for maskers that are relatively short in duration (typically a few hundred milliseconds), and it is limited to signals that occur within about 200 ms of the cessation of the masker.

Although many studies of backward masking have been published, the phenomenon is poorly understood. The amount of backward masking obtained depends strongly on how much practice the subjects have received, and practiced subjects often show little or no backward masking (Miyazaki and Sasaki, 1984; Oxenham and Moore, 1994). The larger masking effects found for unpracticed subjects may reflect some sort of "confusion" of the signal with the masker. In the following paragraphs, I focus on forward masking, which can be substantial even in highly practiced subjects. The main properties of forward masking are as follows:

1. Forward masking is greater the nearer in time to the masker that the signal occurs. This is illustrated in the left panel of Fig. 3.17. When the delay D of the signal after the end of the masker is plotted on a logarithmic scale, the data fall roughly on a straight line. In other words, the amount of forward masking, in dB, is a linear function of $\log(D)$.
2. The rate of recovery from forward masking is greater for higher masker levels. Regardless of the initial amount of forward masking, the masking decays to zero after 100–200 ms.

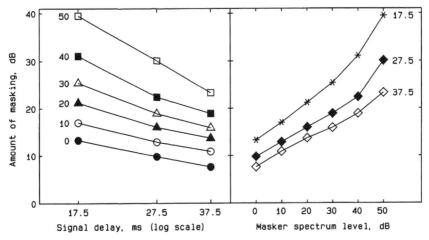

FIGURE 3.17 The left panel shows the amount of forward masking of a brief 4-kHz signal, plotted as a function of the time delay of the signal after the end of the noise masker. Each curve shows results for a different noise spectrum level (10–50 dB). The results for each spectrum level fall roughly on a straight line when the signal delay is plotted on a logarithmic scale, as here. The right panel shows the same thresholds plotted as a function of masker spectrum level. Each curve shows results for a different signal delay time (17.5, 27.5, or 37.5 ms). Note that the slopes of these growth of masking functions decrease with increasing signal delay. Adapted from Moore and Glasberg (1983a).

3. A given increment in masker level does not produce an equal increment in amount of forward masking. For example, if the masker level is increased by 10 dB, the masked threshold may only increase by 3 dB. This contrasts with simultaneous masking, where, at least for wideband maskers, threshold usually corresponds to a constant signal-to-masker ratio. This effect can be quantified by plotting the signal threshold as a function of the masker level. The resulting function is called a growth of masking function. Several such functions are shown in the right panel of Fig. 3.17. In simultaneous masking, such functions would have slopes close to one. In forward masking, the slopes are often less than one, and the slopes decrease as the value of D increases.

4. The amount of forward masking increases with increasing masker duration for durations up to at least 50 ms. The results for greater masker durations vary somewhat across studies. Some studies show an effect of masker duration for durations up to 200 ms (Kidd and Feth, 1982; Zwicker, 1984), while others show little effect for durations beyond 50 ms (Fastl, 1976).

5. Forward masking is influenced by the relation between the frequencies of the signal and the masker (just as in the case of simultaneous masking). This is discussed in more detail in the following section.

The basis of forward masking is still not clear. Five factors may contribute:

1. The response of the BM to the masker continues for some time after the end of the masker, an effect known as "ringing" (see Chapter 1, Section 4, and Fig. 1.13; see also, Chapter 5, Section 3). If the ringing overlaps with the response to the signal, then this may contribute to the masking of the signal. The duration of the ringing is less at places tuned to high frequencies, whose bandwidth is larger than at low frequencies. Hence, ringing plays a significant role only at low frequencies (Duifhuis, 1971, 1973; Plack and Moore, 1990).

2. The masker produces short-term adaptation in the auditory nerve (see Fig. 1.23) or at higher centers in the auditory system, which reduces the response to a signal presented just after the end of the masker (Smith, 1977). It has been argued that the effect in the auditory nerve is too small to account for the forward masking observed behaviorally (Turner et al., 1994), but this argument has been disputed (Meddis and O'Mard, 2005).

3. The neural activity evoked by the masker persists at some level in the auditory system higher than the auditory nerve, and this persisting activity masks the signal (Oxenham, 2001). A model of temporal resolution based on this idea is presented in Chapter 5.

4. The masker may evoke a form of inhibition in the central auditory system, and this inhibition persists for some time after the end of the masker (Brosch and Schreiner, 1997).

5. The masker may activate the efferent system, and this results in reduced gain of the active mechanism, reducing the effective level of the signal (Strickland, 2008). This mechanism probably only operates when the masker duration is greater than a few tens of milliseconds, as it takes this much time for the efferent system to be activated (Backus, 2006; Guinan, 2006).

Oxenham and Moore (1995a) have suggested that the shallow slopes of the growth of masking functions shown in the right panel of Fig. 3.17 can be explained, at least qualitatively, in terms of the compressive input-output function of the BM (see Chapter 1, Section 6B and Fig. 1.12). Such an input-output function is shown schematically in Fig. 3.18. It has a shallow slope for medium input levels, but a steeper slope at very low input levels. Assume that, for a given time delay of the signal relative to the masker, the response evoked by the signal at threshold is directly proportional to the response evoked by

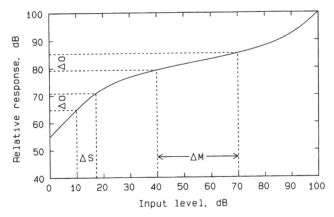

FIGURE 3.18 Illustration of why growth of masking functions in forward masking usually have shallow slopes. The solid curve shows a schematic input-output function on the basilar membrane. The relative response is plotted on a dB scale with an arbitrary origin. When the masker is increased in level by ΔM, this produces an increase in response of ΔO. To restore signal threshold, the response to the signal also has to be increased by ΔO. This requires an increase in signal level, ΔS, that is, markedly smaller than ΔM.

the masker. Assume, as an example, that a masker with a level of 40 dB SPL produces a signal threshold of 10 dB SPL. Consider now what happens when the masker level is increased by 30 dB. The increase in masker level, denoted by ΔM in Fig. 3.18, produces a relatively small increase in response, ΔO. To restore the signal to threshold, the signal has to be increased in level so that the response to it increases by ΔO. However, this requires a relatively small increase in signal level, ΔS, as the signal level falls in the range where the input-output function is relatively steep. Thus, the growth of masking function has a shallow slope.

According to this explanation, the shallow slope of the growth of masking function arises from the fact that the signal level is lower than the masker level, so the masker is subject to more compression than the signal. The input-output function on the BM has a slope that decreases progressively with increasing level over the range 0 to about 50 dB. Hence, the slope of the growth of masking function should decrease with increasing difference in level between the masker and the signal. This can account for the progressive decrease in the slopes of the growth of masking functions with increasing time delay between the signal and the masker (see the right-hand panel of Fig. 3.17); longer time delays are associated with greater differences in level between the signal and the masker. Another prediction is that the growth of masking function for a given signal time delay should increase in slope if the signal level is high enough to fall in the compressive region of the input-output function. Such an effect can be seen in the growth of masking function for the shortest delay time in Fig. 3.17; the function steepens for the highest signal level.

Oxenham and Plack (1997) have investigated forward masking for a 6-kHz sinusoidal masker and a signal of the same frequency. They showed that if the signal is made very brief and the time delay between the signal and the masker is very short, then the level of the signal at threshold is approximately equal to the masker level. Under these conditions, the growth of masking function has a slope of one; each 10-dB increase in masker level is accompanied by a 10-dB increase in signal level. This is consistent with the explanation offered earlier. When they used a masker frequency *below* the signal frequency (3 kHz instead of 6 kHz), the growth of masking function had a slope much *greater* than one; a 10-dB increase in masker level required a 30- to 40-dB increase in signal level. This can be explained in the following way: the signal threshold depends on the response evoked by the masker at the signal CF. The growth of response on the BM for tones well below the CF is almost linear (see Fig. 1.12), at least for high CFs. Thus, the signal is subject to compression while the masker is not (essentially, the opposite of the situation illustrated in Fig. 3.18). This gives rise to the steep growth of masking function.

A method of estimating BM compression using forward masking that has become popular in recent years is based "temporal masking curves" (TMCs, Nelson et al., 2001; Lopez-Poveda et al., 2003). With this method, the brief signal is presented at a fixed low SL, such as 10 dB. This minimizes any off-frequency listening (detection of the signal using an auditory filter that is not centered at the signal frequency). The level of a forward masker needed to mask the signal is measured as a function of the time interval between the masker and the signal. The resulting function is the TMC. The level of the masker required to mask the signal increases with increasing interval, because the forward masking effect decays over time. It is assumed that if the masker is a sinusoid with a frequency well below the signal frequency (called the off-frequency masker), the response to the masker at the place on the BM where the signal is detected is linear. In other words, each 10-dB increase in masker level leads to a 10-dB increase in BM response at that place (this assumption is probably reasonable for medium and high signal frequencies, but not for low frequencies). In contrast, the response on the BM to a sinusoidal masker whose frequency equals the signal frequency (called the on-frequency masker) is expected to be compressive; each 10-dB increase in masker level may lead to only a 2- to 3-dB increase in BM response, for mid-range masker levels. As a result, the masker level has to be increased considerably with increasing masker-signal interval, to compensate for the decay of forward masking and the TMC is much steeper for the on-frequency than for the off-frequency masker, for mid-range masker levels. This is illustrated by the TMCs in the top panel of Fig. 3.19, obtained using a 4-kHz signal (data from Plack *et al.*, 2004).

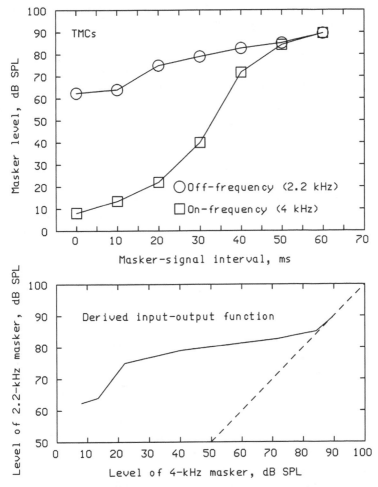

FIGURE 3.19 The top panel shows temporal masking curves (TMCs) obtained in forward masking for a 4-kHz signal and a sinusoidal masker with frequency equal to 4 kHz (squares) or 2.2 kHz (circles). The level of the masker required to mask the signal is plotted as a function of masker-signal interval. The bottom panel shows the derived input-output function of the place on the BM tuned to 4 kHz, obtained by plotting the level of the 2.2-kHz masker against the level of the 4-kHz masker for each masker-signal interval. The dashed line has a slope of 1, for reference.

It is assumed that, for a given masker-signal interval, when the masker is at the level where it just masks the signal, the response on the BM is the same for the on-frequency and the off-frequency maskers. Therefore, by plotting the level of the off-frequency masker against the level of the on-frequency masker for the same masker-signal interval, an estimate of the BM input-output function is obtained. This is illustrated by the solid line in the lower panel of Fig. 3.19. The derived input-output function has a slope near to one for low and high levels, but a shallow slope for mid-range levels, resembling BM input-output functions for a tone with frequency near the CF (see Fig. 1.12).

In summary, the processes underlying forward masking are not fully understood. Contributions from a number of different sources may be important. Temporal overlap of patterns of vibration on the BM may be important, especially for small delay times between the signal and the masker. Short-term adaptation or fatigue in the auditory nerve may also play a role. At higher neural levels, a persistence of the excitation or inhibition evoked by the masker may occur. Also, the masker may activate the efferent system leading in a reduced response to the signal. The form of the growth of masking functions can be explained, at least qualitatively, in terms of the nonlinear input-output functions observed on the BM. Conversely, growth of masking functions and TMCs can be used to estimate input-output functions on the BM in humans.

10 EVIDENCE FOR SUPPRESSION FROM NONSIMULTANEOUS MASKING

The results from experiments on simultaneous masking can generally be explained quite well on the assumption that the peripheral auditory system contains a bank of overlapping band-pass filters that are *approximately* linear. However, measurements from single neurons in the auditory nerve show significant nonlinearities. In particular, the response to a tone of a given frequency can sometimes be suppressed by a tone with a different frequency, giving the phenomenon known as two-tone suppression (see Chapter 1, Section 7F, and Fig. 1.21). For other complex signals, similar phenomena occur and are given the general name lateral suppression or just suppression. This can be characterized in the following way. Strong activity at a given CF can suppress weaker activity at adjacent CFs. As a result, peaks in the excitation pattern are enhanced relative to adjacent dips. The question now arises as to why the effects of suppression are not usually seen in experiments on simultaneous masking.

Houtgast (1972) has argued that simultaneous masking is not an appropriate tool for detecting the effects of suppression because, in the auditory filters and/or neurons used to detect the signal (i.e., those with CFs close to the signal frequency), the masking stimulus and the signal are processed simultaneously. Any suppression at those CFs affects the response to both the signal and the masking noise by the same factor. In other words, the signal-to-noise ratio in a given frequency region is unaffected by suppression, and thus, the threshold of the signal remains unaltered. This argument may not be correct in all cases. Suppression might change the effective signal-to-masker ratio at a given CF if the signal and the masker are widely separated in frequency. However, Houtgast's argument certainly seems reasonable when applied to cases where the signal and the masker have coincident or near coincident frequency components. Say, for example, that the masker consists of two frequency components, at 500 and 2000 Hz, and the signal is a sinusoid at 2000 Hz. If the signal and the masker are presented simultaneously, then the 500-Hz component in the masker may produce suppression at the place on the BM tuned to 2000 Hz (and in neurons with CFs close to 2000 Hz), but that suppression will be applied equally to the 2000-Hz component of the masker and to the 2000-Hz signal, without changing their ratio. If the masking of the signal is determined mainly by the 2000-Hz component of the masker, then the suppression produced by the 500-Hz component will have no measurable effects.

Houtgast suggested that this difficulty could be overcome by presenting the masker and the signal successively (e.g., by using forward masking). If suppression does occur, then its effects will be seen in forward masking provided that (1) in the chain of levels of neural processing, the level at which the suppression occurs is not later than the level at which most of the forward masking effect arises and (2) the suppression built up by the masker has decayed by the time that the signal is presented (otherwise the problems described for simultaneous masking would be encountered).

Houtgast (1972) used a repeated-gap masking technique, in which the masker was presented with a continuous rhythm of 150 ms on, 50 ms off. Signals with a duration of 20 ms were presented in the gaps. In one experiment, he used as maskers high-pass and low-pass noises with sharp spectral cutoffs (96 dB/octave). He anticipated that lateral suppression would result in an enhancement of the neural representation of the spectral edges of the noise. Neurons with CFs well within the passband of the noise should have their responses suppressed by the activity at adjacent CFs. However, for neurons with a CF corresponding to a spectral edge in the noise, there should be a release from suppression, owing to the low activity in neurons with CFs outside the spectral range of the noise. This should be revealed as an increase in the threshold of the signal when its frequency coincided with the spectral edge of each noise band. The results showed the expected edge effects. No such effects were found in simultaneous masking. Thus, nonsimultaneous masking does reveal the type of effects that a suppression process would produce.

Houtgast (1972) also noted a very remarkable feature of the repeated-gap technique that had been reported earlier by Elfner and Caskey (1965): when the bursts of the signal are just above the threshold, they sound like a continuous tone. This is sometimes called the "continuity effect". Only at higher levels of the signal is the percept in accord with the physical time pattern, namely, a series of tone bursts. Houtgast called the level of the signal at which its character changed from continuous to pulsating the pulsation threshold. He showed that the existence of such a pulsation threshold is a very general feature of alternating stimuli and is not restricted to the alternation of two stimuli with a frequency component in common. However, the phenomenon does not occur when the masker contains no frequency component in the neighborhood of the signal. He suggested the following interpretation of the phenomenon: "When a tone and a stimulus S are alternated (alternation cycle about 4 Hz), the tone is perceived as being continuous when the transition from S to tone causes no (perceptible) increase of nervous activity in any frequency region" (Houtgast, 1972). In terms of patterns of excitation, this suggests that "the peak of the nervous activity pattern of the tone at pulsation threshold level just reaches the nervous activity pattern of S". Given this hypothesis, the pulsation threshold for a test tone as a function of frequency can be considered to map out the excitation pattern of the stimulus S. The pulsation threshold curve thus reflects both the quasi-linear filtering revealed in simultaneous masking and the effects of lateral suppression. The pulsation threshold and its interpretation are discussed further in Chapter 8. For the moment, it will be accepted as providing a tool for mapping the representation of sounds in the auditory system. For convenience, I refer to the measurement of the pulsation threshold as a nonsimultaneous masking technique.

Following the pioneering work of Houtgast, many workers have reported that there are systematic differences between the results obtained using simultaneous and nonsimultaneous masking. A good demonstration of this involves a psychophysical analog of neural two-tone suppression. Houtgast (1973, 1974) measured the pulsation threshold for a 1-kHz "signal" alternating with a 1-kHz "masker". He then added a second tone to the "masker" and measured the pulsation threshold again. He found that sometimes the addition of this second tone produced a reduction in the pulsation threshold, and he attributed this to a suppression of the 1-kHz component in the "masker" by the second component. If the 1-kHz component is suppressed, then there will be less activity in the frequency region around 1 kHz, producing a drop in the pulsation threshold. The second tone was most effective as a "suppressor" when it was somewhat more intense than the 1-kHz component and above it in frequency. A "suppression" of about 20 dB could be produced by a "suppressor" at 1.2 kHz. Houtgast mapped out the combinations of frequency and intensity over which the "suppressor" produced a "suppression" exceeding 3 dB. He found two regions, one above 1 kHz and one below, as illustrated in Fig. 3.20. The regions found were similar to the suppression areas that can be observed for single neurons of the auditory nerve (see Fig. 1.21). Similar results have been found using forward masking (Shannon, 1976).

A second major difference between the two types of masking is that the frequency selectivity revealed in nonsimultaneous masking is greater than that revealed in simultaneous masking. An example of this is the PTC, which was discussed in Section 3A. PTCs are obtained by determining the level of a masker required to mask a fixed signal as a function of masker frequency.

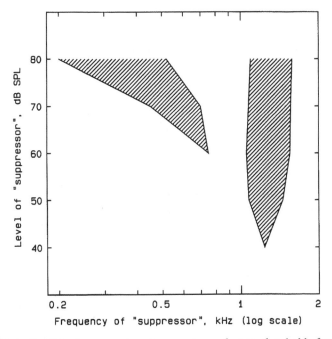

FIGURE 3.20 Results of an experiment measuring pulsation thresholds for a 1-kHz "signal" alternated with a two-component "masker". One component of the masker was a 1-kHz tone that was fixed in level at 40 dB. The second component (the "suppressor") was a tone that was varied both in frequency and in level. The shaded areas indicate combinations of frequency and level where the second tone reduced the pulsation threshold by 3 dB or more. Adapted from Houtgast (1974).

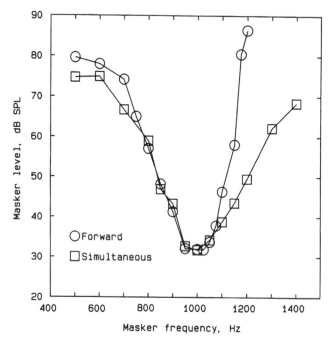

FIGURE 3.21 Comparison of psychophysical tuning curves (PTCs) determined in simultaneous masking (squares) and forward masking (circles). The signal frequency was 1000 Hz. A low-level notched-noise masker was gated with the main narrowband noise masker to restrict off-frequency listening. Data from Moore *et al.* (1984a).

PTCs determined in forward masking, or using the pulsation threshold method, are typically sharper than those obtained in simultaneous masking (Moore, 1978). An example is given in Fig. 3.21 (Moore *et al.*, 1984a). When these data were gathered, a low-level notched-noise masker was gated with the main narrowband noise masker to restrict off-frequency listening. The difference between simultaneous and forward masking is particularly marked on the high-frequency sides of the tuning curves.

Two different explanations have been proposed for the sharper tuning found in forward masking. According to Houtgast (1974), the sharper tuning arises because the internal representation of the masker (its excitation pattern) is sharpened by a suppression process, with the greatest sharpening occurring on the low-frequency side. In simultaneous masking, the effects of suppression are not seen, because any reduction of the masker activity in the frequency region of the signal is accompanied by a similar reduction in signal-evoked activity. In other words, the signal-to-masker ratio in the frequency region of the signal is unaffected by the suppression. In forward masking, on the other hand, the suppression does not affect the signal. For maskers with frequencies above or below that of the signal, the effect of suppression is to sharpen the excitation pattern of the masker, resulting in an increase of the masker level required to mask the signal. Thus, the suppression is revealed as an increase in the slopes of the PTC.

An alternative explanation is that described earlier: in simultaneous masking, the signal may be suppressed by the masker, and this increases the effectiveness of the masker for masker frequencies well above and below the signal frequency. In nonsimultaneous masking, the masker does not suppress the signal, and so, the masker is less effective (Delgutte, 1988, 1990). Hence, when determining a PTC, the masker level has to be increased on the skirts of the PTC.

Whichever of these two explanations is correct, the same inference can be drawn; the tuning curve measured in nonsimultaneous masking gives a more accurate indication of the tuning that occurs for single sinusoids. Thus, the PTC measured in nonsimultaneous masking is likely to be closely related to BM tuning curves and neural tuning curves, while the PTC measured in simultaneous masking is likely to be broader than those curves.

Several other methods of estimating frequency selectivity have indicated sharper tuning in nonsimultaneous masking. For example, for medium signal frequencies, auditory filter shapes estimated in forward masking using a notched-noise masker (as described in Section 3B) have 3-dB bandwidths about 17% less and slopes about 50% greater than those estimated in simultaneous masking (Moore and Glasberg, 1981; Moore et al., 1987). For high signal frequencies, the differences between filter shapes estimated using simultaneous and forward masking are greater (Shera et al., 2002; Oxenham and Shera, 2003; Oxenham and Simonson, 2006).

It can be concluded that results from nonsimultaneous masking do show clearly the types of effects that would be expected if a suppression mechanism were operating. The level at which the effects occur is uncertain, but the most common assumption has been that they arise at a very early stage in auditory processing, probably on the BM (Ruggero et al., 1992).

One question that arises from all of this is: what are the most appropriate psychophysical measures of tuning to compare with measures of tuning obtained from physiological studies of animals. Measures of tuning on the BM or in single neurons of the auditory nerve have often been obtained using sinusoidal stimuli; only one sine wave is presented at any one time (see Chapter 1). Psychophysical measures of tuning obtained from simultaneous masking involve the presentation of more than one sinusoidal component at a time, whereas measures obtained from nonsimultaneous masking, such as PTCs, can involve only one sinusoidal component at a time (e.g., a signal followed by a masker). Therefore, one might argue that measures obtained in forward masking should be more comparable to physiological measures than measures obtained in simultaneous masking (Houtgast, 1973; Shera et al., 2002). However, some researchers have disputed this view (Ruggero and Temchin, 2005).

A related question is whether the sharpness of tuning in humans is similar to that in other mammals. Some authors (Evans et al., 1989; Shera et al., 2002, 2010; Pickles, 2008; Young, 2008) have argued that the auditory filters are sharper in humans than in most other mammals, but Ruggero and Temchin (2005) have argued that the sharpness of tuning in humans is "unexceptional". This remains a matter of controversy, but the weight of evidence seems to favor the idea that humans have sharper tuning than the animals that have been studied the most (cat, guinea pig, and chinchilla).

11 INFORMATIONAL MASKING

The types of simultaneous masking described so far in this chapter can be explained largely in terms of processes occurring in the cochlea and the auditory nerve. Masking of this type is sometimes called (inappropriately) "energetic masking", and it occurs when the response of the auditory nerve to the masker-plus-signal is very similar to the response to the masker alone. However, when a masking sound is highly similar in some way to the signal, and/or when the properties of the masker vary in an unpredictable way from one stimulus to the next, there may be much more masking than would be expected from energetic masking alone. This "extra" masking is called "informational masking". For example, Neff and coworkers (Neff and Green, 1987; Neff and Callaghan, 1988) measured the masking of a 1000-Hz tone produced by a masker composed of multiple (nonharmonic) sinusoidal components. The spectrum of the masker was varied randomly from stimulus to stimulus. The threshold for detecting the signal was much higher than predicted from the amount of masker energy passing through the auditory filter centered at the signal frequency. It is assumed that informational masking occurs because the signal is confused with the masker, because the signal is difficult to perceptually segregate from the masker (see Chapter 8) or because attention is not directed to the most appropriate aspect of the sound (Carhart et al., 1969a; Moore, 1980; Neff and Green, 1987; Freyman et al., 1999; Watson, 2005). Using a task similar to that of Neff, described above, Oxenham et al. (2003) showed that informational masking was smaller for musically trained subjects than for subjects with little or no musical training, perhaps because musicians have more experience in selectively attending to specific spectral and temporal features of sounds.

Informational masking almost certainly involves several different mechanisms, not all of which are understood. Informational masking of speech is discussed in Chapter 9.

12 FREQUENCY SELECTIVITY IN IMPAIRED HEARING

There is now considerable evidence that frequency selectivity is impaired by damage to the cochlea. Chapter 1, Section 6B, reviewed some of the evidence that the tuning of the BM is physiologically vulnerable. Damage to the tuning can be reversed if the damaging agent (e.g., reduced oxygen supply, noise exposure, and drugs such as aspirin) is removed quickly enough. Otherwise, it can be permanent. Evidence for vulnerability of tuning has also been obtained from studies of single neurons (Robertson and Manley, 1974; Evans, 1975; Evans and Harrison, 1976).

There have been many psychophysical studies of frequency selectivity in humans with hearing impairment; for reviews, see Tyler (1986) and Moore (2007). Zwicker and Schorn (1978) measured PTCs for six different groups of subjects: normal hearing; conductive hearing loss, degenerative hearing loss (produced by aging or progressive hereditary loss), noise-induced hearing loss, advanced otosclerosis, and Ménière's disease. They found that the PTCs of the last four groups, where the hearing loss is assumed to involve a defect in the cochlea, were considerably less sharp than those of the first two groups, where no defect of the cochlea is involved. This indicates a loss of frequency selectivity associated with cochlear damage.

Florentine et al. (1980) used several different measures of frequency selectivity and found that, in people with cochlear impairments, all of the measures indicated reduced selectivity. Glasberg and Moore (1986) found that auditory filter shapes estimated using a notched-noise masker (using the same noise level for the normal and the impaired ears) were much broader than normal in cases of cochlear impairment. Some examples are given in Fig. 3.22. Pick et al. (1977) estimated auditory filter shapes in a different way, but came to essentially the same conclusion. Several studies have shown that there is a weak correlation between threshold elevation and filter bandwidth; higher absolute thresholds tend to be associated with broader filters (Tyler, 1986; Moore, 1995; Moore et al., 1999c). The correlation may be weak because the elevation of absolute threshold depends on damage to both OHCs and IHCs, whereas the broadening of the filters depends mainly on damage to the OHCs.

It is worth considering the perceptual consequences of a loss of frequency selectivity. The first major consequence is a greater susceptibility to masking

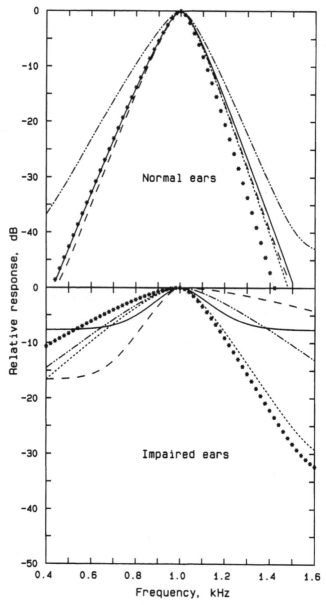

FIGURE 3.22   Auditory filter shapes for a center frequency of 1 kHz, estimated for five subjects, each having one normal ear and one ear with a cochlear hearing loss. The relative response of each filter (in dB) is plotted as a function of frequency. The filter shapes for the normal ears are shown at the top and those for the impaired ears at the bottom. Each line type represents results for one subject. Note that the filters for the impaired ears are broader than normal, particularly on the low-frequency side. Data from Glasberg and Moore (1986).

by interfering sounds. When we are trying to detect a signal in a noisy background, we use the auditory filter(s) giving the best signal-to-noise ratio. In a normal ear, where the auditory filters are relatively narrow, all of the background noise except a narrow band around the signal frequency is attenuated at the filter output. In an impaired ear, where the filters are broader, much more of the noise gets through the filter, and therefore, the detectability of the signal is reduced. Thus, background noises severely disrupt the detection and discrimination of sounds, including speech. This may partly account for the great difficulties experienced by those with cochlear impairments in following speech in noisy situations such as in bars or at parties (Moore, 2007).

A second difficulty arises in the perceptual analysis of complex sounds such as speech or music. As described in Chapter 8, the perception of timbre depends on the ear's frequency selectivity. When frequency selectivity is impaired, the ability to detect differences in the spectral composition of sounds, and hence in timbre, is reduced. Thus, it may be more difficult for the impaired listener to tell the difference between different vowel sounds or to distinguish different musical instruments. Note that the provision of a hearing aid that simply amplifies sound will not overcome any of these difficulties. Such an aid may help to make sounds audible, but it does not correct impaired frequency selectivity.

13 GENERAL CONCLUSIONS

Many of the phenomena discussed in this chapter can be understood by considering the peripheral auditory system as containing a bank of band-pass filters with overlapping passbands. The BM provides the initial basis of the filtering process. The general properties of the frequency analysis carried out by the auditory system are summarized in the critical band concept: listeners' responses to complex stimuli differ depending on whether the components of the stimuli fall within one CB or are spread over a number of CBs. The CB is revealed in experiments on masking, absolute threshold, phase sensitivity, and the audibility of partials in complex tones. However, the auditory filter does not have a rectangular shape; rather, it has a rounded top and sloping sides. The value of the CB should not be regarded as a complete specification of the filter, but merely as a rough indication of its bandwidth.

The auditory filter can be thought of as a weighting function that characterizes frequency selectivity at a particular center frequency. Recent estimates of the bandwidth of the auditory filter are based on its equivalent rectangular bandwidth (ERB). The average value of the ERB at moderate sound levels for normally hearing people is denoted ERB_N. The value of ERB_N for frequencies above 1 kHz is about 10–17% of the center frequency. At moderate sound levels, the auditory filter is roughly symmetric on a linear frequency scale. At high sound levels, the low-frequency side of the filter becomes less steep than the high-frequency side.

The neural excitation pattern of a given sound represents the distribution of activity evoked by that sound as a function of the CF of the neurons stimulated. It resembles a blurred or smeared version of the magnitude spectrum of the sound. In psychophysical terms, the excitation pattern can be defined as the output of each auditory filter as a function of its center frequency. Excitation patterns are usually asymmetric, being less steep on the high-frequency side. The asymmetry increases with increasing sound level. The shapes of excitation patterns are similar to the masking patterns of narrowband maskers.

Simultaneous masking is usually explained in terms of two underlying processes. Masking may correspond to a "swamping" of the neural activity of the signal, a suppression of that activity by the masker, or a mixture of the two. The neural code carrying information about the signal is uncertain. A common assumption is that the *amount* of neural activity in neurons with different CFs is important. Another possibility is that the *time pattern* of neural activity carries information, but this would mainly apply for stimulating frequencies below 4–5 kHz.

Although many phenomena in simultaneous masking can be explained by assuming that the listener monitors the single auditory filter that gives the highest signal-to-masker ratio, some experiments clearly show that listeners can compare the outputs of different auditory filters to enhance signal detection. If the masker is amplitude modulated in such a way that the modulation is coherent or correlated in different frequency bands, a reduction in signal threshold, known as comodulation masking release (CMR), can occur. If the magnitude of the output from any single auditory filter is made an unreliable cue to the presence of the signal, by randomizing the overall sound level of each stimulus, then subjects can still detect the signal by comparing the outputs of different filters, a process called profile analysis.

The processes underlying the phenomena of forward and backward masking are poorly understood. A number of stages can be distinguished in these processes, which may be related to different levels of neural activity. Forward masking may depend on the persistence of responses on the BM (ringing), neural adaptation, or fatigue, the persistence of the neural activity or inhibition evoked by the masker at some level of the auditory system, and activation of the efferent system. The shallow growth of masking that is often found in forward masking can be explained in terms of the nonlinear input-output function of the BM.

Houtgast and others have shown that nonsimultaneous masking reveals suppression effects similar to the suppression observed in primary auditory neurons. These effects are not revealed in simultaneous masking, possibly because suppression at a given CF does not affect the signal-to-masker ratio at that CF. The frequency selectivity measured using forward masking is greater than that measured using simultaneous masking.

There is now a good deal of evidence that part of the ear's frequency selectivity is physiologically vulnerable. This has been shown both in neurophysiological studies using animals and in psychophysical studies using people with hearing impairments of cochlear origin. The broadening of the auditory filter in hearing-impaired people can produce several perceptual deficits that are not corrected by a conventional hearing aid.

14 APPENDIX: SIGNAL DETECTION THEORY

14A INTRODUCTION

A great deal of Chapters 2 and 3 has been concerned with the measurement of thresholds. Classically, a threshold has been considered as that intensity of a stimulus above which it will be detected and below which it will not. It has been known for many years that this viewpoint is unsatisfactory; if the intensity of a stimulus is slowly increased from a very low value, there is no well-defined point at which it suddenly becomes detectable. Rather, there is a range of intensities over which the subject will sometimes report a signal and sometimes will not. Consider a task where on each trial there is a single observation interval, and the subject is required to respond "yes, I heard a signal" or "no, I did not hear a signal". A plot of percentage "yes" responses against the magnitude of the stimulus typically has the form shown in Fig. 3.23; such a plot is called a psychometric function. Note that for low signal magnitudes, the function shows an asymptote at a value greater than zero; the subject sometimes says "yes" even when there is no signal at all. Such responses are called "false positives", and they are discussed further below. Also, a subject's performance may be altered by changing the instructions, while at the same time, the stimulus itself has remained unaltered. Thus, factors not directly associated with the discriminability of the signal may influence the subject's performance. Signal detection theory provides a means of separating factors relating to criterion, motivation, and bias from factors relating to purely sensory capabilities. It also accounts for the fact that responses may vary from trial to trial even when an identical stimulus is presented on each trial.

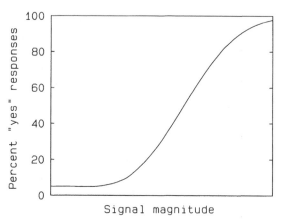

FIGURE 3.23 A typical psychometric function showing how the percentage of "yes" responses varies with signal magnitude.

14B The Basic Idea of Signal Detection Theory

The theory assumes that decisions are based on the value of some internal variable x, called the "decision variable". The nature of x is not precisely specified. One might consider it to correspond to the "sensory impression" evoked by the stimulus, or one might think of it in more physiological terms; x might correspond to the number of neural spikes occurring in a particular channel during the presentation time of the stimulus. The important point is that such a variable exists and that its average value is monotonically related to the magnitude of the stimulus, that is, increases in the magnitude of the stimulus will, on average, increase the value of x. The second assumption of the theory is that the value of x fluctuates from trial to trial, even though the same signal is presented. This variability may arise from two sources. The signal may actually be presented against a variable background, such as a noise, so that fluctuations in physical intensity occur. Alternatively, or in addition, the source of the variability may be neural; neural responses to a fixed stimulus vary from one presentation to the next.

Although the average value of x will depend on whether a signal is present or absent, on any given trial the subject will never be absolutely sure that a signal has occurred, because of the inherent variability of x. Of course, if the signal is sufficiently intense, the increase in x is large compared with this variability, and thus, the uncertainty becomes vanishingly small. But, for faint signals, the best that the subject can do is to make a guess on the basis of the value of x that occurred on that particular trial.

To proceed further, assumptions are needed about the distribution of x. Since x is a random variable, its exact value on any trial cannot be predicted. However, it is possible to specify the probability that x will fall within a specified range of values. One way of doing this is to plot a probability density function, $f(x)$. The expression "$f(x)$" simply implies that f is a function of x. A probability density function, $f(x)$, is defined in such a way that the probability of x lying between x and $x + dx$ (where dx represents a small change in the value of x) is equal to $f(x)$ multiplied by dx. A probability density function is illustrated in Fig. 3.24. The quantity $f(x)dx$ is equal to the area under the curve between the limits x and $x + dx$. More generally, the probability that x lies between two values, x_1 and x_2, is given by the area under the curve between these two points. Since, on any given trial, some value of x must occur, the total area under the curve is equal to 1.

Consider the situation where a subject is given a series of trials, on some of which a signal is present and on some of which it is absent. To describe this situation, two probability density functions must be specified; one describes the distribution of values of x when no signal is present (this is often denoted by $f(x)_N$, the suffix N referring to the "noise", either external or neural, that gives rise to this distribution), and the other describes the distribution of values of x when a signal does occur (often denoted $f(x)_{SN}$). It is usually assumed that these two distributions are normal, or Gaussian, and that they have equal variances. There are some theoretical reasons for making this assumption, but normal distributions are also chosen because results are easier to handle in terms of the mathematics involved. The distributions are plotted with standard deviation units along the abscissa; on such a scale, each

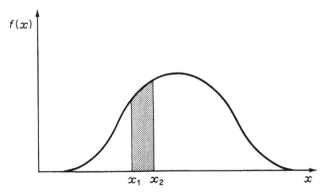

FIGURE 3.24   A probability density function. The probability of x lying between the two values x_1 and x_2 is given by the shaded area under the curve. The total area under the curve is 1.

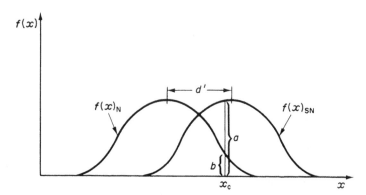

FIGURE 3.25   The two distributions (probability density functions) that occur in response to "noise" alone [f(x)$_N$] and "noise" plus signal [f(x)$_{SN}$]. The separation between the means of the two curves, denoted by d', gives a measure of the discriminability of the signal. The criterion value is labeled x_c, and the ratio of the heights of the two curves at x_c, namely, a/b, gives the likelihood ratio, β.

distribution has a standard deviation corresponding to one unit. They appear as in Fig. 3.25. For each of these two distributions, the mean value of x corresponds to the peak in the distribution, and the separation between the two peaks, denoted by d', gives a measure of the separation of the two distributions and thus of the detectability of the signal.

The theory assumes that the subject establishes a cutoff point corresponding to a particular value of x, denoted the criterion value, x_c. If, on any given trial, the value of x that actually occurs is greater than x_c, the subject reports that a signal was present; otherwise, he or she reports no signal. Just what value of x_c is chosen depends on the instructions to the subject, the probability of a signal, the system of rewards and punishments, previous experience, and motivation. As the exact nature of x is not specified, x_c cannot be given a numerical value. To overcome this problem, a new quantity is introduced: the likelihood ratio, β. This is defined as the ratio of the heights of the two distributions at x_c, that is, as f(x$_c$)$_{SN}$/f(x$_c$)$_N$. In other words, the quantity β is equal to the likelihood ratio that a value of x of magnitude x_c arose from the presentation of a signal plus noise as opposed to noise alone. In Fig. 3.25 β is equal to a/b. In contrast to d', which gives a pure measure of the discriminability of the signal, β is related to the criterion of the subject and gives a measure of his or her degree of caution independent of any changes in sensory capability.

In an experiment, two quantities are measured: the proportion of times the subject responds yes when a signal is present, $P(H)$ (this is called the probability of a hit); and the proportion of times the subject responds yes when a signal is absent, $P(F)$ (this is called the probability of a false positive). From these proportions, and given the assumption that the distributions are normal and of equal variance, it is easy to calculate the values of d' and β. For examples, see Macmillan and Creelman (2005). In practice, the situation is even easier than this, because tables exist giving the values of d' and β for any given values of $P(H)$ and $P(F)$.

The major advantage of signal detection theory is that it makes it possible to separate changes in performance related to purely sensory factors from changes related to motivation or criterion. Notice that this can only be done by measuring the proportion of false positives as well as the proportion of hits. Classical methods of determining thresholds, ignoring as they did the former measure, were not able to achieve this separation. Note further that according to this theory, there is no such thing as a sensory threshold; any given intensity of a signal presented to a subject has associated with it a certain value of d', but there is no particular value of the intensity that corresponds to threshold. In practice, a "threshold" can be defined arbitrarily as the value of the signal needed to produce a particular value of d'.

Yes-no tasks of the type described above are now rarely used. Instead, tasks are used that are intended to eliminate the effects of bias or criterion, so that threshold can be arbitrarily defined as corresponding to a particular percentage correct. One type of task that has proved useful in this respect is the two-alternative forced-choice (2AFC) task, in which there are two observation intervals, only one of which contains the signal. The theory assumes that for each observation interval, a particular value of x occurs, and the subject simply chooses the interval in which the largest value of x occurs. Results in a 2AFC task can be simply related to those in a "single interval" task where the subject is simply required to say whether a signal was present or not on each trial; 76% correct in 2AFC corresponds to a d' of 1.

FURTHER RESOURCES

The following monograph has as its central theme the action of the ear as a frequency analyzer. It is clearly written, and contains a discussion of several aspects of frequency selectivity that are beyond the scope of this book:

Plomp, R. (1976). *Aspects of Tone Sensation.* London: Academic.

A very detailed review of the frequency selectivity of the ear, covering both physiological and psychological aspects, is the following collection of edited chapters:
Moore, B. C. J. (1986). *Frequency Selectivity in Hearing.* London: Academic.

For a more up to date review, see

Oxenham, A. J., and Wojtczak, M. (2010). Frequency selectivity and masking. In C. J. Plack (Ed.), *The Oxford Handbook of Auditory Science: Hearing.* Oxford: Oxford University Press.

Demonstrations 1-3, 9-11, and 32-34 of Auditory Demonstrations on CD are relevant to the contents of this chapter (see list of further reading for Chapter 1).

Computer programs for deriving auditory filter shapes from notched-noise data and for calculating excitation patterns can be downloaded from:

http://hearing.psychol.cam.ac.uk/Demos/demos.html

Software for measuring psychophysical tuning curves using a PC with a good-quality sound card can be downloaded from:

http://hearing.psychol.cam.ac.uk/SWPTC/SWPTC.htm

A comprehensive review of profile analysis is:

Green, D. M. (1988). *Profile Analysis.* New York: Oxford University Press.

A review of across-channel processes in masking, including CMR and MDI, can be found in the chapter by Hall, Grose, and Eddins in:

Moore, B. C. J. (1995). *Hearing.* San Diego, CA: Academic Press.

A comprehensible primer of signal detection theory may be found in:

McNicol, D. (2004). *A Primer of Signal Detection Theory.* Mahwah, NJ: Lawrence Erlbaum.

Signal detection theory and its applications are covered in detail in:

Green, D. M., and Swets, J. A. (1974). *Signal Detection Theory and Psychophysics.* New York: Kreiger.

Macmillan, N. A., and Creelman, C. D. (2005). *Detection Theory: A User's Guide* (2nd Ed.). New York: Erlbaum.

An interactive demonstration of the principles of signal detection theory can be found at:

http://cog.sys.virginia.edu/csees/SDT/index.html

Reviews of the effects of cochlear hearing loss on frequency selectivity may be found in:

Moore, B. C. J. (1995). *Perceptual Consequences of Cochlear Damage.* Oxford: Oxford University Press.

Moore, B. C. J. (2007). *Cochlear Hearing Loss: Physiological, Psychological and Technical Issues* (2nd Ed.). Chichester: Wiley.

Simulations of the effects of reduced frequency selectivity on the perception of music and speech are available on a CD called "Perceptual Consequences of Cochlear Damage" that may be obtained by writing to B. C. J. Moore, Department of Experimental Psychology, University of Cambridge, Downing Street, Cambridge, CB2 3EB, England, and enclosing a check for 25 dollars or a cheque for 12 pounds sterling, made payable to B. C. J. Moore.

CHAPTER 4

The Perception of Loudness

1 INTRODUCTION

The human ear can respond over a remarkable range of sound intensities. The most intense sound we can hear without immediately damaging our ears has a level about 120 dB above that of the faintest sound we can detect. This corresponds to a ratio of intensities of 1,000,000,000,000:1. One aim of this chapter is to discuss the ways in which this range is achieved.

Loudness is defined as that attribute of auditory sensation in terms of which sounds can be ordered on a scale extending from quiet to loud. A second aim of this chapter is to discuss how the loudness of sounds depends on frequency and intensity and to relate this to the way in which the sounds are coded or represented in the auditory system. A problem in studying the loudness of sounds is that loudness is a subjective quantity and, as such, cannot be measured directly. This problem has been tackled in a number of different ways: sometimes subjects are asked to match the loudness of a sound to that of some standard comparison stimulus (often a 1000-Hz tone); in other experiments subjects are asked to rate loudness on a numerical scale, a technique known as magnitude estimation. There are problems associated with each of these methods.

A third area of discussion is that of loudness adaptation, fatigue, and damage risk. In general, adaptation and fatigue in the auditory system are much less marked than in the visual system, and the effects also have different time courses. In certain types of hearing loss, adaptation effects become more marked. I discuss how this and the phenomenon of recruitment (see Section 9) can be used in the differential diagnosis of hearing disorders.

2 LOUDNESS LEVEL AND EQUAL-LOUDNESS CONTOURS

There are many occasions when engineers and acousticians require a subjective scale corresponding to the loudness of a sound. Since complex sounds are often analyzed in terms of their individual frequency components, a useful first step is to derive such a scale for pure tones. One way of doing this is to use the technique of magnitude estimation to determine the relationship between physical intensity and loudness. However, the validity of this technique has been questioned, and before discussing it (Section 3), I consider an alternative measure of loudness that is not at first sight as straightforward, but that nevertheless has proved useful in practice and is not quite so controversial. The alternative is the loudness level, which indicates not how loud a tone is, but rather the level that a 1000-Hz tone must have in order to sound equally loud. To determine the loudness level of a given sound, the subject is asked to adjust the level of a 1000-Hz tone until it has the same loudness as the test sound. The 1000-Hz tone and the test sound are presented alternately rather than simultaneously. The level of the 1000-Hz tone that gives equal loudness is the loudness level of the test sound, measured in "phons". By definition, the loudness level of a 1000-Hz tone is equal to its sound pressure level in dB SPL.

In a variation of this procedure, the 1000-Hz tone may be fixed in level and the test sound adjusted to give a loudness match. If this is repeated for various different frequencies of a sinusoidal test sound, an equal-loudness contour is generated (Fletcher and Munson, 1933). For example, if the 1000-Hz sinusoid is fixed in level at 40 dB SPL, then the 40-phon equal-loudness contour is generated. The shapes of equal-loudness contours depend on the method used to measure them and vary markedly across studies (Gabriel et al., 1997). The ISO standard equal-loudness contours (ISO 226, 2003), shown in Fig. 4.1, are based on extensive measurements from several laboratories, as described by Suzuki and Takeshima (2004). The figure shows equal-loudness contours for binaural listening for loudness levels from 10 to 100 phons, and it

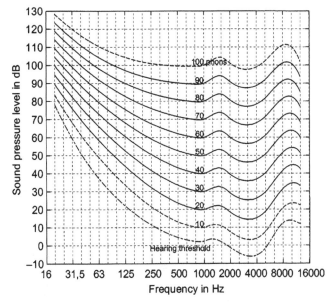

FIG. 4.1   Equal-loudness contours for loudness levels from 10 to 100 phons for sounds presented binaurally from the frontal direction. The absolute threshold curve (the MAF) is also shown. The curves for loudness levels of 10 and 100 phons are dashed, as they are based on interpolation and extrapolation, respectively.

also includes the absolute threshold (MAF) curve. The listening conditions were the same as those for determining the MAF curve, namely, that the sound came from a frontal direction in a free field (i.e., in a situation where there was no reflected sound from walls, floor, or ceiling).

The equal-loudness contours are of similar shape to the MAF curve, but they tend to become flatter at high loudness levels. This means that the rate of growth of loudness differs for tones of different frequency. For example, the absolute threshold for a 100-Hz tone is about 24 dB above that for a 1000-Hz tone (thresholds at about 26 and 2 dB SPL). But for the 100-phon contour, the levels at 100 and 1000 Hz differ much less (106 and 100 dB SPL). For the same range of loudness levels, from threshold to 100 phons, the level of the 1000-Hz tone must be increased by 98 dB, while that of the 100-Hz tone must be increased by only 80 dB. Thus, the rate of growth of loudness level with increasing level is greater for low frequencies (and to some extent for very high frequencies) than for middle frequencies.

The shapes of equal-loudness contours have implications for the reproduction of sound; the relative loudness of the different frequency components in a sound changes as a function of the overall level, so unless the sounds are reproduced at the same level as the original, the "tonal balance" is altered. This is one of the reasons why human voices often sound "boomy" when reproduced at high levels via loudspeakers; the ear becomes relatively more sensitive to low frequencies at high intensities. Conversely, at low levels we are less sensitive to the very low and very high frequencies. To compensate for this, many amplifiers incorporate a "loudness" control that boosts the bass (and to some extent the treble) at low listening levels. Such controls are of limited use, since they take no account of loudspeaker efficiency (see Chapter 10, Section 3C) and size of room.

The shapes of equal-loudness contours have been used in the design of sound level meters. These are intended to give an approximate measure of the loudness of complex sounds. The meters contain weighting networks, so that the meter does not simply sum the intensities at all different frequencies, but rather weights the intensity at each frequency according to the shapes of the equal-loudness contours before doing the summation across frequency. The weighting networks actually used, however, only poorly approximate the shapes of equal-loudness contours. At low sound levels, low-frequency components contribute little to the total loudness of a complex sound, so an "A" weighting is used that reduces the contribution of low frequencies to the final meter reading. The "A" weighting is based roughly on the 30-phon equal-loudness contour. At high levels, all frequencies contribute more or less equally to the loudness sensation (the equal-loudness contours being approximately flat), so a more nearly linear weighting characteristic, the "C" network, is used. The "B" weighting is used for intermediate levels; it is based on the 70-phon equal-loudness contour. Sound levels measured with these meters are usually specified in terms of the weighting used. Thus, a given level might be specified as 35 dBA, meaning that the meter gave a reading of 35 dB when the "A" weighting was used.

There are a number of problems associated with the use of sound level meters. First, they can only be reliably used with steady sounds of relatively long duration; the responses to transient sounds do not correspond to subjective impressions of the loudness of such sounds. Second, they do not provide a satisfactory way of summing the loudness of components in widely separated frequency bands. As described later in this chapter, the loudness of a complex sound with a given amount of energy depends on whether that energy is contained within a narrow range of frequencies or is spread over a wide range of frequencies.

Finally, it should not be assumed that sound level meters give a direct estimate of the perceived loudness of a given sound. The readings obtained are closely related to the decibel scale, which is a scale of physical magnitude rather than a scale of subjective sensation. Thus it would be quite wrong to say that a sound giving a reading of 80 dB was twice as loud as a sound giving a reading of 40 dB; the 80-dB sound would actually appear to be about 16 times as loud as the 40-dB sound (see Section 3). However, the meters do make it possible roughly to compare the loudness of different complex sounds. I discuss below models that provide more satisfactory estimates of the loudness of complex sounds.

3 THE SCALING OF LOUDNESS

In this section, I briefly discuss attempts to derive scales relating the physical magnitudes of sounds to their subjective loudness. The development of scales of loudness and other sensory dimensions was pioneered by S. S. Stevens, and the reader is referred to his work for further details (Stevens, 1957, 1972). Two methods have been commonly used to derive scales of loudness. In one, called magnitude estimation, sounds with various different levels are presented, and the subject is asked to assign a number to each one according to its perceived loudness. Sometimes a reference sound (called the "modulus" or "standard") is presented, and the subject is asked to judge the loudness of each test sound relative to that of the standard. However, some authors have argued that it is better not to use a standard but to allow listeners to use any numbers that they like in making their judgments (Hellman, 1976). In a second method, called magnitude production, the subject is asked to adjust the level of a test sound until it has a specified loudness, either in absolute terms or relative to that of a standard, for example, twice as loud, four times as loud, half as loud, and so on.

Stevens suggested that perceived loudness, L, was a power function of physical intensity, I:

$$L = kI^{0.3}$$

where k is a constant depending on the subject and the units used. In other words, the loudness of a given sound is proportional to its intensity raised to the power 0.3. A simple approximation to this is that a twofold change in loudness is produced by a 10-fold change in intensity, corresponding to a 10-dB change in level. This rule can also be expressed in terms of amplitude or sound pressure; the loudness of a given sound is proportional to its RMS pressure raised to the power 0.6. Stevens proposed the "sone" as the unit of loudness. One sone is defined arbitrarily as the loudness of a 1000-Hz tone at 40 dB SPL, presented binaurally from a frontal direction in free field. A 1000-Hz tone with a level of 50 dB SPL is usually judged as about twice as loud as a 40-dB SPL tone and has a loudness of 2 sones. This simple relationship does not hold for sound levels below 40 dB SPL. At low levels, the loudness changes more rapidly with sound level than implied by the above equation. Figure 4.2 shows the average relationship between loudness in sones and loudness level in phons for a 1000-Hz sinusoid presented binaurally in free field to subjects with "normal" hearing. If a sound is presented to one ear only, the loudness in sones is about 0.67 times that for binaural presentation, although estimates of the ratio of monaural to binaural loudness vary markedly across studies (Moore and Glasberg, 2007; Sivonen and Ellermeier, 2011).

The power law relationship between intensity and loudness has been confirmed in a large number of experiments using a variety of techniques. However, there have also been criticisms of loudness scaling. The techniques used are very susceptible to bias effects, and results are affected by factors such as: (1) the range of stimuli presented; (2) the first stimulus presented; (3) the instructions to the subject; (4) the range of permissible responses; (5) the symmetry of the response range (judgments tend to be biased towards the middle of the range available for responses); and (6) various other factors related to experience, motivation, training, and attention (Poulton, 1979).

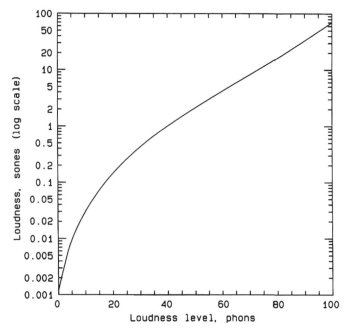

FIG. 4.2 The relationship between loudness in sones and loudness level in phons for a 1000-Hz sinusoid. The curve is based on the loudness model of Moore et al. (1997).

Very large individual differences are observed, and consistent results are only obtained by averaging many judgments of a large number of subjects. Warren (1970a) attempted to eliminate known bias effects by obtaining just a single judgment from each subject. He found that half-loudness corresponds to a 6-dB reduction in level, rather than the 10 dB suggested by Stevens. However, considerable variability is also apparent in his data.

Some researchers object to the whole concept of asking a listener to judge the magnitude of a sensation. What we do in everyday life is to judge the "loudness" of sound sources. Our estimate is affected by the apparent distance of the sound source (Mershon et al., 1981), the context in which it is heard, and the nature of the sound (e.g., whether it is meaningful or not). In other words, we are attempting to make an estimate of the properties of the source itself. Introspection as to the magnitude of the sensation evoked may be an unnatural and difficult process. This point of view has been well expressed by Helmholtz (quoted in Warren, 1981), who said that:

> we are exceedingly well trained in finding out by our sensations the objective nature of the objects around us, but we are completely unskilled in observing these sensations per se; and the practice of associating them with things outside of us actually prevents us from being distinctly conscious of the pure sensations.

4 MODELS OF LOUDNESS

Although the scaling of loudness is fraught with difficulty, there are many practical situations where it would be useful to have some way of estimating the loudness of sounds. Unfortunately, the mechanisms underlying the perception of loudness are not fully understood. A common assumption is that loudness is somehow related to the total neural activity evoked by a sound. If this is the case, then the loudness of a sinusoidal tone is determined not only by activity in neurons with characteristic frequencies (CFs) close to the frequency of the tone, but also by the spread of activity to neurons with adjacent CFs. Put another way, loudness may depend on a summation of neural activity across different frequency channels (critical bands).

Models incorporating this basic concept have been proposed by Fletcher and Munson (1937), Zwicker (1958; Zwicker and Scharf, 1965), and Moore and co-workers (Moore and Glasberg, 1996; Moore et al., 1997; Glasberg and Moore, 2002; Moore and Glasberg, 2007). The models attempt to calculate the average loudness that would be perceived by a large group of listeners with normal hearing under conditions where biases are minimized as far as possible. The models proposed by Moore et al. have the form illustrated in Fig. 4.3. The first stage is a fixed filter to simulate the transmission of sound

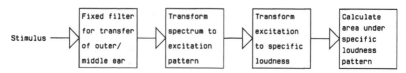

FIG 4.3   Basic structure of models used for the calculation of loudness.

through the outer and middle ear. The next stage is the calculation of an excitation pattern for the sound under consideration; the excitation pattern is calculated as described in Chapter 3, Section 5.

The next stage is the transformation from excitation level (in dB) to specific loudness, which is a kind of "loudness density", representing the loudness per critical band or per ERB_N. This transformation involves a compressive nonlinearity; for example, a 10-fold increase in sound intensity, corresponding to a 10-dB increase in level, produces less than a 10-fold change in specific loudness. Although the models are based on psychoacoustical data, this transformation can be thought of as representing the way that physical excitation is transformed into neural activity; the specific loudness is probably related to the amount of neural activity at the corresponding CF. The compression in the transformation partly reflects the compression that occurs on the basilar membrane (BM), as described in Chapter 1 (see Section 6B and Fig. 1.12). The overall loudness of a given sound, in sones, is assumed to be proportional to the total area under the specific loudness pattern. One might think of this area as approximately proportional to the total neural activity evoked by a sound.

Loudness models of this type have been rather successful in accounting for experimental data on the loudness of both simple and complex sounds (Zwicker and Scharf, 1965; Moore and Glasberg, 1996; Moore et al., 1997; Glasberg and Moore, 2010). They have also been incorporated into "loudness meters" that can give an appropriate indication of the loudness of sounds even when they fluctuate over time (Fastl, 1993; Stone et al., 1997; Zwicker and Fastl, 1999; Glasberg and Moore, 2002).

5 THE EFFECT OF BANDWIDTH ON LOUDNESS

Consider a complex sound of fixed energy (or intensity) having a bandwidth W, which is systematically varied. For such a sound, the noise power density is halved each time the bandwidth, W, is doubled. If W is less than a certain bandwidth, called the critical bandwidth for loudness, CB_L, then the loudness of the sound is almost independent of W; the sound is judged to be about as loud as a pure tone or narrow band of noise of equal intensity lying at the center frequency of the band. However, if W is increased beyond CB_L, the loudness of the complex sound begins to increase. This has been found to be the case for bands of noise (Zwicker et al., 1957; Zwicker and Fastl, 1999) and for complex sounds consisting of pure tones whose frequency separation is varied (Scharf, 1961, 1970). An example for bands of noise is given in Fig. 4.4. The CB_L for the data in Fig. 4.4 is about 250–300 Hz for a center frequency of 1420 Hz, although the exact value of CB_L is hard to determine. The value of CB_L is similar to, but a little greater than, the ERB_N of the auditory filter, as described in Chapter 3. Thus, for a given amount of energy, a complex sound is louder if its bandwidth exceeds one ERB_N than if its bandwidth is less than one ERB_N.

The pattern of results shown in Fig. 4.4 can be understood in terms of the loudness models described earlier. The reason that loudness remains constant for bandwidths less than CB_L can be understood by considering how the specific loudness patterns change with bandwidth. This is illustrated in Fig. 4.5, which shows excitation patterns and specific loudness patterns for a sinusoid and for bands of noise of various widths, all with a level of 60 dB SPL, calculated using the model of Moore et al. (1997). With increasing bandwidth up to CB_L, the specific loudness patterns become lower at their tips, but broader; the decrease in area around the tip is almost exactly canceled by the

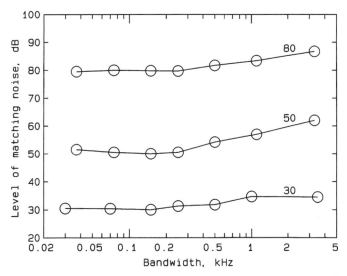

FIG. 4.4 The level of a 210-Hz-wide noise required to match the loudness of a noise of variable bandwidth is plotted as a function of the variable bandwidth; the bands of noise were geometrically centered at 1420 Hz. The number by each curve is the overall noise level in dB SPL. Data from Zwicker et al. (1957).

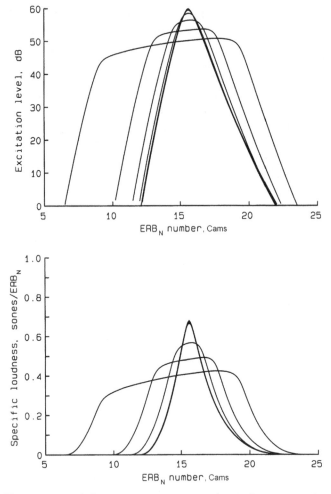

FIG. 4.5 The upper panel shows excitation patterns for a 1-kHz sinusoid with a level of 60 dB SPL (the narrowest pattern with the highest peak) and for noise bands of various widths, all centered at 1 kHz and with an overall level of 60 dB SPL. The frequency scale has been transformed to an ERB_N-number scale; see Chapter 3, Section 3B. The noise bands have widths of 20, 60, 140, 300, 620, and 1260 Hz. As the bandwidth is increased, the patterns decrease in height but spread over a greater number of Cams. The lower panel shows specific loudness patterns corresponding to the excitation patterns in the upper panel. For bandwidths up to 140 Hz, the area under the specific loudness patterns is constant. For greater bandwidths, the total area increases.

increase on the skirts, so the total area remains almost constant. When the bandwidth is increased beyond CB_L, the increase on the skirts is greater than the decrease around the tip, and so the total area, and hence the predicted loudness, increases. Since the increase depends on the summation of specific loudness at different CFs, the increase in loudness is often described as "loudness summation".

At low SLs (around 10–20 dB SL), the loudness of a complex sound is roughly independent of bandwidth. This can also be explained in terms of the loudness models described earlier. At these low levels, specific loudness changes rapidly with excitation level, and so does loudness. As a result, the total area under the specific loudness pattern remains almost constant as the bandwidth is altered, even for bandwidths greater than CB_L. Thus, loudness is independent of bandwidth. When a narrowband sound has a very low SL (below 10 dB), then if the bandwidth is increased keeping the total energy constant, the energy in each critical band becomes insufficient to make the sound audible. Accordingly, near threshold, loudness must decrease as the bandwidth of a complex sound is increased from a small value. As a consequence, if the intensity of a complex sound is increased slowly from a subthreshold value, the rate of growth of loudness is greater for a wideband sound than for a narrowband sound.

6 TEMPORAL INTEGRATION OF LOUDNESS

Chapter 2 described how the absolute threshold for detecting sounds is affected by duration. The effect of duration on loudness has also been measured extensively, but the results show considerable variability except for a general agreement that, at a given intensity, loudness increases with duration for durations up to 100–200 ms. As a very rough summary of the data, it may be stated that, for durations up to about 80 ms, constant energy leads to constant loudness. For reviews, see Scharf (1978) and Buus et al. (1997).

7 THE DETECTION OF INTENSITY CHANGES AND THE CODING OF LOUDNESS

The smallest detectable change in intensity has been measured for many different types of stimuli by a variety of methods. It is common for a two-interval, 2-alternative forced-choice (2AFC) procedure to be used. Two successive stimuli are presented that differ in intensity or in the presence/absence of amplitude modulation. The order of presentation of the two stimuli in a trial is randomly varied. The threshold is usually defined as the stimulus difference that produces 75% correct responses, but other criteria (e.g., 71% correct or 79% correct) may be used. The three main methods for measuring intensity discrimination are:

1. *Modulation detection.* In one interval the stimulus is unmodulated and in the other it is amplitude modulated (i.e., made to vary in amplitude) at a slow regular rate (see Fig. 3.7). The subject is required to indicate which interval contained the modulation.
2. *Increment detection.* A continuous background stimulus is presented and an increment in level is imposed on the background in one of the two possible intervals, usually indicated by lights. The subject is required to indicate which interval contained the increment.
3. *Intensity discrimination of gated or pulsed stimuli.* Two separate pulses of sound are presented successively, one being more intense than the other, and the subject is required to indicate which was the more intense.

Although there are some differences in the experimental results for the different methods, the general trend is similar. Thresholds for detecting intensity changes are often specified in decibels, i.e., as the change in level at threshold, ΔL. For example, in method (3), if one sound has intensity I, and the other sound has intensity $I + \Delta I$, then the value of ΔL is given by

$$\Delta L = 10\log_{10}\{(I + \Delta I)/I\}$$

Sometimes, the threshold is expressed as $\Delta I/I$, or as this ratio expressed in decibels, $10\log_{10}(\Delta I/I)$.

For wideband noise, or for bandpass-filtered noise, the smallest detectable intensity change is approximately a constant fraction of the intensity of the stimulus. In other words, $\Delta I/I$ is roughly constant. This is an example of Weber's law, which states that the smallest detectable change in a stimulus is proportional to the magnitude of that stimulus. The value of $\Delta I/I$ is called the Weber fraction. If the smallest detectable change is expressed as the change in level in decibels, i.e., as ΔL, then this too is constant, regardless of the absolute level, and for wideband noise it has a value of about 0.5–1 dB. This holds from about 20 dB above threshold to 100 dB above threshold (Miller, 1947). The value of ΔL increases for sounds with levels that are close to the absolute threshold.

For pure tones, Weber's law does not hold (Riesz, 1928; Harris, 1963; Viemeister, 1972; Jesteadt *et al.*, 1977; Florentine, 1983; Florentine *et al.*, 1987; Viemeister and Bacon, 1988; Wojtczak and Viemeister, 1999). Instead, if ΔI (in dB) is plotted against I (also in dB), a straight line is obtained with a slope of about 0.9; Weber's law would give a slope of 1.0. Thus discrimination, as measured by the Weber fraction, improves at high levels. This has been termed the "near miss" to Weber's law. The Weber fraction may increase somewhat at very high sound levels (above 100 dB SPL) (Viemeister and Bacon, 1988).

Consider the implications of these findings in terms of the physiological coding of intensity in the auditory system. The three major phenomena to be explained are: (1) the auditory system is capable of detecting changes in level for a range of levels—the dynamic range—of at least 120 dB; (2) Weber's law holds for the discrimination of bursts of noise; and (3) discrimination of the level of pure tones improves (relative to Weber's law) with increasing sound level up to about 100 dB SPL.

7A THE DYNAMIC RANGE OF THE AUDITORY SYSTEM

For many years the wide dynamic range of the auditory system was considered to be difficult to explain in terms of the properties of neurons in the auditory nerve. For example, following a survey of a large number of neurons, Palmer and Evans (1979) concluded that the proportion with wide dynamic ranges (say 60 dB or more) is only about 10%. Further, when stimulated with a tone close to CF at sound levels above about 60 dB SPL, all neurons showed a substantial reduction in the slope of the rate versus intensity function. Thus changes in intensity resulted in only small changes in firing rate. If intensity discrimination were based on changes in the firing rates of neurons with CFs close to the stimulus frequency, we would expect intensity discrimination to worsen at sound levels above 60 dB SPL, whereas in fact it does not.

These findings suggested that there might be some other mechanism for the coding of intensity changes at high intensities. One possibility lies in the way the excitation pattern of the stimulus would spread with increasing intensity (illustrated schematically in Fig. 4.6). At high intensities, the majority of neurons at the center of the pattern would be saturated, but changes in intensity could still be signaled by changes in the firing rates of neurons at the edges of the pattern.

At first sight, it appears that this argument could not hold for the discrimination of wideband stimuli, such as white noise. In theory the excitation pattern for white noise has no edges, so all neurons ought to be saturated by a noise of high intensity. However, we are not equally sensitive to all frequencies, as absolute threshold curves and equal-loudness contours indicate. Thus, although neurons with mid-range CFs would be saturated by an intense white noise, this might not be the case for neurons with very low and very high CFs.

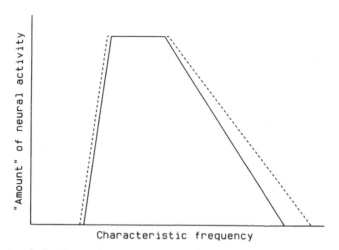

FIG. 4.6   An idealized neural excitation pattern for a tone at a high level (solid line). An increase in level, indicated by the dashed lines, produces no change in activity for the neurons in the center of the pattern, since these are saturated. However, changes in neural activity do occur at the edges of the pattern. Note the greater growth of activity that occurs on the high-frequency side.

The role of spread of excitation has been tested by measuring intensity discrimination in the presence of background noise chosen to mask the edges of the excitation pattern of the signal. For example, Viemeister (1972) investigated the intensity discrimination of pulsed 950-Hz sinusoids in the presence of various types of filtered noise. He found little effect with a lowpass noise, whose cutoff frequency was 800 Hz, but a bandpass noise centered at 1900 Hz or a highpass noise with a cutoff at 1900 Hz both slightly degraded performance at high levels. With the latter stimulus Weber's law was obtained. Moore and Raab (1974) investigated the intensity discrimination of 1000-Hz tone bursts in the presence of highpass noise with a cutoff frequency at 2000 Hz and bandstop noise with cutoff frequencies at 500 and 2000 Hz. Performance was not impaired by the noise at low levels of the tone and noise, but it was impaired at high levels. This confirms that information at CFs remote from the stimulus frequency is important. The bandstop noise, which disrupted both sides of the excitation pattern of the tone, had a greater effect than the highpass noise, which only disrupted information on the high-frequency side. This indicates that information on both the high- and low-frequency sides of the excitation pattern affects intensity discrimination at high levels.

Although these experiments indicate that spread of excitation may play a role in intensity discrimination, they also show that reasonable performance is possible even when the edges of the excitation pattern are masked by noise. In other words, spread of excitation is not essential for maintaining the wide dynamic range of the auditory system. The small effect of masking the edges of the excitation pattern indicates that it may be necessary to invoke some further mechanism for intensity discrimination.

One possibility is that the timing of neural spikes provides a cue to the intensity of a tone in a noise background. When a tone is above threshold but is presented against a noise background, some neurons phase lock to the tone, whereas neurons with CFs far from that of the tone are driven mainly by the noise and have a more random pattern of neural firing. When the tone is increased in intensity, more of the neurons become phase locked to it, and furthermore the degree of temporal regularity in the firing of neurons that are already phase locked increases, since the noise now produces relatively less "jitter". Thus, a change in temporal regularity of the patterns of neural firing could signal the intensity change of the tone. Such a mechanism could operate over a wide range of intensities and would not be affected by saturation effects; temporal patterns of firing can alter even for neurons that are saturated. The mechanism would, however, be limited to frequencies below about 4–5 kHz (see Chapter 1).

Phase locking might be particularly important for coding the relative levels of components in complex sounds. As described in Chapter 1, Section 7, neurons with a given CF tend to phase lock to the stimulus components that are most effective at that CF. When the level of a component is increased relative to that of the other components, the degree of phase locking to that component increases. In general, any change in the spectral composition of a complex sound results in a change in the pattern of phase locking as a function of CF, provided the spectral change is in the frequency region below 4–5 kHz (Young, 2008).

The possibility that phase locking plays a role in intensity discrimination has been tested using stimuli containing components whose frequencies all lie above the range where phase locking occurs. In the most critical experiments, the stimuli have been presented in a background of bandstop noise so that information from the spread of the excitation pattern was also eliminated. Viemeister (1983) measured the intensity discrimination of 200-ms bursts of bandpass noise, with a passband from 6 to 14 kHz. The noise was presented in a background noise with a bandstop in the range 6–14 kHz. He found that intensity discrimination remained relatively good (values of ΔL were about 2 dB) over a wide range of sound levels. This suggests that phase locking is not essential for intensity discrimination. Carlyon and Moore (1984) investigated the intensity discrimination of sinusoidal tone bursts in the presence of a background noise with a bandstop centered on the frequency of the tone. Performance was compared for high- and low-frequency tones.

When the tones were of long duration (225 ms), there was little effect of the overall level of the sounds, although there was a slight deterioration in intensity discrimination for high-frequency (6500 Hz) tones at moderate sound levels (55–70 dB SPL). When the tones were of short duration (30 ms), the deterioration at high frequencies and moderate sound levels became more pronounced. This was called the "severe departure" from Weber's law, although it has also been called the "mid-level hump".

Carlyon and Moore (1984) suggested that, at low frequencies, intensity discrimination depends on both the spread of excitation and phase locking. One or both of these types of information are always available, even in the presence of bandstop noise. At high frequencies, where phase locking does not occur, spread of excitation becomes relatively more important. However, even when the edges of the excitation pattern are masked by bandstop noise, good intensity discrimination is still possible for long-duration stimuli. This indicates that information from the small number of unsaturated neurons with CFs close to the stimulus frequency is sufficient for good intensity discrimination. It is only when the stimulus is of short duration that an impairment in intensity discrimination is observed, and then it is at medium levels rather than at high levels. The mid-level impairment may be related to the fact that compression on the BM is greatest for medium levels (Baer et al., 1999). A result of the compression is that a given change in level of a sound, say 2 dB, results in a smaller change in response on the BM at medium levels than at high or low levels.

A different way of viewing the "problem" of the wide dynamic range of the auditory system has come from studies of the capacity of single neurons to carry information about intensity changes. This capacity depends both on the shape of the rate versus level function and on the statistical properties of the neural responses, particularly their variability at each level (Teich and Khanna, 1985). For example, if the variability in firing rate is very low, even a small change in mean firing rate in response to a change in intensity will be sufficient to "code" the intensity change. The ability of a single neuron to code intensity changes can be quantified by a task comparable to the 2AFC task that is often used in psychoacoustic studies. Two successive stimuli differing in intensity are presented, and the number of spikes evoked by each stimulus is measured. This is repeated for a series of "trials", with the order of the stimuli (soft-loud or loud-soft) randomly varied. If the number of spikes is greater for the more intense stimulus, this counts as a "correct" response from the neuron. By adjusting the intensity difference between the two stimuli, a "threshold" can be measured at which the neuron is correct on, say, 75% of trials. Typically, the intensity discrimination threshold of a given neuron is a U-shaped function of sound level (Delgutte, 1987). The threshold is high at low levels because stimuli close to or below the absolute threshold of the neuron result in minimal changes in firing rate. The threshold is high at high levels because of neural saturation. However, at intermediate levels, the threshold change in level, ΔL, can be as low as 2–3 dB. The level at which the threshold is lowest varies from one neuron to another and a few neurons do not show saturation even for sound levels above 80 dB SPL (Winter *et al.*, 1990).

Studies of this type have indicated that the performance of humans in intensity discrimination tasks can be accounted for if it is assumed that information is combined optimally from a relatively small number of single neurons (Delgutte, 1987; Viemeister, 1988). The number required seems to be about 100. Indeed, if the information contained in the firing rates of all the 30,000 neurons in the auditory nerve were used optimally, then intensity discrimination would be much better than it actually is. For example, ΔL for 1000-Hz tone bursts would be less than 0.1 dB at medium to high levels (Delgutte, 1987). Thus, the "problem" of the dynamic range of the auditory system has changed. Rather than having to explain how intensity discrimination is possible over a wide range of sound levels, it is necessary to explain why intensity discrimination is not better than observed. It appears that, for most stimuli, intensity discrimination is not limited by the information carried in the auditory nerve, but by the use made of that information at more central levels of processing (Carlyon and Moore, 1984; Plack and Carlyon, 1995). It is only when the information in the auditory nerve is highly impoverished that impaired intensity discrimination is observed. This may happen for brief high-frequency tones presented in bandstop noise.

In summary, it seems likely that a number of different mechanisms play a role in intensity discrimination. Intensity changes can be signaled both by changes in the firing rates of neurons at the center of the excitation pattern and by the spreading of the excitation pattern, so that more neurons are brought into operation. However, the spread of excitation is not critical for maintaining performance at high sound levels. In addition, cues related to phase locking may play a role in intensity discrimination. This may be particularly important for complex stimuli, for which the relative levels of different components may be signaled by the degree of phase locking to the components. However, phase locking is also not critical, since good intensity discrimination is possible for stimuli whose frequency components are restricted to the high-frequency range where phase locking does not occur. It appears that the information carried in the firing rates of neurons in the auditory nerve is more than sufficient to account for intensity discrimination. Thus, intensity discrimination appears normally to be limited by the capacity of more central parts of the auditory system to make use of the information in the auditory nerve.

7B Weber's Law

At one time it was thought that Weber's law held for bands of noise because the inherent fluctuations in the noise limit performance. For example, in a task involving the intensity discrimination of bursts of noise, a device that chooses the burst containing the greater energy on each trial would conform to Weber's law (Green, 1960). However, it has been found that Weber's law holds even for "frozen" noise, i.e., noise that is identical from one trial to the next and that does not have random fluctuations in energy (Raab and Goldberg, 1975; Buus, 1990). This indicates that Weber's law must arise from the operation of the auditory system, rather than from the statistical properties of the stimuli.

As mentioned above, the intensity discrimination "threshold" measured in a single neuron is a U-shaped function of sound level. In other words, thresholds measured from single neurons do not conform to Weber's law. Weber's law can be predicted by models that combine the firing rate information from a relatively small number of neurons (about 100) whose thresholds and dynamic ranges are appropriately staggered so as to cover the dynamic range of the auditory system (Delgutte, 1987; Viemeister, 1988). In models of this type, it is generally assumed that the combination is done on a localized basis. In other words, information from neurons with similar CFs is combined, and there are many independent "frequency channels" (comparable to critical bands), each responding to a limited range of CFs. Weber's law is assumed to hold for each frequency channel. Thus, information about the levels of components in complex sounds can be coded over a wide range of overall sound levels. This assumption, that there are many frequency channels each of which conforms to Weber's law, has been widespread in psychophysics for many years. However, there is some evidence to the contrary (Buus and Florentine, 1995).

7C The Near Miss to Weber's Law

Consider the differences between the intensity discrimination of pure tones and of bursts of noise. Accepting that Weber's law reflects the normal mode of operation of a given frequency channel, it is necessary to explain why the intensity discrimination of pure tones deviates from Weber's law. In fact, the deviation occurs both for sinusoids and for narrow bands of noise, especially when the noise is "frozen" (Buus, 1990).

There are probably at least two factors contributing to the improvement in intensity discrimination of pure tones and narrow bands of frozen noise at high sound levels. The first was described by Zwicker (1956, 1970), who studied modulation detection for pure tones. He suggested that a change in intensity can be detected whenever the excitation pattern evoked by the stimulus changes somewhere by (approximately) 1 dB or more. In other words, he assumed that Weber's law held for all frequency channels and that the Weber fraction was about 1 dB for each channel. The high-frequency side of the excitation pattern grows in a nonlinear way with increasing intensity; a 10-dB change in stimulus level gives rise to a change greater than 10 dB on the high-frequency side of the pattern. This is deduced from changes in the shapes of masking patterns for tones in noise as a function of intensity (see Chapter 3, Figs. 3.10 and 3.12). This nonlinear growth in the excitation pattern means that a 1-dB change in excitation on the high-frequency side will be produced by relatively smaller stimulus increments at high levels. As the stimulus level is increased, the excitation pattern spreads more and more. For a given change in stimulus level, the greatest change in excitation level occurs at the highest-frequency part of the pattern (see Fig. 3.12). In support of this idea, Zwicker reported that the addition of a highpass noise, which masks the high-frequency side of the excitation pattern but does not actually mask the tone, causes the threshold for detecting amplitude modulation at high levels to approach that found at low levels.

As described in Chapter 3, the nonlinearity in the excitation pattern is now thought of in a different way. With increasing level, the excitation pattern of a sinusoid grows in a compressive way close to its center, but in a more linear way on its high-frequency side (Nelson and Schroder, 1997). The end result is, however, similar; the rate of growth of response with increasing input level is greater on the high-frequency side of the excitation pattern than around its center.

The second factor contributing to the near miss to Weber's law has been described by Florentine and Buus (1981). They suggested that subjects do not make use of information only from a single channel (i.e., the output of one auditory filter). Rather, they combine information across all the excited channels, i.e., across the whole of the excitation pattern. As the level of a tone is increased, more channels become active, and the increase in the number of active channels allows improved performance. They presented a model based on this idea and showed that it was able to account for the near miss to Weber's law and for the effects of masking noise on intensity discrimination.

In summary, the near miss to Weber's law for pure tones can be accounted for by two factors: the nonlinear changes in excitation patterns with level and the ability of subjects to combine information from different parts of the excitation pattern.

8 LOUDNESS ADAPTATION, FATIGUE, AND DAMAGE RISK

It is a property of all sensory systems that exposure to a stimulus of sufficient duration and intensity produces changes in responsiveness. Some changes occur during the presentation of the stimulus, so that its apparent magnitude decreases (as for exposure to bright lights) or it disappears completely (as sometimes happens for olfactory stimuli). Other changes are apparent after the end of the stimulus; for example, shifts in threshold may occur. In general, such effects are much less marked in the auditory system than they are in other sensory systems, although large threshold shifts may be observed after exposure to stimuli of very high intensity.

Hood (1950, 1972) has distinguished between auditory *fatigue* and auditory *adaptation*. The essential feature of fatigue is that it "results from the application of a stimulus which is usually considerably in excess of that required to sustain the normal physiological response of the receptor, and it is measured after the stimulus has been removed" (Hood, 1972). For example, a subject's absolute threshold at a particular frequency might be measured, after which the subject would be exposed to a fatiguing tone of a particular frequency and intensity for a period of time. The threshold would then be measured again, and the shift in threshold would be taken as a measure of fatigue. Notice that this procedure is concerned with "the effect of an excessive stimulus upon a small and finite group of receptors, namely those which are normally brought into activity at near threshold intensities" (Hood, 1972). Auditory fatigue defined in this way is often referred to as post-stimulatory auditory fatigue, and the shift in threshold is called temporary threshold shift (TTS). The word "temporary" implies that the absolute threshold returns to its pre-exposure value after a sufficient time. Sometimes, this does not happen, and a permanent threshold shift (PTS) occurs (Davis *et al.*, 1950).

Auditory adaptation has as its essential feature the process of "equilibration". The response of a receptor to a steady stimulus declines as a function of time until it reaches a steady value at which the energy expended by the receptor is just balanced by the metabolic energy that is available to sustain it. In individual neurons, the effect can be seen as a decrease in firing rate over time in response to a stimulus of constant amplitude; see Chapter 1, Section 7H, and Fig. 1.23. The psychological counterpart of this is a decline in the apparent magnitude of a stimulus (e.g., its loudness) during the first few minutes of presentation, followed by a period in which the apparent magnitude remains roughly constant.

I will not attempt to give a detailed account of the physiological processes involved in fatigue and adaptation or of the factors that affect these. For a review of these, the reader is referred to Elliot and Fraser (1970); for recent data see Salvi et al. (1996).

8A POST-STIMULATORY AUDITORY FATIGUE

The most common index of auditory fatigue is TTS, whose measurement was described earlier. One problem with measuring TTS is that the recovery process may be quite rapid, so a threshold measurement has to be obtained as quickly as possible; but this in turn can lead to inaccuracies in the measurement. A common method is to give the subject a means of controlling the signal level, and asking the subject to adjust the level so that the signal is just audible. Sometimes continuous tones are used as signals but, since subjects often have difficulty in tracking these, pulsed tones are generally preferred.

There are five major factors that influence the size of TTS:

1. the intensity of the fatiguing stimulus (I),
2. the duration of the fatiguing stimulus (D),
3. the frequency of the fatiguing (exposure) stimulus (F_e),
4. the frequency of the test stimulus (F_t), and
5. the time between cessation of the fatiguing stimulus and the post-exposure threshold determination, called the recovery interval (RI).

TTS generally increases with I, the intensity of the fatiguing stimulus. At low intensities TTS changes relatively slowly as a function of I, and TTS only occurs for test tones with frequencies F_t close to F_e. As I increases, TTS increases, the frequency range over which the effects occur increases, with the greatest increase above F_e, and the frequency of the maximum TTS shifts a half-octave or more above F_e. At high levels, and when F_t is above F_e, TTS grows very rapidly as a function of I. For fatiguing intensities above about 90–100 dB SPL, TTS rises precipitously (Fig. 4.7), and it has been suggested that this indicates a change from fatigue that is transient and physiological in nature to fatigue that is more permanent and pathological in nature (Davis et al., 1950; Hood, 1950; Hirsh and Bilger, 1955). The upward frequency shift in F_t at which the maximum TTS occurs is not fully understood, but it may be related to the properties of the BM. There is evidence that the vibration pattern on the BM shifts toward the basal (high-frequency) end with increasing amplitude of a sinusoidal stimulus (Rhode, 1971; McFadden, 1986; Ruggero et al., 1997; Moore et al., 2002). For example, at a very high level a 1000-Hz tone may produce its maximum amplitude of vibration at a place that, at low levels, would be tuned to about 1400 Hz. Hence, when the

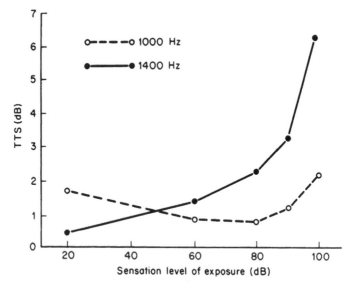

FIG. 4.7 Increases in temporary threshold shift (TTS) with increases in the level of the 1000-Hz fatiguing tone. Test tones of 1000 and 1400 Hz were used. The exposure duration D was 3 min. Note that, for high exposure levels, the function accelerates and that the TTS is greater for a frequency above that of the fatiguing tone than for a tone at that frequency. From Hirsh and Bilger (1955), by permission of the authors and *J. Acoust. Soc. Am.*

threshold is measured using a low-level test tone, the maximum TTS occurs for a 1400-Hz test tone.

Fatigue generally increases with exposure duration, D, and a number of workers have reported that TTS is linearly related to $\log D$ (Hood, 1950; Ward *et al.*, 1958). However, for low frequencies, particularly when the fatiguing stimulus is noise or a rapidly interrupted tone (Ward, 1963), the growth rate is reduced, probably because the middle ear reflex (see Chapter 1, Section 6A) reduces sound transmission at low frequencies. The $\log D$ function probably does not extend to values of D less than 5 min.

Fatigue effects are generally more marked at high frequencies, at least up to 4 kHz. When the fatiguing stimulus is a broadband noise, maximum TTS occurs between 4 and 6 kHz. It is also the case that permanent hearing losses resulting from exposure to intense sounds tend to be greatest in this region.

TTS generally decreases with increasing RI, although for many conditions the recovery curve is diphasic; recovery from the large TTS immediately following exposure is often followed by a "bounce", particularly at high frequencies. Thus, a valley at $RI = 1$ min is often followed by a bounce at $RI = 2$ min (Fig. 4.8). The diphasic nature of the recovery curve has led to the

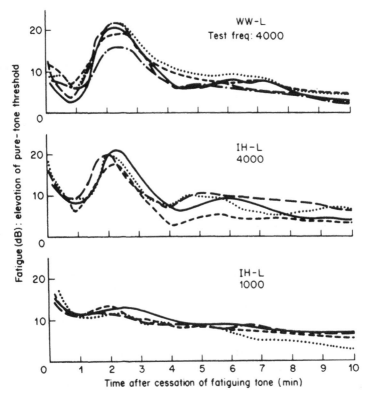

FIG. 4.8 Recovery curves illustrating the elevation in threshold produced by a fatiguing tone of 500 Hz at 120 dB SPL for 3 min. Test tones of 4000 (two subjects) and 1000 Hz (one subject) were used, and each set of curves represents retests under identical conditions. Note the "bounce" that occurs at 2 min for the 4000-Hz test tones. From Hirsh and Ward (1952), by permission of the authors and *J. Acoust. Soc. Am.*

suggestion that two processes are involved: a short-lived recovery process that may correspond to neural activity, and a longer process that involves hair cell and metabolic changes (Salt, 2004). For *RI*s greater than 2 min, recovery is approximately linearly related to log *RI*. Furthermore, for a given amount of TTS, the recovery proceeds at a similar rate regardless of how that amount of TTS was produced. This seems to hold for *RI*s from 2 up to about 112 min (Ward *et al.*, 1958). However, when the TTS at 2 min (denoted TTS2) is greater than 40–50 dB, recovery may be much slower. Even when TTS2 does not exceed 40 dB, recovery times may be as long as 16 h. Recovery over such longtime intervals may indicate that permanent damage has occurred. Physiological studies have indicated that full recovery from TTS does not necessarily indicate that no damage has been done; substantial auditory-nerve degeneration has been found in animals exposed to a noise producing a TTS (Kujawa and Liberman, 2009).

A number of studies have appeared reporting the effects of exposure to environmental noise of various kinds, including rock music. Harris (1972) in a review of these concluded that

> the quieter bands may be harmless, but if the amplification/reverberation condition reaches 110 dBA, a sizeable fraction of persons would be adversely affected probably permanently; while a 120 dBA level, at which some music groups have registered, would create havoc with most audiograms.

In fact, since 1972 sound levels have tended to increase, as amplifiers have become more powerful and loudspeakers more efficient. Nowadays, many rock bands produce sound levels reaching 120 dB SPL among the audience.

Surprisingly, Axelsson et al. (1995) reported that many pop/rock musicians who had been performing for many years had essentially normal hearing, and only a few had a mild high-frequency loss. They speculated that there might be a protective effect of the "generally positive attitude of the musicians toward their performance". Similarly, in a review, Dibble (1995) concluded that "The weight of evidence suggests that music ... is nowhere near as damaging as ... conventional industrial noise". He remarks further that "there is also a body of evidence to support the ... notion that sound which is pleasing, and therefore less stressful, may also be less damaging". It should be noted, however, that musicians who develop hearing loss often stop practicing as musicians. Therefore, the musicians studied by Axelsson et al. may have been a biased sample.

Although music may be less damaging than "noise", there are nevertheless clear indications that music can damage hearing if the sound level is great enough and the exposure is long enough. There is increasing concern about possible damage to hearing caused by prolonged use of personal music players (Fligor and Cox, 2004; Kim et al., 2009; Vinay and Moore, 2010). Many professional musicians now take the precaution of wearing earplugs, especially when rehearsing. For musicians, or indeed generally when listening to high-level music, it is beneficial to use special earplugs that attenuate sounds almost equally at all frequencies (Killion et al., 1988); this gives a natural sound quality, in contrast to conventional earplugs, which attenuate high frequencies more than low frequencies giving a muffled quality. Such "flat response" earplugs are manufactured by Etymōtic Research.

To a first approximation, the permanent damage caused by exposure to intense sounds is related to the total energy received by the ear over a given period. An exposure to a sound level of 85 dBA for 8 h per day is considered to be safe. If the exposure duration is halved, the permissible sound intensity is doubled, corresponding to a 3-dB increase in level. Thus, 88 dB is permissible for 4 h, 91 dB for 2 h, 94 dB for 1 h, 97 dB for 30 min, 100 dB for 15 min, and so on. The "safe" exposure time for sound levels over 110 dBA is very short!

8B AUDITORY ADAPTATION

Early studies of auditory adaptation made use of loudness balance tests, and in particular a test known as the simultaneous dichotic loudness balance (SDLB). For example, a tone of fixed level, say 80 dB SPL, would be applied to one ear (the test ear), and a loudness balance made with a comparison tone of the same frequency but variable level applied to the other ear (the control ear). For a normal subject, this balance is obtained with a level of about 80 dB SPL. The tone in the control ear is now removed, but that in the test ear is continued for a further 3 min. Following this adaptation period, a loudness balance is established once again. It is generally found that the tone in the control ear now produces a loudness match at a lower level, say 60 dB SPL. Thus, the amount of adaptation corresponds to a change in level of 20 dB. Notice that the measurement of the decrement of response takes place while the adapting stimulus is being applied.

Other techniques have tended to show much less adaptation. If the test conditions are designed to avoid presentation of an intermittent tone that is close in frequency to the adapting tone, then supra-threshold loudness adaptation is essentially absent (Bray et al., 1973). One technique makes use of a comparison tone whose frequency differs considerably from that of the adapting tone. The adapting tone is presented continuously to one ear, while the comparison tone is presented intermittently either to the same ear or to the other ear. Another technique requires the subject to adjust the intensity of a continuously presented sound so as to maintain it at constant loudness. If the subject increases the intensity of the sound with increasing duration of presentation, then this indicates that adaptation is occurring. Most workers using these techniques have reported that there is no significant loudness adaptation for adapting tones with levels between 50 and 90 dB SPL.

In a review of loudness adaptation, Scharf (1983) has presented data obtained with a method of successive magnitude estimation. The listener is required to assign numbers to express the loudness of a sound at successive time intervals (see Section 3 for a description of loudness scaling). The results indicate that adaptation occurs only for low-level tones, below about 30 dB SL. Scharf's main conclusions were as follows:

> A sound presented alone adapts only if it is below 30 dB SL. High-frequency pure tones adapt more than low-frequency tones or than noises, whether broadband or narrow-band. Steady sounds adapt more than modulated sounds, and if the sound amplitude is modulated sufficiently adaptation may disappear altogether as when

two tones beat together. People differ widely with respect to the degree of adaptation they experience. While most people hear the loudness of a high-frequency, low-level tone decline by at least half within one min, some others report no change in loudness and still others report that the tone disappears. No relation has been found, however, between the degree to which a person adapts and such individual characteristics as threshold, age, and sex, although there is some evidence that children under 16 years adapt less than adults. Free field listening may produce less adaptation than earphone listening.

Bacon and Viemeister (1994) and Miskiewicz *et al.* (1993) have reported that marked adaptation occurs for high-frequency tones, close to the upper frequency limit of hearing, when those tones are presented at low or moderate levels. The tones often become completely inaudible with prolonged exposure. However, such adaptation does not occur for tones at lower frequencies.

It is curious that marked perceptual adaptation does not occur for low- and mid-frequency tones, since adaptation in response to such sounds does occur in single neurons in the auditory nerve (Javel, 1996). Presumably the central auditory system somehow compensates for the decreasing neural responses rates in the auditory periphery when a steady sound is presented.

9 ABNORMALITIES OF LOUDNESS PERCEPTION IN IMPAIRED HEARING

9A LOUDNESS RECRUITMENT

One phenomenon that often occurs when there are defects in the cochlea is loudness recruitment. This refers to an unusually rapid growth of loudness level as the SL of a tone is increased, and it might be observed as follows. Suppose that a person has a hearing loss at 4000 Hz of 60 dB in one ear only. If a 4000-Hz tone is introduced into his or her normal ear at 100 dB SPL (which would also be about 100 dB above threshold for that ear), then the tone that sounds equally loud in the impaired ear will also have a level of about 100 dB SPL. Thus, a tone that is only 40 dB above threshold in the impaired ear may sound as loud as a tone that is 100 dB above threshold in the normal ear; the ear with recruitment seems to "catch up" with the normal ear in loudness. Notice that, although loudness recruitment is normally regarded as pathological, a phenomenon very much like it occurs in normal listeners for tones of very low frequency. The loudness of these tones grows more rapidly per decibel than does the loudness for tones of middle frequencies (see Fig. 4.1).

One method for measuring loudness recruitment is the alternate binaural loudness balance (ABLB) test, which can be applied when only one ear is affected. A tone of a given level in the normal ear is alternated with a variable tone of the same frequency in the impaired ear (or vice versa), and the level of the tone is adjusted to give a loudness match. This is repeated at a number of different levels, so that the rate of growth of loudness in the impaired ear can be compared with that in the normal ear. Figure 4.9 shows the results of measurements of this type obtained by Moore (2004) for a subject with a hearing loss in the right ear and nearly normal hearing in the left ear. At the test frequency of 2.5 kHz, the absolute threshold was 71.4 dB SPL for the right ear and 27.2 dB SPL for the left ear. Sinusoidal 2.5-kHz tone bursts were presented in alternation to the normal and impaired ears. The mean level of

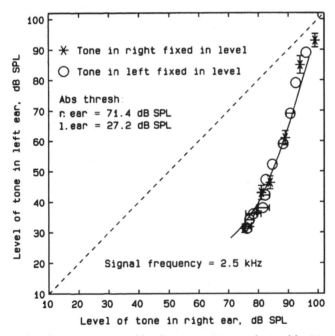

FIG 4.9 Results of measurements of loudness recruitment obtained by Moore (2004) for a subject with a unilateral cochlear hearing loss. A 2.5-kHz tone was presented in alternation to the impaired ear (right) and the normal ear (left). The subject was asked to adjust the level of the tone in one ear until the sounds appeared equally loud in the two ears. The mean matching level in the normal ear is plotted as a function of the level in the impaired ear. The solid line shows predictions of a loudness model (Moore and Glasberg, 2004). The dashed line shows where the matches would be expected to lie for a subject with completely normal hearing in both ears.

the loudness match in the left ear is plotted as a function of the level in the right ear. Loudness matches were made with the tone fixed in level in the right ear and adjusted in the left ear (asterisks), and with the tone fixed in level in the left ear and adjusted in the right ear (circles). The solid line shows a fit to the data obtained using a loudness model (Moore and Glasberg, 2004). The dashed line shows where the matches would be expected to lie for a person with two completely normal ears.

For the subject with the unilateral hearing loss, the slope of the loudness-matching function was greater than one. A level of 80 dB SPL in the impaired ear was matched by a level of about 38 dB SPL in the normal ear, reflecting the elevation in absolute threshold in the impaired ear. However, at high sound levels, the discrepancy in level between the normal and impaired ears was much reduced. A level of 98 dB SPL in the impaired ear was matched by a level of about 93 dB SPL in the normal ear. If higher levels had been used, the loudness in the impaired ear would probably have "caught up" completely with that in the normal ear. However, the sounds started to become uncomfortably loud at levels above those shown.

A second method for detecting recruitment is based on the assumption that, if loudness is increasing more rapidly than normal as the stimulus intensity is increased, then a smaller than normal intensity change will be required for a just-noticeable difference in loudness. Thus, the difference limen (DL) for intensity should be abnormally small, particularly at low SLs, where the rate of growth of loudness level is most rapid. This reasoning gives the basis for clinical tests for recruitment, based on the assumption that a smaller than normal DL will indicate the presence of recruitment. The most widely used test is called the short-increment sensitivity index (SISI) test (Jerger et al., 1959), which involves the detection of brief 1-dB increments in level superimposed on a continuous background. Buus et al. (1982) reviewed this test and concluded that subjects with cochlear impairment show higher SISI scores (i.e., they detect a greater number of the increments) than normal listeners when compared at equal SL, i.e., equal amounts above absolute threshold. However, when compared at equal SPL, the performance of subjects with cochlear damage is not better than normal and may be worse than normal. This conclusion is generally supported by more recent data (Bacon and Gleitman, 1992; Florentine et al., 1993; Stillman et al., 1993; Schlauch, 1994).

It seems clear that intensity discrimination is affected not only by the slope of the loudness-growth function, but also by internal variability or "noise" (Zwislocki and Jordan, 1986). This variability may well be increased in hearing-impaired ears, and the increased variability partially or completely offsets the potential improvement in intensity discrimination that might be gained from the steeper growth of loudness.

In spite of the difficulties of interpretation, a small size of the DL is sometimes associated with recruitment, especially for stimuli at low SLs. When a small intensity DL is found, this is usually indicative of a cochlear hearing loss. In cases where the hearing disorder is in the auditory nerve rather than in the cochlea (and recruitment is generally not seen), the intensity DL may be considerably larger than normal (Fastl and Schorn, 1981).

A third test for recruitment involves the measurement of loudness discomfort levels (LDLs). For most people with normal hearing, a tone becomes uncomfortably loud when its level reaches 100–110 dB SPL. For a person with a nonrecruiting hearing loss (e.g., a conductive loss), the LDL may be much higher, whereas, if recruitment is present, the LDL will fall within the range for normal subjects. In general, if the range between the absolute threshold and the LDL is reduced compared to normal, this is indicative of loudness recruitment.

The phenomenon of loudness recruitment probably accounts for a statement that is often heard from people with this type of hearing loss: "Don't shout; you're talking loud enough, but I can't understand what you are saying!" The person may not be able to hear very faint sounds, but sounds of high intensity are just as loud as for a normal listener. However, sounds that are easily audible may not be easily intelligible.

Loudness recruitment occurs consistently in disorders of the cochlea and is usually absent in conductive deafness and in retrocochlear deafness. It is probably connected with hair cell damage, and in particular with damage to the outer hair cells. However, there have been reports (Dix and Hood, 1973) of recruitment caused by brainstem disorders.

Kiang et al. (1970) and Evans (1975) suggested that reduced sharpness of tuning (as illustrated in Fig. 1.11) might be the main factor contributing to loudness recruitment. For a sinusoidal stimulus, this leads to an excitation pattern that is broader (spreads over a greater range of CFs) in an impaired than in a normal ear. They suggested that, once the level of a sound exceeds the detection threshold, the excitation in an ear with cochlear damage spreads more rapidly than normal across the array of neurons, and this leads to the abnormally rapid growth of loudness with increasing level. However, an experiment of Moore et al. (1985b) failed to support this hypothesis. Moore et al. tested subjects with hearing impairment and loudness recruitment in one ear only, so that loudness matches could be made between the normal and impaired ears. The tone in the impaired ear was presented in a bandstop noise that would have masked the edges of the excitation pattern of the tone. If Evans' hypothesis were correct, this noise should have reduced or abolished the loudness recruitment. In fact, the loudness of the tone in the impaired ear was almost unaffected by the bandstop noise. This indicates that abnormal spread of excitation is not the cause of loudness recruitment. A similar conclusion has been reached by others who have studied the role of spread of excitation in loudness (Hellman, 1978; Hellman and Meiselman, 1986; Zeng and Turner, 1991).

An alternative explanation for loudness recruitment is that it results from damage to or loss of the active process in the cochlea that enhances sensitivity for low input sound levels (see Chapter 1). This process is nonlinear, and it results in an amplification of the BM response to low-level sounds, while leaving the response to high-level sounds relatively unamplified. If the active process is lost, then the response to low-level sounds is not amplified, and the absolute threshold is elevated. However, the response to high-level sounds remains roughly the same as normal. This is illustrated in Fig. 4.10 (Ruggero and Rich, 1991), which shows results obtained from a single point on the BM of a chinchilla. The solid curve with black squares, labeled "Before", shows the input–output function of the BM obtained when the cochlea was in good condition; the stimulus was a 9000-Hz tone, corresponding to the CF of the place on the BM being studied. The curve shows a compressive nonlinearity for input sound levels between about 30 and 90 dB SPL. In contrast, the response to a tone with a frequency of 1000 Hz, well below the CF, is steeper and is almost linear (solid curve with open circles).

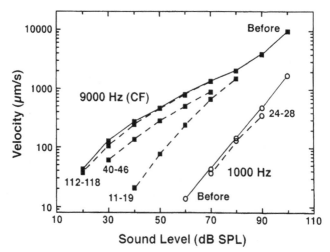

FIG. 4.10 Input–output functions on the BM immediately preceding (solid lines) and following (broken lines) an intravenous furosemide injection. The numbers by each curve indicate the time in minutes after injection of the drug when the data were obtained. See text for details. Redrawn from Ruggero and Rich (1991).

To manipulate the functioning of the cochlea, the animal was injected with furosemide, a diuretic that is known to disrupt the functioning of both inner and outer hair cells. The dashed curves in Fig. 4.10 were obtained at various times after injection of the drug; the time is indicated by a range in minutes next to each curve. Shortly after the injection (11–19 min) the input–output function for the CF tone was markedly altered. The biggest alteration was at low sound levels. To produce a given response on the BM (say, 40 μm/s), the input level had to be increased by about 25 dB relative to the level measured before the injection. However, the response to a CF tone at a high level (80 dB SPL) was almost normal. This is consistent with the idea that the contribution of the active mechanism reduces progressively as the sound level is increased above about 40 dB SPL. After a sufficiently long time (112–118 min), the input–output function returned to normal. Thus, in this case, the cochlear damage was reversible. Larger doses of the drug, or treatment with other drugs, can result in permanent cochlear damage.

In summary, recruitment can be explained by a steepening of the input–output function of the BM that occurs when the cochlea is damaged. This explanation is attractive since it can explain why, in patients with impairment in one ear only, the loudness in the recruiting ear generally "catches up with" and matches the loudness in the normal ear at high sound levels. However, findings from animal models have led some to question this way of accounting for loudness recruitment (Heinz et al., 2005).

9B PATHOLOGICAL ADAPTATION

Abnormal metabolic processes in the cochlea or auditory nerve sometimes result in a very rapid decrease in neural responses, although the response to the onset of a sound may be normal or near normal. The perceptual correlate of this is adaptation that is more extreme and more rapid than normal. This effect is sometimes associated with a tumor (called an acoustic neuroma or vestibular schwannoma) growing near and pressing on the auditory nerve and so pathological adaptation has been used in the differential diagnosis of cochlear and retrocochlear disorders (Jerger and Jerger, 1975).

There are several ways of studying this phenomenon, including the SDLB procedure described earlier. However, since pathological adaptation occurs at all sound levels, it can conveniently be studied with tones close to threshold. One way of doing this is to measure the difference in absolute threshold for continuous and interrupted tones. For people with conductive hearing loss, or for normally hearing people, there is little difference between the two types of threshold. For a person with a retrocochlear loss, the absolute threshold for a continuous tone may be considerably higher than that for an interrupted tone.

One very striking way of demonstrating this is first to determine the threshold for an interrupted tone. The sound level is then raised by 5 dB and the tone is presented continuously. After 5 or 6 s the sensation of tone will disappear completely, although for the normal listener the sensation would persist indefinitely. It is often necessary to raise the level of the tone by 20–30 dB before the sensation persists indefinitely for people with retrocochlear losses. It is easy to confirm that the effect is pathological adaptation rather than fatigue by interrupting the tone at any time during the test: the original threshold is restored at once. These tests are known as tone decay tests (Jerger and Jerger, 1975).

It should be noted that, although tone decay tests have been used to differentiate cochlear and retrocochlear disorders, marked tone decay can occur for people with hearing impairment of cochlear origin, when the hearing loss exceeds about 55 dB (Huss and Moore, 2003). Thus, caution is needed in applying these tests to people with substantial hearing loss. In practice, the diagnosis of a tumor growing near the auditory nerve is usually made nowadays using magnetic resonance imaging (MRI).

10 GENERAL CONCLUSIONS

This chapter has discussed a number of different aspects of the perception of loudness and the way it is coded in the auditory system. Equal-loudness contours allow comparison of the loudness of sinusoids of different frequencies. The shapes of equal-loudness contours are similar to that of the absolute threshold (MAF) curve at low levels, but they become flatter at high levels. Thus, at high levels it is roughly true that tones of equal SPL sound equally loud regardless of frequency over the frequency range 100–10,000 Hz. The shapes of equal-loudness contours indicate that loudness grows more rapidly with increasing level for low frequencies than for middle frequencies. This means that the tonal balance of recorded sounds such as speech or music may be affected by the level at which the sounds are reproduced. Equal-loudness contours are used in the design of sound level meters, so that the readings obtained give a better indication of the perceived loudness than would readings based simply on physical intensity.

The techniques of loudness scaling—magnitude estimation and magnitude production—allow the construction of "psychological" scales of loudness, the most common one being the sone scale suggested by S. S. Stevens (1957). Such scales are supposed to relate the perceived loudness of a given sound to its physical characteristics (such as intensity), and they have been utilized in models that allow the calculation of the loudness of any complex sound.

Loudness meters based on these models give a better indication of subjective loudness than conventional sound level meters.

The loudness of sounds depends on duration. The loudness of short-duration sounds may depend roughly on their total energy, but the results vary considerably across studies.

We are able to detect relatively small changes in sound level (0.3–2 dB) for a wide range of levels and for many types of stimuli. In general, discrimination performance, as measured by the Weber fraction ($\Delta I/I$), is independent of level for bands of noise, but improves at high levels for pure tones. Various psychoacoustic experiments indicate that, at high levels, information from neurons with CFs above and (to a lesser extent) below the frequency of the test tone contributes to intensity discrimination, but is not essential for it. In other words, spread of excitation is not essential for maintaining the wide dynamic range of the auditory system. Similarly, psychophysical experiments suggest that phase locking may play a role in intensity discrimination, but it is not essential.

Recordings from single neurons in the auditory nerve indicate that the information contained in the firing rates of auditory neurons is more than sufficient to account for human intensity discrimination. Indeed, the information from only about 100 of the 30,000 neurons would, in principle, be sufficient. Thus, it appears that intensity discrimination is not limited by the information carried in the auditory nerve, but rather by the use made of that information at higher levels in the auditory system.

Exposure to sounds may produce two changes in the responsiveness of the auditory system: the apparent magnitude of the stimulus may decrease, a process known as adaptation, and the absolute threshold measured after exposure may increase, a process known as fatigue. Fatigue, as measured by TTS, is generally small for low exposure levels, but increases rapidly when the level of the fatiguing stimulus is above about 90–100 dB SPL. This may indicate a division between fatigue that is physiological and transient in nature and fatigue that is more permanent and pathological in nature. TTS generally decreases with increasing recovery time, although a "bounce" sometimes occurs about 2 min after cessation of the fatiguing stimulus. This may indicate that more than one process is involved in recovery. Recovery times vary considerably, but may be 16 h or more following exposure to very intense sounds. The fact that the absolute threshold recovers to its pre-exposure value after a recovery period does not necessarily indicate that there is no damage to the auditory system. Sound levels above 110–120 dB SPL may produce permanent hearing losses, particularly if the exposure is of long duration. Such sound levels are not uncommonly produced by rock and pop groups, and they may be easily obtained by many of the sets of headphones that are available on the domestic market.

Adaptation effects measured with the SDLB technique are generally quite rapid, the greatest adaptation occurring within 1 or 2 min of exposure. Adaptation measured in this way occurs at both high and low sound levels. In contrast, studies that avoid binaural interaction have shown that adaptation occurs only for low-level tones (below 30 dB SL) and is strongest at high frequencies. The reasons for the discrepancies between the different methods remain to be explained.

In some cases of hearing loss, particularly when there is pathology of the cochlea, loudness recruitment may occur. Recruitment is an abnormally rapid growth of loudness level with increasing level: the sufferer may have an elevated absolute threshold, but intense sounds are as loud as for a normal listener. One method of detecting recruitment is based on the assumption that it will be associated with an abnormally small intensity DL, but this assumption does not appear to be well founded. However, the detection of brief increments in sound level often is better than normal at low SLs. When only one ear is affected, recruitment can be detected by direct comparison with the normal ear using a loudness balancing technique. When both ears are affected, recruitment may be revealed by a normal loudness discomfort level, but an elevated absolute threshold. Recruitment may be associated with damage to the outer hair cells and a consequent steepening of the input–output function of the BM. It does not seem to be caused by an abnormal spread of excitation.

Pathological adaptation may occur when there are abnormal metabolic processes in the cochlea or auditory nerve, although the effect is usually greater in the latter case. The adaptation is more rapid and more extreme than normal, and it is most easily measured for tones close to threshold; a continuous tone just above threshold may fade after a time and eventually become completely inaudible. The tone may be made audible once again by interrupting it. However, tone decay is not restricted to cases of retrocochlear hearing loss; marked tone decay can occur for people with cochlear hearing loss greater than about 55 dB.

FURTHER RESOURCES

An extensive review of the perception of loudness may be found in:
Florentine, M., Popper, A. N., and Fay, R. R. (2011). *Loudness*. New York: Springer.

Other reviews are:
Plack, C. J., and Carlyon, R. P. (1995). Loudness perception and intensity coding. In B. C. J. Moore (Ed.), *Handbook of Perception and Cognition, Volume 6. Hearing*. Orlando, FL: Academic Press.
Epstein, M., and Marozeau, J. (2010). Loudness and intensity coding. In C. J. Plack (Ed.), *Oxford Handbook of Auditory Science: Hearing*. Oxford: Oxford University Press.

A review and summary of the literature on loudness adaptation may be found in:
Scharf, B. (1983). Loudness adaptation. In J. V. Tobias & E. D. Schubert (Eds.), *Hearing Research and Theory, Volume 2*. New York: Academic Press.

A review of the effects of cochlear hearing loss on loudness perception can be found in:
Moore, B. C. J. (2007). *Cochlear Hearing Loss: Physiological, Psychological and Technical Issues* (2nd Ed.). Chichester: Wiley.

Demonstrations 4 and 6–8 of auditory demonstrations on CD are relevant to the contents of this chapter (see list of further reading for Chapter 1).

Simulations of the effects of loudness recruitment on the perception of music and speech are available on a CD called "Perceptual Consequences of Cochlear Damage" that may be obtained by writing to Prof. B. C. J. Moore, Department of Experimental Psychology, University of Cambridge, Downing Street, Cambridge, CB2 3EB, England, enclosing a check for 25 dollars or a cheque for 12 pounds sterling, made payable to B. C. J. Moore.

CHAPTER 5

Temporal Processing in the Auditory System

1 INTRODUCTION

This chapter describes certain aspects of the perception of time varying sounds, concentrating especially on limits in the ability to detect changes over time. Time is a very important dimension in hearing, since almost all sounds fluctuate over time. Furthermore, for sounds that convey information, such as speech and music, much of the information appears to be carried in the changes themselves, rather than in the parts of the sounds that are relatively stable. This point is expanded in Chapters 8 and 9. It is important to distinguish between temporal resolution (or acuity) and temporal integration (or summation). The former refers to the ability to detect changes in stimuli over time, for example, to detect a brief gap between two stimuli or to detect that a sound is modulated in some way. The latter refers to the ability of the auditory system to add up information over time to enhance the detection or discrimination of stimuli, and it has been described already in connection with absolute thresholds and loudness (Chapter 2, Section 6, and Chapter 4, Section 6). As pointed out by Viemeister and Plack (1993), it is also important to distinguish the rapid pressure variations in a sound (the "temporal fine structure") from the slower overall changes in the amplitude of those fluctuations (the "envelope"); for example, in Fig. 3.7 (upper panel) the temporal fine structure corresponds to the carrier frequency and the envelope to the modulating frequency. Temporal resolution normally refers to the resolution of changes in the envelope, not in the temporal fine structure.

In characterizing temporal resolution in the auditory system, it is important to take account of the filtering that takes place in the peripheral auditory system. Temporal resolution depends on two main processes: analysis of the time pattern occurring within each frequency channel and comparison of the time patterns across channels. This chapter concentrates mainly on within-channel processes, since these have been studied extensively, but across-channel processes are briefly discussed.

A major difficulty in measuring the temporal resolution of the auditory system is that changes in the time pattern of a sound are generally associated with changes in its magnitude spectrum. Thus, the detection of a change in time pattern can sometimes depend not on temporal resolution *per se*, but on the detection of the spectral change. As an example, consider the task of distinguishing a single brief click from a pair of clicks separated by a short time interval. Assume that the energy of the single click is the same as that of the pair of clicks, so that the two sounds are similar in loudness. At first sight, this task appears to give a direct measure of temporal resolution. The results show that subjects can distinguish the single click from the click pair when the gap between the two clicks in a pair is only a few tens of microseconds (Leshowitz, 1971). This appears to indicate remarkably fine temporal resolution.

The interpretation is not, however, so straightforward. The magnitude spectrum of a pair of clicks is different from the magnitude spectrum of a single click; at some frequencies the single click has more energy and at others it has less energy. Subjects are able to detect these spectral differences, either by monitoring the energy within a single critical band, or by detecting the differences in spectral shape of the two sounds (as occurs in profile analysis; see Chapter 3). The spectral differences in this case are most easily detected at high frequencies. When a noise is added to mask frequencies above 10 kHz, the threshold value of the gap increases dramatically. Thus, the results of this experiment cannot be taken as a direct measure of temporal resolution.

There have been two general approaches to getting around this problem. One is to use signals whose magnitude spectrum is not changed when the time pattern is altered. For example, the magnitude spectrum of white noise remains flat if the noise is interrupted, i.e., if a gap is introduced into the noise. The second approach uses stimuli whose spectra are altered by the change in time pattern, but extra background sounds are added to mask the spectral changes. Both approaches are described.

2 TEMPORAL RESOLUTION MEASURED BY THE DISCRIMINATION OF STIMULI WITH IDENTICAL MAGNITUDE SPECTRA: BROADBAND SOUNDS

2A THE DETECTION OF GAPS IN BROADBAND NOISE

As mentioned above, the long-term magnitude spectrum of broadband white noise remains the same if the noise is briefly interrupted. Thus, the threshold for detecting a gap in a broadband noise provides a simple and convenient measure of temporal resolution. Usually a 2-alternative forced-choice (2AFC) procedure is used: the subject is presented with two successive bursts of noise and either the first or the second burst (at random) is interrupted to produce the gap. The task of the subject is to indicate which burst contained the gap. The gap threshold is typically 2–3 ms (Plomp, 1964b; Penner, 1977). The threshold increases at very low sound levels, when the level of the noise approaches the absolute threshold, but is relatively invariant with level for moderate to high levels.

2B THE DISCRIMINATION OF TIME-REVERSED SIGNALS

The long-term magnitude spectrum of a sound is not changed when that sound is time reversed (played backward in time). Thus, if a time-reversed sound can be discriminated from the original, this must reflect a sensitivity to the difference in time pattern of the two sounds. This was exploited by Ronken (1970), who used as stimuli pairs of clicks differing in amplitude. One click, labeled A, had an amplitude greater than that of the other click, labeled B. Typically the amplitude of A was twice that of B. Subjects were required to distinguish click pairs differing in the order of A and B: either AB or BA. The ability to do this was measured as a function of the time interval or gap between A and B. Ronken found that subjects could distinguish the click pairs for gaps down to 2–3 ms. Thus, the limit to temporal resolution found in this task is similar to that found for the detection of a gap in broadband noise. It should be noted that, in this task, subjects do not hear the individual clicks within a click pair. Rather, each click pair is heard as a single sound with its own characteristic quality. For example, the two click pairs AB and BA might sound like "tick" and "tock".

Ronken's experiment has been repeated several times, mostly with similar results. However, Resnick and Feth (1975) showed that the inter-click interval required for threshold varied systematically as a function both of overall sound level and of the relative level of the clicks within a pair; the thresholds ranged from 0.5 to 1.8 ms. Also, one study has shown much greater temporal acuity. Henning and Gaskell (1981), using very brief clicks (20 μs), found that the order of the click pairs could be discriminated for click pair durations down to 0.25 ms. The reasons for the discrepancies between the different results are unclear.

2C Temporal Modulation Transfer Functions

The experiments described above each give a single number to describe temporal resolution. A more comprehensive approach is to measure the threshold for detecting changes in the amplitude of a sound as a function of the rapidity of the changes. In the simplest case, white noise is sinusoidally amplitude modulated, and the threshold for detecting the modulation is determined as a function of modulation rate. The function relating threshold to modulation rate is known as a temporal modulation transfer function (TMTF). Modulation of white noise does not change its long-term magnitude spectrum. An example of the results is shown in Fig. 5.1; data are taken from

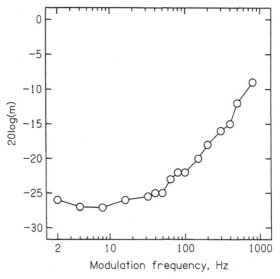

FIG. 5.1   A temporal modulation transfer function (TMTF). A broadband white noise was sinusoidally amplitude modulated, and the threshold amount of modulation required for detection is plotted as a function of modulation rate. The amount of modulation is specified as $20\log(m)$, where m is the modulation index (see Chapter 3, Section 4C). The higher the sensitivity to modulation, the more negative is this quantity. Data from Bacon and Viemeister (1985b).

Bacon and Viemeister (1985b). For low modulation rates, performance is limited by the amplitude resolution of the ear, rather than by temporal resolution. Thus, the threshold is independent of modulation rate for rates up to about 16 Hz. As the rate increases beyond 16 Hz, temporal resolution starts to have an effect; the threshold increases, and for rates above about 1000 Hz the modulation cannot be detected at all. Thus, sensitivity to amplitude modulation (AM) decreases progressively as the rate of modulation increases. The shapes of TMTFs do not vary much with overall sound level, but the ability to detect the modulation does worsen at low sound levels.

A problem with the use of broadband noise as a carrier is that the inherent random amplitude fluctuations in the noise can influence performance (Dau et al., 1997b). This is discussed in more detail later on.

3 TEMPORAL RESOLUTION MEASURED BY THE DISCRIMINATION OF STIMULI WITH IDENTICAL MAGNITUDE SPECTRA: EFFECTS OF CENTER FREQUENCY

The experiments described in Section 2 used broadband stimuli. Thus, they provide no information regarding the question of whether the temporal resolution of the ear varies with center frequency. It has often been suggested that, in theory, temporal resolution should be poorer at low frequencies than at high. This idea is based on the assumption that temporal resolution is limited partly by the response time of the auditory filters. For example, if a stimulus is turned off and on again to form a temporal gap, ringing in the auditory filters (see Chapter 1, Section 4) would partially fill in the gap, so the envelope of the output of the auditory filters would show only a small dip. This is illustrated in Fig. 5.2, which shows the response of a simulated auditory filter to a sinusoid containing a brief gap. The narrower the bandwidth of a filter, the longer is its response time (see Fig. 1.7). The auditory filters have narrower bandwidths at low frequencies than at high. Thus, if the responses of the auditory filters limit temporal resolution, resolution should be worse at low frequencies than at high. The experiment described below provides an initial test of this idea.

Green (1973) used time-reversed stimuli like those of Ronken (1970) to measure temporal resolution, but instead of clicks he used brief pulses of a sinusoid. Each stimulus consisted of a brief pulse of a sinusoid in which the level of the first half of the pulse was 10 dB different from that of the second half. Subjects were required to distinguish two signals, differing in whether the half with the high level was first or second. Green measured performance as a function of the total duration of the stimuli. The threshold, corresponding

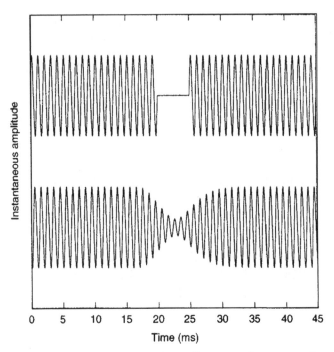

FIG. 5.2   The response of a simulated auditory filter to a 1-kHz sinusoid containing a 5-ms gap. The upper trace shows the input to the filter, and the lower trace shows the output. The filter was centered at 1 kHz, and its characteristics were chosen to simulate those of a human auditory filter with the same center frequency. Only the portions of the waveforms immediately before and after the gap are shown. Note that the gap is partially filled in by the ringing in the filter.

to 75% correct discrimination, was similar for center frequencies of 2 and 4 kHz and was between 1 and 2 ms. However, the threshold was slightly higher for a center frequency of 1 kHz, being between 2 and 4 ms. Thus, these data suggest that the response time of the auditory filters was not important above 2 kHz, but may have played a role below that.

It is interesting that performance in this task was actually a nonmonotonic function of duration. Performance was good for durations in the range 2–6 ms, worsened for durations around 16 ms, and then improved again as the duration was increased beyond 16 ms. For the very short durations, subjects listened for a difference in quality between the two sounds—rather like the "tick" and "tock" described earlier for Ronken's stimuli. At durations around 16 ms, the tonal quality of the bursts became more prominent, and the quality differences were harder to hear. At much longer durations, the soft and loud segments could be separately heard, in a distinct order. It appears, therefore, that performance in this task was determined by two separate mechanisms.

4 MEASUREMENT OF TEMPORAL RESOLUTION USING NARROWBAND SOUNDS

This section considers the temporal resolution of narrowband sounds. For such sounds, changing the time pattern changes the spectrum. For example, the introduction of a gap results in spectral splatter; energy is spread outside the nominal bandwidth of the sound (see Chapter 1, Section 2B). To prevent the splatter from being detected, the sounds are presented in a background sound, usually a noise, designed to mask the splatter. Unfortunately, the noise used to mask the splatter also has effects within the frequency band of interest, making the gap harder to detect. Thus, the level and spectrum of the noise have to be carefully chosen so as to be sure that the splatter is masked while minimizing within-band masking effects.

4A Detection of Gaps in Bands of Noise

One might expect that gap thresholds for noise bands would depend on two factors: the inherent fluctuations in the noise and the effects of the auditory filters. This is illustrated in Fig. 5.3. Each panel of the figure shows a sample of noise containing a gap (upper trace) and the output of a simulated auditory filter in response to that noise (lower trace). The filter is always centered on the passband of the noise. The rapidity of the random fluctuations in the noise increases with increasing bandwidth. This can be seen by comparing the upper trace in the left panel (a 50-Hz-wide noise) and the upper trace in the right panel (a 500-Hz-wide noise). It has been suggested that gap thresholds for noise bands may be partly limited by the inherent fluctuations in the noise (Shailer and Moore, 1983, 1985; Green, 1985; Eddins and Green, 1995). Randomly occurring dips in the noise may be "confused" with the gap to be detected.

When the noise bandwidth is less than the auditory filter bandwidth (left panel), the temporal pattern of the fluctuation in the noise is hardly changed by the auditory filter. Ringing in the filter has the effect of partially filling in the gap, but it does not fill the gap completely. The gap threshold then depends primarily on the confusability of the gap with the inherent fluctuations of the noise itself. Narrow bandwidths lead to slower fluctuations, which in turn lead to larger gap thresholds. Thus, the gap threshold would be expected to decrease with increasing noise bandwidth.

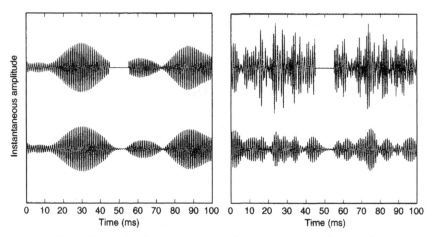

FIG. 5.3 In each panel, the upper trace shows a sample of narrowband noise containing a 10-ms gap, and the lower trace shows the output of a simulated auditory filter in response to that noise. The noises and the filter are centered at 1 kHz. In the left panel, the noise bandwidth is 50 Hz, which is less than the filter bandwidth of 130 Hz. In the right panel, the noise bandwidth is 500 Hz.

When the noise bandwidth is greater than the auditory filter bandwidth (right panel), the fluctuations at the output of the filter are slower than those at the input. For a gap to be reliably detected by monitoring the output of a single auditory filter, it has to be longer than a typical dip in the output of the filter. Now, the filter bandwidth rather than the input noise bandwidth is the factor limiting performance. Thus, if subjects monitored just a single auditory filter, the effect of the filter would be to impair gap detection.

Based on these ideas, one can make the following predictions, assuming that just a single auditory filter is monitored. The detection of temporal gaps in noise bands should be worse at low center frequencies than at high center frequencies, because the bandwidths of the auditory filters are smaller at lower center frequencies. Smaller bandwidths should lead to slower fluctuations and hence to larger gap thresholds. In addition, gap thresholds should decrease with increasing noise bandwidth, but only when the noise bandwidth is less than the bandwidth of the widest auditory filter stimulated by the noise. Further increases in noise bandwidth should not lead to an improvement in the gap threshold.

In fact, the empirical data do not show the expected pattern. Gap thresholds for narrowband noises do decrease with increasing noise bandwidth, but they continue to decrease even when the noise bandwidth exceeds the bandwidth of any single auditory filter stimulated by the noise (Shailer and Moore, 1983, 1985; Glasberg and Moore, 1992; Eddins *et al.*,

1992). Furthermore, gap thresholds measured with noise bands of fixed width show only small effects of center frequency or of upper cutoff frequency (Shailer and Moore, 1985; Eddins *et al.*, 1992; Snell *et al.*, 1994). This is illustrated in Fig. 5.4, which shows data from Eddins *et al.* (1992). The data of Snell *et al.* (1994) using a fixed bandwidth of 1 kHz show the smallest gap thresholds for center frequencies of 2 and 4 kHz, gap thresholds increasing somewhat at both higher and lower center frequencies.

It appears that subjects make use of the output of more than one auditory filter to detect temporal gaps in broadband noises (Grose, 1991; Eddins *et al.*, 1992; Eddins and Green, 1995). When a gap is introduced into a noise band with a large width, the gap creates a dip that is synchronous at the outputs of all the auditory filters that are excited by the noise. In contrast, the randomly occurring dips in the noise are independent at the outputs of auditory filters with substantially different center frequencies. By comparing the outputs of several auditory filters, the confusion of the random dips in the noise with the imposed gap can be greatly reduced. This leads to better gap detection than

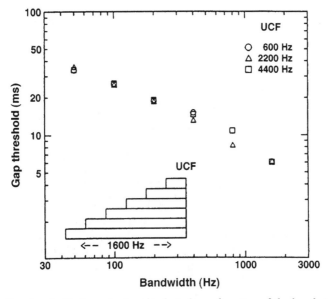

FIG. 5.4   Gap thresholds for noise bands plotted as a function of the bandwidth of the noise bands. The upper cutoff frequency (UCF) of the noise bands was fixed at one of three values: 600, 2200, and 4400 Hz. The inset bars illustrate schematically how the bandwidth was varied keeping the UCF fixed. Gap thresholds decrease progressively with increasing bandwidth, but are almost independent of UCF. The data are from Eddins *et al.* (1992).

would be obtained if only one filter were monitored. Thus, the gap thresholds decrease (improve) with increasing noise bandwidth, even when the bandwidth is much greater than the bandwidth of any single auditory filter that is excited by the noise. Because information can be combined across filters, the auditory filter does not play an obvious role in limiting gap detection, and there is not much effect of center frequency or upper cutoff frequency.

Gap thresholds for narrowband noises tend to decrease with increasing sound level for levels up to about 30 dB above absolute threshold, but remain roughly constant after that.

4B Detection of Gaps in Sinusoids

Shailer and Moore (1987) studied the detection of temporal gaps in sinusoids. The sinusoids were presented in a continuous noise with a spectral notch (bandstop) at the frequency of the sinusoids, in order to mask spectral splatter. The results were strongly affected by the phase at which the sinusoid was turned off and on to produce the gap. The three phase conditions used are illustrated in Fig. 5.5. For all conditions, the portion of the sinusoid preceding the gap ended with a positive-going zero-crossing. In other words, the

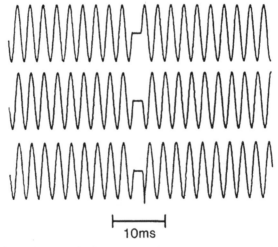

FIG. 5.5   The three phase conditions used by Shailer and Moore (1987) to measure gap detection thresholds for sinusoids. For each condition, the stimulus shown is a 400-Hz sinusoid with a 1.9-ms gap. The three conditions are standard phase (top), reversed phase (middle), and preserved phase (bottom).

sinusoid was turned off as the waveform was about to change from negative to positive values. The three conditions differed in the phase at which the sinusoid was turned on at the end of the gap: for the "standard" phase condition (top trace), the sinusoid started at a positive-going zero-crossing; for the "reversed" phase condition (middle trace), the sinusoid started at a negative-going zero-crossing; and for the "preserved" phase condition (bottom trace) the sinusoid started at the phase it would have had if it had continued without interruption. Thus, for the preserved-phase condition it was as if the gap had been "cut out" from a continuous sinusoid.

Examples of psychometric functions for the three conditions are shown in Fig. 5.6. The frequency of the sinusoid was 400 Hz. A 2AFC task was used, so chance performance corresponds to 50% correct. For the preserved-phase

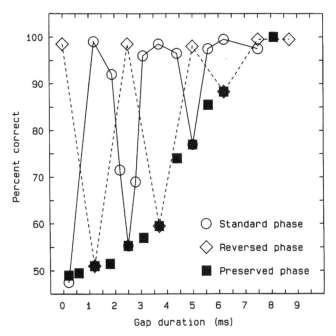

FIG. 5.6   An example of the results of Shailer and Moore (1987), showing data for one subject for a signal frequency of 400 Hz. Psychometric functions for gap detection are plotted for the standard-phase (circles), reversed-phase (diamonds), and preserved-phase (filled squares) conditions. When the gap duration is an integer multiple of the signal period, P ($= 2.5$ ms), the standard-phase condition is identical to the preserved-phase condition. Similarly, when the gap duration is $(n + 0.5)P$, where n is an integer, the reversed-phase condition is identical to the preserved-phase condition. Adapted from Shailer and Moore (1987).

condition, performance improved monotonically with increasing gap duration, as might be expected. However, for the other two conditions, the psychometric functions were distinctly nonmonotonic. For the standard-phase condition, the gap was difficult to detect when its duration was an integer multiple of the period (P) of the signal, i.e., 2.5 and 5 ms. Conversely, the gap was easy to detect when its duration was $(n + 0.5)P$, where $n = 0$ or 1. The psychometric function for the reversed-phase condition showed poor performance when the gap duration was $(n + 0.5)P$, where $n = 0$ or 1, and good performance when the gap duration was nP.

Shailer and Moore (1987) explained these results in terms of ringing in the auditory filter. Their argument is illustrated in Fig. 5.7, which shows responses of a simulated auditory filter with a center frequency of 400 Hz to a series of stimuli from the standard-phase condition, with gap durations ranging from 1.2 to 3.7 ms. When the sinusoid is turned off at the start of the gap, the filter continues to respond or ring for a certain time. If the gap duration is 2.5 ms, corresponding to one whole period of the sinusoid, the sinusoid following the gap is in phase with the ringing response. In this case the output of the filter shows only a small dip, and we would expect gap detection to be difficult. This is exactly what is observed. For a gap duration of 1.2 or 3.7 ms, the sinusoid

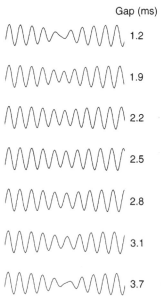

FIG. 5.7 The output of a simulated auditory filter centered at 400 Hz in response to 400-Hz sinusoids containing gaps ranging in duration from 1.2 to 3.7 ms, for the standard-phase condition.

following the gap is out of phase with the ringing response. Now the output of the filter passes through zero before returning to its steady value. The resulting dip in the filter output is larger and is much easier to detect. This explains why the psychometric function is nonmonotonic for the standard-phase condition. Similar arguments explain the nonmonotonicities for the reversed-phase condition. For the preserved-phase condition, the sinusoid following the gap is always in phase with the ringing response of the auditory filter. Thus, the dip in the output of the auditory filter increases monotonically with increasing gap duration, and the psychometric function is monotonic.

The results for the preserved-phase condition can be used to estimate the gap threshold corresponding to 75% correct. For the data shown in Fig. 5.6, the gap threshold is about 4.5 ms. Shailer and Moore (1987) found that the gap threshold was roughly constant at about 5 ms for center frequencies of 400, 1000, and 2000 Hz. Moore et al. (1993a) measured gap thresholds for center frequencies of 100, 200, 400, 800, 1000, and 2000 Hz, using a condition similar to the preserved-phase condition of Shailer and Moore. The gap thresholds were almost constant, at 6–8 ms over the frequency range 400–2000 Hz, but increased somewhat at 200 Hz and increased markedly, to about 18 ms, at 100 Hz. Individual variability also increased markedly at 100 Hz.

Overall, while the auditory filter seems to play a role in determining the form of the results for the standard- and reversed-phase conditions, gap thresholds estimated from the preserved-phase condition do not show a strong effect of center frequency, except at very low frequencies (200 Hz and below). It appears that ringing in the auditory filter only limits gap detection for sine waves at very low center frequencies.

4C Temporal Modulation Transfer Functions for Sinusoidal Carriers

The measurement of TMTFs using sinusoidal carriers is complicated by the fact that the modulation introduces spectral sidebands, which may be detected as separate components if they are sufficiently far in frequency from the carrier frequency; see Chapter 3, Sections 4C and 4D. Also, even when the frequency separation of the carrier and sidebands is very small, subjects may make use of the outputs of auditory filters tuned well above the signal frequency (the high-frequency side of the excitation pattern), for which there is less compression than for filters tuned close to the signal frequency. The effective modulation depth would be greater on the high-frequency side of the excitation pattern, as described in Chapter 4, Section 7C. However, since the compression appears to be very fast-acting (Robles et al., 1986; Recio et al.,

1998), this would not be expected to influence the shape of the TMTF, at least for the range of modulation frequencies where sidebands are not detectable.

When the carrier frequency is high, the effect of resolution of sidebands is likely to be small for modulation frequencies up to a few hundred Hertz. For example, for a carrier frequency of 5000 Hz, the value of ERB_N is about 560 Hz (Glasberg and Moore, 1990), and the "edge" components in complex tones need to be separated by more than about $0.75ERB_N$ from neighboring components to be "heard out" as separate tones, even when all components have equal amplitude (Moore and Ohgushi, 1993). Thus, the results obtained for modulation frequencies less than about $0.5ERB_N$ are likely to reflect temporal resolution rather than spectral resolution. Consistent with this, TMTFs for high carrier frequencies generally show an initial flat portion (sensitivity independent of modulation frequency), then a portion where threshold increases with increasing modulation frequency, presumably reflecting the limits of temporal resolution, and then a portion where threshold decreases again, presumably reflecting the detection of spectral sidebands (Kohlrausch et al., 2000). Some examples are shown in Fig. 5.8. For the carrier frequency of 10 kHz (pentagons), the portion of the curve where threshold increases extends to a modulation rate of about 500 Hz. For the 3-kHz carrier (squares), the rising portion extends to about 250 Hz, while for the 1-kHz carrier (circles), there is no rising portion at all.

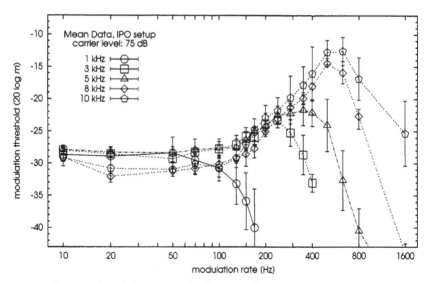

FIG. 5.8 Temporal modulation transfer functions for sinusoidal carriers with various different frequencies, as indicated in the key. From Kohlrausch et al. (2000), with permission of the authors.

The initial flat portion of the TMTF extends to about 100–120 Hz for sinusoidal carriers, but only to 50 or 60 Hz for a broadband noise carrier (compare Figs. 5.1 and 5.8). It has been suggested that the discrepancy occurs because of the inherent amplitude fluctuations in a noise carrier, which limit the detectability of the imposed modulation (Fleischer, 1982; Dau *et al.*, 1997a,b, 1999). The effect of the inherent fluctuations depends on their similarity to the imposed modulation. When a narrowband noise carrier is used, which has relatively slow inherent amplitude fluctuations, TMTFs show the poorest sensitivity for low modulation frequencies (Fleischer, 1982; Dau *et al.*, 1997a); this is described in more detail in Section 6B. In principle, then, TMTFs obtained using sinusoidal carriers provide a better measure of the inherent temporal resolution of the auditory system than TMTFs obtained using noise carriers, provided that the modulation frequency is within the range where spectral resolution does not play a major role.

5 MODELING TEMPORAL RESOLUTION

Although there is evidence that the auditory filter plays a role in some measures of temporal resolution, its influence is seen mainly at low center frequencies. The response of the auditory filter at high center frequencies is too fast for it to be a limiting factor in most tasks involving temporal resolution. This has led to the idea that there is a process at levels of the auditory system higher than the auditory nerve that is "sluggish" in some way, thereby limiting temporal resolution. Models of temporal resolution are especially concerned with this process. The models assume that the internal representation of stimuli is "smoothed" over time, so that rapid temporal changes are reduced in magnitude but slower ones are preserved. Although this smoothing process almost certainly operates on neural activity, the most widely used models are based on smoothing a simple transformation of the stimulus, rather than its neural representation. This is done for simplicity and mathematical convenience, even though it is not very realistic. An example of a model of temporal resolution is illustrated in Fig. 5.9. Each stage of the model is discussed below.

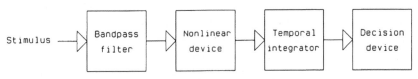

FIG. 5.9   A block diagram of a model of temporal resolution.

5A Bandpass Filtering

There is an initial stage of bandpass filtering, reflecting the action of the auditory filters. For simplicity, only one filter is shown; in reality there is an array of parallel channels, each like that shown in the figure. However, for many of the tasks considered so far in this chapter, the results can be modeled by considering only a single channel.

5B The Nonlinearity

Each filter is followed by a nonlinear device. This nonlinear device is meant to reflect the operation of several processes that occur in the peripheral auditory system. For example, nerve spikes tend to occur at a specific phase of the stimulating waveform on the BM. An effect resembling this can be achieved by a nonlinear process called half-wave rectification; in this process, only the parts of the waveform with a specific polarity (e.g., the positive parts) are passed, while the parts of the waveform with opposite polarity are set to zero. Another significant nonlinearity is the compressive input–output function of the BM; see Chapter 1 and Fig. 1.12. In recent models of temporal resolution, the nonlinear device includes these two processes, i.e., rectification and a compressive nonlinearity, resembling the compressive input–output function on the BM (Oxenham and Moore, 1994, 1997; Moore et al., 1996; Plack and Oxenham, 1998). It is unrealistic to treat the filtering on the BM and the compressive nonlinearity as separate stages, but this probably does not seriously undermine the usefulness of the model. A method for determining the characteristics of the nonlinearity is described later in this chapter.

5C The Sliding Temporal Integrator

The output of the nonlinear device is fed to a "smoothing" device, which can be implemented either as a lowpass filter (Viemeister, 1979) or as a sliding temporal integrator (Moore et al., 1988; Plack and Moore, 1990). The device determines a kind of weighted average of the output of the compressive nonlinearity over a certain time interval or "window". The weighting function is often modeled as a pair of back-to-back exponential functions, as illustrated in Fig. 5.10. This weighting function is sometimes called the "shape" of the temporal window. Most weight is given to the output of the nonlinear device at times close to the temporal center of the window, and progressively less

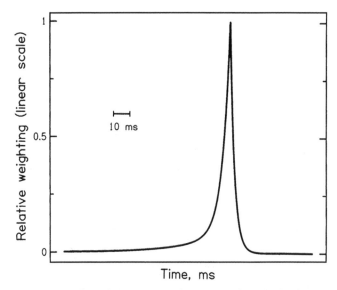

FIG. 5.10 The "shape" of the sliding temporal integrator (window). This is a weighting function applied to the output of the nonlinear device. It performs a weighted running average of the output of the nonlinear device. The shape is plotted on a linear scale as a function of time.

weight is given to the output at times farther from the center. The window itself is assumed to slide in time, so that the output of the temporal integrator is like a weighted running average of the input. This has the effect of smoothing rapid fluctuations while preserving slower ones. When a sound is turned on abruptly, the output of the temporal integrator takes some time to build up. Similarly, when a sound is turned off, the output of the integrator takes some time to decay.

It is often assumed that backward and forward masking depend on the process of build up and decay. For example, if a brief signal is rapidly followed by a masker (backward masking), the response to the signal may still be building up when the masker occurs. If the masker is sufficiently intense, then its internal effects may "swamp" those of the signal. Similarly, if a brief signal follows soon after a masker (forward masking), the decaying response to the masker may swamp the response to the signal.

The operation of the sliding temporal integrator is illustrated in Fig. 5.11. The panels on the left-hand side show several different signals applied to the input of the integrator. These signals can be thought of as corresponding to the envelopes of audio signals, not the waveforms themselves. On the right is shown the output of the sliding temporal integrator. In response to a brief

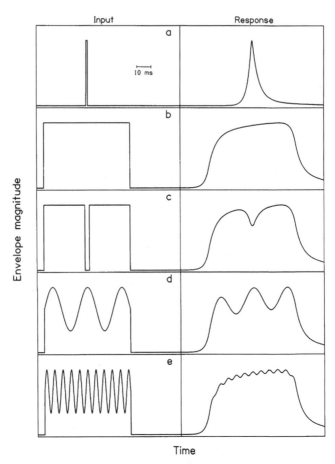

FIG. 5.11 Examples of the influence of the sliding temporal integrator on the envelopes of sounds. The panels on the left show inputs to the sliding temporal integrator. The panels on the right show the corresponding outputs.

pulse (panel a), the output builds up and then decays. The build up is more rapid than the decay, because the window shape is asymmetric in time. In fact, the impulse response shown in the right-hand part of panel (a) is simply the window shape played backward in time. The asymmetry assumed for the window shape makes it possible to account for an asymmetry between forward and backward masking; when the time interval between the masker and the signal is increased, backward masking decreases more rapidly than forward masking (Oxenham and Moore, 1994). In response to an input with a rectangular envelope (panel b), the output builds up, stays at a steady value for some time, and then decays. In response to an input with a temporal gap (panel c), the output shows a build up, a steady part, a dip, another steady part, and then a decay. The dip corresponds to the gap, but it is like a partially filled in representation of the gap. In response to an input with a slow sinusoidal fluctuation, such as might be produced by an amplitude-modulated tone (panel d), the output also shows a sinusoidal modulation; slow fluctuations are preserved at the output of the sliding temporal integrator. In response to an input with a fast sinusoidal fluctuation (panel e), the output shows a much reduced amount of fluctuation; fast fluctuations are attenuated at the output of the sliding temporal integrator.

5D THE DECISION DEVICE

The output of the sliding temporal integrator is fed to a decision device. The decision device may use different "rules" depending on the task required. For example, if the task is to detect a brief temporal gap in a signal, the decision device might look for a "dip" in the output of the temporal integrator. If the task is to detect AM of a sound, the device might assess the amount of modulation at the output of the sliding temporal integrator (Viemeister, 1979).

5E CHARACTERIZING THE NONLINEAR DEVICE AND THE SLIDING TEMPORAL INTEGRATOR

In the model, the characteristics of the auditory filters are based on auditory filter shapes derived from masking experiments, as described in Chapter 3. However, it is also necessary to define the characteristics of the nonlinearity and the sliding temporal integrator. An approach to this problem was described by Oxenham and Moore (1994). They performed an experiment in which they used a noise masker and a brief 6-kHz signal. In one set of conditions, the signal was presented after the masker (forward masking). In another set it was presented before the masker (backward masking). In a third set of conditions, the signal was presented between two bursts of the masker; this involves a combination of forward and backward masking. As described earlier, forward and backward masking can be accounted for in terms of the build up and decay processes at the output of the sliding temporal integrator.

An interesting effect is observed in cases when forward and backward maskers are combined. It might be thought that, if two different maskers are equally effective (i.e., each produces the same amount of masking), then the combination of the two maskers would result in a doubling of the signal energy required for threshold (Green and Swets, 1974); this corresponds to an increase in the signal level at threshold of 3 dB. In fact, the signal threshold often increases by more than this. The amount by which signal threshold exceeds the prediction is referred to as "excess masking". Combining two equally effective nonsimultaneous maskers (one forward and one backward) *consistently* results in excess masking, usually of 7–12 dB at moderate sound levels (Wilson and Carhart, 1971; Cokely and Humes, 1993).

This excess masking can be explained if it is assumed that each stimulus (the forward masker, signal, and backward masker) is subjected to a compressive nonlinearity before the effects of the stimuli are combined in a linear temporal integrator (Penner, 1980; Penner and Shiffrin, 1980), as assumed in the model of temporal resolution shown in Fig. 5.9. To understand how the compressive nonlinearity accounts for excess masking, consider the following. Imagine that two equally effective nonsimultaneous maskers (one forward and one backward) are presented together. At the output of the temporal integrator, the decay of response to the forward masker is summed with the build up of response to the backward masker. It is assumed that, at the time when the brief signal produces its own maximum response at the output of the temporal integrator, the effects of the forward and backward maskers are equal (as they are equally effective maskers). The integrator itself is a linear device, and so the internal effect evoked by the two maskers is simply double the effect evoked by either alone. Thus, in order to reach threshold, the level of the signal has to be increased relative to the level required for a single masker. In fact, to reach the signal threshold, the *internal* effect of the signal must also be doubled. This requires more than a 3-dB increase in signal threshold because the signal itself is independently compressed.

Oxenham and Moore (1994) showed that their results could be used to separate the effects of the temporal integrator and the compressive nonlinearity prior to the integrator. A good fit to their forward and backward masking data was obtained when the stimulus intensity at the output of the simulated auditory filter was raised to a power between 0.25 and 0.35. If, for example, the intensity is raised to the power 0.3, then a tenfold increase in power (corresponding to 10 dB) would be needed to double the internal effect of the signal. Thus, for two equally effective maskers, one forward and one backward, excess masking of 7 dB is predicted.

Oxenham and Moore (1994) also used their data to derive the weighting characteristic or "shape" of the temporal window (see the schematic illustration in Fig. 5.10), following an approach proposed by Moore *et al.* (1988). However, the derivation is rather complex and is beyond the scope of this book. The reader is referred to the original publications for details. In fact, the weighting function shown in Fig. 5.10 corresponds to that derived by Oxenham and Moore.

6 A MODULATION FILTER BANK?

Some researchers have suggested that the analysis of sounds that are amplitude modulated depends on a specialized part of the brain that contains an array of neurons, each tuned to a different modulation rate (Kay, 1982). Each neuron can be considered as a filter in the modulation domain, and the array of neurons is known collectively as a "modulation filter bank". Neurons with appropriate properties have been found in the cochlear nucleus (Møller, 1976) and the inferior colliculus (Rees and Møller, 1983; Schreiner and Langner, 1988; Lorenzi *et al.*, 1995). For a review see Palmer (1995). The modulation filter bank has been suggested as a possible explanation for certain perceptual phenomena, some of which are described below. It should be emphasized, however, that this is still a controversial concept.

6A MASKING IN THE MODULATION DOMAIN WITH BROADBAND CARRIERS

The threshold for detecting AM of a given carrier generally increases if additional AM is superimposed on that carrier. This effect has been called "modulation masking". Houtgast (1989) studied the detection of sinusoidal AM of a pink noise carrier. Thresholds for detecting the modulation were measured when no other modulation was present and when a "masker" modulator was present in addition. In one experiment, the masker modulation was a half-octave-wide band of noise, with a center frequency of 4, 8, or 16 Hz. The results are illustrated in Fig. 5.12. For each masker, the masking pattern showed a peak at the masker frequency. This could be interpreted as indicating selectivity in the modulation-frequency domain, analogous to the frequency selectivity in the audio-frequency domain that was described in Chapter 3.

In a second experiment, Houtgast (1989) conducted an experiment analogous to the classic band-widening experiment of Fletcher (1940), as described in Chapter 3. The masker modulator was a band of noise of variable width centered at 8 Hz. The signal was sinusoidal AM at 8 Hz. The spectral density of the modulator was held constant as the bandwidth was varied, so the power in the modulator increased as the bandwidth increased. The results are shown in Fig. 5.13. The threshold for detecting the signal AM

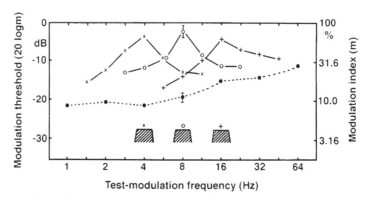

FIG. 5.12 The dashed curve shows the threshold for detecting sinusoidal amplitude modulation of a pink noise carrier in the absence of any masker modulation, plotted as a function of modulation frequency. The solid curves show the modulation detection thresholds obtained in the presence of masking modulators centered at three different frequencies, 4, 8, and 16 Hz. The spectra of the modulators are illustrated schematically at the bottom of the panel. Redrawn from Houtgast (1989).

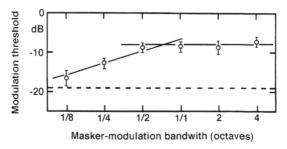

FIG. 5.13 The modulation detection threshold of 8-Hz signal modulation of a pink noise carrier, plotted as a function of the bandwidth of a masking modulator centered at 8 Hz. The spectral density of the masker modulation was held constant as the bandwidth was varied. The dashed line indicates the modulation detection threshold in the absence of a masker. Redrawn from Houtgast (1989).

at first increased as the masker bandwidth increased and then leveled off when the bandwidth was greater than about 1/2 octave. Again, these results could be interpreted as indicating selectivity in the modulation-frequency domain. If the signal modulation was detected by monitoring the output of a modulation filter tuned to 8 Hz, then the threshold would not increase once the masker modulator bandwidth exceeded the bandwidth of the modulation filter.

Bacon and Grantham (1989) measured thresholds for detecting sinusoidal AM of a broadband white noise carrier in the presence of sinusoidal masker AM. When the masker AM frequency was 16 or 64 Hz, most modulation masking occurred when the signal modulation frequency was near the masker frequency. In other words, the masking patterns were roughly bandpass, although they showed an increase for very low signal frequencies. For a 4-Hz masker, the masking patterns had a lowpass characteristic, i.e., there was a downward spread of modulation masking.

6B Forward Masking in the Modulation Domain

Wojtczak and Viemeister (2005) showed that forward masking could occur in the modulation domain: the threshold amount of modulation required for detection of AM of a broadband noise carrier (the signal) was raised by preceding AM (the masker) applied to the same carrier. They demonstrated that this effect showed tuning in the modulation domain. They measured masked-threshold patterns in the modulation domain by keeping the signal AM frequency fixed (at 20, 40, or 80 Hz) and measuring the modulation detection threshold for the signal as a function of the AM frequency of the masker. The masker modulation depth was fixed at 100%. The results for four subjects are shown in Fig. 5.14. The masked-threshold patterns showed a peak close to the signal frequency and the amount of forward masking decreased almost to zero when the masker AM frequency was 1–2 octaves above or below the signal AM frequency.

Wojtczak and Viemeister (2005) suggested that their results were consistent with the idea of modulation filters. They proposed that the forward-masking effect was mediated either by persistence of the neural activity evoked by the AM masker or adaptation produced by the AM masker in these modulation filters.

Although this experiment and the experiments described in the previous section support the idea of frequency selectivity in the modulation domain, the hypothetical modulation filters appear to be much less sharply tuned than the auditory filters in the audio-frequency domain. The bandwidths of the modulation filters have been estimated as between 0.4 and 1 times the center frequency (Dau et al., 1997a; Ewert and Dau, 2000; Lorenzi et al., 2001; Sek and Moore, 2003; Wojtczak and Viemeister, 2005; Moore et al., 2009). The modulation filters, if they exist, are not highly selective.

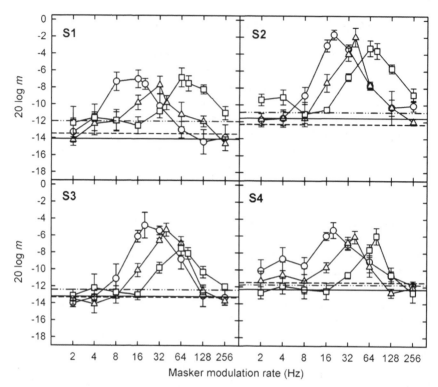

FIG. 5.14 Thresholds for four individual subjects (S1–S4) for the detection of signal AM, plotted as a function of the frequency of the preceding masker AM. The masker was 100% modulated ($m = 1$). The signal AM frequency was 20 (circles), 40 (triangles), or 80 Hz (squares). Thresholds for detecting the signal AM in the absence of any masker AM are also shown: 20 (solid line), 40 (dashed line), and 80 Hz (dashed-dotted line). Redrawn from Wojtczak and Viemeister (2005).

6C THE ABILITY TO HEAR OUT COMPONENT AM

Sek and Moore (2003) examined the ability to "hear out" the modulation frequency of the central component of a three-component modulator applied to a 4-kHz sinusoidal carrier. The task was similar to the tasks that have been used to examine the ability to hear out partials in complex tones in the audio-frequency domain, as described in Chapter 3, Section 4D. On each trial, three successive modulated stimuli were presented. The modulator of the first stimulus contained three sinusoidal components. Within a run the frequencies of the outer two components were fixed and the frequency of the central ("target") component was drawn randomly from one of five values.

The modulators of second and third stimuli contained one sinusoidal component. One had a frequency equal to that of the target and the other, comparison, stimulus had a frequency randomly selected from one of the other possible values. Subjects indicated whether the target corresponded to the second or third stimulus. Scores were around 80% correct when the components in the three-component modulator were widely spaced and when the AM frequencies of the target and comparison stimuli differed sufficiently. Thus, subjects did have some ability to hear out the target component AM. However, the ability to hear out components in the modulation-frequency domain was much poorer than the ability to hear out components in the audio-frequency domain, consistent with the idea that the modulation filters are broadly tuned.

6D TMTFs Obtained Using Narrowband Noise Carriers

Dau et al. (1997a) examined the ability to detect sinusoidal AM of narrowband noise carriers centered at 5 kHz. A high center frequency was chosen so that the AM would not result in detectable spectral changes. The noise carrier had a bandwidth of 3, 31, or 314 Hz. The rapidity of the inherent random amplitude fluctuations in the noise carriers increased with increasing bandwidth. Their results are illustrated in Fig. 5.15. For the 3-Hz-wide carrier (circles), modulation detection thresholds were highest for the lowest modulation frequency tested (3 Hz), and thresholds decreased with increasing modulation frequency up to 100 Hz. For the 31-Hz-wide carrier (squares), modulation detection thresholds were highest for modulation frequencies in the range 5–15 Hz and decreased on either side of this. For the 314-Hz-wide carrier, thresholds were highest at the highest modulation frequency tested (100 Hz). Generally, these results can be described by saying that detection of the signal AM was hardest when its frequency fell within the range of the random AM inherent in the carriers. Dau et al. were able to explain their results quantitatively in terms of a model based on a modulation filter bank. Models of the type described in Section 5 are not able to explain these results.

6E Modulation Detection Interference

As was briefly mentioned in Chapter 3, the detection or discrimination of AM of a sinusoidal carrier can be impaired by the presence of one or more modulated sounds with different carrier frequencies. This effect is called "modulation detection interference" or "modulation discrimination interference", both given the acronym MDI. For example, Yost and Sheft (1989)

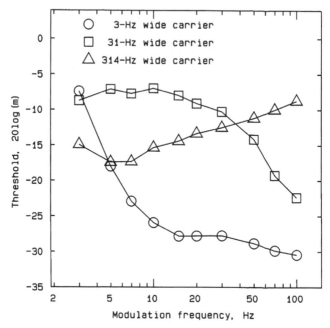

FIG. 5.15 Temporal modulation transfer functions obtained using narrowband noise carriers, with a bandwidth of 3 (circles), 31 (squares), or 314 Hz (triangles). The center frequency of the carrier was 5 kHz. Data from Dau *et al.* (1997a).

showed that the threshold for detecting sinusoidal AM of a sinusoidal carrier was increased in the presence of another carrier amplitude modulated at the same rate, even when the second carrier was remote in frequency from the first. They found that MDI did not occur if the second carrier was unmodulated, although other researchers have sometimes found small effects of unmodulated carriers. Wilson *et al.* (1990) demonstrated a similar phenomenon for the detection of frequency modulation (FM). They showed that the threshold for detecting sinusoidal FM of a given carrier frequency could be elevated in the presence of a second carrier that was also frequency modulated. The effect showed some tuning for carrier frequency, being greater when the carrier frequencies of the target and interfering sounds were close, but it persisted even when the carriers were widely separated in frequency (by more than one octave). The effect also showed tuning for modulation rate, being greatest when the modulation rates of the target and interfering sounds were close.

Moore *et al.* (1991b) determined how thresholds for detecting an increase in modulation depth (sinusoidal AM or FM) of a 1000-Hz carrier frequency (the target) were affected by modulation of carriers (interference) with frequencies of 230 and 3300 Hz. They found that modulation increment thresholds were increased (worsened) when the remote carriers were modulated. This MDI effect was greatest when the target and interference were modulated at similar rates, but the effect was broadly tuned for modulation rate. Moore *et al.* also found cross-modal interference effects; the detection of an increment in AM depth was adversely affected by FM interference, and vice versa. Moore *et al.* suggested that this could be explained by the transformation of FM to AM in the peripheral auditory system; when a sinusoid is frequency modulated, the outputs of auditory filters tuned below and above the sinusoid are amplitude modulated (see Chapter 6).

It has been suggested that MDI occurs because the target and interferer modulation are processed together in a modulation filter bank, where each filter is tuned for modulation rate, but responds to a broad range of carrier frequencies (Yost *et al.*, 1989; Yost and Sheft, 1989; Dau and Verhey, 1999). It is necessary to assume broad tuning in the carrier-frequency domain to explain the fact that MDI can occur when the target and interfering carriers are widely separated in frequency. However, this concept does not fit in very well with the physiological data; these show that most neurons with tuning in the modulation-frequency domain are also tuned in the carrier-frequency domain (Palmer, 1995). Another possible explanation for MDI is that it results from perceptual grouping of the target and interfering carriers. This explanation is discussed in Chapter 8. For more extensive reviews, see Moore (1992) and Hall *et al.* (1995).

6F ACCOUNTING FOR TMTFS WITH A MODULATION FILTER BANK

The shape of the TMTF for a broadband noise carrier (Fig. 5.1) has usually been explained in terms of models incorporating a lowpass filter or a sliding temporal integrator, as described in Section 5. However, Dau *et al.* (1997a,b) have suggested an alternative approach based on a modulation filter bank. Modulation at a specific frequency is assumed to be detected by monitoring the output of a modulation filter tuned close to that frequency. The ability to detect the modulation is assumed to be partly limited by the inherent random amplitude fluctuations in the noise as they appear at the output of the modulation filter. The modulation masking data reviewed above suggest that the bandwidth of the modulation filters, expressed in Hz, increases with increasing center frequency. For a white noise carrier, the power of the random modulation appearing at the output of a modulation filter increases with increasing filter bandwidth. Thus, more random modulation appears at the outputs of modulation filters tuned to higher frequencies, and this makes it progressively harder to detect modulation as the modulation frequency increases.

This explanation cannot apply to TMTFs measured with sinusoidal carriers, since such carriers have no inherent random fluctuations. It has been proposed that the reduced sensitivity to AM for modulation frequencies above about 120 Hz, as measured using sinusoidal carriers, could be explained using the idea that the center frequencies of the modulation filters span a limited range, extending up to about 120 Hz (Dau, 1996). AM with a frequency above 120 Hz may be detected via the output of the modulation filter with the highest CF (the "top" filter), and the roll-off of AM sensitivity may reflect the characteristics of the top filter. Evidence consistent with this idea has been presented by Moore et al. (2009). They measured AM forward masking with a similar method to that of Wojtczak and Viemeister (2005), but using an 8-kHz sinusoidal carrier rather than a noise carrier. The signal AM frequency was 80, 120, or 180 Hz and the masker AM frequencies covered a range above and below each signal frequency. Four highly trained listeners were tested. For the 80-Hz signal, the signal threshold was usually maximal when the masker frequency equaled the signal frequency, as expected. In contrast, for the 180-Hz signal, the signal threshold was maximal when the masker frequency was *below* the signal frequency. This could be explained if the signal were being detected via the top modulation filter, if this had a center frequency below 180 Hz; the masking of the signal would be maximal when the masker frequency was equal to the center frequency of this top filter. For the 120-Hz signal, two listeners showed the former pattern, and two showed the latter pattern. The results support the idea that the highest modulation filter has a center frequency in the range 100-120 Hz.

7 DURATION DISCRIMINATION

Several studies have examined the ability to detect a change in duration of auditory stimuli. Typically, two successive sounds have been presented that have the same power spectrum but differ in duration. The subject is required to indicate which sound had the longer duration. Both Creelman (1962) and Abel (1972b) found that the smallest detectable increase in duration, ΔT, increased with the baseline duration T. The data of Abel showed that, for $T = 10$, 100, and 1000 ms, ΔT was about 4, 15, and 60 ms, respectively. Thus, the Weber fraction, $\Delta T/T$, decreased with increasing T. The results were relatively independent of the overall level of the stimuli and were similar for noise bursts of various bandwidths and for bursts of a 1000-Hz sine wave.

Abel (1972a) reported somewhat different results for the discrimination of the duration of the silent interval between two "markers". For silent durations, T, less than 160 ms, the results showed that discrimination improved as the level of the markers increased. The function relating $\Delta T/T$ to T was nonmonotonic, reaching a local minimum for $T = 2.5$ ms and a local maximum for $T = 10$ ms. The values of ΔT ranged from 6 to 19 ms for a base duration of 10 ms and from 61 to 96 ms for a base duration of 320 ms.

Divenyi and Danner (1977) required subjects to discriminate the duration of the silent interval defined by two 20-ms sounds. When the markers were identical high-level (86 dB SPL) bursts of sinusoids or noise, performance was similar across markers varying in center frequency (500–4000 Hz) and bandwidth. In contrast to the results of Abel (1972a), $\Delta T/T$ was almost independent of T over the range of T from 25 to 320 ms. Thresholds were markedly lower than those reported by Abel (1972a), being about 1.7 ms at $T = 25$ and 15 ms at $T = 320$ ms. This may have been a result of the extensive training of the subjects of Divenyi and Danner. For bursts of a 1-kHz sinusoid, performance worsened markedly when the level of the markers was decreased below 25 dB SL. Performance also worsened markedly when the two markers on either side of a silent interval were made different in level or frequency.

In summary, all studies show that, for values of T exceeding 10 ms, ΔT increases with T and ΔT is roughly independent of the spectral characteristics of the sounds. This is true both for the duration discrimination of sounds and for the discrimination of silent intervals bounded by acoustic markers, provided that the markers are identical on either side of the interval. However, ΔT increases at low sound levels, and it also increases when the markers differ in level or frequency on either side of the interval. The mechanisms underlying duration discrimination are poorly understood, and discussion of them is beyond the scope of this book. The interested reader is referred to Divenyi and Danner (1977).

8 TEMPORAL ANALYSIS BASED ON ACROSS-CHANNEL PROCESSES

Studies of the ability to compare timing across different frequency channels can give very different results depending on whether the different frequency components in the sound are perceived as part of a single sound or as part of more than one sound. Also, it should be realized that subjects may be able to *distinguish* different time patterns, for example, a change in the relative onset time of two different frequencies, without the subjective impression of a change in time pattern; some sort of change in the quality of the sound may be all that is heard. The studies described next indicate the limits of the ability to compare timing across channels, using highly trained subjects.

8A THE DISCRIMINATION OF HUFFMAN SEQUENCES

Patterson and Green (1970) and Green (1973) have studied the discrimination of a class of signals that have the same long-term magnitude spectrum, but that differ in their short-term spectra. These sounds are called Huffman sequences. Essentially, they are brief broadband sounds, like clicks, except that the energy in a certain frequency region is delayed relative to that in other regions. The amount of the delay, the center frequency of the delayed frequency region, and the width of the delayed frequency region can all be varied. If subjects can distinguish a pair of Huffman sequences differing, for example, in the amount of delay in a given frequency region, this implies that they are sensitive to the difference in time pattern. Green (1973) measured the ability of subjects to detect differences in the amount of delay in three frequency regions: 650, 1900, and 4200 Hz. He found similar results for all three center frequencies: subjects could detect differences in delay time of about 2 ms regardless of the center frequency of the delayed region.

It should be noted that subjects did not report hearing one part of the sound after the rest of the sound. Rather, the differences in time pattern were perceived as subtle changes in sound quality. Further, some subjects required extensive training to achieve the fine acuity of 2 ms, and even after this training the task required considerable concentration.

8B DETECTION OF ONSET AND OFFSET ASYNCHRONY IN MULTICOMPONENT COMPLEXES

Zera and Green (1993) measured thresholds for detecting asynchrony in the onset or offset of complex signals composed of many sinusoidal components. The components were either uniformly spaced on a logarithmic frequency scale or formed a harmonic series. In one stimulus, the standard, all components started, and stopped synchronously. In the "signal" stimulus, one component was presented with an onset or offset asynchrony. The task of the subjects was to discriminate the standard stimulus from the signal stimulus. They found that onset asynchrony was easier to detect than offset asynchrony. For harmonic signals, onset asynchronies of less than 1 ms could generally be detected, whether the asynchronous component was leading or lagging the other components (although, in the latter case, thresholds increased markedly for delays in the higher harmonics, presumably because for the higher harmonics several harmonics fall within the passband of a single auditory filter and produce a masking effect on the asynchronous component). Thresholds for detecting offset asynchronies were larger, being about 3–10 ms when the asynchronous component ended after the other components and 10–30 ms when the asynchronous component ended before the other components. Thresholds for detecting asynchronies in logarithmically spaced complexes were generally 2–50 times larger than for harmonic complexes.

The difference between harmonically and logarithmically spaced complexes may be explicable in terms of perceptual grouping (see Chapter 8 for more details). The harmonic signal was perceived as a single sound source, i.e., all of the components appeared to belong together. The logarithmically spaced complex was perceived as a series of separate tones, like many notes being played at once on an organ. It seems that it is difficult to compare the timing of sound elements that are perceived as coming from different sources, a point that will be expanded in Chapter 8. The high sensitivity to onset asynchronies for harmonic complexes is consistent with the finding that the perceived timbres of musical instruments are partly dependent on the exact onset times and rates of rise of individual harmonics within each musical note (Risset and Wessel, 1999).

Overall, the two sets of experiments reviewed above indicate that remarkably small asynchronies between frequency channels can be detected, both for short-duration sounds (Huffman sequences) and for asynchronies in the onsets of longer duration sounds (complex tones).

8C Judgment of Temporal Order

The ability to judge the temporal order of a sequence of sounds depends strongly on whether the task requires *identification* of the order of individual elements or whether it can be performed by *discrimination* of different orders or by attaching well-learned labels to different orders. In the latter case, resolution can be rather fine. With extended training and feedback, subjects can learn to distinguish between and identify orders within sequences of non-related sounds lasting only 10 ms or less (Warren, 1974). For sequences of tones, the component durations necessary for labeling different orders may be as low as 2–7 ms (Divenyi and Hirsh, 1974). This is the type of acuity that would be expected for speech sounds, since these consist of well-learned sequences to which consistent labels have been attached.

When the task is to identify the order of sounds in a sequence, performance is generally markedly worse. For example, Hirsh (1959) found that, for pairs of unrelated items, trained subjects required durations of about 20 ms per item for correct order identification. When the number of items in the sequence is increased, the durations required for order identification tend to increase also. Temporal order judgments are discussed further in Chapter 8.

9 GENERAL CONCLUSIONS

In characterizing temporal resolution in the auditory system, it is important to take account of the filtering that takes place in the peripheral auditory system. Temporal resolution depends on two main processes: analysis of the time pattern occurring within each frequency channel and comparison of the time patterns across channels.

Within-channel temporal resolution can be measured with many different types of signals and in a variety of tasks. In all cases, it is important to ensure that cues in the long-term magnitude spectrum of the stimuli are not being used to perform the task.

For broadband noises, the threshold for detecting a temporal gap is typically 2–3 ms, except at very low levels, where the threshold increases. For pairs of clicks differing in amplitude, the threshold value of the gap between the clicks required to distinguish their order is also about 2–3 ms, although some experiments have given smaller thresholds. The threshold for detecting sinusoidal AM of broadband noise varies with the modulation frequency; the threshold is low at low modulation frequencies and increases with increasing modulation frequency. The function describing modulation thresholds as a function of modulation rate is known as a temporal modulation transfer function (TMTF).

Narrowband sounds allow the measurement of temporal resolution at different center frequencies. We might expect temporal resolution to be poorer at low center frequencies because of ringing in the auditory filters; the filters at low center frequencies have narrow bandwidths and they therefore have a long response time. However, most experiments do not show the expected effect, except at very low frequencies (200 Hz and below).

Thresholds for the discrimination of time-reversed sinusoids are typically in the range 2–3 ms and vary only slightly with center frequency. Thresholds for detecting gaps in bands of noise decrease with increasing noise bandwidth. This probably occurs because randomly occurring dips in the noises may be confused with the gap to be detected; small bandwidths lead to slow random fluctuations and to large gap thresholds. When the bandwidth is held constant, gap thresholds hardly vary with center frequency. Gap thresholds for noises with large bandwidths probably depend on subjects combining information across auditory filters.

The detection of a gap in a sinusoid is strongly affected by the phase at which the sinusoid is turned off and on to produce the gap. The psychometric functions for some conditions show distinct nonmonotonicities that can be explained in terms of ringing in the auditory filter. Gap thresholds for sinusoids do not vary markedly with center frequency for frequencies above about 400 Hz, but increase at very low center frequencies. Overall, the results for different types of narrowband signals suggest that the auditory filter may affect temporal resolution at low frequencies, but it has little effect for center frequencies above a few hundred Hertz.

Most models to account for temporal resolution assume that there is a process that smoothes the internal representation of auditory stimuli, but the models differ in the way that the smoothing is implemented. The models have a number of stages, including a bandpass filter (the auditory filter), a nonlinear device (a rectifier and compressive nonlinearity), a smoothing device (lowpass filter or temporal integrator), and a decision device. Temporal resolution can be affected by all of the stages of the models. Such models are successful in accounting for certain aspects of the data, but none accounts for all aspects.

There is some evidence that amplitude-modulated sounds are processed in a modulation filter bank. Such a concept can be used to explain data on modulation masking in simultaneous and forward masking and modulation detection interference. The modulation filter bank can also provide an alternative explanation for the shape of the TMTF and for why the shape of the TMTF differs depending on whether the carrier is broadband noise, narrowband noise, or a sinusoid.

Studies of duration discrimination have shown that, for values of the baseline duration, T, exceeding 10 ms, the threshold, ΔT, increases with T. ΔT is roughly independent of the spectral characteristics of the sounds. This is true both for the duration discrimination of sounds and for the discrimination of silent intervals bounded by acoustic markers, provided that the markers are identical on either side of the interval. However, ΔT increases at low sound levels, and it also increases when the markers differ in level or frequency on either side of the interval.

Some tasks require a comparison of the timing of events in different frequency channels. Acuity in such tasks, such as the discrimination of Huffman sequences, does not seem to vary markedly with center frequency. Onset asynchronies between components in complex sounds can be detected more readily than offset asynchronies.

Other aspects of temporal resolution are discussed later. Specifically, Chapter 7, Section 12, discusses temporal resolution in binaural processing, and Chapter 8, Section 4C, provides further information about judgments of the temporal order of sounds.

FURTHER READING

The following book is the proceedings of a conference on temporal resolution. The chapters by Green and by Buus and Florentine are of particular relevance to this chapter.

Michelsen, A. (1985). *Time Resolution in Auditory Systems.* Berlin: Springer.

For recent reviews, see:

Viemeister, N. F., and Plack, C. J. (1993). Time analysis. In W. A. Yost, A. N. Popper & R. R. Fay (Eds.), *Human Psychophysics.* New York: Springer.

Eddins, D. A., and Green, D. M. (1995). Temporal integration and temporal resolution. In B. C. J. Moore (Ed.), *Hearing.* San Diego: Academic Press.

For a review of the effects of cochlear hearing impairment on temporal resolution, see:

Moore, B. C. J. (2007). *Cochlear Hearing Loss: Physiological, Psychological and Technical Issues* (2nd Ed.). Chichester: Wiley.

CHAPTER **6**

Pitch Perception

1 INTRODUCTION

This chapter describes the perception of the pitch of both pure and complex tones. Pitch may be defined as "that attribute of auditory sensation in terms of which sounds may be ordered on a scale extending from low to high" (ANSI, 1994b). Variations in pitch create a sense of melody. Pitch is related to the repetition rate of the waveform of a sound; for a pure tone, this corresponds to the frequency and for a periodic complex tone to the fundamental frequency. There are, however, exceptions to this simple rule, as will be described later. As pitch is a subjective attribute, it cannot be measured directly. Assigning a pitch value to a sound is generally understood to mean specifying the frequency of a pure tone that has the same subjective pitch as the sound.

2 THEORIES OF PITCH PERCEPTION

For many years, there have been two theories of pitch perception. One, the "place" theory of hearing, has two distinct postulates. The first is that the stimulus undergoes a spectral analysis in the cochlea: different frequencies (or frequency components in a complex stimulus) excite different places along the basilar membrane (BM), and hence neurons with different CFs (this is called tonotopic organization; see Chapter 1, Section 7B). The second is that the pitch of a stimulus is related to the pattern of excitation produced by that stimulus; for a pure tone, the pitch is generally assumed to correspond to the position of maximum excitation. The first of these two postulates is now well established and has been confirmed in a number of independent ways, including direct observation of the movement of the BM (see Chapter 1). The second is still a matter of dispute.

An alternative to the place theory, the "temporal" theory, is based on the assumption that the pitch of a stimulus is related to the time pattern of the neural spikes evoked by that stimulus. Nerve spikes tend to occur at a particular phase of the waveform on the BM (this is called phase locking; see Chapter 1, Section 7E), and thus, the time intervals between successive spikes approximate integer multiples of the period of the waveform. Phase locking becomes very weak for sinusoids with frequencies above about 5 kHz, although the exact upper limit in humans is not known. However, the tones produced by musical instruments, the human voice, and most everyday sound sources all have fundamental frequencies below 5 kHz.

A difficulty for the place theory is raised by the pitch of complex tones. These produce patterns of excitation along the BM that do not show a single maximum; rather, there is a distribution of excitation with many maxima. The largest maximum may not be at the CF corresponding to the fundamental component. However, the perceived pitch, in general, still corresponds to this component. I describe later how the place theory can be modified to account for this.

3 THE PERCEPTION OF THE PITCH OF PURE TONES

This section discusses theories that attempt to explain how we perceive and discriminate the frequency of pure tones. The main topics are the size of the frequency difference limen (DL, the smallest detectable change in frequency); changes in the size of the DL with frequency; the perception of musical intervals as a function of frequency; and changes in pitch with sound level. It is important to distinguish between frequency selectivity and frequency discrimination. The former refers to the ability to resolve the frequency components of a complex sound, as discussed in Chapter 3. The latter refers to the ability to detect changes in frequency over time. As explained below, for the place theory, frequency selectivity and frequency discrimination are closely connected; frequency discrimination depends upon the filtering that takes place in the cochlea. For the temporal theory, frequency selectivity and frequency discrimination are not necessarily closely connected.

3A The Frequency Discrimination of Pure Tones

There have been two common ways of measuring frequency discrimination. One involves the presentation of two successive steady tones with slightly different frequencies. The subject is asked to judge whether the first or the second has the higher pitch. The order of the tones is varied randomly from trial to trial, and the frequency DL is usually taken as that frequency separation between the pulses for which the subject achieves a certain percentage of correct responses, such as 75%. This measure will be called the difference limen for frequency (DLF). A second measure uses tones that are frequency modulated (FM) at a low rate. Usually, two successive tones are presented, one modulated and the other unmodulated, and the subject has to indicate whether the first or the second tone is modulated. The amount of modulation required for detection of the modulation is determined. This measure will be called the frequency modulation detection limen (FMDL) (Fig. 6.1).

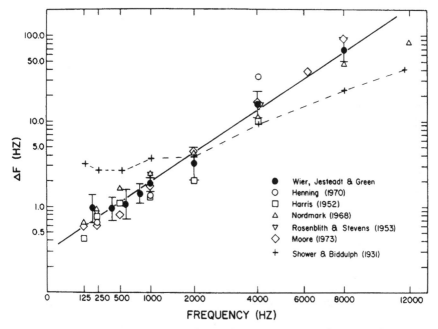

FIGURE 6.1 Summary of the results of several studies measuring frequency discrimination thresholds. The thresholds, ΔF, are plotted in Hertz as a function of frequency. All of the studies measured DLFs except that of Shower and Biddulph; they measured FMDLs. From Wier et al. (1977), by permission of the authors and J. Acoust. Soc. Am.

A summary of the results of some studies measuring frequency discrimination is given in Fig. 6.1, taken from Wier *et al.* (1977). They found that the data describing the DLF as a function of frequency fell on a straight line when plotted as log(DLF) against $\sqrt{}$ (frequency); the axes are scaled in this way in Fig. 6.1. The theoretical significance of this is not clear. Results of a more recent study, in which the same subjects were tested using both types of measure, are shown in Fig. 6.2 (Sek and Moore, 1995). Expressed in Hertz (as in Fig. 6.1), the DLF is smallest at low frequencies and increases monotonically with increasing frequency. Expressed as a proportion of center frequency (as in Fig. 6.2), the DLF tends to be smallest for middle frequencies and larger for very high and very low frequencies. FMDLs, shown as the dashed lines in Figs. 6.1 and 6.2, vary less with frequency than do

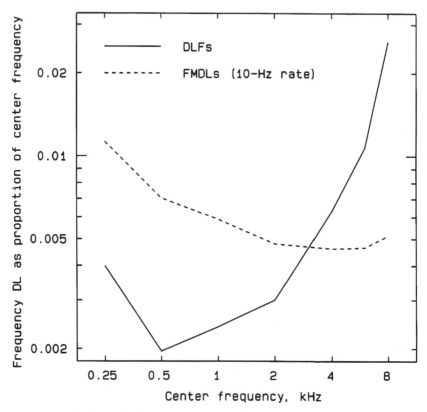

FIGURE 6.2 DLFs and FMDLs for a 10-Hz modulation rate, measured in the same subjects and plotted as a proportion of center frequency. Data from Sek and Moore (1995).

DLFs, both when expressed in Hertz and when expressed as a proportion of center frequency. DLFs and FMDLs tend to get somewhat smaller as the sound level increases (Nelson *et al.*, 1983).

A basic problem for any theory of hearing is to account for the remarkably small size of the frequency DLs; for a frequency of 1000 Hz and at a moderate sound level (60–70 dB SPL), the DLF is about 2–3 Hz. Zwicker (1970) proposed that frequency discrimination is based on changes in the excitation pattern evoked by the stimulus when the frequency is altered. This is a place model. Zwicker inferred the shapes of the excitation patterns from masking patterns such as those shown in Fig. 3.10 (see Chapter 3 for details). In his original formulation of the model, Zwicker intended it to apply only to FMDLs; others have tried to apply the model to account for DLFs.

According to Zwicker's model, a change in frequency can be detected whenever the excitation level at some point on the excitation pattern changes by more than a certain threshold value. Zwicker suggested that this value was about 1 dB. The change in excitation level is greatest on the steeply sloping low-frequency side of the excitation pattern (see Fig. 6.3). Thus, according to

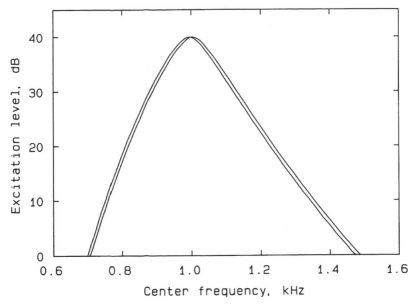

FIGURE 6.3 Schematic representation of the patterns of excitation evoked by two tones of slightly different frequency; the frequencies of the tones are 995 and 1005 Hz and their level is 40 dB SPL. The greatest difference in excitation level for the two patterns occurs on the steeply sloping, low-frequency side.

this model, the detection of a change in frequency is functionally equivalent to the detection of a change in level on the low-frequency side of the excitation pattern. The steepness of the low-frequency side is roughly constant when expressed in units of ERB_N, rather than in terms of linear frequency; the slope is about 27 dB/ERB_N. Thus, Zwicker's model predicts that the frequency DL at any given frequency should be a constant fraction of ERB_N at that frequency. FMDLs do conform fairly well to this prediction of the model when the modulation rate is fairly high (10 Hz or above), as illustrated by the dashed line in Fig. 6.4. However, DLFs vary more with frequency than predicted by the model (Moore, 1974; Moore and Glasberg, 1986, 1989; Sek and Moore, 1995); see Fig. 6.4 (solid line).

Henning (1966) has pointed out a problem with the measurement of frequency DLs at high frequencies; the frequency changes may be accompanied by correlated loudness changes. These occur because the frequency response of headphones is often irregular at high frequencies, and there is also a loss of absolute sensitivity at high frequencies (see the right-hand half of Fig. 2.1). These loudness changes may provide usable cues in the

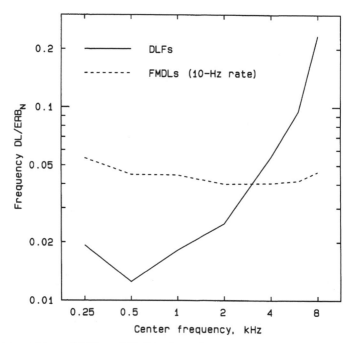

FIGURE 6.4   Values of DLFs and FMDLs for a 10-Hz rate, expressed as a proportion of ERB_N at the same center frequency.

detection of frequency changes. To prevent subjects from using these cues, Henning (1966) measured DLFs for tones whose level was varied randomly from one stimulus to the next. The random variation in level produced changes in loudness that were large compared with those produced by the frequency changes. Henning found that DLFs at high frequencies (4 kHz and above) were markedly increased by the random variation in level, whereas those at low frequencies were not.

Although Henning's experiment was carried out primarily to assess the importance of loudness cues in frequency discrimination, his data also provide a test of Zwicker's model. If the detection of frequency changes were based on the detection of changes in excitation level on the low-frequency side of the excitation pattern, then the introduction of random variations in level should markedly impair frequency discrimination; the small change in excitation level produced by a given frequency change would now be superimposed on much larger random changes in level. This predicted impairment of frequency discrimination was found only at high frequencies. Thus, Henning's data are consistent with Zwicker's model for high frequencies but not for low frequencies. However, Emmerich et al. (1989) repeated Henning's experiment and found that random variations in level did result in larger DLFs at low frequencies (0.5–4.0 kHz). Although these data appear to support Zwicker's model, Emmerich and coworkers argued that this was not necessarily true. They presented evidence that the impairment produced by the randomization of level could be attributed to slight changes in the pitches of the sinusoidal signals with changes in level (see Section 3C for a description of such changes).

Moore and Glasberg (1989) also measured DLFs for tones whose level was randomized from one stimulus to the next, but they randomized the level over a relatively small range (6 dB instead of 20 dB as used by Henning and Emmerich et al.), to minimize changes of pitch with level. The 6-dB range was still large relative to the changes in excitation level produced by small frequency changes. They found only a very small effect of the randomization of level; the DLFs were, on average, only 15% larger than those measured with the level fixed. The DLFs measured with the level randomized were smaller than predicted by Zwicker's model for frequencies from 0.5 to 4.0 kHz. At 6.5 kHz (the highest frequency tested), the data were not inconsistent with the model.

An alternative way of testing Zwicker's model is to use a stimulus that has energy distributed over a range of frequencies and whose magnitude spectrum has a certain slope. The slope of the excitation pattern of such a stimulus should not be steeper than the slope of the physical spectrum. This approach was adopted by Moore (1972, 1973a). He measured DLFs for tone pulses of various durations. For a short-duration tone pulse, the spectrum contains energy at frequencies other than the nominal frequency of the tone pulse (see Chapter 1, Section 2B). The shorter the tone pulse is made, the wider the range of frequencies over which the energy is spread. Below some critical duration, the slope of the spectral envelope becomes less than the slope of the excitation pattern evoked by a long-duration pure tone. Thus, if Zwicker's model is correct, this physical slope should limit performance at short durations. The DLFs measured by Moore are shown by symbols and solid lines in Fig. 6.5. The dashed line shows the performance predicted from Zwicker's model for the 6.25-ms signal duration, assuming that a 2-dB change in excitation level would have been detectable; 2 dB corresponds roughly to the smallest detectable change in level for brief tone pulses (Florentine, 1986). At short durations, the subjects did better than predicted for all

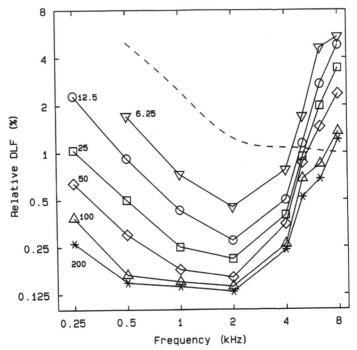

FIGURE 6.5 Values of the DLF plotted as a function of center frequency and expressed as a percentage of center frequency (log scale). The number by each curve is the duration of the tone pulses in milliseconds. Notice the sharp increase in the size of the DLFs that occurs around 5 kHz. The dashed line shows predictions based on Zwicker's (1956, 1970) model for the 6.25-ms duration; see text for details.

frequencies up to 5 kHz. At about this frequency, the DLFs showed a sharp increase in value.

In summary, Zwicker's model predicts that frequency DLs should vary with frequency in the same way as ERB_N. It also predicts that random variations in level should markedly increase frequency DLs. The results for DLFs are not consistent with these predictions. DLFs vary more with frequency than ERB_N, and the effect of randomizing level is smaller than predicted, except at high frequencies. Furthermore, DLFs for short-duration tones are smaller than predicted by Zwicker's model, except above 5 kHz. Other data, reviewed in Moore and Glasberg (1986), also suggest that Zwicker's model does not adequately account for DLFs.

Although I have concentrated on Zwicker's model, other place models (Corliss, 1967; Henning, 1967; Siebert, 1968, 1970; Heinz et al., 2001a,b) also have difficulty in accounting for DLFs. All place models predict that frequency discrimination should be related to frequency selectivity; the sharper the tuning of peripheral filtering mechanisms, the smaller the frequency DL should be. Thus, all place models predict that the frequency DL should vary with frequency in the same way as ERB_N. The failure of this prediction suggests that some other mechanism is involved.

The results for FMDLs are generally consistent with Zwicker's model, especially for relatively high modulation rates (10 Hz and above). However, Moore and Sek (1992, 1994) have shown that Zwicker's model does not account adequately for the results of experiments where subjects are required to detect a mixture of AM and FM (this is called mixed modulation, MM). They proposed an alternative model, but one also based on the concept of the excitation pattern. In this model, listeners do not monitor just a single point on the excitation pattern; rather, information is combined from all parts of the excitation pattern that are above absolute threshold. This is referred to as the "multichannel excitation pattern model". Moore and Sek showed that this model could account for results on the detection of MM at a 10-Hz rate. However, they have also presented evidence that the multichannel model does not work well when the modulation rate is very low (around 2 Hz) (Moore and Sek, 1995b, 1996; Sek and Moore, 1995, 2000). For example, the ratio $FMDL/ERB_N$ is not constant across frequency for a 2-Hz modulation rate, but increases with increasing frequency. They proposed that, at this very low rate, FM is detected by virtue of the changes in phase locking to the carrier that occur over time. They suggested that the mechanism for decoding the phase-locking information was "sluggish" and could not follow rapid oscillations in frequency. Hence, it played little role for high modulation rates. The concept of "sluggishness" has also been used to explain the pitch of musical tones with vibrato; see Section 7C.

Overall, the results are consistent with the idea that DLFs, and FMDLs for very low modulation rates, are determined by temporal information (phase locking) for frequencies up to about 4–5 kHz. The precision of phase locking decreases with increasing frequency above 1–2 kHz, and it is very weak above about 5 kHz. This can explain why DLFs increase markedly above this frequency. Goldstein and Srulovicz (1977) have shown that it is possible to predict the dependence of the DLF on frequency and duration by assuming that the auditory system processes the time intervals between successive nerve impulses; see also Heinz et al. (2001a,b).

FMDLs for medium to high modulation rates may be determined by a place mechanism, that is, by the detection of changes in the excitation pattern. This mechanism may also account for DLFs and for FMDLs for low modulation rates, when the carrier frequency is above about 5 kHz.

3B The Perception of Musical Intervals

If a tone evokes a pitch, then a sequence of tones with appropriate frequencies can evoke the percept of a melody. One way of measuring this aspect of pitch perception is to require subjects to make judgments about the musical relationship of a sequence of two or more pure tones. For example, two tones that are separated in frequency by an interval of one octave (i.e., one has twice the frequency of the other) sound similar. They are judged to have the same name on the musical scale (e.g., C or D). This has led several theorists to suggest that there are at least two dimensions to musical pitch (Ruckmick, 1929). One aspect is related monotonically to frequency (for a pure tone) and is known as "tone height". The other is related to pitch class (i.e., name note) and is called "tone chroma" (Bachem, 1950).

If subjects are presented with a pure tone of frequency, f_1, and are asked to adjust the frequency, f_2, of a second tone so that it appears to be an octave higher in pitch, they generally adjust f_2 to be roughly twice f_1 (but see Section 3D). However, when f_1 lies above 2.5 kHz, so that f_2 would lie above 5 kHz, octave matches become very erratic (Ward, 1954). It appears that the musical interval of an octave is only clearly perceived when both tones have frequencies below 5 kHz.

Other aspects of the perception of pitch also change for frequencies above 5 kHz. For example, a sequence of pure tones above 5 kHz does not produce a clear sense of melody. This has been shown by experiments involving musical transposition. For example, Attneave and Olson (1971) asked subjects to reproduce sequences of tones (e.g., the NBC chimes) at different points along the frequency scale. Their results showed an abrupt break point at about 5 kHz, above which transposition behavior was erratic. Also, subjects with absolute pitch (the ability to assign name notes without reference to other notes; see Section 7B) are very poor at naming notes above 4–5 kHz (Ohgushi and Hatoh, 1991).

In summary, it appears that only pure tones with frequencies below 5 kHz have a pitch in the sense that a sequence of tones can evoke a clear sense of musical interval or melody; that is, only tones below 5 kHz have tone chroma. A sequence of pure tones above 5 kHz does not evoke a clear sense of melody, although differences in frequency can be heard. This is consistent with the idea that the pitch of pure tones is determined by different mechanisms above and below 5 kHz, specifically, by temporal mechanisms at low frequencies and place mechanisms at high frequencies.

3C THE VARIATION OF PITCH WITH LEVEL

The pitch of a pure tone is primarily determined by its frequency. However, sound level also plays a small role. On average, the pitch of tones with frequencies below about 2 kHz decreases with increasing level, whereas the pitch of tones with frequencies above about 4 kHz increases with increasing sound level. The early data of Stevens (1935) showed rather large effects of sound level on pitch, but later data generally showed much smaller effects (Terhardt, 1974b; Verschuure and van Meeteren, 1975). For tones with frequencies between 1 and 2 kHz, changes in pitch with level are equivalent to a change in frequency of less than 1%. For tones with lower and higher frequencies, the changes can be larger (up to 5%). There are also considerable individual differences, both in the size of the pitch shifts with level and in the direction of the shifts.

It has sometimes been argued that pitch shifts with level are inconsistent with the temporal theory of pitch; neural inter-spike intervals (ISIs) are hardly affected by changes in sound level over a wide range. However, changes in pitch with level could be explained by the place theory, if shifts in level were accompanied by shifts in the position of maximum excitation on the BM. On closer examination, these arguments turn out to be rather weak. Although the temporal theory is based on the assumption that pitch depends on the temporal pattern of nerve spikes, it is also assumed that the temporal information is "decoded" at some level in the auditory system. In other words, the time intervals between neural spikes are measured and transformed into another representation. It is quite possible that the mechanism that does this is affected by which neurons are active and by the spike rates in those neurons; these in turn depend on sound level.

The argument favoring the place mechanism is also weak. The results of physiological experiments using animals and forward-masking experiments using human subjects (see Chapter 3, Section 9) suggest that the peak in the excitation pattern evoked by medium- and high-frequency tones shifts towards the base of the cochlea with increasing sound level (Moore *et al.*, 2002). The base is tuned to higher frequencies, so the basal-ward shift should correspond to hearing an increase in pitch. At high sound levels, the basal-ward shift corresponds to a shift in frequency of one-half octave or more. Thus, the place theory predicts that the pitch of a medium- or high-frequency tone should increase with increasing sound level, and the shift should correspond to half an octave or more at high sound levels. In fact, the shift in pitch is always much less than half an octave. Another problem for an explanation in terms of place theory comes from the observation of Thurlow (1943) that the pitch of a tone presented to one ear can be changed by presenting a tone of the same frequency to the other ear, provided that both tones are of fairly high intensity. The change in pitch is in the same direction as that produced by a physical increase in intensity. The pitch shift may have more to do with the loudness of the tone (which depends on information from both ears) than with the intensity in each ear (which determines the position of the peak excitation on the BM).

At present, there is no generally accepted explanation for the shifts in pitch with level. Given this, the existence of these pitch shifts cannot be used to draw any strong conclusions about theories of pitch.

3D THE STRETCHED OCTAVE

If subjects are asked to adjust the frequency of a pure tone so that it sounds one octave higher than a reference pure tone with a frequency of, say, 1000 Hz, they typically adjust the tone to have a frequency a little greater than 2000 Hz. In other words, the perceived octave actually corresponds to a frequency ratio slightly greater than 2:1 (Ward, 1954). This is sometimes referred to as the "octave-enlargement effect" or the "stretched" octave. Ohgushi (1983) offered an explanation of this effect in terms of a temporal theory of pitch. His explanation is based on ISIs in response to a pure tone, such as those shown in Fig. 1.20. Assume that the signal is a 1000-Hz pure tone. The ISIs cluster around integer multiples of the period of this tone ($P = 1$ ms), namely, 1, 2, 3, 4, 5 ... ms. However, the shorter ISIs actually deviate significantly from P, $2P$, and $3P$, due to refractory effects: the neuron has a reduced probability of producing a spike for a short time after a spike has occurred. Thus, a pitch extracted from these intervals will differ slightly from what would occur in the absence of refractory effects. By considering how the deviations of the ISIs from integer multiples of the period vary with frequency, based on neurophysiological data, Ohgushi was able to account for the octave-enlargement effect.

3E The Scaling of Pitch and the Mel Scale

Several researchers have attempted to determine the relationship between the pitch of a pure tone and its frequency. One method of doing this is through magnitude estimation (Beck and Shaw, 1961), as described for loudness in Chapter 4, Section 3. Another method, used by Stevens et al. (1937), is to ask the subject to adjust the frequency of a comparison tone until its pitch appears to be twice or half that of a comparison tone whose frequency is set by the experimenter. The scale obtained in this way is described as the mel scale (where mel comes from melody). Stevens et al. defined the pitch value of a 1000-Hz pure tone as 1000 mels. Hence, a tone whose pitch sounds twice as high as that of a 1000-Hz tone should have a pitch of 2000 mels. Pitch in mels is not simply related to linear frequency or the logarithm of frequency. Instead, pitch in mels appears to be related to the Bark (critical band) scale mentioned in Chapter 3, Section 3B; 1 Bark is about 100 mels (Zwicker and Feldtkeller, 1967).

Although the mel scale is still quite widely used by acoustical engineers and speech researchers, the validity of the scale is questionable, as highly differing patterns of results have been obtained depending on the exact method and the subjects used (Beck and Shaw, 1961; Siegel, 1965). Indeed, the concept of scaling the magnitude of pitch seems dubious, as pitch, unlike loudness, does not vary in amount; when frequency is varied, one pitch is substituted for another, much as perceived hue changes when the wavelength of light is varied.

3F General Conclusions on the Pitch Perception of Pure Tones

Several lines of evidence suggest that place mechanisms are not adequate to explain the frequency discrimination of pure tones. Contrary to the predictions of place theories, the DLF does not vary with frequency in the same way as ERB_N. Also, the DLF for short-duration tones is smaller than predicted by place theories except for frequencies above 5 kHz. This suggests that the DLF is determined by temporal mechanisms at low frequencies and by residual temporal information or place mechanisms at high frequencies.

The perception of sequences of pure tones also changes above 4–5 kHz. It seems that a sequence of tones only evokes a sense of musical interval or melody when the tones lie below 4–5 kHz, in the frequency range where temporal mechanisms probably operate. However, FM for rates of 10 Hz and above may be coded by the changes in the excitation pattern that are evoked by the FM; this is a place mechanism. The octave-enlargement effect can be explained in terms of a temporal mechanism.

4 THE PITCH PERCEPTION OF COMPLEX TONES

As stated earlier in this chapter, the classical place theory has difficulty in accounting for the perception of complex tones. For such tones, the pitch does not, in general, correspond to the position of maximum excitation on the BM. A striking illustration of this is provided by the "phenomenon of the missing fundamental". Consider, as an example, a sound consisting of short impulses (clicks) occurring regularly 200 times per second. This sound has a pitch that is very close to the pitch of a 200-Hz pure tone, and a sharp timbre. It contains harmonics with frequencies 200, 400, 600, 800, ... Hz. However, if the sound is filtered so as to remove the 200-Hz component, the pitch does not alter; the only result is a slight change in the timbre of the note. Indeed, it is possible to eliminate all except a small group of mid-frequency harmonics, say 1800, 2000, and 2200 Hz, and the low pitch still remains, although the timbre is now markedly different.

Schouten (1940) called the low pitch associated with a group of high harmonics the "residue". He pointed out that hearing a residue pitch is not the same as hearing the fundamental component. It just happens that the pitch of the residue is (almost) the same as the pitch of the fundamental component. The residue is distinguishable, subjectively, from a fundamental component that is physically presented or from a fundamental component that may be generated by nonlinear distortion in the ear. Thus, perception of a residue pitch does not require activity at the point on the BM that would respond maximally to a pure tone of similar pitch. This is confirmed by a demonstration of Licklider (1956). He showed that the low pitch of the residue can be heard even in the presence of low-frequency noise that would mask a component at the fundamental frequency. Thus, low pitches may be perceived through neural channels that normally respond to the high- or middle-frequency components of a signal. Several other names have been used to describe residue pitch, including "periodicity pitch", "virtual pitch", and "low pitch". I shall use the term residue pitch. Even when the fundamental component of a complex tone is present, the pitch of the tone is usually determined by harmonics other than the fundamental. Thus, the perception of a residue pitch should not be regarded as unusual. Rather, residue pitches are what we normally hear when we listen to complex tones.

Several models have been proposed to account for residue pitch. The early models may be divided into two broad classes. The "pattern recognition" models are based on the assumption that the pitch of a complex tone is derived from neural information about the frequencies or pitches of the individual partials. The "temporal" models are based on the assumption that the pitch of a complex tone is related to the time intervals between nerve spikes in the auditory nerve. Each class of model is considered below.

4A PATTERN RECOGNITION MODELS

Pattern recognition models are based on the assumption that the perception of the pitch of a complex tone involves two stages. The first stage is a frequency analysis that leads to estimates of the frequencies (or pitches) of some of the individual sinusoidal components of the complex tone; these are the components that can be resolved (see Chapter 3, Section 4D). The second stage is a pattern recognizer that "calculates" the pitch of the complex from the frequencies of the resolved components. Early models of this type were rather vague about the exact way in which the pattern recognizer might work, but a common idea was that it tried to find a fundamental frequency whose harmonics matched the frequencies of the resolved components of the stimulus as closely as possible (de Boer, 1956; Thurlow, 1963; Whitfield, 1970).

The nature of the pattern recognition process is constrained by the results of experiments of Schouten et al. (1962). They investigated the pitch of amplitude-modulated sine waves, which have just three sinusoidal components. If a carrier with frequency f_c is amplitude modulated by a modulator with frequency g, then the modulated wave contains components with frequencies f_c-g, f_c, and f_c+g (see Chapter 3, Section 4C). For example, a 2000-Hz carrier modulated 200 times per second contains components at 1800, 2000, and 2200 Hz and has a pitch similar to that of a 200-Hz sine wave.

Consider now the effect of shifting the carrier frequency to, say, 2030 Hz. The complex tone now contains components at 1830, 2030, and 2230 Hz. This stimulus would be very unlikely to occur naturally; how will the pattern recognizer choose the appropriate matching pattern? One possibility is that pitch is determined on the basis of the spacing between adjacent partials, in which case the pitch would be unaltered. In fact, the perceived pitch shifts slightly upwards; in this particular case, it corresponds roughly to that of a 203-Hz sinusoid. In addition, there is an ambiguity of pitch. If subjects are asked to adjust the frequency of a sine wave to match the pitch, matches around 184 and 226 Hz are also found.

Terhardt (1972a,b, 1974c) suggested that residue pitch corresponds to a sub-harmonic of a resolved component. A sub-harmonic of a given component has a frequency that is an integer submultiple of the frequency of that component. For example, a 2000-Hz component has sub-harmonics at 1000, 666.7, 500, 400, 333.3, ... Hz. Since speech frequently contains harmonic complex tones (see Chapter 9), we are repeatedly exposed to such tones from the earliest moments in life. Terhardt suggested that as a result of this exposure, we learn to associate a given frequency component with the sub-harmonics of that component; these will occur together in harmonic complex sounds. After the learning phase is completed, stimulation by a single pure tone produces pitch cues corresponding to sub-harmonics of that tone. When a harmonic complex tone is presented, the pitch cues corresponding to these sub-harmonics coincide at certain values. The largest number of coincidences occurs at the fundamental frequency, and this determines the overall pitch of the sound. This is illustrated in Table 6.1 for a complex tone consisting of three components: 800, 1000, and 1200 Hz.

The greatest number of coincidences in the sub-harmonics occurs at 200 Hz, and this corresponds to the perceived pitch. For nonharmonic complex tones, such as those used by Schouten et al. (1962), there are no exact coincidences, but the frequency at which there are several near coincidences predicts the perceived pitch quite well. Notice that this model requires that more than one partial be resolved from the complex tone for a residue pitch to be perceived.

An alternative model, although one still dependent on the resolution of individual frequency components, has been described by Goldstein (1973). In this model, the pitch of a complex tone is derived by a central processor that receives information only about the frequencies, and not about the amplitudes or phases, of individual components. The processor presumes that all stimuli

TABLE 6.1.   Frequencies of the sub-harmonics of the components in a harmonic complex tone

Frequency of component (Hz)			Value of integer divisor
800	1000	1200	
400	500	600	2
266.7	333.3	400	3
200	250	300	4
160	200	240	5
133.3	166.7	200	6

Note: The numbers in bold indicate a subharmonic that is common across the components of the tone.

are periodic and that the spectra comprise successive harmonics (which is the usual situation for naturally occurring sounds). The processor finds the harmonic series that provides the "best fit" to the series of components actually presented. For example, for components at 1830, 2030, and 2230 Hz (as in the experiment of Schouten *et al.* described above), a harmonic complex tone with a fundamental frequency of 203 Hz would provide a good "match"; this would have components at 1827, 2030, and 2233 Hz. The perceived pitch is in fact close to that of a 203-Hz sinusoid. According to this model, errors in estimating the fundamental frequency occur mainly through errors in estimating the appropriate harmonic numbers. In the above example, the presented components were assumed by the processor to be the 9th, 10th, and 11th harmonics of a 203-Hz fundamental. However, a reasonable fit could also be found by assuming the components to be the 8th, 9th, and 10th harmonics of a 225.6-Hz fundamental, or the 10th, 11th, and 12th harmonics of a 184.5-Hz fundamental. Thus, the model predicts the ambiguities of pitch that are actually observed for this stimulus; pitch matches tend to lie in three groups around 184, 203, and 226 Hz. The extent to which such multimodal pitch matches occur is predicted to depend on the accuracy with which the frequencies in the stimulus are represented at the input to the central processor.

All of the models described in this section depend on the resolution of individual components in the stimulus. It is predicted that no residue pitch will be heard if no frequency components can be resolved or "heard out" from the complex. Experimental evidence relating to this is discussed in Section 5A. The mechanism by which the frequencies of individual components would be estimated has not generally been specified, although Terhardt (1972a,b) has suggested that this could operate through an extended place principle and that the basic determinant of the pitch of a complex sound is the spatial pattern of activity on the BM. This is not a necessary assumption for these models. Indeed, Goldstein (1973) was careful to state that

> ... the concept that the optimum processor operates on signals representing the constituent frequencies of complex-tone stimuli does not necessarily imply the use of tonotopic or place information per se as the measure of frequency. For example, temporal periods of pure tones are not ruled out as the measure of frequency.

As explained in Section 3, there is quite good evidence that temporal mechanisms play a part in our perception of pure tones, at least for frequencies up to 5 kHz. Thus, it is likely that the resolution of partials in a complex tone, and the determination of their frequencies, relies at least in part on temporal mechanisms, as described in Chapter 3, Section 4D. Given this assumption, these models could still hold, but the basic data on which they operated would be the temporal patterns of firing in different groups of auditory neurons. I discuss later some of the experimental evidence relevant to these models. I turn now to the second main class of model, the "temporal" models.

4B TEMPORAL MODELS

Consider again the example of a pulse train with repetition rate 200 pulses/s, containing harmonics at 200, 400, 600, ... Hz. Fig. 6.6 shows a simulation of the response of the BM to this sound. The lower harmonics in this sound each produce a peak at a specific location on the BM. Effectively, the lower harmonics are resolved. For example, the 600-Hz harmonic produces a local peak at the place tuned to 600 Hz. The timing of the neural spikes derived from such a place relates to the frequency of the individual harmonic rather than to the repetition rate of the complex as a whole. For example, in neurons with CFs close to 600 Hz, the ISIs are close to integer multiples of 1.667 ms. However, at places on the BM responding to the higher harmonics, the harmonics are not resolved. The excitation pattern does not show local peaks corresponding to individual harmonics. In this case, the waveform on the BM results from the interference of a number of harmonics and shows a periodicity the same as that of the input waveform. The timing of neural impulses derived from such a region is related to the repetition rate of the original input waveform, that is, ISIs close to the repetition period are prominent.

These considerations led to a theory whose development is mainly due to Schouten (1940, 1970). He proposed that residue pitches are produced by the upper harmonics, which are not well resolved by the ear, but interfere on the BM. The pitch value was assumed to be determined by the periodicity of the total waveform of the high harmonics. In other words, the pitch is determined by the time pattern of the waveform at the point on the BM where the harmonics interfere. Thus, a low pitch may be signaled through neural channels that normally respond to the high- or middle-frequency components of a complex sound.

Notice a major difference between this model and the pattern recognition models. The pattern recognition models require that one or more components in the complex sound should be resolved for a residue pitch to be heard, whereas Schouten's model requires that at least two components interact for a residue pitch to be heard. According to Schouten's model, a residue pitch may still be heard when none of the individual components is resolvable.

Consider how Schouten's model deals with the complex tone discussed earlier in relation to the pattern recognition models; this contained

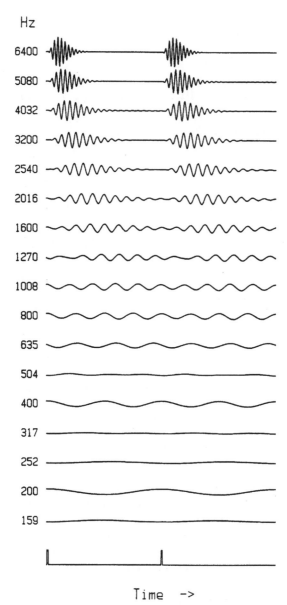

Time ->

FIGURE 6.6 A simulation of the responses on the basilar membrane to periodic impulses of rate 200 pulses/s. Each number on the left represents the frequency that would maximally excite a given point on the basilar membrane. The waveform that would be observed at that point, as a function of time, is plotted opposite that number.

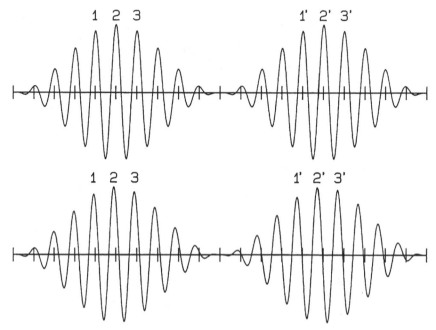

FIGURE 6.7 Waveforms for two amplitude-modulated sine waves. In the upper waveform, the carrier frequency (2000 Hz) is an integer multiple of the modulation frequency (200 Hz). Thus, the time intervals between corresponding peaks in the fine structure, 1-1', 2-2', 3-3', are 5 ms, the period of the modulation frequency. In the lower waveform, the carrier frequency is shifted slightly upwards, to 2030 Hz. Thus, 10 complete cycles of the carrier occur in slightly less than 5 ms, and the time intervals between corresponding points in the waveform, 1-1', 2-2', and 3-3', are slightly shorter than 5 ms. The lower waveform has a slightly higher pitch to than the upper waveform.

components at 1830, 2030, and 2230 Hz. Fig. 6.7 compares the waveform of this signal and the waveform of a signal containing components at 1800, 2000, and 2200 Hz. As these signals contain only a narrow range of frequency components, the waveforms on the BM would not be greatly different from those of the physically presented signals (Rhode and Recio, 2001); the BM would not separate the individual components to any great extent. Although the envelope repetition rates of the two waveforms are the same, the time intervals between corresponding peaks in the temporal fine structure (TFS) are slightly different. Thus, if nerve spikes tend to occur at peaks in the TFS of the waveform close to envelope maxima, the timing of the spikes will convey slightly different pitches for the two stimuli. These differences in the time pattern of spikes have been observed by Javel (1980).

Nerve spikes can occur at any of the prominent peaks in the waveform, labeled 1, 2, 3 and 1′, 2′, 3′. Thus, the time intervals between successive nerve spikes fall into several groups, corresponding to the intervals 1-1′, 1-2′, 1-3′, 2-1′, and so on. This can account for the fact that the pitches of these stimuli are ambiguous. For the signal containing components at 1830, 2030, and 2230 Hz, several of these time intervals fall close to 4.93 ms, corresponding to a pitch of about 203 Hz, which is what is normally heard.

These considerations led to a refinement of Schouten's original theory. The pitch of the residue is assumed to be determined by the time interval between peaks in the TFS of the waveform (on the BM) close to adjacent envelope maxima. If more than one possible time interval is present, the pitch corresponds, in general, to the interval that is most prominent, although sometimes ambiguity of pitch may occur. Note that the time intervals between nerve spikes rather than the overall rate of firing are important. If the system were simply counting the number of impulses per second, then the pitch shifts observed by Schouten and coworkers would not occur.

Moore and Moore (2003) pointed out a potential problem in interpreting the results of experiments using stimuli like those illustrated in Fig. 6.7. When all components are shifted upwards in frequency, the position of maximum excitation on the BM would also shift, even if all components were unresolved. Thus, the shift in pitch might somehow be linked to the shift in the excitation pattern. To assess this possibility, Moore and Moore generated complex tones with many components and then passed the components through a fixed band-pass filter centered on the high (unresolved) components. For tones generated in this way, the position of maximum excitation on the BM does not shift when all frequency components are shifted upwards in frequency. To ensure that components falling on the sloping passband of the filter were not audible, Moore and Moore added a broadband background noise. This noise also served to mask combination tones produced in the auditory system. Pitch matches were obtained to harmonic complex tones and to frequency-shifted tones. The results showed that when there was at least one component with a rank below 14 within the passband of the filter (e.g., a component at 2800 Hz for a fundamental frequency of 200 Hz), then the residue pitch shifted when all frequency components were shifted, suggesting a sensitivity to the TFS of the sound. However, when all components in the passband had ranks above 14, no pitch shift occurred, although pitch matches could still be made. It seems that, when only harmonics above the 14th are audible, residue pitch is determined by the envelope repetition rate of the waveform on the BM, and not by the time intervals between prominent peaks in the TFS.

5 EXPERIMENTAL EVIDENCE RELEVANT TO THE PATTERN RECOGNITION AND TEMPORAL MODELS

5A The "Existence Region" of the Tonal Residue

According to the pattern recognition theories, a residue pitch should only be heard when at least one of the sinusoidal components of the stimulus can be heard out. Chapter 3 discussed Plomp's (1964a) experiments, which showed that for a partial within a multitone complex, only the first five to eight harmonics can be heard out. Thus, a residue pitch should not be heard for stimuli containing only harmonics above about the eighth.

Ritsma (1962) investigated the audibility of residue pitches for amplitude-modulated sinusoids (as mentioned earlier, the spectra of such sounds contain three sinusoidal components) as a function of the modulation rate and the harmonic number (carrier frequency divided by modulation rate). Later (Ritsma, 1963), he extended the results to complexes with a greater number of components. He found that the tonal character of the residue pitch existed only within a limited frequency region, referred to as the "existence region". When the harmonic number was too high (above about 20), only a kind of high buzz of undefinable pitch was heard. He found, further, that some harmonics below 5 kHz had to be present for a residue pitch to be heard and that the modulation rate had to be below about 800 Hz. Other workers (Plomp, 1967; Moore, 1973b; Oxenham et al., 2011) have found, using complex tones with a greater number of components, that residue pitches can be perceived for periodic sounds with repetition rates up to about 1400 Hz. Also, Oxenham et al. (2011) have shown that a residue pitch can be perceived when all of the harmonics have frequencies above 5 kHz. The pitch is sufficiently strong to allow the identification of simple melodies and musical intervals. The stimuli used by Oxenham et al. contained relatively low-numbered harmonics, which were presumable partly resolved along the BM. Since phase locking is usually assumed to be very weak for frequencies above 5 kHz, their findings may indicate that phase locking to individual resolved harmonics is not necessary for perception of a residue pitch. However, an alternative possibility is that phase locking above 5 kHz, while weak, is still sufficient to allow extraction of a residue pitch when the phase-locking information can be combined across several harmonics.

A problem with Ritsma's results is that they were probably influenced by the presence of combination tones in the frequency region below the lowest components in the complex tones, as has since been pointed out by Ritsma (1970) himself. A combination tone is a perceived tone not present in the sensations produced by the constituent components of the stimulus when they are presented singly. Certain combination tones, described in Chapter 1 (Section 6D), have pitches corresponding to frequencies $f_1 - K(f_2 - f_1)$, where f_1 and f_2 are the frequencies of the tones that are physically presented and K is an integer. They correspond to lower partials of the complex that is physically presented. For example, if two tones with frequencies 1800 and 2000 Hz are presented, the combination tone for $K = 1$ has a frequency of 1600 Hz [$(2 \times 1800) - 2000$]. Combination tones of this type, and particularly those with a pitch corresponding to frequency $2f_1 - f_2$, are audible even at moderate intensities (Plomp, 1965, Goldstein, 1967). Smoorenburg (1970) suggested that these combination tones, rather than the physically presented partials, are dominant in determining the pitch of a complex tone containing only high harmonics. Thus, in Ritsma's experiments, the effective harmonic number would have been lower than the nominal harmonic number.

Moore and Rosen (1979) attempted to determine more clearly whether a residue pitch can be heard when no individual components are resolvable. They investigated subjects' abilities to identify simple melodies "played" by varying the repetition rate of pulse trains. The pulse trains were filtered so as to contain only high, unresolvable harmonics, and a low-frequency noise was present to mask combination tones. To determine whether these stimuli evoked a sense of musical interval, performance was compared with that obtained when the tunes were played as a pattern of sinusoidal frequencies in which the pitch changes were clearly audible, but the musical intervals had been distorted; the musical scale was either "compressed" or "expanded". This preserves the pitch contour but makes the musical intervals sound "wrong". Moore and Rosen found that performance was superior for the high-pass-filtered pulse trains and concluded that stimuli containing only high, unresolvable harmonics can evoke a sense of musical interval, and hence of pitch.

Houtsma and Smurzynski (1990) studied musical interval recognition by musically trained subjects, using complex tones with 11 successive harmonics. A background noise was used to mask combination tones. They found that performance worsened when the harmonic number of the lowest harmonic was increased from 7 to 11, but leveled off beyond that. Even when the harmonics extended from the 20th to the 30th, performance was well above chance. These harmonic numbers are well above the range where individual harmonics are resolvable.

Overall, these results indicate that residue pitch can be heard when no individual harmonic can be resolved. The pattern recognition models cannot account for this. It should be noted, however, that the pitches of sounds containing only very high harmonics are less clear than the pitches heard when lower harmonics are present.

5B The Principle of Dominance

According to pattern recognition theories, the lower resolvable harmonics should be the most important for determining pitch. For temporal theories, the higher, unresolved harmonics should be the most important, because interference of harmonics is essential for the extraction of residue pitch. Ritsma (1967b) carried out an experiment to determine which components in a complex sound are most important in determining its pitch. He presented complex tones in which the frequencies of a small group of harmonics were integer multiples of a fundamental frequency that was slightly higher or lower than the fundamental frequency of the remainder. The subject's pitch judgments were used to determine whether the pitch of the complex as a whole was affected by the shift in the group of harmonics. Ritsma found that

> For fundamental frequencies in the range 100 Hz to 400 Hz, and for sensation levels up to at least 50 dB above threshold of the entire signal, the frequency band consisting of the third, fourth and fifth harmonics tends to dominate the pitch sensation as long as its amplitude exceeds a minimum absolute level of about 10 dB above threshold.

Thus Ritsma (1970) introduced the concept of dominance:

> ... if pitch information is available along a large part of the basilar membrane the ear uses only the information from a narrow band. This band is positioned at 3–5 times the pitch value. Its precise position depends somewhat on the subject.

This finding has been broadly confirmed in other ways (Bilsen and Ritsma, 1967; Ritsma, 1967a), although the data of Moore et al. (1984b, 1985a) show that there are large individual differences in which harmonics are dominant, and for some subjects, the first two harmonics play an important role. Other data show that the dominant region is not fixed in terms of harmonic number but also depends somewhat on absolute frequency (Plomp, 1967; Patterson and Wightman, 1976; Dai, 2000). For high fundamental frequencies (above about 1000 Hz), the fundamental is usually the dominant component, while for very low fundamental frequencies, around 50 Hz, harmonics above the fifth may be dominant (Moore and Glasberg, 1988b). For center frequencies above 250 Hz, ERB_N is greater than 50 Hz, so individual components in the dominant region would not be resolvable for a 50-Hz fundamental frequency (Moore and Glasberg, 1988b).

On the whole, these results support the pattern recognition theories. The third, fourth, and fifth harmonics are relatively well resolved on the BM and are usually separately perceptible. However, for very low fundamental frequencies, around 50 Hz, the harmonics in the dominant region would not be resolvable, and only temporal analysis would appear to be possible.

5C Evidence for the Role of Central Mechanisms in the Perception of Complex Tones

Houtsma and Goldstein (1972) conducted an experiment demonstrating that a residue pitch may be heard when there is no possibility of an interaction of components in the cochlea. They investigated the perception of stimuli comprising just two adjacent harmonics, for example, the fourth and fifth or the seventh and eighth harmonics of a (missing) fundamental. On each trial, their musically trained subjects were presented with two successive two-component complexes with different (missing) fundamentals and were required to identify the musical interval corresponding to the fundamentals. Harmonic numbers were randomized from note to note, so that the subjects could not use cues associated with the pitches of individual harmonics to extract the musical interval. They found that performance was good for low harmonic numbers, but fell to chance level for harmonic numbers above about 10–12. They found further that subjects were able to identify melodies when the stimuli were presented dichotically (one harmonic to each ear). At high sound levels, monaural performance was superior to dichotic, whereas at low levels (20 dB SL), there was no difference between the two conditions. Houtsma and Goldstein suggested that the differences at high levels resulted from the influence of combination tones, which would lower the effective harmonic number and which only occur when both tones are presented to the same ear. They considered that if an allowance were made for the effect of combination tones, then there would be essentially no difference between the monaural and the dichotic conditions.

These results cannot be explained in terms of Schouten's model or indeed in terms of any model that requires an interaction of components on the BM. They imply that "the pitch of these complex tones is mediated by a central processor operating on neural signals derived from those effective stimulus harmonics which are tonotopically resolved" (Houtsma and Goldstein, 1972). In other words, these experiments clearly indicate that the pitch of a complex tone can be mediated by some sort of pattern recognition process. However, the pitch of a two-component complex is not very clear; indeed, many listeners do not hear a single low pitch, but rather perceive the component tones individually (Smoorenburg, 1970; Houtsma and Fleuren, 1991). Residue pitches are generally much more distinct when greater numbers of harmonics are present. It does seem to be the case that two-tone complexes only produce a residue pitch for harmonic numbers below about 10, whereas the limit is somewhat higher for multitone complexes (see Section 5A). Thus, some factor other than the ability to resolve individual components affects the upper limit of the existence region.

Houtgast (1976) has reported an even more extreme example of hearing a residue pitch in the absence of interaction of components. He showed that if a context was provided to focus the attention of the subject on pitches in a particular range, a single harmonic was capable of evoking the perception of a low residue pitch. He set up his experiment as follows. Subjects were presented with two successive harmonic complex signals that differed in fundamental frequency by 3%. On each trial, the subject had to say whether the pitch of the second signal was higher or lower than that of the first. The signals did not have any harmonics in common, so subjects could not base their judgments on the pitches of the individual harmonics. The first signal always contained six harmonics (harmonics 2–4 and 8–10) and had a clear unambiguous pitch. The second signal initially had three harmonics (harmonics five to seven), but after a certain number of trials, this number was reduced to two, and finally to one. In the absence of any background noise, performance was very poor and was at chance level (50%) for the one-component signal. Thus, a single sinusoidal component in quiet does not lead to the percept of a residue pitch. However, when the experiment was conducted with a background noise, performance improved considerably; a score of 80% was obtained for the one-component signal. It appears that a single sinusoidal component has the potential to evoke sub-harmonic pitches. When the sensory information is made ambiguous by the presence of a background noise, these potential pitches are more likely to be perceived. If the subject's attention is focused in a particular pitch range, then the sub-harmonic pitch in this range may be the dominant percept.

Yet another demonstration that interaction of components is not essential for the perception of a residue pitch is provided by an experiment of Hall and Peters (1981). They investigated the pitch associated with stimuli consisting of three harmonics that were presented successively in time rather than simultaneously. Each sinusoidal component lasted 40 ms, and there was a 10-ms pause between components. They found that in the absence of a background noise, only pitches corresponding to the individual components were heard. However, when a background noise was present, a pitch corresponding to the missing fundamental was heard. This result resembles that of Houtgast (1976), except that it was not necessary to provide a prior context to direct the subject's attention. It appears that noise enhances a synthetic mode of pitch perception, in which information is combined over different frequency regions and over time to produce a residue pitch. In quiet, an analytic mode of perception is more likely, so that the individual components are heard separately.

It may be concluded that the pitch of a complex tone can be derived from neural signals corresponding to individual partials in the complex, at least for stimuli with low harmonics and containing only a small number of harmonics.

5D IS RESOLVABILITY SUFFICIENT FOR GOOD PITCH PERCEPTION?

I described earlier the experiment of Houtsma and Goldstein (1972), which showed that the perception of the pitch of two-component complex tones deteriorated when the lowest harmonic was above the 10th, even when the harmonics were presented one to each ear. This suggests that presence of resolved harmonics is not sufficient to ensure good pitch perception.

Bernstein and Oxenham (2003) have also presented evidence suggesting that resolvability *per se* is not the critical factor determining whether pitch discrimination is relatively good (when low harmonics are present) or relatively poor (when only high harmonics are present). They measured thresholds for detecting a change in fundamental frequency (F0DLs) for complex tones with successive harmonics of a 100- or 200-Hz fundamental frequency. The number of the lowest harmonic that was present, N, was systematically varied. Also, the rank of the lowest and highest harmonics in each stimulus was randomly varied over a small range, to encourage performance based on comparisons of the missing fundamental frequency, rather than comparisons of the pitches of individual harmonics. The harmonics were presented either dichotically, with even harmonics to one ear and odd harmonics to the other ear, or diotically, with all harmonics presented to both ears. For the dichotic presentation, it was determined randomly for every stimulus (i.e., separately for each of the two tones in a trial) which ear received the even harmonics and which ear received the odd harmonics. Subjects reported that the harmonics were perceptually fused across ears, and a single pitch was heard. The idea behind the experiment was that, with dichotic presentation, the harmonics in each ear would be more widely separated in frequency than for diotic presentation, making the harmonics more resolvable in the former case. If F0DLs for diotic stimuli with high N (say around 12) are large because the harmonics are unresolved, then dichotic presentation should lead to markedly smaller F0DLs for high N.

Bernstein and Oxenham (2003) found that F0DLs increased when N was above 9 and that the pattern of the results was similar for dichotic and diotic presentation. Thus, the subjects could not take advantage of the greater resolvability of the harmonics that was available with dichotic presentation to improve fundamental frequency discrimination for high N. Bernstein and Oxenham concluded that "harmonic number, regardless of peripheral resolvability, governs the transition between two different pitch percepts, one based on the frequencies of individual resolved harmonics and the other based on the periodicity of the temporal envelope".

5E PITCHES BASED PURELY UPON TIMING INFORMATION

Several researchers have investigated pitches evoked by stimuli that contain no spectral peaks and that therefore would not produce a well-defined maximum on the BM. Such pitches cannot arise on the basis of place information and therefore provide evidence for the operation of temporal mechanisms.

Miller and Taylor (1948) presented random white noise that was turned on and off abruptly and periodically, at various rates. The interrupted noise has a flat long-term magnitude spectrum. They reported that the noise had a pitch-like quality for interruption rates between 100 and 250 Hz. Pollack (1969) has shown that some subjects are able to adjust sinusoids to have the same pitch as the interrupted noise for interruption rates up to 2000 Hz. They adjust the frequency of the sinusoid to be roughly equal to the interruption rate of the noise.

Burns and Viemeister (1976, 1981) showed that noise that was sinusoidally amplitude modulated (SAM) had a pitch corresponding to the modulation rate. As for interrupted noise, the long-term magnitude spectrum of white noise remains flat after modulation. They found that the pitch could be heard for modulation rates up to 800–1000 Hz and that subjects could recognize musical intervals and melodies played by varying the modulation rate.

These experiments support the idea of a temporal pitch mechanism. However, the pitch of interrupted noise or modulated noise is not very clear. This could be because it is only the envelope that is periodic. The TFS of the waveform differs from one envelope period to the next. Many subjects do not report a pitch sensation at all, although most can hear that something pitch-like changes when the interruption rate is changed. This phenomenon, that a pitch is heard more clearly if it is varied, seems to be quite a general one and is often marked for residue pitches.

Several experiments have been reported showing pitch sensations as a result of the binaural interaction of noise stimuli. Cramer and Huggins (1958) fed white noise from the same noise generator to both ears, through headphones. The noise to one ear went through a filter that passed all audible frequency components without change of amplitude, but produced a phase change in a small frequency region. A faint pitch was heard corresponding to the frequency region of the phase transition, although the stimulus presented to each ear alone was white noise and produced no pitch sensation. This pitch is called "Huggins pitch". The pitch was only heard when the phase change was in the frequency range below about 1 kHz. A phase shift of a narrow band of the noise results in that band being heard in a different position in space from the rest of the noise (see Chapter 7). This spatial separation may be responsible for the pitch-like character associated with that narrow band. Akeroyd *et al.* (2001) have shown that Huggins pitch is sufficiently clear to allow relatively untrained subjects to recognize simple melodies played by changing the frequency region of the phase transition.

Fourcin (1970) used two noise sources, denoted n_1 and n_2. n_1 was fed through headphones to the two ears, producing a sound image localized in the middle of the head. n_2 was also fed to both ears, but the input to one ear was delayed by a certain time, producing a second sound image localized to one side (see Chapter 7). Sometimes the listener simply heard two separate sound images, neither of which had a pitch. At other times, however, a faint pitch was heard, whose position was not well defined, but which was generally heard in the middle of the head. This pitch is called "Fourcin pitch".

Bilsen and Goldstein (1974) reported that a pitch may be perceived when just one noise source is used, presented binaurally, but with a delay, T, at one ear. For delays shorter than about 2 ms, a single noise image is reported, whose perceived position depends on the delay. For longer time delays, the image is heard clearly toward the side of the head at which the sound leads in time, but the image becomes more diffuse and, in addition, "a faint but distinct pitch image corresponding to $1/T$ appears in the middle of the head". As for the pitches reported by Fourcin, the effect only occurs at low frequencies; the highest pitches reported by Bilsen and Goldstein correspond to frequencies of about 500 Hz. Other examples of pitches produced by dichotic noise stimuli have been reported by Bilsen (1977), Klein and Hartmann (1981), and Hartmann and McMillon (2001).

The exact mechanism that gives rise to these pitches remains to be elucidated. For theoretical accounts, see Raatgever and Bilsen (1986), Culling *et al.* (1998a,b), and Akeroyd *et al.* (2001). In all of the experiments producing pitches by binaural interaction, the stimuli presented to each ear separately conveyed no spectral information. Therefore, timing information must be used in the creation of a central pattern of neural activity from which the pitch is extracted. In other words, information about the relative phases of components in the two ears must be preserved up to the point in the auditory system where binaural interaction occurs. Chapter 7 presents evidence that humans are only able to use phase differences between the two ears in the localization of sounds for frequencies up to about 1500 Hz, and it seems that pitches perceived by binaural interaction are limited to this region. The necessity for binaural interaction means that there is no good reason to regard 1500 Hz as a limit for temporal coding in general.

6 A SCHEMATIC MODEL FOR THE PITCH PERCEPTION OF COMPLEX TONES

It is clear that the perception of a particular pitch does not depend on a high level of activity at a particular place on the BM or in a particular group of peripheral neurons. The pitch of complex tones is, in general, mediated by harmonics higher than the fundamental, so similar pitches may arise from quite different distributions of neural activity. For stimuli containing a harmonics with a wide range of harmonic numbers, the low harmonics, up to the fifth, tend to dominate the pitch percept. These harmonics lie in the range where it is possible to hear them out as individual tones. This supports the pattern recognition models of pitch perception. However, it is possible to hear a residue pitch when the harmonics are too high to be resolved. This cannot be explained by the pattern recognition models, but can be explained by the temporal models. The temporal models, on the other hand, cannot account for the fact that it is possible to hear a residue pitch when there is no possibility of the components of the complex tone interacting in the peripheral auditory system.

It seems that none of the theories presented so far can account for all of the experimental data. I next present a schematic model that incorporates features of both the temporal models and the pattern recognition models and that can account, in a qualitative way, for all of the data. Since this model was proposed in earlier editions of this book, several similar models have been presented, many of which are more quantitative (van Noorden, 1982; Patterson, 1987b; Meddis and Hewitt, 1991; Meddis and O'Mard, 1997; Bernstein and Oxenham, 2005; Ives and Patterson, 2008). The model is illustrated in Fig. 6.8. The first stage is a bank of band-pass filters with overlapping passbands. These are the auditory filters. The outputs of the filters in response to a complex tone have the form shown in Fig. 6.6. The filters responding to low harmonics have outputs that are approximately sinusoidal in form; the individual harmonics are resolved. The filters responding to higher harmonics have outputs corresponding to the interaction of several harmonics. The waveform is complex, but has a repetition rate corresponding to that of the input.

The next stage in the model is the transformation of the filter outputs to neural spikes. The temporal pattern of firing in a given neuron reflects the temporal structure of the waveform driving that neuron. Say, for example, that the input has a fundamental frequency of 200 Hz. The fourth harmonic, at 800 Hz, is well resolved in the filter bank, and hence the neurons with CFs close to 800 Hz respond as if the input were an 800-Hz sinusoid. The time intervals between successive nerve spikes are close to integer multiples of the period of that tone, that is, 1.25, 2.5, 3.75, 5.0, ... ms (see Fig. 1.20). Neurons

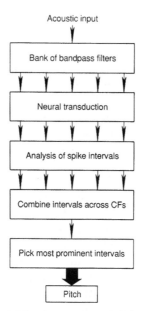

FIGURE 6.8 A schematic model for the perception of the pitch of complex tones. The model depends on both place and timing information.

with higher CFs, say around 2000 Hz, are driven by a more complex waveform. The temporal structure of the response is correspondingly complex. Each peak in the fine structure of the waveform is capable of evoking a spike, so many different time intervals occur between successive spikes. The interval corresponding to the fundamental, 5 ms, is present, but other intervals, such as 4.0, 4.5, 5.5, and 6.0 ms, also occur (Evans, 1978; Javel, 1980; Cariani and Delgutte, 1996a,b).

The next stage in the model is a device that analyzes, separately for each CF, the ISIs that are present. The range of intervals that can be analyzed is probably limited and varies with CF. At a given CF, the device probably operates over a range from about 0.5/CF to 15/CF s. This range is appropriate for the time intervals that would occur most often. The use of such a limit in the model can account for the fact that the perception of pitch worsens when the number of the lowest harmonic is increased above about eight, even under conditions where the harmonics would be resolved (Bernstein and Oxenham, 2003, 2005)

The next stage is a device that compares the time intervals present in the different channels and searches for common time intervals. The device may also integrate information over time. In general, the time interval that is found most often corresponds to the period of the fundamental component (Cariani and Delgutte, 1996a,b). Finally, the time intervals that are most prominently represented across channels are fed to a decision mechanism that selects one interval from among those passed to it. This device incorporates memory and attention processes and may be influenced by immediately preceding stimuli, context, conditions of presentation, and so on. The perceived pitch corresponds to the reciprocal of the final interval selected.

Consider how this model deals with a complex tone composed of a few low harmonics, say the third, fourth, and fifth harmonics of a 200-Hz (missing) fundamental. In those neurons responding primarily to the 600-Hz component, an analysis of time intervals between successive nerve spikes would reveal intervals of 1.67, 3.33, 5.0, 6.67, ... ms, each of which is an integer multiple of the period of that component. Similarly, the intervals in the 800-Hz "channel" are 1.25, 2.5, 3.75, 5.0, ... ms, while those in the 1000-Hz "channel" are 1, 2, 3, 4, 5, ... ms. The only time interval that is in common across all of the channels is 5 ms; this corresponds to the pitch of the missing fundamental. Thus, this stimulus evokes a clear, unambiguous pitch.

Consider next what happens when a small group of high harmonics is presented, say the 12th, 13th, and 14th harmonics of 200 Hz. These harmonics are not resolved in the filter bank, and therefore essentially, only one channel of timing information is available. Furthermore, the time interval information is ambiguous, many values closely spaced around 5 ms being present. Thus, while a pitch corresponding to the missing fundamental may be perceived, that pitch is weak and ambiguous, as is observed psychophysically. This can explain why lower harmonics tend to dominate in the perception of pitch; the temporal information they provide is far less ambiguous, provided that information is combined across channels. The pitch associated with high harmonics can be made more clear by increasing the number of harmonics, because the ambiguities can be reduced by comparing across channels. This also is observed psychophysically.

If a small group of very high harmonics is presented, then they may fail to evoke a sense of musical pitch. This can be explained in terms of the limited range of time intervals that can be analyzed at each CF. For harmonics above about the 15th, the time interval corresponding to the fundamental falls outside the range that can be analyzed in the channel responding to those harmonics (Bernstein and Oxenham, 2005). Alternatively or additionally, it may be the case that the ISIs become too finely spaced for the auditory system to analyze them separately (Moore and Glasberg, 2010). Consider, for example, a stimulus composed of harmonics 19, 20, and 21 of a 100-Hz fundamental. The most prominent time intervals between nerve spikes would cluster around 9.0, 9.5, 10, 10.5, and 11 ms (Javel, 1980). It may be the case that there are errors in the mechanism that extracts the ISIs, so that these intervals become "blurred" together. It may still be possible to extract information from phase locking to the envelope rather than to the TFS, but this does not give a clear pitch. This is one factor contributing to the limited existence region of the tonal residue (Section 5A). The other factor is the upper limit for phase locking. When the harmonics lie above 5 kHz, the TFS of the waveform at the filter output is represented only weakly in the temporal patterning of neural spikes. This seems to lead to a weaker pitch than when harmonics below 5 kHz are present, although a residue pitch can still be perceived, as described earlier (Oxenham et al., 2011).

The way in which the model determines the pitch for a group of low harmonics resembles that proposed by Terhardt (1974c). In his model, each partial gives rise to potential pitches corresponding to sub-harmonics of that partial, and the perceived pitch is that for which the number of coincidences is greatest. In the present model, these sub-harmonic pitches correspond to the ISIs evoked by a given partial. For example, a 1-kHz tone evokes intervals of 1, 2, 3, 4, 5, ... ms, and these correspond to pitches of 1000, 500, 333.3, 250, 200, ... Hz. The differences between the models are as follows. Firstly, Terhardt's model requires a learning phase in which the associations between partials and sub-harmonics are learned, whereas in the present model, the sub-harmonics occur automatically in the temporal patterns of neural firing. Secondly, Terhardt's model cannot explain the pitch produced by high, unresolved harmonics, whereas in the present model, they arise as part of the same process as is used for lower harmonics.

The way that the model deals with the pitch of nonharmonic complex tones depends on the spacing of the components relative to their center frequency. If the components are widely spaced, and therefore resolvable, the pitch of the complex is determined in a similar way to that proposed by Terhardt. Say, for example, that components at 840, 1040, and 1240 Hz are presented. The time intervals in the 840-Hz channel are 1.19, 2.38, 3.57, 4.76, 5.95, ... ms, all of which are integer multiples of the period, 1.19 ms. Similarly, the intervals in the 1040-Hz channel are 0.96, 1.92, 2.88, 3.85, 4.8, 5.76, ... ms, and those in the 1240-Hz channel are 0.81, 1.61, 2.42, 3.22, 4.03, 4.84, ... ms. In this case, there is no time interval that is exactly the same in all channels, but there is a near coincidence at 4.8 ms, the intervals in the three channels being 4.76, 4.8, and 4.84 ms. The perceived pitch thus corresponds to the reciprocal of 4.8 ms, that is, 208 Hz. When the components are closely spaced, and therefore unresolvable, then the pitch is derived from the ISI that is most prominently represented in the pattern of neural spikes. In this case, the model works in the same way as the temporal model outlined in Section 4B. The perceived pitch corresponds to the time interval between peaks in the TFS of the waveform (at the output of the auditory filter) close to adjacent envelope maxima. The pitch is ambiguous because several "candidate" time intervals may be present.

In this model, just as in the models discussed earlier, combination tones may play a role in determining the pitch percept. Their role may be particularly important when the stimulus itself contains only closely spaced components. The combination tones act like lower partials than the partials that are physically present in the stimulus.

The pitches of stimuli without spectral peaks, such as periodically interrupted noise, are explained by the model as arising from the time interval information present primarily in the channels with high CFs, where the filter bandwidths are wider. When a filter has a wide bandwidth, the temporal structure of the input tends to be preserved at the output (see Chapter 1, Fig. 1.7, and Chapter 5). Thus, the temporal patterns of firing reflect the interruption of the noise. However, the time intervals between successive spikes are much less regular than for a periodic sound, because the exact waveform of the noise varies randomly from moment to moment; the only regularity is in the timing of the envelope, not the TFS. Thus, the pitch of interrupted noise is weak.

The model does not account for the pitches evoked by dichotic noise stimuli (Section 5D). However, the models proposed to explain these pitches all depend on the ability to compare the timing of nerve spikes arising from the two ears.

In summary, the model presented here can account for the major features of the pitch perception of complex tones, including the dominant region, the existence region of the residue, and the pitch of nonharmonic complexes. Furthermore, it is consistent with the evidence presented earlier in this chapter that the pitch of pure tones is determined primarily by temporal mechanisms for frequencies up to 5 kHz. Notice, however, that both place and temporal analyses play a crucial role in the model; neither alone is sufficient.

7 THE PERCEPTION OF PITCH IN MUSIC

This topic could easily occupy a book of its own. The discussion here is limited to certain selected aspects related to the rest of this chapter. Other relevant material is presented in Chapter 8.

7A Musical Intervals, Musical Scales, and Consonance

As described in Section 3B, tones that are separated by an octave (i.e., where the frequencies are in the ratio 2/1) sound similar and indeed are given the same name (C, D, etc.) in the traditional musical scale. It is also the case that other musical intervals correspond approximately to simple ratios between the frequencies of the tones. For example, a fifth corresponds to a frequency ratio of 3/2; a major third to 5/4; and a minor third to 6/5. When musical notes in these simple ratios are sounded simultaneously, the sound is pleasant, or consonant, whereas departures from simple, integer ratios, as in certain modern music, tend to result in a less pleasant or even a dissonant sound. This does not always hold for pure tones, a pair of which tend to be judged as consonant as soon as their frequency separation exceeds about one ERB_N (Plomp and Levelt, 1965). However, complex tones blend harmoniously and tend to produce chords only when their fundamental frequencies are in simple ratios. In this situation, several of their harmonics coincide, whereas for non-simple ratios, the harmonics differ in frequency and produce beating sensations. Thus, at least part of the dissonance may be explained in terms of this beating, or interference, of harmonics on the BM when the harmonics are close together, but not identical, in frequency (Helmholtz, 1863; Kameoka and Kuriyagawa, 1969). This cannot account for the whole of the effect, however. Beats do not occur between successive notes; yet, a certain amount of dissonance can be experienced for such notes. Also, beats do not occur when the two notes of an interval are presented one to each ear; yet, some dissonance may be experienced. It is of interest, then, to consider why we prefer certain frequency ratios for both the simultaneous and the successive presentation of tones, why octaves sound so similar, and why some sounds are consonant and others dissonant.

One theory suggests that we learn about octave relationships and about other musical intervals by exposure to harmonic complex sounds (usually speech sounds) from the earliest moments in life. For example, the first two harmonics in a periodic sound have a frequency ratio 2/1, the second and third have a ratio 3/2, the third and fourth 4/3, and so on. By exposure to these sounds, we may learn to associate harmonics with particular frequency ratios. I discussed earlier in this chapter Terhardt's (1974c) suggestion that such a learning process could account for the perception of residue pitch. If judgments of similarity and of consonance or dissonance also depend on familiarity, then a learning process will also account for our perception of musical intervals (Terhardt, 1974c; McDermott et al., 2010).

An alternative theory suggests that we prefer pairs of tones for which there is a similarity in the time patterns of neural discharge. This view was put forward a long time ago by Meyer (1898) and has since been supported by Boomsliter and Creel (1961) and Tramo et al. (2001), among others. If it is the case that the pitch of a complex tone results from an analysis and correlation of the temporal patterns of firing in different groups of auditory neurons, then such an analysis would also reveal similarities between different tones when they are in simple frequency ratios. It is certainly the case that both our sense of musical pitch and our ability to make octave matches weaken above 5 kHz, the frequency at which neural synchrony becomes very weak (see Section 3B). Furthermore, the highest note (fundamental) for instruments in the orchestra lies just below 5 kHz. One could argue from this that our lack of musical pitch at high frequencies is a result of a lack of exposure to tones at these frequencies. However, notes produced by musical instruments do contain harmonics above 5 kHz, so if the learning of associations between harmonics was the only factor involved, there would be no reason for the change at 5 kHz.

It is clear that individual differences and cultural background can influence significantly the musical intervals that are judged to be "pleasant" or otherwise. Thus, for example, Indian musical scales contain "microtones" in which the conventional scale is subdivided into smaller units, producing many musical intervals that do not correspond to simple ratios. Indian music often sounds strange to Western ears, especially on first hearing, but it clearly does not sound strange to Indians; indeed, the microtones, and the various different scales that can be composed from them, are held to add considerably to the richness of the music and to the variety of moods that it can create. Although there is a psychoacoustic basis for consonance and dissonance judgments, these judgments also display individual differences and follow changes in the cultural norm. Modern classical music, for example by Stravinsky and Stockhausen, contains many examples of chords that would have been considered dissonant 20 years ago but that are now enjoyed by many people.

7B ABSOLUTE PITCH

Some people have the ability to recognize and name the pitch of a musical tone without reference to a comparison tone. This faculty is called absolute pitch, or perfect pitch, and it is quite rare, probably occurring in less than 1% of the population (although it is more common in countries where intensive musical education starts early in life, such as Japan). It seems to be distinct from the ability that some people develop to judge the pitch of a note in relation to, say, the lowest note that they can sing. Rakowski (1972) investigated absolute pitch by asking subjects to adjust a variable signal so as to have the same pitch as a standard signal for various time delays between the standard and the variable tones. He used two groups of subjects, one group having been selected for their possession of absolute pitch. For long time delays, the subjects without absolute pitch showed a marked deterioration in performance, presumably because the pitch sensation stored in memory was lost. The subjects with absolute pitch seemed able to recall this memory with the aid of their "imprinted" pitch standards, so that only a small decrement in performance was observed. When the standard tone belonged to the normal musical scale (e.g., $A2 = 110\,Hz$), there was hardly any decrement in performance with increasing time delay. The subjects did not seem able to acquire new standards and never, for example, learned to remember a 1000-Hz tone "as such"; it was always recalled as being a little lower than C6. Attempts to improve absolute pitch identification by intensive training have met with some success (Cuddy, 1968), but the levels of performance achieved rarely equal those found in genuine cases of absolute pitch. It seems likely that absolute pitch is a faculty acquired through "imprinting" in childhood a limited number of standards.

Hsieh and Saberi (2008) have shown that even musicians without absolute pitch seem to have a form of memory for pitch. They compared the performance of two groups of musicians, one composed of subjects with absolute pitch and one composed of subjects without absolute pitch. Subjects were given a note label and were asked to sing the note. Analyses of the sung notes showed that both groups were remarkably accurate, even at the start of the sung note. Hsieh and Saberi concluded that their results supported the existence of two memory retrieval system for pitch: a semantic associative form of memory used by musicians with absolute pitch and a more widespread form of procedural memory that allows access to pitch representations through the vocal-motor system.

7C THE PITCH OF VIBRATO TONES

Many sounds produced by musical instruments or the human voice when singing can be characterized as complex tones in which the fundamental frequency undergoes quasi-periodic fluctuations (vibrato). In other words, the tones are frequency modulated. Often, the FM is accompanied by AM. If the fluctuations are of moderate depth, the fluctuation rate is not too high, and the tones are reasonably long, then the tones are perceived as having a single overall pitch (Miller and Heise, 1950; Shonle and Horan, 1976; d'Alessandro and Castellengo, 1994), which is sometimes referred to as the "principal pitch" (Iwamiya et al., 1983, 1984). It has often been assumed that the overall pitch is a simple average of the pitches derived from brief samples of the sound (Iwamiya et al., 1983), although Feth and his coworkers have proposed that the overall pitch is computed as a weighted average of brief samples; samples with high intensity are weighted more than samples with low intensity (Feth et al., 1982; Stover and Feth, 1983; Anantharaman et al., 1993).

Gockel et al. (2001) have shown that the rate of change of frequency also plays a role in how samples are weighted. They obtained pitch matches between an adjustable unmodulated sinusoid and a sinusoidal carrier that was frequency modulated using a highly asymmetric function with the form of a repeating U (∪ ∪) or inverted U (∩ ∩). The amplitude was constant during the 400-ms presentation time of each stimulus, except for 10-ms onset and offset ramps. They found that the matched frequency was shifted away from the mean carrier frequency, downward for the ∪ ∪ stimuli and upward for the ∩ ∩ stimuli. The shift was typically slightly greater than 1% of the carrier frequency and did not vary markedly with carrier frequency. Gockel et al. proposed that the overall pitch of an FM sound is determined from a weighted average of short-term estimates of the period of the sound. The weight attached to a given estimate is inversely related to the short-term rate of change of period and directly related to the amplitude. In other words, the more rapidly the period (or frequency) is changing during a given brief sample of the sound, the less weight does that sample receive. The reduced weighting for sounds whose period is changing rapidly may be related to the "sluggishness" that was described in Section 3A for the detection of FM. The model proposed by Gockel et al. (2001) can account well for the overall pitch of tones with different types of FM and with combinations of frequency and amplitude modulation.

8 PITCH DISCRIMINATION INTERFERENCE

It is often assumed that human listeners are able to listen selectively in different frequency regions, that is, to the outputs of different auditory filters. This ability is one of the assumptions of the power spectrum model of masking described in Chapter 3. However, in the case of pitch, it appears that we are not always able to do this. Gockel et al. (2004, 2005a) showed that discrimination of the fundamental frequency (F0) of a target complex tone that is filtered into a restricted spectral region can be impaired by the presence of an interfering complex tone with fixed F0 that is filtered into a different spectral region. This interference effect, called pitch discrimination inter-ference (PDI), cannot be explained in terms of energetic masking, because it occurs even when the spectral regions of the target tone and interfering tone are widely separated. In some ways, it resembles modulation detection interference (MDI), as described in Chapter 5.

PDI is greatest when the F0 of the interferer is close to the (mean) F0 of the target, and when the interferer has a higher pitch salience than the interferer. For example, a strong PDI effect is obtained when the target contains only high harmonics while the interferer contains low harmonics (Gockel *et al.*, 2004). Part of the PDI effect may occur because the target and the interfering sounds are perceived as fused, that is, as if they emanated from a single sound source. The processes determining whether sounds are perceived as fused or segregated are discussed in Chapter 8. The tendency for the target and the masker to be perceptually fused is probably stronger when their F0s are similar than when they are different, which explains why PDI is largest when the F0 of the interferer is close to the (mean) F0 of the target. Perceptual fusion of the target and interferer could explain the importance of the relative pitch salience of the target and the interferer. If the two sounds are perceptually fused, then the overall pitch will be dominated by whichever of the two sounds has the most salient pitch. An interferer with high pitch salience but fixed F0 will "dilute" the perceived pitch change produced by the change in F0 of the target, leading to impaired F0 discrimination of the target.

Although perceptual fusion of the target and the interferer can explain part of the PDI effect, it probably cannot explain the whole of the effect, because PDI occurs even under conditions where strong cues are available to promote perceptual segregation of the target and the interferer. For example, PDI is reduced, but not eliminated, by gating the interferer on before and off after the target, or by presenting the interferer continuously (Gockel *et al.*, 2004). Also PDI can occur when the target is presented to one ear and the interferer is presented to the other ear (Gockel *et al.*, 2009). Thus, at least part of the PDI effect must occur at a relatively central level in the auditory system, after the level at which inputs from the two ears are combined.

9 GENERAL SUMMARY

In this chapter, I have discussed how the pitches of stimuli are related to their physical properties and to the anatomical and physiological properties of the auditory system. In principle, there are two ways in which the frequency of a sound may be coded: by the distribution of activity across different auditory neurons (place coding) and by the temporal patterns of firing within and across neurons. It is likely that both types of information are utilized but that their relative importance is different for different frequency ranges and for different types of sounds.

The neurophysiological evidence in animals indicates that the synchrony of nerve impulses to a particular phase of the stimulating waveform weakens above 4–5 kHz. Above this frequency, the ability to discriminate changes in the frequency of pure tones diminishes, and the sense of musical pitch disappears. It is likely that this reflects the use of temporal information in the frequency range below 4–5 kHz. Phase locking is probably used for the frequency discrimination of pulsed tones and for the detection of FM at very low rates, when the carrier frequency is below 4–5 kHz. However, for rates of 10 Hz and above, FM detection probably depends mainly on changes in the excitation pattern, a place mechanism.

For complex tones, two classes of theories have been popular. Temporal theories suggest that the pitch of a complex tone is derived from the time intervals between successive nerve spikes evoked at a point on the BM where adjacent partials are interfering with one another. Pattern recognition theories suggest that pitch is derived by a central processor operating on neural signals corresponding to the individual partials present in the complex sound. In both theories, combination tones in the frequency region below the lowest partial may influence the pitch percept.

The pattern recognition theories are supported by the finding that low, resolvable harmonics tend to dominate the perception of pitch and by the finding that a pitch corresponding to a "missing fundamental" can be perceived when there is no possibility of an interference of partials on the BM. This has been demonstrated by presenting partials dichotically, one to each ear, or successively in time. The temporal theory is supported by the finding that (weak) pitches can be perceived when the harmonics are too close in frequency to be resolved, and also when the stimuli have no well-defined spectral structure (e.g., interrupted noise). Thus, neither of the theories can account for all of the experimental results.

I have described a qualitative model that incorporates features of both the temporal and the pattern recognition models. The model assumes that a complex stimulus first passes through a bank of auditory filters with overlapping passbands. The outputs of the filters produce activity in neurons with corresponding CFs. The temporal pattern of activity in each "channel" is analyzed by a device that measures the time intervals between successive nerve spikes. Then a comparator or correlation device searches across channels looking for common time intervals. The prominent time intervals are fed to a decision device that selects among the intervals. The perceived pitch corresponds to the reciprocal of the interval selected and is usually the same as the pitch corresponding to the fundamental component. This model can account for the majority of experimental results presented in this chapter.

Certain aspects of the perception of music may be related to the basic mechanisms underlying pitch perception. There is some evidence, for example, that we prefer musical intervals, or pairs of tones, for which there is a similarity in the time patterns of neural discharge. On the other hand, it is clear that early experience, individual differences, and cultural background also play a significant role in such judgments.

FURTHER RESOURCES

An extensive review of pitch perception is:
Houtsma, A. J. M. (1995). Pitch perception. In B. C. J. Moore (Ed.), *Hearing*. Orlando, FL: Academic.

The following collection of edited chapters reviews many aspects of pitch perception:
Plack, C. J., Oxenham, A. J., Fay, R. R., and Popper, A. N. (2005). *Pitch Perception*. New York: Springer.

A review of absolute pitch is provided in:
Levitin, D. J., and Rogers, S. E. (2005). Absolute pitch: Perception, coding, and controversies. *Trends Cog. Sci.*, *9*, 26–33.

Demonstrations 12, 13, 15, 17, 20–23, 25, and 26 of Auditory Demonstrations on CD are relevant to this chapter (see the list of further resources for Chapter 1).

CHAPTER 7

Space Perception

1 INTRODUCTION

The ability to localize sound sources is of considerable importance to both humans and animals; it determines the direction of objects to seek or to avoid and indicates the appropriate direction to direct visual attention. Although the most reliable cues used in the localization of sounds depend on a comparison of the signals reaching the two ears, localization can also be partly based on the signal at one ear only.

The term "localization" refers to judgments of the direction and distance of a sound source. Sometimes, when headphones are worn, the sound image is located inside the head. The term "lateralization" is used to describe the apparent location of the sound source within the head. Headphones allow precise control of interaural differences and eliminate effects related to room echoes. Thus, lateralization may be regarded as a laboratory version of localization, providing an efficient means of studying direction perception. The range of possible lateralizations is restricted. Most lateralized sounds are perceived somewhere along an imaginary line joining the two ears.

However, a localized sound can be perceived as coming from any direction and distance.

It is useful to define some common terms used in studies of sound localization. The word "monaural" refers to situations when the sound is delivered to one ear only. The word "binaural" refers to situations where sound is delivered to both ears. When the stimulus arriving at the two ears is identical, this is referred to as "diotic". When the sound is different at the two ears, this is called "dichotic".

The directions of sound sources in space are usually defined relative to the head. For this purpose, three planes are defined, as illustrated in Fig. 7.1 (Blauert, 1997). The horizontal plane passes through the upper margins of the entrances to the ear canals and the lower margins of the eye sockets. The frontal plane lies at right angles to the horizontal plane and intersects the upper margins of the entrances to the ear canals. The median plane lies at right angles to the horizontal and frontal planes; points in the median plane are equally distant from the two ears. The point of intersection of all three planes lies roughly at the center of the head; it defines the origin for a coordinate system for specifying the angles of sounds relative to the head. The direction of a sound can be specified by its azimuth and its elevation. All sounds lying in the median plane have $0°$ azimuth. All sounds lying in the horizontal plane have $0°$ elevation. A sound with $0°$ azimuth and $0°$ elevation lies directly in front of the head. A sound with $90°$ azimuth and $0°$ elevation lies directly opposite the left ear. A sound with $180°$ azimuth and $0°$ elevation lies directly behind the head. A sound with $0°$ azimuth and $90°$ elevation lies directly above the head, while a sound with $0°$ azimuth and $270°$ elevation lies directly below the head. Generally, the azimuth is the angle produced by projection onto the horizontal plane (θ in Fig. 7.1), while the elevation is the angle produced by projection onto the median plane (δ in Fig. 7.1).

There are two aspects of performance in localization of sounds. The first is concerned with how well the perceived direction of a sound source corresponds to its actual direction. The perceived direction generally corresponds reasonably well with the actual direction, although for sinusoidal stimuli errors sometimes occur in judging whether a sound is coming from in front or behind, or from above or below the horizontal (Stevens and Newman, 1936); this point is discussed in more detail later on. The second aspect of localization is concerned with how well subjects can detect a small shift in position of a sound source. This aspect measures the resolution of the auditory system. When resolution is studied using stimuli presented via loudspeakers, the smallest detectable change in angular position, relative to the subject, is referred to as the minimum audible angle (MAA).

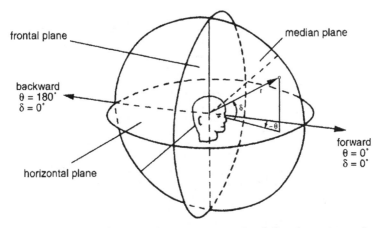

FIGURE 7.1 Illustration of the coordinate system used to define the position of sounds relative to the head. The azimuth is given by the angle θ (positive for left-ward and negative for right-ward directions), and the elevation is given by the angle δ (positive for upward directions and negative for downward directions). Adapted from Blauert (1983). The distance is given by r.

2 THE LOCALIZATION AND LATERALIZATION OF PURE TONES

The cues that allow sound localization vary depending on the nature of the sounds. I consider first steady sinusoidal sounds. Later on I discuss a much more common class of sounds: those that are complex and that change over time.

2A CUES FOR LOCALIZATION

Consider a sinusoidal sound source located to one side of the head in the horizontal plane, for example, with an azimuth of 45° and an elevation of 0°. The sound reaching the farther ear is delayed in time and is less intense than that reaching the nearer ear. There are thus two possible cues as to the location of the sound source: an interaural time difference (ITD) and an interaural intensity difference (IID). When specified in decibels, the IID is referred to as an interaural level difference (ILD). Owing to the physical nature of sounds, ITDs and ILDs are not equally effective at all frequencies.

Low-frequency sounds have a wavelength that is long compared with the size of the head, and so the sound "bends" very well around the head. This process is known as diffraction, and the result is that little or no "shadow" is

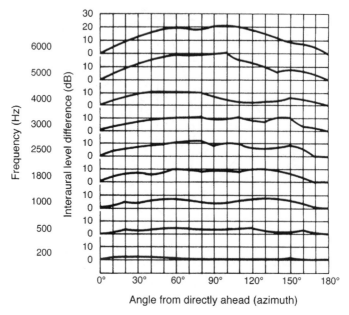

FIGURE 7.2   ILDs for sinusoidal stimuli plotted as a function of azimuth; each curve is for a different frequency. Adapted from Feddersen *et al.* (1957).

cast by the head. On the other hand, at high frequencies, where the wavelength is short compared with the dimensions of the head, little diffraction occurs. A "shadow", almost like that produced by a beam of light, occurs. For sound sources that are distant from the listener, ILDs are negligible below about 500 Hz, but may be as large as 20 dB at high frequencies, as shown in Fig. 7.2, which is adapted from Feddersen *et al.* (1957). The situation is different for sound sources that are very close to the head of the listener. For such sources, considerable ILDs can occur even at low frequencies (Brungart and Rabinowitz, 1999).

ITDs range from 0 (for a sound straight ahead) to about 690 µs for a sound at 90° azimuth (directly opposite one ear). The time difference can be calculated from the path difference between the two ears, as illustrated in Fig. 7.3. The time difference is plotted as a function of azimuth in Fig. 7.4, adapted from Feddersen *et al.* (1957). In practice, the ITD for a given azimuth does vary slightly with frequency, so the function shown in Fig. 7.4 is only an approximation. For a sinusoidal tone, an ITD is equivalent to a phase difference between the two ears, called an interaural phase difference (IPD). For example, for a 200-Hz tone, with a period of 5000 µs, an ITD of 500 µs is equivalent to an IPD of 36° (one-tenth of a cycle). For low-frequency tones,

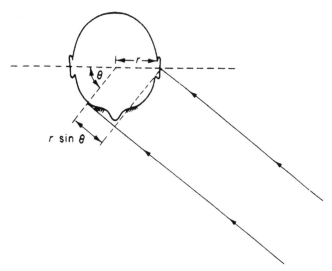

FIGURE 7.3   Illustration of the method for calculating the difference in arrival time at the two ears for a distant sound source at an angle (azimuth) θ radians to the observer. Denoting the radius of the head (about 9 cm) by r, the path difference d between the two ears is given by $d = r\theta + r \sin \theta$. For a sound directly to one side of the observer, $\theta = \pi/2$ radians and $d = (9\pi/2) + (9 \sin(\pi/2)) = 23$ cm. Since sound takes about 30 μs to travel 1 cm, the corresponding time delay is about 690 μs.

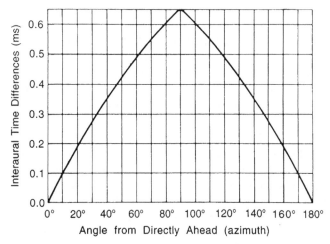

FIGURE 7.4   ITDs plotted as a function of azimuth. Adapted from Feddersen *et al.* (1957).

the IPD provides effective and unambiguous information about the location of the sound. However, for higher-frequency sounds, the IPD provides an ambiguous cue. For example, for a 4000-Hz sinusoid, the period is only 250 μs, and an ITD of 500 μs would result in two whole cycles of IPD. For high-frequency sounds, the auditory system has no way of determining which cycle in the left ear corresponds to a given cycle in the right ear. Ambiguities start to occur when the period of the sound is about twice the maximum possible ITD, i.e., when the period is about 1380 μs and the frequency of the sound is about 725 Hz. A sinusoid of this frequency lying to one side of the head (90° azimuth) produces waveforms at the two ears that are in opposite phase (IPD of 180°). The location of the sound source is now ambiguous, since the waveform at the right ear might be either a half-cycle behind that at the left ear or a half-cycle ahead; a 725-Hz tone at −90° azimuth would produce the same waveforms at the two ears as the same tone at 90° azimuth. Head movements, or movements of the sound source, may resolve this ambiguity, so there is no abrupt upper limit in the ability to use phase differences between the two ears. However, phase differences become highly ambiguous for frequencies above about 1500 Hz.

In summary, for sinusoids, the physical cue of ILD should be most useful at high frequencies, while the cue of ITD should be most useful at low frequencies. The idea that sound localization is based on ILDs at high frequencies and ITDs at low frequencies has been called the "duplex theory" and it dates back to Lord Rayleigh (1907). Although it appears to hold reasonably well for pure tones, it is not strictly accurate for complex sounds, as will be explained later.

2B PERFORMANCE IN LOCALIZATION AND LATERALIZATION TASKS

Studies of localization using sinusoids have usually used tone bursts with gradual onsets and offsets to minimize cues related to the interaural timing of the envelope; envelope cues are discussed in more detail later in this chapter.

Figure 7.5 shows the MAA for sinusoidal signals presented in the horizontal plane, plotted as a function of frequency (Mills, 1958, 1972). Each curve shows results for a different reference azimuth; the task was to detect a shift in position around that azimuth. The MAA is smallest for a reference azimuth of 0°, i.e., for sounds coming from directly in front of the subject. A shift of only about 1° can be detected for frequencies below 1000 Hz. Performance worsens around 1500–1800 Hz. This is consistent with the duplex theory; above 1500 Hz phase differences between the two ears are ambiguous cues for localization, but up to 1800 Hz, ILDs are small and do not change much with azimuth (see Fig. 7.2). Performance worsens markedly when the reference

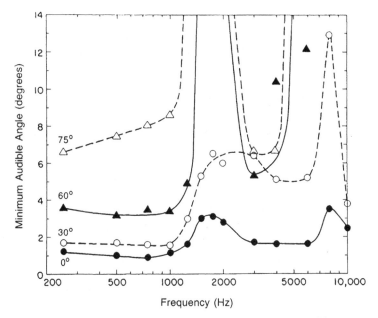

FIGURE 7.5   The MAA for sinusoidal signals plotted as a function of frequency; each curve shows results for a different reference direction. Data from Mills (1958).

azimuth is moved away from 0°. Indeed, for reference azimuths of 60° and 75°, the MAA was so large that it could not be determined when the frequency was around 1800 Hz. This can be understood by consideration of Fig. 7.2. For a frequency of 1800 Hz, there is an ILD of about 10 dB for azimuths from 55° to 140°, but the ILD hardly changes when the azimuth is changed over that range. This leads to a very large MAA.

The MAA is measured using sounds presented using loudspeakers. Such sounds lead to both ITDs and ILDs. When resolution is studied using earphones, it is possible to study the effectiveness of ILDs alone or ITDs alone. In one method, two stimuli are presented successively, one of which is identical at the two ears (diotic) while the other might have an ITD or ILD. The task of the subject is to indicate whether the first stimulus was to the left or the right of the second stimulus. In other words, the task is to identify a shift in location associated with a change in ITD or ILD.

Thresholds for detecting changes in ITD are smallest when the reference ITD is zero, corresponding to a sound heard in the center of the head (Yost, 1974). In this case, a change in ITD of about 10 μs can be detected for a frequency of 900 Hz. Such a change would be produced by moving a sound source through an azimuth of about 1°; this corresponds well with the MAA value described earlier. The smallest detectable ITD increases somewhat at lower frequencies, although the threshold is roughly constant at about 3° when it is expressed as the smallest detectable change in IPD. Above 900 Hz, the threshold ITD increases markedly, and above 1500 Hz changes in ITD are essentially undetectable (this is not true for complex sounds; see Section 3B). The threshold ITD increases for all frequencies when the reference ITD is greater than zero.

Thresholds for detecting changes in ILD are also smallest when the reference ILD is zero. In this case, changes in ILD of about 1 dB can be detected across a wide range of frequencies, although performance worsens slightly for frequencies around 1000 Hz (Mills, 1960; Yost and Dye, 1988). It is interesting that changes in ILD can be detected at low frequencies and are heard as shifts in lateral position, even though such cues only occur in everyday life for sound sources close to the listener (Brungart and Rabinowitz, 1999).

In summary, the resolution of the binaural system for sinusoids is best for sounds that come from directly ahead (0° azimuth). Resolution at low frequencies is based on the use of ITDs. Changes in ITD cannot be detected for frequencies above 1500 Hz. Changes in ILD can be detected over the whole audible frequency range, but, in practice, ILDs sufficiently large to provide useful cues to sound location usually occur only at high frequencies.

2C BINAURAL BEATS

A phenomenon that is related to the ability of the auditory system to process phase differences at the two ears is that of binaural beats. These may be heard when a tone of one frequency is presented to one ear, via headphones, and a tone of slightly differing frequency is presented to the other ear. If the frequency difference is less than about 2 Hz, the sound appears to move right and left across the head. For higher frequency differences, the perception becomes more diffuse and appears to fluctuate in loudness or to be rough. Binaural beats are quite different from the physical beats that are produced when the two tones are mixed in an electrical or acoustical system. Such physical beats or monaural beats occur because the two frequencies are alternately in phase and out of phase and, thus, alternately cancel and reinforce one another; the intensity fluctuates at a rate equal to the frequency difference between the two tones (see Chapter 1, Section 2D). Binaural beats, however, depend on an interaction in the nervous system of the neural output from each ear. They provide a demonstration that the discharges of neurons in the auditory nerve preserve information about the phase of the acoustic stimulus. Neural spikes tend to occur at a particular phase of the stimulating waveform. At points in the auditory system where the signals from the two ears are combined, the trains of neural spikes from the two ears superimpose differently depending on the relative phase of the stimuli at the two ears. There is thus a neural basis for the subjective fluctuations that occur when the relative phase at the two ears fluctuates, as it does when tones with slightly different frequencies are presented to the two ears.

Since binaural beats differ in their origin from monaural beats, it is hardly surprising that the two kinds of beats differ subjectively; binaural beats are never as distinct as monaural beats. Monaural beats can be observed over the entire audible frequency range, whereas binaural beats are essentially a low-frequency phenomenon. Estimates of the highest frequency for which binaural beats can be observed have varied. The beats are heard most distinctly for frequencies between 300 and 600 Hz, but become progressively more difficult to hear at high frequencies. The exact upper limit depends on both the intensity and the experimental technique used, but it is generally agreed that the beats are exceedingly difficult to hear for frequencies above 1000 Hz (Licklider et al., 1950). Monaural beats are most distinctly heard when the two tones are matched for intensity and cannot be heard when the intensities of the two tones differ greatly. Binaural beats, however, can be heard when there are large differences in intensity at the two ears (Tobias, 1963). This is consistent with physiological evidence that phase locking occurs over a wide range of stimulus intensities. It has been claimed that binaural beats can be heard even when the tone to one ear is below absolute threshold (Groen, 1964). However, recent evidence does not support this claim (Gu et al., 1995).

3 THE LATERALIZATION OF COMPLEX SOUNDS

All sounds that occur in nature have onsets and offsets, and many also change their intensity or their spectral structure as a function of time. ITDs of these transients provide cues for localization that are not subject to the phase ambiguities that occur for steady sinusoidal tones. Also, for sounds that cover a reasonable frequency range, phase ambiguities can be resolved by comparisons across frequency; the ITD that is common across all frequency channels must be the "true" ITD (see Section 3G).

3A THE ACUITY OF LATERALIZING TRANSIENTS

Klumpp and Eady (1956) measured thresholds for discriminating ITDs using stimuli delivered via headphones. They compared three types of stimuli: band-limited noise (containing frequencies in the range 150–1700 Hz);

1000-Hz sinusoids with gradual rise and fall times; and clicks of duration 1 ms. The waveform of the first stimulus fluctuates randomly as a function of time and thus provides transient information that is repeated many times during the presentation time of the stimulus; the pure tone provides only information relating to ongoing phase differences, while the click is effectively a single transient. The threshold ITDs were 9, 11, and 28 µs, respectively. The greatest acuity occurred for the noise stimulus, with continuously available transient information, but the tone gave performance that was only slightly worse. The single click gave rise to the poorest performance. It is worth noting, however, that the tones in this experiment were of relatively long duration (1.4 s). For tones of shorter duration, acuity is not so great, and cues related to onset and offset transients (which would be comparable to those provided by the clicks) become relatively more important. Also, threshold ITDs for trains of repeated clicks can be as small as 10 µs (Dye and Hafter, 1984) when the click rate is reasonably low (200 clicks per second or less). For sounds with ongoing transient disparities, such as bursts of noise, the ability to discriminate ITDs improves with duration of the bursts for durations up to about 700 ms, when the threshold reaches an asymptote of about 6 µs (Tobias and Schubert, 1959).

3B ACUITY AS A FUNCTION OF FREQUENCY AND THE USE OF ENVELOPES

Stimuli such as noises and clicks contain energy over a wide range of frequencies. Yost et al. (1971) determined which frequency components were the most important, by studying the lateralization of clicks whose frequency content had been altered by filtering. The subjects were asked to discriminate a centered image (produced by diotic clicks) from a displaced image (produced by delaying the click to the left ear). They found that discrimination deteriorated for clicks that were highpass filtered, so that only energy above 1500 Hz was present, but it was largely unaffected by lowpass filtering. Also, masking with a lowpass noise produced a marked disruption, while a highpass noise had little effect. Thus, the discrimination of lateral position on the basis of ITDs depended largely on the low-frequency content of the clicks, although somewhat poorer discrimination was possible with only high-frequency components.

This finding ties in rather well with the results obtained with pure tones, showing that we cannot compare phases between the two ears for frequencies above 1500 Hz. When a click is presented to the ear, it produces a waveform at a given point on the basilar membrane (BM) looking rather like a decaying sinusoidal oscillation (see Fig. 1.13). The frequency of the oscillation depends on which part of the BM is being observed; at the basal end the frequency is high and at the apical end it is low. For frequencies below 1500 Hz, the phases of these decaying oscillations at the two ears can be compared, thus conveying accurate information about the relative timing of the clicks at the two ears. For frequencies above 1500 Hz, this "temporal fine structure" information is lost; only timing information relating to the envelope of the decaying oscillation is available for binaural processing, and this reduces the accuracy with which the clicks can be localized.

Henning (1974) has provided further evidence for the importance of the amplitude envelope. He investigated the lateralization of high-frequency tones that had been amplitude modulated (see Fig. 3.7). He found that the detectability of ITDs in the envelope of a 3900-Hz carrier modulated at a frequency of 300 Hz was about as good as the detectability of ITDs in a 300-Hz pure tone. However, there were considerable differences among individual subjects; the ITDs necessary for 75% correct detection in his forced-choice task had values of 20, 50, and 65 μs for three different subjects. Henning found that ITD of the envelope rather than ITD of the temporal fine structure within the envelope determines the lateralization. The signals could be lateralized on the basis of ITDs in the envelope even when the carrier frequencies were different in the two ears. Thus, it seems that, for complex signals containing only high-frequency components, listeners extract the envelopes of the signals and make use of the ITDs in the envelopes. However, lateralization performance is best when the carrier frequencies are identical, and poor lateralization results when the complex waveforms at each ear have no frequency component in common. Thus, factors other than the envelope can affect lateralization performance. The fact that ITDs of the envelope can be processed even when the sounds have no components below 1500 Hz indicates that Rayleigh's duplex theory, which was described earlier, is not completely correct.

It has been shown that the ability to discriminate ITDs in the envelopes of high-frequency stimuli can be improved if the temporal structure of the envelope is made "sharper" or more distinct. This has been done using "transposed" stimuli (van de Par and Kohlrausch, 1997). The processing involved is illustrated in Fig. 7.6. A low-frequency sine wave is half-wave rectified, which preserves the positive half cycles while setting the negative half cycles to zero (top trace). The rectified sine wave is then multiplied by a high-frequency carrier (middle trace), giving the transposed stimulus shown in the bottom trace. The envelope of the transposed stimulus would convey similar temporal information in the auditory system to the low-frequency sine wave. Bernstein and Trahiotis (2002) measured thresholds for discriminating changes in ITD for three types of stimuli: (1) low-frequency sine waves;

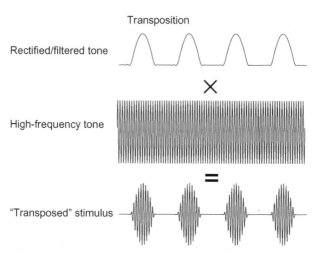

FIGURE 7.6 Illustration of the creation of a "transposed" stimulus. A low-frequency sine wave is half-wave rectified (top trace) and multiplied by a high-frequency sine wave (middle trace) to produce the transposed stimulus (bottom trace). Adapted from Bernstein and Trahiotis (2002).

(2) 100% sinusoidally amplitude-modulated (SAM) high-frequency sine waves, and (3) "transposed" stimuli like those illustrated in Fig. 7.6. The threshold ITDs obtained with the transposed stimuli were generally smaller than those obtained with SAM tones and, for modulation frequencies of 128 and 64 Hz, were equal to or smaller than the threshold ITDs obtained with their low-frequency sinusoidal counterparts. Thus, the binaural system seems to be able to process ITDs carried in the envelopes of high-frequency stimuli with similar precision to that obtained with low-frequency sine waves.

3C ONSET DISPARITIES VERSUS ONGOING DISPARITIES

Tobias and Schubert (1959) investigated the relative importance of onset disparities and ongoing disparities in lateralization judgments by pitting one against the other. They presented bursts of noise via headphones, with a particular onset ITD, and determined the amount of ongoing ITD needed to counteract the onset information and recenter the subjective image. They found that small ongoing ITDs offset much larger onset ITDs and that for durations exceeding 300 ms the onset had no effect. Even for short bursts (10 ms) the ongoing ITD had the greater effect. However, Zurek (1993) pointed out that studies showing that onset ITDs are less important than ongoing ITDs for lateralization all controlled the onset ITD by the gating of the sounds; any ITD in the onset was in the envelope rather than the temporal fine structure. He also pointed out that studies in which the fine structure was delayed showed a greater effect of the onset. This is confirmed by a recent experiment of Akeroyd and Bernstein (2001). They used a method similar to that of Zurek (1980), in which they varied the ITD of a 5-ms section of an otherwise diotic broadband noise of 50-ms duration. Thresholds for detecting the ITD were lowest when the target section was at the start of the sound, deteriorated when it was in the middle, and then got better toward the end. It appears that ITD information in the temporal fine structure is weighted more at the start and end of a sound than in the middle. This may be related to the precedence effect, which is discussed in Section 6 of this chapter.

3D Time-Intensity Trading

If identical clicks are presented to the two ears via headphones, then the sound source is usually located in the middle of the head; the image is said to be centered. If the click in the left ear is made to lead that in the right ear by, say, 100 μs, the sound image moves to the left. However, by making the click in the right ear more intense, it is possible to make the sound image move back toward the right, so that once again the image is centered. Thus, it is possible to trade an ITD for an ILD. The amount of time difference needed to offset a 1-dB difference in level at the two ears is often described as the "trading ratio".

The phenomenon of time-intensity trading led to the theory that ITDs and ILDs are eventually coded in the nervous system in a similar sort of way. In particular, it was suggested that the time required to evoke neural responses was shorter for more intense sounds, so ILDs were transformed into ITDs at the neural level (Deatherage and Hirsh, 1959). This was called the "latency" hypothesis.

More recent work has indicated that things are not so straightforward. Both for low-frequency tones and for clicks, two separate sound images may be heard when ITD and ILD are opposed. For tones, Whitworth and Jeffress (1961) found that one image, the "time image", was little affected by ILDs and showed a trading ratio of about 1 μs/dB. The other, the "intensity image", showed a trading ratio of about 20 μs/dB. For clicks, Hafter and Jeffress (1968) found ratios of 2–35 μs/dB for the "time image" and 85–150 μs/dB for the "intensity image". Hafter and Carrier (1972) have confirmed that listeners are able to detect differences between diotic signals and dichotic signals that have been centered by opposing an ITD with an ILD. These experiments indicate that ITDs and ILDs are not truly equivalent.

3E BINAURAL ADAPTATION

Hafter and his colleagues (Hafter and Dye, 1983; Hafter *et al.*, 1988) have demonstrated a form of adaptation that appears to be specific to binaural processing. They investigated the lateralization of trains of clicks that contained energy only over a limited range of high frequencies, typically around 4 kHz. They measured thresholds for discriminating ITDs or ILDs as a function of the number of clicks in the train (n) and the interval between successive clicks (I). A sample of their results for the discrimination of ILDs is shown in Fig. 7.7. When I was 10 ms, giving a click rate of 100/s, the thresholds decreased progressively with increasing n. The thresholds were inversely proportional to $\sqrt{n}$, which implies that all the clicks in the train provided an equal amount of information (Green and Swets, 1974). However, when I was 1 ms, giving a click rate of 1000/s, the threshold decreased only slightly with increasing n. This implies that the first click provided much more information than the subsequent clicks. The results for values of

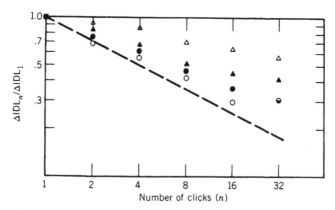

FIGURE 7.7 Thresholds for detecting an interaural difference in level are plotted as a function of the number of clicks, n, in a click train. Each threshold for n clicks (ΔIDL_n) is plotted relative to the threshold for a single click (ΔIDL_1); a log scale is used. The different symbols show data for different interclick intervals: 10 (solid circles), 5 (open circles), 2 (solid triangles), and 1 ms (open triangles). The dashed line has a slope of -0.5 and indicates where the points would lie if each click in the train provided an equal amount of information for localization. From Hafter and Dye (1983), by permission of the authors and *J. Acoust. Soc. Am.*

I between 1 and 10 ms showed that clicks after the first provided progressively less information as *I* was decreased.

In summary, for high click rates, the binaural system appears to process only the onset of the click train; it is as if there is a rapid adaptation at high click rates, so that clicks after the first convey little information for localization. The higher the click rate, the faster is the adaptation. Note that the later clicks can still be heard, even though they do not result in an improvement in localization.

Hafter *et al.* (1988) have presented evidence that a suitable "trigger" stimulus can produce a release from adaptation. Clicks presented after the trigger are more effective for localization than clicks immediately before the trigger. Among suitable triggers are a brief low-intensity burst of noise, a brief tone burst, and a gap in the click train. Hafter and coworkers argued that the recovery from adaptation was the result of an "active release" rather than a simple decay of the adaptation. They suggested that:

> It is as though the auditory system becomes increasingly insensitive to interaural cues past the stimulus onset while continuing to monitor for signs of new conditions. When one occurs, the slate is wiped clean and the spatial environment is sampled again.

From this point of view, the triggers described earlier are successful in producing a release from binaural adaptation because they signal that a change has occurred.

3F BINAURAL INTERFERENCE

McFadden and Pasanen (1976), using stimuli presented via headphones, showed that the ability to discriminate ITDs in a narrowband noise stimulus centered at 4000 Hz was degraded by the presence of a second diotic narrowband noise centered at 500 Hz. Since that time, such interference effects have been demonstrated for a range of stimuli, including sinusoidal tone bursts, amplitude-modulated sine waves, and bands of noise (Trahiotis and Bernstein, 1990; Buell and Hafter, 1991; Stellmack and Dye, 1993; Buell and Trahiotis, 1994; Stellmack, 1994; Heller and Trahiotis, 1995). Interference effects have also been demonstrated for stimuli presented via loudspeakers in an anechoic chamber; the MAA for a narrowband noise target centered at 4000 Hz was higher in the presence of a narrowband noise interferer centered at 500 Hz when the interferer was pulsed on and off with the target (Croghan and Grantham, 2010). These experiments have shown that the ability to detect or discriminate interaural differences in stimuli centered at one frequency is degraded by the presence of conflicting interaural differences in stimuli centered in another frequency region. This across-channel interference effect has been called "binaural interference". In some ways it resembles modulation detection interference, which was described in Chapter 5, and pitch discrimination interference, which was described in Chapter 6.

Binaural interference shows some asymmetry in frequency; generally, low-frequency interferers strongly degrade the lateralization of high-frequency targets, while high-frequency interferers have little effect on the lateralization of low-frequency targets. However, this is not always the case. Heller and Richards (2010) required subjects to discriminate changes in either ITD or ILD of one noise band (the target) in the presence or absence of an uninformative second noise band (the interferer). The noise bands were centered at 500 and 4000 Hz, and either band could be the target. The interferer was presented either diotically, or dichotically with ITDs or ILDs that varied randomly across intervals. For ITD discrimination, interference was greater for the 4000-Hz target than for the 500-Hz target, but for ILD discrimination, interference for the 500-Hz target was comparable to that for the 4000-Hz target. The interference effects were larger when the interferer ITD or ILD was randomly varied than when the interferer was diotic.

One interpretation of binaural interference is that it results from fusion of the target and interfering sounds into a single sound image. The perceived location of the fused image would then depend on some form of average of the positions of the target and interfering sounds. If judgments of lateral position are based upon this fused image, then changes in the position of the target sound will be more difficult to detect when the target is accompanied by an interfering sound that does not change or that changes in an irrelevant way. Low-frequency sounds are weighted more heavily than high-frequency sounds in determining the average (Yost et al., 1971; Zurek, 1985), an effect that has been called "spectral dominance". This can account for the spectral asymmetry that is usually found in the interference effect, although it does not account for the finding of Heller and Richards (2010) that for ILD discrimination, interference for the 500-Hz target was comparable to that for the 4000-Hz target.

The idea that binaural interference results at least partly from perceptual fusion of the target and interfering sounds is supported by the finding that the interference is reduced when the interfering sound is presented continuously, or with an onset asynchrony relative to the target, rather than being turned on and off (gated) synchronously with the target (Stellmack and Dye, 1993; Stellmack, 1994; Heller and Trahiotis, 1995; Croghan and Grantham, 2010). As will be described in Chapter 8, synchronous gating promotes perceptual fusion of different sounds, whereas asynchronous gating promotes perceptual segregation. However, the interference is often not abolished by asynchronous gating, suggesting that perceptual fusion may not provide a complete explanation. For example, Woods and Colburn (1992) measured thresholds for lateralization of a target sinusoid on the basis of its ITD, when it was presented with two interfering sinusoids. The target component started up to 250 ms after the two interfering components. This asynchrony "elicited the percept of two separate sound objects: a rough-timbred object followed by a tone-like object. Each subject reported these perceptions the first time they were exposed to the stimuli" (p. 2897). However, in this condition, the threshold ITD for the target tone was still higher than when that tone was presented in isolation.

3G Across-Frequency Integration and the Effect of Bandwidth

For sounds with a small bandwidth, such as a sinusoid or narrow band of noise, the cue of ITD can be ambiguous. Consider as an example a narrow band of noise centered at 500 Hz. This resembles a 500-Hz sinusoid that is slowly fluctuating in amplitude. If this sound is presented via earphones with an ITD of 1500 µs (which is larger than the largest ITD that would occur in everyday life) with, say, the left ear leading, the sound is heard toward the right rather than toward the left (Jeffress, 1972; Trahiotis and Stern, 1989). The ITD in this case corresponds to an IPD of the fine structure of 270° (0.75 cycle lead in the left ear), but the auditory system appears to give more weight to the smaller possible IPD of −90° (0.25 cycle lead in the right ear). When the IPD is ambiguous, the sound tends to be perceived at a location corresponding to the smallest possible IPD. Ambiguities in IPD can be resolved by increasing the bandwidth of the stimulus so that it produces more or less independent outputs from several auditory filters (Jeffress, 1972; Trahiotis and Stern, 1989; Stern and Trahiotis, 1995). For example, for a broadband noise with a lead at the left ear of 1500 µs, the "true" ITD is common to all of the "channels" (auditory filters) that are excited. In contrast, the smallest IPD in a given channel varies with the center frequency of that channel. For example, for a channel tuned to 400 Hz (period = 2500 µs), the "true" IPD is 216° (corresponding to 0.6 cycle) and the corresponding smaller IPD is 144° (corresponding to 0.4 cycle). For a channel tuned to 800 Hz (period = 1250 µs), the true IPD is 432° (corresponding to 1.2 cycle) and the corresponding smaller IPD is 72° (corresponding to 0.2 cycle). For a stimulus like this, the auditory system determines the location of the sound on the basis of the ITD that is common across channels, rather than on the basis of the smallest IPD, which varies across channels. Thus, the "correct" location is perceived. The bandwidth required for correct localization, for a noise band centered at 500 Hz, is about 400 Hz (Trahiotis and Stern, 1989).

4 THE CONE OF CONFUSION AND THE ROLE OF HEAD MOVEMENTS

Ignoring for the moment the influence of the pinnae, the head may be regarded as a pair of holes separated by a spherical obstacle. If the head is kept stationary, then a given ITD is not sufficient to define uniquely the position of the sound source in space; there is a cone of confusion such that any sound source on the surface of this cone would give rise to the same ITD (see Mills, 1972 and Fig. 7.8).

Ambiguities related to the cone of confusion or to the location of a sound source in the vertical direction may be resolved by head movements. If the head is rotated about a vertical axis by, say, 20°, and this results in a 20° shift in the apparent azimuth of the sound relative to the head, then the sound source is perceived as being in the horizontal plane. If the rotation of the head is accompanied by no change in the position of the auditory image relative to

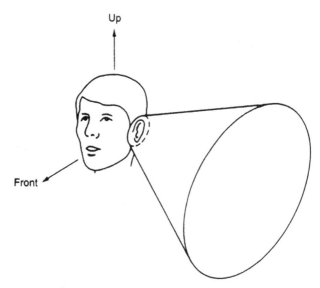

FIGURE 7.8   A cone of confusion for a spherical head and a particular ITD. All sound sources on the surface of the cone would produce that interaural time delay. For details of how to calculate the cone of confusion, see Mills (1972).

the head, then the sound is perceived as located either directly above or below the listener. Intermediate shifts in the location of the auditory image lead to intermediate vertical height judgments (Wallach, 1940).

Hirsh (1971) has reviewed a number of experiments showing improved localization abilities when head movements were allowed. In some cases, monaural localization was as good as binaural localization (Freedman and Fisher, 1968). This suggests that head movements provide cues other than changes in ITD and ILD. For complex sounds, such as white noise, movements of either the head or the sound source produce changes in the spectral patterning at each ear (see Section 5), and these changes provide cues as to the direction of the sound source.

5 MONAURAL LOCALIZATION, THE ROLE OF THE PINNAE AND HRTFS

Although head movements or movements of the sound source are clearly important and can help to resolve ambiguities in vertical direction, our abilities at judging vertical direction are far in excess of what would be predicted if the only information available was related to interaural differences and changes in those differences produced by head movements. For example, we are able to judge the location of a burst of white noise in the median plane when the duration of the burst is too short to allow useful information to be gained from head movements.

Many workers have suggested that the pinnae provide information that is used in judgments of vertical location (Butler, 1969) and for the discrimination of front from back, while others (Batteau, 1967; Freedman and Fisher, 1968) have suggested that the pinnae are important for localization in every direction. To investigate the role of the pinnae, Batteau inserted microphones into casts of actual pinnae held on a bar without a model of the head in between them. The sounds picked up by the microphones were played to the subjects via headphones. The subjects were able to make reasonably accurate judgments of both azimuth and elevation. When the pinnae were removed from the microphones, judgments were quite erratic.

It is noteworthy that, with the artificial pinnae in place, subjects reported that the sounds were localized out "in space" and not, as is usually the case with headphones, lateralized inside the head. This impression persisted even when one microphone was disconnected. The pinnae alter the sound in a way that causes the sounds to be perceived as externalized (although appropriate reverberation is also important).

Gardner and Gardner (1973) investigated localization in the median plane for wideband noise and for bands of noise with various different center frequencies. They found that occlusion of the pinnae cavities by filling them with molded rubber plugs decreased localization abilities, with the largest effects occurring for wideband noise and for the bands of noise with the highest center frequencies (8 and 10 kHz). However, there was still some effect at 3 kHz.

It is now generally accepted that the pinnae modify the spectra of incoming sounds in a way that depends on the angle of incidence of the sound relative to the head. This has been confirmed by measurements in the ear canal of human observers and by measurements using realistic models of the human head (Shaw, 1974; Oldfield and Parker, 1984; Wightman and Kistler, 1989; Kawaura et al., 1991; Wenzel et al., 1993; Blauert, 1997). The sound entering the ear canal arrives both directly from the sound source and after one or more reflections from the pinna. The reflected sound is delayed relative to the direct sound, and when added to the direct sound it cancels the direct sound at some frequencies (when the delayed sound is 180° out of phase with the direct sound) and reinforces the direct sound at other frequencies (when the delayed sound is nearly in phase with the direct sound). Thus, the head and pinna together form a complex direction-dependent filter. The filtering action is often characterized by measuring the spectrum of the sound source and the spectrum of the sound reaching the eardrum. The ratio of these two (usually expressed in decibels) gives what is called the "head-related transfer function" (HRTF). The HRTF shows a complex pattern of peaks and dips that varies systematically with the direction of the sound source relative to the head and that is unique for each direction in space.

The spectral changes produced by the head and pinna can be used to judge the location of a sound source. Since it is the spectral patterning of the sound at the eardrum that is important, the information provided by the pinnae is most effective when the sound has spectral energy over a wide frequency range. High frequencies, above 6 kHz, are especially important, since it is only at high frequencies that the wavelength of sound is sufficiently short for the sound to interact strongly with the pinna.

If diotic narrowband noise signals are presented, their perceived elevation depends on frequency only and not on the direction of sound incidence (Blauert, 1969/1970). Similar results have been found by Butler (1971) for the localization of tone bursts with one ear occluded. The direction perceived corresponds to the direction that would give a peak in the HRTF at that frequency. For example, a diotic narrowband noise or sinusoid with a (center) frequency of 8 kHz is usually localized overhead, regardless of its actual position. This is the precise spatial position that would give a peak in the HRTF at 8 kHz. This suggests that peaks in the spectrum are a major cue for localization. However, other evidence suggests that notches in the spectrum can also play an important role (Bloom, 1977), while some studies suggest that both peaks and notches are important (Watkins, 1978).

Although the spectral changes produced by the pinnae are limited to frequencies above 6 kHz, modification of the spectrum of the stimulus may occur at much lower frequencies than this, because the head and torso, as well as the pinnae, can affect the spectrum. The effects described by Blauert and Butler were found for frequencies between 500 Hz and 16 kHz.

Individuals differ in the shapes and sizes of their heads and pinnae. Hence, HRTFs also differ across individuals. To assess the importance of such individual differences, Wenzel et al. (1993) compared localization accuracy for stimuli presented in free field over loudspeakers and for stimuli presented over earphones. In the latter case, the stimuli were filtered to simulate free-field presentation, using HRTFs; this is often referred to as "virtual localization". The question addressed was: can subjects make effective use of information provided by another person's pinna? To answer this, the accuracy of virtual localization was measured using a "representative" HRTF rather than the listener's own HRTF. The results suggest that cues to horizontal location are robust, but resolution of the cone of confusion is adversely affected by using nonindividualized HRTFs; more errors were made in distinguishing front from back and up from down when free-field listening was simulated using earphones than when true free-field listening was used.

Kawaura et al. (1991) also used virtual localization to study the importance of individual differences in HRTFs. They used three subjects, and each subject was presented with sounds processed using their own HRTFs or processed using the HRTFs of one of the other subjects. Performance was very similar for these two cases, suggesting that individual differences in the HRTFs were not very important. However, in similar experiments, Middlebrooks (1999) and Møller et al. (1996) found that performance was always better when subjects listened via their own HRTFs than when they listened via another person's HRTFs. Middlebrooks also showed that virtual localization could be improved if the HRTFs measured from another person's ears were scaled in frequency to minimize the mismatch between spectral features in the listener's and the other person's HRTFs.

If the listener is to make efficient use of spectral cues associated with the direction of a sound source, then it is necessary to distinguish spectral peaks and dips related to direction from peaks and dips inherent in a sound source or produced by reflections from nearby surfaces. Thus, one might expect that a knowledge of the sound source and room conditions would also be important. However, knowledge of the spectrum of the sound source might not be essential for two reasons. First, the spectral peaks and dips introduced by the pinnae are quite sharp, whereas for many sound sources the spectrum at high frequencies is relatively smooth. Secondly, the two ears provide separate sets of spectral cues, so the difference between the sound at the two eardrums could be used to locate unfamiliar sound sources. Even for sound sources in the median plane, asymmetries in pinna shape may result in interaural disparities that can be used for localization if the stimuli contain frequencies above 8–10 kHz (Searle et al., 1975; Middlebrooks et al., 1989).

Although knowledge of the spectrum of the sound source may not always be necessary to make use of pinna cues, Plenge (1972, 1974) has presented evidence that we do, in fact, make comparisons with stored stimulus patterns in judging the location of a sound source. He showed that if subjects were not allowed to become familiar with the characteristics of the sound source and the listening room then localization was disturbed. In many cases, the sound sources were lateralized in the head rather than being localized externally. This was particularly true for sound in the median plane. However, such familiarity does not seem to require an extended learning process. We become familiar with sound source characteristics and room acoustics within a very few seconds of entering a new situation.

A different aspect of this problem was addressed by Rakerd et al. (1999). They examined how the ability to identify filtered noises on the basis of their spectral shape was affected by spectral variations caused by changes in HRTFs with direction. They found that subjects could accurately identify noises with different spectral peaks and valleys when the source location was fixed. Subjects could also identify noises when the source location was randomly varied (roved) in the median plane, provided that the relevant spectral features were at low frequency. However, subjects failed to identify noises with roved location when the spectral structure was at high frequency, presumably because the spectral structure was confused with the spectral variations caused by different locations. Rakerd et al. concluded that subjects cannot compensate for changes in HRTFs with direction when they try to identify sounds.

6 THE PRECEDENCE EFFECT

In a normal listening environment, the sound from a given source, such as a loudspeaker, reaches the ears via a number of different paths. Some of the sound arrives by a direct path, but a good deal of it only reaches the ears after one or more reflections from the surfaces of the room. In spite of this, we are not normally aware of these reflections, or echoes, and they appear to have little influence on judgments of the direction of the sound source. Thus, we are still able to locate a talker accurately in a reverberant room where the total

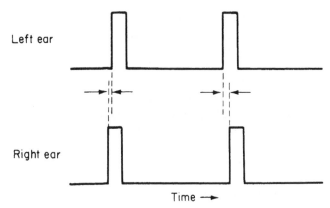

Left ear

Right ear

Time →

FIGURE 7.9 The stimulus sequence used by Wallach *et al.* (1949) to investigate the precedence effect. The first pair of clicks arrives at the ears with a small interaural time disparity, indicated by the arrows. The second pair of clicks simulates a room echo and has a different interaural disparity. The whole stimulus sequence is heard as a single sound whose location is determined primarily by the interaural delay of the leading pair of clicks.

energy in the reflected sound may be greater than that reaching the ears by a direct path.

Wallach *et al.* (1949) investigated the way the auditory system copes with echoes in experiments using both sound sources in free space and sounds delivered by headphones. In the experiments using headphones, pairs of clicks were delivered to each ear (two clicks in each earphone). The delay between the two clicks in a pair and the time of arrival of the first click in a pair could be varied independently (Fig. 7.9). Their results, and the results of more recent experiments (Litovsky *et al.*, 1999), can be summarized as follows:

1. Two brief sounds that reach the ears in close succession are heard as a single sound if the interval between them is sufficiently short. The interval over which fusion takes place is not the same for all types of sounds. The upper limit of the interval is about 5 ms for single clicks, but may be as long as 40 ms for sounds of a complex character, such as speech or music. It is as if the lagging sound, or echo, has been suppressed from conscious perception. This effect has been called "echo suppression". However, the percept does change if the echo is removed; see point 11.

2. If two successive sounds are heard as fused, the location of the total sound is determined largely by the location of the first sound. This is known as the "precedence effect", although it has also been called the "Haas effect", after Haas (1951), and the "law of the first wavefront"

(Blauert, 1997). The effect is reflected in the finding that the ability to detect shifts in the location of the lagging sound (the echo) is reduced for a short time following the onset of the leading sound (Zurek, 1980; Perrott et al., 1989). The reduced ability to lateralize the lagging sound is often taken as a quantitative measure of the precedence effect. Some studies have shown that training can lead to a marked improvement in the ability to detect changes in the ITD of the lagging sound (Saberi and Perrott, 1990), while others have not (Litovsky et al., 2000).

3. The precedence effect is only shown for sounds of a discontinuous or transient character.

4. The lagging sound does have a small influence. If the location of the lagging sound departs more and more from the location of the leading sound, it "pulls" the total sound along with it up to a maximal amount (about 7°) and then it becomes progressively less effective.

5. If the interval between the arrival of the two sounds is 1 ms or less, the precedence effect does not operate; instead, an average or compromise location is heard. This is called "summing localization" (Blauert, 1997).

6. If the lagging sound is made sufficiently intense (10–15 dB higher in level than the leading sound), it overrides the precedence effect and is heard as a separate event. However, it would be very rare in everyday life for an echo to be 10 dB higher in level than the leading sound.

7. It is usually assumed that the precedence effect works most effectively when the leading and lagging sounds are qualitatively similar. However, Divenyi (1992), using sounds presented via headphones, showed that a leading sound could disrupt the lateralization of a lagging sound (on the basis of ITD) even when the two sounds differed markedly in spectrum (the sounds had similar temporal envelopes). In particular, a low-frequency leading sound was very effective in disrupting lateralization of a higher-frequency lagging sound. This was explained in terms of "localization strength"; a leading sound that is localized precisely can have a strong disruptive effect on the localization of a lagging sound that is localized less precisely. A finding apparently contradicting this idea was reported by Yang and Grantham (1997). They showed that, for sounds present via loudspeakers in an anechoic chamber, a leading sound only disrupted localization of a lagging sound when there was spectral overlap of the leading and lagging sounds. They suggested that localization strength is important when sounds are presented via headphones and lateralization is manipulated by changing ITDs. However, for loudspeaker presentation, when both ITD and ILD cues are available, spectral overlap is critical.

8. The precedence effect is usually described as resulting from the processing of ITDs and ILDs. However, Rakerd et al. (2000) have shown that echo suppression occurs when both the leading and lagging sounds are in the median plane. In this case, there is no interaural disparity for either the leading or the lagging sound.

9. The precedence effect can take some time to build up (Freyman et al., 1991). For example, if the leading sound is a single click followed by a simulated echo click with a delay of 8 ms, both clicks are clearly heard. However, if the click pair is presented repeatedly at a rate of, say, 4/s, then after a few presentations the lagging click is no longer heard as a separate event.

10. Changes in the acoustical conditions can cause the precedence effect to break down temporarily (Thurlow and Parks, 1961; Clifton, 1987; Keen and Freyman, 2009). Say, for example, that a leading click is presented from a loudspeaker to the left and a lagging click (simulating an echo) is presented from a loudspeaker to the right. If the click pair is presented repeatedly, the precedence effect builds up, as described earlier. However, if the positions of the leading and lagging sounds are then abruptly swapped, the precedence effect breaks down; each click is heard as a separate event. Then, after a few more presentations, the effect builds up once more, and only a single event is heard. This has been called the "Clifton effect" or the "Keen effect" (since Clifton changed her name to Keen). It may be comparable with the "resetting" of binaural adaptation described in Section 3E.

11. The precedence effect does not involve a complete suppression of information about echoes. Listeners can easily hear the difference between a sound with echoes and one without echoes. Also, changes in the pattern of the echoes can be readily detected. Indeed, the pattern may supply information about room acoustics and the positions of walls and objects in a room (Benade, 1976). Suppression of echoes occurs in two main senses: the echoes are not heard as separate events, and information about the spatial location of the echoes is partially or completely lost.

The phenomena described in 9 and 10 above have led to the suggestion that the precedence effect does not depend on a mechanism that is "hard wired", although physiological correlates of the effect have been reported (Litovsky et al., 1997, 1999; Litovsky, 1998; Xia et al., 2010). The effect may partly reflect relatively high-level cognitive processes (Clifton et al., 1994; Blauert, 1997; Clifton and Freyman, 1997; Hartmann, 1997a; Keen and Freyman, 2009). It appears that echoes are only suppressed when they are consistent with listeners' expectations about the sound source and the room acoustics. These expectations can be influenced by sounds heard previously. Echoes become harder to hear when there is a succession of identical lead-lag events (point 9 above), presumably because each successive pair of events provides additional consistent information about the room acoustics. However, rapid changes in the sounds, such as that produced by switching the positions of the leading and lagging events, create an acoustical situation inconsistent with the built-up expectations and cause the echo to be heard as a separate event. Changes in the spectrum of the echo that signify an unusual change in room acoustics can restore audibility of the echo (Clifton and Freyman, 1997). Also, changes in the direction of incidence of the echo can make the echo audible (Blauert, 1997).

The precedence effect plays an important role in our perception of everyday sounds. It enables us to locate, interpret, and identify sounds in spite of wide variations in the acoustical conditions in which we hear them. Without it, listening in reverberant rooms would be an extremely confusing experience. Sometimes, however, the effect can be an inconvenience! An example of this is found in the stereophonic reproduction of music. The stereo information in conventional recordings is coded almost entirely in terms of intensity differences in the two channels; time disparities are eliminated as far as possible. If the sound originates in one channel only, then the sound is clearly located toward that channel. If the sound is equally intense in both channels, then the sound is located in the center, between the two channels, provided the loudspeakers are equidistant from the listener; this is an example of the summing localization described in point 5 above. If, however, the listener is slightly closer to one loudspeaker than to the other, the sound from that loudspeaker leads in time, and if the time disparity exceeds 1 ms, the precedence effect operates; the sound appears to originate entirely from the nearer loudspeaker. In a normal room this gives the listener a latitude of about 60 cm on either side of the central position. Deviations greater than this produce significant changes in the "stereo image". Almost all of the sound (except that originating entirely from the farther loudspeaker) appears to come from the closer loudspeaker. Thus, the notion of the "stereo seat" is quite close to the truth.

7 GENERAL CONCLUSIONS ON SOUND LOCALIZATION

The auditory system is capable of using a great variety of physical cues to determine the location of a sound source. Time and intensity differences at the two ears, changes in the spectral composition of sounds due to head shadow and pinna effects, and changes in all of these cues produced by head or sound source movements can all influence the perceived direction of a sound source. In laboratory studies, usually just one or two of these cues are isolated. In this way it has been shown that sometimes a single cue may be sufficient for accurate localization of a sound source. In other experiments, one cue has been opposed by another, in order to investigate the relative importance of the cues or to determine whether the cues are encoded along some common neural dimension. These experiments have shown that, in some senses, the cues are not equivalent, but, on the other hand, they may also not be independent.

Wightman and Kistler (1992) conducted an experiment to determine the relative importance of the various cues for localization. Listeners judged the apparent directions of virtual sound sources presented over earphones. The sounds had been processed using measured HRTFs (see Section 5) so as to reproduce at the eardrum the sounds that would be produced by "real" sound sources located in various positions relative to the listener. In a control condition, all of the normal cues for localization were present, i.e., ITDs, ILDs, and spectral cues produced by the pinnae. Under these conditions, the perceived location generally corresponded well to the intended location. When ITDs were processed to oppose interaural intensity and pinna cues, the apparent direction usually followed the ITD cue, as long as the wideband stimuli included low frequencies. With low frequencies removed, apparent direction was determined primarily by ILD and pinna cues. For everyday sounds, which usually include low frequencies, it seems likely that ITDs play a dominant role.

For real sound sources, such as speech or music, all of the cues described earlier may be available simultaneously. However, in this situation they do not provide conflicting cues; rather, the multiplicity of cues makes the location of the sound sources more definite and more accurate.

8 BINAURAL MASKING LEVEL DIFFERENCES

The masked threshold of a signal can sometimes be markedly lower when listening with two ears than when listening with one. Consider the situation shown in Fig. 7.10a. White noise from the same noise generator is fed to both ears via stereo headphones. A pure tone, also from the same signal generator, is fed separately to each ear and mixed with the noise. Thus, the total signals at the two ears are identical. Assume that the level of the tone is adjusted until it is just masked by the noise, i.e., it is at its masked threshold, and let its level at this point be L_0 dB. Assume now that the signal (the tone) at one ear only is inverted, i.e., the waveform is turned upside down. This is equivalent to

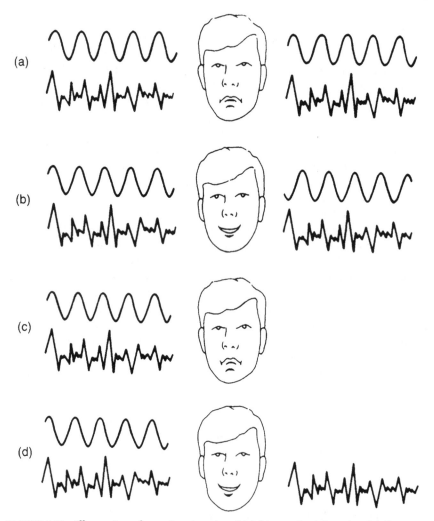

FIGURE 7.10 Illustration of two situations in which binaural masking level differences occur. In conditions (a) and (c) detectability is poor, while in conditions (b) and (d), where the interaural relations of the signal and masker are different, detectability is good (hence the smiling faces).

shifting the phase of the signal by 180° or π radians (see Fig. 7.10b). The result is that the tone becomes audible again. The tone can be adjusted to a new level, L_π, so that it is once again at its masked threshold. The difference between the two levels, $L_0 - L_\pi$ (dB), is known as a masking level difference (MLD), and its value may be as large as 15 dB at low frequencies (around

500 Hz), decreasing to 2–3 dB for frequencies above 1500 Hz (Durlach and Colburn, 1978). Thus, simply by inverting the signal waveform at one ear the signal can be made considerably more detectable.

An example that is perhaps more surprising is given in Fig. 7.10c. The noise and signal are fed to one ear only, and the signal is adjusted to be at its masked threshold. Now the noise alone is added at the other ear; the tone becomes audible once again (Fig. 7.10d)! Thus, by adding noise at the nonsignal ear the tone is made considerably more detectable. Further, the tone disappears when it, too, is added to the second ear, making the sounds at the two ears the same. Notice that it is important that the same noise is added to the nonsignal ear; the noises at the two ears must be derived from the same noise generator. Release from masking is not obtained when an independent noise (derived from a second noise generator) is added to the nonsignal ear.

The phenomenon of the MLD is not limited to pure tones. Similar effects have been observed for complex tones, clicks, and speech sounds. Whenever the phase or level differences of the signal at the two ears are not the same as those of the masker, the ability to detect and identify the signal is improved relative to the case where the signal and masker have the same phase and level relationships at the two ears. Such differences only occur in real situations when the signal and masker are located in different positions in space. Thus, one implication of the MLD phenomenon is that the detection and discrimination of signals, including speech, are improved when the signal and masker are not coincident in space. The MLD thus plays a role in the "cocktail party" effect—the ability to attend to one voice in a situation where many people are talking at once (the cocktail party effect is also strongly influenced by informational masking. The effect of spatial factors on the informational masking of speech is discussed in Chapter 9, Section 8). However, it appears that the MLD is not merely another aspect of our ability to localize sounds, because the largest MLDs occur with the situation of phase inversion (see above), which only occurs naturally for mid-frequency pure tones at highly restricted angular locations. Further, large MLDs occur in situations where the signal and masker are not subjectively well separated in space (see later).

At this point I must introduce some terminology. When the relative phase of the signal at the two ears is the same as the relative phase of the masker, the condition is called "homophasic". When the phase relations are opposite (e.g., one is inverted and the other is not), the term "antiphasic" is used. In general, a particular situation can be described by using the symbols N (for noise) and S (for signal), each being followed by a suffix denoting relative phase at the two ears. A phase inversion is equivalent to a phase shift of $180°$ or π radians. Thus, N_0S_0 refers to the condition where both the noise and the signal are in phase at the two ears (Fig. 7.10a), and N_0S_π refers to the condition where

TABLE 7.1.   Values of the MLD for various interaural relationships of the signal and masker

Interaural condition	MLD (dB)
$N_u S_\pi$	3
$N_u S_0$	4
$N_\pi S_m$	6
$N_0 S_m$	9
$N_\pi S_0$	13
$N_0 S_\pi$	15

These results are typical for broadband maskers and low-frequency signals.

the noise is in phase at the two ears but the signal is inverted in phase (Fig. 7.10(b). N_u means that the noise is uncorrelated at the two ears. The suffix m indicates monaural presentation, i.e., presentation to one ear only. Table 7.1 gives the magnitude of the MLD for a variety of combinations of signal and noise. Four conditions for which there is no binaural advantage, $N_0 S_0$, $N_m S_m$, $N_u S_m$, and $N_\pi S_\pi$, all give about the same "reference" threshold. The MLDs for the conditions shown in the table are obtained by expressing thresholds relative to this reference threshold.

One general finding that has emerged from studies of the MLD is that the largest effects are usually found for low signal frequencies, although large MLDs can occur for high signal frequencies when the masker is a narrowband noise (McFadden et al., 1972). For broadband noise maskers, the MLD falls to 2–3 dB for signal frequencies above about 1500 Hz, and it is noteworthy that this is also the highest frequency for which we are able to compare phases at the two ears in localizing sounds. Thus, it is likely that the MLD depends at least in part on the transmission of temporal information about the stimulus to some higher neural center that compares the temporal information from the two ears.

For a wideband masker, not all of the frequency components are effective; just as was the case for monaural masking (see Chapter 3), only those components in a certain frequency range around the signal frequency are effective in masking it. Further, the release from masking in MLD conditions seems to depend only on the characteristics of the noise in a band around the signal frequency. There has been some disagreement as to whether the binaural critical bandwidth is the same as the monaural critical bandwidth. Some experiments have suggested that the binaural critical bandwidth is greater than the monaural critical bandwidth, while others have shown similar monaural and binaural critical bandwidths (Hall et al., 1983; Hall and Fernandes, 1984; Zurek and Durlach, 1987; Kohlrausch, 1988; Kolarik and

Culling, 2010). Hall *et al.* (1983) suggested that the peripheral auditory filter is the same for monaural and binaural detection, but binaural detection may depend on the output of more than one auditory filter. A similar suggestion has been made by Breebaart *et al.* (2001a).

In addition to improving the detectability of tones, conditions that produce MLDs also favor other aspects of our ability to analyze signals. For example, when speech signals are presented against noisy backgrounds, speech intelligibility is better under antiphasic conditions than under homophasic conditions (Hirsh, 1950; Levitt and Rabiner, 1967). Gebhardt and Goldstein (1972) measured frequency DLs for tones presented against noise backgrounds and found that, for a given signal-to-noise ratio, antiphasic DLs were substantially smaller than homophasic ones when the signals were close to masked threshold. Thus, antiphasic conditions improve our ability to identify and discriminate signals, as well as to detect them.

The relative importance of spatial factors in the MLD was investigated by Carhart *et al.* (1969b). They measured thresholds for identifying one- and two-syllable speech sounds in the presence of four simultaneous maskers. Two of the maskers were modulated white noise and two were whole sentences. They used several different listening conditions, including homophasic, antiphasic, and those where the signal or the maskers were delayed at one ear relative to the other. In these latter conditions, the different maskers were sometimes given opposing time delays, so that some would be located toward one ear and some toward the other. Sometimes the signal was subjectively well separated in location from the masking sounds, and under these conditions subjects reported the task of identifying the signal to be easier. However, the largest MLDs were obtained for the antiphasic condition, where there is no clear separation in the subjective locations; rather, the sound images are located diffusely within the head. Thus, escape from masking and lateralization/localization seem, to some extent, to be separate capacities.

It has been reported that MLDs occur for both forward and backward masking (Dolan and Trahiotis, 1972; Small *et al.*, 1972). Substantial MLDs (4–5 dB) are found for silent intervals between the signal and the masker of up to 40 ms.

9 THE SLUGGISHNESS OF THE BINAURAL SYSTEM

A number of investigators have studied the ability of subjects to follow changes in the location of stimuli over time, i.e., to perceive movements of a sound source. Most of these studies have shown that only rather slow changes in location can be followed consciously, a phenomenon that has been described as "binaural sluggishness". An example is provided by the binaural beats described in Section 2C; for frequency differences between the ears exceeding about 2 Hz, the sound is not heard to move between the two ears, but is heard as a wobbling sound in a fixed location.

Perrott and Musicant (1977) and Grantham (1986) have measured the "minimum audible movement angle" (MAMA), defined as the angle through which a sound source has to move for it to be distinguished from a stationary source. For low rates of movement (15°/s) the MAMA is about 5°, but as the rate of movement increases, the MAMA increases progressively to about 21° for a rate of 90°/s. Thus, the binaural system is relatively insensitive to movements at high rates.

Blauert (1972) used as a stimulus a pulse train of 80 pulses/s, presented binaurally via earphones. Either the ITD or the interaural amplitude difference (IAD) was varied sinusoidally. For low rates of variation, the sound source was heard as moving alternately to the left and right. However, when the rate was increased, the movement could not be followed. Blauert found that the highest rate at which movement could be followed "in detail" was 2.4 Hz for the varying ITD and 3.1 Hz for the varying IAD.

Grantham and Wightman (1978) measured the ability to follow movements in a noise that was lowpass filtered at 3000 Hz. The ITD was varied sinusoidally at a rate f_m. The peak ITD, determining the extent of movement, was varied to determine the threshold for distinguishing the moving stimulus from a stationary reference stimulus. The threshold ITD increased from 30 to 90 μs as f_m increased from 0 to 20 Hz. Again, this indicates that slow movements can be followed well, but rapid movements are more difficult to follow.

The sensitivity to changes in interaural cues has also been determined by measuring MLDs. Grantham and Wightman (1979) measured thresholds for detecting a brief tone that was phase inverted at one ear relative to the other (S_π). The masker was a noise whose correlation between the two ears could be varied continuously between +1 (N_0) and −1 (N_π). The correlation was made to vary sinusoidally at rate f_m. The signal was presented at various points in the masker's modulation cycle. For $f_m = 0$ Hz (fixed interaural correlation), the signal threshold decreased monotonically as the masker's interaural correlation changed from −1 to +1. The decrease, corresponding to an MLD ($N_\pi S_\pi - N_0 S_\pi$), was 20, 16, and 8 dB for signals at 250, 500, and 1000 Hz, respectively. For $f_m > 0$, the function relating signal threshold to the masker's interaural correlation at the moment of signal presentation became progressively flatter with increasing f_m for all signal frequencies. For $f_m = 4$ Hz, the function was flat; there was no measurable effect of masker interaural correlation on the signal threshold. Again, these results indicate that the binaural system is slow in its response to changes in interaural stimulation.

In summary, these and other experiments (Kollmeier and Gilkey, 1990; Culling and Summerfield, 1998; Akeroyd and Summerfield, 1999; Culling and Colburn, 2000) indicate that the binaural system often responds sluggishly to changes in interaural time, intensity, or correlation. However, it seems that the binaural system does not always behave in a sluggish manner. In some tasks, the auditory system appears to respond rapidly to changes in interaural parameters (Akeroyd and Bernstein, 2001; Bernstein et al., 2001; Siveke et al., 2008). Bernstein et al. (2001) suggested that different tasks may result in different time constants because they tap different aspects of binaural temporal processing.

10 MODELS OF BINAURAL PROCESSING

Many different models have been proposed to account for various aspects of binaural processing, including sound localization and MLDs. Some models to account for MLDs have not attempted explanations at the physiological level. Rather they have been "black box" models, assuming that the auditory system is capable of certain types of processing without specifying exactly how it is done. Examples of models of this type are the Webster–Jeffress model (Webster, 1951; Jeffress, 1971, 1972) and the equalization-cancellation model (Durlach, 1963, 1972). Other models have attempted to explain localization and MLDs in terms of neural mechanisms (Colburn, 1977, 1996; Stern and Trahiotis, 1995; Breebaart et al., 2001b). The recent models can account for a great variety of data on binaural processing, including the localization and lateralization of sounds, MLDs, and binaural sluggishness.

These models are complex, and it is beyond the scope of this book to describe them fully. Briefly, they assume that neural spike patterns are compared for neurons with corresponding CFs in the two ears. It is often assumed that, at each CF, there is an array of delay lines that can delay the neural spikes from one ear relative to those from the other; each delay line has a characteristic time delay. These are followed by coincidence detectors, which count the numbers of spikes arriving synchronously from the two ears. If a sound is delayed by a time τ at the left ear relative to the right, then a delay of τ in the neural spikes from the right ear will cause the spikes from the left and right ears to be synchronous at the point of binaural interaction. Thus, the ITD of the signal is coded in terms of which delay line gives the highest response in the coincidence detectors.

This type of model was originally proposed to account for the ability to use ITDs in localizing sounds (Jeffress, 1948), but it has since been extended to account for MLDs and other aspects of binaural processing. It is useful to think of the outputs of the coincidence detectors as providing a kind of two-dimensional display; one of the dimensions is CF and the other is the interaural delay. The response to any stimulus is a pattern of activity in this display. When a signal and a masker have the same ITD, τ, then they produce activity at overlapping points in the pattern; most activity lies around a line of equal delay (τ) versus CF. When a signal and masker have different ITDs, the pattern is more complex. The addition of the signal to the masker may cause activity to appear at points in the pattern where there was little activity for the masker alone. This could enhance the detection of the signal, giving an MLD. For further details, the reader is referred to Colburn (1996) and Stern and Trahiotis (1995).

11 THE INFLUENCE OF VISION ON AUDITORY LOCALIZATION

A stationary sound source is usually perceived as having a fixed position in space. If the head is moved, the sound arriving at the two ears changes, but the sound image remains stationary in space. Somehow, information about the position of the head is combined with information about the sound location relative to the head to arrive at a constant percept. Vision can play an important role in this process by helping to define the position of the head in space. This is vividly illustrated by some experiments of Wallach (1940). His subjects had their heads fixed in the vertical axis of a cylindrical screen that rotated about them. The screen was covered in vertical stripes, and, after watching the movement of these for a few moments, the subjects would perceive themselves as in constant rotation and the screen as at rest. A stationary sound source was then activated straight ahead of the subjects. This sound was perceived as lying directly *above* or *below* the subjects.

The perception seems to result from the brain trying to determine a location of the source that is consistent with all of the sensory evidence. The subjects in this situation perceive themselves as moving, but the sound arriving at the two ears has no interaural disparity and is not changing. This can only occur for a sound source lying directly above or below them. If the sound source is at a constant azimuth (e.g., 20° to the left of the subject), the sound source cannot be interpreted as lying above the subject, since interaural differences of time and intensity now exist. Instead, the source is perceived as rotating with the subject at an elevation that is approximately the complement of the constant azimuth (in this case at an elevation of about 70°). Thus, the interpretation of auditory spatial cues is strongly influenced by perceived visual orientation. Or, more correctly, the highest level of spatial representation involves an integration of information from the different senses.

12 THE PERCEPTION OF DISTANCE

Just as was the case for judgments of lateral position, there are a number of cues that can be used in judging the distance of a sound source; for a review, see Zahorik et al. (2005). For familiar sounds, sound level may give a crude indication of distance from the listener. This cue appears to be most effective when multiple sound sources are present, so that comparison of the levels of different sources is possible (Mershon and King, 1975). Ashmead et al. (1990) have shown that listeners can discriminate differences in the distance of a sound source as well as could be expected from optimal use of intensity cues. Ashmead et al. (1995) have shown that the change in intensity that occurs when a listener walks toward a sound source can provide an absolute cue to distance. This cue is effective even when the overall intensity of the source is varied randomly from trial to trial.

Over moderate distances, the spectrum of a complex sound source may be changed, owing to the absorbing properties of the air; high frequencies are attenuated more than low. The effective use of this cue depends on familiarity with the sounds (Coleman, 1962, 1963). This cue appears to be effective for judging the relative distances of sound sources, but not for judging their absolute distances (Little et al., 1992). For sounds that are close to the head, the larger than normal ILDs (especially at low frequencies) provide a cue for distance (Brungart, 1999; Brungart et al., 1999).

The cues described above could be used to judge the distance of a sound source in free space. Often, we listen in rooms with reflecting walls. In this case, the ratio of direct to reflected sound and the time delay between direct and reflected sound provide cues to distance. Von Békésy (1960) showed that altering these quantities produced the impression of sounds moving toward or away from the listener. The work of Wallach et al. (1949) and others on the precedence effect (Section 6) showed that echoes are not usually perceived as separate sound events; rather they are fused with the leading sound. However, we are still able to use information from echoes to judge distance, in spite of this perceptual fusion. Mershon and Bowers (1979) have shown that the ratio of direct to reflected sound can be used to judge absolute as well as relative distance and that this cue can be used even for the first presentation of an unfamiliar sound in an unfamiliar environment. Also, since reflection from most surfaces is frequency dependent, the spectrum of the reflected sound may differ from that of the direct sound, and this may provide a distance cue (Zahorik, 2002).

It can be concluded that, just as was the case for judgments of the direction of sound sources, judgments of distance may depend on a multiplicity of cues. The results of Zahorik (2002) suggest that information from the different cues is combined, but the perceptual weight assigned to two of the major cues (level and the ratio of direct to reflected sound) varies substantially as a function of both sound source type (noise versus speech) and angular position (0° or 90° azimuth). His results suggest that the cue weighting process is flexible and able to adapt to individual distance cues that vary as a result of source properties and environmental conditions.

Finally, it should be noted that judgments of distance are relatively inaccurate, and errors of the order of 20% are not uncommon for unfamiliar sound sources. Also, for nearby sound sources, the distance tends to be overestimated, while for far away sources the distance tends to be underestimated (Zahorik, 2002).

13 GENERAL CONCLUSIONS

In this chapter, I have discussed the cues and the mechanisms involved in the localization of sounds. Our acuity in locating sounds is greatest in the horizontal plane (azimuth), fairly good in the vertical plane (elevation), and poorest for distance. For each of these, we are able to use a number of distinct cues, although the cues may differ depending on the type of sound.

For localization in the horizontal plane, the cues of interaural time and intensity difference are most important. ITD is most useful at low frequencies, while ILD is most useful at high frequencies. However, transient sounds, or periodic sounds with low repetition rates, can be localized on the basis of ITD even when they contain only high frequencies. For periodic sounds, the binaural system shows a form of adaptation; judgments of position in space depend mostly on the leading part of the sound and less on later parts. This adaptation is more rapid for stimuli with high repetition rates. A recovery from adaptation may be produced by a weak "trigger" whose spectral characteristics differ from those of the test sound.

Judgments of the location of a sound covering a restricted frequency range can be adversely affected by the presence of an interfering sound in a different frequency range, when the interfering sound provides conflicting binaural cues. This binaural interference effect may partly result from perceptual fusion of the target and interfering sounds.

The direction-dependent filtering produced by the pinnae is important for judgments of location in the vertical direction and for front-back discrimination. It is also important for creating the percept of a sound outside the head, rather than inside. Reverberation also contributes to this percept.

The multiplicity of cues to sound location provides a certain redundancy in the system, so that even under very difficult conditions (reverberant rooms or brief sounds) we are still capable of quite accurate localization.

Binaural processing, using information relating to the differences of the signals at the two ears, can improve our ability to detect and analyze signals in noisy backgrounds. This is illustrated by laboratory studies of the binaural MLD. Binaural processing also helps to suppress room echoes and to locate sound sources in reverberant rooms.

The binaural system is often rather sluggish in responding to changes in interaural time or intensity. Thus, we are relatively insensitive to the motion of sound sources. However, in some tasks, the binaural system appears to respond more rapidly.

Judgments of auditory location may be influenced by visual cues. The perceived position of a sound in space is determined by a combination of information from the visual and auditory systems.

Judgments of the distance of sound sources depend on a variety of cues including absolute intensity, changes in intensity with distance (especially dynamic changes), changes in spectrum with distance, enlarged ILDs for sounds close to the head, and the ratio of direct to reverberant sound.

FURTHER RESOURCES

Extensive reviews of data and models related to binaural hearing can be found in:

Durlach, N. I., and Colburn, H. S. (1978). Binaural phenomena. In E. C. Carterette & M. P. Friedman (Eds.), *Handbook of Perception* (Vol. IV). New York: Academic Press.

Colburn, H. S., and Durlach, N. I. (1978). Models of binaural interaction. In E. C. Carterette & M. P. Friedman (Eds.), *Handbook of Perception* (Vol. IV). New York: Academic.

Grantham, D. W. (1995). Spatial hearing and related phenomena. In B. C. J. Moore (Ed.), *Hearing*. New York: Academic.

Stern, R. M., and Trahiotis, C. (1995). Models of binaural interaction. In B. C. J. Moore (Ed.), *Hearing*. New York: Academic.

Blauert, J. (1997). *Spatial Hearing: The Psychophysics of Human Sound Localization*. Cambridge, MA: MIT Press.

Gilkey, R., and Anderson, T. (1997). *Binaural and Spatial Hearing*. Hillsdale, NJ: Erlbaum.

A review of the precedence effect can be found in:

Litovsky, R. Y., Colburn, H. S., Yost, W. A., and Guzman, S. J. (1999). The precedence effect. *J. Acoust. Soc. Am.*, *106*, 1633–1654.

Demonstrations 35–38 of Auditory Demonstrations on CD are relevant to this chapter (see the list of further resources for Chapter 1).

A CD of sound illustrations published as a supplement to Acustica – Acta Acustica (volume 82, number 2, 1996) contains demonstrations of localization, the precedence effect, the Clifton effect, and binaural adaptation. These demonstrations were produced by R. O. Duda.

CHAPTER 8

Auditory Pattern and Object Perception

1 INTRODUCTION

So far I have described several attributes of auditory sensation, such as pitch, subjective location, and loudness, that can be related in a reasonably straightforward way to the physical properties of stimuli. In many cases I have discussed the neural code that may underlie the perception of these attributes. In everyday life, however, we do not perceive these attributes in isolation. Rather, the auditory world is analyzed into discrete sound sources or auditory objects, each of which may have its own pitch, timbre, location, and loudness. Sometimes the source may be recognized as familiar in some way, such as a particular person talking; often the "object" perceived may be identified, for example, as a particular spoken word or a violin playing a specific piece of music. This chapter discusses four related aspects of auditory object and pattern perception: (1) factors involved in the identification of a single object among a large set of possible objects; (2) cues that are used to analyze a complex mixture of sounds into discrete sources; (3) the perception of sequences of sounds; and (4) "rules" that govern the perceptual organization of the auditory world.

2 TIMBRE PERCEPTION AND OBJECT IDENTIFICATION

Many of the attributes of sensation I have described so far, such as pitch and loudness, may be considered as uni-dimensional: if we are presented with a large variety of sounds with different pitches, it is possible to order all of the sounds on a single scale of pitch going from low to high (this is not quite true for complex tones; see Shepard, 1964). Similarly, sounds differing in loudness can be ordered on a single scale going from quiet to loud. Our ability to identify one object from among a large set of objects depends on there being several dimensions along which the objects vary. When a set of stimuli vary along a single dimension, we can only name (attach a verbal label to) the individual stimuli in the set when their number is less than about 5–6. For example, Pollack (1952) investigated the ability of subjects to name musical tones with different pitches, as a function of the number of possible tones. He found that they could only do this reliably when the number of possible tones was less than 5–6. This was true whether the tones were spread over a wide frequency range of several octaves or were concentrated in a relatively narrow range, say, one octave (subjects with absolute pitch do better in this task).

In order to identify more stimuli than this, extra dimensions are required. In hearing, the extra dimensions arise in two main ways. First, for complex stimuli the patterning of energy as a function of frequency is important. Secondly, auditory stimuli typically vary with time, and the temporal patterning can be of crucial importance to perception.

2A TIME-INVARIANT PATTERNS

If a single, steady sinusoid is presented, then the sound pattern can be described by just two numbers specifying frequency and intensity. However, almost all of the sounds that we encounter in everyday life are considerably more complex than this and contain a multitude of frequency components with particular levels and relative phases. The distribution of energy over frequency is one of the major determinants of the quality of a sound or its timbre. Timbre has been defined as "that attribute of auditory sensation which enables a listener to judge that two nonidentical sounds, similarly presented and having the same loudness and pitch, are dissimilar" (ANSI, 1994a).

Differences in timbre enable us to distinguish between the same note played on, say, the piano, the violin, or the flute.

Timbre as defined above depends on more than just the magnitude spectrum of the sound; fluctuations over time can play an important role, and I discuss the effects of these in Section 2B. For the purpose of this section, I adopt a more restricted definition suggested by Plomp (1970): "Timbre is that attribute of sensation in terms of which a listener can judge that two steady complex tones having the same loudness, pitch and duration are dissimilar". Timbre defined in this way depends mainly on the relative magnitudes of the partials of the tones.

Unlike pitch or loudness, which may be considered as uni-dimensional, timbre is multidimensional; there is no single scale along which we can compare or order the timbres of different sounds. Thus, a method is needed for describing the spectrum of a sound that takes into account this multidimensional aspect and that can be related to the subjective timbre. A crude first approach is to look at the overall distribution of spectral energy. For example, complex tones with strong lower harmonics (below the sixth) sound mellow, whereas tones with strong harmonics beyond the sixth or seventh sound sharp and penetrating. However, a much more quantitative approach has been described by Plomp and his colleagues (Plomp, 1970, 1976; Plomp et al., 1967; Pols et al., 1969). They showed that the perceptual differences between different sounds, such as vowels or steady tones produced by musical instruments, were closely related to the differences in the spectra of the sounds, when the spectra were specified as the levels in 18 1/3-octave frequency bands. A bandwidth of 1/3 octave is slightly greater than the critical bandwidth, or the value of ERB_N, over most of the audible frequency range. Thus, timbre is related to the relative level produced by a sound in each critical band. Put another way, the timbre of a sound is related to the excitation pattern of that sound (see Chapter 3).

It is likely that the number of dimensions required to characterize timbre is limited by the number of critical bands required to cover the audible frequency range. This would give a maximum of about 37 dimensions. For a restricted class of sounds, however, a much smaller number of dimensions may be involved. It appears to be generally true, for both speech and nonspeech sounds, that the timbres of steady tones are determined primarily by their magnitude spectra, although the relative phases of the components also play a small role (Plomp and Steeneken, 1969; Darwin and Gardner, 1986; Patterson, 1987a).

2B Time-varying Patterns

Although differences in static timbre may enable us to distinguish between two sounds that are presented successively, they are not always sufficient to allow the absolute identification of an "auditory object", such as a specific musical instrument. One reason for this is that the magnitude and phase spectrum of the sound may be markedly altered by the transmission path and room reflections. In practice, the recognition of a particular timbre, and hence of an "auditory object", may depend upon several other factors. Schouten (1968) has suggested that these include: (1) whether the sound is periodic, having a tonal quality for repetition rates between about 20 and 20,000/s, or irregular, having a noise-like character; (2) whether the waveform envelope is constant or fluctuates as a function of time, and in the latter case what the fluctuations are like; (3) whether any other aspect of the sound (e.g., spectrum or periodicity) is changing as a function of time; and (4) what the preceding and following sounds are like.

The recognition of musical instruments, for example, depends quite strongly on onset transients and on the temporal structure of the sound envelope (Risset and Wessel, 1999). The characteristic tone of a piano depends on the fact that the notes have a rapid onset and a gradual decay. If a recording of a piano is reversed in time, the timbre is completely different. It now resembles that of a harmonium or accordion, in spite of the fact that the long-term magnitude spectrum is unchanged by time reversal. The perception of sounds with temporally asymmetric envelopes has been studied by Patterson (1994a,b). He used sinusoidal carriers that were amplitude modulated by a repeating exponential function. The envelope either increased abruptly and decayed gradually ("damped" sounds) or increased gradually and decayed abruptly ("ramped" sounds). The ramped sounds were time-reversed versions of the damped sounds and had the same long-term magnitude spectrum. The sounds were characterized by the repetition period of the envelope, which was 25 ms, and by the "half-life". For a damped sinusoid, the half-life is the time taken for the amplitude to decrease by a factor of two. Examples of sounds with half-lives of 1, 4, and 16 ms are shown in Fig. 8.1.

Patterson reported that, for half-lives in the range 2–32 ms, the ramped and damped sounds had different qualities. For a half-life of 4 ms, the damped sound was perceived as a single source rather like a drum roll played on a hollow, resonant surface (like a drummer's wood block). The ramped sound was perceived as two sounds: a drum roll on a nonresonant surface (such as a leather table top) and a continuous tone corresponding to the carrier frequency. Akeroyd and Patterson (1995) used sounds with similar envelopes, but the carrier was broadband noise rather than a sinusoid. They reported that the damped sound was heard as a drum struck by wire brushes. It did not have any hiss-like quality. In contrast, the ramped sound was heard as a noise, with a hiss-like quality, that was sharply cut off in time. These experiments clearly demonstrate the important role of temporal envelope in timbre perception.

Many instruments have noise-like qualities that strongly influence their subjective quality. A flute, for example, has a relatively simple harmonic

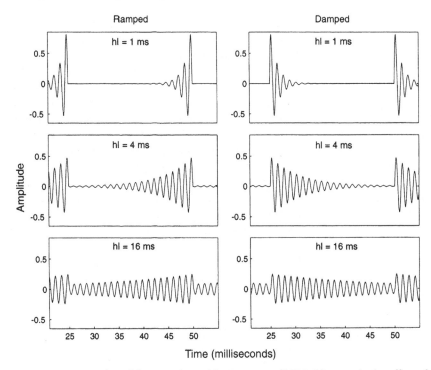

FIGURE 8.1   Examples of the stimuli used by Patterson (1984a,b) to study the effect of temporal envelope on timbre perception.

structure, but synthetic tones with the same harmonic structure do not sound flute-like unless each note is preceded by a small "puff" of noise. In general, tones of standard musical instruments are poorly simulated by the summation of steady component frequencies, since such a synthesis cannot produce the dynamic variation with time characteristic of these instruments. Modern synthesizers shape the envelopes of the sounds they produce and hence are capable of more accurate and convincing imitations of musical instruments. For a simulation to be completely convincing, it is sometimes necessary to give different time envelopes to different harmonics within a complex sound (Handel, 1995; Risset and Wessel, 1999).

3 INFORMATION USED TO SEPARATE AUDITORY OBJECTS

Bregman (1978b) and Bregman and Pinker (1978) have suggested that it is useful to make a distinction between two concepts: source and stream. A source is some physical entity that gives rise to acoustic pressure waves, for example, a violin being played. A stream, on the other hand, is the percept of a group of successive and/or simultaneous sound elements as a coherent whole, appearing to emanate from a single source. For example, it is the percept of hearing a violin being played.

It is hardly ever the case that the sound reaching our ears comes from a single source. Usually the sound arises from several different sources. This is illustrated in Fig. 8.2, which shows the waveforms of several sounds recorded in my laboratory (top four traces) and the waveform resulting from the mixture of those sounds (bottom trace). It is hard to "see" any of the individual sounds in the mixture. However, when listening to all of the sounds together in the laboratory, each can be heard as a separate stream.

As discussed earlier in this book, the peripheral auditory system acts as a frequency analyzer, separating the different frequency components in a complex sound. Somewhere in the brain, the internal representations of these frequency components have to be assigned to their appropriate sources. If the input comes from two sources, A and B, then the frequency components must be split into two groups; the components emanating from source A should be

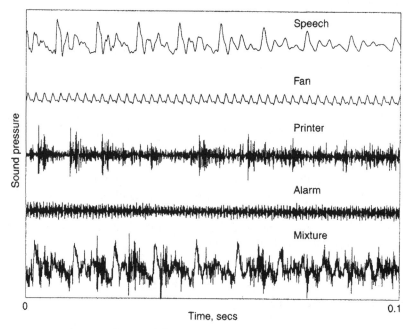

FIGURE 8.2 The waveforms of four individual sounds (top four traces) and the waveform resulting from adding those sounds together.

assigned to one stream and the components emanating from source B should be assigned to another. The process of doing this is often called "perceptual grouping". It is also given the name "parsing" (Bregman and Pinker, 1978) or "auditory scene analysis" (Bregman, 1990). The process of separating the elements arising from two different sources is sometimes called "segregation".

Many different sorts of physical cues may be used to derive separate perceptual streams corresponding to the individual sources that give rise to a complex acoustic input. There are two aspects to this process: "the grouping together of all the simultaneous frequency components that emanate from a single source at a given moment, and the connecting over time of the changing frequencies that a single source produces from one moment to the next" (Bregman and Pinker, 1978). These two aspects are sometimes described as "simultaneous grouping" and "sequential grouping", respectively.

This section considers some of the physical cues that are used to achieve perceptual segregation and grouping, focusing on simultaneous grouping. Section 4 considers cues used for sequential grouping. The physical cues are not completely independent of one another, and no one of them always works perfectly. Section 5 describes the general perceptual rules governing simultaneous and sequential grouping.

One general point should be made about perceptual grouping; it is not an all-or-none process (Darwin and Carlyon, 1995). Most experiments on perceptual grouping are concerned with the effect of one specific attribute of sounds, for example, their pitch, their subjective location, or their timbre, on grouping. These experiments have shown that a cue that is effective for one attribute may be less effective or completely ineffective for another attribute. Also, the effectiveness of the cues may differ for simultaneous and sequential grouping.

3A FUNDAMENTAL FREQUENCY AND SPECTRAL REGULARITY

When we listen to two steady complex tones together (e.g., two musical instruments or two vowel sounds), we do not generally confuse which harmonics belong to which tone. Rather, we hear each tone as a separate source, even though the harmonics may be interleaved and sometimes may even coincide. We can do this only if the two tones have different fundamental frequencies (F0). Broadbent and Ladefoged (1957), in an experiment using synthetic vowels, showed that the normal percept of a single fused voice occurs only if all the harmonics have the same F0. If the harmonics are split into two groups with different F0s, then two separate sounds are heard. Scheffers (1983) has shown that, if two vowels are presented simultaneously, they can be identified better when they have F0s differing by more than 6%

than when they have the same F0. Other researchers have reported similar findings (Assmann and Summerfield, 1990; McKeown and Patterson, 1995).

F0 may be important in several ways. The components in a periodic sound have frequencies that form a simple harmonic series; the frequencies are integer multiples of F0. This property is referred to as "harmonicity". The lower harmonics are resolved in the peripheral auditory system (see Chapter 3, Section 4D). The regular spacing of the lower harmonics may promote their perceptual fusion, causing them to be heard as a single sound. If a sinusoidal component does not form part of this harmonic series, it tends to be heard as a separate sound. This is illustrated by some experiments of Moore *et al.* (1986). They investigated the effect of mistuning a single low harmonic in a harmonic complex tone. When the harmonic was mistuned sufficiently, it was heard as a separate pure tone standing out from the complex as a whole. The degree of mistuning required varied somewhat with the duration of the sounds; for 400-ms tones a mistuning of 3% was sufficient to make the harmonic stand out as a separate tone. Darwin and Gardner (1986) have demonstrated a similar effect for vowel sounds. They also showed that mistuning a harmonic could reduce the contribution of that harmonic to the timbre of the vowel; the effect of the mistuning was similar to the effect of reducing the harmonic in level.

Roberts and Brunstrom (1998, 2001) have presented evidence suggesting that the important feature determining whether a group of frequency components are heard as fused is not harmonicity, but spectral regularity; if a group of components form a regular spectral pattern, they tend to be heard as fused, while if a single component does not "fit" the pattern, it is heard to "pop out". For example, a sequence of components with frequencies 650, 850, 1050, 1250, and 1450 Hz is heard as relatively fused. If the frequency of the middle component is shifted to, say, 1008 or 1092 Hz, that component no longer forms part of the regular pattern, and it tends to be heard as a separate tone, standing out from the complex.

Culling and Darwin (1993, 1994) have suggested that a mechanism other than one based on harmonicity or spectral regularity can play a role in perceptual segregation of lower harmonics. They showed that, for small differences in F0 between two vowels, only the lower frequencies contribute to improved accuracy of vowel identification with increasing difference in F0. They suggested that the improvement occurred because of temporal interactions between the lower harmonics in the two vowels. These interactions, a form of beats (see Chapter 1, Section 2D), have the effect that the neural response to the two vowels is dominated alternately by first one vowel and then the other. The auditory system appears to be able to listen selectively in time to extract a representation of each vowel.

For the higher harmonics in a complex sound, F0 may play a different role. The higher harmonics of a periodic complex sound are not resolved on the basilar membrane, but give rise to a complex waveform with a periodicity equal to F0 (see Fig. 6.6). When two complex sounds with different F0s are presented simultaneously, then each will give rise to waveforms on the basilar membrane with periodicity equal to its respective F0. If the two sounds have different spectra, then each will dominate the response at certain points on the basilar membrane. The auditory system may group together regions with a common F0 and segregate them from regions with a different F0 (Assmann and Summerfield, 1990). It may also be the case that both resolved and unresolved components can be grouped on the basis of the detailed time pattern of the neural spikes (Meddis and Hewitt, 1992).

This process can be explained in a qualitative way by extending the model of pitch perception presented in Chapter 6. Assume that the pitch of a complex tone results from a correlation or comparison of time intervals between successive nerve spikes in neurons with different CFs. Only those "channels" that show a high correlation would be classified as "belonging" to the same sound. Such a mechanism would automatically group together components with a common F0. However, de Cheveigné et al. (1997a) presented evidence against a such a mechanism. They showed that identification of a target vowel in the presence of a background vowel was better when the background was harmonic than when it was inharmonic. In contrast, identification of the target did not depend on whether or not the target was harmonic. de Cheveigné and coworkers (de Cheveigné et al., 1997a,b; de Cheveigné, 1997) proposed a mechanism based on the idea that a harmonic background sound can be "canceled" in the auditory system, thus enhancing the representation of a target vowel. In any case, it should be noted that the ability of the auditory system to segregate a given sound based on F0 information in a given spectral region is limited, as indicated by the phenomenon of pitch discrimination interference (see Chapter 6, Section 8).

3B ONSET DISPARITIES

Rasch (1978) investigated the ability to hear one complex tone in the presence of another. One of the tones was treated as a masker and the level of the signal tone (the higher in F0) was adjusted to find the point where it was just detectable. When the two tones started at the same time and had exactly the same temporal envelope, the threshold of the signal was between 0 and −20 dB relative to the level of the masker (Fig. 8.3a). Thus, when a difference in F0 was the only cue, the signal could not be heard when its level was more than 20 dB below that of the masker.

Rasch also investigated the effect of starting the signal just before the masker (Fig. 8.3b). He found that threshold depended strongly on onset

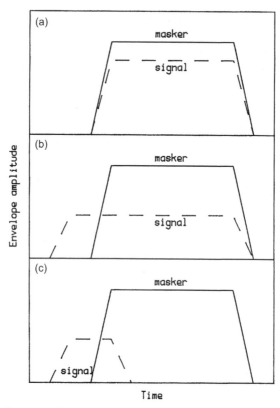

FIGURE 8.3 Schematic illustration of the stimuli used by Rasch (1978). Both the signal and the masker were periodic complex tones, and the signal had a higher fundamental frequency than the masker. When the signal and masker were gated on and off synchronously (panel a), the threshold for detecting the signal was relatively high. When the signal started slightly before the masker (panel b), the threshold was markedly reduced. When the signal was turned off as soon as the masker was turned on (panel c), the signal was perceived as continuing through the masker, and the threshold was the same as when the signal did continue through the masker.

asynchrony, reaching a value of −60 dB for an asynchrony of 30 ms. Thus, when the signal started 30 ms before the masker, it could be heard much more easily and with much greater differences in level between the two tones. It should be emphasized that the lower threshold was a result of the signal occurring for a brief time on its own; essentially performance was limited by backward masking of the 30-ms asynchronous segment, rather than by simultaneous masking. However, the experiment does illustrate the large benefit that can be obtained from a relatively small asynchrony.

Although the percept of his subjects was that the signal continued throughout the masker, Rasch showed that this percept was not based upon sensory information received during the presentation time of the masker. He found that identical thresholds were obtained if the signal was turned off immediately after the onset of the masker (Figure 8.3c). It appears that the perceptual system "assumes" that the signal continues, since there is no evidence to the contrary; the part of the signal that occurs simultaneously with the masker would be completely masked. This effect is related to the continuity phenomenon that was described in Chapter 3, Section 10, and it is discussed further in this chapter (Section 5).

Rasch (1978) showed that, if the two tones have simultaneous onsets but different rise times, this also can give very low thresholds for the signal, provided it has the shorter rise time. Under these conditions and those of onset asynchronies up to 30 ms, the notes sound as though they start synchronously. Thus, we do not need to be consciously aware of the onset differences for the auditory system to be able to exploit them in the perceptual separation of complex tones. Rasch also pointed out that, in ensemble music, different musicians do not play exactly in synchrony even if the score indicates that they should. The onset differences used in his experiments correspond roughly with the onset asynchronies of nominally "simultaneous" notes found in performed music. This supports the view that the asynchronies are an important factor in the perception of the separate parts or voices in polyphonic music.

Onset asynchronies can also play a role in determining the timbre of complex sounds. Darwin and Sutherland (1984) showed that a tone that stops or starts at a different time from a vowel is less likely to be heard as part of that vowel than if it is simultaneous with it. For example, increasing the level of a single harmonic can produce a significant change in the quality (timbre) of a vowel. However, if the incremented harmonic starts before the vowel, the change in vowel quality is markedly reduced. Similarly, Roberts and Moore (1991) showed that extraneous sinusoidal components added to a vowel could influence vowel quality, but the influence was markedly reduced when the extraneous components were turned on before the vowel or turned off after the vowel.

3C Contrast with Previous Sounds

The auditory system seems well suited to the analysis of changes in the sensory input, and particularly to changes in spectrum over time (Kluender et al., 2003; Moore, 2003b). The changed aspect stands out perceptually from the rest. It is possible that there are specialized central mechanisms for detecting changes in spectrum. Additionally, stimulation with a steady sound may result in some kind of adaptation. When some aspect of a stimulus is changed, that aspect is freed from the effects of adaptation and thus will be enhanced perceptually. Although the underlying mechanism is a matter of debate, the perceptual effect certainly is not.

A powerful demonstration of this effect may be obtained by listening to a stimulus with a particular spectral structure and then switching rapidly to a stimulus with a flat spectrum, such as white noise. A white noise heard in isolation may be described as "colorless"; it has no pitch and has a neutral sort of timbre. However, when a white noise follows soon after a stimulus with spectral structure, the noise sounds "colored". The coloration corresponds to

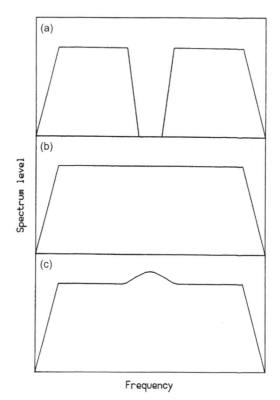

FIGURE 8.4   Schematic illustration of the spectra of stimuli used to demonstrate the effect of contrast with previous sounds. A noise with a spectral notch is presented first (panel a). The stimulus is then changed to a noise with a flat spectrum (panel b). Normally this noise is perceived as "colorless". However, following the noise with the spectral notch it sounds like a noise with a spectral peak, such as that shown in panel c.

the inverse of the spectrum of the preceding sound. For example, if the preceding sound is a noise with a band stop or notch (Fig. 8.4a), the white noise (Fig. 8.4b) has a pitch-like quality, with a pitch value corresponding to the center frequency of the notch (Zwicker, 1964). It sounds like a noise with a small spectral peak (Fig. 8.4c). A harmonic complex tone with a flat spectrum may be given a speech-like quality if it is preceded by a harmonic complex tone with a spectrum that is the inverse of that of a speech sound, such as a vowel (Summerfield et al., 1987).

Another demonstration of the effects of a change in a stimulus can be obtained by listening to a steady complex tone with many harmonics. Usually such a tone is heard with a single pitch corresponding to F0, and the individual harmonics are not separately perceived. However, if one of the harmonics is changed in some way, by altering either its relative phase or its level, then that harmonic stands out perceptually from the complex as a whole. For a short time after the change is made, a pure-tone quality is perceived. The perception of the harmonic then gradually fades, until it merges with the complex once more.

Change detection is obviously of importance in assigning sound components to their appropriate sources. Normally we listen against a background of sounds that may be relatively unchanging, such as the humming of machinery, traffic noises, and so on. A sudden change in the sound is usually indicative that a new source has been activated, and the change detection mechanisms enable us to isolate the effects of the change and interpret them appropriately.

3D Correlated Changes in Amplitude or Frequency

Section 3B described the work of Rasch (1978) showing that the perceptual separation of two complex tones could be enhanced by introducing an onset asynchrony. The threshold of detection of the tone with the higher F0 could be markedly reduced if that tone started 30 ms before the other tone. Rasch also showed that, even when the two tones started synchronously, it was possible to enhance the detection of the tone with higher F0 by frequency modulating it. This modulation was similar to the vibrato that often occurs for musical tones (see Chapter 7, Section 7C), and it was applied so that all the components in the higher tone moved up and down in synchrony. Rasch found that the modulation could reduce the threshold for detecting the higher tone by 17 dB. Thus, when two complex tones are presented simultaneously, the detection of one of the tones can be enhanced if its components are frequency modulated, leaving the other tone steady. A similar effect can be produced by amplitude modulation (AM) of one of the tones. The modulation seems to enhance the salience of the modulated sound, making it appear to stand out from the unmodulated sound.

It seems quite clear that modulation of the components of one sound in amplitude or in frequency can aid the perceptual segregation of that sound from an unchanging background (McAdams, 1982, 1989; Summerfield and Culling, 1992; Moore and Bacon, 1993). What is less clear is whether the perceptual segregation of simultaneous sounds is affected by the coherence of changes in amplitude or frequency when *both* sounds are modulated. Coherence here refers to whether the changes in amplitude or frequency of the two sounds have the same pattern over time or different patterns over time. Several experiments have been reported suggesting that coherence of amplitude changes plays a role; sounds with coherent changes tend to fuse perceptually, whereas sounds with incoherent changes tend to segregate (Bregman et al., 1985; Hall and Grose, 1990; Moore and Shailer, 1991; Moore et al., 1993b). However, Summerfield and Culling (1992) found that the coherence of AM did not affect the identification of pairs of simultaneous vowels when the vowels were composed of components placed randomly in frequency (to avoid effects of harmonicity).

Evidence for a role of FM coherence in perceptual grouping has been more elusive. Although some studies have been interpreted as indicating a weak role for frequency modulation coherence (Cohen and Chen, 1992; Chalikia and Bregman, 1993), the majority of studies have failed to indicate such sensitivity (McAdams, 1989; Carlyon, 1991, 1994; Marin and McAdams, 1991; Summerfield and Culling, 1992; Lyzenga and Moore, 2005). Furukawa and Moore (1996) have shown that the detectability of frequency modulation imposed on two widely separated carrier frequencies is better when the modulation is coherent on the two carriers than when it is incoherent. However, this may occur because the overall pitch evoked by the two carriers fluctuates more when the carriers are modulated coherently than when they are modulated incoherently (Furukawa and Moore, 1997a, 1997b; Carlyon, 2000). There is no clear evidence that the coherence of frequency modulation influences perceptual grouping when both sounds are modulated.

The fusion of components that vary in amplitude in a coherent way can affect the perception of a single harmonic complex tone. Consider a complex tone containing the third, fourth, and fifth harmonics of a 200-Hz F0, namely, 600, 800, and 1000 Hz. This complex tone may be perceived in two ways. We may listen in an analytic mode, hearing the pitches of one or more individual components (Chapter 3, Section 4D), or we may listen in a synthetic mode, hearing a single pitch corresponding to the missing F0 (Chapter 6, Section 4). The analytic mode is more likely if the complex tone is presented continuously or if the complex tone is built up by adding one component at a time. However, the synthetic mode is more likely if all the components in the complex tone are amplitude modulated in the same way; the coherent behavior of the components causes them to be fused into a single percept.

3E SOUND LOCATION

The cues used in sound localization may also help in the analysis of complex auditory inputs. Chapter 7 described a phenomenon that was related to this, namely, the binaural masking level difference (MLD). The phenomenon can be summarized as follows: whenever the phase or level differences of a signal at the two ears are not the same as those of a masker, our ability to detect the signal is improved relative to the case where the signal and masker have the same phase and level relationships at the two ears. The practical implication is that a signal is easier to detect when it is located in a different position in space from the masker. Although most studies of the MLD have been concerned with threshold measurements, it seems clear that similar advantages of binaural listening can be gained in the identification and discrimination of signals presented against a background of other sound.

An example of the use of binaural cues in separating an auditory "object" from its background comes from an experiment by Kubovy et al. (1974). They presented eight continuous sinusoids to each ear via earphones. The sinusoids had frequencies corresponding to the notes in a musical scale, the lowest having a frequency of 300 Hz. The input to one ear, say the left, was presented with a delay of 1 ms relative to the input to the other ear, so the sinusoids were all heard toward the right side of the head. Then, the phase of one of the sinusoids was advanced in the left ear, while its phase in the right ear was delayed, until the input to the left ear led the input to the right ear by 1 ms; this phase-shifting process occurred over a time of 45 ms. The phase remained at the shifted value for a certain time and was then smoothly returned to its original value, again over 45 ms. During the time that the phase shift was present, the phase-shifted sinusoid appeared toward the opposite (left) side of the head, making it stand out perceptually. A sequence of phase shifts in different components was clearly heard as a melody. This melody was completely undetectable when listening to the input to one ear alone. Kubovy et al. interpreted their results as indicating that differences in relative phase at the two ears can allow an auditory "object" to be isolated in the absence of any other cues.

Culling (2000) performed a similar experiment to that of Kubovy et al. (1974), but he examined the importance of the phase transitions. He found that, when one component of a complex sound changed rapidly but smoothly in ITD, it perceptually segregated from the complex. When different components were changed in ITD in succession, a recognizable melody was heard, as reported by Kubovy et al. However, when the transitions were replaced by silent intervals, leaving only "static" ITDs as a cue, the melody was much less salient. Thus, transitions in ITD seem to be more important than static differences in ITD in producing segregation of one component from a background of other components. Nevertheless, static differences in ITD do seem to be sufficient to produce segregation, as illustrated by an experiment of Akeroyd et al. (2001). They investigated the ability of relatively untrained subjects to identify simple melodies created using the "Huggins" pitch described in Chapter 6, Section 5E; noise derived from the same noise generator was fed to each ear of each subject, and the pitch of a "note" was created by introducing a phase shift in a specific frequency region to the stimulus delivered to one ear only; this is equivalent to introducing an ITD in that frequency region. The pitch is presumably heard because the noise components in the phase-shifted frequency region segregate from the remaining components. Each "note" involved a static interaural phase shift, there was a silent interval between successive notes, and the frequency region of the phase shift was changed across "notes" to create the melody. The great majority of subjects could identify the melodies with high accuracy, indicating that static differences in interaural phase (equivalent to ITDs) were sufficient to cause a group of components in the noise to segregate from the remainder, allowing the pitch to be heard.

Other experiments suggest that binaural processing often plays a relatively minor role in simultaneous grouping. For example, when a single component in a harmonic complex tone is mistuned upward or downward by a small amount, this results in a shift of the pitch of the whole complex sound in the same direction (Moore et al., 1985a). Darwin and Ciocca (1992) reported that the pitch shift was almost as large when the mistuned component was presented to the opposite ear as when it was presented to the same ear as the rest of the components. Apparently, segregation by ear did not prevent the mistuned component from contributing to the pitch of the complex sound. However, Gockel et al. (2005b) found that the pitch shift produced by a mistuned component was smaller when that component was presented to the opposite ear than when it was presented to the same ear as the rest of the components, suggesting that segregation by ear did reduce the contribution of the mistuned component to pitch.

Gockel and Carlyon (1998) investigated the ability to detect mistuning of a single component in a harmonic complex sound. They used a two-interval forced-choice task. In the "standard" interval, all components were frequency modulated in phase by a 5-Hz sinusoid in such a way that the components remained harmonically related. In the "signal" interval, the "target" component was modulated with opposite phase to the remaining (nontarget) components; when the target frequency was moving upward, the frequencies of the nontarget components were moving downward, and vice versa. The out-of-phase modulation thus introduced a mistuning proportional to the depth of the FM. The task of the subjects was to identify the signal interval. Gockel and Carlyon suggested that the mistuning "was detected by hearing out the target component"; that component appeared to "pop out" from the rest of the complex. They reasoned that any manipulation of the stimuli that would make the target component pop out in *both* intervals of a trial would make performance worse. In one experiment, they achieved this by presenting the nontarget components in the opposite ear to the target component. As expected, this made performance worse than when all components were presented to one ear. In a second experiment, the nontarget components were presented to both ears. In the ear receiving the target, each component had a level of 45 dB SPL. In the opposite ear, the nontarget components were presented at a level of 65 dB SPL per component. As a result of the interaural level difference (ILD) of the nontarget components, they were perceived as being at the ear contralateral to the ear receiving the target. Performance in this condition was only slightly worse than when the nontarget components were presented only to the same ear as the target (at 45 dB SPL per component) and was much better than when the nontarget components were presented only to the contralateral ear. It seems that segregation of the target from the nontarget components was stronger when they were presented to opposite ears than when they were merely perceived at opposite ears due to an ILD.

Shackleton and Meddis (1992) investigated the ability to identify each vowel in pairs of concurrent vowels. They found that a difference in F0 between the two vowels improved identification by about 22%. In contrast, a 400-μs ITD in one vowel (which corresponds to an azimuth of about 45°) improved performance by only 7%. Culling and Summerfield (1995) investigated the identification of concurrent "whispered" vowels, synthesized using bands of noise. They showed that listeners were able to identify the vowels accurately when each vowel was presented to a different ear. However, they were unable to identify the vowels when they were presented to both ears but with different ITDs. In other words, listeners could not group the noise bands in different frequency regions with the same ITD and thereby separate them from noise bands in other frequency regions with a different ITD.

In summary, when two simultaneous sounds differ in their ILD or ITD, this can contribute to the perceptual segregation of the sounds and enhance their detection and discrimination. However, such binaural processing is not always effective, and in some situations it appears to play little role. The role of differences in spatial location in the perceptual segregation of speech in a background of speech is described in Chapter 9, Section 7.

4 THE PERCEPTION OF SEQUENCES OF SOUNDS

It is beyond the scope of this book to review the extensive literature on the perception of temporal patterns and rhythm. The interested reader is referred to the reviews of Fraisse (1982) and Clarke (1999). The following selective review focuses on the perceptual organization of sequences of sounds.

4A STREAM SEGREGATION

When we listen to rapid sequences of sounds, the sounds may be grouped together (i.e., perceived as if they come from a single source, called fusion or coherence), or they may be perceived as different streams (i.e., as coming from more than one source, called fission or stream segregation) (Miller and Heise, 1950; Bregman and Campbell, 1971; van Noorden, 1975; Bregman, 1990). The term "streaming" is used to denote the processes determining whether one stream or multiple streams are heard. Van Noorden (1971) investigated this phenomenon using a sequence of pure tones where every second B was omitted from the regular sequence ABABAB ..., producing the sequence ABA ABA ... He found that this could be perceived in two ways, depending on the frequency separation of A and B. For small separations, a single rhythm, resembling a gallop, is heard (fusion). For large separations, two separate tone sequences are heard, one of which (A A A) is running twice as fast as the other (B B B) (fission). Bregman (1978b) suggested that each stream corresponds to an auditory "object" and that stream segregation reflects the attribution of different components in the sound to different sources. Components are more likely to be assigned to separate streams if they differ widely in frequency or if there are rapid jumps in frequency between them. The latter point is illustrated by a study of Bregman and Dannenbring (1973). They used tone sequences in which successive tones were connected by frequency glides. They found that these glides reduced the tendency for the sequences to split into high and low streams.

The effects of frequency glides and other types of transitions in preventing stream segregation or fission are probably of considerable importance in the perception of speech. Speech sounds may follow one another in very rapid sequences, and the glides and partial glides observed in the acoustic components of speech may be a strong factor in maintaining the percept of speech as a unified stream (see Chapter 9).

Van Noorden found that, for intermediate frequency separations of the tones A and B in a rapid sequence, either fusion or fission could be heard, according to the instructions given and the "attentional set" of the subject.

When the percept is ambiguous, the tendency for fission to occur increases with increasing exposure time to the tone sequence (Bregman, 1978a; Roberts et al., 2008). The auditory system seems to start with the assumption that there is a single sound source, and fission is only perceived when sufficient evidence has built up to contradict this assumption. Sudden changes in a sequence, or in the perception of a sequence, can cause the percept to revert to its initial "default" condition, which is fusion (Rogers and Bregman, 1993, 1998; for a review, see Moore and Gockel, 2002).

For rapid sequences of complex tones, strong fission can be produced by differences in spectrum of successive tones, even when all tones have the same F0 (van Noorden, 1975; Hartmann and Johnson, 1991; Singh and Bregman, 1997; Vliegen et al., 1999). However, when successive complex tones are filtered to have the same spectral envelope, stream segregation can also be produced by differences between successive tones in F0 (Vliegen and Oxenham, 1999; Vliegen et al., 1999), in temporal envelope (Iverson, 1995; Singh and Bregman, 1997), in the relative phases of the components (Roberts et al., 2002; Stainsby et al., 2004), or in localization (Gockel et al., 1999). Stream segregation can also be produced by differences in pitch between tones created by binaural interaction, as Huggin's pitches (Akeroyd et al., 2005); see Chapter 6, Section 5E. Moore and Gockel (2002) proposed that any salient perceptual difference between successive tones may lead to stream segregation. Consistent with this idea, Dowling (1968; 1973) has shown that stream segregation may also occur when successive pure tones differ in intensity or in spatial location. He presented a melody composed of equal-intensity notes and inserted between each note of the melody a tone of the same intensity, with a frequency randomly selected from the same range. He found that the resulting tone sequence produced a meaningless jumble. Making the interposed notes different from those of the melody, in either intensity, frequency range, or spatial location, caused them to be heard as a separate stream, enabling subjects to pick out the melody.

Darwin and Hukin (1999) have shown that sequential grouping can be strongly influenced by ITD. In one experiment, they presented two simultaneous sentences (Fig. 8.5). They varied the ITDs of the two sentences in the range 0 to $\pm 181\,\mu s$. For example, one sentence might lead in the left ear by $45\,\mu s$, while the other sentence would lead in the right ear by $45\,\mu s$ (as in Fig. 8.5). The sentences were based on natural speech but were processed so that each was spoken on a monotone, i.e., with constant F0. The F0 difference between the two sentences was varied from 0 to 4 semitones. Subjects were instructed to attend to one particular sentence. At a certain point, the two sentences contained two different target words aligned in starting time and duration ("dog" and "bird"). The F0s and the ITDs of the two target words were varied independently from those of the two sentences.

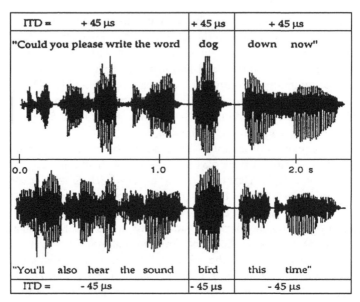

FIGURE 8.5   Example of the stimuli used by Darwin and Hukin (1999) (adapted from their Fig. 8.1).

Subjects had to indicate which of the two target words they heard in the attended sentence. They reported the target word that had the same ITD as the attended sentence much more often than the target word with the opposite ITD. In other words, the target word with the same ITD as the attended sentence was grouped with that sentence. This was true even when the target word had the same ITD as the attended sentence but a different F0. Thus, subjects grouped words across time according to their perceived location, independent of F0 differences. Darwin and Hukin (1999) concluded that listeners who try to track a particular sound source over time direct attention to auditory objects at a particular subjective location. The auditory objects themselves may be formed using cues other than ITD, for example, onset and offset asynchrony and harmonicity.

A number of composers have exploited the fact that stream segregation occurs for tones that are widely separated in frequency. By playing a sequence of tones in which alternate notes are chosen from separate frequency ranges, an instrument such as the flute, which is only capable of playing one note at a time, can appear to be playing two themes at once. Many fine examples of this are available in the works of Bach, Telemann and Vivaldi. There are also cases where composers intend interleaved notes played by different instruments (e.g., the first and second violins) to be heard as a single melody. This only works when the different instruments have similar timbres and locations and play in similar pitch ranges.

4B JUDGMENT OF TEMPORAL ORDER

Judgments of temporal order have already been discussed in Chapter 5, Sections 8B and 8C, where it was pointed out that it may be difficult to judge the temporal order of sounds that appear to come from different sources. An example of this comes from the work of Broadbent and Ladefoged (1959). They reported that extraneous sounds in sentences were grossly mislocated. For example, a click might be reported as occurring a word or two away from its actual position. Surprisingly poor performance was also reported by Warren et al. (1969) for judgments of the temporal order of three or four unrelated items, such as a hiss, a tone, and a buzz. Most subjects could not identify the order when each successive item lasted as long as 200 ms. Naive subjects required that each item last at least 700 ms to identify the order of four sounds presented in an uninterrupted repeated sequence. These durations are well above those that are normally considered necessary for temporal resolution; see Chapter 5.

The poor order discrimination described by Warren et al. is probably a result of stream segregation. The sounds they used do not represent a coherent class. They have different temporal and spectral characteristics, and they do not form a single perceptual stream. Items in different streams appear to float about with respect to each other in subjective time in much the same way as a click superimposed on speech. Thus, temporal order judgments are difficult. It should be emphasized that the relatively poor performance reported by Warren et al. (1969) is found only in tasks requiring absolute identification of the order of sounds and not in tasks that simply require the discrimination of different sequences. Also, as described in Chapter 5, with extended training and feedback subjects can learn to distinguish between and identify orders within sequences of nonrelated sounds lasting only 10 ms or less (Warren, 1974).

To explain these effects, Divenyi and Hirsh (1974) suggested that two kinds of perceptual judgments are involved. At longer item durations the listener is able to hear a clear sequence of steady sounds, whereas at shorter durations a change in the order of items introduces qualitative changes that can be discriminated by trained listeners. Similar explanations have been put forward by Green (1973) and Warren (1974) (see also Chapter 5).

Bregman and Campbell (1971) investigated the factors that make temporal order judgments for tone sequences difficult. They used naive subjects, so performance presumably depended on the subjects actually perceiving the sounds as a sequence, rather than on their learning the overall sound pattern. They found that, in a repeating cycle of mixed high and low tones, subjects could discriminate the order of the high tones relative to one another or of the low tones among themselves, but they could not judge the order of the high tones relative to the low ones. The authors suggested that this was because the two groups of sounds split into separate perceptual streams and that judgments across streams are difficult. Several studies have used tasks involving the discrimination of changes in timing or rhythm as a tool for studying stream segregation (Vliegen *et al.*, 1999; Cusack and Roberts, 2000; Roberts *et al.*, 2002). The rationale of these studies is that, if the ability to judge the relative timing of successive sound elements is good, this indicates that the elements are perceived as part of a single stream, while if the ability is poor, this indicates that the elements are perceived in different streams. This method is especially useful for studying "obligatory" or "automatic" stream segregation, which is segregation that occurs even when the listener is trying to hear the sounds as a single stream.

5 GENERAL PRINCIPLES OF PERCEPTUAL ORGANIZATION

The Gestalt psychologists (Koffka, 1935) described many of the factors that govern perceptual organization, and their descriptions and principles apply reasonably well to the way physical cues are used to achieve perceptual grouping of the acoustic input. It seems likely that the "rules" of perceptual organization have arisen because, on the whole, they tend to give the right answers. That is, use of the rules generally results in a grouping of those parts of the acoustic input that arose from the same source and a segregation of those that did not. No single rule always works, but it appears that the rules can generally be used together, in a coordinated and probably quite complex way, in order to arrive at a correct interpretation of the input. In the following sections, I outline the major principles or rules of perceptual organization. Many, but not all, of the rules apply to both vision and hearing, and they were mostly described first in relation to vision.

5A SIMILARITY

This principle is that elements are grouped if they are similar. In hearing, similarity usually implies closeness of timbre, pitch, loudness, or subjective location. Examples of this principle have already been described in

Section 4A. If we listen to a rapid sequence of pure tones, say 10 tones per second, then tones that are closely spaced in frequency, and are therefore similar, form a single perceptual stream, whereas tones that are widely spaced form separate streams.

For pure tones, frequency is the most important factor governing similarity, although differences in level and subjective location between successive tones can also lead to stream segregation. For complex tones, differences in timbre produced by spectral differences seem to be the most important factor. Again, however, other factors may play a role. These include differences in F0, differences in timbre produced by temporal envelope differences, and differences in perceived location.

5B Good Continuation

This principle exploits a physical property of sound sources, that changes in frequency, intensity, location, or spectrum tend to be smooth and continuous, rather than abrupt. Hence, a smooth change in any of these aspects indicates a change within a single source, whereas a sudden change indicates that a new source has been activated. One example has already been described; Bregman and Dannenbring (1973) showed that the tendency of a sequence of high and low tones to split into two streams was reduced when successive tones were connected by frequency glides.

A second example comes from studies using synthetic speech (see Chapter 9). In such speech, large fluctuations of an unexpected kind in F0 (and correspondingly in the pitch) give the impression that a new speaker has stepped in to take over a few syllables from the primary speaker. However, it appears that, in this case, the smoothness of the F0 contour is not the sole factor determining whether an intrusion is perceived. A single speaker's F0s cover a range of about one octave, but the intrusion effect is observed for much smaller jumps than this, provided they are inconsistent with the changes in F0 required by the linguistic and phonetic context. Thus, it appears that the assignment of incoming spectral patterns to particular speakers is done partly on the basis of F0, but in a manner that requires a knowledge of the "rules" of intonation; only deviations that do not conform to the rules are interpreted as a new speaker.

Darwin and Bethell-Fox (1977) have reported an experimental study of this effect. They synthesized spectral patterns that changed smoothly and repeatedly between two vowel sounds. When the F0 of the sound patterns was constant they were heard as coming from a single source, and the speech sounds heard included glides (l as in let) and semivowels ("w" as in we). When a discontinuous, step-like F0 contour was imposed on the patterns, they were perceived as two perceptually distinct speech streams, and the speech was perceived as containing predominantly stop consonants (e.g., "b" as in "be" and "d" as in "day") (see Chapter 9 for a description of the characteristics of these speech sounds). A given group of components is usually only perceived as part of one stream (see Section 5D). Thus, the perceptual segregation produces illusory silences in each stream during the portions of the signal attributed to the other stream, and these silences are interpreted, together with the gliding spectral patterns in the vowels, as indicating the presence of stop consonants (see Chapter 9). It is clear that the perception of speech sounds can be strongly influenced by stream organization.

5C Common Fate

The different frequency components arising from a single sound source usually vary in a highly coherent way. They tend to start and finish together, change in intensity together, and change in frequency together. This fact is exploited by the perceptual system and gives rise to the principle of common fate: if two or more components in a complex sound undergo the same kinds of changes at the same time, then they are grouped and perceived as part of the same source.

Two examples of common fate were described earlier. The first concerns the role of the onsets of sounds. Components are grouped together if they start and stop synchronously; otherwise they form separate streams. The onset asynchronies necessary to allow the separation of two complex tones are not large, about 30 ms being sufficient. The asynchronies observed in performed music are typically as large as or larger than this, so when we listen to polyphonic music we are easily able to hear separately the melodic line of each instrument. Secondly, components that are amplitude modulated in a synchronous way tend to be grouped together. There is at present little evidence that the coherence of modulation in frequency affects perceptual grouping, although frequency modulation of a group of components in a complex sound can promote the perceptual segregation of those components from an unchanging background.

5D Disjoint Allocation

Broadly speaking, this principle, also known as "belongingness", is that a single component in a sound can only be assigned to one source at a time. In other words, once a component has been "used" in the formation of one stream, it cannot be used in the formation of a second stream. For certain types of stimuli, the perceptual organization may be ambiguous, there being more than one way to interpret the sensory input. When a given component might belong to one of a number of streams, the percept may alter depending on the stream within which that component is included.

An example is provided by the work of Bregman and Rudnicky (1975). They presented a sequence of four brief tones in rapid succession. Two of the tones, labeled X, had the same frequency, but the middle two, A and B, had different frequencies. The four-tone sequence was either XABX or XBAX. The listeners had to judge the order of A and B. This was harder than when the tones AB occurred in isolation (Fig. 8.6a) because A and B were perceived as part of a longer four-tone pattern, including the two "distractor" tones, labeled

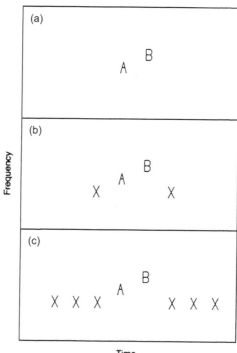

Time

FIGURE 8.6   Schematic illustration of the stimuli used by Bregman and Rudnicky (1975). When the tones A and B are presented alone (panel a), it is easy to tell their order. When the tones A and B are presented as part of a four-tone complex XABX (panel b), it is more difficult to tell their order. If the four-tone complex is embedded in a longer sequence of X tones (panel c), the Xs form a separate perceptual stream, and it is easy to tell the order of A and B.

X (Fig. 8.6b). They then embedded the four-tone sequence into a longer sequence of tones, called "captor" tones (Fig. 8.6c). When the captor tones had frequencies close to those of the distractor tones, they "captured" the distractors into a separate perceptual stream, leaving the tones AB in a stream of their own. This made the order of A and B easy to judge. It seems that the tones X could not be perceived as part of both streams. When only one stream is the subject of judgment and hence of attention, the other one may serve to remove distractors from the domain of attention.

It should be noted that the principle of disjoint allocation does not always work, particularly in situations where there are two or more plausible perceptual organizations (Bregman, 1987). In such situations, a sound element may sometimes be heard as part of more than one stream. Some examples are given in Chapter 9, Section 3F.

5E CLOSURE

In everyday life, the sound from a given source may be temporarily masked by other sounds. During the time that the masking sound is present there may be no sensory evidence that can be used to determine whether the masked sound has continued or not. Under these conditions the masked sound tends to be perceived as continuous. The Gestalt psychologists called this process "closure".

A laboratory example of this phenomenon is the continuity effect described in Chapter 3, Section 10. When a sound A is alternated with a sound B, and B is more intense than A, then A may be heard as continuous, even though it is interrupted. The sounds do not have to be steady. For example, if B is noise and A is a tone that is gliding upward in frequency, the glide is heard as continuous even though certain parts of the glide are missing (Ciocca and Bregman, 1987). Similarly, when an amplitude- or frequency-modulated tone is interrupted by noise, the modulation is perceived to continue through the noise (Lyzenga et al., 2005). Notice that, for this to be the case, the gaps in the tone must be filled with noise and the noise must be a potential masker of the tone (if they were presented simultaneously). In the absence of noise, continuity is not heard.

The continuity effect also works for speech stimuli alternated with noise. In the absence of noise to fill in the gaps, interrupted speech sounds hoarse and raucous. When noise is presented in the gaps, the speech sounds more natural and continuous (Miller and Licklider, 1950). For connected speech at moderate interruption rates, the intervening noise actually leads to an improvement in intelligibility (Dirks and Bower, 1970). This may occur because the abrupt switching of the speech produces misleading cues as to which speech sounds were present (Chapter 9). The noise serves to mask these misleading cues.

It is clear from these examples that the perceptual filling in of missing sounds does not take place solely on the basis of evidence in the acoustic waveform. Our past experience with speech, music, and other stimuli must play a role, and the context of surrounding sounds is obviously important. However, the filling in only occurs when one source is perceived as masking or occluding another. This percept must be based on acoustic evidence that the occluded sound has been masked. Thus, if a gap is not filled by a noise or other sound, the perceptual closure does not occur; a gap is heard.

5F The Figure-ground Phenomenon and Attention

Several times in this chapter I have referred to the role of attention. It seems that we are not generally capable of attending to every aspect of the auditory input (or indeed of other sensory inputs); rather, certain parts are selected for conscious analysis. In principle, we might think it possible to attend to and compare any arbitrary small group of elements in a complex acoustic signal. However, this does not appear to be the case. Rather, it appears that the complex sound is analyzed into streams, and we attend primarily to one stream at a time. This attended stream then stands out perceptually, while the rest of the sound is less prominent. The Gestalt psychologists called the separation into attended and unattended streams the "figure-ground phenomenon".

At a crowded cocktail party, we attend to one conversation at a time, and the other conversations form a kind of background. Similarly, when we listen to a piece of polyphonic music, we attend primarily to one melodic line at a time. We can, of course, switch attention from one conversation to another or from one melodic line to another, and we may have some awareness of the other voices, but it appears that one stream at a time is selected for a complete conscious analysis. Neisser (1967) has suggested that attention may be brought to bear after the preliminary analysis into streams has occurred. The "pre-attentive" processes involved thus place constraints upon attention: it is difficult to attend simultaneously to, or to make relative judgments about, elements that form parts of two separate perceptual streams.

Although the formation of auditory streams places constraints upon attention, this should not be viewed as a one-way process; attention may also influence the formation of streams (Ihlefeld and Shinn-Cunningham, 2008a). For example, when we listen to a sequence of alternating tones, with an interval of about seven semitones between the tones, we may hear either fission or fusion depending on our attentional "set" (van Noorden, 1975). We can listen selectively, trying to hear either the upper tones or the lower tones, or we can listen comprehensively, trying to hear all the tones together. The associated percepts seem to be mutually exclusive. When we listen without any particular set, we may hear first one percept and then the other. The change occurs at irregular intervals and appears spontaneous (Pressnitzer and Hupe, 2006). This is an example of a perceptual reversal, resulting from an ambiguity in the interpretation of the sensory input.

Carlyon et al. (2001) investigated the role of attention in the build up of stream segregation. They used tone sequences of the type ABA ABA ... as described earlier. The tone sequences were presented to the left ear of listeners for 21 s. In a baseline condition, no sounds were presented to the right ear. The main experimental condition ("two-task condition") was designed to draw attention away from the tone sequences presented to the left ear. A series of noise bursts, filtered into a high-frequency region (2–3 kHz), was presented to the right ear for the first 10 s of the sequence. Each noise burst was either increasing or decreasing in amplitude, and listeners were asked to judge the bursts as either approaching or receding. After 10 s, listeners had to switch task and judge the tone sequence in the left ear. In a control condition, the same stimuli were presented as in the two-task condition, but listeners were instructed to ignore the noise bursts in the right ear and just concentrate on the task and stimuli in the left ear.

For the baseline and the control conditions, results were similar and showed the usual build up of stream segregation with time of exposure to the tone sequence, i.e., the probability of hearing two streams was very small at the beginning of the tone sequence but increased with time, and the build up was quicker the bigger the frequency separation of A and B. However, in the two-task condition *after* switching attention back to the left ear, the probability of hearing two streams was significantly smaller than when listeners paid attention to the tone sequence in the left ear over the whole time of presentation. It may be that the build up of stream segregation depends on the listener paying attention to the tone sequence. Alternatively, the act of switching attention from the noise bursts in the right ear to the tone sequence in the left ear may cause a kind of resetting of the build up of stream segregation; the effect could be similar to what occurs when the characteristics of the sequence are changed suddenly, as described earlier.

The importance of changes in stimuli (Section 3C) can be interpreted in the context of the figure-ground phenomenon. Whenever some aspect of a sound changes, while the rest remains relatively unchanging, then that aspect is drawn to the listener's attention: it becomes the figure, while the steady part forms the background. This is of practical value since events of significance in the world are usually associated with a change of some kind. Our sensitivity to change provides a way of directing our attention to new and potentially important events in the environment.

Finally, it should be noted that our ability to direct attention to one stream among a number, and indeed to form the stream in the first place, does not depend only on information available in the acoustic waveform. The Gestalt rules themselves constitute a form of knowledge, but other sources of information or knowledge may also be involved. An example of this comes from the "cocktail party" phenomenon. We can follow a conversation more successfully if the subject matter of that conversation is different from that of the other conversations. Clearly, this involves relatively high-level processes. This point is discussed further in Chapter 9.

6 GENERAL CONCLUSIONS

In everyday life, the sound reaching our ears generally arises from a number of different sound sources. The auditory system is usually able to parse the acoustic input, so that the components deriving from each source are grouped together and form part of a single perceptual stream. Thus, each source may be ascribed its own pitch, timbre, loudness, and location, and sometimes a source may be identified as familiar.

The identification of a particular sound source depends on the recognition of its timbre. For steady sounds, the timbre depends primarily on the distribution of energy over frequency. The perceptual differences in the timbres of sounds are related to differences in their spectra when analyzed using filters whose bandwidths approximate the critical bandwidths of the ear. The time structure of sounds can also have an influence on their timbre; onset transients and the temporal envelope are particularly important.

Many different physical cues can be used to achieve the perceptual separation of the components arising from different sources. These include differences in fundamental frequency, onset disparities, contrast with previous sounds, changes in frequency and intensity, and sound location. No single cue is effective all of the time, but used together they generally provide an excellent basis for the parsing of the acoustic input.

When we listen to rapid sequences of sounds, the sounds may be perceived as a single perceptual stream, or they may split into a number of perceptual streams, a process known as stream segregation or fission. Fission is more likely to occur if the elements making up the sequence differ markedly in frequency, amplitude, location, or spectrum. Such elements would normally emanate from more than one sound source. When two elements of a sound are grouped into two different streams, it is more difficult to judge their temporal order than when they form part of the same stream.

The general principles governing the perceptual organization of the auditory world correspond well to those described by the Gestalt psychologists. The principle of similarity is that sounds are grouped into a single perceptual stream if they are similar in pitch, timbre, loudness, or subjective location. The principle of good continuation is that smooth changes in frequency, intensity, location, or spectrum are perceived as changes in a single source, whereas abrupt changes indicate a change in source. The principle of common fate is that, if two components in a sound undergo the same kinds of changes at the same time, then they are grouped and perceived as part of a single source; however, this principle appears to apply strongly only to onset asynchronies and not, for example, to frequency changes. The principle of disjoint allocation is that a given element in a sound can only form part of one stream at a time. The principle of closure is that, when parts of a sound are masked or occluded, that sound is perceived as continuous, provided there is no direct sensory evidence to indicate that it has been interrupted.

Usually we attend primarily to one perceptual stream at a time. That stream stands out from the background formed by other streams. Stream formation places constraints upon attention, but attention may also influence the formation of streams. Stream formation may also depend upon information not directly available in the acoustic waveform.

FURTHER RESOURCES

The following book by Bregman provides a comprehensive review of the phenomena described in this chapter:

Bregman, A. S. (1990). *Auditory Scene Analysis: The Perceptual Organization of Sound.* Cambridge, MA: Bradford Books, MIT Press.

The following provide useful additional material or alternative viewpoints:

Hartmann, W. M. (1988). Pitch Perception and the Segregation and Integration of Auditory Entities. In G. M. Edelman, W. E. Gall & W. M. Cowen (Eds.), New York: Wiley.
Yost, W. A., and Watson, C. S. (1987). *Auditory Function – Neurobiological Bases of Hearing.* Hillsdale, NJ: Erlbaum.
Darwin, C. J., and Carlyon, R. P. (1995). Auditory grouping. In B. C. J. Moore (Ed.), *Hearing.* San Diego, FL: Academic Press.
Handel, S. (1989). *Listening: An Introduction to the Perception of Auditory Events.* Cambridge, MA: MIT Press.
Handel, S. (1995). Timbre perception and auditory object identification. In B. C. J. Moore (Ed.), *Hearing.* San Diego, FL: Academic Press.
Plomp, R. (2002). *The Intelligent Ear.* Mahwah, NJ: Erlbaum.

Demonstrations 19 and 28–30 of Auditory Demonstrations on CD are relevant to the contents of this chapter (see list of further resources for Chapter 1).

The following compact disc has a large variety of demonstrations relevant to perceptual grouping:

Bregman, A. S. and Ahad, P. (1995). *Demonstrations of Auditory Scene Analysis: The Perceptual Organization of Sound* (Auditory Perception Laboratory, Department of Psychology, McGill University). Distributed by MIT Press, Cambridge, MA.
It can be ordered from The MIT Press, 55 Hayward St., Cambridge, MA 02142, USA.

Further relevant demonstrations can be found at:
http://www.design.kyushu-u.ac.jp/~ynhome/ENG/index.html

CHAPTER 9

Speech Perception

1 INTRODUCTION

This chapter is concerned with the problem of how the complex acoustical patterns of speech are interpreted by the brain and perceived as linguistic units. The details of this process are still not fully understood, despite a large amount of research carried out over the past 50 years. What has become clear is that speech perception does not depend on the extraction of simple invariant acoustic patterns directly available in the speech waveform. This has been illustrated both by perceptual studies and by attempts to build machines that recognize speech (Holmes, 1988). A given speech sound is not represented by a fixed acoustic pattern in the speech wave; instead, the speech sound's acoustic pattern varies in a complex manner according to the preceding and following sounds.

For continuous speech, perception does not depend solely on cues present in the acoustic waveform. Part of a word that is highly probable in the context of a sentence may be "heard" even when the acoustic cues for that part are minimal or completely absent (Bagley, 1900–1901). For example, Warren

(1970b) has shown that when an extraneous sound (such as a cough) completely replaces a speech sound in a recorded sentence, listeners report that they hear the missing sound. This phenomenon is probably related to the continuity effect described in Chapters 3 and 8; when a weak sound is alternated with a stronger sound of similar frequency, the weak sound may appear continuous even though it is, in fact, pulsating. The effect reported by Warren has been shown to depend on similar factors; the missing sound is only heard if the cough is relatively intense and contains frequency components close to those of the missing sound. This kind of filling-in process often occurs when listening in noisy environments, and it illustrates the importance of non-acoustic cues in speech perception. On the other hand, we are able to identify nonsense syllables spoken in isolation, provided they are clearly articulated, so linguistic context is not a necessary requirement for the perception of speech.

It is beyond the scope of this book to give more than a brief description of certain selected aspects of speech perception. I will not emphasize the aspects of speech recognition related to semantic cues (the meaning of preceding and following words and the subject matter), syntactic cues (grammatical rules), and circumstantial cues (speaker identity, listening environment, etc.), even though these may be of considerable importance, especially in noisy environments. I will concentrate rather on the perceptual processing of patterns in the acoustic waveform.

The study of the perception of acoustic patterns in speech has been greatly aided by the use of speech synthesizers. These devices allow the production of acoustic waveforms resembling real speech to varying degrees; the closeness of the resemblance depends upon the complexity of the device and the trouble to which the experimenter is prepared to go. In contrast to real speech, synthesized speech has controlled and precisely reproducible characteristics. Using a speech synthesizer, the experimenter can manipulate certain aspects of the speech waveform, leaving all the other characteristics unchanged, making it possible to investigate what aspects of the waveform determine how it is perceived. The results of such experiments have been instrumental in the formulation of theories of speech perception.

2 THE NATURE OF SPEECH SOUNDS

2A UNITS OF SPEECH

The most familiar units of speech are words. These can often be broken down into syllables. However, linguists and phoneticians have often assumed that syllables can in turn be analyzed in terms of sequences of smaller units—the speech sounds or phonemes. To clarify the nature of phonemes, consider the following example. The word "bit" is argued to contain three phonemes: an initial, a middle, and a final phoneme. By altering just one of these phonemes at a time, three new words can be created: "pit", "bet", and "bid". Thus, for the linguist or phonetician, the phonemes are the smallest units of sound that in any given language differentiate one word from another. Phonemes on their own do not have a meaning or symbolize an object (some are not even pronounceable in isolation), but in relation to other phonemes they distinguish one word from another, and in combination they form syllables and words. Note that phonemes are defined in terms of what is perceived, rather than in terms of acoustic patterns. Thus, they are abstract, subjective entities, rather like pitch. However, they are also sometimes specified in terms of the way they are produced.

Not all researchers accept that it is appropriate to consider phonemes as "the basic units" of speech perception (Mehler, 1981), and some deny that the phoneme has any perceptual reality as a unit (Warren, 1976; Repp, 1981; Plomp, 2002). However, the analysis of speech in terms of phonemes has been widespread and influential, and I will continue to use the concept for the purposes of discussion. English has around 40 different phonemes, which are represented by a set of symbols specified by the International Phonetic Association (IPA). Some symbols are the letters of the Roman alphabet, and others are special characters. When a character is used to represent a phoneme, this is indicated by a slash (/) before and after the character. For example, /s/ is the first and /i/ is the final phoneme of the word "see".

A simple view of speech perception would hold that speech is composed of a series of acoustic patterns or properties and that each pattern or set of patterns corresponds to a particular phoneme. Thus, the acoustic patterns would have a one-to-one correspondence with the phonemes, and a sequence of patterns would be perceived as a sequence of phonemes, which would then be combined into words and phrases. Unfortunately, this view is not tenable. To understand why, the characteristics of speech sounds must be examined in more detail.

2B Speech Production and Speech Acoustics

Speech sounds are produced by the vocal organs, namely, the lungs, the trachea (windpipe), the larynx (containing the vocal folds), the throat or pharynx, the nose and nasal cavities, and the mouth. The part of this system lying above the larynx is called the vocal tract, and its shape can be varied extensively by movements of various parts such as the tongue, the lips and the jaw.

The space between the vocal folds is called the glottis. The vocal folds can open and close, varying the size of the glottis. This affects the flow of air from the lungs. The term "glottal source" refers to the sound energy produced by the flow of air from the lungs past the vocal folds as they open and close quite rapidly in a periodic or quasi-periodic manner. Sounds produced while the vocal folds are vibrating are said to be "voiced". The glottal source is a periodic complex tone with a relatively low F0, whose spectrum contains harmonics covering a wide range of frequencies, but with more energy at low frequencies than at high (see Fig. 9.1a). This spectrum is subsequently modified by the vocal tract. The vocal tract behaves like a complex filter, introducing resonances (called formants) at certain frequencies. The formants are numbered, the one with the lowest frequency being called the first formant

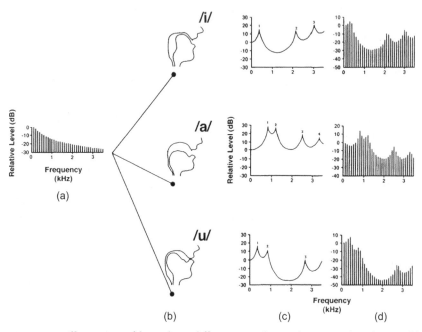

FIGURE 9.1   Illustration of how three different vowel sounds are produced. Part (a) shows the spectrum of the sound produced by vibration of the vocal folds. It consists of a series of harmonics whose levels decline with increasing frequency. Part (b) shows schematic cross sections of the vocal tract in the positions appropriate for the three vowels. Part (c) shows the filter functions or transfer functions associated with those positions of the vocal tract. Part (d) shows the spectra of the vowels resulting from passing the glottal source in panel (a) through the filter functions in panel (c). Adapted from Bailey (1983) by permission of the author.

(F1), the next the second (F2), and so on. The center frequencies of the formants differ according to the shape of the vocal tract.

The speech sounds that are characterized most easily are the vowels. These are usually voiced (but they can be whispered, in which case they are noise-like), and they have formants that are relatively stable over time, when spoken in isolation. Figure 9.1b shows cross sections of the vocal tract for three different vowels, and Fig. 9.1c shows the filter functions or transfer functions for those vocal tract shapes. Figure 9.1d shows the spectra of the vowels resulting from passing the glottal source through the vocal tract. Notice that the vowels contain peaks in their spectra at the frequencies corresponding to the formants.

Consonant speech sounds are produced by a narrowing or constriction of the vocal tract at some point along its length. Such sounds are classified into a number of different types according to the degree and nature of the constriction. The major types are fricatives, stops, affricates, nasals, and approximants.

Fricatives are produced by forcing air past a narrow constriction, which gives a turbulent air flow. They have a noise-like quality and may consist of that noise alone (as in /s/ and /f/), or may consist of that noise together with a glottal source, as in /z/ and /v/, the voiced counterparts of /s/ and /f/.

Stops are produced by making a complete closure somewhere in the vocal tract. The closing and opening are rapid. The closure stops the flow of air for a certain time, with an associated reduction or cessation of acoustic energy, after which the airflow and acoustic energy abruptly resume. As with fricatives, stops may be voiced (as in /b/, /d/, or /g/) or voiceless (as in their counterparts /p/, /t/, or /k/). For a voiced stop, the vocal folds are vibrating at or close to the moment when the release of the closure occurs; they may also vibrate during the closure. For voiceless stops, the vocal folds stop vibrating during closure and usually for some time after the release.

Affricates are like a combination of stop and fricative; they are characterized by a closure, giving silence, followed by a narrow constriction, giving turbulence. An example is /tʃ/, as in the first and last sounds of "church".

Many voiceless sounds do not show a distinct pattern of formants, particularly when they are produced by a constriction close to the outer end of the vocal tract (e.g., /f/). However, they do generally have a distinct spectral shape, which is determined by the shape of the vocal tract during their articulation, and this determines how they sound.

Nasals, such as /m/ and /n/, are produced by allowing air and sound to flow through the nasal passages, keeping the oral cavity completely closed. The closure is produced by the lips for /m/ and by pressing the tongue against the roof of the mouth for /n/. The coupling of the nasal passages can produce one or more extra resonances and also an anti-resonance. The latter reduces the energy of the glottal source over a certain frequency range. The net effect is a broad, low-amplitude, low-frequency spectral prominence.

Approximants are sounds produced by an incomplete constriction of the vocal tract; the degree of constriction is still greater than for vowels. Examples are /w/ as in "we", /j/ as in "you", and /r/ as in "ran".

The different classes of consonants described above differ from each other in the *manner* in which they are produced. The manner of articulation refers to the degree and type of constriction of the vocal tract. In addition, there are, within each class, differences in the *place* of articulation (the place at which maximum constriction occurs, e.g., teeth, lips, roof of the mouth). All of these differences are reflected in the acoustic characteristics of the speech wave, as revealed by the spectrum. However, for nearly all speech sounds, the spectra are not static, but change as a function of time. For further details of the relationship between articulation and the acoustic characteristics of speech, the reader is referred to Pickett (1980) (an introductory text) and Fant (1970) (a technical treatment of the subject).

Speech, then, is composed of acoustic patterns that vary over time in frequency and intensity. In order to show these variations, a display known as the spectrogram is used. In this display the amount of energy in a given frequency band is plotted as a function of time. Essentially, the short-term spectrum is determined for a series of successive samples of the speech. Time is represented on the abscissa, frequency on the ordinate, and intensity by the darkness or color used. In a display like this, it is impossible to have high resolution both in frequency and in time; one is traded against the other (see Chapter 1, Section 2B). For example, if an analyzing bandwidth of 100 Hz is used, the time resolution is about 1/100 s (10 ms). In a "wideband" spectrogram, the bandwidth of analysis is typically 300 Hz. This gives good time resolution, often showing individual glottal pulses of voiced speech (each glottal pulse corresponds to one period of vocal fold vibration) but not the individual harmonics of the F0 (when the F0 is below 300 Hz; exceptions may occur for children and the upper ranges of women's voices). Wideband spectrograms are often used for observing formant patterns. In a "narrowband" spectrogram the bandwidth of analysis is typically 45 Hz. This is usually sufficient to resolve individual harmonics, but it gives poorer resolution in time and does not usually show individual glottal pulses.

An example of a wideband spectrogram is given in Fig. 9.2. Very dark areas indicate high concentrations of energy at particular frequencies, while very light areas indicate an absence of energy. At times when voicing occurs, vertical striations can be seen. Each striation corresponds to one period of vocal fold vibration. Dark bands running roughly horizontally can be clearly seen; these correspond to the formants. Several formants are visible in this example, but experiments using synthetic speech suggest that the first three are the most important for the purpose of identifying speech sounds. Some researchers consider that the frequencies of the formants, and not some other

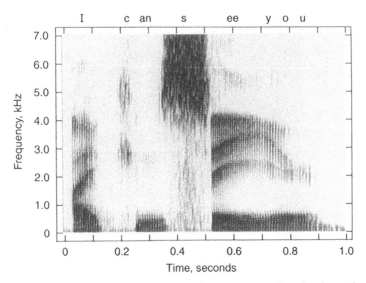

FIGURE 9.2   A wideband spectrogram for "I can see you", spoken by the author. The analyzing filters had a fixed bandwidth of 300 Hz. Dark regions indicate concentrations of energy. These mostly correspond to formant frequencies, except for the /s/ sound. Note the lack of silent intervals between successive words. The vertical striations correspond to individual periods of vocal fold vibration, and their spacing depends on the rate of this vibration.

characteristic such as their bandwidths or amplitudes, are the most important determinant of vowel quality (Klatt, 1982), while others consider that overall spectral shape is important (Beddor and Hawkins, 1990). There are, of course, other ways of analyzing vowel sounds, as described in Chapter 8, but analysis in terms of formants has been by far the most common and most influential technique.

Neither wideband nor narrowband spectrograms are representative of the way that the ear analyzes sounds; the bandwidths of the auditory filters vary with center frequency (see Chapter 3), whereas the spectrogram usually uses a fixed bandwidth and a linear frequency scale. A different form of spectrogram uses a representation more like that of the auditory system; it is called an "auditory spectrogram" (Carlson and Granström, 1982). In the auditory spectrogram, the bandwidths of the analyzing filters vary with center frequency in the same way that the bandwidth of the auditory filter varies with center frequency (see Chapter 3, Section 3B and Fig. 3.5). Also, the frequency scale is transformed so that a constant distance on the transformed scale represents a constant step in Cams (ERB$_N$ number, see Chapter 3, Section 3B). Figure 9.3 compares a conventional wideband spectrogram (top panel) and an auditory

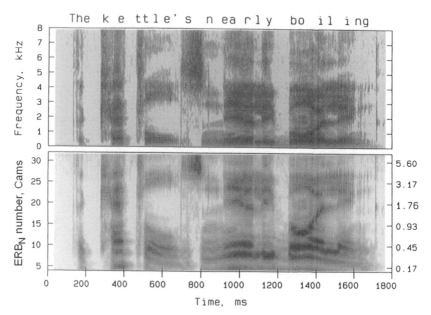

FIGURE 9.3   The upper panel shows a wideband spectrogram for a male talker saying "The kettle's nearly boiling". The lower panel shows an auditory spectrogram for the same utterance. For the latter, the bandwidths of the analyzing filters varied with frequency in the same way as the ERB_N of the auditory filter, and the frequency scale was transformed to an ERB_N-number scale (see Chapter 3). The corresponding frequencies in kilohertz are shown on the right-hand side of the panel.

spectrogram (bottom panel). In the auditory spectrogram, the horizontal bands at lower center frequencies (the first four or five bands) correspond to individual harmonics rather than to formants. Notice also that vertical striations corresponding to voicing are visible in the upper frequency regions of the auditory spectrogram (where the bandwidths of the analyzing filters are relatively large), but not in the lower frequency regions (where the bandwidths of the analyzing filters are small). In the wideband spectrogram, vertical striations are visible over the whole frequency range when voicing occurs.

A marked characteristic of speech sounds is that there are often rapid changes in the frequency of a given formant or set of formants. These changes, known as formant transitions, reflect the changes in the shape of the vocal tract as the articulators move from one position to another. For some speech sounds, such as stop consonants, formant transitions are an inherent property of the sounds; stops are produced by rapid movements of the articulators. The formant transitions in such sounds are important acoustic cues for determining their identity. For other sounds, the formant transitions occur as a consequence of the smooth movement of the articulators from the position appropriate for one sound to the position appropriate for another. In Fig. 9.2, this can be seen in the part of the spectrogram corresponding to the /i/ in "see" and the /u/ in "you". This is one manifestation of coarticulation, which refers to the fact that the articulation of a speech sound is affected by the articulation of neighboring sounds. A consequence of coarticulation is that the acoustic properties of a given speech sound are influenced by the preceding and following sounds. Another example is that an /h/ in "who" is acoustically different from an /h/ in "he", because at the time that the /h/ is produced the articulators are already in the position appropriate for the vowel sound.

The spectrogram of a complete sentence may show a number of time intervals where there is little or no spectral energy. However, these silent intervals do not generally correspond to "spaces" between words, as we do not pause between each word when speaking. Rather, the silent intervals usually indicate the presence of particular types of speech sounds, particularly the stop consonants and affricates; see, for example, the time just before the /k/ in "kettle" in Fig. 9.3. Thus, another problem is to explain how the sequence of sounds is segmented into individual words. This has turned out to be a major difficulty for models of speech perception and also for attempts to build machines to recognize speech. For example, most such machines would have great difficulty in distinguishing the utterances "recognize speech" and "wreck a nice beach" if these were spoken in a normal conversational manner.

3 SPEECH PERCEPTION—WHAT IS SPECIAL ABOUT SPEECH?

Some researchers have argued that special mechanisms have evolved for the perception of speech sounds, and that the perception of speech differs in significant ways from the perception of non-speech sounds. In particular, it has been argued that there is a special "speech mode" of perception that is engaged automatically when we listen to speech sounds. In this section, I compare some aspects of the perception of speech and non-speech sounds and evaluate the extent to which speech perception appears to require special decoding mechanisms.

3A THE RATE AT WHICH SPEECH SOUNDS OCCUR

Liberman *et al.* (1967) pointed out that in rapid speech as many as 30 phonemes per second may occur. It was argued that this would be too fast for resolution in the auditory system; the sounds would merge into an unanalyzable buzz and so a special decoding mechanism would be required. However, evidence does not support this point of view. Chapters 5 and 8 described how listeners can, in fact, learn to identify sequences of non-speech sounds when the individual items are as short as 10 ms (corresponding to a rate of 100 items per second). At these short durations, the listeners do not perceive each successive item separately but rather learn the overall sound pattern. It is likely that for continuous speech something similar occurs. The successive acoustic patterns in speech are probably not perceived as discrete acoustic events. Rather the listener recognizes the sound pattern corresponding to a group of acoustic patterns. The size of this larger sound pattern remains unclear, but it might, for example, correspond to a whole syllable, a word, or even a phrase.

3B The Variable Nature of Acoustic Cues

A central problem in understanding speech perception is the variable nature of the acoustic patterns that can be perceived as any particular phoneme. Consider as an example the phoneme /d/ as in "dawn". A major cue for the perception of /d/ is the form of the second formant transition that occurs at the release of the sound. Consider the highly simplified synthetic spectrographic patterns shown in Fig. 9.4. When these are converted into sound, the first formant transition (the change in frequency of the lowest formant at the

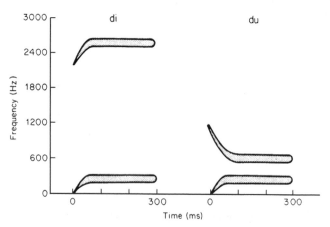

FIGURE 9.4 Highly simplified spectrographic patterns that are perceived as /di/ and /du/ when they are converted into sound. From Liberman *et al.* (1967), by permission of the authors and the American Psychological Association.

beginning of the sound) indicates that the sound is one of the voiced stops /b, d, g/; the first formant transition is very similar for /b/, /d/, and /g/. Some other aspect of the sounds determines which of these three is actually heard. The sounds illustrated are actually identified as /di/ and /du/ when presented to listeners. On the basis of a number of perceptual experiments using such synthetic speech sounds, Liberman et al. (1967) concluded that the second formant transitions in the patterns are the cues for the perception of /d/ as opposed to /b/ or /g/. Notice that, although listeners identify both /di/ and /du/ as beginning with the phoneme /d/, the acoustic patterns at the beginning of the sounds are vastly different for the two sounds. For /di/, the second formant rises from about 2200 to 2600 Hz, while for /du/ it falls from 1200 to 700 Hz. These differences are an example of coarticulation. At the release of the sound, when the /d/ is produced, the lips are already in the position appropriate for the following vowel. Different vowels inevitably give rise to different formant transitions. Thus, the same phoneme can be cued, in different contexts, by acoustic patterns that are vastly different.

It should be noted that highly simplified patterns such as those in Fig. 9.4 do not produce very convincing speech sounds; the /di/ and /du/ are not clearly heard. In natural speech, there may be many cues other than the second formant transition to signal the distinction between the two sounds. I return to this point later.

Liberman et al. (1985) have argued that the context-dependent restructuring of the acoustic patterns seen here for the /d/ phoneme occurs quite generally for consonant sounds. It is rarely possible to find invariant acoustic cues corresponding to a given consonant. For steady vowels, the frequencies of the formants do provide more or less invariant cues, but vowels are rarely steady in normal speech. Usually vowels are articulated between consonants at rather rapid rates, so that "vowels also show substantial restructuring—that is, the acoustic signal at no point corresponds to the vowel alone, but rather shows, at any instant, the merged influences of the preceding or following consonant" (Liberman et al., 1967). The general conclusion is that a single stretch of acoustic signal may carry information about several neighboring phonemes. Thus, there is a complex relation between acoustic pattern and phoneme. Liberman and his colleagues have argued that this implies that phoneme perception requires a special decoder. Liberman et al. (1967) refer to those phonemes whose acoustic patterns show considerable context-dependent restructuring as "encoded", while those phonemes for which there is less restructuring are called "unencoded". They suggested that the perception of encoded phonemes (such as stops) differs from the perception of unencoded phonemes (such as vowels) and from the perception of non-speech sounds. However, it is generally held that there is no clear dichotomy between encoded and unencoded phonemes. Encodedness can be regarded as a dimension going from more contextually dependent to less contextually dependent.

It should be noted that the arguments of Liberman and coworkers are partly based on the assumption that phonemes are basic units of perception, an assumption that is questioned (Plomp, 2002). If perception is based on the analysis of larger units, such as syllables or words, then the difference between the /d/ in /di/ and the /d/ in /du/ becomes largely irrelevant. Also, there is evidence that coarticulation actually improves the ability to identify speech sounds. For example, the ability to identify vowels can be better for vowels in consonant-vowel-consonant words than for vowels presented in isolation (Strange and Bohn, 1998).

3C CATEGORICAL PERCEPTION

For highly encoded phonemes, certain small changes to the acoustic signal may make little or no difference to the way the sound is perceived, while other equally small changes produce a distinct change, altering the phoneme identity. Liberman *et al.* (1967) demonstrated this using simplified synthetic speech signals in which the second formant transition was varied in small, acoustically equal steps through a range sufficient to produce the percept of the three syllables /bi/, /di/, and /gi/. Subjects did not hear a series of small changes in the acoustic signal, but "essentially quantal jumps from one perceptual category to another" (Liberman *et al.*, 1967). It was found that subjects did not hear changes within one phoneme category, but only changes from one phoneme to another. This was called categorical perception. Notice that categorical perception does not normally occur for non-speech sounds. For an acoustic signal varying along a single dimension, such as frequency, it is normally possible to discriminate many more stimuli than can be identified absolutely (see Chapter 8, Section 2).

To demonstrate categorical perception in the laboratory, both identification and discrimination tasks must be performed. The identification task establishes the boundaries between phonetic categories. In the discrimination task, three or four successive stimuli are presented, one of which is different from the others. The listener is required to pick the odd one out. For the ideal case of categorical perception, discrimination would be high for stimuli that straddle category boundaries (i.e., that are labeled differently), but would drop to chance level for pairs of stimuli falling within one category. In practice the situation is rarely as straightforward as this, but, whenever discrimination of acoustic changes is good across phoneme boundaries and poor within phoneme categories, this is taken as evidence of categorical perception.

The perception of steady vowels is very different. Small physical changes in the acoustic stimulus are easily perceived, one vowel may be heard to shade into another, and many intra-phonemic variations may be heard. Liberman *et al.* (1967) suggested that this is because vowels are much less encoded than consonants, so they may be perceived in the same way as non-speech sounds. However, as noted above, vowel sounds in rapidly articulated speech do show restructuring, and there is evidence (Stevens, 1968) that perception of certain vowels in their proper dynamic context is more nearly categorical than is found for steady vowels.

Although categorical perception has been considered to reflect the operation of a special speech decoder, there is evidence that categorical perception can occur for non-speech signals (Locke and Kellar, 1973; Miller *et al.*, 1976; Burns and Ward, 1978). For example, Miller *et al.* (1976) presented a low-level noise stimulus whose onset could occur at various times in relation to the onset of a more intense buzz stimulus (a filtered square wave). In one part of the experiment, subjects labeled single stimuli with either of two responses: "no noise" or "noise". They found that labeling shifted abruptly around a noise lead time of about 16 ms: when the noise onset occurred more than 16 ms before that of the buzz, the label "noise" was applied, otherwise the label "no noise" was applied. Subjects were also required to discriminate among stimuli differing in relative noise onset time. They found that discrimination was best for pairs of stimuli that lay on either side of the 16-ms boundary. These findings resemble the categorical perception found for synthetic speech stimuli.

Demonstrations of categorical perception for non-speech stimuli indicate that the phenomenon is not unique to speech and that its explanation does not depend on the existence of a special speech decoder. However, it appears to occur commonly for speech sounds, whereas it is rare for non-speech sounds. How, then, can it be explained? I consider three explanations, which are not mutually exclusive.

The first explanation is that the differences in perception that are observed for "encoded" consonants and relatively "unencoded" vowels or non-speech sounds may be explained in terms of differences in the extent to which the acoustic patterns can be retained in auditory memory (Pisoni, 1973; Darwin and Baddeley, 1974). The acoustic patterns corresponding to the consonant parts of speech sounds often have a lower intensity than those for vowel sounds. In addition, the acoustic patterns associated with consonants fluctuate more rapidly and often last for a shorter time than those for vowels. Consequently, auditory memory for the acoustic patterns of consonants may decay rapidly. It may be that, by the time these acoustic patterns have been processed in the identification of the phoneme, they are lost from auditory memory. Thus, finer discrimination of stimuli within phoneme categories is not possible. However, for longer and more intense speech sounds such as vowels, the acoustic patterns may be retained in auditory memory for longer periods, so additional discriminations, based upon these stored patterns, can be made.

A second possible explanation for categorical perception is that categories and boundaries in speech have evolved in order to exploit the natural sensitivities of the auditory system (Stevens, 1981). Thus, the boundaries that separate one speech sound from another tend to lie at a point along the acoustic continuum where discrimination is optimal. Demonstrations of categorical perception using synthetic speech stimuli typically use a series of stimuli that vary in "acoustically equal steps". However, the definition of "acoustically equal" is somewhat arbitrary. Steps that are physically equal on some arbitrary scale may not be equal in perceptual terms. At category boundaries, "physically equal" steps may be larger than average in perceptual terms.

A third explanation for categorical perception is that it arises from extensive experience with our own language. When we learn to understand the speech of a particular language, we learn to attend to acoustic differences that affect the meanings of words and to ignore acoustic differences that do not affect word meanings. Once we have learned to do this, it may be difficult to hear acoustic differences that do not affect word meanings. Categorical perception will arise as a natural consequence of this. Consistent with this explanation, Samuel (1977) found that training could substantially improve the discrimination of stimuli that differed acoustically but were labeled as the same stop consonant. Also consistent with this explanation is the fact that it is sometimes difficult to hear differences between phonemes of an unfamiliar language, differences that are perfectly obvious to a native speaker. For example, native Japanese speakers usually have difficulty distinguishing /r/ and /l/, since the acoustic patterns that distinguish these for an English listener are not used for phonetic distinctions in Japanese.

Evidence relevant to these explanations comes from studies of the development of speech perception. Kuhl (1993) has shown that infants are born with innate language-relevant abilities that seem to depend on general mechanisms of auditory perception. Infants show an ability to categorize stimuli, and they perceive similarities among discriminably different speech sounds that belong to the same phonetic category. However, they initially do this in a way that is not specific to any particular language. By the age of six months, infants' perception of speech is altered by exposure to a specific language. For example, there are demonstrable differences between infants reared in America and in Sweden. Certain phonetic boundaries may disappear, and the ones that disappear vary across languages. These results suggest that both innate sensitivities and learning play a strong role.

Kuhl (1993, 2009) has proposed a theory of the development of speech perception called the Native Language Magnet (NLM) theory. The theory proposes that infants' initial perceptual abilities allow a rough division of speech stimuli into phonetic categories. Exposure to a specific language results in the formation of stored representations of phonetic categories in that language. The categories depend strongly on best exemplars or "prototypes" of each category. The prototypes act like perceptual magnets; each one perceptually attracts stimuli with similar acoustic properties, so that nearby stimuli are perceived as more like the prototype. This causes certain perceptual distinctions to be minimized (those between sounds close to a prototype) and others to be maximized (between sounds that are not close to any prototype, but lie on opposite sides of a boundary between categories). Categorical perception is a natural consequence.

3D Evidence for Brain Specialization

One line of evidence indicating that the perception of speech is special is provided by studies establishing that different regions in the brain play a role in the perception of speech and non-speech sounds. These studies are based on the assumption that the crossed neural pathways from the ear to the brain (i.e., from the right ear to the left cerebral cortex, and vice versa) are generally more effective than the uncrossed pathways. If competing stimuli are presented simultaneously to the two ears (e.g., two different spoken messages), then (for most people) speech stimuli presented to the right ear are better identified than those presented to the left, while the reverse is true for melodies (Broadbent and Gregory, 1964; Kimura, 1964). This suggests that speech signals are more readily decoded in the left cerebral hemisphere than in the right. Studies of deficiencies in speech perception and production for people with brain lesions have also indicated that the left hemisphere plays a primary role in speech perception (Broadbent and Ladefoged, 1959).

It is hardly surprising that there are areas of the brain specialized for dealing with speech. We have to learn the phonemes, words, and grammar of our own language, and this knowledge has to be used in understanding speech. However, it could still be the case that the initial auditory processing of speech sounds is similar to that of non-speech sounds.

3E Evidence for a Speech Mode from Sine Wave Speech and Other Phenomena

When we listen to sounds with the acoustical characteristics of speech, we seem to engage a special way of listening, called the "speech mode". Evidence for this comes from studies of the perception and identification of sounds that vary in the extent to which their acoustic characteristics approach those of speech. House *et al.* (1962) required subjects to learn to associate members of various ensembles of acoustic stimuli with buttons on a response box. They found that stimuli with spectral and temporal properties similar to those of speech were learned more readily than simpler stimuli, but only if the speech-like stimuli were actually identified by the listener as speech. Thus, as Stevens and House (1972) have put it, although one can imagine an acoustic continuum in which the sounds bear a closer and closer relation to speech, there is no such continuum as far as the perception of the sounds is concerned—the perception is dichotomous. Sounds are perceived either as linguistic or as nonlinguistic entities.

In some cases, the speech mode can be engaged by highly unnatural signals, provided those signals have the temporal patterning appropriate for speech. An example is provided by the work of Remez and his colleagues on "sine wave speech" (Remez *et al.*, 1981). They analyzed sentences to determine how the frequencies and amplitudes of the first three formants varied over time. They then generated synthetic signals consisting of just three sinusoids. The frequencies and amplitudes of the sinusoids were set equal to those of the first three formants of the original speech and changed over time in the same way. Such signals are quite different from natural speech, lacking the harmonic structure of speech and not having the pulsing structure associated with voicing.

Remez *et al.* (1981) found that these artificial signals could be perceived in two ways. Listeners who were told nothing about the stimuli heard science-fiction-like sounds, electronic music, computer beeps, and so on. Listeners who instead were instructed to transcribe a "strangely synthesized English sentence" were able to do so. They heard the sounds as speech, even though the speech sounded unnatural. Apparently, instructions to the listener can help to engage the speech mode. However, once that mode is engaged, it is difficult to reverse the process. Listeners who have heard the stimuli as speech tend to continue to do so. It should be emphasized that the temporal patterning of the sine waves is critical. Speech is not heard if isolated steady "vowels" are presented as sine wave speech.

In summary, when we are presented with speech-like sounds, there is a perceptual dichotomy: either the sounds are perceived as speech or they are not. Stevens and House (1972) suggested that "the listener need not be set for speech prior to his hearing the signal; his prepared state is triggered by the presence of a signal that has appropriate acoustic properties". There is a strong involuntary component to this "triggering" of the speech mode; no matter how hard we try, when we listen to natural (as opposed to synthetic) speech, it is impossible to hear it in terms of its acoustical characteristics, i.e., as a series of hisses, whistles, buzzes, etc. Rather we perceive a unified stream of speech sounds.

Like most of the other phenomena indicating that speech perception is "special", listening in a specific perceptual mode is not unique to speech perception. For example, Chapters 3, 6, and 8 (Section 3A) described how a harmonic complex tone can be perceived in two modes. We may listen in an analytic mode, hearing the pitches of one or more individual harmonics, or we may listen in a synthetic mode, hearing a single pitch corresponding to the F0. The latter is the more usual mode of perception. However, the speech mode is unusual in that it operates for an entire class of highly complex and varied acoustic signals, whose main common feature is that they were produced by a human vocal tract.

3F DUPLEX PERCEPTION

This phenomenon was first described by Rand (1974), and it has been explored subsequently by Liberman and his colleagues (Liberman, 1982a; Mann and Liberman, 1983). Consider the simplified synthetic stimuli whose spectrograms are shown in Fig. 9.5. The upper part shows the case where the same stimuli are presented to the two ears. All stimuli are identical in their first and second formants, including the formant transitions. The transition in the third formant can be varied to produce the percept of either /da/ or /ga/ (as described earlier, a transition in the second formant can also be varied to produce a percept of /da/ or /ga/, but in this experiment the second formant transition was fixed at a value that did not clearly indicate a /da/ or /ga/). Consider now the case shown in the lower part of the figure. The stimulus is split into two parts. One part, the "base", consists of the first and second formants with their transitions plus the steady part of the third formant. The base is presented to one ear only. The other part consists of the isolated third formant transition. This is presented to the other ear.

These stimuli are perceived in two ways at the same time. A complete syllable is perceived, either /da/ or /ga/ depending on the form of the isolated formant transition, and it is heard at the ear to which the base is presented. Simultaneously a non-speech chirp is heard at the other ear. Thus, the transition is heard separately, but at the same time it is combined with the base to give the percept of a syllable; it has a duplex role in forming the percept. Note that the base on its own sounds like a stop-vowel syllable that is ambiguous between /da/ and /ga/.

Other examples of duplex perception can be found in the work of Darwin and his coworkers. Gardner and Darwin (1986) showed that frequency modulation of a single harmonic near to a formant frequency made that

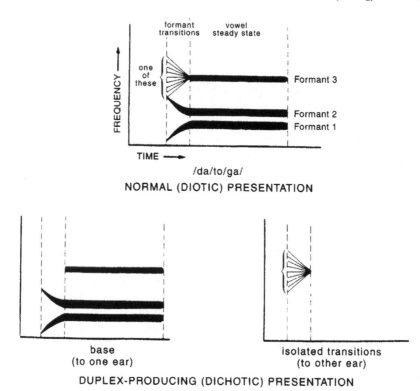

FIGURE 9.5 Schematic spectrograms of the stimuli used to demonstrate "duplex perception". The upper section shows the spectrogram of a complete sound, which is presented diotically (the same sound to each ear). By varying the transition in the third formant, the percept can be changed from /ba/ to /ga/. In the lower section the stimulus is separated into two parts. The "base", consisting of the first and second formants with their transitions and the steady part of the third formant, is presented to one ear. The transition in the third formant is presented to the other ear. Adapted from Mann and Liberman (1983), by permission of the authors and Elsevier Sequoia.

harmonic appear to stand out as a separate tone. However, this did not prevent that harmonic from contributing to the identity of the vowel. Thus, a harmonic can be heard separately but still contribute to vowel quality.

If the formants of a speech sound are separated into two groups with different F0s, then listeners normally report hearing two sounds with different pitches. The sounds are grouped by F0, as described in Chapter 8, Section 3A. However, it has been shown (Darwin, 1981; Gardner *et al.*, 1989) that the phonetic identity of the sound is not always altered by this perceptual segregation. Listeners sometimes report two sound images but only one speech sound.

The phenomenon of duplex perception has aroused considerable interest, partly because it violates the principle of disjoint allocation described in Chapter 8, Section 5D. This principle states that a given acoustic element cannot be assigned to more than one source at a time. The violation was thought to indicate that there are specialized and separate "modules" for dealing with speech and non-speech sounds (Liberman and Mattingly, 1985). The principle of disjoint allocation would then apply within a module, but it would be possible for different modules to share the same acoustic element. In fact, Bregman (1987) has pointed out that the principle of disjoint allocation does not always apply even for non-speech stimuli (or visual stimuli). For example, if a single low harmonic in a complex tone is mistuned in frequency by more than about 3%, it tends to be heard as a pure tone standing out from the complex tone as a whole (Moore et al., 1986). However, that harmonic may still make a contribution to the residue pitch of the whole sound (Moore et al., 1985a). As discussed in Chapter 8, the "rules" of perceptual organization do not always work. However, violations seem more common for speech sounds than for non-speech sounds. It appears that the speech perception mechanism sometimes groups acoustic elements together even when the acoustic properties of the elements suggest that they come from different sources (Darwin and Carlyon, 1995).

One interesting aspect of duplex perception has been revealed by studies of the ability to discriminate changes in the isolated third formant transition (Mann and Liberman, 1983). When listeners are asked to attend to the speech percept, discrimination is best for stimuli that straddle the phoneme boundary. In other words, categorical perception occurs. When listeners are asked to attend to the non-speech chirp, there is no peak in the discrimination function. Thus, the same stimuli are discriminated differently depending on whether listeners are attending to the speech or the non-speech percept.

3G Cue Trading

Some of the synthetic signals described in this chapter contain only a single cue to signal the phonetic contrast between two sounds, such as the third formant transition distinguishing /da/ and /ga/ in the experiment of Mann and Liberman (1983). However, in natural speech almost every phonetic contrast is cued by several distinct acoustic properties of the speech signal (Bailey and Summerfield, 1980). Within limits, a change in the setting or value of one cue, which leads to a change in the phonetic percept, can be offset by an opposed setting of a change in another cue so as to maintain the original phonetic percept. This is known as "cue trading" or "phonetic trading". It has been argued (Repp, 1982) that the properties of cue trading can only be explained by assuming that listeners make use of their tacit knowledge of speech patterns.

Studies of particular interest are those where different patterns of results are obtained depending on whether the same stimuli are perceived as speech or non-speech. For example, Best *et al.* (1981) constructed analogs of a "say"-"stay" continuum by following a noise burst resembling an /s/ with varying periods of silence and then three sinusoids imitating the first three formants of the periodic portion of the speech signal (/ei/). They investigated the trading relation between two cues to the distinction between "say" and "stay". The first cue is the length of the silent interval. The second cue is the initial frequency of the tone simulating the first formant (F1); a high onset indicates "say" and a low onset indicates "stay". A sequence of three stimuli—AXB—was presented on each trial. A and B were analogs of a clear "say" (no silence, high F1 onset) and a clear "stay" (long silence, low F1 onset). The stimulus X contained various combinations of the duration of silence and the F1 onset frequency, and subjects were required to say whether X sounded more like A or more like B. Several subjects were tested, and it was found after the experiment that they could be divided into two groups: those who reported that the stimuli were heard as "say" and "stay", and those who reported various non-speech impressions or inappropriate speech percepts. Only the subjects in the first group showed a trading relation between the silent interval and the F1 onset frequency. The other subjects based their judgments either on the duration of silence or on the F1 onset frequency. It seems that a trading relation only occurred with these stimuli when the subjects were listening in the speech mode.

It should not be assumed that trading relations never occur for non-speech stimuli. For example, Parker *et al.* (1986) have shown that trading relations can be found for stimuli that have some speech-like properties but are not actually perceived as speech. Similarly, Chapter 7 described how interaural time differences may be traded for interaural level differences in sound localization. However, the fact that trading relations differ according to whether stimuli are perceived as speech or non-speech provides support for the concept of a special speech mode of perception.

3H AUDIOVISUAL INTEGRATION

The movements of a speaker's face and lips can have a strong influence on our perception of speech signals; what we hear is influenced by what we see. A dramatic example of this is provided by the work of McGurk and MacDonald (1976). They prepared video recordings of a person saying bisyllables such as "baba" and "mama". The video and audio were then rearranged such that the audio recording of one bisyllable was synchronized with the video recording of a different bisyllable. Most observers perceived syllables that were not present in either the audio or the video recordings. For example, the combination of acoustical "mama" and optical "tata" was typically perceived as "nana". Most observers were not aware of the conflict between auditory and visual cues. They "heard" the sound "nana" and were surprised when they closed their eyes and the percept changed to "mama".

The interpretation of these results is not clear. The auditory and visual information are combined in a complex manner that is not always easy to account for; for reviews, see Summerfield (1987) and Massaro (1999). Some authors have argued that audiovisual integration provides evidence for a speech-specific mode of perception that makes use of articulatory information (Repp, 1982; Liberman and Mattingly, 1985). However, it should be remembered that audiovisual integration can occur for non-speech sounds. For example, Chapter 7 (Section 11) described how sound localization can be influenced by vision.

3I INTERIM SUMMARY OF WORK ON THE SPECIAL NATURE OF SPEECH PERCEPTION

I have described several phenomena that have been used to support the argument that speech perception is special. Some of these phenomena were thought to be unique to the perception of speech stimuli when they were first discovered. However, subsequent work, or further consideration of existing work, has indicated that comparable phenomena often exist for the perception of non-speech sounds. Nevertheless, the evidence for the existence of a special speech mode of perception is compelling. It is also clear that certain areas of the brain are specialized for dealing with speech sounds and that speech itself is special by virtue of the special way in which it is produced.

4 MODELS OF SPEECH PERCEPTION

There are many models of speech perception, but no model is generally accepted and few models are complete enough to account for all aspects of speech perception. It is beyond the scope of this book to describe any of these models in detail, but I briefly describe three influential models that may be considered as representative.

4A THE MOTOR THEORY

The "motor theory" of speech perception was proposed by Liberman and his colleagues (Liberman et al., 1967; Liberman and Mattingly, 1985). In its most recent form, the model claims that "the objects of speech perception are the intended phonetic gestures of the speaker, represented in the brain as invariant motor commands that call for movements of the articulators through certain linguistically significant configurations" (Liberman and Mattingly, 1985). In other words, we perceive the articulatory gestures the speaker is intending to make when producing an utterance. The intended gestures "are not directly manifested in the acoustic signal or in the observable articulatory units". A second claim of the motor theory is that speech perception and speech production are intimately linked and that this link is innately specified. Perception of the intended gestures occurs in a specialized speech mode whose main function is to make the conversion from acoustic signal to articulatory gesture automatically.

The proponents of this theory have argued that it can account for a large body of phenomena characteristic of speech perception, including the variable relationship between acoustic patterns and perceived speech sounds, categorical perception, duplex perception, cue trading, evidence for a speech mode, and audiovisual integration (Liberman and Mattingly, 1985). However, the model is incomplete in that it does not specify how the translation from the acoustic signal to the perceived gestures is accomplished. In this sense, it is more a philosophy than a theory of speech perception (Klatt, 1989).

4B INVARIANT FEATURE OR CUE-BASED APPROACHES

A very different type of model proposes that the acoustic speech signal is processed to yield a discrete representation of the speech stream in terms of a sequence of segments, each of which is described by a set (or bundle) of binary distinctive features (Stevens, 2002). These distinctive features specify the phonemic contrasts that are used in a given language, such that a change in the value of a feature can potentially generate a new word. The processing of the signal proceeds in three steps: (1) Detection of peaks, valleys, and discontinuities in particular frequency ranges of the signal leads to identification of acoustic landmarks. The type of landmark provides evidence for features called "articulator-free" features, which identify broad classes of speech sounds (e.g., vowel, consonant, or continuant). (2) Acoustic cues are extracted from the signal near the landmarks to provide evidence for the actions of particular articulators, such as the lips and tongue. (3) The cues obtained in step (2) are combined, taking context into account, to provide estimates of "articulator-bound" features associated with each landmark (e.g., whether the lips or the nasal passages were involved in production of the sound). These articulator-bound features, combined with the articulator-free features in (1), constitute the sequences of feature bundles that are used to derive words. It is assumed that there is a mental lexicon in which words are stored as sequences of segments, each of which is described as a group of distinctive features. The pattern of feature bundles is compared with items in the lexicon, and a few "candidate" sequences of words are selected. A final feedback stage synthesizes certain aspects of the sound pattern that could result from each candidate sequence and selects the word sequence that provides the best match to the original acoustic pattern.

The philosophy underlying this model is that it should be possible to find a relatively invariant mapping between acoustic patterns and perceived speech sounds, provided the acoustic patterns are analyzed in an appropriate way. This point is elaborated in Section 5.

4C THE TRACE MODEL

The TRACE model (McClelland and Elman, 1986; Elman, 1989) is a connectionist model, based on "neural networks". It assumes that there are three levels of representation, each of which contains highly interconnected processing units called nodes. In the lowest level, the nodes represent phonetic features. In the next, they represent phonetic segments, and in the next, words. Each node represents a hypothesis about a particular feature, phoneme, or word. A node "fires" when a particular level of activation is reached, and this signifies confirmation of that hypothesis, i.e., it indicates that a specific feature, phoneme, or word is present. The nodes can be regarded as detectors of specific features, phonemes, or words.

At the feature level there are several banks of detectors, one for each of several dimensions of speech sounds (such as voicing or the onset frequency of F1). Each bank is replicated for several successive moments in time or time slices. At the phoneme level, there are detectors for each of the phonemes. Each spans six time slices. A copy of the array of phoneme detectors exists for every three time slices. Thus, nodes that are adjacent in time span overlapping ranges. At the word level there are detectors for each word. Again, the detectors are repeated across time slices and span overlapping ranges of time slices.

When a speech signal is presented to the network, the nodes collect evidence for their own specific hypotheses. When a given node fires, activation is passed along weighted links to connected nodes. Excitatory links exist between nodes at different levels. This can cause a node at the next level to fire. For example, the node corresponding to a specific phoneme may fire following firing of two or three nodes corresponding to features usually associated with that phoneme. There are also inhibitory links between nodes within the same level. This allows highly activated nodes to inhibit competitive nodes with less activity, resulting in a "winner takes all" decision. The flow of activation is not simply from the lowest level (feature detectors) to higher levels (phoneme and word levels). Excitatory activation can flow in both directions. This can allow information accrued at the word level to influence phonetic identification.

It is beyond the scope of this book to describe the model or its implications in detail. However, the model is able to provide an account of many aspects of speech perception, such as the perceptual restoration of "missing" phonemes, categorical perception, and cue trading.

5 THE SEARCH FOR INVARIANT ACOUSTIC CUES AND THE MULTIPLICITY OF CUES

Some workers have suggested that the role of encoded or overlapping cues in speech perception has been somewhat overstated. Cole and Scott (1974) have noted that speech perception involves the simultaneous identification of at least three qualitatively different types of cues: invariant cues, context-dependent cues (e.g., formant transitions) and cues provided by the waveform envelope (see below). In a review of the literature on consonant phonemes, traditionally considered as highly encoded speech sounds, Cole and Scott (1974) concluded that all consonant phonemes are accompanied by invariant acoustic patterns, i.e., by acoustic patterns that accompany a particular phoneme in any vowel environment. In some cases the invariant patterns are sufficient to define the consonant uniquely, while in other cases the invariant patterns limit possible candidates to two or three phonemes. They showed further that context-dependent cues are also present in all consonant-vowel syllables. In other words, any given syllable contains both invariant and context-dependent cues. The context-dependent cues may sometimes be necessary to discriminate between two phoneme candidates that have been indicated by the invariant cues.

Stevens (1980) and Blumstein and Stevens (1979) have pointed out several of the acoustic properties that may be used to distinguish between different phonemes in natural, as opposed to synthetic, speech. Some of these properties are illustrated in Fig. 9.6, which shows several representations of the acoustic attributes of the utterance "The big rabbits". The stops, fricatives, affricates, and nasal consonants, such as /p, d, s, z, tʃ, m/, are characterized by a rapid change in spectrum over a time period of 10–30 ms. This is shown in the top left of the figure for the consonant /b/. Approximants such as /w/, on the other hand, are characterized by much slower changes in the spectrum. Thus, rapidity of spectrum change is the crucial property for distinguishing these classes of sounds.

A second property is the abruptness of amplitude change accompanying a consonant. A rapid amplitude change together with a rapid spectrum change is indicative of the stop consonants /p, t, k, b, d, g/. These rapid amplitude changes may be seen in the lower part of Fig. 9.6 for the /b/ and /t/ sounds. Note that stops are also associated with an interval of silence or near silence during the closure.

Periodicity also serves to distinguish between certain pairs of speech sounds. For example, the voiced consonant /b/ in English may be distinguished from the unvoiced consonant /p/ by the presence of low-frequency periodicity during the closure interval (see the /b/ sound at the start of "boiling" in Fig. 9.3). Also, for the unvoiced consonant /p/, noise alone is present for a period of time following the release of closure and then voicing begins. The delay between the release of the consonant and the start of voicing is known as the voice onset time (VOT). Thus, voiced and unvoiced consonants may be distinguished by the presence or absence of low-frequency

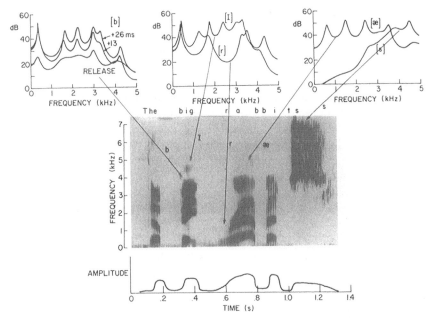

FIGURE 9.6 Several representations of the utterance "The big rabbits". The middle section shows a spectrogram like that in Figure 9.2. At the top are short-term spectra sampled at various points during the utterance. At the bottom is the variation in overall amplitude with time. The spectra have been "pre-emphasized" by boosting the high frequencies relative to the low frequencies. From Stevens (1980), by permission of the author and *J. Acoust. Soc. Am.*

periodicity during the closure interval and by the duration of the VOT. Many other cues to consonant voicing have been described.

For stop consonants, another distinguishing property is the gross shape of the spectrum at the release of the consonant, which can serve to define the place of articulation of the consonant. For example, the spectra for /p/ and /b/ show spectral prominences that are spread out or diffuse in frequency and are flat or falling, as seen in the top left corner of Fig. 9.6. The spectra for /d/ and /t/ show prominences that are spread out, but whose amplitudes increase with increasing frequency, while the spectra for /g/ and /k/ show a distinctive peak in the mid-frequency range, with other spectral peaks being smaller and well separated from the central peak. Blumstein andStevens (1980) showed that sounds with onset spectra having these general shapes are categorized appropriately by human listeners. However, later work (Kewley-Port et al., 1983) showed that dynamic changes in the spectra were more important. It seems that the important property is not simply the gross spectral shape at any one time, but rather the relationship between the spectral shape around the release and the spectral shape of the following sound.

The features described above, when taken together, serve to define uniquely any stop consonant. Thus, the phonemes described by Liberman et al. (1967) as being highly "encoded" do seem to be identifiable from relatively invariant acoustic cues in natural speech.

The bottom part of Fig. 9.6 shows the variation of overall amplitude with time during the utterance. Both amplitude and duration are of considerable importance in determining the prosodic features of speech (those concerned with intonation and stress). A period of silence can provide cues for stress, enabling us to distinguish between such phrases as "lighthouse keeper" and "light housekeeper" (intonation may also play a role). However, such cues are only useful if they are evaluated in relation to duration and amplitude cues from adjacent syllables; speech rates and average intensities vary considerably, so a measure of amplitude or duration taken in isolation would have little significance. Thus, our use of amplitude and duration cues in determining prosodic features indicates that information relating to the waveform envelope can be retained in memory for relatively long time periods.

6 ENVELOPE CUES AND TEMPORAL FINE STRUCTURE CUES

When speech is analyzed in the cochlea, the result is a series of bandpass-filtered signals, each corresponding to one position on the basilar membrane. Each of these signals contains two forms of information; fluctuations in the envelope (the relatively slow variations in amplitude over time) and fluctuations in the temporal fine structure (TFS, the rapid oscillations with rate close to the center frequency of the band). This is illustrated in Fig. 9.7. Information about the TFS is carried in the patterns of phase locking in the auditory nerve (Young, 2008).

The role of envelope cues in speech perception has been studied by filtering the speech into several contiguous frequency bands (each like one of the bands shown in Fig. 9.7) and processing the signal in each band so as to preserve only envelope cues. This is done using what is called a "vocoder" (Dudley, 1939). The envelope in each band is extracted and used to amplitude modulate a noise band (for a noise vocoder) or sinusoid (for a tone vocoder) centered at the same frequency as the band from which the envelope was derived. The resulting signal for each band is passed through a second bandpass filter with the same characteristics as the original filter for that band; this restricts the spectrum of the modulated band signal to the intended frequency range. The modified signals in each band are then added together.

With a moderate number of bands (4–16), vocoded speech in quiet is usually highly intelligible (Shannon, 1995; Loizou, 1999). This demonstrates

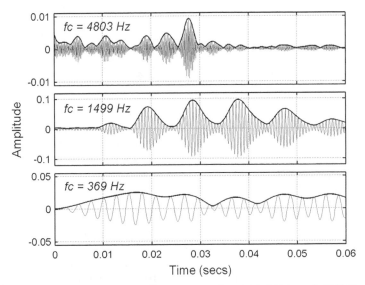

FIGURE 9.7 Outputs of bandpass filters centered at 336, 1416, and 4561 Hz (from bottom to top) in response to a segment of a speech signal, the sound "en" in "sense". The bandwidth of each filter was one ERB_N. For each center frequency, the signal can be considered as a slowly varying envelope imposed on a more rapid temporal fine structure. The envelope for each band signal is shown by the thick line.

that envelope cues in a few frequency bands are sufficient for good intelligibility of speech in quiet. However, when speech in the presence of background sounds is vocoded, intelligibility is much poorer, especially when a fluctuating background sound such as a single talker or an amplitude-modulated noise is used (Nelson, 2003; Qin, 2003; Stone, 2003). This suggests that envelope cues alone are not sufficient to provide good intelligibility of speech in background sounds.

Hopkins *et al.* (2008) extended the approach using vocoders to assess the importance of TFS information in speech perception. They measured speech reception thresholds (SRTs: the speech-to-background ratio required for 50% correct key words in sentences) for target sentences presented in a background talker. The mixture was filtered into 32 bands, each with a

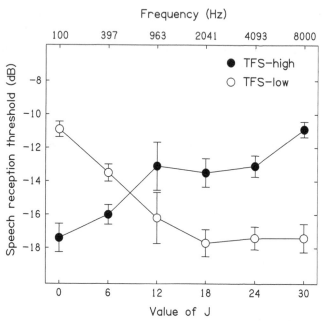

FIGURE 9.8 Results of Hopkins and Moore (2010), showing the speech reception threshold (SRT) for sentences in a background talker, plotted as a function of *J*. For condition TFS-low, bands containing temporal fine structure information were added from the low frequencies, so the number of bands with temporal fine structure information increased as *J* was increased. For condition TFS-high, bands containing temporal fine structure information were added from the high frequencies, so the number of bands with temporal fine structure information decreased as *J* was increased. Error bars indicate ± one standard error of the mean. The frequency corresponding to *J* is shown at the top.

width of one ERB_N. Bands up to and including band number J were unprocessed, and hence contained intact TFS and envelope information. Bands above the Jth were noise or tone vocoded, so that they conveyed only envelope information. The SRT was measured as a function of J; J was varied from 0 to 32. The SRT declined considerably and progressively, i.e., performance improved, as the value of J was increased from 0 (fully vocoded signal) to 32 (fully intact signal).

In a similar experiment using 30 bands, Hopkins and Moore (2010) explored the effect of adding bands with TFS information either starting from low frequencies (condition TFS-low, the same as described above) or starting from high frequencies (condition TFS-high). For condition TFS-high, the signal was fully intact for $J = 0$ and fully vocoded for $J = 30$. The mean results for seven normal-hearing subjects, obtained using a tone vocoder, are shown in Fig. 9.8. Performance improved as TFS information was added, either starting from the low frequencies (TFS-low, open circles) or starting from the high frequencies (TFS-high, filled circles). These and other results (Hopkins and Moore, 2010) suggest that TFS information plays a considerable role in the ability to identify speech in a fluctuating background, and that TFS information is usable over a wide frequency range.

7 THE RESISTANCE OF SPEECH TO CORRUPTING INFLUENCES

It is clear that in the perception of speech the human listener makes use of a great variety of types of information that are available in the speech wave. Many different cues may be available to signal a given phoneme, but the cues may not be constant and may differ in relative importance from utterance to utterance. Many kinds of context-dependent variations in the acoustic cues occur, and accurate speech recognition depends upon the listener's ability to allow for the effects of context. The multidimensional nature of the acoustic cues allows for a high level of redundancy in the speech wave; there may be several different acoustic cues for a given phoneme, of which just one or two might be sufficient for recognition. This redundancy can be used to overcome the ambiguities inherent in the speech, to lessen the effects of interfering stimuli, to compensate for distortions in the signal (e.g., when the speech is transmitted over a telephone line), and to allow for poor articulation on the part of the speaker. At a higher level of processing, errors made in identifying a speech sound from its acoustic pattern can be corrected using knowledge of the kinds of speech signals that can be produced by the human vocal tract, phonological, syntactic, and semantic knowledge, the "sense" of the message, and knowledge of the characteristics of the speaker, e.g., his or her accent or gender.

One way to assess the degree of redundancy in speech is to eliminate or distort certain features and to determine the effect on the intelligibility of the speech. The results of such experiments have indicated that speech is remarkably resistant to many kinds of quite severe distortions.

One factor that can affect speech intelligibility is the amount of background noise. For accurate communication, the average speech level should exceed that of the noise by 6 dB (i.e., the S/N ratio should be +6 dB). When speech and noise levels are equal (0 dB S/N ratio), the word intelligibility score usually reaches about 50% (Kryter, 1962). However, speech may be intelligible at negative S/N ratios (where the speech level is below that of the noise) for connected speech, particularly if the listener is familiar with the subject matter or if the speech and the noise come from different directions in space (Plomp and Mimpen, 1979). In many real-life situations, the noise is intermittent rather than continuous. This decreases the effectiveness of the noise in masking the speech by an amount depending on the on-off ratio of the noise and the interruption rate (Miller and Licklider, 1950). At high interruption rates (above about 200/s), the noise has effects similar to those of continuous noise. At rates between 1 and 200/s, it is possible to patch together the bits of speech heard between the noise, so that the noise is not a very effective masker. At very slow interruption rates whole words or groups of words may be masked, while others are heard perfectly. Thus, intelligibility drops once more.

A second factor that may affect speech intelligibility is a change in frequency spectrum. Many transmission systems (e.g., a telephone line) pass only a limited range of frequencies. Some of the first investigations of speech intelligibility were conducted by engineers of the Bell Telephone Laboratories, in an attempt to assess the importance of frequency range. Experiments using filters with variable cutoff frequencies have shown that no particular frequency components are essential for speech recognition. For example, if a lowpass filter is used to remove all frequency components above 1800 Hz, then the syllable intelligibility score is about 67%, while normal conversation is fully intelligible. However, speech is equally intelligible if instead a highpass filter is used to remove all frequency components below 1800 Hz. Experiments using bandpass filters have shown that, over a fairly wide range of center frequencies, a surprisingly narrow band of frequencies is sufficient for satisfactory recognition. For example, a band of frequencies from 1000 to 2000 Hz is sufficient for sentences to be about 90% intelligible. Clearly, the information carried by the speech wave is not confined to any particular frequency range. This fits in very well with the notion that there are normally multiple acoustic cues to signal phonetic distinctions in speech.

A third kind of disrupting influence that commonly occurs is peak clipping. If an amplifier or other part of a transmission system is overloaded, then the peaks of the waveform may be flattened off or clipped (see Chapter 1, Section 3, and Fig. 1.5). In severe cases the clipping level can be only 1 or 2% of the original speech wave's peak values, with the result that the original speech wave, with its complex waveform shape, is transformed into a series of rectangular pulses. This severe distortion does degrade the quality and naturalness of speech, but it has surprisingly little effect on intelligibility; word intelligibility scores of 80 or 90% are still obtained (Licklider and Pollack, 1948).

In summary, speech is intelligible under a wide variety of conditions where poor performance might have been expected. Speech remains intelligible in the presence of large amounts of background noise, when all but a small part of the speech spectrum is removed, and when time–amplitude variations in the waveform are destroyed by peak clipping. Once again the conclusion is that no single aspect of the speech wave is essential for speech perception; the speech wave is highly redundant. Each of the distortions described destroys some of the cues carried in the speech waveform, but the remaining cues are sufficient to convey the message. This is of great practical advantage. If speech perception depended on a near-perfect transmission of sound from speaker to listener, then speech communication in most real-world situations would become extremely difficult, and devices like the telephone would have to be much more elaborate and costly than they are. Nature has designed the speech communication process so that it can operate under a great variety of adverse conditions.

8 INFORMATIONAL MASKING OF SPEECH

As described in Chapter 3, Section 11, masking can be of two types: "energetic" masking occurs when the neural activity evoked by the signal plus masker is very similar to that evoked by the masker alone; "informational" masking occurs when the signal is confused with the masker in some way. If a speech signal is represented by a spectrogram, preferably an auditory spectrogram that reflects how the sound is represented in the auditory system (see Fig. 9.3, lower panel), it is apparent that the signal has a sparse representation in the auditory system; the energy is high in only a few spectrotemporal regions, with low energy elsewhere (Darwin, 2009). As a result, when the speech of two talkers is mixed, there is often relatively little overlap between the spectrotemporal regions dominated by one talker and the regions dominated by the other talker. In this situation, the ability to identify the speech of the target talker is limited by informational masking, rather than by energetic masking (Brungart et al., 2001). The problem for the listener is to decide which spectrotemporal regions emanated from one talker and which from the other.

One way of demonstrating this is to analyze the mixture of target and interfering talkers using a representation similar to an auditory spectrogram. The representation is divided into many discrete spectrotemporal regions, which will be called pixels. Spectrograms for the target alone and the interferer alone are also constructed and used to identify pixels where the target-to-interferer ratio in the mixture is high. This information is used to construct an "ideal binary mask" (Brungart et al., 2006; Wang et al., 2009); pixels with a high target-to-interferer ratio are retained and pixels with a low target-to-interferer ratio are removed. A sound is then created from the retained pixels, i.e., from spectrotemporal regions when the target is dominant. The intelligibility of this sound can be very high even when the target talker has a much lower level than the interferer. Also, intelligibility is much higher than obtained using the original mixture of talker and interferer (Brungart et al., 2006; Wang et al., 2009). Thus, artificial segregation of the target and masker using a priori knowledge can lead to improved intelligibility.

The effects of informational masking on speech perception have been studied by manipulating the characteristics of the interferer. Brungart et al. (2001) found that the recognition of speech in multi-talker environments generally worsened when the target and interferers had similar voice characteristics. The target was more intelligible when the interfering talker had a different gender from the target than when their genders were the same. Several studies have shown that speech recognition is a non-monotonic function of the number of interfering talkers. When the test materials were sentences, performance was poorest with two competing talkers (Freyman et al., 1999, 2001; Rakerd et al., 2006). Brungart et al. (2001) found that listeners performed better when they were exposed to the characteristics of the target voice prior to the presentation of the stimulus. Thus, familiarity with the talker can help the listener to segregate the target from the interference.

The informational masking of speech is strongly influenced by whether or not the target and background are perceived to come from the same location in space. This is illustrated by experiments of Freyman et al. (1999, 2001). In one of their experiments, listeners were asked to identify nonsense syllables spoken by a female talker in the presence of a background of either noise with the same average spectrum as the speech or a second female talker. In one pair of conditions, the target and masker were both presented from two loudspeakers, one located directly in front of the listener (0° azimuth) and one located 60° to the right. The target speech from the loudspeaker at 0° was presented slightly earlier in time than the target speech from the loudspeaker at 60°, which made the target speech appear to come from in front, due to the precedence effect (see Chapter 7, Section 6). In one condition (the coincident condition), the background sound was presented in the same way, so that it too was heard as coming from in front. In a second condition (called the separated condition), the background sound was presented slightly earlier in time from the loudspeaker at 60° than from the loudspeaker at 0°, which made the background appear to come from the right. The long-term average spectra of the target and background at the two ears were essentially the same for the two conditions. For the noise background, the percentage of key words identified was only 5–10% better for the separated than for the coincident condition. However, for the female-talker background, the corresponding difference was 15–30%. The greater effect for the speech masker was probably due to a release from informational masking caused by the perceived spatial separation of the target speech and the background.

In everyday life, it is common for background talkers to be located at different azimuths from the talker we are trying to attend to. The experiments of Freyman et al. (1999; 2001) and other related experiments (Wu et al., 2005; Rakerd et al., 2006; Ihlefeld and Shinn-Cunningham, 2008b) show that this spatial separation helps to overcome at least part of the effect of informational masking.

9 GENERAL CONCLUSIONS

Speech is a multidimensional stimulus varying in a complex way in both frequency and time. Although the speech wave can be described in terms of amplitude and time, this does not seem to be the most appropriate description from the point of view of the auditory system; nor is a description in terms of static spectra satisfactory. To achieve a description consistent with the known functioning of the auditory system, the dimensions of intensity, frequency, and time should be shown simultaneously. A display of this type that has been widely used is the spectrogram, which shows how the short-term spectrum of the speech, usually plotted on a linear frequency scale, varies with time. However, displays that take into account the frequency-resolving power of the auditory system may be more appropriate.

A problem in the study of speech perception is to relate the properties of the speech wave to specific linguistic units. It is not clear whether the basic unit of perception is the word, the syllable, the phoneme, or some other unit such as the phonetic feature. Indeed, it is not clear whether it even makes sense to talk about basic units of speech perception. For rapid connected speech, psychoacoustic evidence indicates that the acoustic patterns signaling individual phonetic features or phonemes would occur too rapidly to be separately perceived in correct temporal order. Thus, the recognition of the overall sound pattern corresponding to a longer segment, such as a syllable or word, is more likely. Whatever units are involved, it is clear that information is extracted over relatively long stretches of sound.

A second problem is that of finding cues in the acoustic waveform that indicate a particular linguistic unit unambiguously. It is possible to find a number of relatively invariant cues for phonemes or phonetic features in single words or syllables articulated clearly in isolation, but these cues are not so apparent in rapid connected speech. In many cases a phoneme will only be correctly identified if information obtained from a whole syllable or even a group of several words is utilized. The complex relationship between the speech wave and the linguistic units of speech has been one of the central problems in the study of speech perception and has had a powerful influence on the development of theories of speech perception.

There is good evidence that speech is a special kind of auditory stimulus and that speech stimuli are perceived and processed in a different way from non-speech stimuli; there is a special "speech mode" of perception. The evidence includes: categorical perception, the phenomenon that speech sounds can be better discriminated when they are identified as being phonetically different; studies of cerebral asymmetry, which indicate that certain parts of the brain are specialized for dealing with speech; duplex perception, which demonstrates that a single acoustic pattern such as a formant transition can be heard both as part of a speech sound and as a separate non-speech sound; the fact that cue trading has different properties depending on whether signals are perceived as speech or as non-speech; studies of audiovisual integration, showing that the perceived identity of speech sounds is influenced both by what is heard and by what is seen on the face of the talker; and the finding that speech-like sounds are perceived either as speech or as something completely nonlinguistic. An example of this latter effect is provided by "sine wave speech" in which the first three formants are replaced by sinusoids at the formant frequencies. These are heard either as artificial non-speech sounds or as speech. Many of these phenomena are not unique to speech, but taken together they provide good evidence for a special mode of speech perception.

The complex and variable relationship between the acoustic waveform and the phoneme and the various phenomena indicating that speech perception is "special" have led to the development of the "motor theory". This holds that speech perception depends on the listener inferring the intended articulatory gestures of the talker. However, there are many alternative models. One assumes analysis through a sequence of stages, including analysis in the peripheral auditory system, an array of acoustic property detectors, and an array of phonetic feature detectors. This type of model emphasizes the fact that some invariant acoustic cues do exist if the signal is analyzed appropriately and if the analysis takes into account the relational properties of the signal as it changes over time. Another model is the TRACE model, which is a connectionist model with three layers of representation and extensive interactions between levels.

It is clear that speech perception involves processing at many different levels and that separate information at each level may be used to resolve ambiguities or to correct errors that occur at other levels. The initial analysis of speech sounds into features, phonemes, syllables, or words can be checked and readjusted using knowledge of the ways in which speech sounds can follow one another. Our knowledge of syntax (grammatical rules) and semantics (word meanings) allows further adjustments and corrections, while situational cues such as speaker identity and previous message content provide yet further information. It is likely that the processing of speech does not occur in a hierarchical way from one level to the next, but that there are extensive links between each level. Thus, the information at any level may be reanalyzed on the basis of information from other levels. Some details of the speech wave itself may be retained for a short time in "echoic memory" so that the signal can be reanalyzed.

When listening to one talker in a background of a few other talkers, informational masking may limit the ability to understand the target talker. The effects of informational masking can be reduced or eliminated by differences in the voice characteristics of the target and interferer and by spatial separation of the target and interferer.

The multidimensional nature of speech sounds and the large amount of independent information that is available at different levels of processing produce a high level of redundancy in speech. This is reflected in the finding that speech intelligibility is relatively unaffected by severe distortions of the signal. Speech can be accurately understood in the presence of large amounts of background noise or when it is severely altered by filtering, interruption, or peak clipping. Thus, speech is a highly efficient method of communication that remains reliable under difficult conditions.

FURTHER READING

The following provide comprehensive reviews of phenomena and issues in speech perception, each from a slightly different viewpoint:

Repp, B. H. (1982). Phonetic trading relations and context effects: New experimental evidence for a speech mode of perception. *Psychol. Bull.*, *92*, 81–110.

Pisoni, D. B., and Luce, P. A. (1987). Acoustic-phonetic representations in word recognition. *Cognition, 25,* 21–52.

Jusczyk, P. (1987). Speech perception. In *Handbook of Perception and Human Performance. Vol. II. Cognitive Processes and Performance.* New York, NY: Wiley.

Nygaard, L. C., and Pisoni, D. B. (1995). Speech perception: New directions in research and theory. In J. L. Miller & P. D. Eimas (Eds.), *Speech, Language and Cognition.* San Diego, CA: Academic Press.

Hawkins, S., and Smith, R. (2001). Polysp: A polysystemic, phonetically-rich approach to speech understanding. *Ital. J. Linguistics-Rivista di Linguistica, 13,* 99–188.

Jusczyk, P. W., and Luce, P. A. (2002). Speech perception and spoken word recognition: Past and present. *Ear Hear, 23,* 2–40.

Moore, B. C. J., Tyler, L. K., and Marslen-Wilsen, W. D. (2009). *The Perception of Speech: From Sound to Meaning.* Oxford: Oxford University Press.

The following chapter provides a detailed review and evaluation of models of speech perception:

Klatt, D. (1989). Review of selected models of speech perception. In W. D. Marlsen-Wilson (Ed.), *Lexical Representation and Process.* Cambridge, MA: MIT Press.

The following chapter reviews the role of frequency selectivity in speech perception, for both normal and impaired hearing:

Rosen, S., and Fourcin, A. (1986). Frequency selectivity and the perception of speech. In B. C. J. Moore (Ed.), *Frequency Selectivity in Hearing.* London: Academic.

CHAPTER 10

Practical Applications

1 INTRODUCTION

This chapter describes some practical applications of auditory research. The topics chosen are by no means exhaustive, but are meant to illustrate the range of possible applications.

2 APPLICATIONS OF PSYCHOACOUSTIC RESEARCH IN THE ALLEVIATION OF HEARING LOSS

2A HEARING AID DESIGN

Psychoacoustic research can help in the design of hearing aids to compensate for some of the abnormalities of perception that occur in the impaired ear. These abnormalities include loudness recruitment (Chapter 4, Section 9A) and reduced frequency selectivity (Chapter 3, Section 12); for a review, see Moore (2007). Psychoacoustics has two roles to play in this. The first is in the characterization of the perceptual abnormalities. This is important for deciding what type of compensation should be used. The second is in the design and evaluation of particular compensation schemes.

An example of this approach is found in attempts to compensate for loudness recruitment. In an ear with recruitment, the absolute threshold is elevated, but the level at which sounds become uncomfortably loud may be almost normal. That is, the growth of loudness level with increasing level is more rapid than normal. A hearing aid that amplifies all sounds equally is not satisfactory for a person with recruitment. If the gain of the aid (the amount by which it amplifies, usually specified in decibels) is set so as to make faint sounds audible, then more intense sounds are overamplified and are uncomfortably loud.

One method of compensating for loudness recruitment is to use a hearing aid that amplifies low-level sounds more than high-level sounds (Steinberg and Gardner, 1937). In some early hearing aids, this was done in a crude way by limiting the maximum voltage that could be generated by the output amplifier, but this introduced a considerable amount of distortion (see Fig. 1.5), it sounded very unpleasant, and it led to reduced speech intelligibility (Crain and van Tasell, 1994). An alternative method is to use an amplifier whose gain is adjusted automatically according to the level of the input, averaged over a certain period of time. This is often called automatic gain control (AGC) and is also referred to as "compression", because a wide range of levels at the input is compressed into a smaller range at the output. AGC is widely used in modern hearing aids. Although the idea of AGC appears simple, it has turned out to be rather difficult to design effective AGC systems for hearing aids. To understand why, it is helpful to consider the types of variations in sound level that occur in everyday life.

The average level of speech varies from one situation to another over a range of at least 30 dB (Killion, 1997). A person with recruitment may only be able to hear comfortably over a much smaller range of sound levels. This problem can be dealt with by using slow-acting AGC, for which the gain changes slowly from one situation to another. Unfortunately, it is also necessary for the gain to be rapidly reduced in response to a sudden intense sound such as a door slamming or a cup being dropped. If the gain takes a long time to recover after a brief intense sound, as is the case with slow-acting AGC, the aid appears to be "dead" for a certain time, which is very annoying for the user. Moore and coworkers (Moore and Glasberg, 1988a; Moore et al., 1991a; Stone et al., 1999) have described an AGC system that changes gain slowly from one situation to another, but can rapidly reduce the gain for sudden intense sounds. After cessation of a brief intense sound, the gain returns quickly to what it was before the intense sound occurred. This type of AGC is very effective in dealing with variations in overall sound level from one situation to another, and it has been incorporated in several commercial hearing aids (and cochlear implants, which are described later).

Even for speech at a constant average level, individual acoustic elements may vary over a range of 30 dB or more (Dunn and White, 1940; Moore *et al.*, 2008). Typically, the acoustic elements associated with vowels are more intense than those associated with consonants. Thus, a person with severe recruitment may be able to hear the vowel sounds, but weaker consonants may be inaudible. To deal with this, it is necessary to use AGC whose gain changes rapidly, so that the levels of weak consonants can be increased relative to those of vowels. This is often called "syllabic compression". A problem with syllabic compression is that it introduces "cross-modulation" (Stone and Moore, 2003, 2004). Consider a situation where two people are talking at once. The amplitude fluctuations in the speech are largely independent for the two talkers. However, when syllabic compression is applied, the time-varying gain is applied to the mixture of the two speech signals, and therefore, their amplitude fluctuations become partly correlated; this is the cross-modulation effect. The effect makes it harder to perceptually segregate the two voices, because common amplitude modulation is interpreted by the auditory system as indicating that sounds emanate from a common source; see Chapter 8, Section 3D.

When implementing AGC, it is important to take into account the fact that the amount of recruitment is usually not constant as a function of frequency. For example, the threshold elevation is often greater for high-frequency sounds than for low-frequency sounds. Consequently, the rate of growth of loudness with intensity may be almost normal at low frequencies, but markedly abnormal at high frequencies. Thus, the compression appropriate at one frequency is inappropriate at other frequencies. One way of dealing with this is to split the input into a number of frequency bands, using several band-pass filters, and to apply the appropriate amount of compression to the output of each filter. The compressed signals are then combined for presentation to the ear.

Evaluations of multiband compression systems have given mixed results. Some studies have shown distinct advantages for multiband compression (Villchur, 1973), while others have shown no advantage (Barford, 1978). However, many studies have used speech stimuli in which the range of levels has been very restricted. When the speech used for testing covers a range of sound levels, as would occur in everyday life, multiband compression does have advantages (Lippmann *et al.*, 1981; Moore *et al.*, 1992; Hickson, 1994; Moore, 1995).

Almost all modern hearing aids incorporate some form of multiband compression, but they vary in whether the compression is slow-acting, fast-acting, or a combination of the two. There is still controversy as to the "best" compression speed, if there is such a thing (Moore, 2008). There may be individual differences, some hearing-impaired people performing better with slow compression and some performing better with fast compression (Gatehouse et al., 2006a,b). The underlying reasons for these individual differences remain unclear, but cognitive abilities may play some role (Gatehouse et al., 2006b; Lunner and Sundewall-Thoren, 2007).

2B HEARING AID FITTING

Hearing aids with multiband compression are rather complex to fit to the individual person. Many such aids have a large number of frequency bands (up to 24), and it is possible to adjust the gain and amount of compression independently in each band or in small groups of bands. This means that there are many parameters to adjust. One approach to this problem has been to try to quantify the loudness recruitment of the patient at different center frequencies by obtaining loudness judgments as a function of level for stimuli such as tones or bands of noise (Allen et al., 1990). The results of the loudness scaling judgments can be used to calculate the level-dependent gains required at each frequency to restore loudness perception to "normal". However, the reliability of loudness scaling procedures has been questioned (Elberling, 1999), and this approach is not often used nowadays.

An alternative approach is to use a model of loudness to estimate the required settings from the audiogram of the patient. Models of loudness of the type described in Chapter 4 (Section 4) have been modified to account for and predict the perception of loudness by hearing-impaired people (Florentine and Zwicker, 1979; Moore and Glasberg, 1997, 2004). The model described by Moore and Glasberg (2004) makes it possible to predict the loudness of a sound from the spectrum of the sound and the audiogram of the hearing-impaired person.

Loudness models can be used in a variety of ways for fitting hearing aids. One approach is to attempt to restore loudness perception to "normal". With this approach, the frequency-dependent gain for any given sound should be such that the loudness perceived by the hearing-impaired listener is the same as would be perceived by a normally hearing listener without amplification. In one implementation of this approach, the loudness model is used to calculate the required gain in each band of a multiband aid on a moment-by-moment basis. This requires that the loudness model is built into the hearing aid, which is possible with modern digital hearing aids (Kollmeier and Hohmann, 1995; Launer and Moore, 2003). Another approach is to use the loudness model to determine the level-dependent and frequency-dependent gains that would be required to restore loudness to normal for steady sounds with spectra resembling the long-term average spectra of speech. These gains can then be programmed into the hearing aid (Moore, 2000).

Yet another approach is to apply frequency-selective amplification so as to make the loudness of speech equal (as far as possible) in different frequency bands over the frequency range that is most important for speech intelligibility (roughly 500–5000 Hz). This is equivalent to creating a "flat" specific loudness pattern over that frequency range (see Chapter 4, Section 4). This approach was widely used for the fitting of linear hearing aids, in which the gain does not vary with level (Byrne and Dillon, 1986). The basic idea was to place as much of the speech spectrum as possible above absolute threshold for a given overall loudness and to prevent "self-masking" (where one part of the speech spectrum is masked by an adjacent part). The required gains can again be determined using a loudness model (Moore and Glasberg, 1998). However, for linear hearing aids, a flat specific loudness pattern can only be produced for one input speech level. Usually, the goal has been to make the specific loudness pattern flat for a speech level of 65 dB SPL, which is a typical level for conversational speech. This approach can be extended to hearing aids with multiband compression by using the loudness model to calculate the frequency-dependent gains required to give a flat specific loudness pattern over a wide range of speech levels (Moore et al., 1999a,b, 2010). Evaluations of this approach (Moore et al., 2001; Marriage et al., 2004; Füllgrabe et al., 2010) have indicated that it gives satisfactory initial fittings for many hearing-impaired people, although some further "fine tuning" is often necessary.

2C COCHLEAR IMPLANTS

Conventional hearing aids are of very limited effectiveness for people with profound hearing loss, and they are of no use at all for people with total hearing loss. In a large proportion of these people, the disorder is in the cochlea rather than in the central nervous system, and the auditory nerve is partially intact (but degenerated to some extent). In such people, it is possible to create a sensation of sound by electrical stimulation of the auditory nerve. This occurs because of the way in which the auditory nerve is connected to the central nervous system; nerve spikes in the auditory nerve lead to activity in those parts of the brain that are normally concerned with the analysis and perception of sounds and are interpreted as having arisen from acoustic stimulation.

There are several commercially available systems that restore some useful hearing to people with total or profound deafness by electrical stimulation of the auditory nerve. These systems are known as cochlear implants. Usually, the electrical stimuli have the form of brief pulses of electric current.

The design of cochlear implants has been strongly influenced by psychoelectrical studies, that is, by studies of the ability to detect and discriminate electrical stimuli. For stimuli applied to a single electrode, the most important findings are as follows. "Sounds" can be heard for a wide range of electrical rates of stimulation (number of pulses per second). The apparent pitch of electrical stimuli increases monotonically with rate of stimulation for rates up to 300–600 Hz, but then flattens off, although some people hear pitch increases for rates up to 900 or 1000 Hz (Carlyon et al., 2010; Kong and Carlyon, 2010; Macherey et al., 2011). The smallest detectable change in rate varies considerably from person to person. Some people can detect changes of 5% or less for rates up to a few hundred Hertz, others require changes of around 30%, and a few appear to have hardly any ability to detect rate changes (Merzenich et al., 1973; Fourcin et al., 1979); for a review, see Moore and Carlyon (2005). Some postlingually deafened people can recognize simple melodies or musical intervals played as a pattern of electrical rate changes (Pijl and Schwarz, 1995; McDermott and McKay, 1997; Pijl, 1997; McDermott, 2004). The range of currents between the threshold for detection and the point at which the stimulus becomes uncomfortable is very small, especially for high stimulation rates. Thus, an extreme form of loudness recruitment is present.

Most modern systems use several electrodes implanted within the cochlea. The electrode array is usually inserted at the basal end, through the round window, and does not reach the apical part of the cochlea. The use of several electrodes makes it possible selectively to stimulate groups of neurons within the auditory nerve. Stimulation of neurons in the base of the cochlea gives a sensation described as "sharp", whereas stimulation of neurons closer to the apex gives a "dull" sensation (Clark et al., 1987). Thus, different places of stimulation are associated with different timbres. Unfortunately, it is difficult to restrict the current produced by an active electrode to the neurons closest to that electrode; there is always a spread of current to adjacent neurons. This limits the effective number of separate "channels" for electrical stimulation, although electrode arrays have been developed that lie closer to the neurons being stimulated, and these appear to give more selective stimulation (Cohen et al., 2001; Zwolan et al., 2001).

The discrimination of electrical stimuli by a deaf person is generally much less acute than the discrimination of acoustical stimuli by a normally hearing person (Moore, 2003a). This means that careful thought has to be given to the way in which speech should be "coded" into electrical form, so as to convey as much information as possible. Several different speech-coding strategies are currently in use. For most of these, the speech is passed through an AGC system (Boyle et al., 2009) and then passed through a bank of band-pass filters intended roughly to approximate the filtering that takes place in a normal cochlea. The output from each filter is used to derive a signal that is fed to the appropriate electrode in a multi-electrode array; signals derived from filters with low center frequencies are fed to electrodes close to the apex of the cochlea, while signals from filters with high center frequencies are fed to electrodes at the base. This mimics the frequency-to-place mapping of the normal cochlea. The goal of most coding strategies is to provide information about the short-term spectrum of sounds and about the way that the spectrum changes over time. In one strategy, not now widely used, the analog waveform at the output of each filter is fed directly to one of the stimulating electrodes. In another strategy, called continuous interleaved sampling (CIS) (Wilson et al., 1991), each electrode is stimulated continuously by brief pulses presented at a relatively high rate (typically about 800 pulses per second per electrode, although higher rates are sometimes used). The pulses are interleaved in time across electrodes, so no two electrodes are ever stimulated simultaneously; this minimizes interactions between electrodes. The envelope of the output of each filter is extracted, compressed using fast-acting AGC, and used to control the amplitudes (or durations) of the pulses delivered to a particular electrode; the pulses are amplitude (or duration) modulated by the compressed envelope. Another scheme is called the Spectral Maxima Sound Processor (SMSP) (McDermott et al., 1992). The processor incorporates 16 (digital) band-pass filters with center frequencies spaced from 250 to 5400 Hz. Every 4 ms, the six filters with the largest outputs are selected and six corresponding electrodes are stimulated by current pulses whose amplitudes are determined by the respective filter outputs. The Spectral Peak (SPEAK) strategy (Seligman and McDermott, 1995) is similar to the SMSP strategy, but the signal is processed using a bank of 20 filters (rather than 16 in SMSP). The SPEAK processor continuously estimates the outputs of the 20 filters and selects the ones with the largest amplitudes. The number selected varies from 5 to 10 depending on the spectral composition of the input signal, with an average number of six. The Advanced Combination Encoder (ACE) (Vandali et al., 2000) is a hybrid of the SPEAK and the CIS strategies and allows stimulation of up to 20 electrodes out of 22 at rates up to 720 pps/ electrode.

Results obtained using cochlear implants vary widely across patients even for a single type of processing scheme. However, it is remarkable that, for each of the different processing schemes described above, many patients have achieved good levels of speech understanding without lipreading. Almost all patients find that the quality of their lives has been improved by the implants. Some can understand speech reasonably well even in moderate levels of background noise. Indeed, results with multichannel systems have been so encouraging that implants are now being used for people with significant residual (acoustic) hearing. The implant can then be used in combination with a hearing aid (either in the same ear or the opposite ear). Combined electrical and acoustic stimulation gives significant advantages over electrical or acoustic stimulation alone (Dorman *et al.*, 2008). Also, cochlear implants are being increasingly used in young children, for whom they can be of considerable assistance in enhancing speech production, speech perception, and the acquisition of language (McCormick *et al.*, 1994; Dorman *et al.*, 2000).

3 THE PSYCHOACOUSTICS OF HI-FI SOUND REPRODUCTION

The objective of high fidelity (hi-fi) can be defined as the reproduction of sounds corresponding as closely as possible to the intention of the record producer/performer. Thus, the emphasis is on accuracy or fidelity of reproduction.

Any hi-fi reproduction system contains several different devices, each of which may alter or distort signals in various ways. Common system devices include a compact disc (CD) player, personal music player (PMP), a tuner (radio), an amplifier, and loudspeakers (usually two). Each of these can distort the signal in one or more ways, and for any particular type of distortion, the performance of the chain as a whole is determined by the performance of its weakest link. In the following sections, I describe the ways in which the performance of hi-fi devices is specified and give some guidelines as to the perceptual relevance of these specifications. I then consider in turn each of the major devices in a sound-reproducing system, emphasizing those aspects of performance that are likely to be most important in determining how the system sounds.

3A The Interpretation of Specifications

One specification that is commonly quoted is frequency response. This is measured by using as input to the device a sine wave of constant amplitude but variable frequency. Ideally, the output of the device should not vary as a function of frequency, so all frequencies are reproduced to an equal extent. In practice, there is a limit to the range of frequencies that the device reproduces, and there may also be some irregularities in the response. The degree to which the response differs from the ideal response can be specified by using as a reference level the output in response to a given frequency (often 1 kHz). The output at other frequencies can then be specified relative to this level, and the overall response can be specified in terms of the range of frequencies over which the variations in output level fall within certain limits. Thus, the frequency response for a loudspeaker might be stated as 50–15,000 Hz ±5 dB.

This would mean that the sound level did not vary over more than a 10-dB range for any frequency from 50 Hz to 15,000 Hz.

Two aspects of the response are of perceptual relevance. The first is the overall frequency range. There is little point in having a response that extends below about 30 Hz, because there is little audible energy in music below that frequency, except for some organ sounds or synthesized sounds. The desirable upper limit is the subject of some controversy. Most people cannot hear sinusoids with frequencies above about 20 kHz (Ashihara, 2006; Ashihara et al., 2006), and the absolute threshold for detecting sounds usually increases markedly above about 15 kHz (see Fig. 2.1). Consistent with this, most people cannot detect the effect of low-pass filtering recorded speech or music at 16 kHz (Muraoka et al., 1981; Ohgushi, 1984). Despite this, "super audio" has been introduced, which involves the use of special equipment and recording media (the super audio CD or special versions of the DVD) to reproduce frequencies up to about 48 kHz. Proponents of "super audio" claim that some listeners can hear the difference between music containing frequencies up to 48 kHz and music that is low-pass filtered to remove frequencies above about 20 kHz. However, it appears that the audible effect, when it occurs, is due to distortion in the sound-reproduction equipment, particularly the loudspeakers (Ashihara and Kiryu, 2000). Distortion is caused by the presence of frequency components in the music above 20 kHz, and some of the frequency components resulting from the distortion fall in the range below 20 kHz and can therefore be heard (distortion of this type is discussed below; see also Chapter 1, Section 3). Hence, the reproduction of frequencies above 20 kHz can be regarded as having a harmful effect on fidelity. In any case, it should be noted that frequencies above 20 kHz are strongly attenuated by the middle ear, which effectively acts as a low-pass filter (Puria et al., 1997; Aibara et al., 2001). Thus, in the absence of distortion in the equipment, it seems very unlikely that frequencies above 20 kHz make any contribution to the perceived quality of sounds. A frequency response extending from 30 to 16,000 Hz is perfectly adequate for hi-fi reproduction.

The other important aspect of the response is its regularity. If the frequency response has large peaks and dips, then these affect the timbre of the reproduced sound, introducing "coloration" (Moore and Tan, 2003). Psychoacoustic studies suggest that, under ideal conditions, subjects can detect changes in spectral shape when the level in a given frequency region is increased or decreased by 1–2 dB relative to the level in other frequency regions (Bucklein, 1962; Green, 1988; Moore et al., 1989). Thus, a response flat within ±1 dB will not be detectably different from a perfectly flat response. Even ripples in the frequency response of ±2.5 dB have only a small effect on sound quality (Moore and Tan, 2003).

To summarize, the important features to look for in a frequency response are: ideally the response should be flat within ±1 dB over the range

30–16,000 Hz. A response flat within ± 2 dB over the range 40–14,000 Hz would still be very good.

Most devices distort signals to some extent. In other words, they are not completely linear systems (see Chapter 1, Section 3). Usually the distortion is specified in terms of the extent to which frequency components are present at the output that were not present at the input. Unfortunately, distortion is not usually specified in a way that allows an easy estimate of its audibility. The most common method is to specify harmonic distortion. A sine wave of a particular frequency is used as input to the device. If the device distorts the signal, the output is not exactly sinusoidal, but is a periodic waveform with the same repetition rate as the input. This periodic waveform can be expressed as a fundamental component (with frequency equal to that of the input sinusoid) and a series of harmonics. The total amplitude of the second and higher harmonics, expressed as a percentage of the amplitude of the fundamental, is called the "total harmonic distortion" (THD).

The audibility of harmonic distortion is not predictable from the THD, because audibility depends on the distribution of energy among the different harmonics. If the energy of the distortion products is mainly in the second and the third harmonics, then these harmonics will be masked to some extent by the fundamental component, and if the signal is a piece of music, they will in any case be masked by the harmonics that are normally present in the input signal. In this case, distortion of 2–3% would not normally be noticed. If, on the other hand, the distortion produces high harmonics, then these are much more easily audible and subjectively more objectionable. Distortion in this case should be kept below about 0.1%.

An additional way of measuring distortion is to apply two tones of differing frequency to the input of the device and to measure the amplitudes of other frequencies (distortion products) at the output. Again, the amplitudes of the distortion products are usually expressed as a percentage of the amplitudes of the primary tones. Each tone produces its own harmonic distortion products, but, in addition, there are frequency components produced by the nonlinear interaction of the two tones. If the frequencies of the two input tones are f_1 and f_2, then "combination" products are produced with frequencies such as $f_1 - f_2$, $f_1 + f_2$, $2f_1 - f_2$, $2f_2 + f_1$. This type of distortion is called "intermodulation distortion" (note that the auditory system produces similar distortion products, particularly $2f_1 - f_2$; see Chapters 1, 3, and 6). Once again, it is difficult to predict the audibility of a given percentage of intermodulation distortion in a normal listening situation, because the figures quoted by a manufacturer depend on the exact frequencies and relative levels of the tones chosen for the test. In general, intermodulation distortion is more easily audible than harmonic distortion, but values of less than 0.5% are unlikely to be detected. Methods for calculating the audibility of distortion based on auditory models have been developed, but are beyond the scope of this chapter (Tan *et al.*, 2004).

Many devices add a certain amount of undesired noise to the signal. This noise usually takes the form of a low-frequency hum (related to the frequency of the alternating current power supply) and a high-frequency hiss. The performance of a device in this respect is usually specified as the ratio of the output power with a relatively high-level input signal to the output power due to hum and noise alone. The ratio is normally expressed in decibels. Sometimes the hum and noise are "weighted" to reflect the sensitivity of the ear to different frequencies. This is rather like the weighting used in the sound level meters described in Chapter 4, and it usually results in a higher signal-to-noise ratio. A ratio of 70 dB unweighted or 80 dB weighted is adequate for listening to music at moderate sound levels, although for source material with a very wide dynamic range (as is sometimes found on CDs), and when high listening levels are used, higher ratios are desirable (Stuart, 1994).

3B Amplifiers

The basic performance of even a moderately priced hi-fi amplifier is likely to be so good that improvements in technical specification would make little audible difference. For example, a moderately good amplifier will have a frequency response from 20 to 20 000 Hz ± 1 dB, distortion less than 0.1%, and a signal-to-noise ratio greater than 90 dB (for input signals with a reasonably high level, such as from a CD player). These values are better than the limits required by the ear. Nevertheless, some aspects of performance are worth considering.

The necessary power output of an amplifier can only be determined in relation to the loudspeakers with which it will be used. For most transistor amplifiers, the distortion increases very rapidly once a certain power output is exceeded. If the amplifier power is inadequate, then distortion will be easily heard during more intense passages. Loudspeakers vary considerably in the efficiency with which they convert electrical energy into sound energy; "horn" loudspeakers may have efficiencies of 30% or more, while "transmission line" loudspeakers may convert less than 1% of the electrical energy into sound. Thus, it is nonsense to say, as one manufacturer has done, that an amplifier produces "forty-four watts of pure sound". In fact, even one acoustic watt, in a normal-sized room, would correspond to an extremely loud sound. There are many loudspeakers available that produce high sound levels (in excess of 90 dB SPL at a distance of 1 m) with quite moderate electrical inputs, say 1 W. In other words, given loudspeakers of reasonable efficiency, it is quite unnecessary to spend a lot of money on a high-power amplifier. Additionally, it is worth remembering that a doubling of power (which might mean a doubling in price) produces only a 3-dB increase in sound level, which is only just noticeable (see Chapter 4). However, with loudspeakers of low efficiency, a high-power amplifier may be necessary to produce adequate sound levels without significant distortion.

3C LOUDSPEAKERS

Efficiency is an important aspect of loudspeaker performance. As mentioned in the previous section, loudspeakers vary considerably in the efficiency with which they convert electrical energy into sound energy. A common way of specifying efficiency is in terms of the electrical input (in watts) required to produce a sound level of 90 dB SPL at a distance of 1 m from the loudspeaker. An alternative is to specify the sound level produced at a distance of 1 m by an input of 1 W. This level can vary from as little as 77 to over 100 dB SPL. A 200-W amplifier would be needed to produce the same sound level in the first case as a 1-W amplifier in the second case.

Most loudspeakers have frequency responses that are considerably less regular than those of amplifiers. Many loudspeakers are so bad that the manufacturers do not specify decibel limits when quoting a "frequency range" for their loudspeakers. A frequency response without decibel limits is meaningless.

The frequency response of a loudspeaker is normally measured in an anechoic chamber, so that there is no reflected sound from walls, ceiling, or floor. In domestic situations, reflected sound is always present and influences the perceived sound quality to some extent. High frequencies are usually absorbed more than low frequencies, so the relative level of the low frequencies is boosted. Additionally, at certain low frequencies, room resonances may occur, making bass notes sound "boomy". Finally, at high frequencies, complex interference patterns are set up, and therefore the sound entering the ears depends strongly on the exact position of the head.

Given that room acoustics must have an influence on the "effective" frequency response of a loudspeaker, one might think that the response of a loudspeaker measured in an anechoic chamber is not particularly relevant to how the loudspeaker will sound. This is not in fact the case, because peaks and dips in the "anechoic" frequency response combine with peaks and dips produced by room acoustics to produce an overall response that is more irregular than either alone. To minimize this irregularity, the "anechoic" frequency response should be as smooth as possible. In addition, listeners appear to compensate for the characteristics of a room (or of transmission channels in general) in judging the nature of sound sources (Watkins and Makin, 1996; Watkins, 1998; Toole, 2008).

The frequency response of a loudspeaker is usually measured with a microphone directly in front of the loudspeaker, a position known as "on axis". If the microphone is placed "off axis", at some angle to the loudspeaker but at the same distance from it, the measured output often falls. This is because the sound is "beamed" forward by the loudspeaker, rather than being propagated equally in all directions. A very narrow beam at any given frequency is undesirable, because the character of the reproduced sound would be strongly influenced by listening position. For conventional loudspeakers, the degree of beaming depends on the size of the transducer (the vibrating area) relative to the wavelength of the sound being reproduced. The smaller the transducer and the lower the frequency, the wider is the beam. Thus, for a single transducer, the beam gets narrower as the frequency increases. This means that, if the frequency response is flat on axis, it will fall with increasing frequency off axis. Toole (1986a,b) has shown that listeners prefer a frequency response that is the same (i.e., flat) on axis and off axis. In other words, the beaming should not vary with frequency, which means that the total power radiated into the room is independent of frequency. Most manufacturers have dealt with this problem by using more than one transducer, each of which produces a reasonably wide beam over the range of frequencies it reproduces. However, because the angle of dispersion for each transducer varies with frequency, the response off axis tends to be a lot less regular than the response on axis. A frequency response of 50–15,000 Hz ± 3 dB, both on axis and at $\pm 45°$ off axis, would be exceptionally good, and, provided other aspects of its performance were also good, a loudspeaker with this response would add little of its own quality to the reproduced sound; it would be an accurate transducer.

For a waveform to be reproduced accurately, not only should all the frequency components be reproduced at the correct relative amplitudes, but also the relative phases of the components should be preserved. This is equivalent to saying that, at the listener's ear, the time delay of all frequency components should be equal. Changes in the relative phases of the components can produce marked changes in a waveform. Loudspeaker manufacturers have not paid much attention to this, because it has generally been assumed that the ear is insensitive to changes in relative phase. The statement that the ear is "phase deaf" is often ascribed to Helmholtz (1863, 1954), who experimented with harmonic complex tones containing harmonics 1–8. In fact, Helmholtz did not exclude the possibility that phase changes were detectable for high harmonics, beyond the sixth to eighth, and more recent work has shown that phase changes produce both changes in timbre (Plomp and Steeneken, 1969; Patterson, 1988; Roberts et al., 2002) (see Chapters 3 and 8) and changes in the clarity of pitch (Bilsen, 1973; Moore, 1977; Lundeen and Small, 1984) (see Chapter 6). The effects for steady tones are, however, often rather small. This is not particularly surprising, because, for steady sounds, room reflections produce marked alterations in the relative phases of components, and, as discussed earlier, room reflections have relatively little effect on the perceived quality of reproduced sounds.

The situation is rather different for transient or short-duration sounds, which are, of course, common in speech and music. The results of a number of experiments have indicated that we can discriminate between sounds differing only in the relative phases of the components (and not in the amplitudes of the components), even when those sounds have durations as small as 2–3 ms (Patterson and Green, 1970) (see also Chapter 5). When such sounds are reproduced by loudspeakers, any given sound is completed before any reflected sounds (echoes) reach the ears, provided the head of the listener is more than 60–90 cm from any room surface and the loudspeaker is not too close to a wall. Thus, room reflections have little effect on our ability to discriminate between short-duration sounds differing in the relative phases of the components. This has been confirmed by Hansen and Madsen (1974) and Flanagan et al. (2005).

What these results mean is that the phase response of a loudspeaker can be important in determining the subjective quality of the reproduced sound. Changes in the relative phases of components are much more noticeable when those components are close together in frequency than when they are widely separated (see Chapter 3, Section 4D), so phase changes that occur abruptly as a function of frequency have a larger subjective effect than phase changes that occur gradually over a wide frequency range. Unfortunately, the former is the more common situation. Most modern "hi-fi" loudspeakers contain two or more transducers to deal with different parts of the frequency range. A "woofer" is used for low frequencies and a "tweeter" for high. The electronic input to the loudspeaker is split into high- and low-frequency bands by electronic filters known as crossover networks, and the transition frequency between a high band and a low band is known as the crossover frequency. It is in the region of the crossover frequency that rapid phase changes often occur, and thus, the crossover network is a source of phase distortion. One solution to this problem is to use digital filters, which can be designed to have a linear phase response and avoid rapid phase changes. In addition, certain cabinet designs, such as the vented enclosure or reflex cabinet, introduce marked phase changes in particular frequency regions. It is noteworthy that loudspeakers that avoid rapid changes in phase as a function of frequency, such as the Quad electrostatic, tend to be judged as reproducing sounds with greater clarity and realism than those that have a rapidly changing or irregular phase response. Unfortunately, it is difficult to isolate this aspect of performance from other differences between loudspeakers, so it has not yet been conclusively demonstrated that a given loudspeaker sounds better because of its superior phase response.

Blauert and Laws (1978) investigated the audibility of phase distortion by taking a variety of complex sounds, including speech, music, noise, and brief impulses, and delaying a group of frequency components with respect to the remainder. They found that the minimum detectable delay was about 400 µs when the frequencies delayed were in the range 1–4 kHz, although Flanagan et al. (2005) found somewhat higher thresholds (1400–2000 µs). Blauert and Laws also measured the delays that actually occurred for several loudspeakers and headphones. For the headphones, the worst case corresponded to a delay of 500 µs, which is close to the threshold for detection. For the loudspeakers, delays up to 1500 µs were found. These are close to or above the threshold for detection and might therefore have an effect on the perceived quality of the sound reproduced by the loudspeakers. It is to be hoped that in the future the aspects of phase response that are subjectively important will become more clearly defined.

Loudspeakers often give rise to significant amounts of harmonic and intermodulation distortion (Czerwinski et al., 2001). THD amounts of 1–2% are quite common, especially when the input frequency is low, but there is considerable variation across loudspeakers. Such amounts of distortion are far higher than those introduced by amplifiers or CD players. Thus, loudspeakers are often the "weakest link" in this respect.

Finally, there is one myth about loudspeaker performance that should be laid to rest. Occasionally in technical and hi-fi magazines, the phrase "Doppler distortion" is used. This distortion arises because the cone in a loudspeaker has to reproduce more than one frequency simultaneously. Consider a high-frequency tone together with a low one. When the phase of the low tone is such that the cone is moving toward the listener, this produces an upward shift in the apparent frequency of the high tone. Conversely, when the phase of the low tone is such that the cone is moving away from the listener, the apparent frequency of the high tone is lowered. These Doppler shifts are similar to the shift in pitch of a train whistle as the train passes you at a station. In principle, therefore, the low-frequency tone produces a slight frequency modulation of the high tone, which might be heard as a distortion. In fact, Villchur and Allison (1980) have shown, both by listening tests and by a theoretical analysis, that Doppler distortion is completely inaudible for any practical cone velocity.

3D Compact Disc Players and Other Digital Systems

Many systems for the digital storage and retrieval of audio signals work in a similar way. Examples are CD players, PMPs, DVD players, and hard disc systems. These systems depend on the sound being coded or stored as a sequence of numbers. Provided that the numbers are stored and retrieved accurately, the performance of such systems is independent of the medium used for storage.

Digital recording systems are of two types. "Lossless" systems are designed to represent all aspects of the signal as faithfully as possible. "Lossy" systems attempt to reduce the amount of stored information by discarding parts of the signal that would not be audible; these are discussed in the next section. Lossless systems generally work in the following way. The sound is picked up by a microphone, which converts the time-varying pressure to a time-varying voltage. The voltage is low-pass filtered, usually with a cutoff frequency of about 20 kHz. The filtered voltage is sampled repetitively at a high regular, rate. For CD, the sampling rate is 44.1 kHz, while for DVD, it is usually 48 kHz. The analog voltage of each sample is converted to digital form (i.e., a number) using an analog-to-digital converter (ADC). The number is in binary format, that is, it is a series of "zeros" and "ones". Each binary digit is called a "bit". The greater the number of bits that are used, the higher is the precision with which the analog voltage can be represented. The CD uses 16-bit numbers, which means that 65,536 different uniformly spaced voltages can be represented. However, recording studios may use ADCs with 18–24 bits to produce a master digital recording.

When a CD or a DVD is played, the sequence of digits is read from the disc, and converted to a time-varying analog voltage using a digital-to-analog converter (DAC). The output of the DAC is not a smoothly varying voltage, but looks rather like a staircase; the voltage shows abrupt steps as it changes from one sampled value to another. However, the output of the DAC is low-pass filtered, usually with a cutoff frequency of about 20 kHz, and this creates a smoothly varying voltage, resembling the voltage originally generated by the microphone.

The range of frequencies that can be reproduced by a digital system is slightly less than one-half of the sampling rate. Thus, a rate of 44.1 kHz is adequate to give a bandwidth of about 20 kHz. The range of sound levels that can be reproduced (referred to as the dynamic range) is determined by the number of bits used to represent each sample. As a rough rule of thumb, each bit gives 6 dB of dynamic range, so a 16-bit system has a dynamic range of about 96 dB. At the lowest level that can be coded, a sine wave would be represented as a sequence of numbers alternating between two discrete values, corresponding to the least significant bit. Thus, the sine wave would be transformed to a square wave and considerable distortion would be introduced. In practice, this distortion is reduced and the dynamic range is extended by adding a low-level noise called "dither" before the ADC (Vanderkooy and Lipshitz, 1984). This noise has a level about 96 dB below the maximum level that can be coded, so the maximum signal-to-noise ratio in a 16-bit system is about 96 dB. In practice, the dither can have its spectrum "shaped" so as to reduce its audibility (Wannamaker, 1992; Stuart, 1994; Stuart and Wilson, 1994). This is done by placing most of the energy of the dither at high frequencies (between 15 and 20 kHz), where the ear is less sensitive (see Chapter 2, Fig. 2.1). This can give an "effective" signal-to-noise ratio and dynamic range that are both greater than 96 dB.

CD and DVD players generally have a specification that is far better than that of loudspeakers. Essentially, the output signal that they provide is indistinguishable from the signal obtained from the master recording produced by the recording studio (studio recordings are now usually digital recordings). Thus, provided such a CD or DVD player is working according to specification, it will produce no noticeable degradation in sound quality. It follows from this that most hi-fi CD players and DVD players sound the same.

This statement should be qualified by saying that CD and DVD players do differ somewhat in their error-correction capabilities; errors occur when numbers are not retrieved correctly from the disc. Thus, it may sometimes be possible to detect slight differences between players in how well they deal with badly damaged or defective discs. However, most CD and DVD players cope very effectively with the errors that are typically present. It is also possible for CD and DVD players to have faults that can produce very noticeable effects. Finally, some manufacturers have produced CD players that have poor DACs and/or poor output amplifiers. This is especially true of cheap portable CD players or CD players incorporated in "boom boxes" or personal computers. Such CD players generally have a poorer than usual specification (e.g., the signal-to-noise ratio may be markedly less than 90 dB), and they may produce some degradation of sound quality. The take-home message is buy a CD or DVD player that has the facilities you require, buy from a reputable manufacturer, and beware of the very cheapest models. On the other hand, there is usually little advantage to be gained in sound quality from spending more than about 200 pounds or 300 dollars on a CD player.

3E Perceptual Coders

Digital recordings require the storage of huge amounts of data. For example, on the CD, two 16-bit samples are stored 44,100 times per second (giving a "bit rate" of 1411.2 kbits/s), so the total storage requirement for a 70-min CD is 5,927,040,000 bits. In practice, the requirement is even greater than this, because extra bits are used for keeping track of time and for error correction (compensation for "missing bits" caused by faults on the disc). The high bit rate is a problem if it is required to broadcast digitally coded sound, because broadcasting channels generally do not have the capacity to transmit digital information at such high rates. It is also a problem if it is desired to store the digital recording on a medium with limited capacity, such as a PMP.

Systems have been developed for digital recording and transmission of sound that can give "hi-fi" sound but with a greatly reduced bit rate (Brandenburg and Stoll, 1994; Gilchrist and Grewin, 1996). These "lossy" systems rely on the masking properties of the human auditory system, and they are given the general name of "perceptual coders". With these systems, the reproduced signal contains considerable noise and distortion, but the noise and the distortion are inaudible to human listeners because they are masked by the "desired" signal. Examples of systems using perceptual coders are "NICAM", which is widely used for television sound in Europe; MP3, which is widely used for Internet transmission of sound files and in PMPs; Digital Audio Broadcasting (DAB); and cinema sound coded using the Dolby AC3 system or the Digital Theatre System (DTS). These systems vary in their exact mode of operation but work roughly in the following way.

The signal is filtered into a number of adjacent frequency bands called sub-bands. Each band is represented as a sequence of numbers, just as the broadband signal is represented on CD or DVD. The sampling rate required for each band is slightly more than twice the width of the band. If each band were coded with 16-bit resolution, this would not give any saving in the bit rate compared to a "conventional" system such as CD. However, it is not necessary to code each band with the full 16-bit resolution. When the width of a band is similar to the ERB_N of the auditory filter at the same center frequency, the signal within that band can be represented by a relatively small number of bits (typically 5–6) over a short time frame, provided that the overall level in that band is separately coded. Only 5 or 6 bits are needed because noise and distortion introduced by the limited number of bits are not detectable when their level is more than about 30 dB below the level of the original signal, provided that their spectrum overlaps with that of the signal. This is achieved because out-of-band distortion and noise are filtered out at the stage when the digital signal is converted to analog form. In practice, the bands used in perceptual coders have widths that are greater than ERB_N at low center frequencies (this is done because filters with very narrow bandwidths tend to introduce unacceptably long time delays). Hence, the low-frequency bands need to be coded with more than 5–6 bits. However, the high-frequency bands can be coded with a relatively small number of bits.

To achieve the saving in number of bits, the sound is divided up into "blocks" (typically lasting 1.5–12 ms). For each band and each block, a scale factor is determined, which codes the overall level in that band and block. This scale factor is transmitted or recorded along with the digital code for the signal in each band. However, the scale factors do not take up much capacity in terms of bit rate, because they are only updated once per block.

A further saving in number of bits can be made in the following way. For each block, a calculation is made of the amount by which the signal in each band is above the masked threshold produced by the signals in adjacent bands. The calculation is based on masking patterns for human listeners, as described in Chapter 3. The number of bits allocated to a given band increases with the amount by which the level in that band exceeds the calculated masked threshold. The absolute threshold may also be taken into account. If the signal in a given band is below the calculated threshold, then no bits at all are allocated to that band (except for the scale factor specifying the level in that band). If the signal level is far above the calculated threshold, then more bits are allocated. The allocation of bits is altered dynamically from block to block. In the replay system, the bands are recombined to give the desired broadband signal.

Such systems can typically reduce the bit rate by about a factor of 5 to 10 (compared to a lossless system) without audible degradation of the signal. Objective analysis, using instruments such as spectrum analyzers, can reveal the considerable noise introduced by perceptual coders. When a given band is coded with a small number of bits, or no bits at all, the signal-to-noise ratio in that band is extremely poor. Nevertheless, listening tests with the better coding systems have revealed that the great majority of human listeners cannot distinguish a perceptually coded signal from the original signal (Gilchrist and Grewin, 1996).

3F Loudspeaker Cables and Optical Cables

Some manufacturers have claimed that sound quality can be improved by the use of special cables between the amplifier and the loudspeakers. It is true that some loudspeakers work best if the resistance of the cable is low. However, this does not require the use of special cable. It merely means that if a long cable is used, then it should be thick so that the overall resistance does not exceed about 0.5 ohm. Ignore claims that exotic cables can give "fuller bass" or "brighter highs"; such claims are without foundation.

Many modern digital devices can be connected via a digital optical cable, for example, between a DVD player and an amplifier. Claims are sometimes made that the quality of the optical cable affects performance and that high-quality (and high-expense) cables are necessary. Again, such claims are without foundation. The basic optical cable that is typically supplied with a CD player or DVD player is perfectly adequate.

4 THE EVALUATION OF CONCERT HALL ACOUSTICS

This topic is one of great complexity, and it is beyond the scope of this book to cover it in any detail. The interested reader is referred to Ando (1985), Barron (1993), Tohyama *et al.* (1995), and Beranek (2008) for further details. Judgments of the acoustic quality of concert halls, and comparisons between different concert halls, are difficult for two reasons. Firstly, the perceived quality at a given performance depends as much on the manner of playing of the musicians and their seating arrangements as on the characteristics of the hall itself. Secondly, long-term acoustical memory is relatively poor, and so many of the subtleties of acoustical quality are not recalled by the time a listener has traveled from one hall to another. Ultimately, the consensus of opinion of a large number of listeners determines whether a hall is "good" or "bad", but it is not easy to define the crucial features that influence such judgments or to derive general rules that could be applied in the design of new halls. Indeed, many new halls are simply modeled on other halls that have been judged as good.

Schroeder *et al.* (1974) have developed recording and reproduction techniques that make possible immediate comparisons of the acoustic qualities of different halls under realistic free field conditions on the basis of identical musical source material. The first step was to make a recording of an orchestra in an anechoic chamber, so that the acoustics of the recording room were not superimposed on those of the hall to be evaluated. This also ensured that the musical material was always identical. The recording was replayed from the stage of the hall that was to be evaluated. Schroeder *et al.* (1974) used a two-channel recording, replayed through two loudspeakers on the stage of the hall, so as to simulate in a crude way the spatial extent of the orchestra. However, there is no reason why the technique should not be extended to multichannel recordings, which would mimic more accurately the sounds radiated by a live orchestra.

The next step was to record the signals using microphones at the "eardrums" of a dummy head. This is a model of a human head and torso with realistic pinnae and ear canals, whose acoustical properties match those of an "average" head as closely as possible. Two different positions were used for each hall, both corresponding to places that would normally be occupied by a listener's head.

The next step was to present the dummy head recordings to listeners for evaluation. To present the signals in a realistic way, the dummy head recordings were electronically processed so that, when played back over two selected loudspeakers in an anechoic chamber, the recorded signals were recreated at the eardrums of a human listener. Schroeder *et al.* (1974) explain the technique as follows.

The sound radiated from each loudspeaker goes into both ears and not just the "near" ear of the listener as would be desired. In other words, there is "crosstalk" from each loudspeaker to the "far" ear. However, by radiating properly mixed and filtered compensation signals from the loudspeakers, the unwanted "crosstalk" can be cancelled out.

The appropriate filter responses in the compensation scheme were computed from measurements obtained by applying short electrical impulses to one of the two loudspeakers and recording the resulting microphone signals from the ears of a dummy head at some distance in front of the loudspeakers. For further details, the reader is referred to the original article and to Schroeder and Atal (1963).

Using this technique, Schroeder and coworkers asked subjects to indicate preferences for different concert halls presented in pairs, one after the other. For the halls with reverberation times less than 2 s, reverberation time was highly correlated with preference; the greater the reverberation time, the greater was the preference. However, for the halls with reverberation times greater than 2 s, the reverberation time was slightly negatively correlated with preference. One factor that showed a strong negative correlation with preference, for halls with both long and short reverberation times, was the interaural coherence. This is a measure of the correlation of the signals at the two ears. Listeners prefer halls that produce a low interaural coherence, meaning that the signals at the two ears are relatively independent of one another. Schroeder et al. (1974) suggested that "This effect might be mediated by a more pronounced feeling—of being immersed in the sound—that presumably occurs for less coherent ear signals". Interaural coherence can be manipulated by sound diffusers on the walls and ceiling of the concert hall.

Finally, for the halls with longer reverberation times, which also tended to be the larger halls, the volume of the halls showed a strong negative correlation with preference. Thus, once a hall has reached a certain size, further increases in size result in a worsening of the perceived acoustic quality.

5 GENERAL SUMMARY AND CONCLUDING REMARKS

In this chapter, I have described some practical applications of auditory research. Hearing aids that process sounds before delivery to an impaired ear can partially compensate for some of the abnormalities of perception that are associated with the impairment. For example, hearing aids incorporating AGC can help to compensate for loudness recruitment. Models of loudness perception for hearing-impaired people can be useful tools in fitting hearing aids to the individual. For people who are totally or profoundly deaf, cochlear implants can provide a means of restoring a limited, but useful, form of hearing.

In the reproduction of sounds, particularly music, the transducers in the reproduction system, especially the loudspeakers, have the greatest influence on the overall sound quality. Unfortunately, the aspects of performance that determine how good a system will sound are often poorly specified. Amplifiers, CD players, and DVD players are usually sufficiently good that they have little or no influence on sound quality. Digital sound recording and transmission systems are becoming increasingly based on perceptual coders, which reduce the required bit rate by exploiting the masking properties of the auditory system.

Recordings made using a dummy head provide a way of comparing the acoustics of different concert halls. The factors correlating most strongly with preference are reverberation time and interaural coherence.

Many other practical applications may occur to the reader. A bottle of fine wine will be given to the reader who suggests the most interesting new applications for inclusion in the next edition of this book.

REFERENCES

Abel, S. M. (1972a). Discrimination of temporal gaps. *J. Acoust. Soc. Am.*, 52, 519–524.

Abel, S. M. (1972b). Duration discrimination of noise and tone bursts. *J. Acoust. Soc. Am.*, 51, 1219–1223.

Abeles, M., and Goldstein, M. H. (1972). Responses of single units in the primary auditory cortex of the cat to tones and to tone pairs. *Brain Res.*, 42, 337–352.

Aibara, R., Welsh, J. T., Puria, S., and Goode, R. L. (2001). Human middle-ear sound transfer function and cochlear input impedance. *Hear. Res.*, 152, 100–109.

Akeroyd, M. A., and Bernstein, L. R. (2001). The variation across time of sensitivity to interaural disparities: behavioral measurements and quantitative analyses. *J. Acoust. Soc. Am.*, 110, 2516–2526.

Akeroyd, M. A., Carlyon, R. P., and Deeks, J. M. (2005). Can dichotic pitches form two streams? *J. Acoust. Soc. Am.*, 118, 977–981.

Akeroyd, M. A., Moore, B. C. J., and Moore, G. A. (2001). Melody recognition using three types of dichotic-pitch stimulus. *J. Acoust. Soc. Am.*, 110, 1498–1504.

Akeroyd, M. A., and Patterson, R. D. (1995). Discrimination of wideband noises modulated by a temporally asymmetric function. *J. Acoust. Soc. Am.*, 98, 2466–2474.

Akeroyd, M. A., and Summerfield, A. Q. (1999). A binaural analog of gap detection. *J. Acoust. Soc. Am.*, 105, 2807–2820.

Alcántara, J. I., Moore, B. C. J., and Vickers, D. A. (2000). The relative role of beats and combination tones in determining the shapes of masking patterns at 2 kHz: I. Normal-hearing listeners. *Hear. Res.*, 148, 63–73.

Alcántara, J. I., Moore, B. C. J., Glasberg, B. R., Wilkinson, A. J. K., and Jorasz, U. (2003). Phase effects in masking: within- versus across-channel processes. *J. Acoust. Soc. Am.*, *114*, 2158–2166.

Allen, J. B., Hall, J. L., and Jeng, P. S. (1990). Loudness growth in 1/2-octave bands (LGOB); a procedure for the assessment of loudness. *J. Acoust. Soc. Am.*, *88*, 745–753.

Anantharaman, J. N., Krishnamurthy, A. K., and Feth, L. L. (1993). Intensity-weighted average of instantaneous frequency as a model for frequency discrimination. *J. Acoust. Soc. Am.*, *94*, 723–729.

Anderson, C. M. B., and Whittle, L. S. (1971). Physiological noise and the missing 6 dB. *Acustica*, *24*, 261–272.

Ando, Y. (1985). *Concert Hall Acoustics*. New York: Springer.

ANSI. (1994a). *American National Standard Acoustical Terminology, ANSI S1.1-1994*. New York: American National Standards Institute.

ANSI. (1994b). *ANSI S1.1-1994. American National Standard Acoustical Terminology*. New York: American National Standards Institute.

Arthur, R. M., Pfeiffer, R. R., and Suga, N. (1971). Properties of 'two-tone inhibition' in primary auditory neurones. *J. Physiol.*, *212*, 593–609.

Ashihara, K. (2006). Hearing threshold for pure tones above 16 kHz. *J. Acoust. Soc. Am.*, *122*, EL52–EL57.

Ashihara, K., and Kiryu, S. (2000). Influence of expanded frequency band of signals on non-linear characteristics of loudspeakers. *J. Acoust. Soc. Jap. (J)*, *56*, 549–555.

Ashihara, K., Kurakata, K., Mizunami, T., and Matsushita, K. (2006). Hearing threshold for pure tones above 20 kHz. *Acoust. Sci. Tech.*, *27*, 12–19.

Ashmead, D. H., Davis, D., and Northington, A. (1995). The contribution of listeners' approaching motion to auditory distance perception. *J. Exp. Psychol.: Human Percept. Perf.*, *21*, 239–256.

Ashmead, D. H., LeRoy, D., and Odom, R. D. (1990). Perception of the relative distances of nearby sound sources. *Percept. Psychophys.*, *47*, 326–331.

Ashmore, J. F. (1987). A fast motile response in guinea pig outer hair cells: the cellular basis of the cochlear amplifier. *J. Physiol.*, *388*, 323–347.

Assmann, P. F., and Summerfield, A. Q. (1990). Modeling the perception of concurrent vowels: vowels with different fundamental frequencies. *J. Acoust. Soc. Am.*, *88*, 680–697.

Attneave, F., and Olson, R. K. (1971). Pitch as a medium: a new approach to psychophysical scaling. *Am. J. Psychol.*, *84*, 147–166.

Avan, P., and Bonfils, P. (2005). Distortion-product otoacoustic emission spectra and high-resolution audiometry in noise-induced hearing loss. *Hear. Res.*, *209*, 68–75.

Axelsson, A., Eliasson, A., and Israelsson, B. (1995). Hearing in pop/rock musicians: a follow-up study. *Ear Hear.*, *16*, 245–253.

Bachem, A. (1950). Tone height and tone chroma as two different pitch qualities. *Acta Psych.*, *7*, 80–88.

Backus, B. C., and Guinan, J. J., Jr. (2006). Time-course of the human medial olivocochlear reflex. *J. Acoust. Soc. Am.*, *119*, 2889–2904.

Bacon, S. P. (1990). Effect of masker level on overshoot. *J. Acoust. Soc. Am.*, *88*, 698–702.

Bacon, S. P., and Gleitman, R. M. (1992). Modulation detection in subjects with relatively flat hearing losses. *J. Speech Hear. Res.*, *35*, 642–653.

Bacon, S. P., and Grantham, D. W. (1989). Modulation masking: effects of modulation frequency, depth and phase. *J. Acoust. Soc. Am.*, *85*, 2575–2580.

Bacon, S. P., and Liu, L. (2000). On the decline in overshoot at high masker levels [letter]. *J. Acoust. Soc. Am.*, *107*, 2295–2297.

Bacon, S. P., and Moore, B. C. J. (1986a). Temporal effects in masking and their influence on psychophysical tuning curves. *J. Acoust. Soc. Am.*, *80*, 1638–1644.

Bacon, S. P., and Moore, B. C. J. (1986b). Temporal effects in simultaneous pure-tone masking: effects of signal frequency, masker/signal frequency ratio, and masker level. *Hear. Res.*, *23*, 257–266.

Bacon, S. P., and Moore, B. C. J. (1987). "Transient masking" and the temporal course of simultaneous tone-on-tone masking. *J. Acoust. Soc. Am.*, *81*, 1073–1077.

Bacon, S. P., and Viemeister, N. F. (1985a). The temporal course of simultaneous tone-on-tone masking. *J. Acoust. Soc. Am.*, *78*, 1231–1235.

Bacon, S. P., and Viemeister, N. F. (1985b). Temporal modulation transfer functions in normal-hearing and hearing-impaired subjects. *Audiology*, *24*, 117–134.

Bacon, S. P., and Viemeister, N. F. (1994). Intensity discrimination and increment detection at 16 kHz. *J. Acoust. Soc. Am.*, *95*, 2616–2621.

Baer, T., Moore, B. C. J., and Glasberg, B. R. (1999). Detection and intensity discrimination of Gaussian-shaped tone pulses as a function of duration. *J. Acoust. Soc. Am.*, *106*, 1907–1916.

Bagley, W. C. (1900–1901). The apperception of the spoken sentence: a study in the psychology of language. *Am. J. Psychol.*, *12*, 80–130.

Bailey, P. J., and Summerfield, Q. (1980). Information in speech: observations on the perception of [s]-stop clusters. *J. Exp. Psychol.: Human Percept. Perform.*, *6*, 536–563.

Baker, R. J., and Rosen, S. (2006). Auditory filter nonlinearity across frequency using simultaneous notched-noise masking. *J. Acoust. Soc. Am.*, *119*, 454–462.

Baker, R. J., Rosen, S., and Darling, A. M. (1998). An efficient characterisation of human auditory filtering across level and frequency that is also physiologically reasonable. In A. R. Palmer, A. Rees, A. Q. Summerfield & R. Meddis (Eds.), *Psychophysical and Physiological Advances in Hearing*. London: Whurr.

Barford, J. (1978). Multichannel compression hearing aids: Experiments and considerations on clinical applicability. In C. Ludvigsen & J. Barford (Eds.), *Sensorineural Hearing Impairment and Hearing Aids*. Scand. Audiol., Suppl.6.

Barron, M. (1993). *Auditorium Acoustics and Architectural Design*. London: Chapman and Hall.

Batteau, D. W. (1967). The role of the pinna in human localization. *Proc. Roy. Soc. B.*, *168*, 158–180.

Beck, J., and Shaw, W. A. (1961). The scaling of pitch by the method of magnitude-estimation. *Am. J. Psychol.*, *74*, 242–251.

Beddor, P. S., and Hawkins, S. (1990). The influence of spectral prominence on perceived vowel quality. *J. Acoust. Soc. Am.*, *87*, 2684–2704.

Benade, A. (1976). *Fundamentals of Musical Acoustics*. Oxford: Oxford University Press.

Bendor, D., and Wang, X. (2005). The neuronal representation of pitch in primate auditory cortex. *Nature*, *436*, 1161–1165.

Benser, M. E., Marquis, R. E., and Hudspeth, A. J. (1996). Rapid, active hair bundle movements in hair cells from the bullfrog's sacculus. *J. Neurosci.*, *16*, 5629–5643.

Beranek, L. L. (2008). Concert hall acoustics—2008. *J. Audio Eng. Soc.*, *56*, 532–544.

Bernstein, J. G., and Oxenham, A. J. (2003). Pitch discrimination of diotic and dichotic tone complexes: harmonic resolvability or harmonic number? *J. Acoust. Soc. Am.*, *113*, 3323–3334.

Bernstein, J. G., and Oxenham, A. J. (2005). An autocorrelation model with place dependence to account for the effect of harmonic number on fundamental frequency discrimination. *J. Acoust. Soc. Am.*, *117*, 3816–3831.

Bernstein, L. R., and Trahiotis, C. (2002). Enhancing sensitivity to interaural delays at high frequencies by using "transposed stimuli". *J. Acoust. Soc. Am.*, *112*, 1026–1036.

Bernstein, L. R., Trahiotis, C., Akeroyd, M. A., and Hartung, K. (2001). Sensitivity to brief changes of interaural time and interaural intensity. *J. Acoust. Soc. Am.*, *109*, 1604–1615.

Best, C. T., Morrongiello, B., and Robson, R. (1981). Perceptual equivalence of acoustic cues in speech and nonspeech perception. *Percept. Psychophys.*, *29*, 191–211.

Bilsen, F. A. (1973). On the influence of the number and phase of harmonics on the perceptibility of the pitch of complex signals. *Acustica*, *28*, 60–65.

Bilsen, F. A. (1977). Pitch of noise signals: evidence for a central spectrum. *J. Acoust. Soc. Am.*, *61*, 150–161.

Bilsen, F. A., and Goldstein, J. L. (1974). Pitch of dichotically delayed noise and its possible spectral basis. *J. Acoust. Soc. Am.*, *55*, 292–296.

Bilsen, F. A., and Ritsma, R. J. (1967). Repetition pitch mediated by temporal fine structure at dominant spectral regions. *Acustica*, *19*, 114–116.

Blauert, J. (1970). Sound localization in the median plane. *Acustica*, *22*, 205–213.

Blauert, J. (1972). On the lag of lateralization caused by interaural time and intensity differences. *Audiology*, *11*, 265–270.

Blauert, J. (1983). *Spatial Hearing*. Cambridge, MA: MIT Press.

Blauert, J. (1997). *Spatial Hearing: The Psychophysics of Human Sound Localization*. Cambridge, MA: MIT Press.

Blauert, J., and Laws, P. (1978). Group delay distortions in electroacoustical systems. *J. Acoust. Soc. Am.*, *63*, 1478–1483.

Bloom, P. J. (1977). Creating source elevation illusions by spectral manipulation. *J. Audio. Eng. Soc.*, *25*, 560–565.

Blumstein, S. E., and Stevens, K. N. (1979). Acoustic invariance in speech production: evidence from measurements of the spectral characteristics of stop consonants. *J. Acoust. Soc. Am.*, *66*, 1001–1017.

Blumstein, S. E., and Stevens, K. N. (1980). Perceptual invariance and onset spectra for stop consonants in different vowel environments. *J. Acoust. Soc. Am.*, *67*, 648–662.

Boomsliter, P., and Creel, W. (1961). The long pattern hypothesis in harmony and hearing. *J. Music Theory*, *5*, 2–31.

Boyle, P. J., Büchner, A., Stone, M. A., Lenarz, T., and Moore, B. C. J. (2009). Comparison of dual-time-constant and fast-acting automatic gain control (AGC) systems in cochlear implants. *Int. J. Audiol.*, *48*, 211–221.

Brandenburg, K., and Stoll, G. (1994). ISO-MPEG-1 audio: a generic standard for coding of high-quality digital audio. *J. Audio Eng. Soc.*, *42*, 780–792.

Bray, D. A., Dirks, D. D., and Morgan, D. E. (1973). Perstimulatory loudness adaptation. *J. Acoust. Soc. Am.*, *53*, 1544–1548.

Breebaart, D. J., van de Par, S., and Kohlrausch, A. (2001a). An explanation for the apparently wider critical bandwidth in binaural experiments. In D. J. Breebaart, A. J. M. Houtsma, A. Kohlrausch, V. F. Prijs & R. Schoonhoven (Eds.), *Physiological and Psychophysical Bases of Auditory Function*. Maastricht: Shaker.

Breebaart, J., van de Par, S., and Kohlrausch, A. (2001b). Binaural processing model based on contralateral inhibition. I. Model structure. *J. Acoust. Soc. Am.*, *110*, 1074–1088.

Bregman, A. S. (1978a). Auditory streaming is cumulative. *J. Exp. Psychol.: Human Percept. Perf.*, *4*, 380–387.

Bregman, A. S. (1978b). The formation of auditory streams. In J. Requin (Ed.), *Attention and Performance VII*. Hillsdale, NJ: Erlbaum.

Bregman, A. S. (1987). The meaning of duplex perception: sounds as transparent objects. In M. E. H. Schouten (Ed.), *The Psychophysics of Speech Perception*. Dordrecht: Martinus Nijhoff.

Bregman, A. S. (1990). *Auditory Scene Analysis: The Perceptual Organization of Sound*. Cambridge, MA: Bradford Books, MIT Press.

Bregman, A. S., and Campbell, J. (1971). Primary auditory stream segregation and perception of order in rapid sequences of tones. *J. Exp. Psychol.*, *89*, 244–249.

Bregman, A. S., and Dannenbring, G. (1973). The effect of continuity on auditory stream segregation. *Percept. Psychophys.*, *13*, 308–312.

Bregman, A. S., and Pinker, S. (1978). Auditory streaming and the building of timbre. *Canad. J. Psychol.*, *32*, 19–31.

Bregman, A. S., and Rudnicky, A. (1975). Auditory segregation: stream or streams? *J. Exp. Psychol.: Human Percept. Perf.*, *1*, 263–267.

Bregman, A. S., Abramson, J., Doehring, P., and Darwin, C. J. (1985). Spectral integration based on common amplitude modulation. *Percept. Psychophys.*, *37*, 483–493.

Broadbent, D. E., and Gregory, M. (1964). Accuracy of recognition for speech presented to the right and left ears. *Q. J. Exp. Psychol.*, *16*, 359–360.

Broadbent, D. E., and Ladefoged, P. (1957). On the fusion of sounds reaching different sense organs. *J. Acoust. Soc. Am.*, *29*, 708–710.

Broadbent, D. E., and Ladefoged, P. (1959). Auditory perception of temporal order. *J. Acoust. Soc. Am.*, *31*, 151–159.

Brosch, M., and Schreiner, C. E. (1997). Time course of forward masking tuning curves in cat primary auditory cortex. *J. Neurophysiol.*, *77*, 923–943.

Brownell, W. E. (1983). Observations on a motile response in isolated outer hair cells. In W. R. Webster & L. M. Aitkin (Eds.), *Mechanisms of Hearing*. Clayton, Victoria, Australia: Monash University Press.

Brugge, J. F., and Merzenich, M. M. (1973). Responses of neurones in auditory cortex of macaque monkey to monaural and binaural stimulation. *J. Neurophysiol.*, *36*, 1138–1158.

Brugge, J. F., Anderson, D. J., Hind, J. E., and Rose, J. E. (1969). Time structure of discharges in single auditory nerve fibres of the Squirrel Monkey in response to complex periodic sounds. *J. Neurophysiol.*, *32*, 386–401.

Brungart, D. S. (1999). Auditory localization of nearby sources. III. Stimulus effects. *J. Acoust. Soc. Am.*, *106*, 3589–3602.

Brungart, D. S., and Rabinowitz, W. M. (1999). Auditory localization of nearby sources. Head-related transfer functions. *J. Acoust. Soc. Am.*, *106*, 1465–1479.

Brungart, D. S., Durlach, N. I., and Rabinowitz, W. M. (1999). Auditory localization of nearby sources. II. Localization of a broadband source. *J. Acoust. Soc. Am.*, *106*, 1956–1968.

Brungart, D. S., Chang, P. S., Simpson, B. D., and Wang, D. (2006). Isolating the energetic component of speech-on-speech masking with ideal time-frequency segregation. *J. Acoust. Soc. Am.*, *120*, 4007–4018.

Brungart, D. S., Simpson, B. D., Ericson, M. A., and Scott, K. R. (2001). Informational and energetic masking effects in the perception of multiple simultaneous talkers. *J. Acoust. Soc. Am.*, *110*, 2527–2538.

Bucklein, R. (1962). Hörbarkeit von Unregelmässigkeiten in Frequenzgängen bei akustischer Übertragung. *Frequenz*, *16*, 103–108.

Buell, T. N., and Hafter, E. R. (1991). Combination of binaural information across frequency bands. *J. Acoust. Soc. Am.*, *90*, 1894–1900.

Buell, T. N., and Trahiotis, C. (1994). Detection of interaural delay in bands of noise: effects of spectral interference combined with spectral uncertainty. *J. Acoust. Soc. Am.*, *95*, 3568–3573.

Burns, E. M., and Viemeister, N. F. (1976). Nonspectral pitch. *J. Acoust. Soc. Am.*, *60*, 863–869.

Burns, E. M., and Viemeister, N. F. (1981). Played again SAM: further observations on the pitch of amplitude-modulated noise. *J. Acoust. Soc. Am.*, *70*, 1655–1660.

Burns, E. M., and Ward, W. D. (1978). Categorical perception—phenomenon or epiphenomenon: evidence from experiments in the perception of melodic musical intervals. *J. Acoust. Soc. Am.*, *63*, 456–468.

Burns, E. M., Keefe, D. H., and Ling, R. (1998). Energy reflectance in the ear canal can exceed unity near spontaneous otoacoustic emission frequencies. *J. Acoust. Soc. Am.*, *103*, 462–474.

Butler, R. A. (1969). Monaural and binaural localization of noise bursts vertically in the median sagittal plane. *J. Aud. Res.*, *3*, 230–235.

Butler, R. A. (1971). The monaural localization of tonal stimuli. *Percept. Psychophys.*, *9*, 99–101.

Buus, S. (1985). Release from masking caused by envelope fluctuations. *J. Acoust. Soc. Am.*, *78*, 1958–1965.

Buus, S. (1990). Level discrimination of frozen and random noise. *J. Acoust. Soc. Am.*, *87*, 2643–2654.

Buus, S., and Florentine, M. (1995). Sensitivity to excitation-level differences within a fixed number of channels as a function of level and frequency. In G. A. Manley, G. M. Klump, C. Köppl, H. Fastl & H. Oekinghaus (Eds.), *Advances in Hearing Research*. Singapore: World Scientific.

Buus, S., Florentine, M., and Poulsen, T. (1997). Temporal integration of loudness, loudness discrimination, and the form of the loudness function. *J. Acoust. Soc. Am.*, *101*, 669–680.

Buus, S., Florentine, M., and Redden, R. B. (1982). The SISI test: a review. Part II. *Audiology*, *21*, 365–385.

Buus, S., Zhang, L., and Florentine, M. (1996). Stimulus-driven, time-varying weights for comodulation masking release. *J. Acoust. Soc. Am.*, *99*, 2288–2297.

Buus, S., Schorer, E., Florentine, M., and Zwicker, E. (1986). Decision rules in detection of simple and complex tones. *J. Acoust. Soc. Am.*, *80*, 1646–1657.

Byrne, D., and Dillon, H. (1986). The National Acoustic Laboratories' (NAL) new procedure for selecting the gain and frequency response of a hearing aid. *Ear Hear.*, *7*, 257–265.

Carhart, R., Tillman, T., and Greetis, R. (1969a). Perceptual masking in multiple sound backgrounds. *J. Acoust. Soc. Am.*, *45*, 694–703.

Carhart, R., Tillman, T. W., and Greetis, E. S. (1969b). Release from multiple maskers: effects of interaural time disparities. *J. Acoust. Soc. Am.*, *45*, 411–418.

Cariani, P. A., and Delgutte, B. (1996a). Neural correlates of the pitch of complex tones. I. Pitch and pitch salience. *J. Neurophysiol.*, *76*, 1698–1716.

Cariani, P. A., and Delgutte, B. (1996b). Neural correlates of the pitch of complex tones. II. Pitch shift, pitch ambiguity, phase invariance, pitch circularity, rate pitch and the dominance region for pitch. *J. Neurophysiol.*, *76*, 1717–1734.

Carlson, R., and Granström, B. (1982). Towards an auditory spectrograph. In R. Carlson & B. Granström (Eds.), *The Representation of Speech in the Peripheral Auditory System*. Amsterdam: Elsevier.

Carlyon, R. P. (1991). Discriminating between coherent and incoherent frequency modulation of complex tones. *J. Acoust. Soc. Am.*, *89*, 329–340.

Carlyon, R. P. (1994). Further evidence against an across-frequency mechanism specific to the detection of frequency modulation (FM) incoherence between resolved frequency components. *J. Acoust. Soc. Am.*, *95*, 949–961.

Carlyon, R. P. (2000). Detecting coherent and incoherent frequency modulation. *Hear. Res.*, *140*, 173–188.

Carlyon, R. P., and Moore, B. C. J. (1984). Intensity discrimination: a severe departure from Weber's Law. *J. Acoust. Soc. Am.*, *76*, 1369–1376.

Carlyon, R. P., Buus, S., and Florentine, M. (1989). Comodulation masking release for three types of modulator as a function of modulation rate. *Hear. Res.*, *42*, 37–46.

Carlyon, R. P., Deeks, J. M., and McKay, C. M. (2010). The upper limit of temporal pitch for cochlear-implant listeners: stimulus duration, conditioner pulses, and the number of electrodes stimulated. *J. Acoust. Soc. Am.*, *127*, 1469–1478.

Carlyon, R. P., Cusack, R., Foxton, J. M., and Robertson, I. H. (2001). Effects of attention and unilateral neglect on auditory stream segregation. *J. Exp. Psychol.: Human Percept. Perf.*, *27*, 115–127.

Carney, L. H., Heinz, M. G., Evilsizer, M. E., Gilkey, R. H., and Colburn, H. S. (2002). Auditory phase opponency: a temporal model for masked detection at low frequencies. *Acta Acust. United Ac.*, *88*, 334–346.

Chalikia, M. H., and Bregman, A. S. (1993). The perceptual segregation of simultaneous vowels with harmonic, shifted, and random components. *Percept. Psychophys.*, *53*, 125–133.

Cheatham, M. A., and Dallos, P. (2001). Inner hair cell response patterns: implications for low-frequency hearing. *J. Acoust. Soc. Am.*, *110*, 2034–2044.

Cheung, S. W., Bedenbaugh, P. H., Nagarajan, S. S., and Schreiner, C. E. (2001). Functional organization of squirrel monkey primary auditory cortex: responses to pure tones. *J. Neurophysiol.*, *85*, 1732–1749.

Ciocca, V., and Bregman, A. S. (1987). Perceived continuity of gliding and steady-state tones through interrupting noise. *Percept. Psychophys.*, *42*, 476–484.

Clark, G. M., Blamey, P. J., Brown, A. M., Gusby, P. A., Dowell, R. C., Franz, B. K.-H., and Pyman, B. C. (1987). *The University of Melbourne-Nucleus Multi-Electrode Cochlear Implant*. Basel: Karger.

Clarke, E. F. (1999). Rhythm and timing in music. In D. Deutch (Ed.), *The Psychology of Music* (2nd Ed.). San Diego, CA: Academic Press.

Clifton, R. K. (1987). Breakdown of echo suppression in the precedence effect. *J. Acoust. Soc. Am.*, *82*, 1834–1835.

Clifton, R. K., and Freyman, R. L. (1997). The precedence effect: beyond echo suppression. In R. Gilkey & T. Anderson (Eds.), *Binaural and Spatial Hearing in Real and Virtual Environments*. Hillsdale, NJ: Erlbaum.

Clifton, R. K., Freyman, R. L., Litovsky, R. Y., and McCall, D. (1994). Listeners' expectations about echoes can raise or lower echo threshold. *J. Acoust. Soc. Am.*, *95*, 1525–1533.

Cohen, L. T., Saunders, E., and Clark, G. M. (2001). Psychophysics of a prototype perimodiolar cochlear implant electrode array. *Hear. Res.*, *155*, 63–81.

Cohen, M. F., and Chen, X. (1992). Dynamic frequency change among stimulus components: effects of coherence on detectability. *J. Acoust. Soc. Am.*, *92*, 766–772.

Cohen, M. F., and Schubert, E. D. (1987). Influence of place synchrony on detection of a sinusoid. *J. Acoust. Soc. Am.*, *81*, 452–458.

Cokely, C. G., and Humes, L. E. (1993). Two experiments on the temporal boundaries for the nonlinear additivity of masking. *J. Acoust. Soc. Am.*, *94*, 2553–2559.

Colburn, H. S. (1977). Theory of binaural interaction based on auditory-nerve data: II. Detection of tones in noise. *J. Acoust. Soc. Am.*, *61*, 525–533.

Colburn, H. S. (1996). Computational models of binaural processing. In H. Hawkins & T. McMullin (Eds.), *Auditory computation*. New York: Springer-Verlag.

Cole, R. A., and Scott, B. (1974). Towards a theory of speech perception. *Psychol. Rev.*, *81*, 348–374.

Coleman, P. D. (1962). Failure to localize the source distance of an unfamiliar sound. *J. Acoust. Soc. Am.*, *34*, 345–346.

Coleman, P. D. (1963). An analysis of cues to auditory depth perception in free space. *Psychol. Bull.*, *60*, 302–315.

Cooper, N. P. (1999). An improved heterodyne laser interferometer for use in studies of cochlear mechanics. *J. Neurosci. Methods*, *88*, 93–102.

Cooper, N. P., and Rhode, W. S. (1995). Nonlinear mechanics at the apex of the guinea-pig cochlea. *Hear. Res.*, *82*, 225–243.

Corliss, E. L. R. (1967). Mechanistic aspects of hearing. *J. Acoust. Soc. Am.*, *41*, 1500–1516.

Craig, J. H., and Jeffress, L. A. (1962). Effect of phase on the quality of a two-component tone. *J. Acoust. Soc. Am.*, *34*, 1752–1760.

Crain, T. R., and van Tasell, D. J. (1994). Effect of peak clipping on speech recognition threshold. *Ear Hear.*, *15*, 443–453.

Cramer, E. M., and Huggins, W. H. (1958). Creation of pitch through binaural interaction. *J. Acoust. Soc. Am.*, *30*, 413–417.

Creelman, C. D. (1962). Human discrimination of auditory duration. *J. Acoust. Soc. Am.*, *34*, 582–593.

Croghan, N. B., and Grantham, D. W. (2010). Binaural interference in the free field. *J. Acoust. Soc. Am.*, *127*, 3085–3091.

Cuddy, L. L. (1968). Practice effects in the absolute judgment of pitch. *J. Acoust. Soc. Am.*, *43*, 1069–1076.

Culling, J. F. (2000). Auditory motion segregation: a limited analogy with vision. *J. Exp. Psychol.: Human Percept. Perf.*, *26*, 1760–1769.

Culling, J. F., and Colburn, H. S. (2000). Binaural sluggishness in the perception of tone sequences and speech in noise. *J. Acoust. Soc. Am.*, *107*, 517–527.

Culling, J. F., and Darwin, C. J. (1993). Perceptual separation of simultaneous vowels: within and across-formant grouping by F$_0$. *J. Acoust. Soc. Am.*, *93*, 3454–3467.

Culling, J. F., and Darwin, C. J. (1994). Perceptual and computational separation of simultaneous vowels: cues arising from low-frequency beating. *J. Acoust. Soc. Am.*, *95*, 1559–1569.

Culling, J. F., and Summerfield, A. Q. (1998). Measurements of the binaural temporal window using a detection task. *J. Acoust. Soc. Am.*, *103*, 3540–3553.

Culling, J. F., and Summerfield, Q. (1995). Perceptual separation of concurrent speech sounds: absence of across-frequency grouping by common interaural delay. *J. Acoust. Soc. Am.*, *98*, 785–797.

Culling, J. F., Marshall, D. H., and Summerfield, A. Q. (1998a). Dichotic pitches as illusions of binaural unmasking. II. The Fourcin pitch and the dichotic repetition pitch. *J. Acoust. Soc. Am.*, *103*, 3527–3539.

Culling, J. F., Summerfield, A. Q., and Marshall, D. H. (1998b). Dichotic pitches as illusions of binaural unmasking. I. Huggins' pitch and the "binaural edge pitch". *J. Acoust. Soc. Am.*, *103*, 3509–3526.

Cusack, R., and Roberts, B. (2000). Effects of differences in timbre on sequential grouping. *Percept. Psychophys.*, *62*, 1112–1120.

Czerwinski, E., Voishvillo, A., Alexandrov, S., and Terekhov, A. (2001). Multitone testing of sound system components—Some results and conclusions. Part 1. History and theory. *J. Audio Eng. Soc*, *49*, 1011–1048.

Dai, H. (2000). On the relative influence of individual harmonics on pitch judgment. *J. Acoust. Soc. Am.*, *107*, 953–959.

d'Alessandro, C., and Castellengo, M. (1994). The pitch of short-duration vibrato tones. *J. Acoust. Soc. Am.*, *95*, 1617–1630.

Darwin, C. J. (1981). Perceptual grouping of speech components differing in fundamental frequency and onset time. *Q. J. Exp. Psychol.*, *33A*, 185–287.

Darwin, C. J. (2009). Listening to speech in the presence of other sounds. In B. C. J. Moore, L. K. Tyler & W. D. Marslen-Wilsen (Eds.), *The Perception of Speech: From Sound to Meaning.* Oxford: Oxford University Press.

Darwin, C. J., and Baddeley, A. D. (1974). Acoustic memory and the perception of speech. *Cog. Psychol.*, 6, 41–60.

Darwin, C. J., and Bethell-Fox, C. E. (1977). Pitch continuity and speech source attribution. *J. Exp. Psychol.: Hum. Perc. Perf.*, 3, 665–672.

Darwin, C. J., and Carlyon, R. P. (1995). Auditory grouping. In B. C. J. Moore (Ed.), *Hearing*. San Diego, CA: Academic Press.

Darwin, C. J., and Ciocca, V. (1992). Grouping in pitch perception: effects of onset asynchrony and ear of presentation of a mistuned component. *J. Acoust. Soc. Am.*, 91, 3381–3390.

Darwin, C. J., and Gardner, R. B. (1986). Mistuning a harmonic of a vowel: grouping and phase effects on vowel quality. *J. Acoust. Soc. Am.*, 79, 838–845.

Darwin, C. J., and Hukin, R. W. (1999). Auditory objects of attention: the role of interaural time differences. *J. Exp. Psychol.: Human Percept. Perf.*, 25, 617–629.

Darwin, C. J., and Sutherland, N. S. (1984). Grouping frequency components of vowels: when is a harmonic not a harmonic? *Q. J. Exp. Psychol.*, 36A, 193–208.

Dau, T. (1996). Modeling auditory processing of amplitude modulation. Ph.D. Thesis, University of Oldenburg, Germany.

Dau, T., and Verhey, J. L. (1999). Modelling across-frequency processing of amplitude modulation. In T. Dau, V. Hohmann & B. Kollmeier (Eds.), *Psychophysics, Physiology and Models of Hearing*. Singapore: World Scientific.

Dau, T., Ewert, S., and Oxenham, A. J. (2009). Auditory stream formation affects comodulation masking release retroactively. *J. Acoust. Soc. Am.*, 125, 2182–2188.

Dau, T., Kollmeier, B., and Kohlrausch, A. (1997a). Modeling auditory processing of amplitude modulation. I. Detection and masking with narrowband carriers. *J. Acoust. Soc. Am.*, 102, 2892–2905.

Dau, T., Kollmeier, B., and Kohlrausch, A. (1997b). Modeling auditory processing of amplitude modulation. II. Spectral and temporal integration. *J. Acoust. Soc. Am.*, 102, 2906–2919.

Dau, T., Verhey, J. L., and Kohlrausch, A. (1999). Intrinsic envelope fluctuations and modulation-detection thresholds for narrow-band noise carriers. *J. Acoust. Soc. Am.*, 106, 2752–2760.

Davis, A. (1995). *Hearing in Adults*. London: Whurr.

Davis, H., Morgan, C. T., Hawkins, J. E., Jr., Galambos, R., and Smith, F. W. (1950). Temporary deafness following exposure to loud tones and noise. *Acta Otolaryngol.*, 88(Supplement), 1–56.

de Boer, E. (1956). On the "residue" in hearing. Ph.D. Thesis, University of Amsterdam, Amsterdam.

de Cheveigné, A. (1997). Concurrent vowel identification. III. A neural model of harmonic interference cancellation. *J. Acoust. Soc. Am.*, 101, 2857–2865.

de Cheveigné, A., McAdams, S., and Marin, C. M. H. (1997a). Concurrent vowel identification. II. Effects of phase, harmonicity and task. *J. Acoust. Soc. Am.*, 101, 2848–2856.

de Cheveigné, A., Kawahara, H., Tsuzaki, M., and Aikawa, K. (1997b). Concurrent vowel identification. I. Effects of relative amplitude and F_0 difference. *J. Acoust. Soc. Am.*, 101, 2839–2847.

Deatherage, B. H., and Hirsh, I. J. (1959). Auditory localization of clicks. *J. Acoust. Soc. Am.*, *31*, 486–492.

Delgutte, B. (1987). Peripheral auditory processing of speech information: implications from a physiological study of intensity discrimination. In M. E. H. Schouten (Ed.), *The Psychophysics of Speech Perception*. The Netherlands: Nijhoff, Dordrecht.

Delgutte, B. (1988). Physiological mechanisms of masking. In H. Duifhuis, J. W. Horst & H. P. Wit (Eds.), *Basic Issues in Hearing*. London: Academic Press.

Delgutte, B. (1990). Physiological mechanisms of psychophysical masking: observations from auditory-nerve fibers. *J. Acoust. Soc. Am.*, *87*, 791–809.

Delgutte, B. (1996). Physiological models for basic auditory percepts. In H. L. Hawkins, T. A. McMullen, A. N. Popper & R. R. Fay (Eds.), *Auditory Computation*. New York: Springer.

Dibble, K. (1995). Hearing loss and music. *J. Audio Eng. Soc.*, *43*, 251–266.

Dirks, D., and Bower, D. (1970). Effects of forward and backward masking on speech intelligibility. *J. Acoust. Soc. Am.*, *47*, 1003–1008.

Divenyi, P. L. (1992). Binaural suppression of nonechoes. *J. Acoust. Soc. Am.*, *91*, 1078–1084.

Divenyi, P. L., and Danner, W. F. (1977). Discrimination of time intervals marked by brief acoustic pulses of various intensities and spectra. *Percept. Psychophys.*, *21*, 125–142.

Divenyi, P. L., and Hirsh, I. J. (1974). Identification of temporal order in three-tone sequences. *J. Acoust. Soc. Am.*, *56*, 144–151.

Dix, M. R., and Hood, J. D. (1973). Symmetrical hearing loss in brain stem lesions. *Acta Otolaryngol.*, *75*, 165–177.

Dolan, T. R., and Trahiotis, C. (1972). Binaural interaction in backward masking. *Percept. Psychophys.*, *11*, 92–94.

Dorman, M. F., Gifford, R. H., Spahr, A. J., and McKarns, S. A. (2008). The benefits of combining acoustic and electric stimulation for the recognition of speech, voice and melodies. *Audiol. Neurotol.*, *13*, 105–112.

Dorman, M. F., Loizou, P. C., Kemp, L. L., and Kirk, K. I. (2000). Word recognition by children listening to speech processed into a small number of channels: data from normal-hearing children and children with cochlear implants. *Ear Hear.*, *21*, 590–596.

Dowling, W. J. (1968). Rhythmic fission and perceptual organization. *J. Acoust. Soc. Am.*, *44*, 369.

Dowling, W. J. (1973). The perception of interleaved melodies. *Cognitive Psychol.*, *5*, 322–337.

Dubno, J. R., and Dirks, D. D. (1989). Auditory filter characteristics and consonant recognition for hearing-impaired listeners. *J. Acoust. Soc. Am.*, *85*, 1666–1675.

Duifhuis, H. (1970). Audibility of high harmonics in a periodic pulse. *J. Acoust. Soc. Am.*, *48*, 888–893.

Duifhuis, H. (1971). Audibility of high harmonics in a periodic pulse II. Time effects. *J. Acoust. Soc. Am.*, *49*, 1155–1162.

Duifhuis, H. (1973). Consequences of peripheral frequency selectivity for nonsimultaneous masking. *J. Acoust. Soc. Am.*, *54*, 1471–1488.

Dunn, H. K., and White, S. D. (1940). Statistical measurements on conversational speech. *J. Acoust. Soc. Am.*, *11*, 278–288.

Durlach, N. I. (1963). Equalization and cancellation theory of binaural masking-level differences. *J. Acoust. Soc. Am.*, 35, 1206–1218.

Durlach, N. I. (1972). Binaural signal detection: equalization and cancellation theory. In J. V. Tobias (Ed.), *Foundations of Modern Auditory Theory* (Vol. 2). New York: Academic Press.

Durlach, N. I., and Colburn, H. S. (1978). Binaural phenomena. In E. C. Carterette & M. P. Friedman (Eds.), *Handbook of Perception* (Vol. IV). New York: Academic Press.

Dye, R. H., and Hafter, E. R. (1984). The effects of intensity on the detection of interaural differences of time in high-frequency trains of clicks. *J. Acoust. Soc. Am.*, 75, 1593–1598.

Eddins, D. A., and Green, D. M. (1995). Temporal integration and temporal resolution. In B. C. J. Moore (Ed.), *Hearing*. San Diego, CA: Academic Press.

Eddins, D. A., Hall, J. W., and Grose, J. H. (1992). Detection of temporal gaps as a function of frequency region and absolute noise bandwidth. *J. Acoust. Soc. Am.*, 91, 1069–1077.

Egan, J. P., and Hake, H. W. (1950). On the masking pattern of a simple auditory stimulus. *J. Acoust. Soc. Am.*, 22, 622–630.

Eguiluz, V. M., Ospeck, M., Choe, Y., Hudspeth, A. J., and Magnasco, M. O. (2000). Essential nonlinearities in hearing. *Phys. Rev. Lett.*, 84, 5232–5235.

Elberling, C. (1999). Loudness scaling revisited. *J. Am. Acad. Audiol.*, 10, 248–260.

Elfner, L. F., and Caskey, W. E. (1965). Continuity effects with alternately sounded noise and tone signals as a function of manner of presentation. *J. Acoust. Soc. Am.*, 38, 543–547.

Elliot, D. N., and Fraser, W. R. (1970). Fatigue and adaptation. In J. V. Tobias (Ed.), *Foundations of Modern Auditory Theory*. New York: Academic Press.

Elman, J. L. (1989). Connectionist approaches to acoustic/phonetic processing. In W. D. Marslen-Wilsen (Ed.), *Lexical Representation and Process*. Cambridge, MA: MIT Press.

Emmerich, D. S., Ellermeier, W., and Butensky, B. (1989). A re-examination of the frequency discrimination of random-amplitude tones, and a test of Henning's modified energy-detector model. *J. Acoust. Soc. Am.*, 85, 1653–1659.

Evans, E. F. (1968). Cortical representation. In A. V. S. de Reuck & J. Knight (Eds.), *Hearing Mechanisms in Vertebrates*. London: Churchill.

Evans, E. F. (1975). The sharpening of frequency selectivity in the normal and abnormal cochlea. *Audiology*, 14, 419–442.

Evans, E. F. (1978). Place and time coding of frequency in the peripheral auditory system: some physiological pros and cons. *Audiology*, 17, 369–420.

Evans, E. F., and Harrison, R. V. (1976). Correlation between outer hair cell damage and deterioration of cochlear nerve tuning properties in the guinea pig. *J. Physiol.*, 252, 43–44p.

Evans, E. F., Pratt, S. R., and Cooper, N. P. (1989). Correspondence between behavioural and physiological frequency selectivity in the guinea pig. *Br. J. Audiol.*, 23, 151–152.

Ewert, S. D., and Dau, T. (2000). Characterizing frequency selectivity for envelope fluctuations. *J. Acoust. Soc. Am.*, 108, 1181–1196.

Exner, S. (1876). Zur Lehre von den Gehörsempfindungen. *Pflügers Archiv*, 13, 228–253.

Fant, G. C. M. (1970). *Acoustic Theory of Speech Production*. The Hague: Mouton.

Fantini, D. A., Moore, B. C. J., and Schooneveldt, G. P. (1993). Comodulation masking release as a function of type of signal, gated or continuous masking, monaural or dichotic presentation of flanking bands, and center frequency. *J. Acoust. Soc. Am.*, 93, 2106–2115.

Fastl, H. (1976). Temporal masking effects: I. Broad band noise masker. *Acustica*, 35, 287–302.

Fastl, H. (1993). Loudness evaluation by subjects and by a loudness meter. In R. T. Verrillo (Ed.), *Sensory Research—Multimodal Perspectives*. Hillsdale, NJ: Erlbaum.

Fastl, H., and Schorn, K. (1981). Discrimination of level differences by hearing impaired patients. *Audiology*, 20, 488–502.

Feddersen, W. E., Sandel, T. T., Teas, D. C., and Jeffress, L. A. (1957). Localization of high-frequency tones. *J. Acoust. Soc. Am.*, 29, 988–991.

Feth, L. L., O'Malley, H., and Ramsey, J. J. (1982). Pitch of unresolved, two-component complex tones. *J. Acoust. Soc. Am.*, 72, 1403–1412.

Fine, P. A., and Moore, B. C. J. (1993). Frequency analysis and musical ability. *Music Percept.*, 11, 39–53.

Flanagan, S., Moore, B. C. J., and Stone, M. A. (2005). Discrimination of group delay in click-like signals presented via headphones and loudspeakers. *J. Audio Eng. Soc.*, 53, 593–611.

Fleischer, H. (1982). Modulationsschwellen von Schmalbandrauschen (Modulation detection thresholds for narrowband noise). *Acustica*, 51, 154–161.

Fletcher, H. (1940). Auditory patterns. *Rev. Mod. Phys.*, 12, 47–65.

Fletcher, H., and Munson, W. A. (1933). Loudness, its definition, measurement and calculation. *J. Acoust. Soc. Am.*, 5, 82–108.

Fletcher, H., and Munson, W. A. (1937). Relation between loudness and masking. *J. Acoust. Soc. Am.*, 9, 1–10.

Fligor, B. J., and Cox, L. C. (2004). Output levels of commercially available portable compact disc players and the potential risk to hearing. *Ear Hear.*, 25, 513–527.

Florentine, M. (1983). Intensity discrimination as a function of level and frequency and its relation to high-frequency hearing. *J. Acoust. Soc. Am.*, 74, 1375–1379.

Florentine, M. (1986). Level discrimination of tones as a function of duration. *J. Acoust. Soc. Am.*, 79, 792–798.

Florentine, M., and Buus, S. (1981). An excitation-pattern model for intensity discrimination. *J. Acoust. Soc. Am.*, 70, 1646–1654.

Florentine, M., and Zwicker, E. (1979). A model of loudness summation applied to noise-induced hearing loss. *Hear. Res.*, 1, 121–132.

Florentine, M., Buus, S., and Mason, C. R. (1987). Level discrimination as a function of level for tones from 0.25 to 16 kHz. *J. Acoust. Soc. Am.*, 81, 1528–1541.

Florentine, M., Fastl, H., and Buus, S. (1988). Temporal integration in normal hearing, cochlear impairment, and impairment simulated by masking. *J. Acoust. Soc. Am.*, 84, 195–203.

Florentine, M., Buus, S., Scharf, B., and Zwicker, E. (1980). Frequency selectivity in normally-hearing and hearing-impaired observers. *J. Speech Hear. Res.*, *23*, 643–669.

Florentine, M., Reed, C. M., Rabinowitz, W. M., Braida, L. D., Durlach, N. I., and Buus, S. (1993). Intensity perception. XIV. Intensity discrimination in listeners with sensorineural hearing loss. *J. Acoust. Soc. Am.*, *94*, 2575–2586.

Fourcin, A. J. (1970). Central pitch and auditory lateralization. In R. Plomp & G. F. Smoorenburg (Eds.), *Frequency Analysis and Periodicity Detection in Hearing*. Sijthoff: Leiden.

Fourcin, A. J., Rosen, S. M., Moore, B. C. J., Douek, E. E., Clark, G. P., Dodson, H., and Bannister, L. H. (1979). External electrical stimulation of the cochlea: clinical, psychophysical, speech-perceptual and histological findings. *Br. J. Audiol.*, *13*, 85–107.

Fraisse, P. (1982). Rhythm and tempo. In D. Deutsch (Ed.), *The Psychology of Music*. New York: Academic Press.

Freedman, S. J., and Fisher, H. G. (1968). The role of the pinna in auditory localization. In S. J. Freedman (Ed.), *Neuropsychology of Spatially Oriented Behaviour*. Illinois: Dorsey Press.

Freyman, R. L., Balakrishnan, U., and Helfer, K. S. (2001). Spatial release from informational masking in speech recognition. *J. Acoust. Soc. Am.*, *109*, 2112–2122.

Freyman, R. L., Clifton, R. K., and Litovsky, R. Y. (1991). Dynamic processes in the precedence effect. *J. Acoust. Soc. Am.*, *90*, 874–884.

Freyman, R. L., Helfer, K. S., McCall, D. D., and Clifton, R. K. (1999). The role of perceived spatial separation in the unmasking of speech. *J. Acoust. Soc. Am.*, *106*, 3578–3588.

Füllgrabe, C., Baer, T., Stone, M. A., and Moore, B. C. J. (2010). Preliminary evaluation of a method for fitting hearing aids with extended bandwidth. *Int. J. Audiol.*, *49*, 741–753.

Furukawa, S., and Moore, B. C. J. (1996). Across-frequency processes in frequency modulation detection. *J. Acoust. Soc. Am.*, *100*, 2299–2312.

Furukawa, S., and Moore, B. C. J. (1997a). Dependence of frequency modulation detection on frequency modulation coherence across carriers: effects of modulation rate, harmonicity and roving of the carrier frequencies. *J. Acoust. Soc. Am.*, *101*, 1632–1643.

Furukawa, S., and Moore, B. C. J. (1997b). Effect of the relative phase of amplitude modulation on the detection of modulation on two carriers. *J. Acoust. Soc. Am.*, *102*, 3657–3664.

Gabriel, B., Kollmeier, B., and Mellert, V. (1997). Influence of individual listener, measurement room and choice of test-tone levels on the shape of equal-loudness level contours. *Acta Acust. Acust.*, *83*, 670–683.

Gaese, B. H. (2001). Population coding in the auditory cortex. *Prog. Brain. Res.*, *130*, 221–230.

Gardner, M. B., and Gardner, R. S. (1973). Problem of localization in the median plane: effect of pinnae cavity occlusion. *J. Acoust. Soc. Am.*, *53*, 400–408.

Gardner, R. B., and Darwin, C. J. (1986). Grouping of vowel harmonics by frequency modulation: absence of effects on phonemic categorization. *Percept. Psychophys.*, *40*, 183–187.

Gardner, R. B., Gaskill, S. A., and Darwin, C. J. (1989). Perceptual grouping of formants with static and dynamic differences in fundamental frequency. *J. Acoust. Soc. Am.*, *85*, 1329–1337.

Garner, W. R., and Miller, G. A. (1947). The masked threshold of pure tones as a function of duration. *J. Exp. Psychol.*, *37*, 293–303.

Gässler, G. (1954). Über die Hörschwelle für Schallereignisse mit verschieden breitem Frequenzspektrum. *Acustica*, *4*, 408–414.

Gatehouse, S., Naylor, G., and Elberling, C. (2006a). Linear and nonlinear hearing aid fittings—1. Patterns of benefit. *Int. J. Audiol.*, *45*, 130–152.

Gatehouse, S., Naylor, G., and Elberling, C. (2006b). Linear and nonlinear hearing aid fittings—2. Patterns of candidature. *Int. J. Audiol.*, *45*, 153–171.

Gebhardt, C. J., and Goldstein, D. P. (1972). Frequency discrimination and the M.L.D. *J. Acoust. Soc. Am.*, *51*, 1228–1232.

Gifford, R. H., and Bacon, S. P. (2000). Contributions of suppression and excitation to simultaneous masking: effects of signal frequency and masker-signal frequency relation. *J. Acoust. Soc. Am.*, *107*, 2188–2200.

Gilchrist, N., and Grewin, C. (1996). *Collected Papers on Digital Audio Bit Rate Reduction*. New York: Audio Engineering Society.

Glasberg, B. R., and Moore, B. C. J. (1986). Auditory filter shapes in subjects with unilateral and bilateral cochlear impairments. *J. Acoust. Soc. Am.*, *79*, 1020–1033.

Glasberg, B. R., and Moore, B. C. J. (1990). Derivation of auditory filter shapes from notched-noise data. *Hear. Res.*, *47*, 103–138.

Glasberg, B. R., and Moore, B. C. J. (1992). Effects of envelope fluctuations on gap detection. *Hear. Res.*, *64*, 81–92.

Glasberg, B. R., and Moore, B. C. J. (2000). Frequency selectivity as a function of level and frequency measured with uniformly exciting notched noise. *J. Acoust. Soc. Am.*, *108*, 2318–2328.

Glasberg, B. R., and Moore, B. C. J. (2002). A model of loudness applicable to time-varying sounds. *J. Audio Eng. Soc.*, *50*, 331–342.

Glasberg, B. R., and Moore, B. C. J. (2005). Development and evaluation of a model for predicting the audibility of time-varying sounds in the presence of background sounds. *J. Audio Eng. Soc.*, *53*, 906–918.

Glasberg, B. R., and Moore, B. C. J. (2006). Prediction of absolute thresholds and equal-loudness contours using a modified loudness model. *J. Acoust. Soc. Am.*, *120*, 585–588.

Glasberg, B. R., and Moore, B. C. J. (2010). The loudness of sounds whose spectra differ at the two ears. *J. Acoust. Soc. Am.*, *127*, 2433–2440.

Glasberg, B. R., Moore, B. C. J., and Nimmo-Smith, I. (1984). Comparison of auditory filter shapes derived with three different maskers. *J. Acoust. Soc. Am.*, *75*, 536–544.

Gockel, H., and Carlyon, R. P. (1998). Effects of ear of entry and perceived location of synchronous and asynchronous components on mistuning detection. *J. Acoust. Soc. Am.*, *104*, 3534–3545.

Gockel, H., Carlyon, R. P., and Micheyl, C. (1999). Context dependence of fundamental-frequency discrimination: lateralized temporal fringes. *J. Acoust. Soc. Am.*, *106*, 3553–3563.

388

Gockel, H., Carlyon, R. P., and Moore, B. C. J. (2005a). Pitch discrimination interference: the role of pitch pulse asynchrony. *J. Acoust. Soc. Am.*, *117*, 3860–3866.

Gockel, H., Carlyon, R. P., and Plack, C. J. (2004). Across-frequency interference effects in fundamental frequency discrimination: questioning evidence for two pitch mechanisms. *J. Acoust. Soc. Am.*, *116*, 1092–1104.

Gockel, H., Carlyon, R. P., and Plack, C. J. (2005b). Dominance region for pitch: effects of duration and dichotic presentation. *J. Acoust. Soc. Am.*, *117*, 1326–1336.

Gockel, H., Moore, B. C. J., and Carlyon, R. P. (2001). Influence of rate of change of frequency on the overall pitch of frequency modulated tones. *J. Acoust. Soc. Am.*, *109*, 701–712.

Gockel, H., Moore, B. C. J., and Patterson, R. D. (2002). Asymmetry of masking between complex tones and noise: the role of temporal structure and peripheral compression. *J. Acoust. Soc. Am.*, *111*, 2759–2770.

Gockel, H. E., Hafter, E. R., and Moore, B. C. J. (2009). Pitch discrimination interference: the role of ear of entry and of octave similarity. *J. Acoust. Soc. Am.*, *125*, 324–327.

Gold, T. (1948). Hearing. II. The physical basis of the action of the cochlea. *Phil. Trans. R. Soc. B*, *135*, 492–498.

Goldstein, J. L. (1967). Auditory nonlinearity. *J. Acoust. Soc. Am.*, *41*, 676–689.

Goldstein, J. L. (1973). An optimum processor theory for the central formation of the pitch of complex tones. *J. Acoust. Soc. Am.*, *54*, 1496–1516.

Goldstein, J. L., and Srulovicz, P. (1977). Auditory-nerve spike intervals as an adequate basis for aural frequency measurement. In E. F. Evans & J. P. Wilson (Eds.), *Psychophysics and Physiology of Hearing*. London: Academic Press.

Gorga, M. P., Neely, S. T., Ohlrich, B., Hoover, B., Redner, J., and Peters, J. (1997). From laboratory to clinic: a large scale study of distortion product otoacoustic emissions in ears with normal hearing and ears with hearing loss. *Ear Hear.*, *18*, 440–455.

Grandori, F., and Lutman, M. (1999). The European consensus development conference on neonatal hearing screening (Milan, May 15-, 16, 1998). *Am. J. Audiol.*, *8*, 19–20.

Grantham, D. W. (1986). Detection and discrimination of simulated motion of auditory targets in the horizontal plane. *J. Acoust. Soc. Am.*, *79*, 1939–1949.

Grantham, D. W., and Wightman, F. L. (1978). Detectability of varying interaural temporal differences. *J. Acoust. Soc. Am.*, *63*, 511–523.

Grantham, D. W., and Wightman, F. L. (1979). Detectability of a pulsed tone in the presence of a masker with time-varying interaural correlation. *J. Acoust. Soc. Am.*, *65*, 1509–1517.

Green, D. M. (1960). Auditory detection of a noise signal. *J. Acoust. Soc. Am.*, *32*, 121–131.

Green, D. M. (1973). Temporal acuity as a function of frequency. *J. Acoust. Soc. Am.*, *54*, 373–379.

Green, D. M. (1985). Temporal factors in psychoacoustics. In A. Michelsen (Ed.), *Time Resolution in Auditory Systems*. New York: Springer-Verlag.

Green, D. M. (1988). *Profile Analysis*. Oxford: Oxford University Press.

Green, D. M., and Swets, J. A. (1974). *Signal Detection Theory and Psychophysics.* New York: Krieger.

Greenwood, D. D. (1961a). Auditory masking and the critical band. *J. Acoust. Soc. Am.,* 33, 484–501.

Greenwood, D. D. (1961b). Critical bandwidth and the frequency coordinates of the basilar membrane. *J. Acoust. Soc. Am.,* 33, 1344–1356.

Greenwood, D. D. (1990). A cochlear frequency-position function for several species—29 years later. *J. Acoust. Soc. Am.,* 87, 2592–2605.

Groen, J. J. (1964). Super- and subliminal binaural beats. *Acta Otolaryngol.,* 57, 224–231.

Grose, J. H. (1991). Gap detection in multiple narrow bands of noise as a function of spectral configuration. *J. Acoust. Soc. Am.,* 90, 3061–3068.

Grose, J. H., and Hall, J. W. (1989). Comodulation masking release using SAM tonal complex maskers: effects of modulation depth and signal position. *J. Acoust. Soc. Am.,* 85, 1276–1284.

Gu, X., Wright, B. A., and Green, D. M. (1995). Failure to hear binaural beats below threshold. *J. Acoust. Soc. Am.,* 97, 701–703.

Guinan, J. J., Jr. (2006). Olivocochlear efferents: anatomy, physiology, function, and the measurement of efferent effects in humans. *Ear Hear.,* 27, 589–607.

Haas, H. (1951). Über den Einfluss eines Einfachechos an die Hörsamkeit von Sprache. *Acustica,* 1, 49–58.

Hafter, E. R., and Carrier, S. C. (1972). Binaural interaction in low-frequency stimuli: the inability to trade time and intensity completely. *J. Acoust. Soc. Am.,* 51, 1852–1862.

Hafter, E. R., and Dye, R. H. (1983). Detection of interaural differences of intensity in trains of high-frequency clicks as a function of interclick interval and number. *J. Acoust. Soc. Am.,* 73, 644–651.

Hafter, E. R., and Jeffress, L. A. (1968). Two-image lateralization of tones and clicks. *J. Acoust. Soc. Am.,* 44, 563–569.

Hafter, E. R., Buell, T. N., and Richards, V. M. (1988). Onset-coding in lateralization: its form, site, and function. In G. M. Edelman, W. E. Gall & M. W. Cowan (Eds.), *Auditory Function: Neurobiological Bases of Hearing.* New York: Wiley.

Haggard, M. P., Hall, J. W., and Grose, J. H. (1990). Comodulation masking release as a function of bandwidth and test frequency. *J. Acoust. Soc. Am.,* 88, 113–118.

Hall, D. A., Hart, H. C., and Johnsrude, I. S. (2003). Relationships between human auditory cortical structure and function. *Audiol. Neurootol.,* 8, 1–18.

Hall, J. W., and Fernandes, M. A. (1984). The role of monaural frequency selectivity in binaural analysis. *J. Acoust. Soc. Am.,* 76, 435–439.

Hall, J. W., and Grose, J. H. (1988). Comodulation masking release: evidence for multiple cues. *J. Acoust. Soc. Am.,* 84, 1669–1675.

Hall, J. W., and Grose, J. H. (1990). Comodulation masking release and auditory grouping. *J. Acoust. Soc. Am.,* 88, 119–125.

Hall, J. W., and Peters, R. W. (1981). Pitch for nonsimultaneous successive harmonics in quiet and noise. *J. Acoust. Soc. Am.,* 69, 509–513.

Hall, J. W., Grose, J. H., and Haggard, M. P. (1990). Effects of flanking band proximity, number, and modulation pattern on comodulation masking release. *J. Acoust. Soc. Am.*, 87, 269–283.

Hall, J. W., Grose, J. H., and Mendoza, L. (1995). Across-channel processes in masking. In B. C. J. Moore (Ed.), *Hearing*. San Diego, CA: Academic Press.

Hall, J. W., Haggard, M. P., and Fernandes, M. A. (1984). Detection in noise by spectro-temporal pattern analysis. *J. Acoust. Soc. Am.*, 76, 50–56.

Hall, J. W., Tyler, R. S., and Fernandes, M. A. (1983). Monaural and binaural auditory frequency resolution measured using bandlimited noise and notched-noise masking. *J. Acoust. Soc. Am.*, 73, 894–898.

Handel, S. (1995). Timbre perception and auditory object identification. In B. C. J. Moore (Ed.), *Hearing*. San Diego, CA: Academic Press.

Hansen, V., and Madsen, E. R. (1974). On aural phase detection. *J. Audio Eng. Soc.*, 22, 10–14.

Harris, J. D. (1963). Loudness discrimination, *J. Speech. Hear. Disord.* Monographs, Suppl. 11, 1–63.

Harris, J. D. (1972). Audition. *Ann. Rev. Psychol.*, 23, 313–346.

Hartmann, W. M. (1997a). Listening in a room and the precedence effect. In R. Gilkey & T. Anderson (Eds.), *Binaural and Spatial Hearing in Real and Virtual Environments*. Hillsdale, NJ: Erlbaum.

Hartmann, W. M. (1997b). *Signals, Sound, and Sensation*. Woodbury, NY: AIP Press.

Hartmann, W. M., and Hnath, G. M. (1982). Detection of mixed modulation. *Acustica*, 50, 297–312.

Hartmann, W. M., and Johnson, D. (1991). Stream segregation and peripheral channeling. *Music Percept.*, 9, 155–184.

Hartmann, W. M., and McMillon, C. D. (2001). Binaural coherence edge pitch. *J. Acoust. Soc. Am.*, 109, 294–305.

Heinz, M. G., Colburn, H. S., and Carney, L. H. (2001a). Evaluating auditory performance limits: I. One-parameter discrimination using a computational model for the auditory nerve. *Neur. Comput.*, 13, 2273–2316.

Heinz, M. G., Colburn, H. S., and Carney, L. H. (2001b). Evaluating auditory performance limits: II. One-parameter discrimination with random level variation. *Neur. Comput.*, 13, 2317–2339.

Heinz, M. G., Colburn, H. S., and Carney, L. H. (2002). Quantifying the implications of nonlinear cochlear tuning for auditory-filter estimates. *J. Acoust. Soc. Am.*, 111, 996–1011.

Heinz, M. G., Issa, J. B., and Young, E. D. (2005). Auditory-nerve rate responses are inconsistent with common hypotheses for the neural correlates of loudness recruitment. *J. Assoc. Res. Otolaryngol.*, 6, 91–105.

Heller, L. M., and Richards, V. M. (2010). Binaural interference in lateralization thresholds for interaural time and level differences. *J. Acoust. Soc. Am.*, 128, 310–319.

Heller, L. M., and Trahiotis, C. (1995). Interference in detection of interaural delay in a sinusoidally amplitude-modulated tone produced by a second, spectrally remote sinusoidally amplitude-modulated tone. *J. Acoust. Soc. Am.*, 97, 1808–1816.

Hellman, R. P. (1976). Growth of loudness at 1000 and 3000 Hz. *J. Acoust. Soc. Am.*, *60*, 672–679.

Hellman, R. P. (1978). Dependence of loudness growth on skirts of excitation patterns. *J. Acoust. Soc. Am.*, *63*, 1114–1119.

Hellman, R. P., Meiselman, C. H. (1986). Is high-frequency hearing necessary for normal loudness growth at low frequencies?, *12th ICA* Paper B11-5.

Helmholtz, H. L. F. (1863). *Die Lehre von den Tonempfindungen als physiologische Grundlage für die Theorie der Musik [On the Sensations of Tone as a Physiological Basis for the Theory of Music]*. Braunschweig: F. Vieweg.

Helmholtz, H. L. F. (1954). *On the Sensations of Tone*. New York: Dover.

Henning, G. B. (1966). Frequency discrimination of random amplitude tones. *J. Acoust. Soc. Am.*, *39*, 336–339.

Henning, G. B. (1967). A model for auditory discrimination and detection. *J. Acoust. Soc. Am.*, *42*, 1325–1334.

Henning, G. B. (1974). Detectability of interaural delay in high-frequency complex waveforms. *J. Acoust. Soc. Am.*, *55*, 84–90.

Henning, G. B., and Gaskell, H. (1981). Monaural phase sensitivity measured with Ronken's paradigm. *J. Acoust. Soc. Am.*, *70*, 1669–1673.

Hickson, L. M. H. (1994). Compression amplification in hearing aids. *Am. J. Audiol.*, *3*, 51–65.

Hind, J. E., Rose, J. E., Brugge, J. F., and Anderson, D. J. (1967). Coding of information pertaining to paired low-frequency tones in single auditory nerve fibres of the squirrel monkey. *J. Neurophysiol.*, *30*, 794–816.

Hirsh, I. J. (1950). The relation between localization and intelligibility. *J. Acoust. Soc. Am.*, *22*, 196–200.

Hirsh, I. J. (1959). Auditory perception of temporal order. *J. Acoust. Soc. Am.*, *31*, 759–767.

Hirsh, I. J. (1971). Masking of speech and auditory localization. *Audiology*, *10*, 110–114.

Hirsh, I. J., and Bilger, R. C. (1955). Auditory-threshold recovery after exposures to pure tones. *J. Acoust. Soc. Am.*, *27*, 1186–1194.

Hirsh, I. J., and Ward, W. D. (1952). Recovery of the auditory threshold after strong acoustic stimulation. *J. Acoust. Soc. Am.*, *24*, 131–141.

Holmes, J. (1988). *Speech Synthesis and Recognition*. London: Van Nostrand Reinhold.

Hood, J. D. (1950). Studies in auditory fatigue and adaptation. *Acta Otolaryngol.*, *92*(Suppl.), 1–57.

Hood, J. D. (1972). Fundamentals of identification of sensorineural hearing loss. *Sound*, *6*, 21–26.

Hopkins, K., and Moore, B. C. J. (2010). The importance of temporal fine structure information in speech at different spectral regions for normal-hearing and hearing-impaired subjects. *J. Acoust. Soc. Am.*, *127*, 1595–1608.

Hopkins, K., Moore, B. C. J., and Stone, M. A. (2008). Effects of moderate cochlear hearing loss on the ability to benefit from temporal fine structure information in speech. *J. Acoust. Soc. Am.*, *123*, 1140–1153.

Horst, J. W., Javel, E., and Farley, G. R. (1990). Coding of spectral fine structure in the auditory nerve. II. Level-dependent nonlinear responses. *J. Acoust. Soc. Am.*, *88*, 2656–2681.

House, A. S., Stevens, K. N., Sandel, T. T., and Arnold, J. B. (1962). On the learning of speechlike vocabularies. *J. Verb. Learn. Verb. Behav.*, *1*, 133–143.

Houtgast, T. (1972). Psychophysical evidence for lateral inhibition in hearing. *J. Acoust. Soc. Am.*, *51*, 1885–1894.

Houtgast, T. (1973). Psychophysical experiments on 'tuning curves' and 'two-tone inhibition'. *Acustica*, *29*, 168–179.

Houtgast, T. (1974). Lateral suppression in hearing. Ph.D. Thesis, Free University of Amsterdam, Amsterdam.

Houtgast, T. (1976). Subharmonic pitches of a pure tone at low S/N ratio. *J. Acoust. Soc. Am.*, *60*, 405–409.

Houtgast, T. (1989). Frequency selectivity in amplitude-modulation detection. *J. Acoust. Soc. Am.*, *85*, 1676–1680.

Houtsma, A. J. M., and Fleuren, J. F. M. (1991). Analytic and synthetic pitch of two-tone complexes. *J. Acoust. Soc. Am.*, *90*, 1674–1676.

Houtsma, A. J. M., and Goldstein, J. L. (1972). The central origin of the pitch of complex tones: evidence from musical interval recognition. *J. Acoust. Soc. Am.*, *51*, 520–529.

Houtsma, A. J. M., and Smurzynski, J. (1990). Pitch identification and discrimination for complex tones with many harmonics. *J. Acoust. Soc. Am.*, *87*, 304–310.

Hsieh, I. H., and Saberi, K. (2008). Dissociation of procedural and semantic memory in absolute-pitch processing. *Hear. Res.*, *240*, 73–79.

Hubel, D. H., and Wiesel, T. N. (1968). Receptive fields and functional architecture of monkey striate cortex. *J. Physiol.*, *195*, 215–243.

Hudspeth, A. (1997). Mechanical amplification of stimuli by hair cells. *Curr. Opin. Neurobiol.*, *7*, 480–486.

Hughes, J. W. (1946). The threshold of audition for short periods of stimulation. *Phil. Trans. R. Soc. B*, *133*, 486–490.

Huss, M., and Moore, B. C. J. (2003). Tone decay for hearing-impaired listeners with and without dead regions in the cochlea. *J. Acoust. Soc. Am.*, *114*, 3283–3294.

Ihlefeld, A., and Shinn-Cunningham, B. (2008a). Disentangling the effects of spatial cues on selection and formation of auditory objects. *J. Acoust. Soc. Am.*, *124*, 2224–2235.

Ihlefeld, A., and Shinn-Cunningham, B. (2008b). Spatial release from energetic and informational masking in a selective speech identification task. *J. Acoust. Soc. Am.*, *123*, 4369–4379.

ISO 226. (2003). *Acoustics—Normal Equal-Loudness Contours.* Geneva: International Organization for Standardization.

ISO 389-7. (2005). *Acoustics—Reference zero for the calibration of audiometric equipment. Part 7: reference threshold of hearing under free-field and diffuse-field listening conditions.* Geneva: International Organization for Standardization.

Iverson, P. (1995). Auditory stream segregation by musical timbre: effects of static and dynamic acoustic attributes. *J. Exp. Psychol.: Human Percept. Perf.*, *21*, 751–763.

Ives, D. T., and Patterson, R. D. (2008). Pitch strength decreases as F0 and harmonic resolution increase in complex tones composed exclusively of high harmonics. *J. Acoust. Soc. Am.*, *123*, 2670–2679.

Iwamiya, S., Kosugi, K., and Kitamura, O. (1983). Perceived principal pitch of vibrato tones. *J. Acoust. Soc. Jpn. (E)*, 4, 73–82.

Iwamiya, S., Nishikawa, S., and Kitamura, O. (1984). Perceived principal pitch of FM-AM tones when the phase difference between frequency modulation and amplitude modulation is in-phase and anti-phase. *J. Acoust. Soc. Jpn. (E)*, 5, 59–69.

Jacob, S., Johansson, C., Ulfendahl, M., and Fridberger, A. (2009). A digital heterodyne laser interferometer for studying cochlear mechanics. *J. Neurosci. Methods*, 179, 271–277.

Javel, E. (1980). Coding of AM tones in the chinchilla auditory nerve: implications for the pitch of complex tones. *J. Acoust. Soc. Am.*, 68, 133–146.

Javel, E. (1996). Long-term adaptation in cat auditory-nerve fiber responses. *J. Acoust. Soc. Am.*, 99, 1040–1052.

Jeffress, L. A. (1948). A place theory of sound localization. *J. Comp. Physiol. Psychol.*, 41, 35–39.

Jeffress, L. A. (1971). Detection and lateralization of binaural signals. *Audiology*, 10, 77–84.

Jeffress, L. A. (1972). Binaural signal detection: vector theory. In J. V. Tobias (Ed.), *Foundations of Modern Auditory Theory*. New York: Academic Press.

Jerger, J., and Jerger, S. (1975). A simplified tone decay test. *Arch. Otolaryngol.*, 102, 403–407.

Jerger, J., Shedd, J., and Harford, E. (1959). On the detection of extremely small changes in sound intensity. *Arch. Otolaryngol.*, 69, 200–211.

Jesteadt, W., Wier, C. C., and Green, D. M. (1977). Intensity discrimination as a function of frequency and sensation level. *J. Acoust. Soc. Am.*, 61, 169–177.

Johnson, D. L., and Gierke, H. von (1974). Audibility of infrasound. *J. Acoust. Soc. Am.*, 56(Suppl), S37.

Johnson-Davies, D., and Patterson, R. D. (1979). Psychophysical tuning curves: restricting the listening band to the signal region. *J. Acoust. Soc. Am.*, 65, 765–770.

Jurado, C., and Moore, B. C. J. (2010). Frequency selectivity for frequencies below 100 Hz: comparisons with mid-frequencies. *J. Acoust. Soc. Am.*, 128, 3585–3596.

Jurado, C., Pedersen, C. S., and Moore, B. C. J. (2011). Psychophysical tuning curves for frequencies below 100 Hz, *J. Acoust. Soc. Am.*, 129, 3166–3180.

Kaas, J. H., and Collins, C. E. (2001). The organization of sensory cortex. *Curr. Opin. Neurobiol.*, 11, 498–504.

Kameoka, A., and Kuriyagawa, M. (1969). Consonance theory. Part II: consonance of complex tones and its calculation method. *J. Acoust. Soc. Am.*, 45, 1460–1469.

Kawaura, J., Suzuki, Y., Asano, F., and Sone, T. (1991). Sound localization in headphone reproduction by simulating transfer functions from the sound source to the external ear. *J. Acoust. Soc. Jpn. (E)*, 12, 203–216.

Kay, R. H. (1982). Hearing of modulation in sounds. *Physiol. Rev.*, 62, 894–975.

Keen, R., and Freyman, R. L. (2009). Release and re-buildup of listeners' models of auditory space. *J. Acoust. Soc. Am.*, 125, 3243–3252.

Kemp, D. T. (1978). Stimulated acoustic emissions from within the human auditory system. *J. Acoust. Soc. Am.*, 64, 1386–1391.

Kewley-Port, D., Pisoni, D. B., and Studdert-Kennedy, M. (1983). Perception of static and dynamic cues to place of articulation in initial stop consonants. *J. Acoust. Soc. Am.*, 73, 1779–1793.

Khanna, S. M., and Leonard, D. G. B. (1982). Basilar membrane tuning in the cat cochlea. *Science*, 215, 305–306.

Kiang, N. Y. S., Moxon, E. C., and Levine, R. A. (1970). Auditory nerve activity in cats with normal and abnormal cochleas. In G. E. W. Wolstenholme & J. J. Knight (Eds.), *Sensorineural Hearing Loss*. London: Churchill.

Kiang, N. Y.-S., Watanabe, T., Thomas, E. C., and Clark, L. F. (1965). *Discharge Patterns of Single Fibers in the Cat's Auditory Nerve*. Cambridge, MA: MIT Press.

Kidd, G., and Feth, L. L. (1982). Effects of masker duration in pure-tone forward masking. *J. Acoust. Soc. Am.*, 72, 1384–1386.

Kidd, G., Mason, C. R., Brantley, M. A., and Owen, G. A. (1989). Roving level tone-in-noise detection. *J. Acoust. Soc. Am.*, 86, 1310–1317.

Killion, M. C. (1978). Revised estimate of minimal audible pressure: where is the 'missing 6 dB'? *J. Acoust. Soc. Am.*, 63, 1501–1510.

Killion, M. C. (1997). Hearing aids: past, present and future: moving toward normal conversations in noise. *Br. J. Audiol.*, 31, 141–148.

Killion, M. C., DeVilbiss, E., and Stewart, J. (1988). An earplug with uniform 15-dB attenuation. *Hear. J.*, 41, 14–16.

Kim, D. O., and Molnar, C. E. (1979). A population study of cochlear nerve fibres: comparison of spatial distributions of average-rate and phase-locking measures of responses to single tones. *J. Neurophysiol.*, 42, 16–30.

Kim, D. O., Molnar, C. E., and Matthews, J. W. (1980). Cochlear mechanics: nonlinear behaviour in two-tone responses as reflected in cochlear-nerve-fibre responses and in ear-canal sound pressure. *J. Acoust. Soc. Am.*, 67, 1704–1721.

Kim, M. G., Hong, S. M., Shim, H. J., Kim, Y. D., Cha, C. I., and Yeo, S. G. (2009). Hearing threshold of Korean adolescents associated with the use of personal music players. *Yonsei Med. J.*, 50, 771–776.

Kimura, D. (1964). Left-right differences in the perception of melodies. *Q. J. Exp. Psychol.*, 16, 355–358.

Klatt, D. (1982). Speech processing strategies based on auditory models. In R. Carlson & B. Granström (Eds.), *The Representation of Speech in the Peripheral Auditory System*. Amsterdam: Elsevier.

Klatt, D. (1989). Review of selected models of speech perception. In W. D. Marlsen-Wilson (Ed.), *Lexical Representation and Process*. Cambridge, MA: MIT Press.

Klein, M. A., and Hartmann, W. M. (1981). Binaural edge pitch. *J. Acoust. Soc. Am.*, 70, 51–61.

Kluender, K. R., Coady, J. A., and Kiefte, M. (2003). Sensitivity to change in perception of speech. *Speech Comm.*, 41, 59–69.

Kluk, K., and Moore, B. C. J. (2004). Factors affecting psychophysical tuning curves for normally hearing subjects. *Hear. Res.*, 194, 118–134.

Klumpp, R. G., and Eady, H. R. (1956). Some measurements of interaural time difference thresholds. *J. Acoust. Soc. Am.*, 28, 859–860.

Koffka, K. (1935). *Principles of Gestalt Psychology*. New York: Harcourt and Brace.

Kohlrausch, A. (1988). Auditory filter shapes derived from binaural masking experiments. *J. Acoust. Soc. Am.*, *84*, 573–583.

Kohlrausch, A., and Sander, A. (1995). Phase effects in masking related to dispersion in the inner ear. II. Masking period patterns of short targets. *J. Acoust. Soc. Am.*, *97*, 1817–1829.

Kohlrausch, A., Fassel, R., and Dau, T. (2000). The influence of carrier level and frequency on modulation and beat-detection thresholds for sinusoidal carriers. *J. Acoust. Soc. Am.*, *108*, 723–734.

Kolarik, A. J., and Culling, J. F. (2010). Measurement of the binaural auditory filter using a detection task. *J. Acoust. Soc. Am.*, *127*, 3009–3017.

Kollmeier, B., and Gilkey, R. H. (1990). Binaural forward and backward masking: evidence for sluggishness in binaural detection. *J. Acoust. Soc. Am.*, *87*, 1709–1719.

Kollmeier, B., and Hohmann, V. (1995). Loudness estimation and compensation employing a categorical scale. In G. A. Manley, G. M. Klump, C. Köppl, H. Fastl & H. Oeckinghaus (Eds.), *Advances in Hearing Research*. Singapore: World Scientific.

Kong, Y. Y., and Carlyon, R. P. (2010). Temporal pitch perception at high rates in cochlear implants. *J. Acoust. Soc. Am.*, *127*, 3114–3123.

Krumbholz, K., Patterson, R. D., and Pressnitzer, D. (2000). The lower limit of pitch as determined by rate discrimination. *J. Acoust. Soc. Am.*, *108*, 1170–1180.

Kryter, K. D. (1962). Methods for the calculation and use of the articulation index. *J. Acoust. Soc. Am.*, *34*, 467–477.

Kubovy, M., Cutting, J. E., and McGuire, R. M. (1974). Hearing with the third ear: dichotic perception of a melody without monaural familiarity cues. *Science*, *186*, 272–274.

Kuhl, P. K. (1993). Developmental speech perception: implications for models of language impairment. In P. Tallal, A. M. Galaburda, R. R. Llinás & C. von Euler (Eds.), *Temporal Information Processing in the Nervous System: Special Reference to Dyslexia and Dysphasia*. New York: New York Academy of Sciences.

Kuhl, P. K. (2009). Early language acquisition: phonetic and word learning, neural substrates, and a theoretical model. In B. C. J. Moore, L. K. Tyler & W. D. Marslen-Wilsen (Eds.), *The Perception of Speech: From Sound to Meaning*. Oxford: Oxford University Press.

Kujawa, S. G., and Liberman, M. C. (2001). Effects of olivocochlear feedback on distortion product otoacoustic emissions in guinea pig. *J. Assoc. Res. Otolaryngol.*, *2*, 268–278.

Kujawa, S. G., and Liberman, M. C. (2009). Adding insult to injury: cochlear nerve degeneration after "temporary" noise-induced hearing loss. *J. Neurosci.*, *29*, 14077–14085.

Langhans, A., and Kohlrausch, A. (1992). Spectral integration of broadband signals in diotic and dichotic masking experiments. *J. Acoust. Soc. Am.*, *91*, 317–326.

Launer, S., and Moore, B. C. J. (2003). Use of a loudness model for hearing aid fitting. V. On-line gain control in a digital hearing aid. *Int. J. Audiol.*, *42*, 262–273.

Leonard, D. G. B., and Khanna, S. M. (1984). Histological evaluation of damage in cat cochleas used for measurement of basilar membrane mechanics. *J. Acoust. Soc. Am.*, *75*, 515–527.

Leshowitz, B. (1971). Measurement of the two-click threshold. *J. Acoust. Soc. Am.*, *49*, 426–466.

Levitt, H., and Rabiner, L. R. (1967). Binaural release from masking for speech and gain in intelligibility. *J. Acoust. Soc. Am.*, *42*, 601–608.

Liberman, A. M. (1982a). On finding that speech is special. *Am. Psychologist.*, *37*, 148–167.

Liberman, A. M., and Mattingly, I. G. (1985). The motor theory of speech perception revised. *Cognition*, *21*, 1–36.

Liberman, A. M., Cooper, F. S., Shankweiler, D. P., and Studdert-Kennedy, M. (1967). Perception of the speech code. *Psychol. Rev.*, *74*, 431–461.

Liberman, M. C. (1978). Auditory-nerve response from cats raised in a low-noise chamber. *J. Acoust. Soc. Am.*, *63*, 442–455.

Liberman, M. C. (1982b). The cochlear frequency map for the cat: labeling auditory-nerve fibers of known characteristic frequency. *J. Acoust. Soc. Am.*, *72*, 1441–1449.

Liberman, M. C., and Guinan, J. J., Jr. (1998). Feedback control of the auditory periphery: anti-masking effects of middle ear muscles vs. olivocochlear efferents. *J. Commun. Disord.*, *31*, 471–482.

Licklider, J. C., Webster, J. C., and Hedlun, J. M. (1950). On the frequency limits of binaural beats. *J. Acoust. Soc. Am.*, *22*, 468–473.

Licklider, J. C. R. (1956). Auditory frequency analysis. In C. Cherry (Ed.), *Information Theory*. Academic Press: New York.

Licklider, J. C. R., and Pollack, I. (1948). Effects of differentiation, integration and infinite peak clipping upon the intelligibility of speech. *J. Acoust. Soc. Am.*, *20*, 42–52.

Lippmann, R. P., Braida, L. D., and Durlach, N. I. (1981). Study of multi-channel amplitude compression and linear amplification for persons with sensorineural hearing loss. *J. Acoust. Soc. Am.*, *69*, 524–534.

Litovsky, R. Y. (1998). Physiological studies of the precedence effect in the inferior colliculus of the kitten. *J. Acoust. Soc. Am.*, *103*, 3139–3152.

Litovsky, R. Y., Colburn, H. S., Yost, W. A., and Guzman, S. J. (1999). The precedence effect. *J. Acoust. Soc. Am.*, *106*, 1633–1654.

Litovsky, R. Y., Hawley, M. L., Fligor, B. J., and Zurek, P. M. (2000). Failure to unlearn the precedence effect. *J. Acoust. Soc. Am.*, *108*, 2345–2352.

Litovsky, R. Y., Rakerd, B., Yin, T. C. T., and Hartmann, W. M. (1997). Psychophysical and physiological evidence for a precedence effect in the median sagittal plane. *J. Neurophysiol.*, *77*, 2223–2226.

Little, A. D., Mershon, D. H., and Cox, P. H. (1992). Spectral content as a cue to perceived auditory distance. *Perception*, *21*, 405–416.

Locke, S., and Kellar, L. (1973). Categorical perception in a non-linguistic mode. *Cortex*, *9*, 353–369.

Lopez-Poveda, E. A., and Meddis, R. (2001). A human nonlinear cochlear filterbank. *J. Acoust. Soc. Am.*, *110*, 3107–3118.

Lopez-Poveda, E. A., Plack, C. J., and Meddis, R. (2003). Cochlear nonlinearity between 500 and 8000 Hz in listeners with normal hearing. *J. Acoust. Soc. Am.*, *113*, 951–960.

Lorenzi, C., Micheyl, C., and Berthommier, F. (1995). Neuronal correlates of perceptual amplitude-modulation detection. *Hear. Res.*, *90*, 219–227.

Lorenzi, C., Soares, C., and Vonner, T. (2001). Second-order temporal modulation transfer functions. *J. Acoust. Soc. Am.*, *110*, 1030–1038.

Lundeen, C., and Small, A. M. (1984). The influence of temporal cues on the strength of periodicity pitches. *J. Acoust. Soc. Am.*, *75*, 1578–1587.

Lunner, T., and Sundewall-Thoren, E. (2007). Interactions between cognition, compression, and listening conditions: effects on speech-in-noise performance in a two-channel hearing aid. *J. Am. Acad. Audiol.*, *18*, 604–617.

Lutfi, R. A., and Patterson, R. D. (1984). On the growth of masking asymmetry with stimulus intensity. *J. Acoust. Soc. Am.*, *76*, 739–745.

Lyzenga, J., and Moore, B. C. J. (2005). Effect of FM coherence for inharmonic stimuli: FM-phase discrimination and identification of artificial double vowels. *J. Acoust. Soc. Am.*, *117*, 1314–1325.

Lyzenga, J., Carlyon, R. P., and Moore, B. C. J. (2005). Dynamic aspects of the continuity illusion: perception of level and of the depth, rate, and phase of modulation. *Hear. Res.*, *210*, 30–41.

Macherey, O., Deeks, J. M., and Carlyon, R. P. (2011). Extending the limits of place and temporal pitch perception in cochlear implant users. *J. Assoc. Res. Otolaryngol.*, *12*, 233–251.

Macmillan, N. A., and Creelman, C. D. (2005). *Detection Theory: A User's Guide* (2nd ed.). New York: Erlbaum.

Mann, V. A., and Liberman, A. M. (1983). Some differences between phonetic and auditory modes of perception. *Cognition*, *14*, 211–235.

Marin, C. M. H., and McAdams, S. (1991). Segregation of concurrent sounds. II: effects of spectral envelope tracing, frequency modulation coherence, and frequency modulation width. *J. Acoust. Soc. Am.*, *89*, 341–351.

Marriage, J. E., Moore, B. C. J., and Alcántara, J. I. (2004). Comparison of three procedures for initial fitting of compression hearing aids. III. Inexperienced versus experienced users. *Int. J. Audiol.*, *43*, 198–210.

Marshall, L., Lapsley Miller, J. A., Heller, L. M., Wolgemuth, K. S., Hughes, L. M., Smith, S. D., and Kopke, R. D. (2009). Detecting incipient inner-ear damage from impulse noise with otoacoustic emissions. *J. Acoust. Soc. Am.*, *125*, 995–1013.

Massaro, D. W. (1999). Speechreading: illusion or window into pattern recognition. *Trends Cog. Sci.*, *3*, 310–317.

Mayer, A. M. (1894). Research in acoustics. *Lond. Edinb. Dubl. Phil. Mag.*, *ser. 5*, 259–288.

McAdams, S. (1982). Spectral fusion and the creation of auditory images. In M. Clynes (Ed.), *Music, Mind and Brain: The Neuropsychology of Music*. New York: Plenum.

McAdams, S. (1989). Segregation of concurrent sounds. I.: effects of frequency modulation coherence. *J. Acoust. Soc. Am.*, *86*, 2148–2159.

McClelland, J. L., and Elman, J. L. (1986). The TRACE model of speech perception. *Cog. Psychol.*, *18*, 1–86.

McCormick, B., Archbold, S., and Sheppard, S. (1994). *Cochlear Implants for Young Children*. London: Whurr.

McDermott, H. J. (2004). Music perception with cochlear implants: a review. *Trends Amplif.*, *8*, 49–82.

McDermott, H. J., and McKay, C. M. (1997). Musical pitch perception with electrical stimulation of the cochlea. *J. Acoust. Soc. Am.*, *101*, 1622–1631.

McDermott, H. J., McKay, C. M., and Vandali, A. E. (1992). A new portable sound processor for the University of Melbourne/Nucleus limited multielectrode cochlear implant. *J. Acoust. Soc. Am.*, *91*, 3367–3371.

McDermott, J. H., Lehr, A. J., and Oxenham, A. J. (2010). Individual differences reveal the basis of consonance. *Curr. Biol.*, *20*, 1035–1041.

McFadden, D. (1986). The curious half octave shift: evidence for a basalward migration of the travelling-wave envelope with increasing intensity. In R. J. Salvi, D. Henderson, R. P. Hamernik & V. Colletti (Eds.), *Basic and Applied Aspects of Noise-Induced Hearing Loss*. New York: Plenum.

McFadden, D. (1989). Spectral differences in the ability of temporal gaps to reset the mechanisms underlying overshoot. *J. Acoust. Soc. Am.*, *85*, 254–261.

McFadden, D., and Pasanen, E. G. (1976). Lateralization at high frequencies based on interaural time differences. *J. Acoust. Soc. Am.*, *59*, 634–639.

McFadden, D., and Plattsmier, H. S. (1984). Aspirin abolishes spontaneous otoacoustic emissions. *J. Acoust. Soc. Am.*, *76*, 443–448.

McFadden, D., Jeffress, L. A., and Ermey, H. L. (1972). Differences of interaural phase and level in detection and lateralization: 1000 and 2000 Hz. *J. Acoust. Soc. Am.*, *52*, 1197–1206.

McGurk, H., and MacDonald, J. (1976). Hearing lips and seeing voices. *Nature, 264*, 746–748.

McKeown, J. D., and Patterson, R. D. (1995). The time course of auditory segregation: concurrent vowels that vary in duration. *J. Acoust. Soc. Am.*, *98*, 1866–1877.

Meddis, R., and Hewitt, M. (1991). Virtual pitch and phase sensitivity of a computer model of the auditory periphery. I: pitch identification. *J. Acoust. Soc. Am.*, *89*, 2866–2882.

Meddis, R., and Hewitt, M. (1992). Modeling the identification of concurrent vowels with different fundamental frequencies. *J. Acoust. Soc. Am.*, *91*, 233–245.

Meddis, R., and O'Mard, L. (1997). A unitary model of pitch perception. *J. Acoust. Soc. Am.*, *102*, 1811–1820.

Meddis, R., and O'Mard, L. P. (2005). A computer model of the auditory-nerve response to forward-masking stimuli. *J. Acoust. Soc. Am.*, *117*, 3787–3798.

Mehler, J. (1981). The role of syllables in speech processing: infant and adult data. *Phil. Trans. Roy. Soc. B*, *295*, 333–352.

Mehrgardt, S., and Schroeder, M. R. (1983). Monaural phase effects in masking with multicomponent signals. In R. Klinke & R. Hartmann (Eds.), *Hearing— Physiological Bases and Psychophysics*. Berlin: Springer-Verlag.

Mersenne, M. (1636). *Trait des Instrumens*. Paris: Sebastian Cramoisy.

Mershon, D. H., and Bowers, J. N. (1979). Absolute and relative cues for the auditory perception of egocentric distance. *Perception*, *8*, 311–322.

Mershon, D. H., and King, L. E. (1975). Intensity and reverberation as factors in the auditory perception of egocentric distance. *Percept. Psychophys.*, *18*, 409–415.

Mershon, D. H., Desaulniers, D. H., Kiefer, S. A., Amerson, T. L., and Mills, J. T. (1981). Perceived loudness and visually-determined auditory distance. *Perception*, 10, 531–543.

Merzenich, M. M., Michelson, R. P., Schindler, R. A., Pettit, C. R., and Reid, M. (1973). Neural encoding of sound sensation evoked by electrical stimulation of the acoustic nerve. *Ann. Otol.*, 82, 486–503.

Meyer, M. (1898). Zur Theorie der Differenztöne und der Gehörsempfindungen überhaubt. *Beitr. Akust. Musikwiss.*, 2, 25–65.

Middlebrooks, J. C. (1999). Virtual localization improved by scaling nonindividualized external-ear transfer functions in frequency. *J. Acoust. Soc. Am.*, 106, 1493–1510.

Middlebrooks, J. C., Makous, J. C., and Green, D. M. (1989). Directional sensitivity of sound pressure levels in the human ear canal. *J. Acoust. Soc. Am.*, 61, 89–108.

Miller, G. A. (1947). Sensitivity to changes in the intensity of white noise and its relation to masking and loudness. *J. Acoust. Soc. Am.*, 191, 609–619.

Miller, G. A., and Heise, G. A. (1950). The trill threshold. *J. Acoust. Soc. Am.*, 22, 637–638.

Miller, G. A., and Licklider, J. C. R. (1950). The intelligibility of interrupted speech. *J. Acoust. Soc. Am.*, 22, 167–173.

Miller, G. A., and Taylor, W. (1948). The perception of repeated bursts of noise. *J. Acoust. Soc. Am.*, 20, 171–182.

Miller, J. D., Wier, C. C., Pastore, R., Kelly, W. J., and Dooling, R. J. (1976). Discrimination and labelling of noise-burst sequences with varying noise-lead times: an example of categorical perception. *J. Acoust. Soc. Am.*, 60, 410–417.

Mills, A. W. (1958). On the minimum audible angle. *J. Acoust. Soc. Am.*, 30, 237–246.

Mills, A. W. (1960). Lateralization of high-frequency tones. *J. Acoust. Soc. Am.*, 32, 132–134.

Mills, A. W. (1972). Auditory localization. In J. V. Tobias (Ed.), *Foundations of Modern Auditory Theory* (Vol. II). New York: Academic Press.

Miskiewicz, A., Scharf, B., Hellman, R., and Meiselman, C. (1993). Loudness adaptation at high frequencies. *J. Acoust. Soc. Am.*, 94, 1281–1286.

Miyazaki, K., and Sasaki, T. (1984). Pure-tone masking patterns in nonsimultaneous masking conditions. *Jap. Psychol. Res.*, 26, 110–119.

Møller, A. R. (1976). Dynamic properties of primary auditory fibers compared with cells in the cochlear nucleus. *Acta Physiol. Scand.*, 98, 157–167.

Møller, H., and Pedersen, C. S. (2004). Hearing at low and infrasonic frequencies. *Noise Health*, 6, 37–57.

Møller, H., Sørensen, M. S., Jensen, C. B., and Hammershøi, D. (1996). Binaural technique: do we need individual recordings? *J. Audio Eng. Soc.*, 44, 451–469.

Montoya, F. S., Ibarguen, A. M., Vences, A. R., Del Rey, A. S., and Fernandez, J. M. S. (2008). Evaluation of cochlear function in normal-hearing young adults exposed to mp3 player noise by analyzing transient evoked otoacoustic emissions and distortion products. *J. Otolaryngol. Head Neck Surg.*, 37, 718–724.

Moore, B. C. J. (1972). Some experiments relating to the perception of pure tones: possible clinical applications. *Sound*, 6, 73–79.

Moore, B. C. J. (1973a). Frequency difference limens for short-duration tones. *J. Acoust. Soc. Am.*, 54, 610–619.

Moore, B. C. J. (1973b). Some experiments relating to the perception of complex tones. *Q. J. Exp. Psychol.*, 25, 451–475.

Moore, B. C. J. (1974). Relation between the critical bandwidth and the frequency-difference limen. *J. Acoust. Soc. Am.*, 55, 359.

Moore, B. C. J. (1975). Mechanisms of masking. *J. Acoust. Soc. Am.*, 57, 391–399.

Moore, B. C. J. (1977). Effects of relative phase of the components on the pitch of three-component complex tones. In E. F. Evans & J. P. Wilson (Eds.), *Psychophysics and Physiology of Hearing*. London: Academic Press.

Moore, B. C. J. (1978). Psychophysical tuning curves measured in simultaneous and forward masking. *J. Acoust. Soc. Am.*, 63, 524–532.

Moore, B. C. J. (1980). Detection cues in forward masking. In G. van den Brink & F. A. Bilson (Eds.), *Psychophysical, Physiological and Behavioural Studies in Hearing*. Delft: Delft University Press.

Moore, B. C. J. (1986). Parallels between frequency selectivity measured psychophysically and in cochlear mechanics. *Scand. Audiol.*, 25(Supplement), 139–152.

Moore, B. C. J. (1992). Across-channel processes in auditory masking. *J. Acoust. Soc. Jpn. (E)*, 13, 25–37.

Moore, B. C. J. (1995). *Perceptual Consequences of Cochlear Damage*. Oxford: Oxford University Press.

Moore, B. C. J. (2000). Use of a loudness model for hearing aid fitting. IV. Fitting hearing aids with multi-channel compression so as to restore "normal" loudness for speech at different levels. *Br. J. Audiol.*, 34, 165–177.

Moore, B. C. J. (2002). Frequency resolution. In L. Tranebjærg, J. Christensen-Dalsgaard, T. Andersen & T. Poulsen (Eds.), *Genetics and the Function of the Auditory System*. Copenhagen, Denmark: Holmens Trykkeri.

Moore, B. C. J. (2003a). Coding of sounds in the auditory system and its relevance to signal processing and coding in cochlear implants. *Otol. Neurotol.*, 24, 243–254.

Moore, B. C. J. (2003b). Temporal integration and context effects in hearing. *J. Phonetics*, 31, 563–574.

Moore, B. C. J. (2004). Testing the concept of softness imperception: loudness near threshold for hearing-impaired ears. *J. Acoust. Soc. Am.*, 115, 3103–3111.

Moore, B. C. J. (2007). *Cochlear Hearing Loss: Physiological, Psychological and Technical Issues* (2nd ed.). Chichester: Wiley.

Moore, B. C. J. (2008). The choice of compression speed in hearing aids: theoretical and practical considerations, and the role of individual differences. *Trends Amplif.*, 12, 103–112.

Moore, B. C. J., and Bacon, S. P. (1993). Detection and identification of a single modulated component in a complex sound. *J. Acoust. Soc. Am.*, 94, 759–768.

Moore, B. C. J., and Carlyon, R. P. (2005). Perception of pitch by people with cochlear hearing loss and by cochlear implant users. In C. J. Plack, A. J. Oxenham, R. R. Fay & A. N. Popper (Eds.), *Pitch Perception*. New York: Springer.

Moore, B. C. J., and Emmerich, D. S. (1990). Monaural envelope correlation perception, revisited: effects of bandwidth, frequency separation, duration, and relative level of the noise bands. *J. Acoust. Soc. Am.*, 87, 2628–2633.

Moore, B. C. J., and Glasberg, B. R. (1981). Auditory filter shapes derived in simultaneous and forward masking. *J. Acoust. Soc. Am.*, *70*, 1003–1014.

Moore, B. C. J., and Glasberg, B. R. (1983a). Growth of forward masking for sinusoidal and noise maskers as a function of signal delay: Implications for suppression in noise. *J. Acoust. Soc. Am.*, *73*, 1249–1259.

Moore, B. C. J., and Glasberg, B. R. (1983b). Suggested formulae for calculating auditory-filter bandwidths and excitation patterns. *J. Acoust. Soc. Am.*, *74*, 750–753.

Moore, B. C. J., and Glasberg, B. R. (1986). The role of frequency selectivity in the perception of loudness, pitch and time. In B. C. J. Moore (Ed.), *Frequency Selectivity in Hearing*. London: Academic Press.

Moore, B. C. J., and Glasberg, B. R. (1987). Formulae describing frequency selectivity as a function of frequency and level and their use in calculating excitation patterns. *Hear. Res.*, *28*, 209–225.

Moore, B. C. J., and Glasberg, B. R. (1988a). A comparison of four methods of implementing automatic gain control (AGC) in hearing aids. *Br. J. Audiol.*, *22*, 93–104.

Moore, B. C. J., and Glasberg, B. R. (1988b). Effects of the relative phase of the components on the pitch discrimination of complex tones by subjects with unilateral cochlear impairments. In H. Duifhuis, H. Wit & J. Horst (Eds.), *Basic Issues in Hearing*. London: Academic Press.

Moore, B. C. J., and Glasberg, B. R. (1989). Mechanisms underlying the frequency discrimination of pulsed tones and the detection of frequency modulation. *J. Acoust. Soc. Am.*, *86*, 1722–1732.

Moore, B. C. J., and Glasberg, B. R. (1996). A revision of Zwicker's loudness model. *Acta Acust. Acust.*, *82*, 335–345.

Moore, B. C. J., and Glasberg, B. R. (1997). A model of loudness perception applied to cochlear hearing loss. *Auditory Neurosci.*, *3*, 289–311.

Moore, B. C. J., and Glasberg, B. R. (1998). Use of a loudness model for hearing aid fitting. I. Linear hearing aids. *Br. J. Audiol.*, *32*, 317–335.

Moore, B. C. J., and Glasberg, B. R. (2004). A revised model of loudness perception applied to cochlear hearing loss. *Hear. Res.*, *188*, 70–88.

Moore, B. C. J., and Glasberg, B. R. (2007). Modeling binaural loudness. *J. Acoust. Soc. Am.*, *121*, 1604–1612.

Moore, B. C. J., and Glasberg, B. R. (2010). The role of temporal fine structure in harmonic segregation through mistuning. *J. Acoust. Soc. Am.*, *127*, 5–8.

Moore, B. C. J., and Gockel, H. (2002). Factors influencing sequential stream segregation. *Acta Acust. United Ac.*, *88*, 320–333.

Moore, B. C. J., and Ohgushi, K. (1993). Audibility of partials in inharmonic complex tones. *J. Acoust. Soc. Am.*, *93*, 452–461.

Moore, B. C. J., and Oxenham, A. J. (1998). Psychoacoustic consequences of compression in the peripheral auditory system. *Psych. Rev.*, *105*, 108–124.

Moore, B. C. J., and Raab, D. H. (1974). Pure-tone intensity discrimination: some experiments relating to the "near-miss" to Weber's Law. *J. Acoust. Soc. Am.*, *55*, 1049–1054.

Moore, B. C. J., and Rosen, S. M. (1979). Tune recognition with reduced pitch and interval information. *Q. J. Exp. Psychol.*, *31*, 229–240.

Moore, B. C. J., and Sek, A. (1992). Detection of combined frequency and amplitude modulation. *J. Acoust. Soc. Am.*, *92*, 3119–3131.

Moore, B. C. J., and Sek, A. (1994). Effects of carrier frequency and background noise on the detection of mixed modulation. *J. Acoust. Soc. Am.*, *96*, 741–751.

Moore, B. C. J., and Sek, A. (1995a). Auditory filtering and the critical bandwidth at low frequencies. In G. A. Manley, G. M. Klump, C. Köppl, H. Fastl & H. Oeckinghaus (Eds.), *Advances in Hearing Research*. Singapore: World Scientific.

Moore, B. C. J., and Sek, A. (1995b). Effects of carrier frequency, modulation rate and modulation waveform on the detection of modulation and the discrimination of modulation type (AM vs FM). *J. Acoust. Soc. Am.*, *97*, 2468–2478.

Moore, B. C. J., and Sek, A. (1996). Detection of frequency modulation at low modulation rates: evidence for a mechanism based on phase locking. *J. Acoust. Soc. Am.*, *100*, 2320–2331.

Moore, B. C. J., and Shailer, M. J. (1991). Comodulation masking release as a function of level. *J. Acoust. Soc. Am.*, *90*, 829–835.

Moore, B. C. J., and Tan, C. T. (2003). Perceived naturalness of spectrally distorted speech and music. *J. Acoust. Soc. Am.*, *114*, 408–419.

Moore, B. C. J., and Vickers, D. A. (1997). The role of spread of excitation and suppression in simultaneous masking. *J. Acoust. Soc. Am.*, *102*, 2284–2290.

Moore, B. C. J., Alcántara, J. I., and Dau, T. (1998). Masking patterns for sinusoidal and narrowband noise maskers. *J. Acoust. Soc. Am.*, *104*, 1023–1038.

Moore, B. C. J., Alcántara, J. I., and Glasberg, B. R. (2002). Behavioural measurement of level-dependent shifts in the vibration pattern on the basilar membrane. *Hear. Res.*, *163*, 101–110.

Moore, B. C. J., Alcántara, J. I., and Marriage, J. E. (2001). Comparison of three procedures for initial fitting of compression hearing aids. I. Experienced users, fitted bilaterally. *Br. J. Audiol.*, *35*, 339–353.

Moore, B. C. J., Füllgrabe, C., and Sek, A. (2009). Estimation of the center frequency of the highest modulation filter. *J. Acoust. Soc. Am.*, *125*, 1075–1081.

Moore, B. C. J., Glasberg, B. R., and Baer, T. (1997). A model for the prediction of thresholds, loudness and partial loudness. *J. Audio Eng. Soc.*, *45*, 224–240.

Moore, B. C. J., Glasberg, B. R., and Peters, R. W. (1985a). Relative dominance of individual partials in determining the pitch of complex tones. *J. Acoust. Soc. Am.*, *77*, 1853–1860.

Moore, B. C. J., Glasberg, B. R., and Peters, R. W. (1986). Thresholds for hearing mistuned partials as separate tones in harmonic complexes. *J. Acoust. Soc. Am.*, *80*, 479–483.

Moore, B. C. J., Glasberg, B. R., and Roberts, B. (1984a). Refining the measurement of psychophysical tuning curves. *J. Acoust. Soc. Am.*, *76*, 1057–1066.

Moore, B. C. J., Glasberg, B. R., and Schooneveldt, G. P. (1990). Across-channel masking and comodulation masking release. *J. Acoust. Soc. Am.*, *87*, 1683–1694.

Moore, B. C. J., Glasberg, B. R., and Shailer, M. J. (1984b). Frequency and intensity difference limens for harmonics within complex tones. *J. Acoust. Soc. Am.*, *75*, 550–561.

Moore, B. C. J., Glasberg, B. R., and Stone, M. A. (1991a). Optimization of a slow-acting automatic gain control system for use in hearing aids. *Br. J. Audiol.*, *25*, 171–182.

Moore, B. C. J., Glasberg, B. R., and Stone, M. A. (1999a). Use of a loudness model for hearing aid fitting. III. A general method for deriving initial fittings for hearing aids with multi-channel compression. *Br. J. Audiol.*, *33*, 241–258.

Moore, B. C. J., Glasberg, B. R., and Stone, M. A. (2010). Development of a new method for deriving initial fittings for hearing aids with multi-channel compression: CAMEQ2-HF. *Int. J. Audiol.*, *49*, 216–227.

Moore, B. C. J., Oldfield, S. R., and Dooley, G. (1989). Detection and discrimination of spectral peaks and notches at 1 and 8 kHz. *J. Acoust. Soc. Am.*, *85*, 820–836.

Moore, B. C. J., Peters, R. W., and Glasberg, B. R. (1993a). Detection of temporal gaps in sinusoids: effects of frequency and level. *J. Acoust. Soc. Am.*, *93*, 1563–1570.

Moore, B. C. J., Peters, R. W., and Glasberg, B. R. (1996). Detection of decrements and increments in sinusoids at high overall levels. *J. Acoust. Soc. Am.*, *99*, 3669–3677.

Moore, B. C. J., Shailer, M. J., and Black, M. J. (1993b). Dichotic interference effects in gap detection. *J. Acoust. Soc. Am.*, *93*, 2130–2133.

Moore, B. C. J., Alcántara, J. I., Stone, M. A., and Glasberg, B. R. (1999b). Use of a loudness model for hearing aid fitting. II. Hearing aids with multi-channel compression. *Br. J. Audiol.*, *33*, 157–170.

Moore, B. C. J., Glasberg, B. R., Gaunt, T., and Child, T. (1991b). Across-channel masking of changes in modulation depth for amplitude- and frequency-modulated signals. *Q. J. Exp. Psychol.*, *43A*, 327–347.

Moore, B. C. J., Glasberg, B. R., Hess, R. F., and Birchall, J. P. (1985b). Effects of flanking noise bands on the rate of growth of loudness of tones in normal and recruiting ears. *J. Acoust. Soc. Am.*, *77*, 1505–1515.

Moore, B. C. J., Glasberg, B. R., Plack, C. J., and Biswas, A. K. (1988). The shape of the ear's temporal window. *J. Acoust. Soc. Am.*, *83*, 1102–1116.

Moore, B. C. J., Johnson, J. S., Clark, T. M., and Pluvinage, V. (1992). Evaluation of a dual-channel full dynamic range compression system for people with sensorineural hearing loss. *Ear Hear*, *13*, 349–370.

Moore, B. C. J., Poon, P. W. F., Bacon, S. P., and Glasberg, B. R. (1987). The temporal course of masking and the auditory filter shape. *J. Acoust. Soc. Am.*, *81*, 1873–1880.

Moore, B. C. J., Vickers, D. A., Plack, C. J., and Oxenham, A. J. (1999c). Inter-relationship between different psychoacoustic measures assumed to be related to the cochlear active mechanism. *J. Acoust. Soc. Am.*, *106*, 2761–2778.

Moore, B. C. J., Glasberg, B. R., Low, K.-E., Cope, T., and Cope, W. (2006). Effects of level and frequency on the audibility of partials in inharmonic complex tones. *J. Acoust. Soc. Am.*, *120*, 934–944.

Moore, B. C. J., Stone, M. A., Füllgrabe, C., Glasberg, B. R., and Puria, S. (2008). Spectro-temporal characteristics of speech at high frequencies, and the potential for restoration of audibility to people with mild-to-moderate hearing loss. *Ear Hear*, *29*, 907–922.

Moore, G. A., and Moore, B. C. J. (2003). Perception of the low pitch of frequency-shifted complexes. *J. Acoust. Soc. Am.*, *113*, 977–985.

Morosan, P., Rademacher, J., Schleicher, A., Amunts, K., Schormann, T., and Zilles, K. (2001). Human primary auditory cortex: cytoarchitectonic subdivisions and mapping into a spatial reference system. *Neuroimage*, *13*, 684–701.

Muraoka, T., Iwahara, M., and Yamada, Y. (1981). Examination of audio-bandwidth requirements for optimum sound transmission. *J. Audio Eng. Soc.*, *29*, 2–9.

Neff, D. L., and Callaghan, B. P. (1988). Effective properties of multicomponent simultaneous maskers under conditions of uncertainty. *J. Acoust. Soc. Am.*, *83*, 1833–1838.

Neff, D. L., and Green, D. M. (1987). Masking produced by spectral uncertainty with multi-component maskers. *Percept. Psychophys.*, *41*, 409–415.

Neisser, U. (1967). *Cognitive Psychology*. New York: Appleton-Century-Crofts.

Nelson, D. A., and Schroder, A. C. (1997). Linearized response growth inferred from growth-of-masking slopes in ears with cochlear hearing loss. *J. Acoust. Soc. Am.*, *101*, 2186–2201.

Nelson, D. A., Schroder, A. C., and Wojtczak, M. (2001). A new procedure for measuring peripheral compression in normal-hearing and hearing-impaired listeners. *J. Acoust. Soc. Am.*, *110*, 2045–2064.

Nelson, D. A., Stanton, M. E., and Freyman, R. L. (1983). A general equation describing frequency discrimination as a function of frequency and sensation level. *J. Acoust. Soc. Am.*, *73*, 2117–2123.

Ohgushi, K. (1983). The origin of tonality and a possible explanation of the octave enlargement phenomenon. *J. Acoust. Soc. Am.*, *73*, 1694–1700.

Ohgushi, K. (1984). Recent research on hearing in Japan. *J. Acoust. Soc. Jpn. (E)*, *5*, 127–133.

Ohgushi, K., and Hatoh, T. (1991). Perception of the musical pitch of high frequency tones. In Y. Cazals, L. Demany & K. Horner (Eds.), *Ninth International Symposium on Hearing: Auditory Physiology and Perception*. Oxford: Pergamon.

Ohm, G. S. (1843). Über die Definition des Tones, nebst daran geknüpfter Theorie der Sirene und ähnlicher tonbildender Vorrichtungen (On the definition of a tone and related theory of a siren and similar tone-producing devices). *Annalen der Physik und Chemie*, *59*, 513–565.

Oldfield, S. R., and Parker, S. P. A. (1984). Acuity of sound localization: a topography of auditory space. I. Normal hearing conditions. *Perception*, *13*, 581–600.

O'Loughlin, B. J., and Moore, B. C. J. (1981). Improving psychoacoustical tuning curves. *Hear. Res.*, *5*, 343–346.

Oxenham, A. J. (2001). Forward masking: adaptation or integration? *J. Acoust. Soc. Am.*, *109*, 732–741.

Oxenham, A. J., and Dau, T. (2001). Reconciling frequency selectivity and phase effects in masking. *J. Acoust. Soc. Am.*, *110*, 1525–1538.

Oxenham, A. J., and Moore, B. C. J. (1994). Modeling the additivity of nonsimultaneous masking. *Hear. Res.*, *80*, 105–118.

Oxenham, A. J., and Moore, B. C. J. (1995a). Additivity of masking in normally hearing and hearing-impaired subjects. *J. Acoust. Soc. Am.*, *98*, 1921–1934.

Oxenham, A. J., and Moore, B. C. J. (1995b). Overshoot and the "severe departure" from Weber's law. *J. Acoust. Soc. Am.*, 97, 2442–2453.

Oxenham, A. J., and Moore, B. C. J. (1997). Modeling the effects of peripheral nonlinearity in listeners with normal and impaired hearing. In W. Jesteadt (Ed.), *Modeling Sensorineural Hearing Loss*. Hillsdale, NJ: Erlbaum.

Oxenham, A. J., and Plack, C. J. (1997). A behavioral measure of basilar-membrane nonlinearity in listeners with normal and impaired hearing. *J. Acoust. Soc. Am.*, 101, 3666–3675.

Oxenham, A. J., and Shera, C. A. (2003). Estimates of human cochlear tuning at low levels using forward and simultaneous masking. *J. Assoc. Res. Otolaryngol.*, 4, 541–554.

Oxenham, A. J., and Simonson, A. M. (2006). Level dependence of auditory filters in nonsimultaneous masking as a function of frequency. *J. Acoust. Soc. Am.*, 119, 444–453.

Oxenham, A. J., Fligor, B. J., Mason, C. R., and Kidd, G., Jr. (2003). Informational masking and musical training. *J. Acoust. Soc. Am.*, 114, 1543–1549.

Oxenham, A. J., Micheyl, C., Keebler, M. V., Loper, A., & Santurette, S. (2011). Pitch perception beyond the traditional existence region of pitch, *Proc. Natl. Acad. Sci. USA*, 408, 7629–7634.

Palmer, A. R. (1995). Neural signal processing. In B. C. J. Moore (Ed.), *Hearing*. San Diego, CA: Academic Press.

Palmer, A. R., and Evans, E. F. (1979). On the peripheral coding of the level of individual frequency components of complex sounds at high sound levels. In O. Creutzfeldt, H. Scheich & C. Schreiner (Eds.), *Hearing Mechanisms and Speech*. Berlin: Springer-Verlag.

Palmer, A. R., and Russell, I. J. (1986). Phase-locking in the cochlear nerve of the guinea-pig and its relation to the receptor potential of inner hair-cells. *Hear. Res.*, 24, 1–15.

Parker, E. M., Diehl, R. L., and Kleunder, K. R. (1986). Trading relations in speech and nonspeech. *Percept. Psychophys.*, 39, 129–142.

Patterson, J. H., and Green, D. M. (1970). Discrimination of transient signals having identical energy spectra. *J. Acoust. Soc. Am.*, 48, 894–905.

Patterson, R. D. (1976). Auditory filter shapes derived with noise stimuli. *J. Acoust. Soc. Am.*, 59, 640–654.

Patterson, R. D. (1987a). A pulse ribbon model of monaural phase perception. *J. Acoust. Soc. Am.*, 82, 1560–1586.

Patterson, R. D. (1987b). A pulse ribbon model of peripheral auditory processing. In W. A. Yost & C. S. Watson (Eds.), *Auditory Processing of Complex Sounds*. Hillsdale, NJ: Erlbaum.

Patterson, R. D. (1988). Timbre cues in monaural phase perception: distinguishing within-channel cues and between-channel cues. In H. Duifhuis, J. W. Horst & H. P. Wit (Eds.), *Basic Issues in Hearing*. London: Academic Press.

Patterson, R. D. (1994a). The sound of a sinusoid: spectral models. *J. Acoust. Soc. Am.*, 96, 1409–1418.

Patterson, R. D. (1994b). The sound of a sinusoid: time-interval models. *J. Acoust. Soc. Am.*, 96, 1419–1428.

Patterson, R. D., and Henning, G. B. (1977). Stimulus variability and auditory filter shape. *J. Acoust. Soc. Am.*, *62*, 649–664.

Patterson, R. D., and Milroy, R. (1980). The appropriate sound level for auditory warnings on civil aircraft. *J. Acoust. Soc. Am.*, *67*, S58.

Patterson, R. D., and Moore, B. C. J. (1986). Auditory filters and excitation patterns as representations of frequency resolution. In B. C. J. Moore (Ed.), *Frequency Selectivity in Hearing*. London: Academic Press.

Patterson, R. D., and Nimmo-Smith, I. (1980). Off-frequency listening and auditory filter asymmetry. *J. Acoust. Soc. Am.*, *67*, 229–245.

Patterson, R. D., and Wightman, F. L. (1976). Residue pitch as a function of component spacing. *J. Acoust. Soc. Am.*, *59*, 1450–1459.

Patuzzi, R. B. (1992). Effects of noise on auditory nerve fiber response. In A. Dancer, D. Henderson, R. Salvi & R. Hamernik (Eds.), *Noise Induced Hearing Loss*. St. Louis, MO: Mosby Year Book.

Penner, M. J. (1972). Neural or energy summation in a Poisson counting model. *J. Math. Psychol.*, *9*, 286–293.

Penner, M. J. (1977). Detection of temporal gaps in noise as a measure of the decay of auditory sensation. *J. Acoust. Soc. Am.*, *61*, 552–557.

Penner, M. J. (1980). The coding of intensity and the interaction of forward and backward masking. *J. Acoust. Soc. Am.*, *67*, 608–616.

Penner, M. J. (1992). Linking spontaneous otoacoustic emissions and tinnitus. *Br. J. Audiol.*, *26*, 115–123.

Penner, M. J., and Shiffrin, R. M. (1980). Nonlinearities in the coding of intensity within the context of a temporal summation model. *J. Acoust. Soc. Am.*, *67*, 617–627.

Perrott, D. R., and Musicant, A. D. (1977). Minimum auditory movement angle: binaural localization of moving sound sources. *J. Acoust. Soc. Am.*, *62*, 1463–1466.

Perrott, D. R., Marlborough, K., and Merrill, P. (1989). Minimum audible angle thresholds obtained under conditions in which the precedence effect is assumed to operate. *J. Acoust. Soc. Am.*, *85*, 282–288.

Peters, R. W., and Moore, B. C. J. (1992a). Auditory filter shapes at low center frequencies in young and elderly hearing-impaired subjects. *J. Acoust. Soc. Am.*, *91*, 256–266.

Peters, R. W., and Moore, B. C. J. (1992b). Auditory filters and aging: filters when auditory thresholds are normal. In Y. Cazals, L. Demany & K. Horner (Eds.), *Auditory Physiology and Perception*. Oxford: Pergamon.

Pfeiffer, R. R., and Kim, D. O. (1975). Cochlear nerve fibre responses: distribution along the cochlear partition. *J. Acoust. Soc. Am.*, *58*, 867–869.

Pfingst, B. E., and O'Conner, T. A. (1981). Characteristics of neurons in auditory cortex of monkeys performing a simple auditory task. *J. Neurophysiol.*, *45*, 16–34.

Pick, G., Evans, E. F., and Wilson, J. P. (1977). Frequency resolution in patients with hearing loss of cochlear origin. In E. F. Evans & J. P. Wilson (Eds.), *Psychophysics and Physiology of Hearing*. London: Academic Press.

Pickett, J. M. (1980). *The Sounds of Speech Communication*. Baltimore, MD: University Park Press.

Pickles, J. O. (2008). *An Introduction to the Physiology of Hearing* (3rd ed.). Bingley, UK: Emerald.

Pickles, J. O., Osborne, M. P., and Comis, S. D. (1987). Vulnerability of tip links between stereocilia to acoustic trauma in the guinea pig. *Hear. Res.*, 25, 173–183.

Piechowiak, T., Ewert, S. D., and Dau, T. (2007). Modeling comodulation masking release using an equalization-cancellation mechanism. *J. Acoust. Soc. Am.*, 121, 2111–2126.

Pijl, S. (1997). Labeling of musical interval size by cochlear implant patients and normally hearing subjects. *Ear Hear.*, 18, 364–372.

Pijl, S., and Schwarz, D. W. F. (1995). Melody recognition and musical interval perception by deaf subjects stimulated with electrical pulse trains through single cochlear implant electrodes. *J. Acoust. Soc. Am.*, 98, 886–895.

Pisoni, D. B. (1973). Auditory and phonetic memory codes in the discrimination of consonants and vowels. *Percept. Psychophys.*, 13, 253–260.

Plack, C. J., and Carlyon, R. P. (1995). Loudness perception and intensity coding. In B. C. J. Moore (Ed.), *Hearing*. Orlando, FL: Academic Press.

Plack, C. J., and Moore, B. C. J. (1990). Temporal window shape as a function of frequency and level. *J. Acoust. Soc. Am.*, 87, 2178–2187.

Plack, C. J., and Oxenham, A. J. (1998). Basilar-membrane nonlinearity and the growth of forward masking. *J. Acoust. Soc. Am.*, 103, 1598–1608.

Plack, C. J., Drga, V., and Lopez-Poveda, E. A. (2004). Inferred basilar-membrane response functions for listeners with mild to moderate sensorineural hearing loss. *J. Acoust. Soc. Am.*, 115, 1684–1695.

Plenge, G. (1972). Über das Problem der Im-Kopf-Lokalisation. *Acustica*, 26, 213–221.

Plenge, G. (1974). On the differences between localization and lateralization. *J. Acoust. Soc. Am.*, 56, 944–951.

Plomp, R. (1964a). The ear as a frequency analyzer. *J. Acoust. Soc. Am.*, 36, 1628–1636.

Plomp, R. (1964b). The rate of decay of auditory sensation. *J. Acoust. Soc. Am.*, 36, 277–282.

Plomp, R. (1965). Detectability thresholds for combination tones. *J. Acoust. Soc. Am.*, 37, 1110–1123.

Plomp, R. (1967). Pitch of complex tones. *J. Acoust. Soc. Am.*, 41, 1526–1533.

Plomp, R. (1970). Timbre as a multidimensional attribute of complex tones. In R. Plomp & G. F. Smoorenburg (Eds.), *Frequency Analysis and Periodicity Detection in Hearing*. Leiden: Sijthoff.

Plomp, R. (1976). *Aspects of Tone Sensation*. London: Academic Press.

Plomp, R. (2002). *The Intelligent Ear*. Erlbaum: Mahwah, NJ.

Plomp, R., and Levelt, W. J. M. (1965). Tonal consonance and critical bandwidth. *J. Acoust. Soc. Am.*, 38, 548–560.

Plomp, R., and Mimpen, A. M. (1968). The ear as a frequency analyzer II. *J. Acoust. Soc. Am.*, 43, 764–767.

Plomp, R., and Mimpen, A. M. (1979). Speech-reception threshold for sentences as a function of age and noise level. *J. Acoust. Soc. Am.*, 66, 1333–1342.

Plomp, R., and Steeneken, H. J. M. (1969). Effect of phase on the timbre of complex tones. *J. Acoust. Soc. Am.*, *46*, 409–421.

Plomp, R., Pols, L. C. W., and van de Geer, J. P. (1967). Dimensional analysis of vowel tones. *J. Acoust. Soc. Am.*, *41*, 707–712.

Pollack, I. (1952). The information of elementary auditory displays. *J. Acoust. Soc. Am.*, *24*, 745–749.

Pollack, I. (1969). Periodicity pitch for white noise—Fact or artifact? *J. Acoust. Soc. Am.*, *45*, 237–238.

Pols, L. C. W., van der Kamp, L. J. T., and Plomp, R. (1969). Perceptual and physical space of vowel sounds. *J. Acoust. Soc. Am.*, *46*, 458–467.

Poulton, E. C. (1979). Models for the biases in judging sensory magnitude. *Psych. Bull.*, *86*, 777–803.

Pressnitzer, D., and Hupe, J. M. (2006). Temporal dynamics of auditory and visual bistability reveal common principles of perceptual organization. *Curr. Biol.*, *16*, 1351–1357.

Pressnitzer, D., Patterson, R. D., and Krumbholz, K. (2001). The lower limit of melodic pitch. *J. Acoust. Soc. Am.*, *109*, 2074–2084.

Puria, S., Rosowski, J. J., and Peake, W. T. (1997). Sound-pressure measurements in the cochlear vestibule of human-cadaver ears. *J. Acoust. Soc. Am.*, *101*, 2754–2770.

Raab, D. H., and Goldberg, I. A. (1975). Auditory intensity discrimination with bursts of reproducible noise. *J. Acoust. Soc. Am.*, *57*, 437–447.

Raatgever, J., and Bilsen, F. A. (1986). A central spectrum theory of binaural processing: evidence from dichotic pitch. *J. Acoust. Soc. Am.*, *80*, 429–441.

Rabinowitz, W. M., Bilger, R. C., Trahiotis, C., and Neutzel, J. (1980). Two-tone masking in normal hearing listeners. *J. Acoust. Soc. Am.*, *68*, 1096–1106.

Rakerd, B., Aaronson, N. L., and Hartmann, W. M. (2006). Release from speech-on-speech masking by adding a delayed masker at a different location. *J. Acoust. Soc. Am.*, *119*, 1597–1605.

Rakerd, B., Hartmann, W. M., and Hsu, J. (2000). Echo suppression in the horizontal and median sagittal planes. *J. Acoust. Soc. Am.*, *107*, 1061–1064.

Rakerd, B., Hartmann, W. M., and McCaskey, T. L. (1999). Identification and localization of sound sources in the median sagittal plane. *J. Acoust. Soc. Am.*, *106*, 2812–2820.

Rakowski, A. (1972). Direct comparison of absolute and relative pitch. In *Hearing Theory 1972*. Eindhoven, The Netherlands: IPO.

Rand, T. C. (1974). Dichotic release from masking for speech. *J. Acoust. Soc. Am.*, *55*, 678–680.

Rasch, R. A. (1978). The perception of simultaneous notes such as in polyphonic music. *Acustica*, *40*, 21–33.

Rayleigh, L. (1907). On our perception of sound direction. *Phil. Mag.*, *13*, 214–232.

Recio, A., Rich, N. C., Narayan, S. S., and Ruggero, M. A. (1998). Basilar-membrane responses to clicks at the base of the chinchilla cochlea. *J. Acoust. Soc. Am.*, *103*, 1972–1989.

Rees, A., and Møller, A. R. (1983). Responses of neurons in the inferior colliculus of the rat to AM and FM tones. *Hearing. Res.*, *10*, 301–310.

Remez, R. E., Rubin, P. E., Pisoni, D. B., and Carrell, T. D. (1981). Speech perception without traditional speech cues. *Science*, *212*, 947–950.

Repp, B. H. (1981). On levels of description in speech research. *J. Acoust. Soc. Am.*, *69*, 1462–1464.

Repp, B. H. (1982). Phonetic trading relations and context effects: new experimental evidence for a speech mode of perception. *Psych. Bull.*, *92*, 81–110.

Resnick, S. B., and Feth, L. L. (1975). Discriminability of time-reversed click pairs: intensity effects. *J. Acoust. Soc. Am.*, *57*, 1493–1499.

Rhode, W. S. (1971). Observations of the vibration of the basilar membrane in squirrel monkeys using the Mössbauer technique. *J. Acoust. Soc. Am.*, *49*, 1218–1231.

Rhode, W. S., and Cooper, N. P. (1993). Two-tone suppression and distortion production on the basilar membrane in the hook region of the cat and guinea pig cochleae. *Hear. Res.*, *66*, 31–45.

Rhode, W. S., and Cooper, N. P. (1996). Nonlinear mechanics in the apical turn of the chinchilla cochlea *in vivo*. *Auditory Neurosci.*, *3*, 101–121.

Rhode, W. S., and Recio, A. (2001). Basilar-membrane response to multicomponent stimuli in chinchilla. *J. Acoust. Soc. Am.*, *110*, 981–994.

Rhode, W. S., and Robles, L. (1974). Evidence from Mössbauer experiments for nonlinear vibration in the cochlea. *J. Acoust. Soc. Am.*, *55*, 588–596.

Richards, V. M. (1987). Monaural envelope correlation perception. *J. Acoust. Soc. Am.*, *82*, 1621–1630.

Richards, V. M. (1992). The detectability of a tone added to narrow bands of equal-energy noise. *J. Acoust. Soc. Am.*, *91*, 3424–3435.

Richards, V. M., and Nekrich, R. D. (1993). The incorporation of level and level-invariant cues for the detection of a tone added to noise. *J. Acoust. Soc. Am.*, *94*, 2560–2574.

Riesz, R. R. (1928). Differential intensity sensitivity of the ear for pure tones. *Phys. Rev.*, *31*, 867–875.

Risset, J. C., and Wessel, D. L. (1999). Exploration of timbre by analysis and synthesis. In D. Deutsch (Ed.), *The Psychology of Music* (2nd ed.). San Diego, CA: Academic Press.

Ritsma, R. J. (1962). Existence region of the tonal residue. I. *J. Acoust. Soc. Am.*, *34*, 1224–1229.

Ritsma, R. J. (1963). Existence region of the tonal residue. II. *J. Acoust. Soc. Am.*, *35*, 1241–1245.

Ritsma, R. J. (1967a). Frequencies dominant in the perception of periodic pulses of alternating polarity. *IPO Annual Prog. Rep.*, *2*, 14–24.

Ritsma, R. J. (1967b). Frequencies dominant in the perception of the pitch of complex sounds. *J. Acoust. Soc. Am.*, *42*, 191–198.

Ritsma, R. J. (1970). Periodicity detection. In R. Plomp & G. F. Smoorenburg (Eds.), *Frequency Analysis and Periodicity Detection in Hearing*. Leiden: Sijthoff.

Roberts, B., and Brunstrom, J. M. (1998). Perceptual segregation and pitch shifts of mistuned components in harmonic complexes and in regular inharmonic complexes. *J. Acoust. Soc. Am.*, *104*, 2326–2338.

Roberts, B., and Brunstrom, J. M. (2001). Perceptual fusion and fragmentation of complex tones made inharmonic by applying different degrees of frequency shift and spectral stretch. *J. Acoust. Soc. Am.*, *110*, 2479–2490.

Roberts, B., and Moore, B. C. J. (1991). The influence of extraneous sounds on the perceptual estimation of first-formant frequency in vowels under conditions of asynchrony. *J. Acoust. Soc. Am.*, *89*, 2922–2932.

Roberts, B., Glasberg, B. R., and Moore, B. C. J. (2002). Primitive stream segregation of tone sequences without differences in F_0 or passband. *J. Acoust. Soc. Am.*, *112*, 2074–2085.

Roberts, B., Glasberg, B. R., and Moore, B. C. J. (2008). Effects of the build-up and resetting of auditory stream segregation on temporal discrimination. *J. Exp. Psychol.: Human Percept. Perf.*, *34*, 992–1006.

Robertson, D., and Manley, G. A. (1974). Manipulation of frequency analysis in the cochlear ganglion of the guinea pig. *J. Comp. Physiol.*, *91*, 363–375.

Robles, L., and Ruggero, M. A. (2001). Mechanics of the mammalian cochlea. *Physiol. Rev.*, *81*, 1305–1352.

Robles, L., Ruggero, M. A., and Rich, N. C. (1986). Basilar membrane mechanics at the base of the chinchilla cochlea. I. Input-output functions, tuning curves, and response phases. *J. Acoust. Soc. Am.*, *80*, 1364–1374.

Robles, L., Ruggero, M. A., and Rich, N. C. (1991). Two-tone distortion in the basilar membrane of the cochlea. *Nature*, *349*, 413–414.

Rogers, W. L., and Bregman, A. S. (1993). An experimental evaluation of three theories of auditory stream segregation. *Percept. Psychophys.*, *53*, 179–189.

Rogers, W. L., and Bregman, A. S. (1998). Cumulation of the tendency to segregate auditory streams: resetting by changes in location and loudness. *Percept. Psychophys.*, *60*, 1216–1227.

Ronken, D. (1970). Monaural detection of a phase difference between clicks. *Acoust. Soc. Am.*, *47*, 1091–1099.

Rose, J. E., Brugge, J. F., Anderson, D. J., and Hind, J. E. (1968). Patterns of activity in single auditory nerve fibres of the squirrel monkey. In A. V. S. de Reuck & J. Knight (Eds.), *Hearing Mechanisms in Vertebrates*. London: Churchill.

Rosen, S., and Howell, P. (2010). *Signals and Systems for Speech and Hearing* (2nd ed.). Bingley, UK: Emerald.

Rosen, S., Baker, R. J., and Darling, A. (1998). Auditory filter nonlinearity at 2 kHz in normal hearing listeners. *J. Acoust. Soc. Am.*, *103*, 2539–2550.

Rosen, S., Baker, R. J., and Kramer, S. (1992). Characterizing changes in auditory filter bandwidth as a function of level. In Y. Cazals, K. Horner & L. Demany (Eds.), *Auditory Physiology and Perception*. Oxford: Pergamon Press.

Rosowski, J. J. (1991). The effects of external- and middle-ear filtering on auditory threshold and noise-induced hearing loss. *J. Acoust. Soc. Am.*, *90*, 124–135.

Ruckmick, C. A. (1929). A new classification of tonal qualities. *Psych. Rev.*, *36*, 172–180.

Ruggero, M. A. (1992). Responses to sound of the basilar membrane of the mammalian cochlea. *Curr. Opin. Neurobiol.*, *2*, 449–456.

Ruggero, M. A., and Rich, N. C. (1991). Furosemide alters organ of Corti mechanics: evidence for feedback of outer hair cells upon the basilar membrane. *J. Neurosci.*, *11*, 1057–1067.

Ruggero, M. A., and Temchin, A. N. (2005). Unexceptional sharpness of frequency tuning in the human cochlea. *Proc. Natl. Acad. Sci. USA, 102*, 18614–18619.

Ruggero, M. A., Robles, L., and Rich, N. C. (1992). Two-tone suppression in the basilar membrane of the cochlea: mechanical basis of auditory-nerve rate suppression. *J. Neurophysiol., 68*, 1087–1099.

Ruggero, M. A., Robles, L., Rich, N. C., and Costalupes, J. A. (1986). Basilar membrane motion and spike initiation in the cochlear nerve. In B. C. J. Moore & R. D. Patterson (Eds.), *Auditory Frequency Selectivity*. New York: Plenum.

Ruggero, M. A., Rich, N. C., Recio, A., Narayan, S. S., and Robles, L. (1997). Basilar-membrane responses to tones at the base of the chinchilla cochlea. *J. Acoust. Soc. Am., 101*, 2151–2163.

Saberi, K., and Perrott, D. R. (1990). Lateralization thresholds obtained under conditions in which the precedence effect is assumed to operate. *J. Acoust. Soc. Am., 87*, 1732–1737.

Sachs, M. B., and Abbas, P. J. (1974). Rate versus level functions for auditory-nerve fibers in cats: tone-burst stimuli. *J. Acoust. Soc. Am., 56*, 1835–1847.

Sachs, M. B., and Kiang, N. Y. S. (1968). Two-tone inhibition in auditory nerve fibers. *J. Acoust. Soc. Am., 43*, 1120–1128.

Sachs, M. B., and Young, E. D. (1980). Effects of nonlinearities on speech encoding in the auditory nerve. *J. Acoust. Soc. Am., 68*, 858–875.

Salt, A. N. (2004). Acute endolymphatic hydrops generated by exposure of the ear to nontraumatic low-frequency tones. *J. Assoc. Res. Otolaryngol., 5*, 203–214.

Salvi, R. J., Axelsson, A., Henderson, D., and Hamernik, R. (1996). *Effects of Noise on Hearing: Vth International Symposium*. Stockholm: Thieme.

Samuel, A. G. (1977). The effect of discrimination training on speech perception: noncategorical perception. *Percept. Psychophys., 22*, 321–330.

Scharf, B. (1961). Complex sounds and critical bands. *Psychol. Bull., 58*, 205–217.

Scharf, B. (1970). Critical bands. In J. V. Tobias (Ed.), *Foundations of Modern Auditory Theory*. New York: Academic Press.

Scharf, B. (1978). Loudness. In E. C. Carterette & M. P. Friedman (Eds.), *Handbook of Perception, Volume IV. Hearing*. New York: Academic Press.

Scharf, B. (1983). Loudness adaptation. In J. V. Tobias & E. D. Schubert (Eds.), *Hearing Research and Theory* (Vol. 2). New York: Academic Press.

Scheffers, M. T. M. (1983). Sifting vowels: Auditory pitch analysis and sound segregation. Ph.D. Thesis, Groningen University, The Netherlands.

Schlauch, R. S. (1994). Intensity resolution and loudness in high-pass noise. *J. Acoust. Soc. Am., 95*, 2171–2179.

Schmidt, S., and Zwicker, E. (1991). The effect of masker spectral asymmetry on overshoot in simultaneous masking. *J. Acoust. Soc. Am., 89*, 1324–1330.

Schooneveldt, G. P., and Moore, B. C. J. (1987). Comodulation masking release (CMR): effects of signal frequency, flanking-band frequency, masker bandwidth, flanking-band level, and monotic versus dichotic presentation of the flanking band. *J. Acoust. Soc. Am., 82*, 1944–1956.

Schooneveldt, G. P., and Moore, B. C. J. (1989). Comodulation masking release (CMR) as a function of masker bandwidth, modulator bandwidth and signal duration. *J. Acoust. Soc. Am.*, 85, 273–281.

Schorer, E. (1986). Critical modulation frequency based on detection of AM versus FM tones. *J. Acoust. Soc. Am.*, 79, 1054–1057.

Schouten, J. F. (1940). The residue and the mechanism of hearing. *Proc. Kon. Ned. Akad. Wetenschap.*, 43, 991–999.

Schouten, J. F. (1968). The perception of timbre. *6th International Conference on Acoustics*, 1, GP-6-2.

Schouten, J. F. (1970). The residue revisited. In R. Plomp & G. F. Smoorenburg (Eds.), *Frequency Analysis and Periodicity Detection in Hearing*. Leiden: Sijthoff.

Schouten, J. F., Ritsma, R. J., and Cardozo, B. L. (1962). Pitch of the residue. *J. Acoust. Soc. Am.*, 34, 1418–1424.

Schreiner, C. E., and Langner, G. (1988). Coding of temporal patterns in the central auditory system. In G. Edelman, W. Gall & W. Cowan (Eds.), *Auditory Function: Neurobiological Bases of Hearing*. New York: Wiley.

Schroeder, M. R. (1970). Synthesis of low peak-factor signals and binary sequences with low autocorrelation. *IEEE Trans. Inf. Theory IT*, 16, 85–89.

Schroeder, M. R., and Atal, B. S. (1963). Computer simulation of sound transmission in rooms. *IEEE Int. Conv. Rec.*, 7, 150–155.

Schroeder, M. R., Gottlob, D., and Siebrasse, K. F. (1974). Comparative study of European concert halls: correlation of subjective preference with geometric and acoustic parameters. *J. Acoust. Soc. Am.*, 56, 1192–1201.

Schubert, E. D. (1969). On estimating aural harmonics. *J. Acoust. Soc. Am.*, 45, 790–791.

Searle, C. L., Braida, L. D., Cuddy, D. R., and Davis, M. F. (1975). Binaural pinna disparity: another auditory localization cue. *J. Acoust. Soc. Am.*, 57, 448–455.

Sek, A. (1994). Modulation thresholds and critical modulation frequency based on random amplitude and frequency changes. *J. Acoust. Soc. Jpn. (E)*, 15, 67–75.

Sek, A., and Moore, B. C. J. (1994). The critical modulation frequency and its relationship to auditory filtering at low frequencies. *J. Acoust. Soc. Am.*, 95, 2606–2615.

Sek, A., and Moore, B. C. J. (1995). Frequency discrimination as a function of frequency, measured in several ways. *J. Acoust. Soc. Am.*, 97, 2479–2486.

Sek, A., and Moore, B. C. J. (2000). Detection of quasitrapezoidal frequency and amplitude modulation. *J. Acoust. Soc. Am.*, 107, 1598–1604.

Sek, A., and Moore, B. C. J. (2003). Testing the concept of a modulation filter bank: the audibility of component modulation and detection of phase change in three-component modulators. *J. Acoust. Soc. Am.*, 113, 2801–2811.

Seligman, P., and McDermott, H. (1995). Architecture of the Spectra 22 speech processor. *Ann. Otol. Rhinol. Laryngol.*, 166(Suppl.), 139–141.

Sellick, P. M., Patuzzi, R., and Johnstone, B. M. (1982). Measurement of basilar membrane motion in the guinea pig using the Mössbauer technique. *J. Acoust. Soc. Am.*, 72, 131–141.

Sergi, P., Pastorino, G., Ravazzani, P., Tognola, G., and Grandori, F. (2001). A hospital based universal neonatal hearing screening programme using click-evoked otoacoustic emissions. *Scand. Audiol.*, 52(Suppl.), 18–20.

Shackleton, T. M., and Meddis, R. (1992). The role of interaural time difference and fundamental frequency difference in the identification of concurrent vowel pairs. *J. Acoust. Soc. Am.*, *91*, 3579–3581.

Shailer, M. J., and Moore, B. C. J. (1983). Gap detection as a function of frequency, bandwidth and level. *J. Acoust. Soc. Am.*, *74*, 467–473.

Shailer, M. J., and Moore, B. C. J. (1985). Detection of temporal gaps in band-limited noise: effects of variations in bandwidth and signal-to-masker ratio. *J. Acoust. Soc. Am.*, *77*, 635–639.

Shailer, M. J., and Moore, B. C. J. (1987). Gap detection and the auditory filter: phase effects using sinusoidal stimuli. *J. Acoust. Soc. Am.*, *81*, 1110–1117.

Shailer, M. J., Moore, B. C. J., Glasberg, B. R., Watson, N., and Harris, S. (1990). Auditory filter shapes at 8 and 10 kHz. *J. Acoust. Soc. Am.*, *88*, 141–148.

Shannon, R. V. (1976). Two-tone unmasking and suppression in a forward masking situation. *J. Acoust. Soc. Am.*, *59*, 1460–1470.

Shaw, E. A. G. (1974). Transformation of sound pressure level from the free field to the eardrum in the horizontal plane. *J. Acoust. Soc. Am.*, *56*, 1848–1861.

Shepard, R. N. (1964). Circularity in judgements of relative pitch. *J. Acoust. Soc. Am.*, *36*, 2346–2353.

Shera, C. A., Guinan, J. J., Jr., and Oxenham, A. J. (2002). Revised estimates of human cochlear tuning from otoacoustic and behavioral measurements. *Proc. Natl. Acad. Sci. USA*, *99*, 3318–3323.

Shera, C. A., Guinan, J. J., Jr., and Oxenham, A. J. (2010). Otoacoustic estimation of cochlear tuning: validation in the chinchilla. *J. Assoc. Res. Otolaryngol.*, *11*, 343–365.

Shonle, J. I., and Horan, K. E. (1976). Trill threshold revisited. *J. Acoust. Soc. Am.*, *59*, 469–471.

Siebert, W. M. (1968). Stimulus transformations in the peripheral auditory system. In P. A. Kolers & M. Eden (Eds.), *Recognizing Patterns*. Cambridge, MA: MIT Press.

Siebert, W. M. (1970). Frequency discrimination in the auditory system: place or periodicity mechanisms. *Proc. IEEE*, *58*, 723–730.

Siegel, R. J. (1965). A replication of the mel scale of pitch. *Am. J. Psychol.*, *78*, 615–620.

Singh, P. G., and Bregman, A. S. (1997). The influence of different timbre attributes on the perceptual segregation of complex-tone sequences. *J. Acoust. Soc. Am.*, *102*, 1943–1952.

Siveke, I., Ewert, S. D., Grothe, B., and Wiegrebe, L. (2008). Psychophysical and physiological evidence for fast binaural processing. *J. Neurosci.*, *28*, 2043–2052.

Sivonen, V. P., and Ellermeier, W. (2011). Binaural loudness. In M. Florentine, A. N. Popper & R. R. Fay (Eds.), *Loudness*. New York: Springer.

Small, A. M., Boggess, J., Klich, R., Kuehn, D., Thelin, J., and Wiley, T. (1972). MLD's in forward and backward masking. *J. Acoust. Soc. Am.*, *51*, 1365–1367.

Smith, B. K., Sieben, U. K., Kohlrausch, A., and Schroeder, M. R. (1986). Phase effects in masking related to dispersion in the inner ear. *J. Acoust. Soc. Am.*, *80*, 1631–1637.

Smith, R. L. (1977). Short-term adaptation in single auditory-nerve fibers: some poststimulatory effects. *J. Neurophysiol.*, *49*, 1098–1112.

Smith, R. L., and Brachman, M. L. (1980). Operating range and maximum response of single auditory nerve fibers. *Brain Res.*, *184*, 499–505.

Smoorenburg, G. F. (1970). Pitch perception of two-frequency stimuli. *J. Acoust. Soc. Am.*, *48*, 924–941.

Snell, K. B., Ison, J. R., and Frisina, D. R. (1994). The effects of signal frequency and absolute bandwidth on gap detection in noise. *J. Acoust. Soc. Am.*, *96*, 1458–1464.

Soderquist, D. R. (1970). Frequency analysis and the critical band. *Psychon. Sci.*, *21*, 117–119.

Soderquist, D. R., and Lindsey, J. W. (1972). Physiological noise as a masker of low frequencies: the cardiac cycle. *J. Acoust. Soc. Am.*, *52*, 1216–1220.

Spiegel, M. F. (1981). Thresholds for tones in maskers of various bandwidths and for signals of various bandwidths as a function of signal frequency. *J. Acoust. Soc. Am.*, *69*, 791–795.

Spoendlin, H. (1970). Structural basis of peripheral frequency analysis. In R. Plomp & G. F. Smoorenburg (Eds.), *Frequency Analysis and Periodicity Detection in Hearing*. Leiden: Sijthoff.

Stainsby, T. H., Moore, B. C. J., Medland, P. J., and Glasberg, B. R. (2004). Sequential streaming and effective level differences due to phase-spectrum manipulations. *J. Acoust. Soc. Am.*, *115*, 1665–1673.

Steinberg, J. C., and Gardner, M. B. (1937). The dependence of hearing impairment on sound intensity. *J. Acoust. Soc. Am.*, *9*, 11–23.

Stellmack, M. A. (1994). The reduction of binaural interference by the temporal nonoverlap of components. *J. Acoust. Soc. Am.*, *96*, 1465–1470.

Stellmack, M. A., and Dye, R. H. (1993). The combination of interaural information across frequencies: the effects of number and spacing of the components, onset asynchrony, and harmonicity. *J. Acoust. Soc. Am.*, *93*, 2933–2947.

Stern, R. M., and Trahiotis, C. (1995). Models of binaural interaction. In B. C. J. Moore (Ed.), *Hearing*. San Diego, CA: Academic Press.

Stevens, K. N. (1968). On the relations between speech movements and speech perception. *Z. Phonetik Sprachwiss. Kommunikationforsch.*, *21*, 102–106.

Stevens, K. N. (1980). Acoustic correlates of some phonetic categories. *J. Acoust. Soc. Am.*, *68*, 836–842.

Stevens, K. N. (1981). Constraints imposed by the auditory system on the properties used to classify speech sounds. In T. F. Myers, J. Laver & J. Anderson (Eds.), *The Cognitive Representation of Speech*. Amsterdam, The Netherlands: North-Holland.

Stevens, K. N. (2002). Toward a model for lexical access based on acoustic landmarks and distinctive features. *J. Acoust. Soc. Am.*, *111*, 1872–1891.

Stevens, K. N., and House, A. S. (1972). Speech perception. In J. V. Tobias (Ed.), *Foundations of Modern Auditory Theory*. New York: Academic Press.

Stevens, S. S. (1935). The relation of pitch to intensity. *J. Acoust. Soc. Am.*, *6*, 150–154.

Stevens, S. S. (1957). On the psychophysical law. *Psych. Rev.*, *64*, 153–181.

Stevens, S. S. (1972). Perceived level of noise by Mark VII and decibels (E). *J. Acoust. Soc. Am.*, *51*, 575–601.

Stevens, S. S., and Newman, E. B. (1936). The localization of actual sources of sound. *Am. J. Psychol.*, *48*, 297–306.

Stevens, S. S., Volkmann, J., and Newman, E. B. (1937). A scale for the measurement of the psychological magnitude of pitch. *J. Acoust. Soc. Am.*, *8*, 185–190.

Stillman, J. A., Zwislocki, J. J., Zhang, M., and Cefaratti, L. K. (1993). Intensity just-noticeable differences at equal-loudness levels in normal and pathological ears. *J. Acoust. Soc. Am.*, *93*, 425–434.

Stone, M. A., and Moore, B. C. J. (2003). Effect of the speed of a single-channel dynamic range compressor on intelligibility in a competing speech task. *J. Acoust. Soc. Am.*, *114*, 1023–1034.

Stone, M. A., and Moore, B. C. J. (2004). Side effects of fast-acting dynamic range compression that affect intelligibility in a competing speech task. *J. Acoust. Soc. Am.*, *116*, 2311–2323.

Stone, M. A., Moore, B. C. J., and Glasberg, B. R. (1997). A real-time DSP-based loudness meter. In A. Schick & M. Klatte (Eds.), *Contributions to Psychological Acoustics*. Oldenburg: Bibliotheks- und Informationssystem der Universität Oldenburg.

Stone, M. A., Moore, B. C. J., Alcántara, J. I., and Glasberg, B. R. (1999). Comparison of different forms of compression using wearable digital hearing aids. *J. Acoust. Soc. Am.*, *106*, 3603–3619.

Stover, L. J., and Feth, L. L. (1983). Pitch of narrow-band signals. *J. Acoust. Soc. Am.*, *73*, 1701–1707.

Strange, W., and Bohn, O. S. (1998). Dynamic specification of coarticulated German vowels: perceptual and acoustical studies. *J. Acoust. Soc. Am.*, *104*, 488–504.

Strickland, E. A. (2001). The relationship between frequency selectivity and overshoot. *J. Acoust. Soc. Am.*, *109*, 2062–2073.

Strickland, E. A. (2008). The relationship between precursor level and the temporal effect. *J. Acoust. Soc. Am.*, *123*, 946–954.

Stuart, J. R. (1994). Noise: methods for estimating detectability and threshold. *J. Audio Eng. Soc.*, *42*, 124–140.

Stuart, J. R., and Wilson, R. J. (1994). Dynamic range enhancement using noise-shaped dither applied to signals with and without preemphasis. *J. Audio Eng. Soc.*, *42*, 400.

Summerfield, A. Q., Sidwell, A. S., and Nelson, T. (1987). Auditory enhancement of changes in spectral amplitude. *J. Acoust. Soc. Am.*, *81*, 700–708.

Summerfield, Q. (1987). Some preliminaries to a comprehensive account of audio-visual speech perception. In B. Dodd & R. Campbell (Eds.), *Hearing by Eye: The Psychology of Lipreading*. Hillsdale, NJ: Erlbaum.

Summerfield, Q., and Culling, J. F. (1992). Auditory segregation of competing voices: absence of effects of FM or AM coherence. *Phil. Trans. R. Soc. B*, *336*, 357–366.

Summers, V. (2001). Overshoot effects using Schroeder-phase harmonic maskers in listeners with normal hearing and with hearing impairment. *Hear. Res.*, *162*, 1–9.

Summers, V., and Leek, M. R. (1997). Influence of masker phase structure on tone detection by normal-hearing and hearing-impaired listeners. *J. Acoust. Soc. Am.*, *101*, 3148.

Summers, V., and Leek, M. R. (1998). Masking of tones and speech by Schroeder-phase harmonic complexes in normally hearing and hearing-impaired listeners. *Hear. Res.*, *118*, 139–150.

Suzuki, Y., and Takeshima, H. (2004). Equal-loudness-level contours for pure tones. *J. Acoust. Soc. Am.*, *116*, 918–933.

Tan, C. T., Moore, B. C. J., Zacharov, N., and Matilla, V.-V. (2004). Predicting the perceived quality of nonlinearly distorted music and speech signals. *J. Audio Eng. Soc.*, *52*, 699–711.

Teich, M. C., and Khanna, S. M. (1985). Pulse-number distribution for the neural spike train in the cat's auditory nerve. *J. Acoust. Soc. Am.*, *77*, 1110–1128.

Terhardt, E. (1972a). Zur Tonhöhenwahrnehmung von Klängen II. Ein Funktionsschema. *Acustica*, *26*, 187–199.

Terhardt, E. (1972b). Zur Tonhöhenwahrnehmung von Klängen. I. Psychoakustische Grundlagen. *Acustica*, *26*, 173–186.

Terhardt, E. (1974a). On the perception of periodic sound fluctuations (roughness). *Acustica*, *30*, 201–213.

Terhardt, E. (1974b). Pitch of pure tones: its relation to intensity. In E. Zwicker & E. Terhardt (Eds.), *Facts and Models in Hearing*. Berlin: Springer.

Terhardt, E. (1974c). Pitch, consonance, and harmony. *J. Acoust. Soc. Am.*, *55*, 1061–1069.

Thurlow, W. R. (1943). Binaural interaction and perception of pitch. *J. Exp. Psychol.*, *32*, 17–36.

Thurlow, W. R. (1963). Perception of low auditory pitch: a multicue mediation theory. *Psychol. Rev.*, *70*, 461–470.

Thurlow, W. R., and Parks, T. E. (1961). Precedence suppression effects for two-click sources. *Percept. Motor Skills*, *13*, 7–12.

Tian, B., Reser, D., Durham, A., Kustov, A., and Rauschecker, J. P. (2001). Functional specialization in rhesus monkey auditory cortex. *Science*, *292*, 290–293.

Tobias, J. V. (1963). Application of a 'relative' procedure to a problem in binaural beat perception. *J. Acoust. Soc. Am.*, *35*, 1442–1447.

Tobias, J. V., and Schubert, E. D. (1959). Effective onset duration of auditory stimuli. *J. Acoust. Soc. Am.*, *31*, 1595–1605.

Tohyama, M., Susuki, H., and Ando, Y. (1995). *The Nature and Technology of Acoustic Space*. San Diego, CA: Academic Press.

Toole, F. E. (1986a). Loudspeaker measurements and their relationship to listener preferences: Part 1. *J. Audio Eng. Soc.*, *34*, 227–235.

Toole, F. E. (1986b). Loudspeaker measurements and their relationship to listener preferences: Part 2. *J. Audio Eng. Soc.*, *34*, 323–348.

Toole, F. E. (2008). *Sound Reproduction*. Amsterdam: Focal Press, Elsevier.

Trahiotis, C., and Bernstein, L. R. (1990). Detectability of interaural delays over select spectral regions: effects of flanking noise. *J. Acoust. Soc. Am.*, *87*, 810–813.

Trahiotis, C., and Stern, R. M. (1989). Lateralization of bands of noise: effects of bandwidth and differences of interaural time and phase. *J. Acoust. Soc. Am.*, *86*, 1285–1293.

Tramo, M. J., Cariani, P. A., Delgutte, B., and Braida, L. D. (2001). Neurobiological foundations for the theory of harmony in western tonal music. *Ann. New York Acad. Sci.*, *930*, 92–116.

Turner, C. W., Relkin, E. M., and Doucet, J. (1994). Psychophysical and physiological forward masking studies: probe duration and rise-time effects. *J. Acoust. Soc. Am.*, *96*, 795–800.

Tyler, R. S. (1986). Frequency resolution in hearing-impaired listeners. In B. C. J. Moore (Ed.), *Frequency Selectivity in Hearing*. London: Academic Press.

Ulfendahl, M. (1997). Mechanical responses of the mammalian cochlea. *Prog. Neurobiol.*, 53, 331–380.

Unoki, M., Irino, T., Glasberg, B. R., Moore, B. C. J., and Patterson, R. D. (2006). Comparison of the roex and gammachirp filters as representations of the auditory filter. *J. Acoust. Soc. Am*, 120, 1474–1492.

Uppenkamp, S., Fobel, S., and Patterson, R. D. (2001). The effects of temporal asymmetry on the detection and perception of short chirps. *Hear. Res.*, 158, 71–83.

van de Par, S., and Kohlrausch, A. (1997). A new approach to comparing binaural masking level differences at low and high frequencies. *J. Acoust. Soc. Am.*, 101, 1671–1680.

van Noorden, L. P. A. S. (1971). Rhythmic fission as a function of tone rate. *IPO Annual Prog. Rep*, 6, 9–12.

van Noorden, L. P. A. S. (1975). Temporal coherence in the perception of tone sequences. Ph.D. Thesis, Eindhoven University of Technology, Eindhoven.

van Noorden, L. P. A. S. (1982). Two-channel pitch perception. In M. Clynes (Ed.), *Music, Mind and Brain*. New York: Plenum.

Vandali, A. E., Whitford, L. A., Plant, K. L., and Clark, G. M. (2000). Speech perception as a function of electrical stimulation rate: using the Nucleus 24 cochlear implant system. *Ear Hear.*, 21, 608–624.

Vanderkooy, J., and Lipshitz, S. P. (1984). Resolution below the least significant bit in digital systems with dither. *J. Audio Eng. Soc.*, 32, 106–113.

Verhey, J. L., Dau, T., and Kollmeier, B. (1999). Within-channel cues in comodulation masking release (CMR): experiments and model predictions using a modulation-filterbank model. *J. Acoust. Soc. Am.*, 106, 2733–2745.

Verschuure, J., and van Meeteren, A. A. (1975). The effect of intensity on pitch. *Acustica*, 32, 33–44.

Viemeister, N. F. (1972). Intensity discrimination of pulsed sinusoids: the effects of filtered noise. *J. Acoust. Soc. Am.*, 51, 1265–1269.

Viemeister, N. F. (1979). Temporal modulation transfer functions based on modulation thresholds. *J. Acoust. Soc. Am.*, 66, 1364–1380.

Viemeister, N. F. (1983). Auditory intensity discrimination at high frequencies in the presence of noise. *Science*, 221, 1206–1208.

Viemeister, N. F. (1988). Psychophysical aspects of auditory intensity coding. In G. M. Edelman, W. E. Gall & W. A. Cowan (Eds.), *Auditory Function*. New York: Wiley.

Viemeister, N. F., and Bacon, S. P. (1988). Intensity discrimination, increment detection, and magnitude estimation for 1-kHz tones. *J. Acoust. Soc. Am.*, 84, 172–178.

Viemeister, N. F., and Plack, C. J. (1993). Time analysis. In W. A. Yost, A. N. Popper & R. R. Fay (Eds.), *Human Psychophysics*. New York: Springer-Verlag.

Viemeister, N. F., and Wakefield, G. H. (1991). Temporal integration and multiple looks. *J. Acoust. Soc. Am.*, 90, 858–865.

Villchur, E. (1973). Signal processing to improve speech intelligibility in perceptive deafness. *J. Acoust. Soc. Am.*, 53, 1646–1657.

Villchur, E., and Allison, R. F. (1980). The audibility of Doppler distortion in loudspeakers. *J. Acoust. Soc. Am.*, 68, 1561–1569.

Vinay, and Moore, B. C. J. (2010). Effects of the use of personal music players on amplitude modulation detection and frequency discrimination. *J. Acoust. Soc. Am.*, *128*, 3634–3641.

Vliegen, J., and Oxenham, A. J. (1999). Sequential stream segregation in the absence of spectral cues. *J. Acoust. Soc. Am.*, *105*, 339–346.

Vliegen, J., Moore, B. C. J., and Oxenham, A. J. (1999). The role of spectral and periodicity cues in auditory stream segregation, measured using a temporal discrimination task. *J. Acoust. Soc. Am.*, *106*, 938–945.

Vogten, L. L. M. (1974). Pure-tone masking: A new result from a new method. In E. Zwicker & E. Terhardt (Eds.), *Facts and Models in Hearing*. Berlin: Springer-Verlag.

von Békésy, G. (1947). The variations of phase along the basilar membrane with sinusoidal vibrations. *J. Acoust. Soc. Am.*, *19*, 452–460.

von Békésy, G. (1960). *Experiments in Hearing*. New York: McGraw-Hill.

von Klitzing, R., and Kohlrausch, A. (1994). Effect of masker level on overshoot in running- and frozen-noise maskers. *J. Acoust. Soc. Am.*, *95*, 2192–2201.

Wallach, H. (1940). The role of head movements and vestibular and visual cues in sound localization. *J. Exp. Psychol.*, *27*, 339–368.

Wallach, H., Newman, E. B., and Rosenzweig, M. R. (1949). The precedence effect in sound localization. *Am. J. Psychol.*, *62*, 315–336.

Wang, D., Kjems, U., Pedersen, M. S., Boldt, J. B., and Lunner, T. (2009). Speech intelligibility in background noise with ideal binary time-frequency masking. *J. Acoust. Soc. Am.*, *125*, 2336–2347.

Wannamaker, R. A. (1992). Psychoacoustically optimal noise shaping. *J. Audio Eng. Soc.*, *40*, 611–620.

Ward, W. D. (1954). Subjective musical pitch. *J. Acoust. Soc. Am.*, *26*, 369–380.

Ward, W. D. (1963). Auditory fatigue and masking. In J. F. Jerger (Ed.), *Modern Developments in Audiology*. New York: Academic Press.

Ward, W. D., Glorig, A., and Sklar, D. L. (1958). Dependence of temporary threshold shift at 4 kc on intensity and time. *J. Acoust. Soc. Am.*, *30*, 944–954.

Warren, R. M. (1970a). Elimination of biases in loudness judgements for tones. *J. Acoust. Soc. Am.*, *48*, 1397–1413.

Warren, R. M. (1970b). Perceptual restoration of missing speech sounds. *Science*, *167*, 392–393.

Warren, R. M. (1974). Auditory temporal discrimination by trained listeners. *Cognitive Psychol.*, *6*, 237–256.

Warren, R. M. (1976). Auditory perception and speech evolution. *Ann. N. Y. Acad. Sci.*, *280*, 708–717.

Warren, R. M. (1981). Measurement of sensory intensity. *Behav. Brain Sci.*, *4*, 175–189.

Warren, R. M., Obusek, C. J., Farmer, R. M., and Warren, R. P. (1969). Auditory sequence: confusion of patterns other than speech or music. *Science*, *164*, 586–587.

Watkins, A. J. (1978). Psychoacoustical aspects of synthesized vertical locale cues. *J. Acoust. Soc. Am.*, *63*, 1152–1165.

Watkins, A. J. (1998). The precedence effect and perceptual compensation for spectral envelope distortion. In A. R. Palmer, A. Rees, A. Q. Summerfield & R. Meddis (Eds.), *Psychophysical and Physiological Advances in Hearing*. London: Whurr.

Watkins, A. J., and Makin, S. J. (1996). Some effects of filtered contexts on the perception of vowels and fricatives. *J. Acoust. Soc. Am., 99*, 588–594.

Watson, C. S. (2005). Some comments on informational masking. *Acta Acust. Acust., 91*, 502–512.

Webster, F. A. (1951). The influence of interaural phase on masked thresholds: the role of interaural time deviation. *J. Acoust. Soc. Am., 23*, 452–462.

Wegel, R. L., and Lane, C. E. (1924). The auditory masking of one sound by another and its probable relation to the dynamics of the inner ear. *Phys. Rev., 23*, 266–285.

Wenzel, E. M., Arruda, M., Kistler, D. J., and Wightman, F. L. (1993). Localization using nonindividualized head-related transfer functions. *J. Acoust. Soc. Am., 94*, 111–123.

Whitfield, I. C. (1970). Central nervous processing in relation to spatiotemporal discrimination of auditory patterns. In R. Plomp & G. F. Smoorenburg (Eds.), *Frequency Analysis and Periodicity Detection in Hearing*. Leiden: Sijthoff.

Whitfield, I. C., and Evans, E. F. (1965). Responses of auditory cortical neurones to stimuli of changing frequency. *J. Neurophysiol., 28*, 655–672.

Whittle, L. S., Collins, S. J., and Robinson, D. W. (1972). The audibility of low-frequency sounds. *J. Sound Vib., 21*, 431–448.

Whitworth, R. H., and Jeffress, L. A. (1961). Time versus intensity in the localization of tones. *J. Acoust. Soc. Am., 33*, 925–929.

Wier, C. C., Jesteadt, W., and Green, D. M. (1977). Frequency discrimination as a function of frequency and sensation level. *J. Acoust. Soc. Am., 61*, 178–184.

Wightman, F. L., and Kistler, D. J. (1989). Headphone simulation of free field listening I: stimulus synthesis. *J. Acoust. Soc. Am., 85*, 858–867.

Wightman, F. L., and Kistler, D. J. (1992). The dominant role of low-frequency interaural time differences in sound localization. *J. Acoust. Soc. Am., 91*, 1648–1661.

Wightman, F. L., McGee, T., and Kramer, M. (1977). Factors influencing frequency selectivity in normal and hearing-impaired listeners. In E. F. Evans & J. P. Wilson (Eds.), *Psychophysics and Physiology of Hearing*. London: Academic Press.

Wilson, A. S., Hall, J. W., and Grose, J. H. (1990). Detection of frequency modulation (FM) in the presence of a second FM tone. *J. Acoust. Soc. Am., 88*, 1333–1338.

Wilson, B. S., Finley, C. C., Lawson, D. T., Wolford, R. D., Eddington, D. K., and Rabinowitz, W. M. (1991). Better speech recognition with cochlear implants. *Nature, 352*, 236–238.

Wilson, R. H., and Carhart, R. (1971). Forward and backward masking: interactions and additivity. *J. Acoust. Soc. Am., 49*, 1254–1263.

Winter, I. M., Robertson, D., and Yates, G. K. (1990). Diversity of characteristic frequency rate intensity functions in guinea pig auditory nerve fibers. *Hear. Res., 45*, 191–202.

Wojtczak, M., and Viemeister, N. F. (1999). Intensity discrimination and detection of amplitude modulation. *J. Acoust. Soc. Am., 106*, 1917–1924.

Wojtczak, M., and Viemeister, N. F. (2005). Forward masking of amplitude modulation: basic characteristics. *J. Acoust. Soc. Am., 118*, 3198–3210.

Woods, W. S., and Colburn, H. S. (1992). Test of a model of auditory object formation using intensity and interaural time difference discrimination. *J. Acoust. Soc. Am.*, *91*, 2894–2902.

Wright, A., Davis, A., Bredberg, G., Ulehlova, L., and Spencer, H. (1987). Hair cell distributions in the normal human cochlea. *Acta Otolaryngol.*, *444*(Suppl.), 1–48.

Wu, X., Wang, C., Chen, J., Qu, H., Li, W., Wu, Y., Schneider, B., and Li, L. (2005). The effect of perceived spatial separation on informational masking of Chinese speech. *Hear. Res.*, *199*, 1–10.

Xia, J., Brughera, A., Colburn, H. S., and Shinn-Cunningham, B. (2010). Physiological and psychophysical modeling of the precedence effect. *J. Assoc. Res. Otolaryngol.*, *11*, 495–513.

Yang, X., and Grantham, D. W. (1997). Cross-spectral and temporal factors in the precedence effect: discrimination and suppression of the lag sound in free field. *J. Acoust. Soc. Am.*, *102*, 2973–2983.

Yates, G. K. (1990). Basilar membrane nonlinearity and its influence on auditory nerve rate-intensity functions. *Hear. Res.*, *50*, 145–162.

Yates, G. K. (1995). Cochlear structure and function. In B. C. J. Moore (Ed.), *Hearing.* San Diego, CA: Academic Press.

Yost, W. A. (1974). Discrimination of interaural phase differences. *J. Acoust. Soc. Am.*, *55*, 1299–1303.

Yost, W. A., and Dye, R. (1988). Discrimination of interaural differences of level as a function of frequency. *J. Acoust. Soc. Am.*, *83*, 1846–1851.

Yost, W. A., and Sheft, S. (1989). Across-critical-band processing of amplitude-modulated tones. *J. Acoust. Soc. Am.*, *85*, 848–857.

Yost, W. A., Sheft, S., and Opie, J. (1989). Modulation interference in detection and discrimination of amplitude modulation. *J. Acoust. Soc. Am.*, *86*, 2138–2147.

Yost, W. A., Wightman, F. L., and Green, D. M. (1971). Lateralization of filtered clicks. *J. Acoust. Soc. Am.*, *50*, 1526–1531.

Young, E. D. (2008). Neural representation of spectral and temporal information in speech. *Phil. Trans. R. Soc. B*, *363*, 923–945.

Young, E. D., and Sachs, M. B. (1979). Representation of steady-state vowels in the temporal aspects of the discharge patterns of populations of auditory-nerve fibres. *J. Acoust. Soc. Am.*, *66*, 1381–1403.

Zahorik, P. (2002). Assessing auditory distance perception using virtual acoustics. *J. Acoust. Soc. Am.*, *111*, 1832–1846.

Zahorik, P., Brungart, D. S., and Bronkhorst, A. W. (2005). Auditory distance perception in humans: a summary of past and present research. *Acta Acust. United Ac.*, *91*, 409–420.

Zeki, S. (2001). Localization and globalization in conscious vision. *Ann. Rev. Neurosci.*, *24*, 57–86.

Zeng, F. G., and Turner, C. W. (1991). Binaural loudness matches in unilaterally impaired listeners. *Q. J. Exp. Psychol.*, *43A*, 565–583.

Zera, J., and Green, D. M. (1993). Detecting temporal onset and offset asynchrony in multicomponent complexes. *J. Acoust. Soc. Am.*, *93*, 1038–1052.

Zhang, X., Heinz, M. G., Bruce, I. C., and Carney, L. H. (2001). A phenomenological model for the responses of auditory-nerve fibers: I. Nonlinear tuning with compression and suppression. *J. Acoust. Soc. Am.*, *109*, 648–670.

Zhou, B. (1995). Auditory filter shapes at high frequencies. *J. Acoust. Soc. Am.*, *98*, 1935–1942.

Zurek, P. M. (1980). The precedence effect and its possible role in the avoidance of interaural ambiguities. *J. Acoust. Soc. Am.*, *67*, 952–964.

Zurek, P. M. (1981). Spontaneous narrowband acoustic signals emitted by human ears. *J. Acoust. Soc. Am.*, *69*, 514–523.

Zurek, P. M. (1985). Spectral dominance in sensitivity to interaural delay for broadband stimuli. *J. Acoust. Soc. Am.*, *78*(Suppl), S18.

Zurek, P. M. (1993). A note on onset effects in binaural hearing. *J. Acoust. Soc. Am.*, *93*, 1200–1201.

Zurek, P. M., and Durlach, N. I. (1987). Masker-bandwidth dependence in homophasic and antiphasic tone detection. *J. Acoust. Soc. Am.*, *81*, 459–464.

Zwicker, E. (1952). Die Grenzen der Hörbarkeit der Amplitudenmodulation und der Frequenzmodulation eines Tones (The limits of audibility of amplitude modulation and frequency modulation of a pure tone). *Acustica*, *2*, 125–133.

Zwicker, E. (1954). Die Verdeckung von Schmalbandgeräuschen durch Sinustöne. *Acustica*, *4*, 415–420.

Zwicker, E. (1956). Die elementaren Grundlagen zur Bestimmung der Informations-kapazität des Gehörs (The foundations for determining the information capacity of the auditory system). *Acustica*, *6*, 356–381.

Zwicker, E. (1958). Über psychologische und methodische Grundlagen der Lautheit (On the psychological and methodological bases of loudness). *Acustica*, *8*, 237–258.

Zwicker, E. (1961). Subdivision of the audible frequency range into critical bands (Frequenzgruppen). *J. Acoust. Soc. Am.*, *33*, 248.

Zwicker, E. (1964). 'Negative afterimage' in hearing. *J. Acoust. Soc. Am.*, *36*, 2413–2415.

Zwicker, E. (1965). Temporal effects in simultaneous masking by white-noise bursts. *J. Acoust. Soc. Am.*, *37*, 653–663.

Zwicker, E. (1970). Masking and psychological excitation as consequences of the ear's frequency analysis. In R. Plomp & G. F. Smoorenburg (Eds.), *Frequency Analysis and Periodicity Detection in Hearing*. Leiden: Sijthoff.

Zwicker, E. (1984). Dependence of post-masking on masker duration and its relation to temporal effects in loudness. *J. Acoust. Soc. Am.*, *75*, 219–223.

Zwicker, E., and Fastl, H. (1999). *Psychoacoustics—Facts and Models* (2nd ed.). Berlin: Springer-Verlag.

Zwicker, E., and Feldtkeller, R. (1967). *Das Ohr als Nachtrichtenempfänger (The Ear as a Receiver of Information)*. Stuttgart: Hirzel-Verlag.

Zwicker, E., and Scharf, B. (1965). A model of loudness summation. *Psych. Rev.*, *72*, 3–26.

Zwicker, E., and Schorn, K. (1978). Psychoacoustical tuning curves in audiology. *Audiology*, *17*, 120–140.

Zwicker, E., and Terhardt, E. (1980). Analytical expressions for critical band rate and critical bandwidth as a function of frequency. *J. Acoust. Soc. Am.*, *68*, 1523–1525.

Zwicker, E., Flottorp, G., and Stevens, S. S. (1957). Critical bandwidth in loudness summation. *J. Acoust. Soc. Am.*, *29*, 548–557.

Zwislocki, J. J. (1960). Theory of temporal auditory summation. *J. Acoust. Soc. Am.*, *32*, 1046–1060.

Zwislocki, J. J., and Jordan, H. N. (1986). On the relations of intensity jnds to loudness and neural noise. *J. Acoust. Soc. Am.*, *79*, 772–780.

Zwolan, T., Kileny, P. R., Smith, S., Mills, D., Koch, D., and Osberger, M. J. (2001). Adult cochlear implant patient performance with evolving electrode technology. *Otol. Neurotol.*, *22*, 844–849.

Glossary

This glossary defines most of the technical terms that appear in the text. Sometimes the definitions are specific to the context of the book and do not apply to everyday usage of the terms. The glossary also defines some terms not used in the text but that may be found in the literature on hearing. When a definition uses text in italics, this indicates that this text is itself an entry in the glossary.

Absolute threshold The minimum detectable level of a sound in the absence of any other external sounds. The manner of presentation of the sound and the method of determining detectability must be specified.

Amplitude The instantaneous amplitude of an oscillating quantity (e.g., sound pressure) is its value at any instant, while the peak amplitude is the maximum value that the quantity attains. Sometimes the word peak is omitted when the meaning is clear from the context.

Amplitude modulation (AM) The process whereby the amplitude of a carrier is made to change as a function of time.

Audiogram A graph showing absolute threshold for pure tones as a function of frequency. It is usually plotted as hearing loss (deviation from the average threshold for young normally hearing people) in decibels as a function of frequency, with increasing loss plotted in the downward direction.

Auditory filter One of an array of bandpass filters that are assumed to exist in the peripheral auditory system. The characteristics of the filters are often estimated in masking experiments.

Aural harmonic A harmonic generated in the auditory system.

Azimuth The angle of a sound relative to the center of a listener's head, projected onto the horizontal plane. It is represented by θ in Fig. 7.1.

Bandwidth A term used to refer to a range of frequencies. The bandwidth of a bandpass filter is often defined as the difference between the two frequencies at which the response of the filter has fallen by 3 dB (i.e., to half power).

Basilar membrane A membrane inside the cochlea that vibrates in response to sound and whose vibrations lead to activity in the auditory pathways (see Chapter 1).

Beats Periodic fluctuations in peak amplitude that occur when two sinusoids with slightly different frequencies are superimposed.

Bel A unit for expressing the ratio of two powers. The number of bels is the logarithm to the base 10 of the power ratio.

Best frequency See *Characteristic frequency*.

Binaural A situation involving listening with two ears.

Binaural masking level difference (BMLD or MLD) This is a measure of the improvement in detectability of a signal that can occur under binaural listening conditions. It is the difference in threshold of the signal (in dB) for the case where the signal and masker have the same phase and level relationships at the two ears and the case where the interaural phase and/or level relationships of the signal and masker are different.

Cam The unit of ERB_N *number*.

Categorical perception A type of perception where stimuli are distinguished much better if they are identified as belonging to a different category than if they are identified as belonging to the same category. It occurs commonly for speech sounds, but is not unique to speech.

CB See *Critical bandwidth*.

Characteristic frequency (CF), best frequency The frequency at which the threshold of a given single neuron is lowest, i.e., the frequency at which it is most sensitive. CF is also used to describe the frequency to which a given place on the basilar membrane is most sensitive.

Combination tone A tone perceived as a component of a complex stimulus that is not present in the sensations produced by the constituent components of the complex when they are presented alone.

Comodulation masking release (CMR) The release from masking that can occur when the components of a masker have the same amplitude modulation pattern in different frequency regions.

Complex tone   A tone composed of a number of sinusoids of different frequencies.

Component   One of the sinusoids composing a complex sound. Also called a frequency component. In Chapter 10, the section on hi fi uses the word component to describe one of the pieces of equipment making up a hi-fi system.

Compressive nonlinearity   A form of nonlinearity in which the range of amplitudes or levels at the output of a system is smaller than the range of amplitudes or levels at the input.

Critical bandwidth (CB)   A measure of the "effective bandwidth" of the auditory filter. It is often defined empirically by measuring some aspect of perception as a function of the bandwidth of the stimuli and trying to determine a "break point" in the results. However, such break points are rarely clear.

Cycle   That portion of a periodic function that occurs in one period.

Decibel   One-tenth of a bel, abbreviated dB. The number of dB is equal to 10 times the logarithm of the ratio of two intensities, or 20 times the logarithm of the ratio of two amplitudes or pressures.

Dichotic   A situation in which the sounds reaching the two ears are not the same.

Difference limen (DL)   Also called the just-noticeable difference (JND) or the differential threshold. The smallest detectable change in a stimulus. The method of determining detectability must be specified.

Diotic   A situation in which the sounds reaching the two ears are the same.

Diplacusis   Binaural diplacusis describes the case when a tone of fixed frequency evokes different pitches in the left and right ears.

Elevation   The angle of a sound relative to the center of a listener's head, projected onto the median plane. It is represented by δ in Fig. 7.1.

Energetic masking   Masking that occurs because the neural response to the signal plus masker is similar to the neural response to the masker alone.

Envelope   The envelope of any function is the smooth curve passing through the peaks of the function.

Equal-loudness contours   Curves plotted as a function of frequency showing the sound pressure level required to produce a given loudness level.

Equivalent rectangular bandwidth (ERB)   The ERB of a filter is the bandwidth of a rectangular filter that has the same peak transmission as that filter and that passes the same total power for a white noise input. The ERB of the auditory filter is often used as a measure of the critical bandwidth.

ERB   See   *Equivalent   rectangular bandwidth.*

ERB$_N$ The average value of the equivalent rectangular bandwidth of the auditory filter at moderate sound levels for young listeners with no known hearing defect.

ERB$_N$-number scale (Cam)   A scale in which the frequency axis has been converted into units based on *ERB$_N$*. Each 1-Cam step corresponds to a distance of about 0.89 mm on the basilar membrane.

Excitation pattern   A term used to describe the pattern of neural activity evoked by a given sound as a function of the *characteristic frequency* (CF) of the neurons being excited. Sometimes the term is used to describe the effective level of excitation (in dB) at each CF. Psychoacoustically, the excitation pattern of a sound can be defined as the output of the auditory filters as a function of center frequency.

F0   See *Fundamental frequency.*

Filter   A device that modifies the frequency spectrum of a signal, usually while it is in electrical form.

Formant   A resonance in the vocal tract that is usually manifested as a peak in the spectral envelope of a speech sound.

Free field   A field or system of waves free from the effects of boundaries.

Frequency   For a sine wave the frequency is the number of periods occurring in 1 s. The unit is cycles per second or Hertz (Hz). For a complex periodic sound, the term "repetition rate" is used to describe the number of periods per second (pps).

Frequency modulation (FM)   The process whereby the frequency of a carrier is made to change as a function of time.

Frequency threshold curve   See *Tuning curve.*

Fundamental frequency (F0)   The fundamental frequency of a periodic sound is the frequency of that sinusoidal component of the sound that has the same period as the periodic sound. It is often abbreviated F0.

Harmonic   A harmonic is a component of a complex tone whose frequency is an integer multiple of the fundamental frequency of the complex.

Horizontal plane   The plane passing through the upper margins of the entrances to the ear canals and the lower margins of the eye sockets.

Hz   See *Frequency.*

Informational masking   Masking that is produced by confusion of a signal with a masker or difficulty in perceptual segregation of a signal and masker. It is contrasted with *energetic masking*, which occurs when the neural response to the signal plus masker is similar to the neural response to the masker alone.

Intensity Intensity is the sound power transmitted through a given area in a sound field. Units such as watts per square meter are used. The term is also used as a generic name for any quantity relating to amount of sound, such as power or energy, although this is not technically correct.

Level The level of a sound is specified in dB in relation to some reference level. See *Sensation level* and *Sound pressure level*.

Linear A linear system is a system that satisfies the conditions of superposition and homogeneity (see Chapter 1, Section 3).

Loudness This is the intensive attribute of an auditory sensation, in terms of which sounds may be ordered on a scale extending from quiet to loud.

Loudness level The loudness level of a sound, in phons, is the sound pressure level in dB of a pure tone of frequency 1 kHz that is judged to be equivalent in loudness.

Loudness recruitment See *Recruitment*.

Masked audiogram See *Masking pattern*.

Masking Masking is the amount (or the process) by which the threshold of audibility for one sound is raised by the presence of another (masking) sound.

Masking level difference (MLD) See *Binaural masking level difference*.

Masking pattern, masked audiogram This is a graph of the amount of masking (in dB) produced by a given sound (the masker) as a function of the frequency of the masked sound (the signal). It may also be plotted as the masked threshold of the signal as a function of signal frequency.

MDI See *Modulation detection interference* and *modulation discrimination interference*.

Median plane The plane containing all points that are equally distant from the two ears.

Modulation Modulation refers to a change in a particular dimension of a stimulus. For example, a sinusoid may be modulated in frequency or in amplitude.

Modulation detection interference (MDI) A reduced ability to detect modulation of a given carrier frequency when a modulated carrier with a different center frequency is present.

Modulation discrimination interference (MDI) A reduced ability to discriminate changes in the modulation of a given carrier frequency when a modulated carrier with a different center frequency is present.

Monaural A situation in which sounds are presented to one ear only.

Noise Noise in general refers to any unwanted sound. White noise is a sound whose power per unit bandwidth is constant, on average, over the range of audible frequencies. It usually has a normal (Gaussian) distribution of instantaneous amplitudes.

Octave An octave is the interval between two tones when their frequencies are in the ratio 2/1.

Partial A partial is any sinusoidal frequency component in a complex tone. It may or may not be a harmonic.

Peak factor The ratio of the maximum amplitude of a waveform to its RMS value.

Period The period of a periodic function is the smallest time interval over which the function repeats itself.

Periodic sound A periodic sound is one whose waveform repeats itself regularly as a function of time.

Phase The phase of a periodic waveform is the fractional part of a period through which the waveform has advanced, measured from some arbitrary point in time.

Phase locking This is the tendency for nerve firings to occur at a particular phase of the stimulating waveform on the basilar membrane.

Phon The unit of loudness level.

Pink noise This is a noise whose spectrum level decreases by 3 dB for each doubling of frequency.

Pitch Pitch is that attribute of auditory sensation in terms of which sounds may be ordered on a musical scale.

Pitch discrimination interference (PDI) The phenomenon whereby the ability to detect a change in fundamental frequency of a complex tone filtered into one frequency region is adversely affected by the presence of another complex tone with fixed fundamental frequency filtered into a different frequency region.

Power Power is a measure of energy per unit time. It is difficult to measure the total power generated by a sound source, and it is more common to specify the magnitudes of sounds in terms of their *intensity*, which is the sound power transmitted through a unit area in a sound field.

Psychophysical tuning curve (PTC) A curve showing the level of a narrowband masker needed to mask a fixed sinusoidal signal, plotted as a function of masker frequency.

Pure tone A sound wave whose instantaneous pressure variation as a function of time is a sinusoidal function. Also called a simple tone.

Recruitment This refers to a more rapid than usual growth of loudness level with increase in stimulus level. It occurs for people with cochlear hearing loss.

Rectification A process whereby all negative values of the instantaneous amplitude of a waveform are converted to positive values.

Residue pitch Also known as virtual pitch, low pitch, and periodicity pitch. The low pitch heard when a group of partials is perceived as a coherent whole. For a harmonic complex tone, the residue pitch is usually close to the pitch of the fundamental component, but that component does not have to be present for a residue pitch to be heard.

Resonance An enhancement of the intensity of a sound that occurs when its frequency equals or is close to the natural frequency of vibration of an acoustic system or air-filled cavity. The word is also used to describe the process by which the enhancement occurs.

Sensation level This is the level of a sound in decibels relative to the threshold level for that sound for the individual listener.

Simple tone See *Pure tone*.

Sine wave, sinusoidal vibration A waveform whose variation as a function of time is a sine function. This is the function relating the sine of an angle to the size of the angle.

Sone A unit of subjective loudness. A 1-kHz sinusoid presented binaurally in free field from a frontal direction is defined as having a loudness of 1 sone when its level is 40 dB SPL. The loudness in sones roughly doubles for each 10-dB increase in sound level above 40 dB SPL.

Sound pressure level This is the level of a sound in decibels relative to an internationally defined reference level. The latter corresponds to an intensity of 10^{-12} W/m^2, which is equivalent to a sound pressure of 20 µPa.

Spectrogram A display showing how the short-term spectrum of a sound changes over time. The abscissa is time, the ordinate is frequency, and the amount of energy is indicated by the lightness or darkness of shading. Spectrograms are often used in the analysis of speech sounds.

Spectrum The spectrum of a sound wave is the distribution in frequency of the magnitudes (and sometimes the phases) of the components of the wave. It can be represented by plotting power, intensity, amplitude, or level as a function of frequency.

Spectrum level This is the level of a sound in decibels measured in a 1-Hz-wide band. It is often used to characterize sounds with continuous spectra such as noises. A white noise has a long-term average spectrum level that is independent of frequency. A pink noise has a spectrum level that decreases by 3 dB for each doubling of frequency.

Spike A single nerve impulse or action potential.

Suppression The process whereby excitation or neural activity at one characteristic frequency is reduced by the presence of excitation or neural activity at adjacent characteristic frequencies.

Temporal masking curve (TMC) The level of a forward masker required to mask a signal of fixed level, plotted as a function of the silent interval between the masker and signal.

Temporal modulation transfer function (TMTF) The modulation depth required for detection of sinusoidal modulation of a carrier, plotted as a function of modulation frequency.

Threshold-equalizing noise (TEN) Noise whose spectrum is shaped so that the detection threshold for a sinusoidal tone presented in the noise is the same for all signal frequencies.

Timbre Timbre is that attribute of auditory sensation in terms of which a listener can judge that two sounds similarly presented and having the same loudness and pitch are dissimilar. Put more simply, it relates to the quality of a sound.

TMC See *Temporal masking curve*.

TMTF See *Temporal modulation transfer function*.

Tone A tone is a sound wave capable of evoking an auditory sensation having pitch.

Tuning curve For a single nerve fiber this is a graph of the lowest sound level at which the fiber will respond, plotted as a function of frequency. Also called a frequency threshold curve (FTC). See also *Psychophysical tuning curve*.

Virtual pitch See *Residue pitch*.

Waveform Waveform is a term used to describe the form or shape of a wave. It may be represented graphically by plotting instantaneous amplitude or pressure as a function of time.

White noise A noise with a spectrum level that does not vary as a function of frequency.

INDEX